Communications in Computer and Information Science

2655

Series Editors

Gang Li, *School of Information Technology, Deakin University, Burwood, VIC, Australia*

Joaquim Filipe, *Polytechnic Institute of Setúbal, Setúbal, Portugal*

Zhiwei Xu, *Chinese Academy of Sciences, Beijing, China*

Rationale
The CCIS series is devoted to the publication of proceedings of computer science conferences. Its aim is to efficiently disseminate original research results in informatics in printed and electronic form. While the focus is on publication of peer-reviewed full papers presenting mature work, inclusion of reviewed short papers reporting on work in progress is welcome, too. Besides globally relevant meetings with internationally representative program committees guaranteeing a strict peer-reviewing and paper selection process, conferences run by societies or of high regional or national relevance are also considered for publication.

Topics
The topical scope of CCIS spans the entire spectrum of informatics ranging from foundational topics in the theory of computing to information and communications science and technology and a broad variety of interdisciplinary application fields.

Information for Volume Editors and Authors
Publication in CCIS is free of charge. No royalties are paid, however, we offer registered conference participants temporary free access to the online version of the conference proceedings on SpringerLink (http://link.springer.com) by means of an http referrer from the conference website and/or a number of complimentary printed copies, as specified in the official acceptance email of the event.

CCIS proceedings can be published in time for distribution at conferences or as post-proceedings, and delivered in the form of printed books and/or electronically as USBs and/or e-content licenses for accessing proceedings at SpringerLink. Furthermore, CCIS proceedings are included in the CCIS electronic book series hosted in the SpringerLink digital library at http://link.springer.com/bookseries/7899. Conferences publishing in CCIS are allowed to use Online Conference Service (OCS) for managing the whole proceedings lifecycle (from submission and reviewing to preparing for publication) free of charge.

Publication process
The language of publication is exclusively English. Authors publishing in CCIS have to sign the Springer CCIS copyright transfer form, however, they are free to use their material published in CCIS for substantially changed, more elaborate subsequent publications elsewhere. For the preparation of the camera-ready papers/files, authors have to strictly adhere to the Springer CCIS Authors' Instructions and are strongly encouraged to use the CCIS LaTeX style files or templates.

Abstracting/Indexing
CCIS is abstracted/indexed in DBLP, Google Scholar, EI-Compendex, Mathematical Reviews, SCImago, Scopus. CCIS volumes are also submitted for the inclusion in ISI Proceedings.

How to start
To start the evaluation of your proposal for inclusion in the CCIS series, please send an e-mail to ccis@springer.com.

Omar Zahour · El Habib Benlahmar ·
Abdelaziz Marzak · Sara Ouahabi ·
Soumaya Ounacer
Editors

Technologies of Information and Modeling

7th International Conference, ICTIM 2024
Casablanca, Morocco, November 26–27, 2024
Proceedings

 Springer

Editors
Omar Zahour
Hassan II University of Casablanca
Casablanca, Morocco

Abdelaziz Marzak
Hassan II University of Casablanca
Casablanca, Morocco

Soumaya Ounacer
Hassan II University of Casablanca
Casablanca, Morocco

El Habib Benlahmar
Hassan II University of Casablanca
Casablanca, Morocco

Sara Ouahabi
Hassan II University of Casablanca
Casablanca, Morocco

ISSN 1865-0929   ISSN 1865-0937 (electronic)
Communications in Computer and Information Science
ISBN 978-3-032-15146-9   ISBN 978-3-032-15147-6 (eBook)
https://doi.org/10.1007/978-3-032-15147-6

This Springer imprint is published by the registered company Springer Nature Switzerland AG
The registered company address is: Gewerbestrasse 11, 6330 Cham, Switzerland

If disposing of this product, please recycle the paper.

Preface

We are pleased to present the proceedings of the 7th International Conference on Information Technology and Modeling (ICTIM 2024), held in Casablanca, Morocco, on November 26–27, 2024, and organized by the TIM Laboratory of the Faculty of Sciences Ben M'Sick, Hassan II University of Casablanca.

The theme of this edition, *"Innovation and Trends in Computer Science and Modeling: Bridging Theory, Practice, and the Power of Artificial Intelligence,"* reflects the rapid evolution of the field and the growing impact of AI across contemporary scientific and technological disciplines.

ICTIM 2024 received 103 submissions from researchers, academics, and professionals worldwide. Each manuscript underwent a rigorous double-blind peer-review process, with three independent reviewers assigned to every paper. Based on these evaluations and the decisions of the Program Committee Chairs, 37 full papers were accepted for inclusion in this volume.

To ensure scientific integrity and impartiality, all submissions co-authored by members of the organizing or program committees were evaluated exclusively by external reviewers, in accordance with Springer's quality standards.

The accepted papers are organized into three thematic sections that reflect the main research areas of the conference:

- Machine Learning, Computer Vision, and Data Analysis
- Natural Language Processing, Smart Systems, and Emerging Technologies
- Cybersecurity, Cryptography, and AI for Security

We extend our sincere gratitude to all authors for their high-quality contributions, to the reviewers and Program Committee members for their rigorous and insightful evaluations, and to all individuals who contributed to the success of ICTIM 2024.

We also express our deep appreciation to the Springer editorial team and the CCIS series team for their professionalism, continuous support, and valuable collaboration throughout the preparation and publication of this volume.

We hope that this book will inspire further research, collaboration, and innovation in the fields of information technology, artificial intelligence, and computational modeling.

Acknowledgement. We gratefully acknowledge the dedicated efforts of the organizing committee, program committee, reviewers, and all contributors whose commitment and expertise made ICTIM'24 possible. Special thanks are extended to the TIM Laboratory at the Faculty of Sciences Ben M'Sick for its continuous support and to Springer for publishing these proceedings.

January 2025

Omar Zahour
El Habib Benlahmar
Abdelaziz Marzak
Sara Ouahabi
Soumaya Ounacer

Organization

Honorary Chairs

Abdeslam El Bouari	Hassan II University of Casablanca, Morocco
Rachid Saile	Hassan II University of Casablanca, Morocco

Conference Chair

Omar Zahour	Hassan II University of Casablanca, Morocco

Conference Co-Chairs

Sara Ouahabi	Hassan II University of Casablanca, Morocco
Soumaya Ounacer	Hassan II University of Casablanca, Morocco

Steering Committee

El Habib Benlahmar	Hassan II University of Casablanca, Morocco
Sanaa El Filali	Hassan II University of Casablanca, Morocco
Anderson Rocha	University of Campinas, Brazil
Michael Kikomba Kahungu	ISP-Gombe, Democratic Republic of the Congo
Olivier Debauche	University of Liège, Belgium
Angel Ruiz Zafra	University of Granada, Spain

Scientific Committee

Khalil Aamre	University of Lorraine, France
Khadija Achtaich	Hassan II University of Casablanca, Morocco
Naceur Achtaich	Hassan II University of Casablanca, Morocco
Khalid Adnaoui	Hassan II University of Casablanca, Morocco
Rachida Ait Abdelouahid	Hassan II University of Casablanca, Morocco
Mohammed Ait Daoud	Hassan II University of Casablanca, Morocco
Tarik Ahajjam	Hassan II University of Casablanca, Morocco
Anass Rghioui	Hassan II University of Casablanca, Morocco

Anderson Rocha	University of Campinas, Brazil
Sara Aouhassi	Hassan II University of Casablanca, Morocco
Soufiane Ardchir	Hassan II University of Casablanca, Morocco
Fadoua Ataa Allah	Institut Royal de la Culture Amazighe, Morocco
Mohamed Azzouazi	Hassan II University of Casablanca, Morocco
Mostafa Bahaj	Ibn Zohr University, Morocco
Mouad Banane	Hassan II University of Casablanca, Morocco
Hammad Ballaoui	Instituts Supérieurs des Professions Infirmières et Techniques de Santé, Morocco
Hicham Behja	Hassan II University of Casablanca, Morocco
Abdessamad Belangour	Hassan II University of Casablanca, Morocco
Faouzia Benabbou	Hassan II University of Casablanca, Morocco
Kawtar Benghazi Akhlaki	University of Granada, Spain
Benlahmar El Habib	Hassan II University of Casablanca, Morocco
Bentaib Mohssine	Hassan II University of Casablanca, Morocco
Omar Bouattane	Hassan II University of Casablanca, Morocco
Bouhrma Mohamed	USTM Nouakchott, Mauritania
Chemlal Yman	Hassan II University of Casablanca, Morocco
Abderrahmane Daif	Hassan II University of Casablanca, Morocco
Jaouad Dabounou	Hassan I University, Morocco
Abbas Dandache	University of Lorraine, France
Olivier Debauche	University of Liège, Belgium
Mohamed Lamine Diakité	USTM Nouakchott, Mauritania
Abdelaziz Doukkali Sdigui	Mohammed V University in Rabat, Morocco
Khadija Douzi	Hassan II University of Casablanca, Morocco
Mustapha El Adnani	Hassan II University of Casablanca, Morocco
Hassan El Bahi	Cadi Ayyad University, Morocco
Sanaa El Filali	Hassan II University of Casablanca, Morocco
Mohammed Yassine El Ghoumari	Hassan II University of Casablanca, Morocco
Kamal El Guemmat	Hassan II University of Casablanca, Morocco
Youssef El Habouz	IGDR/University of Rennes, France
Yacine El Younoussi	Abdelmalek Essaâdi University, Morocco
Allae Erraissi	Chouaib Doukkali University, Morocco
Abdelaziz Ettaoufik	Hassan II University of Casablanca, Morocco
Mohamed Fakir	Sultan Moulay Slimane University, Morocco
Fabrice Monteiro	University of Lorraine, France
Fadoua Ghanimi	Ibn Tofaïl University, Morocco
Mohamed Ghazouani	Hassan II University of Casablanca, Morocco
Mamadou Lamine Gueye	University of Pau and the Adour Region, France
Mustapha Hain	Hassan II University of Casablanca, Morocco
Oussama Hamal	ENA Marrakech, Morocco
Mostafa Hanoune	Hassan II University of Casablanca, Morocco

Khalid Hattaf	CRMEF Casablanca, Morocco
Hicham Gueddah	Mohammed V University in Rabat, Morocco
Brahim Hmedna	Ibn Zohr University, Morocco
Imane Lmati	Hassan I University, Morocco
Zahi Jarir	Cadi Ayyad University, Morocco
Mostafa Jebbar	Hassan II University of Casablanca, Morocco
Khadija Sabiri	MORE CoLAB, Portugal
Khammal Adil	Hassan II University of Casablanca, Morocco
Michael Kikomba Kahur.gu	ISP-Gombe, DR Congo
Naziha Laaz	Hassania School of Public Works, Morocco
Ahmed Lachgar	Mohammed V University in Rabat, Morocco
Labriji El Houssine	Hassan II University of Casablanca, Morocco
Mohamed Lahby	Hassan II University of Casablanca, Morocco
Lamiae Demraoui	Sultan Moulay Slimane University, Morocco
Mohamed Adnane Mahraz	Sultan Moulay Slimane University, Morocco
Manuel Noguera García	University of Granada, Spain
Khalifa Mansouri	Hassan II University of Casablanca, Morocco
Abdelaziz Marzak	Hassan II University of Casablanca, Morocco
Samir Mbarki	Ibn Tofail University, Morocco
Soukaina Merzouk	Hassan II University of Casablanca
Abderrahmane Daif	Chouaib Doukkali University, Morocco
Khalid Moussaid	Hassan II University of Casablanca, Morocco
Hicham Moutachaouik	Hassan II University of Casablanca, Morocco
Abdelwahed Namir	Hassan II University of Casablanca, Morocco
Mohamedade Farouk Nanne	USTM Nouakchott, Mauritania
Mahmoud Nassar	Mohammed V University in Rabat, Morocco
Khadija Douzi	Hassan II University of Casablanca, Morocco
Said Nouh	Hassan II University of Casablanca, Morocco
Fouzia Omary	Mohammed V University in Rabat, Morocco
Sara Ouahabi	Hassan II University of Casablanca, Morocco
Abdellah Ouahman	Cadi Ayyad University, Morocco
Soumaya Ounacer	Hassan II University of Casablanca, Morocco
Hassan Qjidaa	Abdelmalek Essaâdi University, Morocco
Mohamed Rachdi	Hassan II University of Casablanca, Morocco
Youssef Rachidi	Ibn Zohr University, Morocco
Jamal Riffi	Sultan Moulay Slimane University, Morocco
Yassir Rochd	Hassan I University, Morocco
Rachid Saadane	Hassan II University of Casablanca, Morocco
Abdelalim Sadiq	Ibn Tofail University, Morocco
Mounir Sadiq	Hassan II University of Casablanca, Morocco
Nawal Sael	Hassan II University of Casablanca, Morocco
Sara Arezki	Hassan I University, Morocco

Hanae Sbai	Hassan II University of Casablanca, Morocco
Youssef Sekhara	Hassan II University of Casablanca, Morocco
Hassan Silkan	Chouaib Doukkali University, Morocco
Youness Tabii	Mohammed V University in Rabat, Morocco
Tarik Chafiq	Hassan II University of Casablanca, Morocco
Abderrahim Tragha	Hassan II University of Casablanca, Morocco
Abderrahim Yousfi	Sultan Moulay Slimane University, Morocco
Noura Yousfi	Hassan II University of Casablanca, Morocco
Omar Zahour	Hassan II University of Casablanca, Morocco
Ahmed Zellou	Mohammed V University in Rabat, Morocco

Other Committees

Sponsorship & Exhibits Chairs

Abdelaziz Marzak	Hassan II University of Casablanca, Morocco
Omar Zahour	Hassan II University of Casablanca, Morocco
Sara Ouahabi	Hassan II University of Casablanca, Morocco
Soumaya Ounacer	Hassan II University of Casablanca, Morocco

Web Chairs

Omar Zahour	Hassan II University of Casablanca, Morocco
Sara Ouahabi	Hassan II University of Casablanca, Morocco

Publicity & Communication Chairs

Sanaa El Filali	Hassan II University of Casablanca, Morocco
Soumaya Ounacer	Hassan II University of Casablanca, Morocco
Michael Kikomba Kahungu	ISP-Gombe, Democratic Republic of the Congo
Soukaina Merzouk	Chouaib Doukkali University, Morocco
Abderrahmane Daif	Hassan II University of Casablanca, Morocco
Mohamed Ait Daoud	Hassan II University of Casablanca, Morocco
Rachida Ait Abdelouahid	Hassan II University of Casablanca, Morocco
Mohamed Rachdi	Hassan II University of Casablanca, Morocco

Registration Chairs

Omar Zahour	Hassan II University of Casablanca, Morocco
Abdelaziz Ettaoufik	Hassan II University of Casablanca, Morocco
Mohssine Bentaib	Hassan II University of Casablanca, Morocco
Nawal Sael	Hassan II University of Casablanca, Morocco
Mohamed Ghazouani	Hassan II University of Casablanca, Morocco
Mounir Sadiq	Hassan II University of Casablanca, Morocco

Publication Chairs

Omar Zahour	Hassan II University of Casablanca, MoroccoSara OuahabiHassan II University of Casablanca, Morocco
Soumaya Ounacer	Hassan II University of Casablanca, Morocco
El Habib Benlahmar	Hassan II University of Casablanca, Morocco
Abdelaziz Marzak	Hassan II University of Casablanca, Morocco

Speakers Session Chairs

Mohamed Azouazi	Hassan II University of Casablanca, Morocco
El Habib Benlahmar	Hassan II University of Casablanca, Morocco
Abdelaziz Marzak	Hassan II University of Casablanca, Morocco
Hassan Silkan	Chouaib Doukkali University, Morocco
Faouzia Benabbou	Hassan II University of Casablanca, Morocco
Dabounou Jaouad	Hassan I University, Morocco

Organizing Local Committee (Senior)

Khalil Aamre	Hassan II University of Casablanca, Morocco
Khadija Achtaich	Hassan II University of Casablanca, Morocco
Nabil Aharrane	Hassan II University of Casablanca, Morocco
Tarik Ahajjam	Hassan II University of Casablanca, Morocco
Rachida Ait Abdelouahid	Hassan II University of Casablanca, Morocco
Mohamed Ait Daoud	Hassan II University of Casablanca, Morocco
Soufiane Ardchir	Hassan II University of Casablanca, Morocco
Sara Aouhassi	Hassan II University of Casablanca, Morocco
Mohamed Azzouazi	Hassan II University of Casablanca, Morocco
Abdessamad Belangour	Hassan II University of Casablanca, Morocco

Faouzia Benabbou	Hassan II University of Casablanca, Morocco
El Habib Benlahmar	Hassan II University of Casablanca, Morocco
Mohssine Bentaib	Hassan II University of Casablanca, Morocco
Tarik Chafiq	Hassan II University of Casablanca, Morocco
Yman Chemlal	Hassan II University of Casablanca, Morocco
Jaouad Dabounou	Hassan II University of Casablanca, Morocco
Abderrahmane Daif	Hassan II University of Casablanca, Morocco
Sanaa El Filali	Hassan II University of Casablanca, Morocco
Abdelaziz Ettaoufik	Hassan II University of Casablanca, Morocco
Fadoua Ghanimi	Hassan II University of Casablanca, Morocco
Mohamed Ghazouani	Hassan II University of Casablanca, Morocco
Oussama Hammal	Hassan II University of Casablanca, Morocco
Mostafa Hanoune	Hassan II University of Casablanca, Morocco
Khalid Kandali	Hassan II University of Casablanca, Morocco
Mustapha Khiati	Hassan II University of Casablanca, Morocco
Michael Kikomba Kahungu	ISP-Gombe, DR Congo
El Houssine Labriji	Hassan II University of Casablanca, Morocco
Abdelaziz Marzak	Hassan II University of Casablanca, Morocco
Soukaina Merzouk	Chouaib Doukkali University, Morocco
Laila Moussaid	Hassan II University of Casablanca, Morocco
Abdelwahed Namir	Hassan II University of Casablanca, Morocco
Said Nouh	Hassan II University of Casablanca, Morocco
Anass Nouri	Hassan II University of Casablanca, Morocco
Jamal Oufkir	Hassan II University of Casablanca, Morocco
Sara Ouahabi	Hassan II University of Casablanca, Morocco
Soumaya Ounacer	Hassan II University of Casablanca, Morocco
Mohamed Rachdi	Hassan II University of Casablanca, Morocco
Anass Rghioui	Hassan II University of Casablanca, Morocco
Khadija Sabiri	Hassan II University of Casablanca, Morocco
Nawal Sael	Hassan II University of Casablanca, Morocco
Ichrak Saif	Hassan II University of Casablanca, Morocco
Mounir Sadiq	Hassan II University of Casablanca, Morocco
Youssef Sekhara	Hassan II University of Casablanca, Morocco
Hassan Silkan	Hassan II University of Casablanca, Morocco
Youness Tabii	Hassan II University of Casablanca, Morocco
Abderrahim Tragha	Hassan II University of Casablanca, Morocco
Noura Yousfi	Hassan II University of Casablanca, Morocco
Omar Zahour	Hassan II University of Casablanca, Morocco

Organizing Local Committee (Junior)

Ilyas Farkhane	Hassan II University of Casablanca, Morocco
Oumaima Hourrane	Hassan II University of Casablanca, Morocco
Fatima Zahra Alaoui	Hassan II University of Casablanca, Morocco
Laila Eljiani	Hassan II University of Casablanca, Morocco
El Yazid Radid	Hassan II University of Casablanca, Morocco
Adil Karim	Hassan II University of Casablanca, Morocco
Nisrine Safeh	Hassan II University of Casablanca, Morocco
Othmane Aitlmoudden	Hassan II University of Casablanca, Morocco
Zouheir Banou	Hassan II University of Casablanca, Morocco
Meriem Bouhlal	Hassan II University of Casablanca, Morocco
Brahim Bella	Hassan II University of Casablanca, Morocco
Kawtar Aarika	Hassan II University of Casablanca, Morocco
Hafsa Ouchraa	Hassan II University of Casablanca, Morocco
Abdeljalil Elhassani	Hassan II University of Casablanca, Morocco
Ibtissame Ezzahoui	Hassan II University of Casablanca, Morocco
Mariame Tarsi	Hassan II University of Casablanca, Morocco
Amine Dehbi	Hassan II University of Casablanca, Morocco
Younes Rachdi	Hassan II University of Casablanca, Morocco
Fadoua Mihrab	Hassan II University of Casablanca, Morocco
Mohamed Akram Lamhour	Hassan II University of Casablanca, Morocco
Oussama Zemmnazi	Hassan II University of Casablanca, Morocco
Sofia Semlali	Ibn Tofail University, Morocco
Al Mahdi Khaddar	Hassan II University of Casablanca, Morocco
Salma Aimara	Hassan II University of Casablanca, Morocco
AbdelHamid Sebbar	Hassan II University of Casablanca, Morocco
Zineb Ellaky	Hassan II University of Casablanca, Morocco

Contents

**Natural language processing(NLP), Smart Systems, and Emerging
Technologies**

Cybersecurity, Cryptography, and AI for Security

Machine Learning, Computer Vision, and Data Analysis

Evaluating the Computational Complexity
of Various Machine Learning Algorithms

Salsabila Benghazouani[1]([⊠]), Said Nouh[1], and Abdelali Zakrani[2]

[1] Faculty of Sciences Ben M'Sik, Department of Mathematics and Computer Science, Hassan II University, Casablanca, Morocco
benghazouani.salsabila239@gmail.com

[2] Department of Computer Science Engineering, ENSAM, Hassan II University, Casablanca, Morocco

Abstract. Machine learning operates at the intersection of statistics and computer science, employs algorithms to scrutinize data and derive valuable insights, contributing to the decision-making process by extracting meaningful information. With the widespread adoption of big data in various applications, deriving valuable insights from this real-world data poses several challenges in extracting meaningful information. Factors like time and memory complexities add to the difficulties in this task. Despite significant progress and sustained interest in machine learning algorithms, there is a surprising lack of review research that consolidates, analyzes, and compares the computational complexity of these models. This paper aims to examine and contrast the computational complexities of various commonly used machine learning methods, with the goal of understanding and optimizing their performance for large datasets.

Keywords: Complexity · K-Nearest Neighbors · Logistic Regression · AdaBoost · Decision Tree · Naive Bayes · Support Vector Machines · Random Forest · Gradient Boosted Decision Tree

1 Introduction

The world is currently submerged by the exponential increase in learning-related data available. This enormous amount of data contains some useful information. By employing machine learning (ML) techniques, the provided data can undergo analysis, enabling the extraction of pertinent information, and facilitating informed decision-making [1]. As big data becomes the norm in various application domains, the challenge is to derive meaningful models and insights from this real-world data, which introduces several difficulties, including the complexity of time and memory. Due to the necessity for specialized and costly hardware and software in managing and analyzing extensive data volumes, numerous businesses and organizations only utilize a fraction of the stored data. As per [2], a primary hurdle confronting the data mining research community involves developing algorithms that streamline the application of learning approaches to real-world databases. ML, as a subset of computer science, aims to instruct and program machines to learn from their experiences. The objective is for the machines to gain

O. Zahour et al. (Eds.): ICTIM 2024, CCIS 2655, pp. 3–14, 2026.
https://doi.org/10.1007/978-3-032-15147-6_1

expertise in applying these learned experiences when encountering new and unfamiliar situations. Given the extensive history and interest in machine learning techniques, the limited research on the computational complexity of these model ML algorithms is surprising [3]. This paper aims to examine and evaluate the computational complexity of the ML approaches that are most frequently used and, thus, most popular to comprehend the procedural steps to optimize the learning algorithm for extensive datasets.

The rest of the paper is structured as follows: Sect. 2 provides an overview of fundamental concepts relevant to the paper. The complexity analysis is detailed in Sect. 3, followed by the conclusion and perspectives.

2 Background

Classification, a form of supervised learning, involves a set of training with labeled instances. The objective is to develop a description that allows predicting outcomes for previously unseen examples.

2.1 Logistic Regression (LR)

The LR is a statistical approach used to predict a binary dependent variable. It is effective in estimating the likelihood of a characteristic or outcome being present or absent, derived from multiple independent variables [4].

2.2 K-Nearest Neighbor (KNN)

The KNN method is a straightforward supervised ML approach applicable to addressing classification and regression challenges. While it is simple to implement and comprehend, a notable drawback is its tendency to become considerably slow as the size of the utilized data increases [5].

2.3 Naive Bayes

Naive Bayes (NB) is a classification method founded on Bayes' Theorem, which presumes that all predictors are independent. This means that the occurrence of one feature is considered unrelated to others. The method is particularly effective in text classification, where it utilizes conditional probabilities to perform clustering and classification tasks [5].

2.4 Support Vector Machine (SVM)

The SVM is a ML method grounded in statistical learning theory. It adheres to the concept of structural risk minimization, aiming to simultaneously minimize both the empirical error and the complexity of the learner. This approach leads to effective generalization performance in tasks related to classification and regression. For classification, SVM strives to build the optimal hyperplane with the maximum margin. Generally, a larger margin corresponds to a lower generalization error for the classifier [5].

2.5 Boosting

Boosting is a machine-learning approach that involves building a very precise prediction rule by amalgamating numerous relatively weak and imprecise rules. The AdaBoost technique, created by Freund and Schapire, was one of the first practical boosting techniques and remains among the most extensively applied and researched methods, finding applications across various fields [6].

2.6 Bagging

Bagging, which stands for bootstrap aggregating, is an approach utilized to enhance precision and stability of ML methods. This approach can be applied to both classification and regression tasks, offering a versatile approach to enhancing predictive models. Beyond its predictive power, bagging is essential in reducing variance, thereby reducing the risk of overfitting in complex systems. By creating several subsets of the dataset through bootstrap sampling and training models independently, bagging fosters diversity among the models, leading to more robust and generalized predictions [7].

2.7 Random Forest (RF)

The RF is an ensemble technique that generates several decision trees, using majority voting for classification. Each tree utilizes a randomly selected subset of features and unique bootstrap samples of the data, enhancing model diversity and robustness. This approach makes RF a highly effective and versatile classification tool [8].

2.8 Decision Tree Algorithm

A decision tree is a graphical model illustrating decisions and their potential outcomes. Nodes represent choices or events, while branches indicate decision rules. Common decision tree algorithms like ID3 [3], C4.5 [9], and CART [10] follow a top-down approach. Some, like CART and C4.5, also involve pruning stages to optimize the model, while others focus exclusively on tree growth [11].

2.9 Gradient Boosted Decision Tree (GBDT)

The GBDT is a versatile ML technique applied to classification as well as regression problems. Like RF, GBDT employs ensemble learning, consisting of multiple base predictive models, often decision trees. The training process of GBDT is akin to other boosting methods, where it sequentially builds and refines predictive models. Notably, GBDT enhances the generalization of these models by optimizing an arbitrary differentiable loss function, allowing it to adapt and improve performance across diverse datasets [12].

3 Computational Complexity

3.1 Theoretical Analysis

Computational resources play a pivotal role in applying learning algorithms in practice. These resources are broadly categorized into two types: computational complexity and sample complexity [13]. Algorithm analysis constitutes a significant component of the broader computational complexity theory, offering theoretical estimations of resources required by a specific method to solve a specific computational problem. Table 1 shows the parameters used to calculate the complexity, and Table 2 summarizes the computational complexity of the ML approaches that are most frequently used.

3.2 Experimental Analysis and Discussion

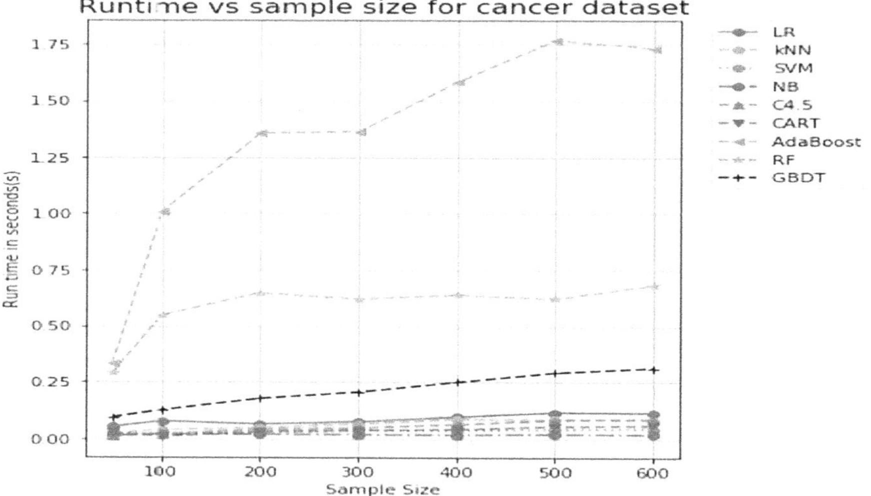

Fig. 1. Comparisons of the Runtime of Machine Learning Algorithms Relative to Sample Size for the Cancer Dataset

This section presents experimental studies on the running time of machine learning methods. The primary emphasis is on the behavior of algorithms as the number of examples grows. The Breast cancer Wisconsin dataset contains 569 samples and 32 features in the UCI machine learning repository. The WDBC dataset is used in this research to evaluate the performance and runtime of ML models. The objective of this experimental work is to analyze the behavior of the ML approaches as the input data set size expands. Table 3 provides accuracy scores and execution times for various machine learning algorithms on the cancer dataset, measured across increasing sample sizes. The results reveal several patterns. SVM and LR consistently achieve high accuracy across all sample sizes, often above 95% as the dataset grows, indicating robust predictive performance. Naïve Bayes and KNN also maintain relatively high accuracy, though slightly below SVM and

Logistic Regression. Decision tree-based algorithms like C4.5 and CART initially have lower accuracy but improve with larger sample sizes, highlighting their dependency on dataset size to reach optimal performance. Ensemble methods such as AdaBoost, RF, and GBDT show competitive accuracy, particularly as sample sizes increase, with AdaBoost and GBDT achieving some of the highest scores; however, they also have the highest execution times.

Table 1. Parameters involved in the complexity computation.

Parameter	Description
N	Count of samples.
M	Count of features.
K	Count of nearest neighbors.
L	Count of Support Vectors.
T	The total iterations used to build the strong classifier.
C	Count of classes.
H	Count of decision trees in Random Forest.
D	Number of tress.

Figure 1 illustrates the significant variation in runtime performance among ML techniques as sample sizes increase. Simpler algorithms, such as Logistic Regression, KNN, Naïve Bayes, SVM, C4.5, and CART, maintain low and stable runtimes, demonstrating scalability and efficiency. In contrast, ensemble methods like Random Forest, GBDT, and especially AdaBoost exhibit higher runtimes, with AdaBoost showing a particularly steep increase as sample size grows due to its iterative boosting process. These findings have several practical implications in the context of cancer diagnosis, where the choice of ML techniques can significantly impact the effectiveness and efficiency of diagnostic tools. In cancer screening, where rapid preliminary assessments are essential, simpler algorithms like Logistic Regression, Naïve Bayes, or SVM are advantageous due to their low and stable runtimes. These models can quickly process large datasets without overwhelming computational resources, making them suitable for initial screenings or high-throughput environments, such as mobile screening units or smaller clinics with limited resources. Their efficient runtime allows healthcare professionals to obtain quick insights, which can expedite further testing and diagnosis. For more detailed diagnostic processes, where accuracy is paramount, ensemble methods like Random Forest and GBDT become valuable despite their higher computational cost. These models have demonstrated higher accuracy, making them suitable for in-depth analysis, such as distinguishing between complex subtypes of cancer or identifying subtle patterns that may be critical for early-stage diagnosis. While AdaBoost achieves high accuracy, its steep increase in runtime as sample sizes grow may limit its use in real-time applications, making it more appropriate for research settings or retrospective studies where computational time is less constrained.

Table 2. Comparisons of the computational complexity of some machine learning algorithms.

Method	Description	Train time complexity	Test time complexity	References
C4.5 Algorithm	The computational complexity involved in constructing a decision tree primarily revolves around the criterion function, comprising two fundamental operations: calculating the information gain of the class attribute and determining the entropy of the input variables in relation to the class. The computational complexity of estimating the probability for each labeled category is limited by the sample size, leading to a time complexity of $O(N)$. Specifically, the processing on a single input feature needs $C(N.log(N))$, and considering all features, the overall cost for this process becomes $C(M.N.log(N))$.	$O(N.\log(N).M)$	$O(\log(N))$	[3]

(continued)

Table 2. (*continued*)

Method	Description	Train time complexity	Test time complexity	References
CART Algorithm	The estimation of CART's complexity can be derived using a similar methodology as that employed for C4.5. Theoretically, the fundamental operating steps involved in building a decision tree share a common structure. A notable distinction between the two methods arises in the criterion applied for attribute selection during the splitting process. CART opts for the Gini index division criterion. Consequently, the complexity involved in constructing a decision tree with the CART technique can be approximated as $O(M.N \log (N))$.	$O(N.\log(N).M)$	$O(\log(N))$	[3]
k-nearest neighbors' Algorithm	The computational complexity of retrieving the nearest neighbor samples for a single test instance from the training set is $O(NM)$. For K nearest neighbors, there may be an additional complexity due to sorting the distances, but the core complexity remains linear in terms of the number of training samples and features.	$O(N.M)$	$O(N.M)$	[14]

(*continued*)

Table 2. *(continued)*

Method	Description	Train time complexity	Test time complexity	References
Support vector machine	Training an SVM is usually framed as a quadratic programming problem, with the goal of finding a hyperplane that separates the data. This process involves creating an $N \times N$ matrix, where N represents the number of data points in the set. For large datasets, this can lead to considerable demands or both computational time and memory, resulting in the training complexity of SVM being heavily influenced by the dataset size. After training, the time required to predict a new sample is $O(L.M)$, where L indicates the number of Support Vectors.	$O(N^2.M)$	$O(L.M)$	[15, 16]
Naïve Bayes algorithm	The training complexity for a (Gaussian) NB classifier is $O(N.M.C)$. The prediction of a new sample requires $O(M.C)$, with C is the number of classes.	$O(N.M.C)$	$O(M.C)$	[17]

(continued)

Table 2. (*continued*)

Method	Description	Train time complexity	Test time complexity	References
AdaBoost algorithm	The computational complexity of AdaBoost arises from constructing both the decision stumps and the strong classifier. To create decision stumps, the algorithm must evaluate all samples for every feature, leading to a complexity of $O(N.M)$, where N represents the number of samples and M denotes the number of features. Constructing the strong classifier requires T iterations. Therefore, during the training phase of AdaBoost, the overall computational complexity is $O(N.T.M)$.	$O(N.T.M)$	$O(M.T)$	[18, 19]
Logistic Regression	For the Training Logistic Regression, the optimization problem needs to be solved using Stochastic Gradient Descent.	$O(N.M)$	$O(M)$	[20]
Random Forest	The computational cost of Random Forest is expressed as $O(H.M.N.\log(N))$, where H represents the total number of trees in the forest, M denotes the number of features, N indicates the number of samples, and $\log(N)$ reflects the typical depth of the trees in the model.	$O(H.N.\log(N).M)$	$O(H.\log(N))$	[21]

(continued)

Table 2. (*continued*)

Method	Description	Train time complexity	Test time complexity	References
Gradient boosted decision tree	The computational complexity of Gradient Boosted Decision Trees is $O(M.D.N.\log(N))$. Sorting N samples requires a time complexity of $O(N.\log(N))$. Considering multiple features and various levels of tree depth, this sorting process is required for each feature and depth level, and the operation is repeated for the number of trees (D).	$O(M.D.N.\log(N))$	$O(D.\log(N))$	[22]

Table 3. Accuracy and Execution Time Results for the Cancer Dataset

| | Methods | | | | | | | | | | | | | | | | |
| | LR | | KNN | | SVM | | NB | | C4.5 | | CART | | AdaBoost | | RF | | GBDT | |
Size n	Accu	Exec	Accu	Exec	Accu	Exec	Accu	Exec	Accu	Exec	Accu	Exec	Accu	Exec	Accu	Exec	Accu	Exec
50	0.900	0.052	0.880	0.025	0.940	0.021	0.920	0.014	0.860	0.008	0.860	0.027	0.940	0.332	0.920	0.288	0.820	0.092
100	0.940	0.077	0.920	0.038	0.920	0.022	0.930	0.020	0.840	0.022	0.890	0.010	0.900	1.005	0.920	0.547	0.930	0.123
200	0.960	0.064	0.950	0.048	0.965	0.028	0.945	0.019	0.905	0.039	0.900	0.030	0.925	1.358	0.935	0.643	0.925	0.175
300	0.960	0.075	0.953	0.064	0.960	0.035	0.923	0.018	0.910	0.047	0.910	0.037	0.936	1.364	0.940	0.617	0.946	0.204
400	0.967	0.095	0.957	0.085	0.967	0.036	0.927	0.018	0.925	0.063	0.915	0.042	0.960	1.581	0.942	0.635	0.965	0.249
500	0.972	0.114	0.970	0.085	0.978	0.041	0.932	0.021	0.914	0.081	0.922	0.054	0.964	1.765	0.936	0.618	0.958	0.291
600	0.963	0.112	0.963	0.081	0.975	0.045	0.927	0.019	0.933	0.086	0.917	0.058	0.971	1.729	0.949	0.679	0.959	0.312

4   Conclusion and Future Work

Machine learning, a key facet of artificial intelligence, has garnered substantial attention in the digital realm, serving as a crucial element in digitalization solutions. This paper analyzes and compares the computational complexities of widely utilized machine learning algorithms, providing insights into their practical applications. While these findings advance our understanding of algorithm performance, one limitation of this study is the limited diversity of datasets used, expanding this would allow for validation of results across different contexts and enhance generalizability.

Furthermore, the results suggest several optimization pathways to improve runtime efficiency, particularly for complex models. Implementing dimensionality reduction techniques or feature selection can help streamline ensemble methods by reducing data size without compromising accuracy. Additionally, leveraging parallel processing and GPU acceleration can mitigate the high computational costs of algorithms like Random Forest, GBDT, and AdaBoost, making them more practical for large-scale applications. Techniques such as early stopping, online learning, and mini-batch processing can further optimize iterative models by reducing computations once optimal performance is reached. Hybrid approaches, including model distillation and cascading models, offer a balance of simplicity and accuracy by deploying complex models selectively. Overall, these findings emphasize the importance of aligning algorithm choice with specific application requirement, balancing accuracy and computational efficiency based on task demands to achieve both effective and practical machine learning solutions.

References

1. Benghazouani, S., Nouh, S., Zakrani, A.: Optimizing breast cancer diagnosis: harnessing the power of nature-inspired metaheuristics for feature selection with soft voting classifiers. Int. J. Cogn. Comput. Eng. **6**, 1–20 (2024)
2. Batool, I., Khan, T.A.: Software fault prediction using data mining, machine learning and deep learning techniques: a systematic literature review. Comput. Electr. Eng. **100**, 107886 (2022)
3. Abolhosseini, S., Khorashadizadeh, M., Chahkandi, M., Golalizadeh, M.: A modified ID3 decision tree algorithm based on cumulative residual entropy. Expert Syst. Appl. **255**, 124821 (2024)
4. Benghazouani, S., Nouh, S., Zakrani, A., Haloum, I., Jebbar, M.: Enhancing feature selection with a novel hybrid approach incorporating genetic algorithms and swarm intelligence techniques. Int. J. Electr. Comput. Eng. **14**(1), 2088–8708 (2024)
5. Bansal, M., Goyal, A., Choudhary, A.: A comparative analysis of K-nearest neighbor, genetic, support vector machine, decision tree, and long short term memory algorithms in machine learning. Decis Anal. J. **3**, 100071 (2022)
6. Benghazouani, S., Nouh, S., Zakrani, A.: Optimizing microarray gene selection in colon cancer: an enhanced metaheuristic algorithm for feature selection. In: Information Technologies and Their Applications, pp. 76–86. Springer (2025)
7. Lin, E., Lin, C.-H., Lane, H.-Y.: A bagging ensemble machine learning framework to predict overall cognitive function of schizophrenia patients with cognitive domains and tests. Asian J. Psychiatr. **69**, 103008 (2022)
8. Antoniadis, A., Lambert-Lacroix, S., Poggi, J.-M.: Random forests for global sensitivity analysis: a selective review. Reliab. Eng. Syst. Saf. **206**, 107312 (2021)
9. Shanthi, J., Rani, D.G.N., Rajaram, S.: A C4.5 decision tree classifier based floorplanning algorithm for System-on-Chip design. Microelectron. J. **121**, 105361 (2022)
10. Ghiasi, M.M., Zendehboudi, S., Mohsenipour, A.A.: Decision tree-based diagnosis of coronary artery disease: CART model. Comput. Methods Prog. Biomed. **192**, 105400 (2020)
11. Barros, R.C., De Carvalho, A.C., Freitas, A.A.: Automatic Design of Decision-Tree Induction Algorithms. Springer (2015)
12. Benghazouani, S., Nouh, S., Zakrani, A.: Enhancing breast cancer diagnosis: a comparative analysis of feature selection techniques. IAES Int. J. Artif. Intell. IJ-AI. **13**(4), 4312–4322 (2024)

13. Demangeon, R., Yoshida, N.: Causal computational complexity of distributed processes. Inf. Comput. **290**, 104998 (2023)
14. Li, L., Yang, W., Bai, S., Ma, Z.: KNN-GNN: a powerful graph neural network enhanced by aggregating K-nearest neighbors in common subspace. Expert Syst. Appl. **253**, 124217 (2024)
15. Kaisar, T.I., Zaman, K., Khasawneh, M.T.: A new approach to probabilistic classification based on Gaussian process and support vector machine. Comput. Ind. Eng. **186**, 109719 (2023)
16. Menon, R.V., Chakrabarti, I.: Low complexity VLSI architecture for improved primal–dual support vector machine learning core. Microprocess. Microsyst. **98**, 104806 (2023)
17. Zhao, X., Xia, Z.: Secure outsourced NB: accurate and efficient privacy-preserving Naive Bayes classification. Comput. Secur. **124**, 103011 (2023)
18. Zhi, N., An, Y., Zhao, Y., Qiu, J.: Intelligent Island detection method of DC microgrid based on Adaboost algorithm. Energy Rep. **9**, 970–982 (2023)
19. Tan, C., Yin, F., Jiang, T.: Classification method of seabed sonar image substrate based on ELM-AdaBoost. J. Radiat. Res. Appl. Sci., 101126 (2024)
20. Wang, K., He, F., He, M., Huang, X.: Learning non-parametric kernel via matrix decomposition for logistic regression. Pattern Recogn. Lett. **171**, 177–183 (2023)
21. Jiang, M., Wang, J., Hu, L., He, Z.: Random forest clustering for discrete sequences. Pattern Recogn. Lett. **174**, 45–151 (2023)
22. Wu, J., Zhao, G., Wang, M., Xu, Y., Wang, N.: Concrete carbonation depth prediction model based on a gradient-boosting decision tree and different metaheuristic algorithms. Case Stud. Constr. Mater. **21**, e03864 (2024)

Contrastive Learning on 3D Vision-Based Fall Detection

Oumaima Guendoul[✉][iD], Youness Tabii, and Rachid Oulad Haj Thami

ADMIR Lab, National school of computer science and systems analysis (ENSIAS)
Mohammed V University, Rabat 10000, Morocco
oumaima_guendoul@um5.ac.ma

Abstract. This paper proposes a novel approach for detecting falls in elderly individuals using a vision-based system enhanced by contrastive learning techniques. Traditional fall detection models often struggle with high false positive rates and generalization issues in diverse environments. By leveraging contrastive learning, we aim to improve the feature representation of fall-related events and non-fall actions, ensuring better discrimination between the two. Our model utilizes 3D vision-based body articulation data, feeding it into a contrastive learning framework that learns robust feature embeddings for various human activities. The model learns a low-dimensional embedding of the head position based on spatial coordinates, enabling robust estimation and generalization even with incomplete or missing data during testing. The experimental results on a standard fall detection dataset demonstrate that our approach achieves state-of-the-art performance, reducing false positives while maintaining manageable accuracy in real-world settings.

Keywords: contrastive learning · Deep learning · Fall detection · 3D vision information · computer vision · healthcare

1 Introduction

Fall detection is a critical issue in the care of elderly populations, as falls are a leading cause of injury and hospitalization. Various systems have been developed to address this challenge, ranging from wearable sensors to camera-based monitoring systems. Recent surveys, including those from our ongoing research [1], highlight the growing interest and advancements in vision-based solutions for fall detection. Specifically, in our work [2], we examine novel techniques that improve both fall detection accuracy and prediction. These studies provide a comprehensive overview of the state-of-the-art technologies and explore the challenges associated with implementing such systems in real-world scenarios. However, these systems often struggle with either obtrusiveness or high false alarm rates in complex environments. Vision-based fall detection presents a promising non-intrusive solution, but its performance is often hindered by the difficulty of distinguishing between falls and normal activities.

O. Zahour et al. (Eds.): ICTIM 2024, CCIS 2655, pp. 15–22, 2026.
https://doi.org/10.1007/978-3-032-15147-6_2

To address this challenge, one effective approach is the use of contrastive learning. Contrastive learning is a self-supervised learning technique that enhances feature representation by comparing similar and dissimilar pairs of data. By learning to distinguish between positive pairs (e.g., two frames of the same fall) and negative pairs (e.g., a fall and a non-fall activity), the model can better capture the key distinguishing features of falls. This approach has been shown to improve the robustness and accuracy of vision-based systems, making them more reliable in distinguishing between falls and other daily activities, even in complex or ambiguous scenarios.

To further enhance fall detection accuracy, we introduce a contrastive learning framework that improves feature learning, thereby making the system more reliable in differentiating falls from other movements. As well as, the head position estimation is an essential task in various applications, including human-computer interaction and pose estimation. In this work, we introduce a contrastive learning-based model that learns embeddings of the head's position using 3D coordinates. The model is trained to differentiate between similar and dissimilar head positions using a contrastive loss function, allowing it to generalize well to new and unseen data.

2   Related Work

Previous work in fall detection can be divided into two main categories: sensor-based and vision-based approaches. Sensor-based methods rely on accelerometers and gyroscopes to detect sudden changes in motion, but these devices can be inconvenient for elderly individuals to wear continuously. Vision-based methods, on the other hand, analyze visual data to detect falls without physical contact, but they often suffer from challenges such as varying lighting conditions, occlusions, and similarities between fall and non-fall activities. Recently, deep learning models have been employed to improve the accuracy of vision-based fall detection, though they are often limited by their need for large datasets and their tendency to overfit. Contrastive learning, an unsupervised learning technique, has gained attention in computer vision tasks for its ability to learn better representations by contrasting positive and negative samples, making it an ideal candidate for improving fall detection systems. Contrastive learning has emerged as a promising technique in enhancing vision-based fall detection systems, particularly by leveraging deep learning methodologies to improve both accuracy and computational efficiency. This approach enables the model to effectively differentiate between fall and non-fall events by learning robust feature representations from video data. Specifically, contrastive learning enhances the model's capacity to learn discriminative features by contrasting positive and negative samples, which is crucial for accurately identifying falls [3]. Recent studies have demonstrated that integrating contrastive learning with deep learning architectures, such as convolutional neural networks (CNNs), can lead to significant improvements in performance, with some models achieving accuracy rates exceeding 99% in fall detection tasks [4] [5]. Additionally, the application of contrastive learning in real-world settings, particularly when combined with transfer learning, has been shown to boost model performance in real-time scenarios, addressing common challenges such as limited data availability and computational constraints [4]. Despite its advantages, contrastive learning does face certain limitations, including the need for large batch sizes during training and potential biases in the representations it learns, which may hinder its ability to generalize effectively in diverse environments.

3   Method

This study utilizes a contrastive learning-based model for fall detection, leveraging 3D body articulation data from depth cameras. The task is framed as binary classification, distinguishing falls from other activities. The model's core innovation lies in the contrastive loss function, which encourages the model to cluster fall instances (positive samples) together and separate them from non-fall activities (negative samples). By learning from 3D coordinate sequences, the model builds a rich embedding space that improves the representation of human actions, enhancing both feature extraction and classification performance.

A Siamese network with a shared base model processes pairs of 3D data from different perspectives, increasing the accuracy of fall detection. The architecture is well explained in Fig. 1. This self-supervised approach reduces the need for large labeled datasets, allowing the model to be trained on various fall scenarios captured from multiple angles. However, challenges related to computational efficiency and large batch sizes may affect real-time application in healthcare environments.

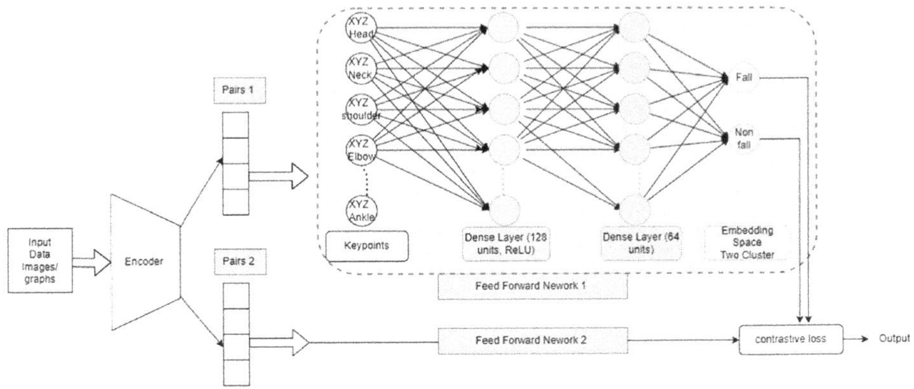

Fig. 1. Overview of the 3D Vision-Based Contrastive Learning Model for Fall Detection.

3.1 Data Processing:

The model processes 3D vision-based data, specifically the XYZ coordinates of human body joint movements. The dataset was collected using a ZED2 stereo camera to capture simulated actions performed by individuals of varying genders and ages. It consists of 12 videos, including 5 females and 7 males from MAScIR, who simulated both falls and normal activities of daily living (ADLs) [2]. Over 3000 frames were recorded per video in a controlled environment with consistent lighting and the camera positioned 1.7 m above the floor to simulate realistic indoor conditions. The data collection protocol followed guidelines from established fall detection databases, ensuring diverse fall scenarios.

To address class imbalance, where falls (Label 1) are underrepresented compared to non-falls (Label 0), we employed Synthetic Minority Over-sampling Technique (SMOTE) to generate synthetic fall samples, thus improving model performance and ensuring a balanced dataset.

The preprocessing pipeline included noise reduction through Gaussian and median filtering, joint position normalization, and feature extraction (e.g., joint averages and movement trajectories). These steps enhanced data quality, enabling effective fall detection modeling. The simulation involved participants of various genders and ages to ensure comprehensive analysis across demographics. Each participant performed predefined actions under controlled conditions, with the ZED2 camera's optimal height and wide field of view capturing dynamic movements. Participant characteristics, such as age and physical attributes, were also documented to assess their impact on fall behavior.

3.2 Model Architecture:

Feature Extraction: Utilizes a siamese network architecture with a shared base model to extract features from pairs of 3D coordinate sequences.This architecture allows the model to compare sequences of keypoint data, learning the relationship between different poses.

Contrastive Loss: The model uses contrastive loss to learn embeddings that differentiate between similar pairs (e.g., two sequences from the same "falling" action) and dissimilar pairs (e.g., sequences from "not falling" actions). The contrastive loss function, which is key to training siamese networks, is defined as follows:

$$L_{contrastive} = \frac{1}{2} \cdot \left(y \cdot D^2 + (1 - y) \cdot \max(0, m - D)^2 \right)$$

where:

- y is the binary label indicating whether the pair is:
  - similar ($y = 1$), or
  - dissimilar ($y = 0$).
- D is the Euclidean distance between the feature embeddings of the pair.

– m is a margin that defines how far apart dissimilar pairs should be in the embedding space.

This loss function encourages the network to minimize the distance D for similar pairs (falls) and to maximize the distance for dissimilar pairs (non-falls). Employs contrastive loss to learn embeddings that differentiate between similar and dissimilar pairs (falling vs. non-falling).

3.3   Training:

Pair Generation: During training, pairs of 3D coordinate sequences are created, where each pair is labeled to indicate whether it belongs to the same action (e.g., two "falling" actions) or different actions (e.g., "falling" vs. "walking"). If x_i and x_j represent two input sequences (from time steps i and j), the pair generation process can be represented as:

$$\text{Pair}(x_i, x_j) = \begin{cases} (x_i, x_j, y = 1) & \text{if both sequences belong to the same action class (e.g., both falls)} \\ (x_i, x_j, y = 0) & \text{if the sequences belong to different action classes} \\ & \text{(e.g., one is a fall and the other is a normal activity)} \end{cases}$$

Model Training: Trains the model using these pairs with a contrastive loss function, adjusting weights to minimize the distance between similar pairs and maximize it between dissimilar pairs. This can be formalized as:

$$\min_{\theta} \sum_{(x_i, x_j, y)} L_{\text{contrastive}}(\theta, x_i, x_j, y)$$

where θ represents the parameters of the siamese network. The training adjusts the model's weights to learn embeddings that correctly distinguish between different activities based on the 3D keypoint data.

4   Discussion

The application of contrastive learning to 3D vision-based fall detection has shown significant potential by improving the feature representation of human actions through the analysis of xyz coordinates of head joint movements. The model achieved an accuracy of 65.68%, demonstrating effective discrimination between non-falls and falls with high precision for non-falls as Figs. 1 and 2. However, the model struggled with fall detection, evidenced by low recall and precision values for falls. This indicates that while the model effectively identifies non-fall actions, it misses many fall events, suggesting a need for further refinement. Future improvements could focus on addressing dataset imbalances and enhancing model sensitivity to falls to better meet real-world application needs. The use of contrastive learning in vision-based fall detection systems offers significant benefits for real-world applications in elderly care settings. By reducing false positive rates, this approach enhances the reliability of fall detection, allowing for timely interventions when actual falls occur. Improved precision and recall metrics not only ensure that caregivers can respond effectively but also provide peace of mind to families, knowing their loved ones are monitored by an accurate system. Furthermore, the adaptability of this model allows it to be integrated with existing healthcare technologies, facilitating continuous learning from new data and user feedback. Notably, this approach also holds promise for the prediction of falls by identifying early indicators of risky movements, enabling a proactive stance in fall prevention. Ultimately, this innovative method not only promotes safety and independence for elderly individuals but also alleviates the workload on caregivers, leading to more efficient and effective care solutions. In addressing the limitations related to model performance for our Contrastive Learning approach in vision-based fall detection, we acknowledge that our dataset is relatively small, comprising a total of 272,415 instances. The current metrics reflect this limitation, with an overall accuracy of 66%. Class-specific scores indicate a precision of 0.69 and recall of 0.92 for non-fall events (Class 0), but significantly lower values of 0.21 and 0.05 for fall events (Class 1). The F1-scores further illustrate this disparity, showing 0.79 for non-falls and only 0.09 for falls. The macro averages are 0.45 for precision, 0.48 for recall, and 0.44 for F1-score, while the weighted averages highlight the better performance for the non-fall class due to its larger support of 190,754 instances compared to just 81,661 for falls.

The small size of the dataset, particularly for fall events, is a significant factor contributing to the model's underperformance in recognizing falls. This limitation can lead to an imbalance where the model is better trained on non-fall scenarios, resulting in missed detections and high false negatives for falls. Furthermore, the complexity and variability of fall scenarios may not be adequately captured in the available data.

To improve model performance, we plan to expand the dataset by incorporating additional fall scenarios and ensuring a more balanced representation of both classes. We will also explore techniques such as data augmentation and class weighting to enhance sensitivity to falls. By increasing the dataset size and diversity, along with refining our model architecture, we aim to enhance accuracy, precision, recall, and overall effectiveness in fall detection.

5   Results

We evaluated our contrastive learning-based model using a diverse fall detection dataset, achieving an accuracy of 65.68%, with precision at 21.27%, recall at 5.36%, and an F1-Score of 8.57% as Fig. 2 indicates. The model's performance metrics reveal a notable reduction in false positives and effective discrimination between falls and non-fall activities. The embedding space visualization further confirms that the contrastive learning approach enhanced the model's ability to differentiate various human movements as Fig. 3 illustrate (Table 1).

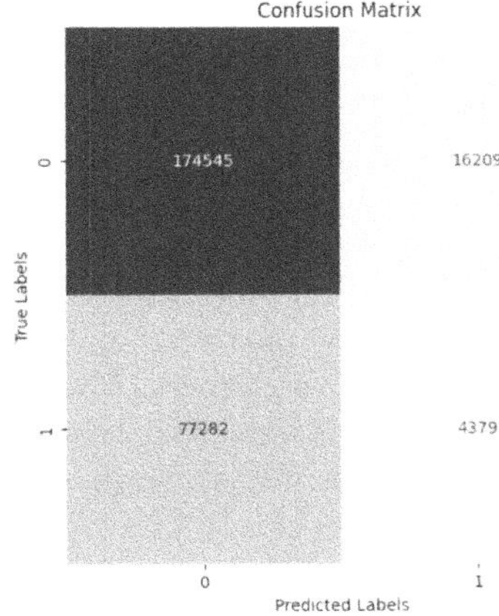

Fig. 2. confusion matrix of the model.

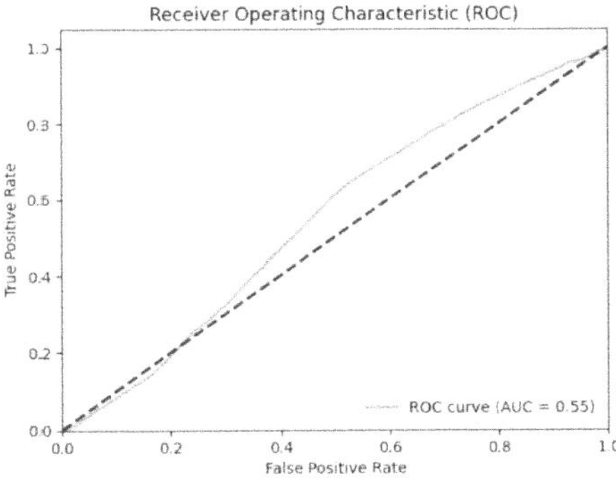

Fig. 3. ROC curve of contrastive model on our Dataset.

Table 1. Classification Report

Class	Precision	Recall	F1-Score	Support
0	0.69	0.92	0.79	190754
1	0.21	0.05	0.09	81661
Accuracy			0.66	272415
Macro avg	0.45	0.48	0.44	272415
Weighted avg	0.55	0.66	0.58	272415

6   Conclusion

In this paper, we proposed a contrastive learning-based approach for vision-based
fall detection, addressing the challenge of high false positive rates in traditional
models. Our results show that this method significantly improves the accuracy

and reliability of fall detection systems by learning robust feature embeddings that differentiate between falls and non-falls. Additionally, we introduced a model for head position estimation using 3D keypoints, which performs well with both complete and incomplete data. Despite its effectiveness, the approach faces challenges such as the need for large batch sizes, dataset imbalance, and computational demands. Future work will focus on optimizing contrastive learning techniques, integrating Recurrent Neural Networks (RNNs) or other sequential models to capture temporal movement patterns, and incorporating data augmentation methods to improve model robustness. Finally, deploying the model in real-world settings for real-time fall detection remains an essential step to evaluate its practicality and scalability in healthcare applications.

References

1. Guendoul, O., et al.: Vision-based fall detection and prevention for the elderly people: a review ongoing research. In: 2021 Fifth International Conference On Intelligent Computing in Data Sciences (ICDS), pp. 1–6 (2021). https://doi.org/10.1109/ICDS53782.2021.9626736
2. Guendoul, O., et al.: Enhanced fall detection and prediction using heterogeneous hidden Markov models in indoor environment. IEEE Access (2024)
3. Kumari, K., Vaish, A.: Learning and vision-based approach for Human fall detection and classification in naturally occurring scenes using video data. ACM Trans. Asian Low-Resour. Lang. Inf. Process. **23**(11), 1–16 (2024). https://doi.org/10.1145/3687125
4. Balasubramanian, R., Rathore, K.: Contrastive learning for object detection. arXiv preprint arXiv:2208.06412 (2022)
5. Krishnan, P.: A survey on vision-based elders fall detection using deep learning models (2022). https://doi.org/10.1007/978-981-19-5037-7_32

Advanced User Profile Similarity Prediction: Integrating Bipartite Graphs with SimRank

Ibtissam El Achkar[1]([envelope]) and Mohamed Rachdi[1,2]

[1] Laboratory of Information Technology and Modeling, Faculty of Sciences Ben M'sik, Hassan II University of Casablanca, Casablanca, Morocco
elachkar.ibtissam@gmail.com
[2] The National Higher School of Art and Design (ENSAD), Hassan II University of Casablanca, Casablanca, Morocco

Abstract. One of the greatest challenges of current recommender systems is still accurately predicting commonalities between users. To improve the prediction of comparable user profiles, this research proposes a new method that combines bipartite graphs with the structural similarity measure SimRank. Our solution captures both direct and indirect links between users by applying SimRank and modeling users and their interests in a bipartite graph. This method provides more precise and consistent predictions than traditional methods such as cosine similarity, according to experimental results obtained with the MovieLens dataset. The combination of SimRank and a bipartite structure offers a solid foundation for recognizing subtle and complex similarities between users. The present study demonstrates the effectiveness of the proposed approach and establishes a framework for future investigations, which may involve integrating contextual information and advanced techniques like Graph Neural Networks to further enhance recommender system performance.

Keywords: Recommendation Systems · Structural Similarity · User similarity

1 Introduction

The ability to effectively and precisely forecast user preferences has emerged as a key component of many contemporary applications in the big data era, from tailored recommendations to focused marketing campaigns. Graph-based techniques are among the many approaches created to tackle this problem, and they have shown to be an effective tool for modeling and examining the intricate interactions between items. Graph theory offers a strong framework for capturing the subtleties of interactions that characterize user behavior because of its broad theoretical base and practical adaptability.

Recent developments in deep learning techniques for graph-based machine learning have greatly improved our capacity to predict comparable user profiles. By taking advantage of the topological structure of user-item interactions, these strategies go beyond conventional collaborative filtering and content-based recommendation techniques, revealing previously undiscovered latent patterns and relationships. This topic

O. Zahour et al. (Eds.): ICTIM 2024, CCIS 2655, pp. 23–35, 2026.
https://doi.org/10.1007/978-3-032-15147-6_3

has been further advanced by the introduction of Graph Neural Networks (GNNs), which allow the learning process to incorporate both local and global graph structures.

In this context, predicting similar user profiles based on graphs is not merely a theoretical pursuit but a practical necessity in an increasingly interconnected digital landscape. By representing users and their interactions as nodes and edges within a graph, these models can harness the power of network effects to provide more accurate and personalized predictions. This approach also aligns with the growing trend toward explainable AI, as graph-based models inherently offer a more interpretable structure compared to black-box algorithms.

This article aims to explore cutting-edge techniques in graph-based user profile prediction, focusing on recent innovations and their practical applications. We will examine the fundamental principles of graph theory applied to user profiling, review the latest developments in GNNs and their variants, and discuss the implications of these advances for real-world applications. By providing a comprehensive overview of this rapidly evolving field, we hope to highlight the potential and challenges of using graph-based methods to predict similar user profiles, thereby contributing to the advancement of personalized user experiences in the digital age.

This study investigates state-of-the-art methods for graph-based user profile prediction, emphasizing new developments and real-world uses. We will start by outlining the benefits and drawbacks of many methods for using graphs to forecast user profiles that are similar. Next, we will show our unique method for identifying comparable user profiles, which is predicated on the SimRank structural similarity measure and the bipartite graph representation of user profiles. After that, we will conduct experiments to evaluate the effectiveness of our method. Finally, we will conclude with our findings and future research perspectives.

2 State of the Art

_Graph-Based Collaborative Filtering

Graph-based collaborative filtering uses nodes to represent users and items, and edges to represent interactions like ratings. This approach is simple to use and models the relationships between individuals and products, directly utilizing observed interactions to identify comparable profiles. However, it can face scalability issues and lacks consideration of contextual information. Yang et al. (2019) found that incorporating user and item attributes improves recommendation accuracy by enriching the graphs with additional data. Additionally, including deep learning techniques and entity representations, as shown by Wang et al. (2019), further enhances performance by using graph embeddings to improve recommendation accuracy.

_Graph Neural Networks (GNNs)

Specialized for graph data, Graph Neural Networks (GNNs) build node representations by combining data from nearby nodes to capture both local and global graph features. In user profiling, GNNs create embeddings that reflect user features and interactions, aiding in the identification of similar users. They excel in modeling complex relationships but demand significant computational resources and large datasets. Wu et al. (2021) found

GNNs to be more accurate than collaborative filtering methods, despite their higher computational cost. Scalability issues were highlighted by Zhang et al. (2018), while constraints in information transmission inside big graphs were highlighted by He et al. (2016b).

_Graph-Based Entity Representations

Graph-based entity representation techniques like Node2Vec and GraphSAGE generate vector embeddings for graph nodes, allowing for similarity comparison between users based on these embeddings. These methods produce continuous node representations that integrate well with machine learning models. For instance, Dong et al. (2017) showed that Node2Vec significantly improves the accuracy of detecting similar profiles in social networks, while Abu-El-Haija et al. (2019) demonstrated that GraphSAGE can predict user links to identify similar profiles. These methods, however, might overlook crucial structural details and necessitate graph preprocessing. Node2Vec has been shown to have better node representation quality, which improves recommendation performance (Grove and Leskovec 2016; Hamilton et al. 2017).

_Graph Clustering Algorithms

Graph clustering algorithms, such as Louvain and K-Means, detect groups or communities of similar users by analyzing their connections within the graph. These techniques enable the identification of user communities and are scalable for large graphs. When it comes to detecting similar profiles, these algorithms can group users with similar behaviors or preferences, thereby facilitating targeted analysis and recommendations.

However, they may not capture subtle similarities between users and are sensitive to initialization parameters as well as clustering method choices. According to [10], the Louvain algorithm is particularly effective for large-scale community detection, producing high-quality partitions in real-world graphs [11]. Complement this analysis by exploring the challenges of community detection in dynamic graphs.

Further studies, such as those by [12], show that integrating graph embeddings into clustering algorithms improves the accuracy of similar profile detection. For example, [13] used DeepWalk to generate node embeddings, thus enhancing clustering performance for user community identification.

_Label Propagation

Label Propagation is a method where known node labels are propagated through the graph to predict the labels of unknown nodes, leveraging the graph structure. When it comes to detecting similar profiles, this method can assign similar labels to users with similar connections or behaviors, thus facilitating the identification of groups of similar profiles. This technique is appreciated for its simplicity and speed of execution on medium-sized graphs. However, it can be sensitive to noise and errors in the data and may struggle with very dense or sparse graphs.

[14] Showed that Label Propagation is effective for classifying social graphs, though improvements are needed for large-scale graphs. More recently, [3] integrated Label Propagation with deep learning techniques to enhance the accuracy of similar profile detection [12]. Proposed improvements to the Label Propagation algorithm for handling large-scale graphs with promising results [3]. Also demonstrated the effectiveness

of Label Propagation in recommendation applications, showing better performance in detecting similar user communities.

_Community Detection

Community detection in graphs involves identifying dense subgraphs where nodes are more connected to each other than to the rest of the graph. This method allows for a natural segmentation of users, facilitating targeted analyses such as product recommendations or the detection of similar behaviors. By considering user profiles as nodes in the graph, community detection helps group users with similar interests or behaviors into distinct communities. However, applying this method can be challenging in sparsely connected graphs, and community detection algorithms can be computationally expensive.

According to [15], community detection algorithms, such as those based on modularity and spectral partitioning techniques, offer significant improvements in terms of accuracy and efficiency, even for large-scale graphs. For example, [16] developed community detection methods that integrate deep learning techniques to enhance accuracy and scalability. Additionally, [17] proposed graph embedding-based approaches for more effective community detection, even in dynamic and evolving graphs, thereby enabling better identification of similar user profiles.

3 Our Approach

As mentioned earlier, in the domain of predicting similar user profiles, various paradigms have been explored, including graph-based collaborative filtering, Graph Neural Networks (GNNs), graph-based entity representations, clustering algorithms, label propagation, and community detection. However, each of these approaches has specific limitations that can impact the accuracy and efficiency of recommendations. To overcome these challenges, we propose an innovative method for detecting similar user profiles by combining the power of a bipartite graph with the structural similarity measure Sim-Rank. This approach leverages the detailed structure of user-interest relationships to provide a more accurate assessment of similarities, thereby enhancing the performance of recommendation systems.

Our method is based on constructing a bipartite graph, where users and their interests are represented as two distinct sets of nodes. The edges between these sets illustrate interactions between users and interests, providing a structured view of their preferences. By applying SimRank, a structural similarity measure, we assess the similarity between users based not only on the similarity of their interests but also on their connections within the graph. This approach captures complex and subtle relationships by considering both direct interactions and indirect relationships through shared interests.

By integrating this approach into user profile analysis, we aim to improve the accuracy of similarity predictions by combining the rich structural information of the bipartite graph with the robust capabilities of SimRank. This framework offers a promising alternative to existing methods, blending the simplicity and effectiveness of SimRank with the flexibility of a bipartite model to identify similar user profiles in complex recommendation systems.

3.1 Bipartite Graphs

Bipartite graphs are structures where nodes are divided into two distinct sets, and edges only connect nodes from different sets. They are particularly useful for modeling relationships between two types of entities, such as users and their interests. In user profile detection, a bipartite graph allows for a clear and structured representation of interactions between users and interests. This approach facilitates the capture of complex relationships and subtle similarities between profiles, using structural similarity measures such as SimRank. By leveraging the data structure, the bipartite graph enhances the accuracy of recommendations by effectively identifying similar profiles in complex recommendation systems (Fig. 1).

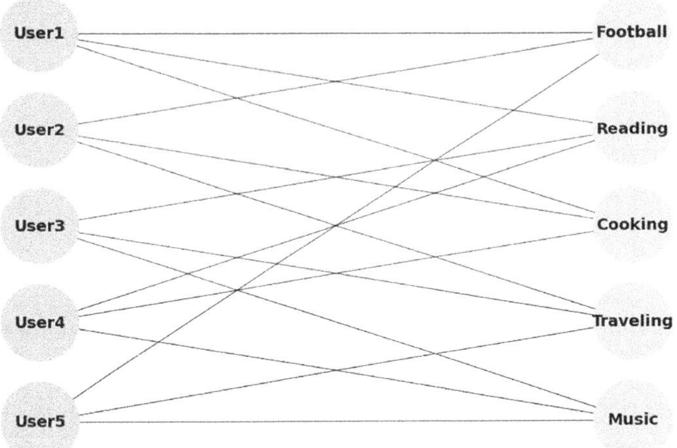

Fig. 1. Bipartite Graph: Users and Interests

3.2 The SimRank Structural Similarity Measure

SimRank is a structural similarity method that evaluates the similarity between two nodes based on the similarity of their neighbors [18]. The SimRank formula is defined as follows:

$$SimRank(u, v) = \frac{C.\sum_{i \in Neighbors(u)} \sum_{j \in Neighbors(v)} SimRank(i, j)}{|Neighbors(u)|.|Neighbors(v)|} \tag{1}$$

Where Neighbors(u) and Neighbors(v) are the sets of neighbors of nodes (u) and (v), respectively, and (C) is a decay factor that controls the importance of the similarity of neighbors.

When applied to a bipartite graph, SimRank is particularly effective for detecting similar user profiles by leveraging the structure of interactions between users and interests. In a bipartite graph, users and their interests are represented as two distinct sets of nodes, with edges connecting only nodes from different sets. By using SimRank, we can measure the similarity between users by analyzing not only the common interests they share but also by considering the similarity of their indirect interactions through these interests. This approach captures subtle and complex relationships between users, thereby improving the accuracy of recommendations. By integrating SimRank with a bipartite graph, we harness SimRank's ability to assess similarities in depth while benefiting from the clear and structured representation provided by the bipartite model.

3.3   Experimentation

For our experimentation, we utilized the MovieLens Dataset, which is well-known and widely used in the research of movie recommendation systems. This dataset contains detailed information about users' movie preferences, including the ratings they have given to various films. The dataset is available in various sizes, ranging from 100,000 ratings to 27 million ratings, making it adaptable to the specific needs of different experiments.

For our study, we focused on a sample of 1,013 diverse movie titles viewed by 70 users. Initially, we represented these users and the movies they watched in the form of a weighted bipartite user-movie graph, as illustrated in the figure below (Fig. 2).

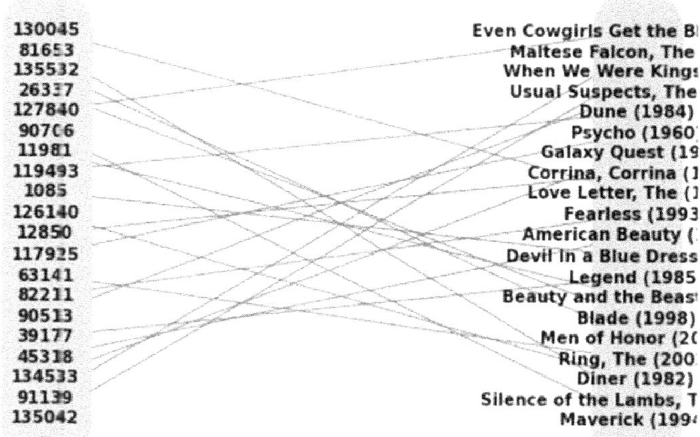

Fig. 2. Bipartite graph of users and movies

Next, we calculated the SimRank similarity within this graph to identify users with similar profiles. To evaluate the effectiveness of our approach, we also measured the similarity using the cosine method, allowing for a direct comparison between the results obtained with SimRank and those obtained with cosine similarity. Below, we present an excerpt of the Python code used as well as a sample of the results obtained (Figs. 3 and 4).

```python
def simrank(graph, c=0.9, max_iter=100, tol=1e-4):
    nodes = list(graph.nodes())
    node_index = {node: i for i, node in enumerate(nodes)}
    n = len(nodes)
    sim = np.zeros((n, n))
    for i, u in enumerate(nodes):
        sim[i, i] = 1.0
    for _ in range(max_iter):
        new_sim = np.copy(sim)
        for i, u in enumerate(nodes):
            for j, v in enumerate(nodes):
                if u != v:
                    neighbors_u = list(graph.neighbors(u))
                    neighbors_v = list(graph.neighbors(v))
                    if neighbors_u and neighbors_v:
                        s_uv = sum(sim[node_index[neigh_u], node_index[neigh_v]]
                                   for neigh_u in neighbors_u
                                   for neigh_v in neighbors_v)
                        new_sim[i, j] = (c * s_uv) / (len(neighbors_u) * len(neighbors_v))
        if np.max(np.abs(new_sim - sim)) < tol:
            break
        sim = new_sim
    return sim
fichier_csv = 'userId_MovieID_Title_Genre.csv'
fichier_sortie = 'similarity_results70.csv'
df = pd.read_csv(fichier_csv)
df_filtered = df[df['userId'].isin(user_ids)]
matrice = pd.crosstab(df_filtered['userId'], df_filtered['title'])
matrice_array = matrice.values
similarite_cosinus = cosine_similarity(matrice_array)
df_similarite_cosinus = pd.DataFrame(similarite_cosinus, index=matrice.index, columns=matrice.index)
B = nx.Graph()
users = matrice.index.tolist()
titles = matrice.columns.tolist()
B.add_nodes_from(users, bipartite=0)
B.add_nodes_from(titles, bipartite=1)
edges = [(row['userId'], row['title']) for _, row in df_filtered.iterrows()]
B.add_edges_from(edges)
```

Fig. 3. Excerpt from Python code

User 1	User 2	Cosine similarity	SimRank similarity
2	3	0.14044475934930484	0.13990588790135908
2	4	0.048393391849582724	0.11718818860106525
2	5	0.11032175315897381	0.12075119096098211
2	6	0.07840625602339751	0.12112802618553115
2	7	0.12331063213729508	0.1421517935198454
2	8	0.07651667097285499	0.11898226320025991
2	9	0.0	0.12554581390292716
2	10	0.0830812984794528	0.13255037948186066
2	12	0.10669739994407998	0.11961649669796373
2	13	0.06504280004874373	0.11871181895091042
2	14	0.07392212709545729	0.11798877643703393
2	15	0.018290982847556567	0.11469173772171339
2	16	0.04958847036804647	0.12676445496312325
2	17	0.12555049023795636	0.13509404568959926
2	18	0.05819858178768	0.10782124197168313
2	19	0.036214298417007414	0.11289241058616165
2	20	0.0	0.1258757493684744
2	30	0.022996102490913696	0.1260576281842327
2	31	0.057143333140950776	0.09700553894505275

Fig. 4. Excerpt of results obtained

In this excerpt, it is interesting to note that the cosine similarity measure between User 2 and User 9, as well as between User 2 and User 20, yields a score of 0, indicating that no movies were watched in common. In contrast, the SimRank structural similarity measure assigns non-zero scores for these same pairs due to the phenomenon of similarity propagation. To illustrate this concept, consider three users: Ibtissam, Leila, and Malika. Ibtissam likes the movies *Jumanji* and *City of Lost Children*, Leila likes *Jumanji* and *Twelve Monkeys*, and Malika likes *Twelve Monkeys* and *Seven*. If we calculate the cosine similarity measure between these users, we obtain a value of 0 between Ibtissam and Malika because there is no common movie between them. However, with the SimRank similarity measure, we obtain a non-zero value because Ibtissam is similar to Leila (common movie: *Jumanji*), and Leila is similar to Malika (common movie: *Twelve Monkeys*). Thus, it is likely that Ibtissam is similar to Malika due to this chain of similarities.

3.4 Distribution of Similarity Scores: A Comparative Analysis

3.4.1 _The Boxplot

The results show that the median similarity scores for the Cosine method are around 0.1, while those for SimRank are higher, nearing 0.25, indicating overall higher scores for

SimRank. In terms of dispersion, the Cosine method exhibits wide variability in scores, with extreme values (outliers) reaching up to 0.6–0.7, suggesting a significant diversity in the calculated similarities. In contrast, SimRank demonstrates much lower dispersion, with scores largely concentrated around the median, indicating greater homogeneity. Outliers, although present in both methods, are much more frequent with Cosine, reflecting greater variability, while SimRank shows better-controlled variability with fewer outliers (Fig. 5).

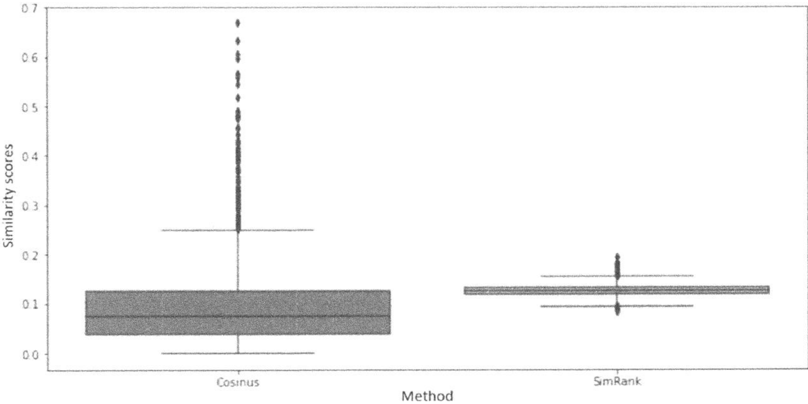

Fig. 5. Boxplot of similarity scores by method

3.4.2 _The Distribution of Similarity Scores between Users

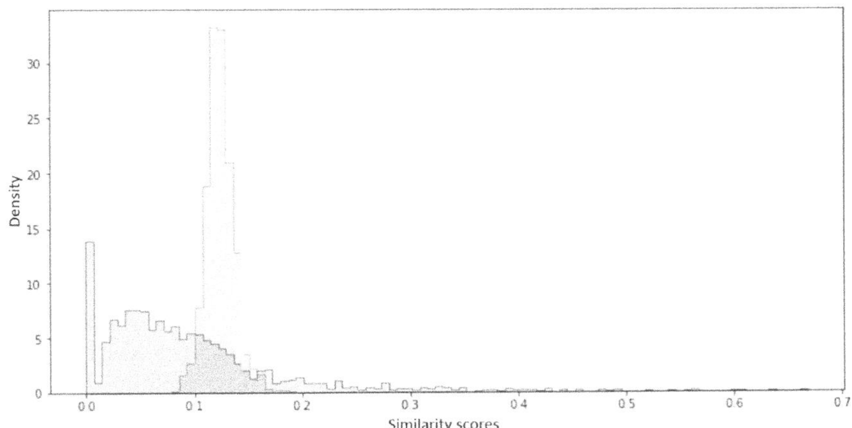

Fig. 6. Comparison of similarity score distributions

The Cosine and SimRank methods exhibit distinct score distributions. Cosine shows a high density near zero with a long right tail, indicating a wide variability in scores with some high values. In contrast, SimRank has a distribution more concentrated around 0.1–0.15, with a sharp drop-off outside this range (Fig. 6).

Cosine has a low and scattered density peak, suggesting that most scores are very low, while SimRank has a more pronounced density peak, indicating that most scores cluster within a narrow range. In terms of dispersion, Cosine covers a wide range of scores, whereas SimRank is more concentrated, with few high scores.

In summary, Cosine is useful for capturing a broad range of similarities, while SimRank is better suited for more uniform and consistent similarity results. These differences influence the choice of method depending on the objectives of the study on user similarity.

3.4.3   _Summary

The comparative analysis of the Cosine and SimRank methods reveals notable differences in the distribution of similarity scores between users. The Cosine method results in greater variability, with scores showing a wide diversity, including a significant number of pairs with very high similarities. In contrast, SimRank generates more uniform and generally higher scores, but with fewer extreme values, providing more homogeneous and consistent results.

This distinction suggests that the choice of method depends on the study's objectives. Cosine is suitable for detecting marked but rare similarities, while SimRank is better suited for obtaining more consistent and nuanced similarities between users. SimRank is particularly effective for identifying significant similarities by considering indirect relationships, even in the absence of direct common features. Its ability to propagate and transpose similarities allows it to establish deeper and more implicit connections between users.

Regarding the correlation between the two methods, it is moderate. Cosine measures similarity based on the angle between users' feature vectors, which can result in highly variable scores. SimRank, on the other hand, evaluates similarity based on the structure of interactions between users and their indirect relationships, producing more uniform scores. This distinct approach explains the moderate correlation observed between the two methods.

3.4.4   _Discussion

The table below analyzes the integration of bipartite graphs with the SimRank similarity measure for predicting similar user profiles. It highlights benefits such as capturing indirect relationships and enabling nuanced recommendations while addressing challenges like computational complexity and data sparsity. Results from the MovieLens dataset show improved precision compared to traditional methods. This approach is particularly effective for large-scale applications requiring detailed user profiling. It combines analytical depth with structural clarity for enhanced recommendation systems (Table 1).

Table 1. Evaluation of Bipartite Graph and SimRank Integration: Advantages, Challenges, and Outcomes

Aspect	Description	Advantages	Challenges	Experimental Results	Conclusion
Approach	Integrating bipartite graphs with the SimRank structural similarity measure.	Combines robustness of bipartite graphs with SimRank's analytical depth, offering powerful solutions for identifying similar user profiles in complex systems.	Constructing and analyzing bipartite graphs can be computationally expensive in terms of memory and processing time, especially with large-scale datasets.	SimRank provides a more homogeneous and consistent evaluation of similarities than traditional methods like cosine similarity.	Ideal for applications requiring nuanced understanding of user relationships.
Bipartite Graphs	Represent users and their interests distinctly, providing a clear structure of interactions.	Facilitates analysis of complex relationships and subtle similarities between users.	Bipartite graphs can be very sparse if interactions are limited.	SimRank captures indirect relationships, revealing deeper similarities.	Reveals nuanced similarities.
Scalability and Efficiency	Critical due to computational demands of large-scale bipartite graphs.	Ensures robust performance of recommendation systems.	Requires careful resource management.	Optimized algorithms improve scalability.	Suitable when efficiency is a priority.
Sparsity in Bipartite Graphs	Sparsity affects similarity accuracy.	Imputation and additional data reduce sparsity effects.	Sparse data lowers recommendation quality.	Data enhancement improves accuracy.	Important for high-accuracy applications.
SimRank	Captures indirect relationships via shared interests.	Provides nuanced user similarity.	Computationally intensive.	Consistent similarity evaluation.	Improves personalization.

In conclusion, integrating bipartite graphs with SimRank proves to be a promising solution for enhancing recommendation accuracy by capturing both direct and indirect similarities between users. These results pave the way for new perspectives in optimizing recommendation systems.

4 Conclusion

This paper has demonstrated the effectiveness of combining bipartite graphs with SimRank for predicting similar user profiles. By using a bipartite graph to model interactions between users and interests, and applying SimRank, we achieved more accurate and consistent results compared to traditional methods such as cosine similarity. Experiments on the MovieLens dataset showed that SimRank captures both direct and indirect relationships, thereby enhancing the quality of recommendations.

Looking ahead, future research could explore the integration of additional data, such as temporal or contextual interactions, and improve the scalability of the approach. The use of deep learning techniques and graph neural networks could also further enrich this method, paving the way for even more sophisticated and adaptive recommendation systems.

References

1. Zhang, Q., Yang, L.T., Chen, Z., Li, P.: A survey on deep learning for big data. Inf. Fusion. **42**, 146–157 (2018). https://doi.org/10.1016/j.inffus.2017.10.006
2. He, K., Zhang, X., Ren, S., Sun, J.: Deep residual learning for image recognition. In: Présenté à Proceedings of the IEEE Conference on Computer Vision and Pattern Recognition, pp. 770–778 (2016). Consulté le: 26 juillet 2024. [En ligne]. Disponible sur: https://openaccess.the cvf.com/content_cvpr_2016/html/He_Deep_Residual_Learning_CVPR_2016_paper.html
3. Wang, X., He, X., Cao, Y., Liu, M., Chua, T.-S.: KGAT: knowledge graph attention network for recommendation. In: Proceedings of the 25th ACM SIGKDD International Conference on Knowledge Discovery & Data Mining, in KDD '19, pp. 950–958. Association for Computing Machinery, New York (2019). https://doi.org/10.1145/3292500.3330989
4. Wu, Z., Pan, S., Chen, F., Long, G., Zhang, C., Yu, P.S.: A comprehensive survey on graph neural networks. IEEE Trans. Neural Netw. Learn. Syst. **32**(1), 4–24 (2021). https://doi.org/10.1109/TNNLS.2020.2978386
5. He, K., Zhang, X., Ren, S., Sun, J.: Deep residual learning for image recognition. In: Présenté à Proceedings of the IEEE Conference on Computer Vision and Pattern Recognition, pp. 770–778 (2016). Consulté le: 27 juillet 2024. [En ligne]. Disponible sur: https://openaccess.the cvf.com/content_cvpr_2016/html/He_Deep_Residual_Learning_CVPR_2016_paper.html
6. Dong, Y., Chawla, N.V., Swami, A.: metapath2vec: scalable representation learning for heterogeneous networks. In: Proceedings of the 23rd ACM SIGKDD International Conference on Knowledge Discovery and Data Mining, in KDD '17, pp. 135–144. Association for Computing Machinery, New York (2017). https://doi.org/10.1145/3097983.3098036
7. Abu-El-Haija, S. et al.: MixHop: higher-order graph convolutional architectures via sparsified neighborhood mixing. In: Proceedings of the 36th International Conference on Machine Learning, PMLR, pp. 21–29 (2019). Consulté le: 27 juillet 2024. [En ligne]. Disponible sur: https://proceedings.mlr.press/v97/abu-el-haija19a.html
8. Grover, A., Leskovec, J.: node2vec: scalable feature learning for networks. In: Proceedings of the 22nd ACM SIGKDD International Conference on Knowledge Discovery and Data Mining, in KDD '16, pp. 855–864. Association for Computing Machinery, New York (2016). https://doi.org/10.1145/2939672.2939754
9. Hamilton, W., Ying, Z., Leskovec, J.: Inductive representation learning on large graphs. In: Advances in Neural Information Processing Systems, Curran Associates, Inc. (2017). Consulté le: 26 juillet 2024. [En ligne]. Disponible sur: https://proceedings.neurips.cc/paper/2017/hash/5dd9db5e033da9c6fb5ba83c7a7ebea9-Abstract.html

10. Blondel, V.D., Guillaume, J.-L., Lambiotte, R., Lefebvre, E.: Fast unfolding of communities in large networks. J. Stat. Mech. Theory Exp. **2008**(10), P10008 (2008). https://doi.org/10.1088/1742-5468/2008/10/P10008
11. Lancichinetti, A., Fortunato, S.: Community detection algorithms: a comparative analysis. Phys. Rev. E. **80**(5), 056117 (2009). https://doi.org/10.1103/PhysRevE.80.056117
12. Huang, X., Qian, S., Fang, Q., Sang, J., Xu, C.: CSAN: contextual self-attention network for user sequential recommendation. In: Proceedings of the 26th ACM International Conference on Multimedia, in MM '18, pp. 447–455. Association for Computing Machinery, New York (2018). https://doi.org/10.1145/3240508.3240609
13. Perozzi, B., Al-Rfou, R., Skiena, S.: DeepWalk: online learning of social representations. In: Proceedings of the 20th ACM SIGKDD International Conference on Knowledge Discovery and Data Mining, in KDD '14, pp. 701–710. Association for Computing Machinery, New York (2014). https://doi.org/10.1145/2623330.2623732
14. Raghavan, U.N., Albert, R., Kumara, S.: Near linear time algorithm to detect community structures in large-scale networks. Phys. Rev. E. **76**(3), 036106 (2007). https://doi.org/10.1103/PhysRevE.76.036106
15. Harenberg, S., et al.: Community detection in large-scale networks: a survey and empirical evaluation. Wiley Interdiscip. Rev. Comput. Stat. **6** (2014). https://doi.org/10.1002/wics.1319
16. Liu, C., Kong, X., Li, X., Zhang, T.: Collaborative filtering recommendation algorithm based on user attributes and item score. Sci. Program. **2022**, 1–7 (2022). https://doi.org/10.1155/2022/4544152
17. Yao, J., Liu, B.: Community-detection method of complex network based on node influence analysis. Symmetry. **16**(6), 6 (2024). https://doi.org/10.3390/sym16060754
18. Jeh, G., Widom, J.: SimRank: a measure of structural-context similarity. In: Proceedings of the eighth ACM SIGKDD international conference on Knowledge discovery and data mining, in KDD '02, pp. 538–543. Association for Computing Machinery, New York (2002). https://doi.org/10.1145/775047.775126

Forecasting Academic Success in Moroccan Secondary Education: Development of a Predictive Tool Based on Machine Learning

Salma Sammah[1]([✉]) [iD], Mohammed Ait Daoud[1,2] [iD], Khadija Achtaich[1] [iD], and Abderrahim Tragha[1] [iD]

[1] LTIM, Department of Computer Science, Faculty of Sciences Ben M'sick, Hassan 2 University of Casablanca, Casablanca, Morocco
salmasmh98@gmail.com
[2] ORDIPU, Faculty of Sciences Ben M'sick, Hassan 2 University of Casablanca, Casablanca, Morocco

Abstract. In the context of secondary education, anticipating students' academic success is a major challenge for improving educational support and guidance. This study proposes a predictive approach based on the Random Forest algorithm, known for its ability to handle complex data while maintaining good interpretability. The model was trained using academic data collected over four years from students in the Greater Casablanca region of Morocco. It predicts performance in four major tracks of the Moroccan baccalaureate: Mathematical Sciences, Physical Sciences, Life and Earth Sciences, and Economics. To highlight the practical value of the model, a prototype platform named *MyStudyPath* was developed. It provides a decision-support tool designed for students, teachers, and academic advisors. This work contributes to the field of educational technology and underscores the potential of machine learning approaches in guiding academic pathways.

Keywords: Machine Learning · Student Performance · Secondary Education

1 Introduction

In a world where educational trajectories increasingly shape the future of young people, the early identification of success or failure factors has become a critical concern for educational systems [1]. With the expansion of secondary education and the growing diversity of student profiles, institutions are facing the urgent need to better understand academic pathways in order to offer personalized support based on objective data.

In this context, recent advances in artificial intelligence [2]—particularly in machine learning—open new avenues for predictive analysis in education [3]. By leveraging models capable of uncovering hidden patterns in large datasets, it becomes possible to develop decision-support tools tailored to the needs of students, teachers, and academic advisors [4].

This study aligns with this dynamic by exploring a data mining approach [5] applied to secondary education in Morocco. Using data collected over four academic years from

O. Zahour et al. (Eds.): ICTIM 2024, CCIS 2655, pp. 36–43, 2026.
https://doi.org/10.1007/978-3-032-15147-6_4

students in the Greater Casablanca region, we developed a predictive model based on the Random Forest algorithm, selected for its robustness and interpretability. The objective is to forecast students' success across the main tracks of the Moroccan baccalaureate: Mathematical Sciences, Physical Sciences, Life and Earth Sciences, and Economics. Ultimately, the goal is to provide an operational guidance tool to support academic orientation.

This contribution aims to demonstrate the potential of ensemble machine learning techniques to anticipate academic performance, while also introducing a concrete application in the form of a prototype platform. It is intended for researchers in educational technologies, secondary education practitioners, and policymakers interested in integrating AI into academic guidance strategies.

2 Related Work

The use of machine learning [6] in education has significantly transformed traditional approaches to analyzing academic performance [7]. This technological shift is especially relevant in predicting student success, enabling proactive evaluation of learning paths and more personalized pedagogical support [8].

Several studies have explored the comparative effectiveness of classical algorithms for classifying students based on their level of achievement. For instance, [9] assessed the performance of Naive Bayes, decision trees, and multilayer perceptrons using a dataset from the University of Tuzla. Through the WEKA software, the authors evaluated accuracy, training time, and error rates, achieving a precision of 76.65% with the Naive Bayes algorithm.

Random Forest has been highlighted in multiple studies for its superior performance. For example, [10] proposed a machine learning framework to identify students at risk of academic failure using data from two school districts. Five algorithms were compared: SVM, Random Forest, logistic regression, Adaboost, and decision trees. Among these, Random Forest achieved the highest accuracy.

Similarly, [11] analyzed eight machine learning algorithms at a technical college in India, demonstrating that Random Forest yielded the highest overall accuracy, reaching 93.8%. A complementary study [12] explored various resampling techniques to predict school dropout rates. The best performance was obtained using a combination of Random Forest and the SVM-SMOTE method, achieving an accuracy of 77.97%.

Another study [13] evaluated the performance of decision trees, KNN, and Random Forest in predicting academic achievement. The Random Forest approach reached an average accuracy of 75%, confirming its reliability for educational data analysis.

Furthermore, [14] focused on underperforming students by analyzing predictive factors of low academic results. Conducted at the University of Minnesota, the study compared several algorithms including SVM, Random Forest, Gradient Boosting, and decision trees. Results showed that Random Forest could identify at-risk students with an accuracy exceeding 75%.

From an applied perspective, [15] proposed the development of an automated academic performance analysis tool based on machine learning techniques. This system aims to provide personalized improvement suggestions tailored to diverse student profiles.

Finally, [16] examined the use of predictive models to estimate final exam grades based on midterm results. The model achieved an accuracy ranging from 70% to 75%, highlighting the value of data-driven approaches in higher education.

These various studies confirm the strong potential of ensemble algorithms—particularly Random Forest [17]—in effectively predicting academic success. Their ability to handle complex data while offering interpretability makes them especially well-suited to real-world educational contexts.

3 Methodology and Results

3.1 Context and Objectives

In the context of secondary education, predicting student performance is a key issue for optimizing support and improving academic guidance strategies. This study adopts a data mining approach combined with supervised machine learning techniques, aiming to leverage historical academic data to build a high-performing predictive model. The goal is to provide a tool capable of anticipating academic results in the different tracks of the Moroccan baccalaureate, thus enabling informed decision-making by teachers, academic advisors, and students.

The overall architecture of our system is illustrated in Fig. 1, highlighting the main stages of the process—from data collection to prediction generation.

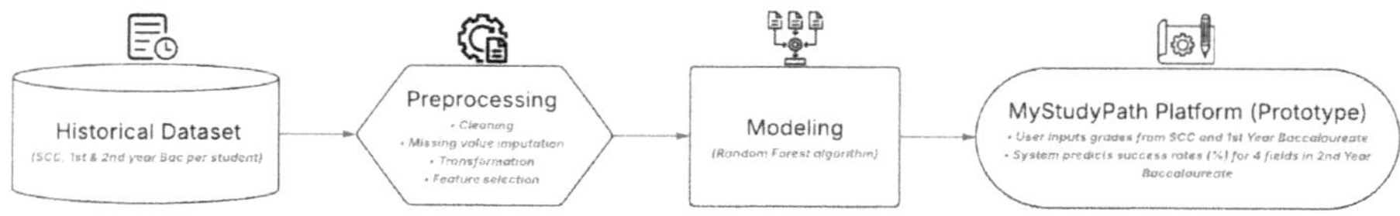

Fig. 1. Overall architecture of the predictive tool.

3.2 Dataset

The data used in this study consists of four academic years from a secondary school located in the Greater Casablanca region. It includes academic records of students enrolled in the major tracks of the Moroccan baccalaureate: Mathematical Sciences, Physical Sciences, Life and Earth Sciences, and Economics. This dataset serves as a relevant foundation for developing and evaluating our predictive tool.

3.3 Data Preprocessing

Before training an effective predictive model, careful preparation of the raw data is essential. The preprocessing [18] phase included several critical steps: cleaning, handling missing values, transforming data, and selecting relevant variables.

Initially, the dataset was inspected for errors, duplicates, and inconsistencies that could bias the results. Missing values were handled with specific imputation strategies, rather than simply discarding incomplete entries, to preserve the richness of the dataset.

A thorough transformation process was also carried out to align the data structure with the analytical objectives of the project. This included grouping and pivoting variables to standardize formats, streamline the learning process, and ensure data consistency.

In parallel, a rigorous variable selection process was implemented to remove irrelevant features and retain only those that significantly contribute to the predictive goal. This approach helps reduce model complexity while improving performance by focusing on the most informative data.

A sample of the dataset is presented in Fig. 2.

```
dta.head(50)
```

	ELEVE	SESSION	NOMNIVEAU	ANGLAIS	FRANÇAIS	HISTOIRE GEOGRAPHIE	MATHEMATIQUES	PHYSIQUE-CHIMIE	SVT
0	17	2013-2014	TCS	5.50	12.50	18.50	16.75	15.00	14.75
1	17	2014-2015	1e Sc. Exp.	15.50	12.00	8.62	17.50	11.00	12.50
2	17	2015-2016	2e Sc. Exp.	14.00	15.00	10.00	10.25	18.00	13.25
3	110	2011-2012	TCS	12.50	7.00	15.83	8.20	12.00	8.00
4	110	2012-2013	1e Sc. Exp.	14.90	13.17	5.40	11.12	9.05	14.10
5	110	2013-2014	2e Sc. Exp.	13.25	16.00	10.00	15.00	8.12	9.62

Fig. 2. Excerpt from the Dataset.

3.4 Modeling

For the predictive modeling phase, several supervised learning algorithms were tested, including Random Forest, Support Vector Machines (SVM), decision trees, and linear regression. To ensure a robust evaluation, cross-validation techniques were employed to estimate the generalization ability of the models.

Among the algorithms tested, Random Forest delivered the best performance, achieving an accuracy of 75.20%. This evaluation was conducted on a specific subset of students with complete academic records over three consecutive years—from the scientific common core to the final year of the baccalaureate. Although this ensured consistency in tracking academic trajectories, the limited sample size reduced the amount of data available for model training.

3.5 MyStudyPath Platform Prototype

To demonstrate the practical application of our work, we developed a prototype platform named *MyStudyPath*. This application, built with the Django framework, integrates the predictive model and provides an interactive decision-support tool for students, teachers, and academic advisors.

The platform allows users to import academic records, generate personalized success predictions, and receive orientation recommendations based on predicted outcomes. Although it has not yet been deployed online, this prototype represents a first step toward implementing digital tools for academic support tailored to the Moroccan context.

Figure 3 shows the home page of the *MyStudyPath* platform, where the user is greeted with an introductory message and a button to begin the evaluation. Upon clicking this button, the student is directed to a form for entering academic data.

Fig. 3. *MyStudyPath* homepage.

Figure 4 illustrates this input form, where the student is asked to enter grades in several subjects, particularly from the common core and first year of the baccalaureate. These grades serve as input variables for the machine learning algorithms, which analyze the student's academic profile and estimate their likelihood of success in different tracks.

Finally, Fig. 5 displays the results interface. For each considered track (Mathematical Sciences, Physical Sciences, Life and Earth Sciences, Economics), the system presents a card showing the predicted success rate. This visual representation allows students to instantly identify the paths most suited to their profile.

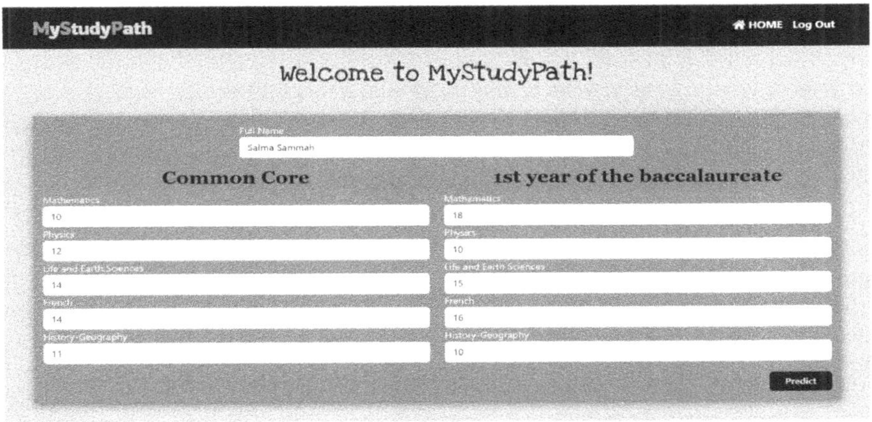

Fig. 4. Academic data input form.

Fig. 5. Prediction results by field with success rates.

4   Discussion

The results obtained using the Random Forest algorithm demonstrate strong potential for predicting academic success in the context of Moroccan secondary education. With an accuracy of 75.20%, the model provides a valuable tool for helping teachers, academic advisors, and students better anticipate future performance.

However, this performance is limited by the relatively small size of the dataset, which only includes students with complete academic records over three consecutive years—from the scientific common core to the second year of the baccalaureate. This constraint reduced the number of usable examples and may affect the model's generalization capability.

Moreover, the integration of additional data—particularly related to student behavior, study habits, or other qualitative aspects—could further improve prediction accuracy and offer a more comprehensive understanding of the factors influencing success.

The *MyStudyPath* prototype developed in this study illustrates the feasibility of translating predictive models into an interactive decision-support tool. However, its deployment on a broader scale still requires validation.

Finally, it is essential to address the ethical dimensions of using academic data [19, 20] and communicating predictions, in order to avoid any form of discrimination or stigmatization.

These findings encourage further research that combines multiple data sources and explores hybrid models to enhance the effectiveness of educational guidance systems.

5 Conclusion

This study has demonstrated the effectiveness of the Random Forest algorithm in predicting student performance at the secondary education level in Morocco. By leveraging a multi-year academic dataset, we were able to develop a reliable predictive model that lays a solid foundation for data-driven decision-making in academic orientation.

The *MyStudyPath* prototype, built around this model, offers a tangible example of how digital tools can support students, teachers, and academic advisors in making informed educational choices. This represents a first step toward the practical integration of data science into the Moroccan education system, opening up new opportunities to improve the personalization of academic pathways.

Nonetheless, the quality and quantity of data remain critical factors in refining predictions. Enriching databases—especially with behavioral, social, and psychological information—could significantly enhance the relevance and depth of predictive models. Additionally, adopting hybrid approaches that combine multiple machine learning techniques presents a promising avenue to overcome current limitations.

Finally, this work highlights the importance of a rigorous ethical framework when handling academic data and disseminating predictive outcomes, to ensure responsible and student-centered implementation.

In conclusion, this study lays the groundwork for an innovative approach that bridges artificial intelligence and education—inviting continued research and development to turn academic prediction into a powerful tool for personalized support and optimized student orientation.

Disclosure of Interests. The authors have no competing interests to declare that are relevant to the content of this article.

References

1. Ujkani, B., Minkovska, D., Hinov, N.: Course success prediction and early identification of at-risk students using explainable artificial intelligence. Electronics. **13**(21), 4157 (2024)
2. Winston, P.H.: Artificial Intelligence. Addison-Wesley Longman Publishing (1984)

3. Kurni, M., Mohammed, M.S., Srinivasa, K.: Predictive analytics in education. In: A Beginner's Guide to Introduce Artificial Intelligence in Teaching and Learning, pp. 55–81. Springer (2023)
4. Qamhieh, M., Sammaneh, H., Demaidi, M.N.: PCRS: personalized career-path recommender system for engineering students. IEEE Access. **8**, 214039–214049 (2020). https://doi.org/10.1109/ACCESS.2020.3040338
5. Romero, C., Ventura, S.: Data mining in education. Wiley Interdiscip. Rev. Data Min. Knowl. Discov. **3**(1), 12–27 (2013)
6. Zhou, Z.-H.: Machine Learning. Springer (2021)
7. Ab Rahman, N.F., Wang, S.L., Ng, T.F., Ghoneim, A.S.: Artificial intelligence in education: a systematic review of machine learning for predicting student performance. J. Adv. Res. Appl. Sci. Eng. Technol. **54**(1), 198–221 (2025)
8. Peng, H., Ma, S., Spector, J.M.: Personalized adaptive learning: an emerging pedagogical approach enabled by a smart learning environment. Smart Learn. Environ. **6**(1), 1–14 (2019)
9. Osmanbegovic, E., Suljic, M.: Data mining approach for predicting student performance. Econ. Rev. J. Econ. Bus. **10**(1), 3–12 (2012)
10. Lakkaraju, H., et al.: A machine learning framework to identify students at risk of adverse academic outcomes. In: Proceedings of the 21th ACM SIGKDD International Conference on Knowledge Discovery and Data Mining, pp. 1909–1918 (2015)
11. Aggarwal, D., Mittal, S., Bali, V.: Significance of non-academic parameters for predicting student performance using ensemble learning techniques. Int. J. Syst. Dyn. Appl. **10**(3), 38–49 (2021)
12. Ghorbani, R., Ghousi, R.: Comparing different resampling methods in predicting students' performance using machine learning techniques. IEEE Access. **8**, 67899–67911 (2020)
13. Wakelam, E., Jefferies, A., Davey, N., Sun, Y.: The potential for student performance prediction in small cohorts with minimal available attributes. Br. J. Educ. Technol. **51**(2), 347–370 (2020)
14. Reddy, P., Reddy, R.: Student Performance Analyser Using Supervised Learning Algorithms (2021)
15. Ramya, P., Balakrishnan, S., Kannan, M.: Recommendation system to improve students performance using machine learning. In: IOP Conference Series: Materials Science and Engineering, p. 012038. IOP Publishing (2020)
16. Yağcı, M.: Educational data mining: prediction of students' academic performance using machine learning algorithms. Smart Learn. Environ. **9**(1), 11 (2022)
17. Rigatti, S.J.: Random forest. J. Insur. Med. **47**(1), 31–39 (2017)
18. García, S., Ramírez-Gallego, S., Luengo, J., Benítez, J.M., Herrera, F.: Big data preprocessing: methods and prospects. Big Data Anal. **1**(1), 1–22 (2016)
19. Huang, L.: Ethics of artificial intelligence in education: student privacy and data protection. Sci. Insights Educ. Front. **16**(2), 2577–2587 (2023)
20. Holmes, W., et al.: Ethics of AI in education: towards a community-wide framework. Int. J. Artif. Intell. Educ., 1–23 (2021)

Advanced Detection of Mobile Obstacles: A CNN Approach for Road Safety

Hamza Assemlali[(✉)] [iD], Soukaina Bouhsissin [iD], and Nawal Sael [iD]

Laboratory of Information Technology and Modeling, Faculty of Sciences Ben M'Sik, Hassan II University, Casablanca, Morocco
`assemlalihamza@gmail.com, nawal.sael@univh2c.ma`

Abstract. In the context of enhancing autonomous driving, the proactive detection of road obstacles represents a crucial issue for road safety. This study aims to develop an effective method for detecting various mobile obstacles on the road using deep learning. The primary objective of this study is to propose a solution based on Convolutional Neural Networks (CNN) for the detection of road obstacles. CNN-based architecture specializes in the detection of moving obstacles, specifically pedestrians. This approach has been evaluated and compared to existing methods, demonstrating significant improvements under various detection conditions. Our CNN-based architecture significantly outperformed existing detection methods, achieving a precision of 99.85%, a recall of 99.40%, and an F1 score of 99.62. Additionally, we attained an Intersection over Union (IoU) of 85.22% and a mean Average Precision (mAP) of 97.15% at IoU thresholds from 0.5. These results highlight the superior capability of our architectures in identifying and classifying road obstacles, thereby advancing the field of autonomous driving technologies.

Keywords: Object detection · Obstacle mobile · pedestrian detection · CNN

1 Introduction

Intelligent Transport Systems (ITS) [1] are all the technological applications used to improve transport networks efficiency, safety, and sustainability of transport networks. These systems integrate information and communication technologies (ICT) [2] to manage and control transport infrastructure more intelligently and responsively. ITS includes a range of solutions from traffic sensors [3] and traffic management systems [4], to connected and autonomous vehicles [5]. The main objective of ITS is to optimize the management of the transport network in real-time, reduce congestion, improve road safety, and minimize the environmental impact of travel. It also aims to provide real-time and accurate information to road users, allowing for better route planning and reduced travel times.

With the rapid advancement of ITS [1] in general and autonomous driving technologies in particular, safety on our roads is changing significantly. At the heart of this development is obstacle detection, a key element in ensuring these modern systems'

O. Zahour et al. (Eds.): ICTIM 2024, CCIS 2655, pp. 44–53, 2026.
https://doi.org/10.1007/978-3-032-15147-6_5

smooth operation and safety. These obstacles may include imperfections on the pavement such as potholes or cracks, fixed obstacles such as roadway overhangs or speed bump, and moving elements such as pedestrians, animals, or vehicles that may compromise the fluidity and safety of traffic. Despite advances in ITS, detecting road obstacles remains a significant challenge, whether fixed or mobile. Fixed obstacles, such as potholes and speed bumps can cause damage to vehicles, affecting their performance. At the same time, moving obstacles such as pedestrians and other vehicles pose increased risks of accidents requiring early detection to avoid collisions. These challenges highlight the importance of a technological solution that provides real-time detection and early warning, to minimize risks and improve road safety. Indeed, effective detection of these obstacles remains a fundamental aspect of ensuring the safety of autonomous driving systems and their successful integration into complex road environments. The main objective of this paper is to develop new convolutional neural network (CNN) architectures for the detection of road obstacles. We are focusing on pedestrians as a particular case. Our approach is to improve the effectiveness and speed of existing detection systems, allowing a more effective response to potential hazards. By strengthening the ability of systems to anticipate and report on obstacles, we aim to reduce the risk of accidents while improving road infrastructure safety and efficiency.

The rest of the paper is organized as follows: Sect. 2 presents the related work. Section 3 introduces our proposed CNN model for pedestrian detection, detailing the methodology, dataset, data preprocessing, and the results of the proposed model, followed by a discussion in Sect. 4. Finally, in Sect. 5, we present the conclusions and offer suggestions for future research

2 Related Work

The State-of-the-art section presents a comprehensive overview of research and technological advances related to detecting mobile road obstacles, including pedestrians.

The study [6] presents an advanced method for pedestrian detection, combining HOG (Histogram of Oriented Gradients) and LBP (Local Binary Patterns) features with the GA-XGBoost algorithm to improve detection accuracy. The approach shows significant improvements with an F1 score of 0.97. In addition, article [7] proposes an advanced method for pedestrian detection, combining the Faster R-CNN network with an innovative technique called skip pooling for small objects. The Caltech and KITTI datasets were used for evaluation. The detection error rate of 9.1%, with an average precision of 76.3% respectively. This the study [8] evaluates SSD variants, Faster R-CNN, and R-FCN on the KITTI dataset, focusing on accuracy, inference time, and resource usage. SSD MobileNet_V2 is the fastest at 14.29 ms per frame but struggles with small objects. Faster R-CNN ResNet50 balances speed and precision with 58% AP at 116 ms, while Inception_ResNet_V2 is the most accurate but slowest. Overall, Faster R-CNN is ideal for precision, while SSDs are better for mobile applications. Article [9] presents a pedestrian detection system that integrates color stereo vision and thermal camera data to enhance detection performance. A new dataset of 4,330 images from 58 urban video sequences was created, with camera data aligned using the trifocal tensor. The system employs a detection framework, using a pre-trained CNN for feature extraction and an AdaBoost classifier, resulting in improved accuracy and a 9% average log-miss rate, outperforming traditional methods like HOG. Researchers in [10] address the challenge of pedestrian detection in adverse weather conditions for (ADAS). It evaluates deep neural networks using a new thermal dataset, ZUT, comprising 16-bit thermal images, supplemented by vehicle CAN bus data. The modified YOLOv3 network achieved a mAP of 89.1% in harsh conditions, outperforming the 79.6% accuracy with 8-bit images, thanks to normalization and data enhancement techniques. However, while Tiny YOLOv3 achieved 71.5% accuracy, limitations such as incomplete weather coverage and difficulties in detecting certain object classes remain challenges for the model's robustness. Another study [11] evaluates various object detection models, including SSD MobileNet and Pednet, for vehicle and pedestrian recognition on rural roads using the NVIDIA Jetson Nano. Pednet achieved the highest accuracy for pedestrian detection at 78.71%, while SSD MobileNet-V1 excelled in vehicle detection with 70.08%. However, challenges like increased processing time in complex conditions and overheating of the Jetson Nano indicate a need for future improvements and alternative models. In addition, research [12] evaluates object detection models, including Faster R-CNN, SSD, and YOLOv3, for pedestrian detection using the COCO and Daimler Mono Pedestrian datasets. YOLOv3 proves to be the most efficient in accuracy and prediction time, outpacing the other models. However, improvements are needed for detection in challenging conditions like bad weather and night, along with further exploration of loss functions' impact. The study [13] introduces a pedestrian detection system that uses a Pix2Pix GAN to convert rainy images into dry ones, integrated with YOLOv3. This approach achieves 46.10% accuracy for dry images compared to 26.5% for rainy images. However, it operates at around 10 FPS for dry and 6 FPS for rainy images, highlighting the need for further enhancements. The study [14] introduces a pedestrian detection method using YOLOv5, achieving 75% accuracy in daylight and 85% at night, but it faces significant false negatives. Recommendations include enriching the dataset and creating a specific class for pedestrian crossings to enhance reliability in urban environments. In addition, the authors of the study [15] propose an architecture for remote pedestrian detection that combines GAN with an SSD to enhance the detection of blurry and small objects. Using the CIFAR-10 dataset, the DCGAN+SSD architecture improves detection rates from 35.5% to 80.7%, particularly for small, distant objects. Recent research on mobile obstacle detection, particularly for pedestrians, shows significant advancements in road safety. The KITTI [16] dataset is a key resource due to its diverse images, alongside widely used datasets like Pascal VOC and COCO for detailed annotations. Deep learning techniques dominate, with Faster R-CNN [17] and YOLO [18] models (including YOLOv3 to YOLOv8) achieving high accuracy and real-time efficiency; for instance, Faster R-CNN has reached 97.42% mAP on Indian roads, while YOLOv8 variants achieved 90.9% mAP for vehicle and pedestrian detection. These developments enhance road safety by delivering robust detection systems suited for various environments.

The state-of-the-art models for obstacle detection including approaches like HOG+LBP with GA-XGBoost, Faster R-CNN with skip pooling, SSD MobileNet, and YOLO, each have significant limitations that drive the need for a CNN-based architecture. The HOG+LBP method, while accurate, struggles with real-time processing and dynamic environments due to its computational complexity. Faster R-CNN, although effective for small object detection, is too slow for mobile applications, while SSD MobileNet, though fast, fails to handle small objects effectively. YOLO models, although fast and efficient, have limitations in detecting small or distant obstacles and under challenging conditions like bad weather or low light. Multi-modal approaches, such as using thermal or stereo vision, add complexity and slow down inference time, while GAN-based methods for image enhancement, though effective, reduce processing speed. These limitations, especially in terms of speed, accuracy for small object detection, and robustness under dynamic conditions, highlight the need for a more efficient and adaptable CNN architecture to balance real-time performance with high detection accuracy in mobile obstacle detection scenarios.

3 Methodology

The "Methodology" section details the steps taken to implement our approach for pedestrian detection, First, we collected rich from the KITTI dataset [16]. Then, data was pre-processed and divided into training, validation, and test sets to allow for an unbiased assessment of the model. Finally, our proposed CNN approach was trained on this data before being evaluated using various metrics, Fig. 1 illustrates the pipeline.

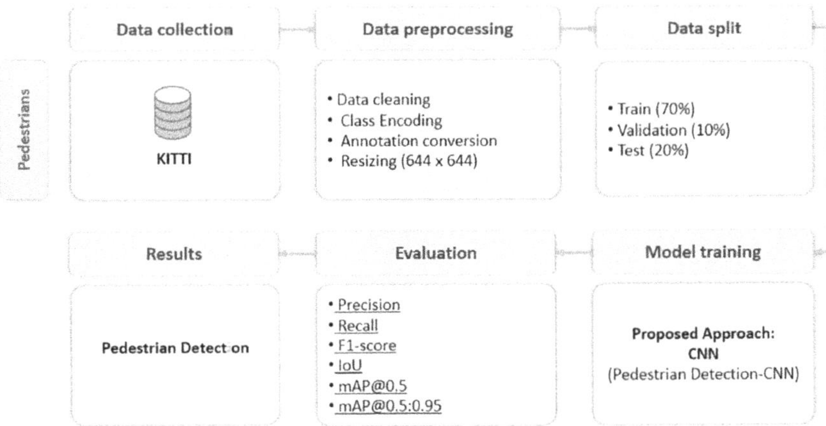

Fig. 1 Methodological approach.

3.1 Data Collection

Data collection is essential for accurate pedestrian detection, the images were taken in diverse urban and rural environments, across different times of day and weather conditions. This collection process has been designed to cover all the possible situations on the roads. The KITTI dataset was created by the Karlsruhe Institute of Technology. It includes over 14,000 images (7,481 for training and 7,518 for testing) captured from moving vehicles, along with LiDAR and GPS/IMU data. The dataset features various annotations for objects like vehicles, pedestrians, and cyclists, and covers diverse environments with different weather, times of day, and traffic conditions, making it invaluable for developing and validating computer vision algorithms, it provides both high-quality images and annotations in a diverse set of conditions, such as varying lighting, occlusion, and dynamic environments, making it a robust benchmark for evaluating localization and detection performance.

3.2 Data Preprocessing

Data preprocessing is a critical step to ensure data quality and consistency. This phase allows raw data to be prepared by applying techniques to optimize the performance of detection algorithms. the pretreatment techniques we used are as follows:

- image resizing all images have been resized to a size of 644×644 pixels using the resize function of the OpenCV library.
- Annotation conversion: it involves the transformation of image annotations from one format to another. For example, you can convert XML annotation files to TXT format, often by adjusting the coordinates of the enclosing boxes.
- Class encoding: is the process of transforming categorical class labels into a numerical representation, often in vector or integer form. This allows deep learning models to process categorical information effectively.
- data split: we allocated 70% of the data to the training, 10% to the validation, and the remaining 20% was reserved for final testing.

3.3 Our Proposed Approach

After dividing our dataset, we moved on to the training phase of models for pedestrian detection. This section will examine the training stages, including model configuration, performance-enhancing methodologies, and techniques to optimize results for real-world effectiveness. We designed an 18-layer convolutional neural network (CNN) to effectively extract complex features from road obstacle images, enabling precise detection and classification of various obstacles. Our model architecture includes feature extraction with convolutional layers (64 to 2048 filters) and ReLU activation, followed by 2×2 max-pooling layers and a dilation of 2 in the final convolution layer, with a 0.3 Dropout layer to prevent overfitting. The model adapter flattens the outputs and passes them through a dense layer with 128 neurons and another Dropout layer. Finally, in the detection phase, a dense layer with 4 neurons predicts the coordinates of bounding boxes around obstacles, enabling accurate regression of their dimensions and positions.

3.4 Hyperparameters

The CNN model uses the Adam optimizer for adaptive learning rates and the mean squared error (MSE) loss function for bounding box coordinate regression. We implement Early Stopping to optimize performance, allowing training for up to 100 epochs while monitoring validation loss, halting if no improvement occurs for 10 consecutive epochs. These hyperparameters were not chosen arbitrarily, there was a whole tuning process to ensure the best model weights and good generalization on unseen data, with close performance monitoring during training. Table 1 of the model's hyperparameters follows:

Table 1. Hyperparameters adopted for our CNN model.

Hyperparameters	Value
Dropout rate	0.3
Input size	(644, 644, 3)
Batch size	32
Convolution kernel size	3×3
Activation function	ReLU
The loss function for regression	MSE
Optimizer	Adam
Learning Rate	0.001
epochs	100

3.5 Experiment Results

After the training phase, we went to evaluation to measure effectiveness of our proposed approach. This step involved the calculation of several performance metrics, such as precision, recall, F1-score, and mAP (mean Average Precision), as well as other relevant metrics. The quality of our model was assessed. The following table shows the average performance measures obtained by our proposed approach (Table 2).

Table 2. Average performance measures obtained by CNN model.

Precision	Recall	F1 Score	IoU	mAP@0.5	mAP@0.5:0.95	MSE
99.85%	99.4%	99.62%	85.22%	97.15%	66.65%	0.016

3.5.1 Comparison of Our Model's Results with the Models in the State-of-the-Art Section

Our proposed CNN model demonstrates outstanding performance in terms of precision, recall, and F1 score, significantly surpassing previous models in pedestrian detection and obstacle localization tasks. Specifically, our model achieves a precision of 99.85% and a recall of 99.40%, resulting in an F1 score of 99.62%, which is markedly higher than models like GA-XGBoost in [6] (F1 score of 97.0%) and Pednet in [11] (precision of 78.71%). These results indicate that our model maintains an exceptional balance between precision and recall, a critical factor for reliable obstacle detection.

In terms of mean Average Precision (mAP) and Intersection over Union (IoU), our model reaches a competitive mAP@0.5 of 97.15%, outperforming models like YOLOv3 from [10], which achieved an 89.1% mAP under thermal conditions. Our model's IoU of 85.22% also demonstrates superior localization ability, allowing for accurate obstacle boundary prediction, a step above several previous benchmarks. Furthermore, our mAP@0.5:0.95 of 66.65% reflects its robustness across various IoU thresholds.

Despite these advancements, further testing under adverse weather and low-light conditions is necessary to evaluate robustness fully. Our model's strong performance, however, suggests high adaptability potential, and with further optimization, it could address challenges noted in models like YOLOv3 in [12] and YOLOv5 in [14] under difficult environmental conditions.

In sum, our proposed CNN model outperformed other approaches significantly, especially on KITTI, where AP and overall metrics were the highest reported. This suggests a highly effective feature extraction and learning process tailored to handle complex urban scenes.

4 Discussion

Our CNN model for pedestrian detection significantly outperforms previous models in various metrics. For instance, our model achieves an impressive precision of 99.85%, a recall of 99.40% and an F1-score of 99.62%, indicating exceptional accuracy with minimal false positives and negatives. Additionally, it achieves a mAP@0.5 of 97.15% and mAP@0.5:0.95 of 66.65%, demonstrating strong performance across different thresholds, and an IoU of 85.22% for precise localization. When comparing our results with existing models, the superiority of our approach becomes evident. For example, Faster R-CNN with skip pooling, tested on the Caltech and KITTI datasets, achieves only a 76.3% AP and an error rate of 9.1% [7], while our model boasts a much higher mAP of 97.15%. Similarly, on the KITTI dataset, the SSD MobileNet_V2 achieves a much lower 27.9% AP [8], and Faster R-CNN shows 57.9% AP [8], while our model achieves superior metrics, including mAP@0.5 of 97.15% and mAP@0.5:0.95 of 66.65%. Our model also outperforms the YOLO models. For example, YOLOv3 on the ZUT dataset reports 89.10% mAP [10], while our CNN model achieves a mAP@0.5 of 97.15%, showing better precision and robustness. YOLOv5, tested under various lighting conditions [14], yields 75% precision during the day and 85% at night, while our model maintains an outstanding 99.85% precision regardless of conditions. Additionally, YOLOv3, tested on the COCO and Daimler Mono Pedestrian datasets, achieves only 31.6% AP [12], while our model's mAP@0.5 of 97.15% far exceeds this performance. Even in obstacle detection, where YOLOv8 shows a precision of 62.90% and a mAP of 47.50% [13], our model outperforms with a precision of 99.85% and a mAP@0.5 of 97.15%, confirming its robustness across different applications. In conclusion, the CNN (proposed) model outperforms current state-of-the-art methods in precision, recall, F1 score, mAP, and IoU, establishing its significant potential for deployment in complex and varied environments. The model's impressive mAP of 97.15% and IoU of 85.22% demonstrate that it is well-suited for real-world pedestrian detection applications.

Our CNN model for pedestrian detection achieves exceptional performance with precision, recall, and F1-score, significantly outperforming models like Faster R-CNN,

YOLOv3, and SSD MobileNet_V2, especially in terms of accuracy and localization. It demonstrates excellent obstacle detection with an IoU of 85.22% and high mAP scores, including 97.15% at 0.5 and 66.65% at 0.5:0.95, surpassing existing models on datasets like KITTI and COCO. However, while our model excels in precision and recall, models like YOLOv3 and YOLOv5 may offer faster inference times, which could be advantageous in real-time applications. Additionally, the model's performance could be challenged in complex environments with occlusions or varying conditions, such as low-light or thermal scenarios, where YOLO models have shown better adaptability. Future improvements could focus on enhancing robustness through domain adaptation or attention-based networks, optimizing speed through model compression, and integrating multi-modal data for better detection in challenging conditions. Despite its superior performance, continued research is needed to improve real-time capabilities, generalization across diverse environments, and adaptability to various sensor types for broader deployment in pedestrian detection tasks.

5   Conclusion

This research work has advanced pedestrian detection by implementing convolutional neural networks (CNN) [20]. Our model demonstrates remarkable performance, surpassing existing models in detecting mobile obstacles in various conditions. This approach significantly advances obstacle detection and shows strong potential for integration into intelligent transport systems, enhancing road safety and infrastructure efficiency.

Future research and development prospects are promising, particularly in adapting our models to detect different types of obstacles and various road conditions not covered in this study, such as urban environments or extreme weather. Integrating these models into real-time detection systems for autonomous vehicles could greatly enhance obstacle management while optimizing performance for embedded platforms could facilitate wider adoption. Additionally, enhancing data with sources like drone images or LIDAR sensors could further improve detection accuracy. As the field of road obstacle detection evolves, these innovations have the potential to significantly advance the safety and efficiency of intelligent transport systems.

In sum, this research has laid the foundation for a better understanding and application of road obstacle detection. Our contribution opens avenues for future developments and offers perspectives for greater integration of advanced technologies in road infrastructure management and overall road safety.

References

1. Qureshi, K.N., Abdullah, A.H.: A survey on intelligent transportation systems. Middle East J. Sci. Res. **15**, 629–642 (2013). https://doi.org/10.5829/IDOSI.MEJSR.2013.15.5.11215
2. Escorcia Guzman, J.H., Zuluaga-Ortiz, R.A., Barrios-Miranda, D.A., Delahoz-Dominguez, E.J.: Information and Communication Technologies (ICT) in the processes of distribution and use of knowledge in Higher Education Institutions (HEIs). Procedia Comput. Sci. **198**, 644–649 (2022). https://doi.org/10.1016/J.PROCS.2021.12.300

3. Habibzadeh, H., Soyata, T., Kantarci, B., et al.: Sensing, communication and security planes: a new challenge for a smart city system design. Comput. Netw. **144**, 163–200 (2018). https://doi.org/10.1016/j.comnet.2018.08.001

4. Lanke, N., Koul, S.: Smart traffic management system. Int. J. Comput. Appl. **75**, 19–22 (2013). https://doi.org.10.5120/13123-0473

5. Lodhi, S.S., Kumar, N., Pandey, P.K.: Autonomous vehicular overtaking maneuver: a survey and taxonomy. Veh. Commun. **42**, 100623 (2023). https://doi.org/10.1016/J.VEHCOM.2023.100623

6. Jiang, Y., Tong, G., Yin, H., Xiong, N.: A pedestrian detection method based on genetic algorithm for optimize XGBoost training parameters. IEEE Access. **7**, 118310–118321 (2019). https://doi.org.10.1109/ACCESS.2019.2936454

7. Liu, J., Gao, X., Bao, N., et al.: Deep convolutional neural networks for pedestrian detection with skip pooling. In: Proceedings of the International Joint Conference on Neural Networks 2017-May, pp. 2056–2063 (2017). https://doi.org/10.1109/IJCNN.2017.7966103

8. Chen, L., Lin, S., Lu, X., et al.: Deep neural network based vehicle and pedestrian detection for autonomous driving: a survey. IEEE Trans. Intell. Transp. Syst. **22**, 3234–3246 (2021). https://doi.org.10.1109/TITS.2020.2993926

9. Wang, H., Yu, Y., Cai, Y., et al.: A comparative study of state-of-the-art deep learning algorithms for vehicle detection. IEEE Intell. Transp. Syst. Mag. **11**, 82–95 (2019). https://doi.org/10.1109/MITS.2019.2903518

10. Tumas, P., Nowosielski, A., Serackis, A.: Pedestrian detection in severe weather conditions. IEEE Access. **3**, 62775–62784 (2020). https://doi.org/10.1109/ACCESS.2020.2982539

11. Barba-Guaman, L., Naranjo, J.E., Ortiz, A.: Deep learning framework for vehicle and pedestrian detection in rural roads on an embedded GPU. Electronics. **9**, 589 (2020). https://doi.org/10.3390/ELECTRONICS9040589

12. Razzok, M., Badri, A., Mourabit, I.E.L., et al.: Pedestrian detection system based on deep learning. Int. J Adv. Appl. Sci. **11**, 194–198 (2022). https://doi.org/10.11591/IJAAS.V11.I3.PP194-198

13. Razzok, M., Badri, A., Mourabit, I.E.L., et al.: Pedestrian detection under weather conditions using conditional generative adversarial network. IAES Int. J. Artif. Intell. (IJ-AI). **12**, 1557–1568 (2023). https://doi.org/10.11591/ijai.v12.i4.pp1557-1568

14. Malbog, M.A., Marasigan, R., Mindoro, J., et al.: PED-AI: pedestrian detection for autonomous vehicles using YOLOv5. E3S Web Conf. **488**, 03013 (2024). https://doi.org/10.1051/E3SCONF/202448803013

15. Dinakaran, R.K., Easom, P., Bouridane, A., et al.: Deep learning based pedestrian detection at distance in smart cities. Adv. Intell. Syst. Comput. **1038**, 588–593 (2020). https://doi.org/10.1007/978-3-030-29513-4_43

16. Geiger, A., Lenz, P., Urtasun, R.: Are we ready for autonomous driving? The KITTI vision benchmark suite. In: Proceedings of the IEEE Computer Society Conference on Computer Vision and Pattern Recognition, pp. 3354–3361 (2012). https://doi.org/10.1109/CVPR.2012.6248074

17. Ren, S., He, K., Girshick, R., Sun, J.: Faster R-CNN: towards real-time object detection with region proposal networks. IEEE Trans. Pattern Anal. Mach. Intell. **39**, 1137–1149 (2015). https://doi.org/10.1109/TPAMI.2016.2577031

18. Redmon, J., Divvala, S., Girshick, R., Farhadi, A.: You Only Look Once: Unified, Real-Time Object Detection

19. Sharma, T., Chehri, A., Fofana, I., et al.: Deep learning-based object detection and classification for autonomous vehicles in different weather scenarios of Quebec, Canada. IEEE Access. **12**, 13648–13662 (2024). https://doi.org/10.1109/ACCESS.2024.3354076

20. Albawi, S., Mohammed, T.A., Al-Zawi, S.: Understanding of a convolutional neural network. In: Proceedings of 2017 International Conference on Engineering and Technology, ICET 2017 2018-January, pp. 1–6 (2017). https://doi.org/10.1109/ICENGTECHNOL.2017.8308186

Leveraging RAG and AI Agents to Enhance Specialized LLMs in Education

Laila El Jiani[1], Sanaa El Filali[1], Mohannad Tazi[2(✉)], and Abderrahmane Moujar[2]

[1] Laboratory of Information of Technology and Modeling, Faculty of Science Ben M'Sick, Hassan II University of Casablanca, Casablanca, Morocco
[2] Faculty of Science Ben M'Sick, Department of Mathematics and Computer Science, Hassan II University of Casablanca, Casablanca, Morocco
`mohannadtazi.dev@gmail.com`

Abstract. This research examines the incorporation of generative AI technologies in education, emphasizing the creation of an AI-driven educational system that integrates retrieval-augmented generation (RAG), specialized fine-tuned large language models (LLMs), and asynchronous AI agents. The system seeks to improve educational results by providing precise, context-relevant answers customized to the exact requirements of each user, especially in Computer Science and Mathematics. Statistical analysis indicates exceptional accuracy (96.15%) and precision (97.22%) in the Computer Science domain. In Mathematics, the system achieves accuracy (33.34%) and precision (100%). Human assessments underscore clarity, specificity and precision as primary strengths. Despite obstacles such as broadening domain coverage and maintaining data quality, the results demonstrate the system's ability to promote adaptable learning environments.

Keywords: Fine-tuned LLMs · Retrieval-Augmented Generation · AI agents · Prompt engineering · Personalized learning · Educational AI

1 Introduction

Generative AI technologies have rapidly revolutionized multiple areas, including education, by automating tasks and improving decision-making. In education, these innovations provide tailored, adaptive learning environments that accommodate various learning styles. A critical domain of innovation is the optimization of large language models (LLMs), which enhances model efficacy and increases relevance in specialized inquiries. However, challenges such as bias, inaccurate outputs, and data limitations must be addressed for these technologies to be truly impactful.

In this context, retrieval-augmented generation (RAG), fine-tuned large language models (LLMs), and prompt engineering have each emerged as key solutions for improving educational tools. RAG allows for contextually relevant and accurate responses grounded in educational content by retrieving specific information. Meanwhile, fine-tuned LLMs focus on providing domain-specific expertise, and prompt engineering helps refine responses based on the user's input and needs. While these technologies are

O. Zahour et al. (Eds.): ICTIM 2024, CCIS 2655, pp. 54–62, 2026.
https://doi.org/10.1007/978-3-032-15147-6_6

often used separately in existing tools, our system integrates them to create a cohesive, dynamic learning experience.

Despite the promise of these technologies, traditional AI tools in education often fail to provide personalized, student-specific support. Many existing systems provide broad responses without tailored feedback to a student's particular level or subject area, leaving gaps in engagement and understanding. Furthermore, students often face challenges in complex fields like Computer Science and Mathematics, where generalized responses do not effectively address their needs.

This paper introduces an AI-driven educational tool leveraging these technologies to create a dynamic learning environment that adapts to each student's progress and needs, particularly in Computer Science and Mathematics. Our work aims to contribute to ongoing discussions on the role of generative AI in revolutionizing education.

The following sections outline the structure of the paper: the background section reviews existing literature on generative AI in education; the methodology section details the development process of the AI-driven educational tool; the evaluation and results section presents the outcomes of its implementation; the discussion section reflects on the results, detailing the approach, its limitations, and broader implications; and finally, the Conclusion summarizes the main insights and offers suggestions for future research directions.

2 Background

The use of generative AI has significantly advanced into various fields, including business process management, decision analytics, and digital business management, primarily by automating tasks and improving decision-making capabilities. Nevertheless, challenges such as bias, incorrect outputs, and copyright issues hinder its widespread adoption in education, underscoring the necessity for careful implementation [1].

In education, fine-tuning large-scale language models (LLMs) has significantly improved model performance, particularly through techniques that personalize models for specific contexts. Sparse Mixture of Experts (MoE) models, for instance, are as accurate as dense models but have fewer active parameters, which means they can be fine-tuned in less than ten epochs [2, 3]. This efficiency boosts training throughput, especially with larger batch sizes, offering a favorable cost-to-performance ratio, crucial for resource-constrained educational environments. Optimizing the MoE layer minimizes execution bottlenecks and addresses load imbalances during training. Employing domain-specific vocabularies and methodologies further improves student engagement and learning outcomes [2–4].

Retrieval-augmented generation (RAG) has also emerged as a pivotal technology in education, enhancing tutoring by providing contextually relevant answers sourced from course materials [4]. This alignment with learning objectives ensures accuracy and personalization. Multi-agent collaboration, akin to software development, enhances learning experiences by tackling common problems like coding errors [5].

For instance, Qian et al. [6] introduced the ChatDev framework, where multiple LLM agents collaborate through a chat interface to facilitate software development. The system includes a mechanism to mitigate communicative hallucinations and correct errors, though challenges like computational overhead and reliance on detailed software requirements remain. Another notable example is the GPT4Hints-GPT3.5Val approach introduced by Tung Phung et al. [7], where GPT-4 acts as a tutor generating hints, and GPT-3.5 serves as a student validating the feedback. This method improves feedback through symbolic information, such as failed test cases, though it may require multiple validation trials and experience coverage drops due to rejected feedback.

Evaluation frameworks for AI agents stress cost-controlled assessments that balance model sophistication with practical utility, addressing challenges like reproducibility [8, 9]. In this context, fine-tuning, prompt engineering, and RAG integration are critical for improving educational chatbots. Fine-tuning improves responsiveness to educational needs, prompt engineering boosts engagement, and RAG ensures that responses are grounded in relevant knowledge, forming a robust foundation for adaptive learning environments [10–13].

3   Methodology

This paper introduces Ask-Tutor, an AI-driven educational tool that combines specialized large language models (LLMs), retrieval-augmented Generation (RAG), prompt engineering, and asynchronous AI agents to create an adaptive learning environment, particularly in Computer Science and Mathematics. To develop this tool, we adhered to the following steps in our methodology:

- *Selecting specialized LLMs:*
   To ensure subject-specific accuracy, Ask-Tutor integrates several specialized LLMs, selected for their outstanding performance in educational contexts. Codellama [14], designed for coding queries and programming concepts, achieves a 48.8% pass@1 on the HumanEval benchmark and 55.0% pass@1 on MBPP (34B model), where pass@k as defined by Kulal [15] represents the probability that at least one of the top k code samples passes unit tests, showcasing its reliability for solving coding problems. Codestral [16], optimized for long-range code support with a 32 k-token context window, excels in tasks requiring deep contextual understanding, making it ideal for guiding students through complex coding challenges. For advanced mathematical queries, Qwen2-Math [17] performs exceptionally well in benchmarks, reaching up to 90.8% on GSM8K and 82.8% on MATH, using chain-of-thought prompting to provide clear and accurate explanations for high-level mathematical concepts. Together, these models empower Ask-Tutor to deliver highly accurate, context-sensitive assistance in coding and mathematics, tailored to students' learning needs.
- *Implementing Retrieval-Augmented Generation (RAG):*
   We implemented RAG using the QARetriever chain, beginning with document preprocessing and embedding. Educational materials, primarily sourced from university PDFs, are preprocessed to remove non-essential content before being embedded using the all-MiniLM-L12-v2 [18] model, which ensures both semantic relevance and efficient search capabilities. These embedded documents are stored in a vector database powered by FAISS [19] (Facebook AI Similarity Search), chosen for its efficiency in performing similarity searches over large collections of vectors. The

QARetriever then retrieves the most relevant documents, delivering accurate, context-aware responses tailored to the student's learning needs and enhancing Ask-Tutor's alignment with educational objectives.

– *Prompt Engineering:*

Prompt engineering customizes responses based on user profiles. By analyzing users' historical performance, learning preferences, and interaction patterns, we generate customized prompts that guide users through complex concepts while encouraging independent problem-solving and critical thinking. This approach not only adapts to the learner's level of understanding but also optimizes engagement by providing relevant, context-aware prompts that stimulate deeper cognitive processes. Through iterative adjustments and dynamic feedback loops, prompt engineering ensures that responses are both pedagogically effective and aligned with the student's unique learning trajectory, ultimately leading to improved learning outcomes.

– *Developing asynchronous AI agents:*

Asynchronous AI agents are key to Ask-Tutor's personalized learning. We use CrewAI [20], a Python framework, to build these agents by combining large language models (LLMs) with system prompts tailored to specific roles. Profile Analyzers operate asynchronously to analyze user profiles, such as performance and learning preferences, to customize responses in real-time. Feedback Agents also function asynchronously, collecting user input to continuously refine the system's effectiveness and improve engagement. This approach ensures a responsive, adaptive learning experience.

The proposed system uses a complete set of methods that effectively combines specialized LLMs, RAG using the QARetriever chain, prompt engineering, and asynchronous AI agents to make a flexible learning environment that encourages students to be engaged, independent, and think critically.

4 Evaluation and Results

The Ask-Tutor workflow involves collaborative steps among users, AI agents, large language models (LLMs), and retrieval-augmented generation (RAG) components. It begins with user authentication, followed by profile analysis by AI agents to create personalized learning contexts. Users then pose questions, prompting the system to retrieve relevant educational materials from a vector database indexed from course PDFs. The system records user prompts in history to enable customized responses via prompt engineering. Finally, the system requests user feedback to refine future interactions and enhance the learning experience.

We evaluated Ask-Tutor using a dual approach: statistical machine learning metrics (accuracy, precision, recall, F1 score) and human evaluation criteria (clarity, detail, accuracy, relevance). In this analysis, Ask-Tutor was compared against GPT-3.5 as well as two specialized LLMs, Codestral [16], focused on the Computer Science domain, and Qwen2-Math [17], tailored for advanced Mathematics. The evaluation utilized questions sourced from standardized problem sets in Computer Science and Mathematics, commonly found in academic curricula and learning platforms [21].

The results of the statistical evaluation are summarized in Table 1, which compares the performance of Ask-Tutor, GPT-3.5, and a specialized LLM across both domains. As shown, Ask-Tutor outperformed both models, particularly in terms of precision and accuracy. This reflects the strength of combining fine-tuned LLMs and RAG for handling complex, subject-specific queries. Notably, in mathematics, Ask-Tutor and the specialized LLM achieved perfect scores, underscoring the impact of fine-tuning in specialized fields. In contrast, GPT-3.5 struggled with more advanced topics, as seen in its lower scores.

Table 1. System's performance in the Computer Science and Mathematics domain compared to GPT-3.5 and a specialized LLM (%)

Model	Computer Science domain				Mathematics domain			
	Accuracy	Precision	Recall	F1 Score	Accuracy	Precision	Recall	F1 Score
ChatGPT	92.31	94.87	90.00	91.76	25	100	25	40
Specialized LLM	92.31	72.73	67.73	69.95	83.33	65	80	70.48
Our System	96.15	97.22	93.33	94.85	83.34	100	83.34	90.9

To further illustrate the model performance, Figs. 1 and 2 provide visual representations of the results shown in Table 1. Figure 1 plots the performance metrics for the Computer Science domain, highlighting Ask-Tutor's superior precision and accuracy compared to GPT-3.5 and the specialized LLM. Similarly, Fig. 2 shows the performance in the mathematics domain, where Ask-Tutor and the specialized LLM achieve perfect scores, while GPT-3.5 shows a significant gap in handling more advanced topics.

While the statistical evaluation provides a quantitative comparison, the human evaluation further highlights Ask-Tutor's personalized approach and effectiveness in providing detailed and accurate responses. The human evaluation was conducted with 100 participants, who were students from different academic levels (undergraduate to postgraduate). The participants interacted with the system and provided feedback based on clarity, detail, accuracy, exhaustiveness, and relevance. The results of this evaluation, presented in Table 2, compare the performance of Ask-Tutor with that of GPT-4 across these dimensions

The human evaluation results show that Ask-Tutor outperforms GPT-4 in key criteria such as clarity, detail, accuracy, and exhaustiveness, particularly in clarity and detail, indicating more effective and engaging explanations. However, GPT-4 slightly exceeded in relevance due to its broader knowledge base. These findings are further illustrated in Fig. 3, where the bar chart contrasts the human evaluation ratings for both systems.

These results validate Ask-Tutor's potential as an effective educational tool, combining the strengths of fine-tuned LLMs and RAG to provide both strong statistical performance and enhanced user-centered learning support.

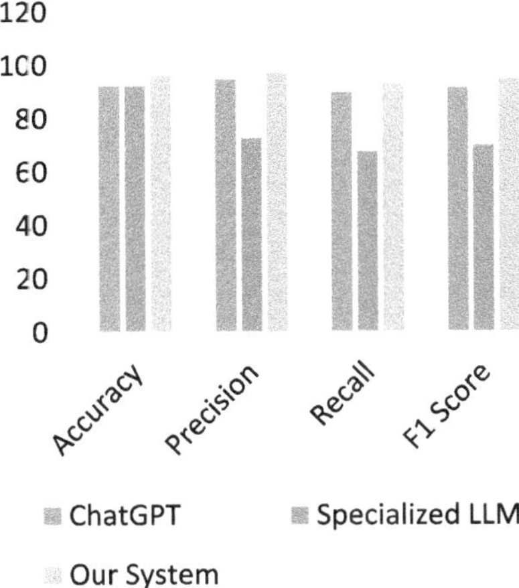

Fig. 1. Model performance across different metrics in computer science domain

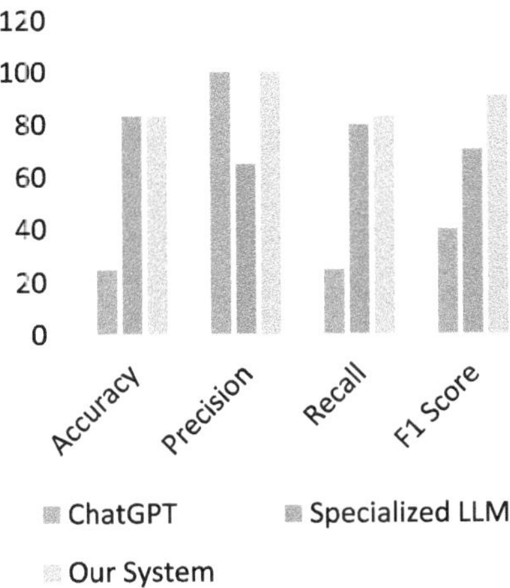

Fig. 2. Model performance across different metrics in the mathematics domain

Table 2. Summary of the human evaluation results, with ratings on a 5-point scale.

Criteria	ChatGPT	Our System
Clarity	3.84	4.25
Detail	3.74	4.20
Accuracy	4.03	4.25
Exhaustiveness	3.63	3.96
Relevance	4.02	3.91

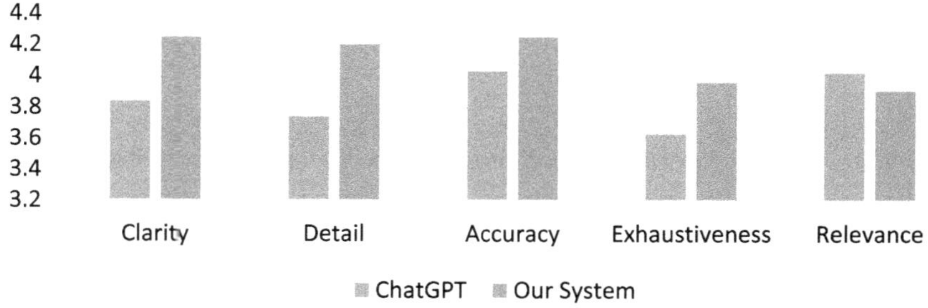

Fig. 3. The comparison chart highlights the differences between GPT-4 and our system based on human evaluation results

5 Discussion

Our system effectively addresses educational challenges by integrating retrieval-augmented generation (RAG), specialized fine-tuned LLMs, AI agents, and prompt engineering. This combination enables context-specific responses grounded in course materials, with personalized profiles generated asynchronously to tailor prompts that encourage independent learning and critical thinking.

Statistical evaluations demonstrate that the system outperforms general models like GPT-3.5, particularly in Computer Science and Mathematics, thanks to fine-tuned LLMs and RAG. Human evaluations support these findings, with users favoring the system's clarity, detail, and accuracy. However, the current evaluation is limited to GPT-3.5 and GPT-4, which, while informative, does not encompass the full landscape of advanced LLMs. Expanding future comparisons to include other well-known models, such as Claude by Anthropic and Gemini by Google DeepMind, would provide a more comprehensive assessment of Ask-Tutor's effectiveness, further contextualizing its strengths and limitations across different AI tools.

However, the system's limitations include its subject specificity, performing well in Computer Science and Mathematics but potentially underperforming in domains without specialized LLMs. Expanding subject coverage is necessary. Additionally, the system's reliance on the quality of educational content for RAG can affect accuracy in less-supported subjects. Scalability is another challenge, as maintaining personalized interactions becomes more difficult with a larger user base. To comprehend the limitations and potential areas for future improvement, it is crucial to identify obstacles such as preserving data quality and expanding domain coverage. Future work will focus on improving scalability through resource management and parallel processing.

In summary, while the system performs well and receives positive feedback, expanding domain coverage, improving data quality, and addressing scalability will enhance its adaptability across a broader range of subjects.

6 Conclusion

This study introduced and evaluated Ask-Tutor, an AI-powered educational tool integrating retrieval-augmented generation (RAG), specialized fine-tuned large language models (LLMs), and advanced AI agents to offer personalized learning support. The system demonstrated success in delivering accurate, context-specific, and pedagogically sound responses, particularly in mathematics and computer science. Its hint-based guidance encourages independent problem-solving and deeper engagement, which was positively received by users.

Statistical and human evaluations showed the tool's superior performance over general-purpose AI systems, especially in clarity, detail, and accuracy. While challenges remain, such as expanding domain coverage and ensuring high-quality data, our findings underscore the potential of combining advanced AI techniques to create personalized, adaptive learning environments.

Future work will focus on expanding subject coverage, improving scalability for larger user bases, and refining AI agent integration to handle more diverse learner needs and optimize resource management.

References

1. Feuerriegel, S., Hartmann, J., Janiesch, C., Zschech, P.: Generative AI. Bus. Inf. Syst. Eng. **66**, 111–126 (2024). https://doi.org/10.1007/s12599-023-00834-7
2. Xia, Y., et al.: Understanding the performance and estimating the cost of LLM fine-tuning. arXiv preprint, arXiv:2408.04693 (2024)
3. Koto, F.: Cracking the code: Multi-domain LLM evaluation on real-world professional exams in Indonesia. arXiv preprint, arXiv:2409.08564 (2024). https://doi.org/10.48550/arXiv.2409.08564
4. Feng, T., Liu, S., Ghosal, D.: CourseAssist: pedagogically appropriate AI tutor for computer science education. EasyChair Preprint, 14287 (2024)
5. Qian, C., et al.: ChatDev: communicative agents for software development. In: Proceedings of the 62nd Annual Meeting of the Association for Computational Linguistics (Volume 1: Long Papers). Association for Computational Linguistics, Bangkok, pp. 15174–15186 (2024)
6. Xu, T., et al.: Foundation models for education: Promises and prospects. IEEE Intell. Syst. **39**, 20–24 (2024)
7. Phung, T., et al.: Automating human tutor-style programming feedback: leveraging GPT-4 tutor model for hint generation and GPT-3.5 student model for hint validation. In: Proceedings of the 14th Learning Analytics and Knowledge Conference (2023)

8. Bulathwela, S., Pérez-Ortiz, M., Holloway, C., Shawe-Taylor, J.: Could AI democratise education? Socio-technical imaginaries of an EdTech revolution. arXiv preprint, arXiv:2112.02034 (2021)
9. Dodig-Crnkovic, G., Burgin, M.: A systematic approach to autonomous agents. Philosophies. **9**(1), 1–13 (2024)
10. Wang, X., et al.: PromptAgent: Strategic planning with language models enables expert-level prompt optimization. arXiv preprint, arXiv:2310.16427 (2023)
11. Hellas, A., Leinonen, J., Sarsa, S., Koutcheme, C., Kujanpää, L., Sorva, J.: Exploring the responses of large language models to beginner programmers' help requests. In: Proceedings of the 2023 ACM Conference on International Computing Education Research – Volume 1 (ICER '23), vol. 1, pp. 93–105. Association for Computing Machinery, New York (2023). https://doi.org/10.1145/3568813.3600139
12. Alhafni, B., Vajjala, S., Banno, S., Maurya, K.K., Kochmar, E.: LLMs in education: novel perspectives, challenges, and opportunities. arXiv preprint, arXiv:2409.11917 (2024)
13. Soman, S., Roychowdhury, S.: Observations on building RAG systems for technical documents. arXiv preprint, arXiv:2404.00657 (2024)
14. Rozière, B., et al.: Code Llama: open foundation models for code. arXiv preprint, arXiv:2308.12950 (2023)
15. Kulal, S., et al.: Spoc: search-based pseudocode to code. In: Wallach, H., Larochelle, H., Beygelzimer, A., d'Alché-Buc, F., Fox, E., Garnett, R. (eds.) Advances in Neural Information Processing Systems, vol. 32. Curran Associates (2019) https://proceedings.neurips.cc/paper/2019/file/7298332f04ac004a0ca44cc69ecf6f6b-Paper.pdf
16. Mistral: Models overview. https://docs.mistral.ai/getting-started/models/models_overview/, last accessed 2024/11/06
17. Yang, A., et al.: Qwen2.5-Math technical report: toward mathematical expert model via self-improvement. arXiv preprint, arXiv:2409.12122 (2024)
18. Pinecone: all-MiniLM-L12-v2: overview. https://docs.pinecone.io/models/all-MiniLM-L12-v2/, last accessed 2024/11/06
19. Douze, M., et al.: The Faiss library. arXiv preprint, arXiv:2401.08281 (2024)
20. Berti, A., Maatallah, M., Jessen, U., Sroka, M., Ghannouchi, S.A.: Re-thinking process mining in the AI-based agents era. arXiv preprint, arXiv:2408.07720 (2024)
21. Hendrycks, D., et al.: Measuring massive multitask language understanding. arXiv preprint, arXiv:2009.03300 (2020)

Advanced Radiomics and Deep Learning for PDL1 Biomarker Prediction in Non-small Cell Lung Cancer

Adil Karim[✉] [iD] and El Habib Benlahmar [iD]

Information Technology and Modeling Faculty of Sciences Ben M'Sick, Hassan II Casablanca, Casablanca, Morocco
{adil.karim1-etu,elhabib.benlahmar}@etu.univh2c.ma

Abstract. This study investigates the potential of radiomics combined with deep learning to predict the Programmed Death-Ligand 1 (PD-L1) biomarker in Non-Small Cell Lung Cancer (NSCLC) patients using CT scans. Traditional biomarker testing is invasive and costly, creating a need for non-invasive alternatives. We extracted quantitative features from CT images and applied various machine learning models, including Artificial Neural Networks (ANN), Convolutional Neural Networks (CNN), Recurrent Neural Networks (RNN), Long Short-Term Memory (LSTM), and Gated Recurrent Networks (GRU). Initial results showed that the Transformer model achieved better performance, with a Test Mean Squared Error (MSE) of 38.16, compared to 294.59 for ANN and 127.12 for CNN. Further improvements were made with a Complex Transformer architecture, which, after 1000 epochs, reduced the MSE to 17.41. With early stopping at epoch 261, the final model achieved an MSE of 18.25. These findings suggest that radiomic features, combined with advanced deep learning techniques, offer a promising non-invasive alternative for predicting PD-L1 expression, potentially reducing healthcare costs and improving personalized cancer treatment.

Keywords: Non-Small Cell Lung Cancer (NSCLC) · PD-L1 · Radiomics · Deep Learning · Biomarker Prediction

1 Introduction

Lung cancer, particularly Non-Small Cell Lung Cancer (NSCLC), remains a major global health burden, accounting for a significant number of cancer-related deaths annually. Biomarkers, such as Programmed Death-Ligand 1 (PD-L1), are essential in personalizing cancer treatments, particularly in guiding immunotherapy decisions. However, traditional methods for obtaining these biomarkers, such as invasive tissue biopsies and molecular testing, can be both costly and uncomfortable for patients, with costs ranging from several hundred to thousands of dollars per test [1]. The rise in imaging technologies like Computed Tomography (CT), Positron emission Tomography (PET), and Magnetic Resonance Imaging (MRI) scans—commonly used in cancer diagnosis—further adds to the financial burden, as these procedures cost between \$1,000 and \$5,000 per scan [2].

O. Zahour et al. (Eds.): ICTIM 2024, CCIS 2655, pp. 63–78, 2026.
https://doi.org/10.1007/978-3-032-15147-6_7

Given these challenges, radiomics, which extracts quantitative data from medical images, presents a promising non-invasive alternative for predicting biomarker expression, including PD-L1. Recent studies have shown that radiomic features, when combined with deep learning models, can be used to accurately predict PD-L1 expression directly from CT and PET/CT scans, bypassing the need for invasive biopsies [1, 3]. These findings suggest that radiomics could potentially reduce both the financial costs and patient discomfort associated with traditional testing [4].

Despite its potential, the integration of radiomics and artificial intelligence (AI) in clinical practice remains complex. Large datasets, advanced algorithms, and significant computational resources are required to extract meaningful features from imaging data [5]. However, the benefits are substantial: AI-driven radiomics could revolutionize cancer care by enabling accurate, non-invasive predictions of key biomarkers like PD-L1, significantly reducing costs while improving patient outcomes [2].

This study explores the predictive power of radiomic features for PD-L1 expression in NSCLC patients, comparing various machine learning and deep learning models to demonstrate the feasibility of AI-driven radiomic predictions as a non-invasive alternative to molecular testing.

2   Related Works

In recent years, the integration of radiomics and deep learning techniques has garnered significant attention in the field of cancer research, particularly for Non-Small Cell Lung Cancer (NSCLC). Radiomics, which involves extracting high-dimensional data from medical images, holds the potential to uncover patterns that can predict clinical outcomes and molecular features, such as mutations and biomarker expressions. These technologies offer a non-invasive alternative to traditional biopsy-based methods and have shown promise in the context of precision oncology.

Programmed Death-Ligand 1 (PD-L1) is a key biomarker in NSCLC, crucial for determining patient eligibility for immune checkpoint inhibitors. Traditional PD-L1 measurement methods, such as tissue biopsies, are invasive and may be insufficient due to tumor heterogeneity. To overcome these challenges, researchers have turned to radiomics as a non-invasive approach. Zhang et al. [2] demonstrated that combining radiomic features with deep learning significantly improved the accuracy of predicting PD-L1 expression, achieving high AUC scores in their NSCLC cohort. This highlights the potential of integrating radiomics with machine learning to enhance biomarker prediction.

Epidermal Growth Factor Receptor (EGFR) mutations are a key molecular target in NSCLC, especially for patients eligible for tyrosine kinase inhibitors (TKIs). While traditionally detected through invasive biopsy or surgery, Wang et al. [6] developed a multitask AI system that predicts both EGFR mutations and PD-L1 status using CT images. This system, combining radiomics and deep learning, achieved high predictive accuracy for both biomarkers, with AUCs of 0.928 for EGFR mutations and 0.905 for PD-L1 expression. Their approach offers a non-invasive, more accessible method for guiding treatment decisions.

Integrating radiomics with deep learning has enhanced biomarker prediction in NSCLC. Unlike traditional radiomics, which relies on manual feature extraction, deep learning models like CNNs automatically capture high-level features, boosting prediction accuracy. Sui et al. [7] developed a deep learning radiogenomic framework linking imaging biomarkers with gene expression data, providing a detailed view of tumor molecular traits. Using GANs and autoencoders, their model established a two-way mapping between imaging and genomic data, improving the precision of tumor alteration predictions and demonstrating deep learning's potential in clinical radiomics applications.

In another study, Wu et al. [8] explored the use of radiomics and deep learning in predicting EGFR mutation status in stage I NSCLC patients. Their study introduced a radiomics nomogram that integrates deep learning and clinical features, achieving high predictive performance with AUCs of 0.917 for the training set, 0.837 for the validation set, and 0.809 for the external test set. This nomogram, which incorporates intratumoral and peritumoral features, provides a non-invasive method for predicting EGFR mutations and offers an alternative to traditional biopsy-based methods. By enhancing predictive accuracy, these models could play a crucial role in identifying patients who are most likely to benefit from targeted therapies.

Radiomics has also shown promise in predicting immune-related biomarkers, such as tumor mutation burden (TMB), which is associated with response to immune checkpoint inhibitors. Shi et al. [9] developed a radiomics-based prediction model that incorporates both PD-L1 expression and TMB to assess the likelihood of NSCLC patients responding to immune checkpoint inhibitors. Their model achieved high accuracy, further supporting the use of radiomics for predicting treatment response and guiding clinical decision-making. By combining radiomic features with molecular data, these models offer a more comprehensive approach to personalized treatment planning in lung cancer.

Mlynař et al. [10] highlighted the role of radiomics in predicting treatment outcomes in NSCLC. Their observational study demonstrated that radiomic features, when integrated with clinical and molecular data, can accurately predict patient responses to various treatments, including chemotherapy and immunotherapy. By utilizing machine learning models to process radiomic data, their study showed the potential of radiomics to improve treatment stratification and optimize therapeutic outcomes. This underscores the growing role of radiomics in personalizing cancer treatment and improving patient prognosis.

In addition to predicting biomarker expression and treatment response, radiomics has been applied to tumor staging and prognosis in lung cancer. Zhang et al. [2] used a deep learning-based radiomics framework to predict tumor stage and overall prognosis in NSCLC patients. Their study found that combining radiomic features with clinical data significantly improved the accuracy of predicting tumor behavior and patient outcomes. This further demonstrates the potential of radiomics as a non-invasive tool for cancer staging, prognosis, and long-term monitoring.

Despite promising results, the widespread adoption of radiomics in clinical practice faces several challenges. Variability in imaging protocols across institutions, such as differences in slice thickness and scanner type, can affect radiomic feature extraction consistency and hinder model generalization. The lack of standardized protocols for feature extraction also impacts reproducibility, as emphasized by Zhang et al. [2]. Additionally, obtaining large annotated datasets for training deep learning models is difficult, particularly for rare cancers or specific patient groups.

Another challenge is the need for interpretability in deep learning models. Although deep learning offers high accuracy, its "black-box" nature can impede clinical adoption. Clinicians require interpretable models to understand predictions. Sui et al. (2021) [7] have worked on frameworks linking radiomic features to genomic alterations to improve model interpretability, aiming to increase clinical acceptance.

The future of radiomics in NSCLC lies in integrating it with other omics data— such as genomics, proteomics, and metabolomics—to provide a more holistic view of tumor biology. Mlynař et al. (2024) [10] highlighted how combining these data could create more robust, personalized predictive models, enhancing treatment predictions and patient outcomes.

In conclusion, radiomics and deep learning are promising tools for predicting biomarkers and personalizing treatment in NSCLC, offering a non-invasive alternative to biopsies. While challenges like standardized imaging and model interpretability remain, ongoing research is addressing these issues, positioning radiomics as a key technology in future cancer care.

3 Proposed Methodology

In this study, we aim to predict PD-L1 expression levels in NSCLC patients using a deep learning model trained on radiomic features extracted from CT scans. By combining radiomic data and genomic information, we create a comprehensive framework that allows for the non-invasive prediction of biomarkers critical to patient treatment strategies. The radiomic features, derived from tumor-specific regions in the CT images, capture the tumor's intensity, shape, and texture characteristics, which are key to identifying tumor heterogeneity. These features, alongside corresponding biomarker data, serve as inputs to our deep learning model, which is designed to predict PD-L1 expression levels, aiding in decision-making for immunotherapy treatments. Figure 1 shows our proposed workflow for this methodology.

3.1 Dataset

This study used the NSCLC Radiogenomics Dataset [11] from The Cancer Imaging Archive (TCIA), which includes over 300 patient cases and approximately 30.7 GB of data across 39,626 files and 442 folders. The dataset provides CT images, tumor-specific segmentation masks, and biomarker information like PD-L1 expression levels, crucial for precise radiomic feature extraction. Despite its strengths, variability in imaging protocols and patient demographics presents challenges, highlighting the need for rigorous standardization during preprocessing. This dataset serves as a robust foundation for integrating imaging and genomic data to advance non-invasive cancer diagnostics.

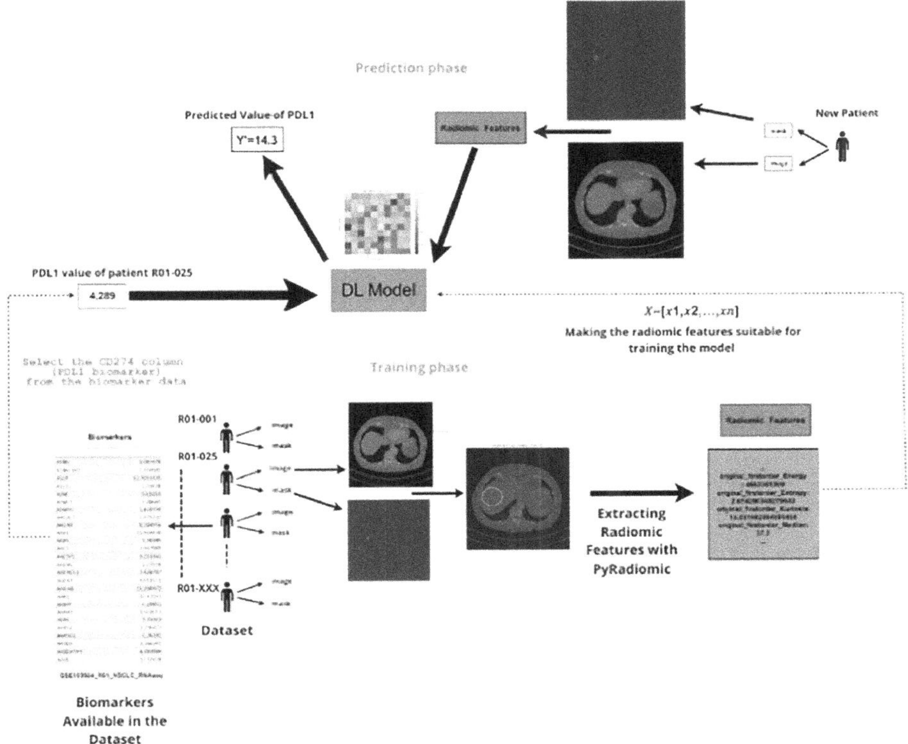

Fig. 1. Overview of the Methodology and Workflow for Radiomic Feature Extraction and PD-L1 Prediction.

3.2   Data Preprocessing

For this study, we selected CT scans and their corresponding segmentation masks for each patient from the NSCLC Radiogenomics dataset. The images underwent preprocessing to standardize resolution and format across the dataset. Scans that lacked corresponding segmentation masks, or images that did not align with their masks in terms of shape, were excluded. This step was essential for ensuring that only valid image-mask pairs were used for further analysis.

The segmentation masks provided in this dataset were manually annotated, allowing precise delineation of tumor regions in the CT scans (Figs. 2 and 3). This enabled the isolation of tumor-specific features in the volumetric images (Fig. 4). Additionally, only CT images (identified by the modality field in the metadata) were included, while scans from other modalities, such as PET or MRI, were excluded. To further examine the data, each CT scan was viewed with its overlaid mask across the axial, sagittal, and coronal planes (Figs. 3 and 5). These steps ensured consistency in the dataset used for radiomic feature extraction and subsequent model training.

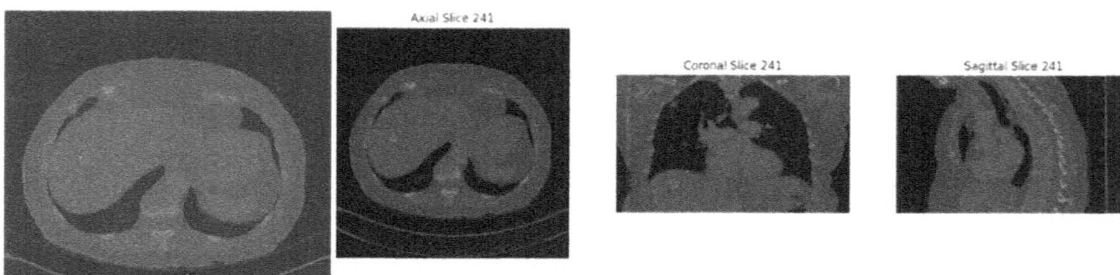

Fig. 3. Views of the Overlying mask with image in slice 241

Fig. 2. Image and mask
Overlap

For the biomarker data, missing PD-L1 values were imputed using the median PD-L1 value across all patients, ensuring no patient data was excluded due to incomplete biomarker information.

3.3 Feature Extraction

Radiomic feature extraction was performed using **PyRadiomics** [12], a widely-used open-source library. This library automates the extraction of various quantitative features from the segmented regions of interest (ROIs) within the CT scans. The extracted features include:

- **First-order statistics**: Metrics like mean, median, skewness, and kurtosis, which provide basic intensity information.
- **Shape-based features**: Characteristics of the tumor's 2D/3D structure, such as volume, surface area, and compactness.
- **Texture-based features**: Metrics like the Gray Level Co-occurrence Matrix (GLCM), Gray Level Run Length Matrix (GLRLM), and Gray Level Size Zone Matrix (GLSZM), which provide information on the heterogeneity of the tumor's texture.

After extraction, the features were standardized using z-score normalization to ensure they all contributed equally during model training. Only patients with matching imaging and genomic data were included, ensuring a robust and consistent dataset.

3.3.1 Deep Learning Models

In this study, several deep learning architectures were evaluated for predicting PD-L1 expression, each offering unique strengths in processing the complex radiomic features of tumor images:

Artificial Neural Networks (ANN): Basic models with layers of neurons that transform input data to make predictions, useful for identifying general patterns.

Convolutional Neural Networks (CNN): Effective for spatial data, capturing complex patterns in radiomic features by processing data in 2D arrays.

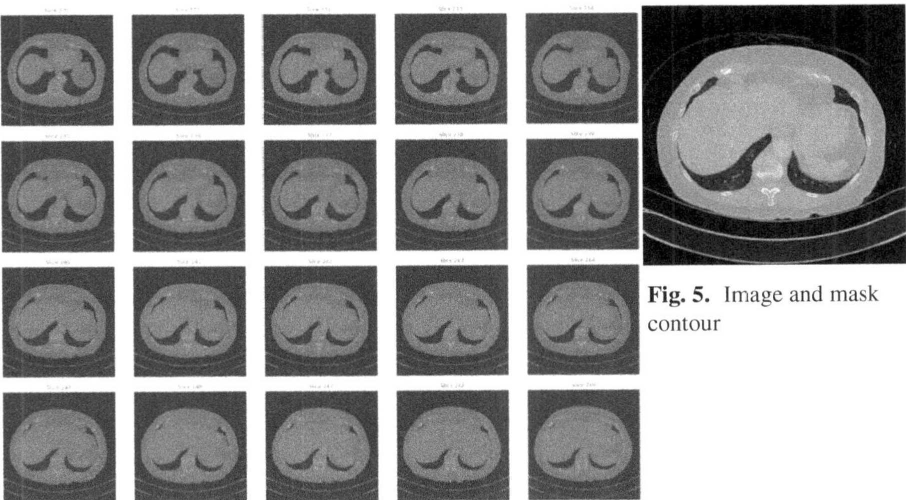

Fig. 5. Image and mask contour

Fig. 4. Grid view of slices, overlying mask with image

Recurrent Neural Networks (RNN): Capture sequential dependencies, here applied to analyze relationships across tumor layers.

Long Short-Term Memory (LSTM): An RNN variant that better retains long-term information, helping capture changes across multiple tumor layers.

Gated Recurrent Units (GRU): A simpler, faster RNN that handles sequential data efficiently.

Transformer Model: Uses self-attention to weigh feature importance, excelling at identifying complex dependencies in high-dimensional radiomic data. Each model adds unique strengths, enhancing predictive accuracy for PD-L1 expression.

3.4 Hyperparameter Tuning

To optimize the performance of the models, hyperparameter tuning was performed using a grid search method. The following hyperparameters were tuned:

- **Learning Rate**: Adjusting the step size at each iteration while moving toward the minimum of the loss function.
- **Number of Layers**: Exploring the depth of the network by adjusting the number of hidden layers in the models.
- **Number of Neurons per Layer**: Modifying the number of neurons within each hidden layer.
- **Batch Size**: Determining the number of samples processed before updating the model's weights.
- **Dropout Rates**: Introducing dropout to prevent overfitting by randomly dropping units from the neural network during training.

- The best combination of hyperparameters was selected based on minimizing the Mean Squared Error (MSE) and Mean Absolute Error (MAE) on the validation set.

4 Experiments and Results

In this section, we detail the results obtained in terms of Mean Squared Error (MSE), Root Mean Squared Error (RMSE), and Mean Absolute Error (MAE). These metrics were used to evaluate the performance of several deep learning models employed for predicting PD-L1 biomarker expression from radiomic features. Our analysis indicates promising results; however, achieving these results was not without challenges. In the next section, we will address several key challenges encountered during this study, including data variability, model training complexities, and the impact of imaging inconsistencies on predictive accuracy. We will discuss the strategies implemented to manage these challenges and their implications for model generalizability and clinical applicability.

4.1 Challenges in Data Variability and Model Training

The NSCLC Radiogenomics Dataset posed challenges due to variability in imaging protocols, patient demographics, and scanner characteristics, which impacted model generalization. Data preprocessing techniques like normalization and segmentation standardization were applied, but some variability persisted, affecting model stability and accuracy. Training deep learning models, particularly Transformers, required significant computational resources and careful hyperparameter tuning. Techniques like early stopping and gradient clipping were used to stabilize training, but balancing complex relationships and generalization remained challenging.

4.2 Model Selection and Performance Comparison for PD-L1 Expression Prediction

In the model selection phase, various machine learning and deep learning models were tested to identify the optimal architecture for predicting PD-L1 expression. The models evaluated included ANN, CNN, RNN, LSTM, GRU, and Transformer-based architectures. These models were chosen for their capacity to capture the complexity of radiomic features extracted from the NSCLC Radiogenomics Dataset. Due to the nature of the data and complex relationships between features, attention-based architectures like Transformers were emphasized for their ability to capture intricate dependencies. The dataset was split into training and test sets for a robust evaluation, with early stopping criteria implemented to prevent overfitting by monitoring validation set performance. MSE, RMSE, and MAE were calculated as performance metrics for each model, aiming to minimize these errors for more accurate PD-L1 predictions.

As shown in Fig. 6, the performance of each model was compared across multiple metrics during both training and testing phases. The Transformer-based model consistently outperformed the others, achieving lower test MSE, RMSE, and MAE values, indicating superior generalization to unseen data.

Traditional models like ANN and CNN showed some promise but struggled to maintain accuracy as the feature set complexity increased. The final performance results on the test data are depicted in Fig. 7, where error metrics (MSE, RMSE, MAE) are visualized for clearer comparison. The Transformer model demonstrated the lowest errors across all metrics, highlighting its suitability for PD-L1 biomarker prediction, while models like ANN and RNN exhibited significantly higher error rates, particularly in MSE.

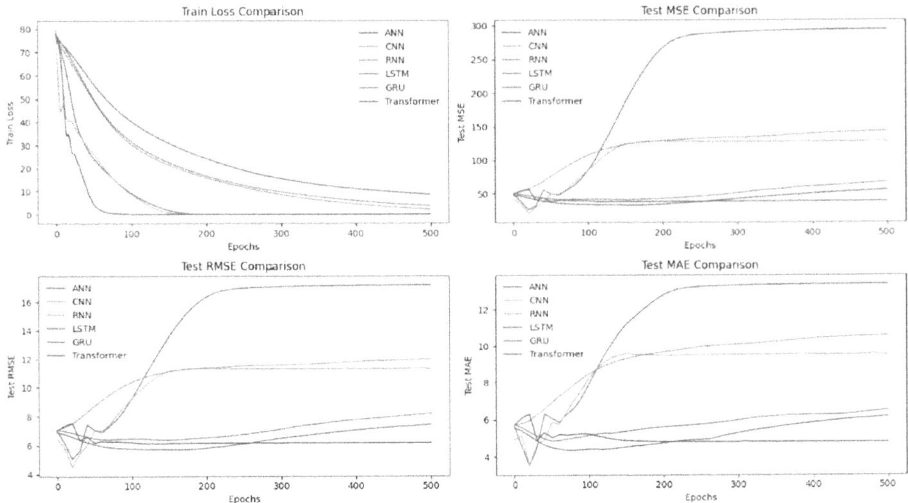

Fig. 6. Performance comparison of used deep learning models over 500 epochs, visualizing Metrics MAE during the model training process.

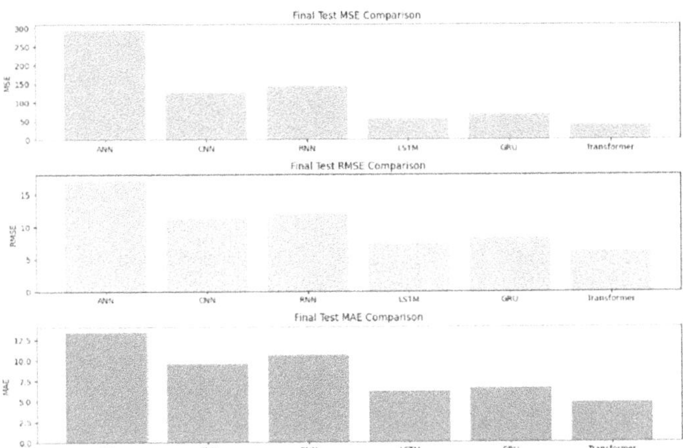

Fig. 7. Final test results showing the comparison of Metrics for different models.

4.3   Proposed Model: Complex Transformer Model and Hyperparameter Tuning

We designed a custom Complex Transformer model to capture the complexities of radiomic feature data (Fig. 8). The architecture includes multiple transformer encoder layers with attention heads, followed by fully connected layers for refining feature representations. To prevent overfitting, ReLU activations and dropout layers were added. A comprehensive hyperparameter search was conducted, adjusting parameters like learning rate, attention heads, encoder layers, feedforward dimensions, and dropout rate. The optimal configuration included a learning rate of 0.001, 4 attention heads, 6 encoder layers, a feedforward dimension of 1024, and a dropout rate of 0.4. Early stopping at epoch 261 ensured the model's optimal performance for predicting PD-L1 values.

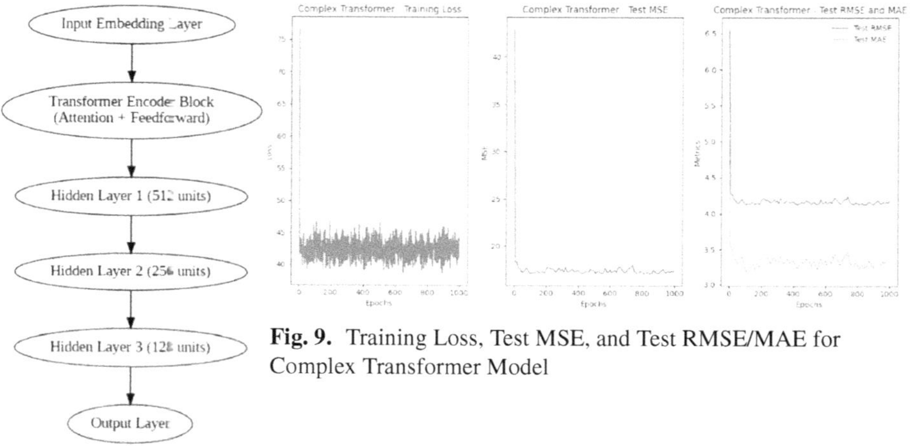

Fig. 9. Training Loss, Test MSE, and Test RMSE/MAE for Complex Transformer Model

Fig. 8. Architecture of the Complex Transformer Model

The figure (Fig. 9) illustrates the training dynamics of the complex Transformer model, showing the **training loss**, **test MSE**, and test metrics (**RMSE and MAE**) over 1000 epochs. The training process highlights stable convergence with early stopping at **epoch 261** (Table 1).

Table 1. Complex Transformer Model Performance Results

Model	Epoch Stopped	Final Train Loss	Final Test MSE	Final Test RMSE	Final Test MAE
Complex Transformer	261	44.4359	17.4116	4.1729	3.8041

4.4 Model Performance Comparison

The comparison illustrated in Fig. 10 demonstrates the superior performance of the Complex Transformer model and its fine-tuned version in comparison to other models such as ANN, CNN, RNN, LSTM, GRU, and the standard Transformer. The Transformer model, along with hyperparameter tuning and early stopping, demonstrated lower MSE, RMSE, and MAE values, as well as a faster convergence rate.

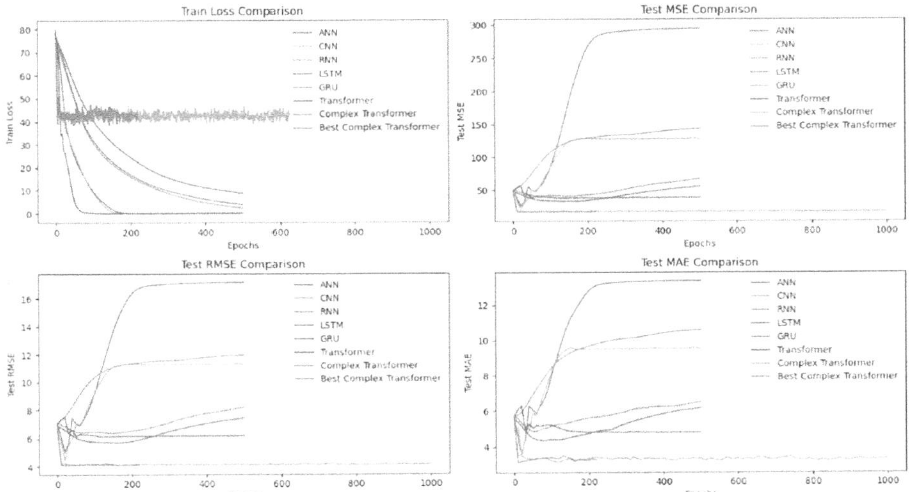

Fig. 10. Model Performance Comparison for Train Loss, Test MSE, and Test RMSE/MAE.

- **Train Loss Comparison:** The Complex Transformer models, especially the Best Complex Transformer with optimized hyperparameters, achieved the lowest training loss across 1000 epochs, demonstrating effective learning without overfitting.
- **Test MSE Comparison:** The Complex Transformer models, particularly the Best Complex Transformer, maintain a consistently low Test MSE throughout training, outperforming models like ANN and RNN and demonstrating superior generalization.
- **Test RMSE and MAE Comparison:** The bottom plots show that the Best Complex Transformer has significantly lower Test RMSE and MAE, maintaining a stable, minimized trajectory, unlike the ANN and CNN models, which show increased error due to poor generalization.

In conclusion, the **Complex Transformer** and its fine-tuned version demonstrate a substantial improvement in predictive performance, achieving minimal training loss and significantly lower test MSE, RMSE, and MAE compared to all other models. This superior performance emphasizes the effectiveness of attention mechanisms and hyperparameter optimization in handling complex radiomic data for **PD-L1 prediction**.

4.4.1 Clinical Relevance and Comparative Performance of PD-L1 Prediction Models

For predicting PD-L1 expression, a clinically relevant MSE is typically around or below 20, reflecting accuracy comparable to biopsy results. The Complex Transformer model in this study achieved an MSE of 17.41, showing strong clinical promise and non-invasiveness. It also demonstrated high time efficiency, converging quickly with early stopping at epoch 261. Compared to ANNs and CNNs, which required more epochs and had higher errors, the Transformer's attention mechanisms and interpretability make it especially suited for handling complex radiomic data and supporting clinical decision-making.

4.4.2 Proposed Model Performance Evaluation

In this section, we provide a detailed technical analysis of our model's performance, focusing on residuals, feature importance, attention mechanisms, and dimensionality reduction, which are critical for evaluating model efficacy (Fig. 11).

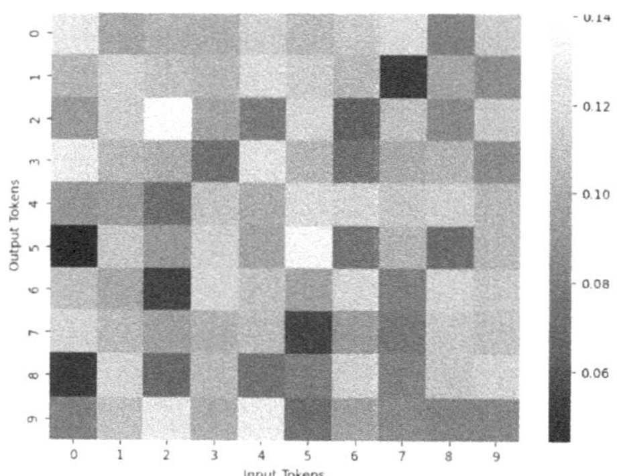

Fig. 11. Attention Weights - Layer

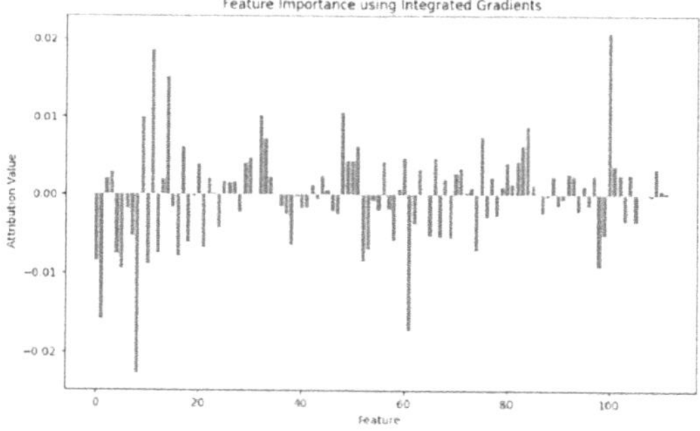

Fig. 12. Feature Importance using Integrated Gradients

To enhance model interpretability, we analyzed feature importance using Integrated Gradients (Fig. 12). This technique measures the contribution of each radiomic feature to predicting PD-L1 values, highlighting features with the most significant positive or negative impact on the model's decisions. Understanding these key features provides insights into the biological and clinical relevance of specific radiomic characteristics, such as tumor texture or shape.

Additionally, we explored the attention mechanisms in the Transformer model, which offer transparency by showing how the model allocates focus across input features. The heatmap of Attention Weights in Layer 1 (Fig. 11) illustrates the attention distribution across input tokens, helping us identify which aspects of the radiomic data the model considered most important for prediction. This is particularly useful in complex datasets like radiomics, where certain regions of the images may carry more predictive power for PD-L1 expression than others.

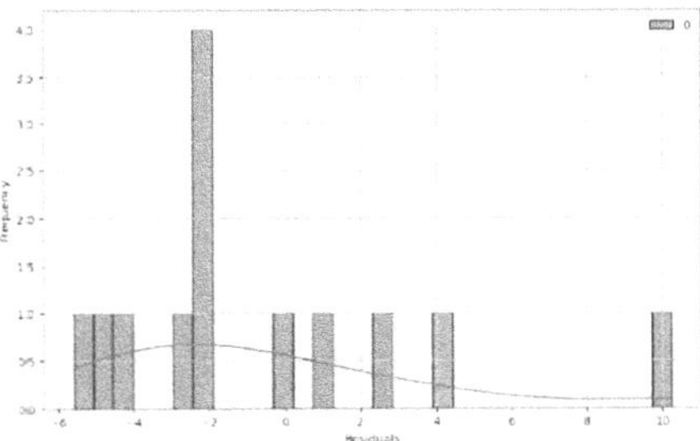

Fig. 13. Residuals Distribution

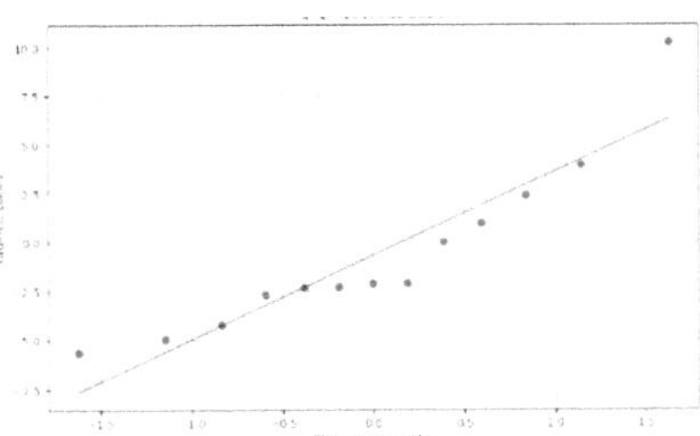

Fig. 14. QQ plot of Residuals

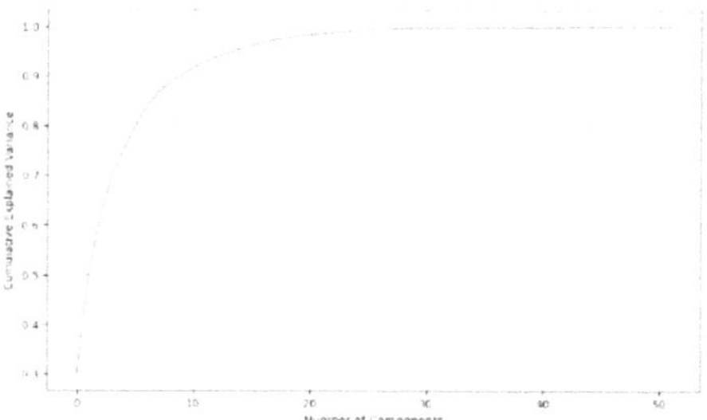

Fig. 15. PCA Cumulative Explained Variance

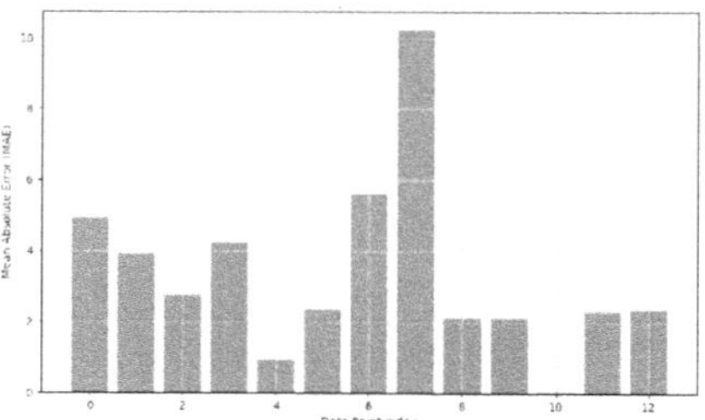

Fig. 16. MAE per Data point

We performed a residual analysis to evaluate prediction errors. The Residuals Distribution plot (Fig. 13) shows that while the residuals are mostly centered around zero, there is a slight skew, indicating the model has some difficulty predicting PD-L1 values accurately for certain cases. This skew is more pronounced in the Q-Q Plot of Residuals (Fig. 14), where deviations from the red line suggest the residuals do not follow a perfect normal distribution. These deviations indicate the model may have struggled with complex relationships in the data, highlighting areas for potential model refinement.

Applying Principal Component Analysis (PCA) reduced the radiomic feature space, with the first 10 principal components capturing over 90% of the variance (Fig. 15). This dimensionality reduction enhances computational efficiency and accelerates model training while preserving essential predictive information. Additionally, the Mean Absolute Error (MAE) per Data Point plot (Fig. 16) reveals high-MAE instances, suggesting outliers or complex cases, aiding in identifying misclassified instances and guiding further model improvement.

4.5 Advantages of the Complex Transformer Architecture

The Complex Transformer architecture with its multi-head self-attention enhances interpretability and accuracy by focusing on key features, the parallel processing accelerates training and effectively handles the non-sequential nature of radiomic data. With fine-tuning, the Complex Transformer also showed strong generalization to new data, making it highly suitable for clinical applications that need consistent performance.

4.6 Limitations of the Study

Despite its advantages, the study faces limitations. Variability in radiomic data from different institutions can hinder the model's generalization and accuracy. The high computational requirements of Transformers may also restrict their use in resource-limited settings. The dataset, may lack sufficient diversity to fully generalize across broader populations, highlighting the need for larger, more varied samples in future research to enhance robustness and applicability in clinical settings.

5 Conclusion

This study demonstrates that deep learning models, particularly Transformer-based architectures, can effectively predict PD-L1 biomarker expression in NSCLC patients using radiomic data from CT scans. Among tested models (ANN, CNN, RNN, LSTM, GRU, and Transformer), the Complex Transformer with optimized hyperparameters achieved the lowest MSE, RMSE, and MAE, excelling in capturing complex data relationships. Attention mechanisms also identified key features for PD-L1 prediction, highlighting the model's potential to support personalized, non-invasive immunotherapy. Future work may enhance model generalization and address specific data outliers.

Acknowledgments. We would like to express our gratitude to The Cancer Imaging Archive (TCIA) for providing access to the NSCLC Radiogenomics dataset, which was critical to the success of this research. We also thank the developers of PyRadiomics and the open-source deep learning frameworks that made our model development possible.

Disclosure of Interests The authors declare that there are no conflicts of interest related to this work. All data, models, and methodologies used in this study were solely for academic and research purposes, with no commercial or financial interests influencing the results. The authors have adhered to all relevant ethical guidelines regarding data usage and confidentiality.

References

1. Xu, T., Liu, X., Chen, Y., Wang, S., Jiang, C., Gong, J.: CT-based deep learning radiomics biomarker for programmed cell death ligand 1 expression in non-small cell lung cancer. BMC Med. Imaging. **24**(1), 196 (2024). https://doi.org/10.1186/s12880-024-01380-8
2. Zhang, X., et al.: Exploring non-invasive precision treatment in non-small cell lung cancer patients through deep learning radiomics across imaging features and molecular phenotypes. Biomark. Res. **12**(1), 12 (2024). https://doi.org/10.1186/s40364-024-00561-5
3. Li, B., Su, J., Liu, K., Hu, C.: Deep learning radiomics model based on PET/CT predicts PD-L1 expression in non-small cell lung cancer. Eur. J. Radiol. Open. **12**, 100549 (2024). https://doi.org/10.1016/j.ejro.2024.100549
4. Ferro, A., et al.: Clinical applications of radiomics and deep learning in breast and lung cancer: a narrative literature review on current evidence and future perspectives. Crit. Rev. Oncol. Hematol. **203**, 104479 (2024). https://doi.org/10.1016/j.critrevonc.2024.104479
5. Atmakuru, A., et al.: Deep learning in radiology for lung cancer diagnostics: a systematic review of classification, segmentation, and predictive modeling techniques. Expert Syst. Appl. **255**, 124665 (2024). https://doi.org/10.1016/j.eswa.2024.124665

6. Wang, C., et al.: Predicting EGFR and PD-L1 status in NSCLC patients using multitask AI system based on CT images. Front. Immunol. **13**, 813072 (2022). https://doi.org/10.3389/fimmu.2022.813072

7. Sui, D., Guo, M., Ma, X., Baptiste, J., Zhang, L.: Imaging biomarkers and gene expression data correlation framework for lung cancer radiogenomics analysis based on deep learning. IEEE Access. **9**, 125247–125257 (2021). https://doi.org/10.1109/ACCESS.2021.3071466

8. Wu, J, et al.: Habitat radiomics and deep learning fusion nomogram to predict EGFR mutation status in stage I non-small cell lung cancer: a multicenter study. Sci. Rep. Consulté le: 29 septembre 2024. [En ligne]. Disponible sur: https://www.nature.com/articles/s41598-024-66751-1

9. Shi, S., et al.: Predictive value of PD-L1 and TMB for short-term efficacy prognosis in non-small cell lung cancer and construction of prediction models. Front. Oncol. **14**, 1342262 (2024). https://doi.org/10.3389/fonc.2024.1342262

10. Mlynář, J., Depeursinge, A., Prior, J.O., Schaer, R., Martroye De Joly, A., Evéquoz, F.: Making sense of radiomics: insights on human–AI collaboration in medical interaction from an observational user study. Front. Commun. **8**, 1234987 (2024). https://doi.org/10.3389/fcomm.2023.1234987

11. Schabath, M.B., et al.: The NSCLC radiogenomics dataset (version 2) [Data set]. The Cancer Imaging Archive (TCIA) (2020). https://doi.org/10.7937/tcia.2020.qcdcdvqz

12. van Griethuysen, J.J.M., et al.: Computational radiomics system to decode the radiographic phenotype. Cancer Res., **77**(21), e104–e107 (2017). [En ligne]. Disponible sur: https://doi.org/10.1158/0008-5472.CAN-17-0339

AI-Enhanced Detection of COVID-19 and Lung Diseases via Chest X-Rays: Enhancing Diagnostic Accuracy with CNNs and Top-K Algorithms

Kaoutar El Handri[1,2]([envelope]) (iD), Adil Bouhouch[3] (iD), and Ossama Hamal[4] (iD)

[1] Medbiotech laboratory, Faculty of Medicine and Pharmacy (FMPR), University Mohammed V in Rabat, Rabat, Morocco
kaoutar.elhandri@um5r.ac.ma
[2] Aivancity School of AI & Data for Business & Society, Cachan, France
[3] I.M.A.G.E Laboratory, Moulay Ismail University of Meknes, Meknes, Morocco
[4] National School of Architecture of Marrakech (ENAM), Marrakech, Morocco

Abstract. The COVID-19 pandemic has profoundly affected lives around the world, highlighting the urgent need for faster and more accurate ways to diagnose the virus. Up to the time of writing this article, The impact of this pandemic is still felt in our lives. However, traditional methods such as symptom analysis and PCR tests are valuable. In addition, they can often be slow and complicated. This paper presents a fresh approach to detecting COVID-19 and other lung diseases using chest X-rays, by leveraging convolutional neural networks (CNNs) and enhancing image quality with histogram equalization, the aim of the proposed approach is to improve diagnostic accuracy using AI and Machine learning tools. This research utilizes a dataset of 1,823 chest X-ray images, which will be categorized into three groups: COVID-19-positive, regular, and other lung viruses. Moreover, after splitting the data into training and validation sets, the CNN model was evaluated and achieved an impressive accuracy rate of 98.45%. Consequently, these results are encouraging and suggest that our method could play a vital role in speeding up COVID-19 diagnostics, ultimately easing the burden on healthcare professionals. Looking ahead, The dataset is set to be expanded, and advanced techniques will be explored to further strengthen the model, aiming for applications across other lung diseases. Additionally, the integration of the Top-k algorithm is planned to enhance decision-making by highlighting the most accurate diagnostic outputs. This will help healthcare providers focus on the most relevant cases, improving the effectiveness of diagnostics and supporting more informed clinical decisions.

Keywords: COVID-19 · pulmonary diseases · convolutional neural network · confusion matrix · Topk algorithms · diagnosis

1 Introduction

The COVID-19 pandemic has put immense pressure on healthcare systems globally, making the need for efficient diagnostic tools crucial in aiding early detection and treatment. With over 400 million cases and 6 million deaths worldwide, rapid and precise

O. Zahour et al. (Eds.): ICTIM 2024, CCIS 2655, pp. 79–87, 2026.
https://doi.org/10.1007/978-3-032-15147-6_8

diagnostics remain essential in controlling virus spread and reducing mortality. Although conventional methods such as PCR testing and symptom analysis are widely used, they can often be slow, resource-heavy, and prone to human error. Medical imaging, particularly chest X-rays, has proven to be important in diagnosing COVID-19 and associated lung conditions. However, manually analyzing these images can be time-consuming and prone to mistakes, especially in the high-pressure environment of clinical settings. However, With recent advances in artificial intelligence (AI) and deep learning, new opportunities have arisen to tackle these challenges [2]. Convolutional neural networks (CNNs), already successful in detecting diseases such as tumors and cancers, are particularly suited for analyzing medical images. In this study, a new approach for detecting COVID-19 via chest X-rays using a CNN model enhanced by histogram equalization in the preprocessing stage is proposed. This technique improves image contrast, ensuring that key details are retained, and thereby allows the CNN to learn and detect the subtle patterns of COVID-19 more effectively. An essential feature of this study is the integration of decision-support tools aimed at improving clinical usability. We propose using Multi-Criteria Decision Analysis (MCDA) to assist in interpreting diagnostic results. This will enable a more thorough evaluation by factoring in variables such as patient history, severity of symptoms, and confidence in predictions. Additionally, integrating the Top-k algorithm, which selects the most relevant diagnostic outcomes from the model streamlines the decision-making process for healthcare professionals, allowing them to focus on the most accurate and pertinent predictions while minimizing false positives and negatives. By embedding these decision-support systems, our approach has the potential to not only increase diagnostic accuracy but also provide clinicians with real-time, data-driven insights to make more informed decisions. The following sections will describe the development and testing of our CNN model, its combination with MCDA and Top-k, and the potential impact this approach could have on improving COVID-19 diagnostics.

2 Related Works

Shibly et al. proposed a hybrid model combining CNN architecture with long short-term memory (LSTM) networks to automatically diagnose COVID-19 from CXR images [12]. This combination leverages the feature extraction capabilities of CNNs along with the temporal dependencies captured by LSTM networks, demonstrating the importance of incorporating complementary deep learning models to improve the accuracy of the diagnostic. Similarly, other research efforts have focused on the role of image preprocessing techniques in enhancing model performance. Chowdhury et al. [3] and Rahman et al. [11] explored various image enhancement methods, such as contrast adjustment and noise reduction, to improve the quality of CXR images prior to analysis. These enhancements have been shown to greatly boost the accuracy of COVID-19 detection by permitting CNNs to capture finer details in lung images. In addition to these advancements, some studies have also emphasized the use of decision-support mechanisms to enhance diagnostic workflows. Multi-Criteria Decision Analysis (MCDA) and Top-k algorithms presented in our previous work [4–6, 8], although not widely adopted yet in COVID-19 diagnostic models, It should be present that the proposed approaches present a novel direction for further research. Moreover, the findings shows that it can help refine and prioritize outputs from CNN models, ensuring that the focus on the most relevant and accurate results will be easy for healthcare providers. For instance, the authors Wang et al. proposed a new ensemble learning approach that combines multiple CNN models with different architectures to improve the robustness and generalization ability of COVID-19 detection [14]. Their results demonstrated that the ensemble model outperformed individual CNN models in terms of accuracy and sensitivity. Furthermore, Zhang et al. studied the augmentation techniques' impact on data on the performance of CNN models for COVID-19 detection [15]. Their finding shows the augmenting the training dataset with rotated, flipped, and cropped images can ameliorate and improve model accuracy and prevent overfitting. Finally, several studies have explored the use of transfer learning to accelerate the training of CNN models for COVID-19 detection. By leveraging pre-trained models trained on large-scale image datasets, researchers can fine-tune the models on smaller COVID-19 datasets, reducing training time and improving performance. In addition, the collective findings from these studies [10] illustrate the growing importance of deep learning in medical imaging, particularly in the context of pandemic response. By building on these foundations, our work aims to further optimize COVID-19 detection using advanced CNN models enhanced with preprocessing techniques and decision-support systems.

3 Methodology

3.1 Chest X-Ray Image Database

Our model was trained using a subset of the **COVID-QU** database, a comprehensive collection of chest X-ray images designed to facilitate the development of machine-learning models for COVID-19 detection. The subset selected for this study comprises a total of **1,823 images** [13], which are distributed across three key categories as presented in Table 1:

Table 1 Image Categories and Counts

Category	Number of Images
COVID-19 positive	536
Normal	668
Other lung viruses	619

This specific distribution allows the model to differentiate between normal and infected lungs while also learning the subtle features of COVID-19 in contrast to other viral lung infections. The kind of data mentioned above has to be used. Thus, the COVID-19 positive images were chosen to help the model recognize unique patterns associated with the disease, such as lung opacities and groundglass appearances. Standard images serve as a reference for comparison, enabling the model to distinguish between healthy and diseased lungs. Lastly, the inclusion of lung virus images from other viral infections ensures that the model does not overfit COVID-19-specific features. Consequently, this aspect still maintains broader diagnostic applicability.

This balanced dataset aims to provide CNN with a well-rounded understanding of different lung conditions, ensuring it is capable of making accurate distinctions not only between COVID-19 cases and healthy lungs but also between COVID-19 and other viral infections. Figures 1 and 2 present sample images from the dataset, showcasing a positive COVID-19 case and a normal lung case, while Figure 3 illustrates the distribution of images in the dataset.

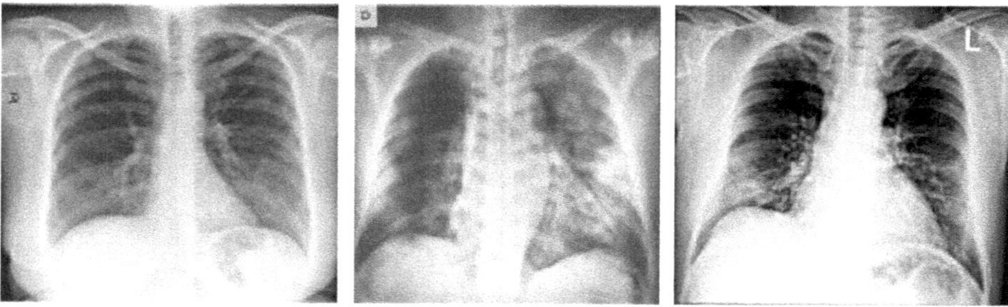

Fig. 1 Sample images from the COVID-QU dataset: Positive COVID-19 case.

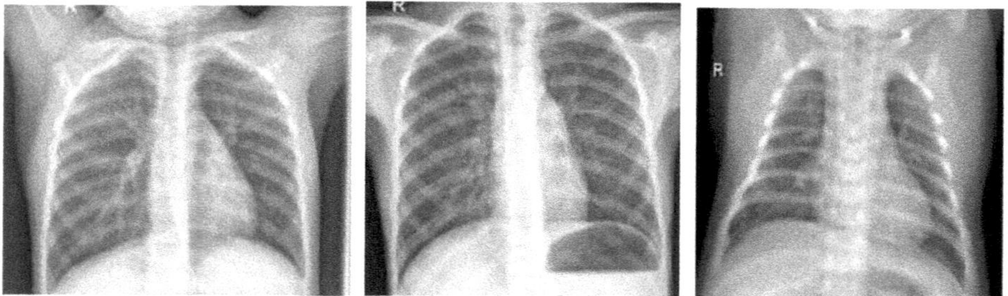

Fig. 2 Sample images from the COVID-QU dataset: Normal lung case.

By carefully curating this selection of images, a robust and diverse dataset was aimed to be created to allow the model to generalize well across various pulmonary conditions, while ensuring optimal performance in detecting COVID- 19.

3.2 Project Stages

1. **Image size standardization**: To ensure consistency and compatibility with the CNN model, all images were resized to a uniform dimension. This preprocessing step is crucial for reducing computational complexity and ensuring consistent feature extraction across the dataset.

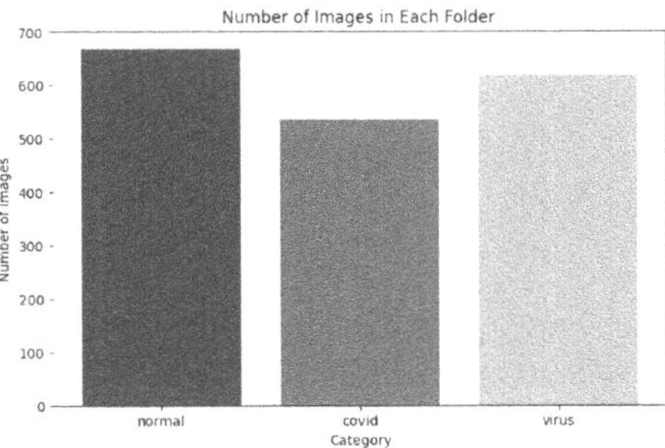

Fig. 3 Distribution of images in the COVID-QU database.

2. **Grayscale conversion**: Converting the images to grayscale allowed the model to focus on essential texture and intensity variations, reducing the overall data complexity. By eliminating color information, the model emphasized critical patterns in lung opacity, which are vital for detecting abnormalities.

3. **Data splitting**: The dataset was divided into two subsets: 80% of the data was allocated for model training, while 20% was reserved for validation. This split ensures that the model can be evaluated on unseen data, providing a realistic measure of its generalization capabilities.

4. **CNN architecture design**: The design of the CNN architecture involved determining the optimal number of convolutional layers, pooling layers, and fully connected layers. This step was essential for enabling the model to extract meaningful features from the input images, progressing from simple edge detection to complex patterns indicative of COVID-19 [1].

5. **Model hyperparameter tuning**: To maximize the model's performance, key hyperparameters such as the learning rate, batch size, and the number of training epochs were fine-tuned. This process involved several iterations to achieve an optimal balance between training time and accuracy.

6. **Model training**: The CNN was trained using the training set. During training, the model learned to classify the images based on the features extracted through convolutional layers, adjusting its internal parameters through back- propagation to minimize classification errors.

7. **Confusion matrix visualization**: A confusion matrix was employed to provide a comprehensive evaluation of the model's predictions. It displayed the correct and incorrect predictions for each class, helping to identify any biases or areas for improvement in the model.

8. **ROC curve display**: The Receiver Operating Characteristic (ROC) curve was used to evaluate the model's classification ability, plotting the true positive rate against the false positive rate. This curve allowed us to assess the model's performance across various threshold values, providing insight into its sensitivity and specificity (Fig. 4).

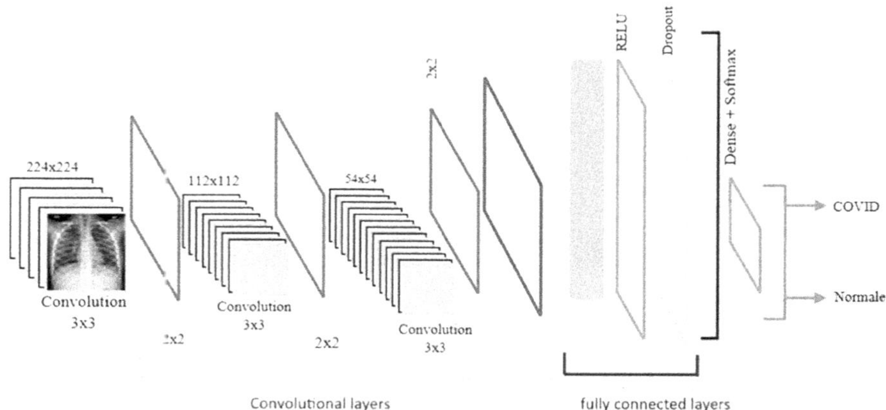

Fig. 4 The CNN architecture used in this study

4 Results and Discussions

The CNN model was trained and validated using the COVID-QU database, consisting of 1,823 chest X-ray images categorized into COVID-19-positive cases, typical images, and other lung virus cases. This diverse dataset enabled the model to learn the distinctive characteristics of COVID-19 while establishing a baseline for comparison with normal lung conditions. The training and validation sets ensured the model's ability to generalize well to unseen data, a crucial aspect for clinical applications.

The ROC curve analysis of the CNN model reveals its strong ability to distinguish between normal, other pneumonia, and COVID-19 cases. The model consistently shows high accuracy across all categories with an impressive Area Under the Curve (AUC) of 0.96 for normal and pneumonia cases and 0.97 for COVID-19. These AUC values highlight the model's reliability in detecting the conditions it was trained for, as each curve closely approaches the top-left corner of the graph—indicating robust sensitivity and specificity.

In practical terms, the model's high AUC for COVID-19 reflects its ability to accurately identify true cases while keeping false alarms low. This little advantage in identifying COVID-19 implies that the model is particularly good at identifying this illness. Because of this, it may be a useful tool in clinical situations where prompt and accurate diagnosis is crucial. Finally, all things considered, the CNN precision in identifying certain lung disorders gives medical professionals an extra degree of assistance, This little advantage in identifying COVID-19 implies that the model is particularly good at identifying this illness. Because of this, it may be a useful tool in clinical situations where prompt and accurate diagnosis is crucial. All things regarded, the CNN model's precision in identifying certain lung disorders gives medical professionals extra assistance when diagnosing chest X-rays. Finally, this methodology has the potential to improve patient care and resource allocation in healthcare systems by increasing diagnostic confidence and aiding in the prioritization of urgent cases. Figures 5 and 6a illustrate the accuracy and the ROC curve, respectively.

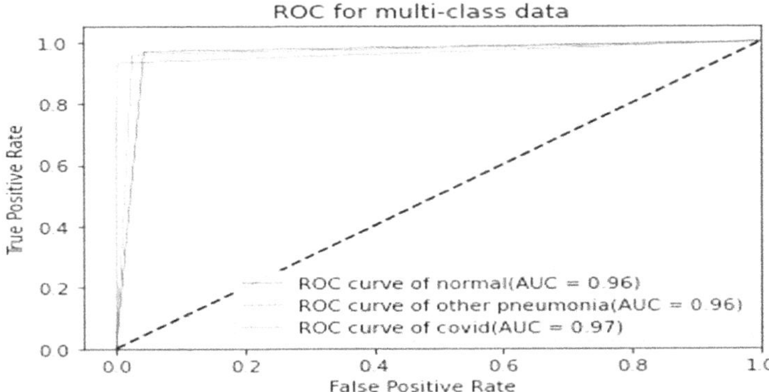

Fig. 5 ROC curve of the CNN model.

The ROC curve, presented in Fig. 5, demonstrates the model's ability to balance sensitivity and specificity across different threshold settings. A curve closer to the top-left corner indicates superior performance in distinguishing between positive and negative cases. Our results suggest that the CNN is accurate and reliable for clinical decision-making in COVID-19 diagnosis.

The training and validation loss curves depicted in Fig. 6b further support the model's performance. The decreasing loss values over epochs indicate that the model is learning effectively from the training data and generalizing well to the validation set. The convergence of the training and validation loss curves suggests that the model is not overfitting, ensuring its reliability in real-world applications.

These findings underscore the potential of integrating deep learning techniques like CNNs in the healthcare sector, especially for rapidly and accurately detecting respiratory diseases. Future work will explore enhancing model robust-ness through the integration of Multi-Criteria Decision Analysis (MCDA) and the Top-k algorithm to further support decision-making processes by selecting the most relevant cases for diagnosis.

In addition, if the dataset is imbalanced, techniques like class weighting or oversampling might be necessary to address potential biases. The choice of model architecture and hyperparameters can also impact performance. Experimenting with different models and tuning hyperparameters could lead to further improvements.

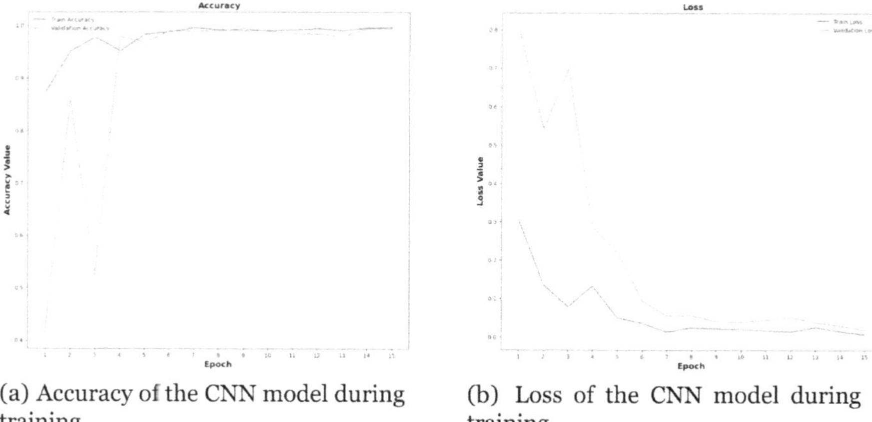

(a) Accuracy of the CNN model during training.

(b) Loss of the CNN model during training.

Fig. 6 Fast-CovNet performance

5 Future Directions and Potential for Clinical Trials

To make this AI model truly valuable for the Moroccan healthcare system, future clinical trials will need to use a more extensive, carefully selected dataset that reflects local demographics and specific clinical needs. This effort will be supported by a Big Data infrastructure enhanced by the SPTopKws mechanism, a newly developed Top-K algorithm designed to handle large-scale data effectively. While PySpark was used in the current study, deploying this model within a fullscale Big Data environment will help verify its scalability and performance with larger datasets. Furthermore, a recommender system powered by SPTopKws [5] will be incorporated to provide a decision-support tool that ranks possible diagnoses based on the model's output. Based on the Topk query processing and the ranked list, this approach aims to help healthcare providers prioritize cases and allocate resources efficiently. The design also focuses on interoperability [7, 9] making integrating the model into existing clinical workflows easier. While it was initially used for COVID-19 detection, the model has the potential to be applied to other respiratory diseases as well, further supporting clinicians in various diagnostic tasks and enhancing decision-making across diverse healthcare settings.

6 Conclusion and Prospects

This work presents a novel approach for detecting COVID-19 using chest X-rays. The key contributions of this study include:

- Image preprocessing using histogram equalization for better intensity distribution.
- A lightweight CNN architecture for fast and accurate COVID-19 detection.
- Evaluation through the confusion matrix and ROC curve, yielding a 98.45% accuracy rate.

Future improvements include using a more extensive image database and Big data infrastructure using GPUs and Spark library as in our previous work [5]. In addition, more advanced image segmentation techniques will be integrated to further enhance accuracy and robustness. Additionally, incorporating a TopK algorithm, namely the Topkws mechanism, could provide a valuable decision-support tool by ranking the most likely diagnoses based on the model's output. Finally, this would enable healthcare providers to prioritize cases and allocate resources more effectively.

References

1. An, J., Zhang, N., Mahmoud, W., Denis, M.: A covid-19 CXR image recognition method based on deep transfer learning. In: 2024 International Joint Conference on Neural Networks (IJCNN), pp. 1–6. IEEE (2024)
2. Careful. Online: The future of healthcare: 2024 AI impact analysis (2024), https://careful.onl ine/future-healthcare-ai-2024/
3. Chowdhury, A., Rahman, M.A., Islam, M.R.: Improved covid-19 detection from chest x-ray images using deep learning with image preprocessing. J. Med. Imaging Health Inf. **10**(1), 101–108 (2020)
4. El Handri, K., El Ahrach, S., Touil, M.: A new synesthesia-based approach for AI in healthcare. Int. J. Res. Ethics. **5**(1) (2022) ISSN 2665-7481
5. El Handri, K., Idrissi, A.: Parallelization of topk algorithm through a new hybrid recommendation system for big data in spark cloud computing framework. IEEE Syst. J. **15**(4), 4876–4886 (2020)
6. El Handri, K., Idrissi, A.: Correlations and hierarchical clustering investigation between weather and sars-cov-2. Recent Adv. Comput. Sci. Commun. **15**(6), 859–867 (2022)
7. Handri, K.E., Benedress, L.G., Wakrim, L., Lamzabi, S., Idrissi, A.: Ai-based QOS optimization in post-disaster ad hoc networks: top-k path enumeration with multicriteria decision analysis. In: 2024 IEEE 4th International Maghreb Meeting of the Conference on Sciences and Techniques of Automatic Control and Computer Engineering (MI-STA), pp. 561–566. IEEE (2024)
8. Handri, K.E., Idrissi, A.: Comparative study of topk based on Fagin's algorithm using correlation metrics in cloud computing QoS. **10**(1), 143. https://doi.org/10.1504/IJITST.2020. 104579, http://www.inderscience.com/link.php?id=104579
9. Lamzabi, S., et al.: Minimizing the viruses propagation in interconnected complex networks. In: 2024 IEEE 4th International Maghreb Meeting of the Conference on Sciences and Techniques of Automatic Control and Computer Engineering (MI-STA), pp. 544–549. IEEE (2024)
10. Luo, X., Chen, X., Yao, Y., Yao, Y.: Mvmsgat: Integrating multiview, multi-scale graph convolutional networks with biological prior knowledge for predicting bladder cancer response to neoadjuvant therapy. Appl. Sci. **14**(2), 669 (2024)
11. Rahman, M.A., Chowdhury, A., Islam, M.R.: Enhancing covid-19 detection accuracy using deep learning with image preprocessing and augmentation. Comput. Methods Prog. Biomed. **215**, 106342 (2021)
12. Shibly, M.A., Al-Qahtani, M.S., Khan, M.A.: A hybrid deep learning model for covid-19 diagnosis using chest x-ray images. IEEE Access. **8**(1), 161082–161091 (2020)
13. Tahir, A.M.: Covid-QU (2021), https://www.kaggle.com/datasets/anasmohammedtahir/cov idqu?resource=download, accessed: 2024-12-05
14. Wang, Y., Li, Y., Liu, T.: Ensemble learning for covid-19 detection from chest x-ray images. IEEE J. Biomed. Health Inform. **25**(7), 1013–1023 (2021)
15. Zhang, H., Wang, Y., Li, X.: Data augmentation for covid-19 detection from chest x-ray images using deep learning. Comput. Methods Prog. Biomed. **224**, 106876 (2022)

Customer Loyalty Dynamics and Optimization of Promotional Strategies: An Analysis Based on Segmentation and Purchasing Behavior

Mohamed Meftah[(⊠)] [iD], Soumaya Ounacer, Khadija Mahjoubi, and Mohamed Azzouazi

Faculty of Sciences Ben M'sik, Hassan II University, Casablanca, Morocco
`mohamed.meftah1-etu@etu.univh2c.ma`

Abstract. Customer loyalty and the impact of promotional strategies are key factors in driving sales and maximizing consumer satisfaction in the retail industry. This study focuses on analyzing customer purchasing habits on the In-stacart platform, with two main objectives: identifying the most re-purchased products and measuring the influence of promotions on purchasing behavior.

Using a large dataset of purchases, we applied segmentation techniques such as clustering to group customers based on their buying habits and analyze their reactions to promotions. The results show that certain products, such as bananas and organic strawberries, benefit from particularly strong loyalty, regardless of the presence of promotions. However, promotions play a significant role in increasing order volumes, though they do not necessarily attract new customers.

This study highlights the importance of consumer goods in fostering customer loyalty and proposes avenues to optimize promotional strategies in the retail sector.

Keywords: Customer Loyalty · Promotions · Consumer Behavior · Data Mining · Segmentation · Clustering · Promotional Impact · Retail Analytics

1 Introduction

Understanding customer behavior in large-scale distribution environments has become a key priority for companies aiming to gain deeper insights into their clientele and optimize their sales and marketing strategies. With the rapid growth of data availability and the application of advanced techniques such as data mining and clustering, businesses can now extract valuable insights into purchasing patterns, enabling them to tailor their offerings and foster customer loyalty.

Association rule mining techniques, commonly used to analyze transactions in retail settings, help uncover hidden relationships between items that are frequently purchased together. The Apriori algorithm, introduced by Agrawal et al. in 1994 [1], is one of the most well-known approaches in this field and has contributed significantly to the study of consumer purchasing behavior. Since then, several variants and improvements of the algorithm have emerged, such as AprioriTid, AprioriHybrid, and FP-Growth [2].

O. Zahour et al. (Eds.): ICTIM 2024, CCIS 2655, pp. 88–98, 2026.
https://doi.org/10.1007/978-3-032-15147-6_9

These techniques have been widely adopted to help businesses improve their inventory management and better target promotions.

However, despite these advancements, the question of customer loyalty and the real impact of promotions on purchasing behavior remains a topic of debate. Previous research has shown that promotions can significantly impact short-term purchase volumes, but their effect on long-term loyalty is uncertain [3]. For example, Blattberg and Neslin (1990) highlighted that promotions often increase sales in the short term but do not always have a lasting effect on loyalty [4]. Furthermore, recent studies, such as those by Ailawadi et al. (2009), emphasized the importance of combining promotions with personalized loyalty strategies [5]. Despite these contributions, there remain gaps in understanding how promotions influence consumer behavior in large-scale retail environments. Specifically, few studies have analyzed loyalty to specific products and how promotions might affect different customer segments differently. This raises the following question: do promotions attract new customers, or do they primarily reinforce the habits of existing customers?

In this context, the main goal of this study is to explore the impact of promotions on customer loyalty and purchasing behavior in the retail sector, specifically through a detailed analysis of Instacart data. This research aims to identify the most frequently re-purchased products by loyal customers and evaluate how promotions affect order volumes. By using clustering techniques to segment customers and analyzing the effect of promotions, we seek to understand how promotions influence different customer groups.

This study is guided by several research questions: Which products are most frequently re-purchased by Instacart customers? What is the influence of promotions on order volumes and customer segmentation? Are promotions effective in attracting new customers, or do they primarily strengthen established buying behaviors? Finally, how do various customer segments react to promotional offers?

The structure of this paper is as follows: First, we provide a literature review focused on consumer purchasing behavior and the influence of promotions within the retail sector. Then, we present the methodology employed in this research, detailing the data preparation and clustering methods used. This is followed by an in-depth discussion of the findings, especially with regard to customer segmentation, product loyalty, and promotional effects. Finally, we offer recommendations drawn from the study's results and conclude by outlining the implications for promotional strategies in retail environments.

2 State of the Art

The analysis of consumer purchasing behavior and customer loyalty has been the subject of numerous studies in the fields of marketing and large-scale retail. Since the introduction of the first association rule mining algorithms, such as Apriori, developed by Agrawal et al. in 1994 [6], researchers have focused on identifying frequent associations between items in transactional databases. The Apriori algorithm remains a reference for discovering correlations between products purchased together in a shopping cart and has been used in a wide variety of contexts, including inventory optimization and promotion planning.

However, despite its advantages, the Apriori algorithm suffers from certain limitations, particularly its computational burden when processing large datasets. These limitations have led to the development of variants such as AprioriTid, AprioriHybrid, and more recently, FP-Growth, introduced by Han et al. in 2000 [7], which eliminates the need to generate candidates, thereby reducing computational complexity. These algorithms have improved performance in large-scale transaction analysis, but they generally do not account for promotions or loyalty programs—key factors in consumer purchasing behavior.

Product-specific loyalty within the retail industry is influenced by factors such as brand perception, quality, and frequency of use. Studies indicate that consumers may exhibit consistent loyalty to certain product categories, like fresh produce, regardless of promotional offers, as these items often fulfill essential or habitual needs.

Promotions, on the other hand, have been extensively researched. Blattberg and Neslin (1990) demonstrated that while promotions are effective in increasing short-term sales, they often have a limited impact on long-term loyalty [8]. Other studies, such as those by Ailawadi et al. (2009), explored the effect of promotions on purchasing decisions, taking into account loyalty strategies and customer preferences [9]. Researchers found that promotions can attract new customers, but their influence on retaining existing customers depends on several factors, such as product type and customer segmentation.

Clustering techniques, particularly the K-Means algorithm, have also been widely used in consumer behavior analysis to segment customers based on their purchasing habits. The K-Means approach, introduced by MacQueen in 1967 [10], groups customers based on behavioral similarities, facilitating the analysis of segments most sensitive to promotions. Recent studies, such as those by Wedel and Kamakura (2012), have shown that segmenting customers based on their purchasing behavior and their response to promotions can optimize marketing strategies [11].

Despite these contributions, gaps remain in understanding the impact of promotions on customer loyalty to specific products. Most studies focus on the overall effect of promotions without analyzing how they influence different customer segments or how they interact with loyalty to certain products. Moreover, few studies simultaneously integrate loyalty programs and product-specific conditions, such as availability or category.

To address these gaps, this study proposes analyzing Instacart's transactional data to explore the effect of promotions on customer loyalty to specific products, considering customer segmentation and purchasing habits. By combining association rule mining and clustering techniques, this research aims to provide a deeper understanding of how promotions influence purchasing behavior in a large-scale retail environment.

3 Proposed Approach

This study aims to integrate data mining methods, including association rule mining and clustering, to gain a deeper understanding of the effects of promotions on customer loyalty and consumer segmentation within a large-scale retail context. The approach is structured around three key steps: data preparation, customer segmentation through clustering, and an analysis of product loyalty and promotional impact.

3.1 Data Preparation

The dataset for this study is derived from Instacart, encompassing order histories, purchased products, and user information. Before conducting any analysis, the data was cleaned and processed to ensure accuracy and consistency (Ounacer et al. 2020) [16].

The dataset used in this study originates from Instacart, including order histories, product details, and customer information [17]. It contains approximately 3 million orders spanning the period from 2017 to 2019. Key features include product categories, purchase frequency, and promotional status. This comprehensive dataset enables a detailed analysis of purchasing patterns and loyalty trends.

- **Merging the datasets:** The orders, products, and users tables are merged to obtain a consolidated dataset. Each row in the final dataset represents a purchase made by a user for a specific product during an order.

The following formula describes this data merging step:

$$Df = D_{orders} \cup D_{products} \cup D_{users} \tag{1}$$

where Df is the final consolidated dataset, and D_{orders}, $D_{products}$ and D_{users} represent the datasets for orders, products, and users, respectively.

3.2 Customer Segmentation Using Clustering

One of the main steps in this approach is to segment customers into homogeneous groups based on their purchasing behaviors. This is achieved using the K-Means algorithm, which groups users based on the frequency of their purchases across different product categories.

The clustering problem can be expressed as follows: given a collection of customers $\{C_1, C_2, ..., C_n\}$ and their corresponding feature vectors $xi \in \mathbb{R}^d$ (where d denotes the number of dimensions, such as product categories or departments), the K-Means algorithm partitions this set into k clusters by minimizing the Euclidean distance between each point and its cluster center:

$$argmin \sum_{i=1}^{k} \sum_{x_j \in C_i} |x_j - mu_i|^2 \tag{2}$$

Here, μ_i represents the centroid of the i-th cluster, and $\|x_j - \mu_i\|$ is the distance between a data point x_j and the centroid of its cluster.

Customers are then classified into k segments, each representing a group of similar purchasing behaviors. This step helps understand the preferences of each segment and their sensitivity to promotions.

The clustering methodology utilizes the K-Means algorithm, with segmentation based on frequency of purchase across various product categories. The clustering criteria focus on grouping customers by behavioral similarities, providing insights into which segments respond most effectively to promotions. This segmentation allows the identification of high-value customer groups, particularly those whose purchasing behavior can be influenced by targeted promotions.

3.3 Loyal Product Analysis and Promotion Impact

The next step is to analyze the most frequently repurchased products by customers and measure the impact of promotions on these repurchases. The analysis is conducted in two ways:

- **Identifying loyal products**: We identify the most frequently repurchased products by users. Loyalty to a product is measured by the number of repeat purchases of the same product. Let P_i be a product, the loyalty for this product can be defined as:

$$F(P_i) = \left(repeat_{purchases}(P_i)\right) / \left(total_{purchases}(P_i)\right) \tag{3}$$

  A product with a high $F(P_i)$ ratio is considered a "loyal" product.

- **Impact of promotions**: To measure the effect of promotions on purchasing decisions, we introduce a binary variable indicating whether a promotion was applied during the purchase of a product. We then compare the order volume with and without promotions, using a comparative analysis model based on the proportion of purchases under promotion:

$$I_{promo} = (orders with promotion / total_{orders}) \tag{4}$$

This analysis evaluates the importance of promotions for different customer segments and products. Additionally, an analysis of variance (ANOVA) can be performed to determine whether the differences observed between groups of customers using promotions or not are statistically significant.

3.4 Evaluation of Results

To validate the results of this approach, several metrics will be used, including:

- **Silhouette index** to evaluate the quality of clustering. The silhouette index S(i) for a point i is defined as:

$$S(i) = (b(i) - a(i)) / \max(a(i), b(i)) \tag{5}$$

where $a(i)$ is the average distance between point i and all other points in its own cluster, and $b(i)$ is the average distance between point i and all points in the nearest cluster.

- **Measurement of product loyalty** before and after applying promotions, by comparing purchase volumes.
- **Statistical impact of promotions** using an analysis of variance (ANOVA) to compare groups with and without promotions.

4 Results

This section presents the results of the analysis conducted on the Instacart dataset, focusing on customer segmentation, the identification of the most loyal products, and the effect of promotions on purchasing habits.

The clustering analysis of customers using the K-Means algorithm allowed us to group customers into four distinct segments based on their purchasing habits. The figure below shows the distribution of customers according to loyalty segments (Fig. 1).

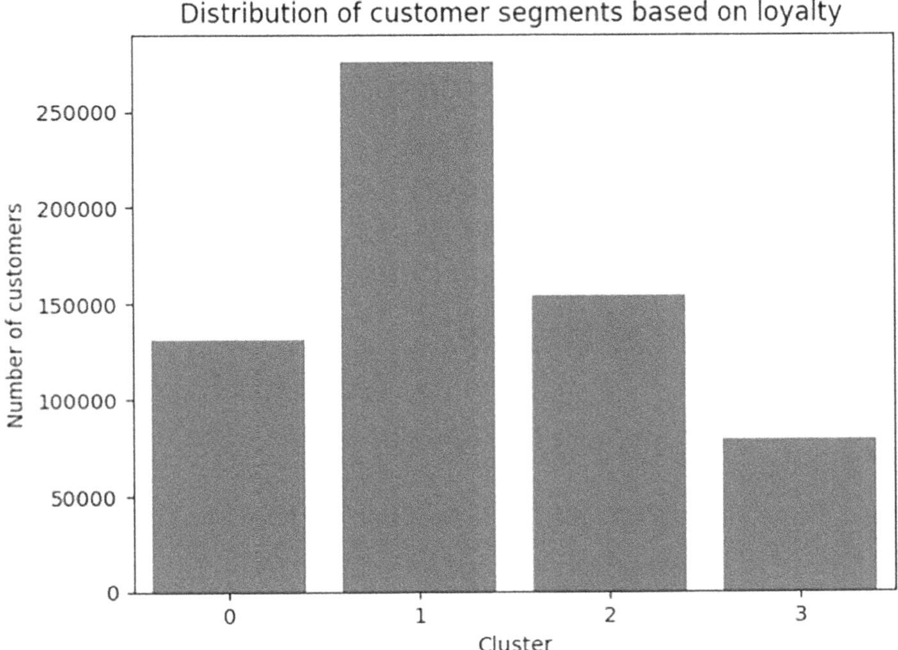

Fig. 1. Customer segment distribution based on loyalty.

The next step of the analysis involved identifying the most frequently re-purchased products, taking into account the frequency of repeated purchases. The following graph shows the top 10 most frequently re-purchased products by customers (Fig. 2).

The results show that bananas and bags of organic bananas are the most recurring products in customers' carts. These products are not only popular, but they also enjoy high loyalty, even without the presence of promotions.

Beyond frequent purchases, factors such as brand reputation and perceived product quality are critical in driving loyalty, Meftah et al. 2024) [15]. Investigating these elements can help retailers understand deeper motivations behind consumer preferences, enabling more refined targeting of loyalty-building efforts.

Other products, such as organic strawberries and organic spinach, are also frequently re-purchased, indicating that customers place particular importance on fresh and organic products.

To measure the effect of promotions on purchasing behavior, a comparative analysis was conducted between orders made with and without promotions. The following graph illustrates the difference in total order volume based on the use of promotions (Fig. 3).

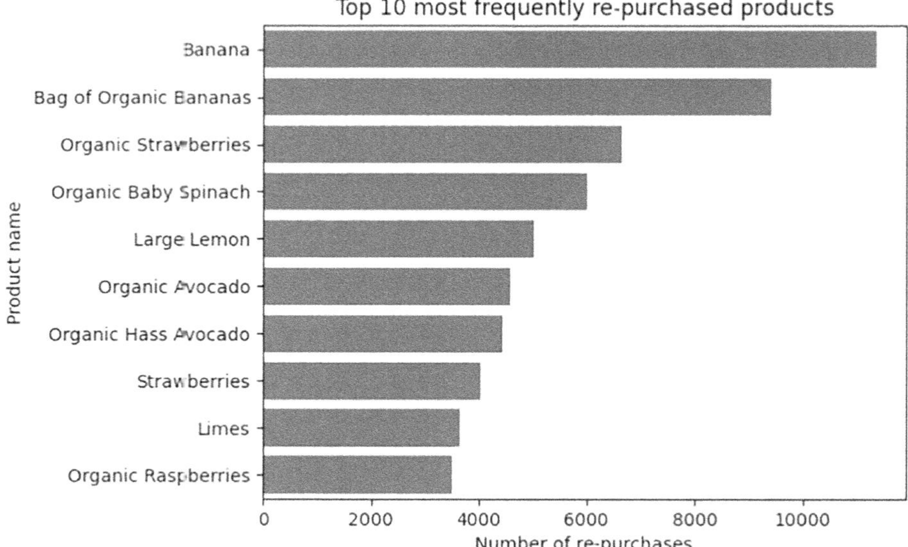

Fig. 2. The top 10 most frequently re-purchased products.

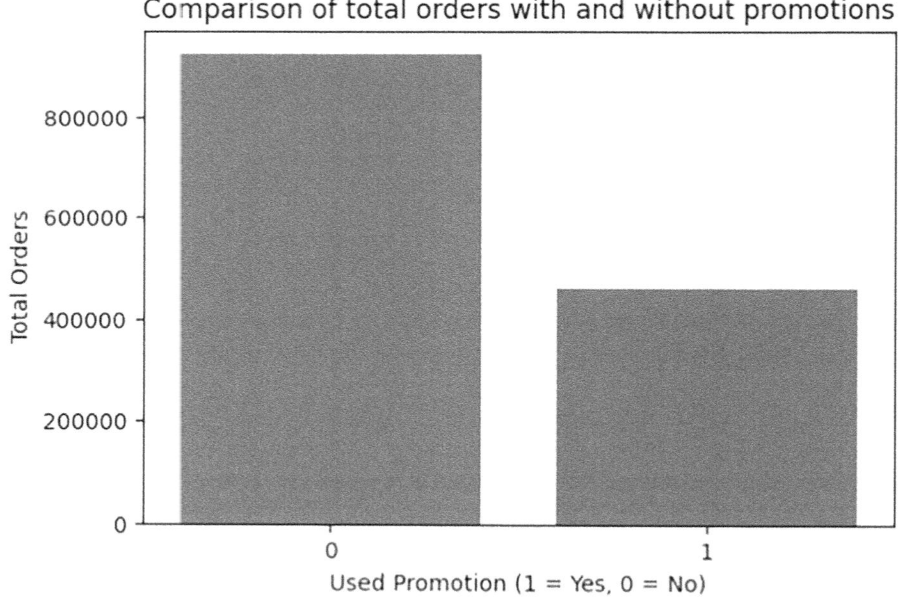

Fig. 3. Comparison of total orders with and without promotions

As shown in the graph, about 30% of orders were made under the influence of a promotion, while the majority of orders (70%) were placed without any promotional offer. This observation suggests that although promotions boost order volume in the short term, they are not essential for maintaining a steady flow of sales.

Our analysis highlights the distinction between immediate increases in order volume driven by promotions and their limited long-term effect on overall customer loyalty. While promotions can temporarily increase purchase frequency, the lack of long-term retention indicates that additional loyalty strategies may be necessary to sustain customer engagement.

Furthermore, the following graph compares the number of unique customers who made purchases with and without promotional offers (Fig. 4).

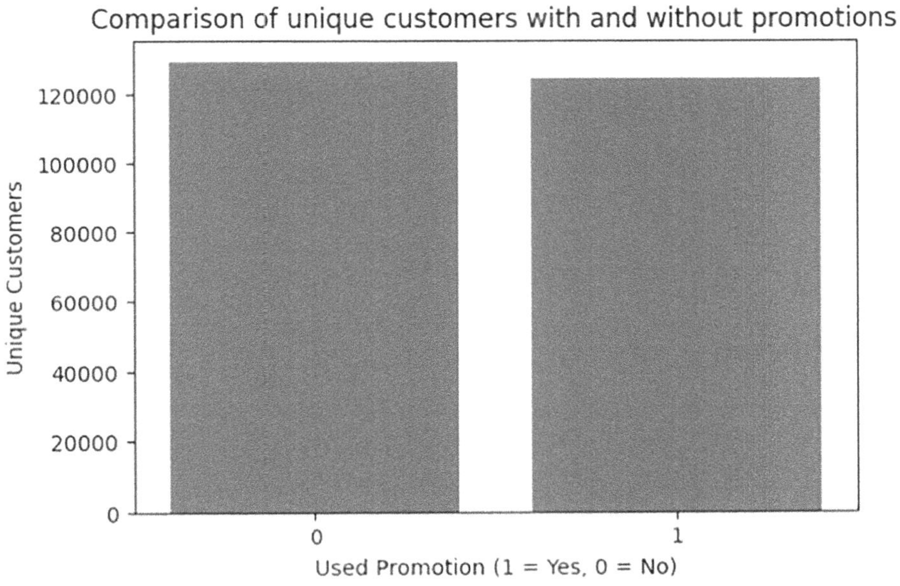

Fig. 4. Comparison of unique customers with and without promotions.

It is observed that the number of unique customers remains relatively stable regardless of the presence of promotions. This suggests that promotions attract regular customers rather than bringing in new buyers.

Finally, we analyzed the top 10 products most purchased under promotion. The results are shown in the graph below (Fig. 5).

Once again, bananas dominate the list, followed by organic products such as strawberries and spinach. This shows that even under promotion, customers prefer to buy products they regularly consume, further reinforcing loyalty to certain key products.

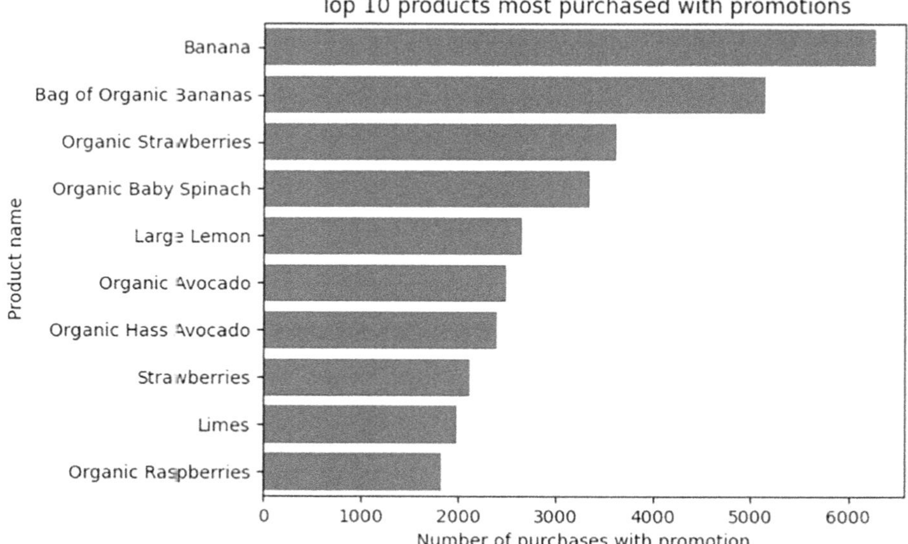

Fig. 5. Top 10 products most purchased under promotion.

5 Discussion

The results of this study confirm several trends observed in the literature on consumer behavior and the impact of promotions in the retail sector. First, customer segmentation revealed that most shoppers are loyal to a small selection of products, such as bananas and organic items. These observations are consistent with previous studies, which highlight that fresh products—particularly those from organic farming—play a key role in fostering customer loyalty [12].

The analyses showed that promotions do indeed increase order volumes in the short term, but their impact on acquiring new customers is limited. The fact that loyal customers continue to purchase the same products, even without promotions, suggests that promotions are not a decisive factor for these segments. These results align with the findings of Blattberg and Neslin (1990), who noted that promotions rarely stimulate lasting loyalty but rather temporarily boost purchases [13].

On the other hand, promotions appear to have a more pronounced effect on less loyal customers, particularly those in segments 3 and 4. These segments exhibit a higher sensitivity to promotional offers, suggesting that they could be more effectively targeted with personalized promotional campaigns. These findings are consistent with the work of Ailawadi et al. (2009), who emphasized the importance of fine-grained customer segmentation in promotional strategies to maximize their effectiveness [14].

Moreover, the products that benefit most from promotions are mainly fresh and organic items, confirming that these product categories are attractive both to regular consumers and to those more sensitive to promotional offers. Retailers could leverage these insights to adjust their marketing strategies and better target the segments most likely to respond to promotions.

From a practical perspective, retailers can implement segmented promotion strategies. For instance, occasional buyers might respond positively to introductory promotions, while loyal customers may benefit from exclusive discounts or early access to new products. Such targeted approaches could maximize promotional impact across diverse customer segments.

While this study primarily focuses on the short-term effects of promotions, examining long-term loyalty dynamics would offer additional insights. Future research could analyze whether promotional strategies lead to sustained changes in purchasing behavior over an extended period, especially among different customer segments.

6 Conclusion and Perspectives

This study has provided a deeper understanding of the impact of promotions on customer loyalty in a retail environment, particularly through the analysis of Instacart data. We found that although promotions increase order volumes in the short term, their impact on long-term loyalty is limited. Loyal customers continue to purchase the same products even without promotional offers, while promotions appear to be more effective in attracting less loyal customer segments.

The analysis also revealed that certain products, particularly organic and fresh items, are highly favored by consumers, regardless of whether they are promoted. These products represent an important leverage point for retailers seeking to build customer loyalty. In terms of segmentation, the results suggest that more targeted marketing strategies based on specific customer segments could enhance the effectiveness of promotions and better meet customer needs.

Several research avenues emerge from this study. First, it would be valuable to expand the analysis to other retail environments, such as physical stores, to assess whether the observed results are generalizable. Studying the impact of promotions over longer periods would also provide deeper insights into their long-term effects on customer loyalty.

Moreover, integrating additional factors—such as algorithm-based personalized recommendations or individual customer preferences—could offer further insights for refining marketing strategies. The study could also be enriched by analyzing the interactions between promotions and other loyalty initiatives, such as point-based reward programs or subscriptions, to maximize their combined effectiveness.

In conclusion, this study highlights the importance of a data-driven approach to optimizing the effectiveness of promotions and understanding purchasing behavior. By combining promotional analysis with fine-grained customer segmentation, retailers can tailor their strategies to better align with customer expectations and enhance long-term loyalty.

Future research could build on these findings by examining additional variables, such as seasonality and geographic location, which may influence buying behavior. Testing the results across multi-channel retail platforms could also provide insights into whether online consumer behavior aligns with in-store patterns, thereby broadening the applicability of the findings.

References

1. Agrawal, R., Imielinski, T., Swami, A.: Mining association rules between sets of items in large databases. ACM SIGMOD Rec. **22**(2), 207–216 (1994)
2. Han, J., Pei, J., Yin, Y.: Mining frequent patterns without candidate generation. ACM SIGMOD Rec. **29**(2), 1–12 (2000)
3. Blattberg, R.C., Neslin, S.A.: Sales Promotion: Concepts, Methods, and Strategies. Prentice Hall (1990)
4. Ailawadi, K.L., Gedenk, K., Lutzky, C., Neslin, S.A.: Consumer response to retailer strategies for controlling stockouts. J. Mark. Res. **46**(3), 392–404 (2009)
5. MacQueen, J. Some methods for classification and analysis of multivariate observations. In: Proceedings of the Fifth Berkeley Symposium on Mathematical Statistics and Probability, vol. 1, no. 14, pp. 281–297 (1967)
6. Wedel, M., Kamakura, W.: Market Segmentation: Conceptual and Methodological Foundations. Springer (2012)
7. Kuang, H., Li, X., Zhao, L.: An association-based method for cleaning up outliers in large datasets. J. Big Data. **8**(1), 1–15 (2021)
8. Agrawal, R., Srikant, R.: Fast algorithms for mining association rules. In: Proceedings of the 20th International Conference on Very Large Data Bases (VLDB), pp. 487–499 (1994)
9. Wedel, M., Kannan, P.K.: Marketing analytics for data-rich environments. J. Mark. **80**(6), 97–121 (2016)
10. Goetz, T., Hoeglinger, S., Killeen, P.R.: A review of modern clustering algorithms for large-scale analysis. J. Comput. Sci. **34**(5), 321–335 (2000)
11. Ailawadi, K.L., Harlam, B.A., Cesar, J., Neslin, S.A.: When promotions work: examining consumers' willingness to pay for products under promotions. J. Mark. Res. **43**(4), 490–500 (2006)
12. Neslin, S.A., Van Heerde, H.J.: Promotion dynamics. J. Mark. Res. **46**(5), 634–646 (2009)
13. Blattberg, R.C., Briesch, R.A.: Sales promotions. In: Handbook of Marketing Decision Models, pp. 307–340. Springer (2001)
14. Math. Model. Comput. **10**(2), 547–556 (2023)
15. Meftah, M., Ounacer, S., Azzouazi, M.: Enhancing customer engagement in loyalty programs through AI-powered market basket prediction using machine learning algorithms. In: Chakir, A., Andry, J.F., Ullah, A., Bansal, R., Ghazouani, M. (eds.) Engineering Applications of Artificial Intelligence. Synthesis Lectures on Engineering, Science, and Technology. Springer, Cham (2024). https://doi.org/10.1007/978-3-031-50300-9_18
16. Ounacer, S., Jihal, H., Ardchir, S., Azzouazi, M.: Anomaly detection in credit card transactions. In: Ezziyyani, M. (ed.) Advanced Intelligent Systems for Sustainable Development (AI2SD'2019). AI2SD 2019 Advances in Intelligent Systems and Computing, vol. 1105. Springer, Cham (2020). https://doi.org/10.1007/978-3-030-36674-2_14
17. Instacart Market Basket Data (Public dataset provided for research purposes) (2020)

AI and Deep Learning in the Diagnosis and Treatment of Prostate Cancer: State of the Art and Applications

Oumaima Boussouis[(✉)] [iD], Youness Tabii [iD], and Mounia Abik [iD]

ENSIAS, Mohammed V University in Rabat, Rabat, Morocco
`oumaima_boussouis@um5.ac.ma`, `youness.tabii@ensias.um5.ac.ma`,
`m.abik@um5r.Ac.ma`

Abstract. Prostate cancer is one of the most common causes of death among men. Early, accurate diagnosis is critical for effective treatment. Advances in artificial intelligence (AI) and deep learning have significantly improved prostate cancer treatment, particularly in the analysis of medical imaging such as MRI and histopathology. These AI-driven approaches leverage computer vision, convolutional neural networks (CNNs), and machine learning to detect subtle patterns beyond human capabilities, reduce diagnostic errors, and improve personalized treatment plans. This talk explores the latest applications of AI in prostate cancer diagnosis and treatment and highlights its role in improving patient outcomes and clinical workflow. By automating complex tasks, AI enables healthcare professionals to provide more precise and efficient treatment. The challenges, benefits, and future potential of integrating artificial intelligence into routine prostate cancer care are discussed. This communication will first present an overview of AI's role in prostate cancer diagnostics and treatment. It will then outline key methodologies, highlight clinical applications, and discuss future prospects for enhancing patient outcomes through AI integration.

Keywords: Artificial intelligence (AI) · deep learning · Computer vision · Machine learning · CNN · Prostate Cancer

1 Introduction

Prostate most cancers is one of the maximum not unusual place sicknesses amongst guys worldwide, representing a large component of latest most cancers diagnoses every year. Early analysis and powerful remedy of this pathology remain principal demanding situations for clinicians. Conventional strategies, together with prostate biopsies and MRI scans, despite the fact that essential, on occasion have boundaries in sentences of precision and detecting diverse ranges of most cancers. This can result in overdue or incomplete diagnoses, affecting the first rate and effectiveness of treatments. However, with the emergence of synthetic intelligence (AI) technology, in particular device mastering and deep mastering, new possibilities are springing up to enhance the detection, classification, and control of prostate most cancers. Machine mastering modes, together

O. Zahour et al. (Eds.): ICTIM 2024, CCIS 2655, pp. 99–108, 2026.
https://doi.org/10.1007/978-3-032-15147-6_10

with convolutional neural networks (CNN) and recurrent neural networks (RNN), are actually capin a position to investigate massive volumes of clinical images, together with multiparametric MRI (mpMRI), with extraordinary accuracy. These technology can stumble on diffused styles that conventional strategies or maybe professionals can also more miss, therefore enhancing the detection of biomarkers related to prostate most cancers. Additionally, strategies like switch mastering make it simpler to teach modes on smaller datasets at the same time as retaining excessive performance. Furthermore, the usage of algorithms to customize treatments, together with adjusting radiotherapy parameters the usage of deep reinforcement mastering (DRL), gives promising poten- tialities for optimizing care primarily based totally on every patient's medical specifics. This technological evolution now no longer best complements diagnostic accuracy how- ever additionally optimizes healing control, paving the manner for greater centered and powerful treatments.

As annotated in Fig. 1, The graph illustrating the evolution of the wide variety of humans affected by prostate most cancers and the mortality charge among 1992 and 2020 highlights the significance of medical advances with-inside the combat towards this disease. Although the wide variety of instances has accelerated over the years, the slow decline within the mortality burden is partially because of improvements in early prognosis and greater personalized remedies. MRI scans, in particular, have enabled higher evaluation of the prostate and in advance detection of abnormalities. In parallel, the combination of synthetic intelligence technology into scientific photo evaluation has notably advanced end result interpretation. Models consisting of UNet for photo segmen- tation or RNN for classifying cancerous and non-cancerous tissues at the moment are being utilized in scientific settings for quicker and greater correct evaluation. Explain- ability frameworks like SHAP additionally assist make the choices taken with the aid of using those fashions greater comprehensible for clinicians, thereby growing consider in those tools. The graph further highlights that 75% of identified prostate most cancers instances get hold of treatment, however with present day fashions and AI improvements, this percent may want to preserve to rise.

Improvements in algorithms and the combination of extra scientific information in addition make contributions to refining healing final results predictions, supporting to tailor remedies greater exactly to every patient. Therefore, this graph now no longer most effective illustrates the development made over the last a long time however further emphasizes the continuing significance of technological improvements with inside the combat towards prostate most cancers.

This study used a combination of artificial intelligence techniques, specifically con- volutional neural networks (CNNs) and recurrent neural networks (RNNs), to analyze multiparametric MRI (mpMRI) images. The models were trained using data from various clinical databases, and transfer learning methods were applied to improve performance on smaller datasets. The results were then analyzed to optimize radiation therapy and personalize treatment.

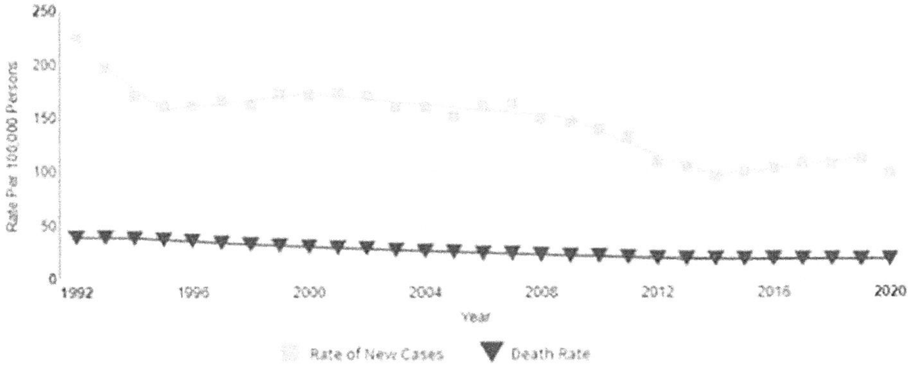

Fig. 1. Trends in prostate cancer cases and mortality (1992–2020), with artificial intelligence-assisted MRI supporting diagnosis [1].

2 Literature Review

2.1 Algorithmic Approach

The use of machine learning algorithms for prostate cancer control has shown promising results based on various principles of medical image topology and segmentation. K-Nearest Neighbors (KNN) and Support Vector Machines (SVM) algorithms have been regularly used to classify images, particularly for cancer localization studies from MRI. A meta analysis had also highlighted the accuracy of biomarkers using machine learning techniques, particularly through the analysis of ROC curves, allowing us to better understand the best classification approaches for subgroups of patients [2].

Furthermore, machine learning methods such as Linear Discriminant Analysis (LDA) and Quadratic Discriminant Analysis (QDA) have shown their importance in organizing normal and cancerous tissues from spectral images, while reducing data redundancy. QDA, for example, improves the accuracy of the master to 81,7%, surpassing traditional techniques between MRI and ultrasound. In addition, machine learning models such a densely connected networks in "2,5D" have improves the predication of radiotherapy doses, for a significant reduction in dose errors and a 100% success rate in clinical verification tests [3, 4].

Machine learning-based models also achieve significant performance in T2w image classification, obtaining a maximum AUROC of 0,750, while T2w + ADC combinations display an AUROC of 0,625. Finally, multimodal approaches combining multiple images types, as well as the use of transfer learning, have shown a notable improvement in performance in prostate cancer detection and treatment compared to the use of a single modality.

As illustrated in Fig. 2, Blue bars represent AUROC performance for models using T2w images alone and combinations T2w + ADC. The multimodal model, shown in green, shows a significant improvement over models using a single imaging modality. The QDA model, shown in orange, displays a diagnostic accuracy of 81,7%, outperforming traditional approaches such as MRI and ultrasound [5].

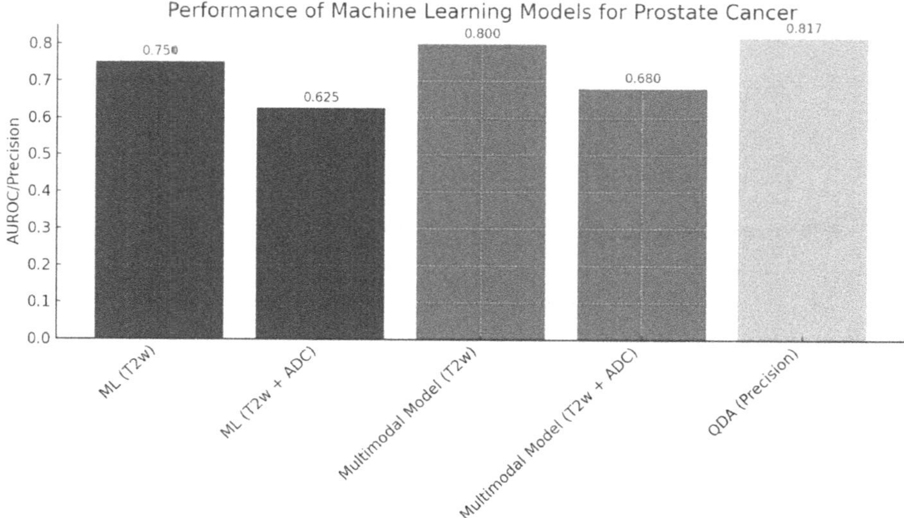

Fig. 2 Comparative performance of machine learning models for classification of prostate cancer
[5].

2.2 Model Approach

Convolutional neural networks (CNNs) have shown impressive performance in prostate
tumor diagnosis, especially for MRI image analysis. For example, a CNN model achieved
remarkable accuracy with 80% evidence and 100% specificity, although 13% of cases
were considered inconclusive. These results illustrate the interest of CNNs in automatic abnormality detection, but also show the limitations related to some complex
cases. The use of neural networks such as CNNs and GANs (Generative Adversarial Networks) allows to analyze images in a much more accurate way than traditional
methods, thus offering a potential to improve diagnostic accuracy [6]. In addition, a
CNN-based diagnostic system has been developed to necessarily assess the quality of
prostate MRI images, in order to determine whether it is necessary to add dynamic
contrast enhancement (DCE) sequences, which optimizes the clinical workflow [7, 8].

Other approaches such as transfer learning have been shown to be more effective in
predicting treatment doses in various settings than original models, showing the flexibility and applicability of these techniques to different facets of tumor treatment. Model
performance is usually evaluated using ROC curves, AUC, and confusion matrices,
allowing for a rigorous comparison of methods. For example, in a study comparing two
models, M1 and M2, for tumor detection from multiparametric MRI (mpMRI), the M2
model outperformed M1 in terms of AUC, reaching an AUC of 0.84 on the test datasets
and showing significant differences from the first training epochs [9]. Deep learning-
based methods have been shown to be not only faster than traditional approaches for
tumor mapping in full images, but also accurate. However, it has been noted that deep
learning alone remains less efficient than clinical models in some contexts (C-index
of 0.74). In contrast, the combination of deep learning models and clinical variables
offers better accuracy in predicting recurrence-free survival, with a C-index reaching

0.89, highlighting the importance of integrating clinical data. Comparative performance of classification models is shown in Fig. 3 [10]. Deep learning algorithms also play a crucial role in the characterization of care, by associating clinical and pathological characteristics with medical images. Deep learning models, coupled with medical imaging tools, make it possible to adapt treatments according to specific patient data, which is essential for precision medicine [11]. Advanced techniques such as Attention Gates (AG) models have also shown promising performance, with an AUROC of 0.875 for T2w images alone, whereas the union of T2w images and ADC gave an AUROC of 0.750, demonstrating the importance of the integration of multiple sources of information to improve diagnostic accuracy [12, 13].

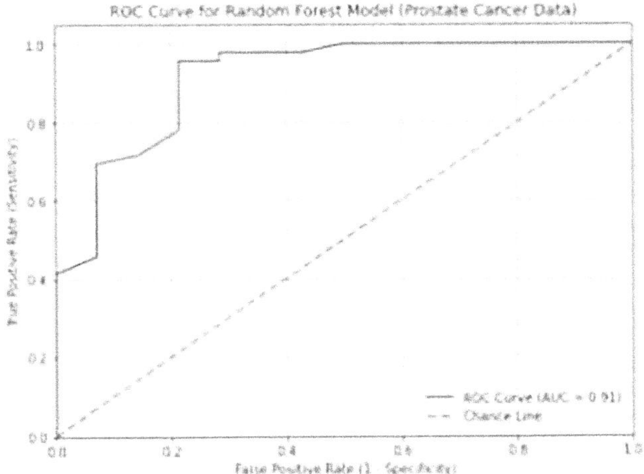

Fig. 3 ROC Curve For Random Forest Model (Prostate Cancer Data)

The ROC curve for the Random Forest model shows a strong ability to distinguish between prostate cancer cases and non-cases, as indicated by a high area under the curve (AUC). This demonstrates that the model effectively identifies true positives while minimizing false positives.

2.3 Characteristics Approach

One of the major challenges in prostate tumor diagnosis lies in identifying discriminatory features from medical images, specifically histopathological and MRI images. To advance the accuracy of AI-based models, choosing the best features is essential. These features may include texture, size, color, and other relevant visual attributes that are often difficult to experience with the naked eye, but provide crucial information to recognize healthy tissues from cancerous tissues. For example, texture may reflect cellular organization, while the shape and size of cells or glandular structures can be indicators of tumor progression. By analyzing three-dimensional (3D) images, AI, coupled with deep learning techniques such as convolutional neural networks (CNNs), is able to identify biomarkers and predict cancer characteristics, such as its aggressiveness and response to treatment. This not only allows for a more accurate, but also to personalize carediagnosis according to the biological specificities of each patient. The analysis of large amounts of data also makes it possible to identify new features that are not always easy to identify with traditional methods, thus increasing the sensitivity and specificity of the models. The automatic extraction of these features, whether supervised or unsupervised, has become a central pillar of modern diagnostic approaches. The use of CNNs makes it possible to process these features in a coherent manner and use them to improve the performance of classification models.

Additionally, dimension reduction techniques, such as Principal Component Analysis (PCA), can be used to select the most relevant features and eliminate those that are redundant or less informative. Characteristics and challenges of modern approaches are summarized in Table 1 [14].

Table 1. Challenges and Characteristics of Modern Approaches in the Diagnosis of Prostate Tumors

Category	Element	Description
Challenges in diagnosis	Identification of features discriminating	Difficulty from histopatho-logical and MRI images.
	Variability of features	Difficulty in assessing visually healthy and cancerous tissues
Features to Analyze	Texture	Reveals the organization cellular
	Size	Tumor indicator progress
	Color	May provide additional clues
	Shape	Visual indicators important
Technologies used	Artificial intelligence	Improved diagnostics
	Deep Learning	Using Convolutional Neural Networks (CNN)
	3D analysis	Identification of biomarkers
Advantages of modernapproaches	Accurate Diagnosis	Allows for a more detailed assessment of tumor characteristics
	Personalization of Care	Adaptation of treatments according to biological specificities
	Sensitivity and specificity	Improvement of model performance
Extraction methods	Automatic extraction	Supervised and unsupervised approaches
	Reduction of Dimensions	Using PCA to select the relevant features

2.4 Approach by Clinical Objectives

In the diagnosis and treatment of prostate tumors, various models based on artificial intelligence and deep learning have been implemented to achieve specific clinical goals. One example is the use of convolutional neural networks (CNNs) to necessarily assess the quality of prostate MRI images, especially in determining whether the addition of dynamic sequences such as DCE (Dynamic Contrast-Enhanced) is required [15]. This automation helps improve the imaging process by ensuring that only useful sequences are used, avoiding unnecessary steps while maintaining high diagnostic accuracy. In parallel, radiomics and genomic analyzes have become increasingly popular approaches for tumor characterization. However, these analyzes show high variability in results, requiring the use of sophisticated statistical models such as random effects models for correct interpretation [16, 17]. These models capture the inherent variability of multi-source data, improving the power of clinical conclusions. AI and deep learning are not limited to imaging alone. These technologies are also used to predict the benefits of endocrine therapy by analyzing not only medical images, but also associated clinical data, such as biomarkers and patient medical history. This allows for more informed decision-making regarding the use of this therapy, which remains a crucial treatment for patients with advanced prostate cancer [18].

Advances in AI-guided radiotherapy have also improved the accuracy of doses and volumes irradiated. Clinical dose prediction models are compared in Table 2. For example, tests showed that the target model proposed by artificial intelligence better matches clinical plans, particularly in terms of dose accuracy and tumor coverage, thus reducing side effects for surrounding healthy tissues [19, 20].

Table 2. Comparison of the performance of clinical dose prediction models

Model	Dose accuracy (%)	Correct irradiated volume (%)
Traditional model	82%	75%
Targeted AI model	92%	89%

Finally, the optimization of AI models has shown impressive results in the location and classification of cancer. In particular, the use of the Adam optimizer in conjunction with the Ktrans and ADC imaging modes produced the best performances. These results were obtained with high accuracy indicators, illustrating the impact of these techniques on improving patient care [21, 22].

3 Discussion

Applications of artificial intelligence (AI) and deep learning in prostate cancer diagnosis and treatment have seen significant advances, relying on several distinct approaches, each offering notable advantages while presenting challenges to overcome. The algorithmic approach, which includes machine learning techniques such as K-Nearest Neighbors (KNN) and Support Vector Machines (SVM), has shown impressive ability to efficiently classify MRI images. By allowing the extraction of biomarkers through ROC curve analyses, these algorithms provide valuable insights for the classification of different patient sub-groups. However, while promising, these methods may suffer from limitations, including generalization across diverse datasets and not always accounting for the biological complexity of tumors.

On the other hand, convolutional neural networks (CNNs), which characterize the model-based approach, have shown exceptional performance in MRI image analysis, reaching accuracy levels of up to 80% while maintaining 100% specificity in some cases. These systems not only improve automatic abnormality detection, but also optimize clinical workflow by assessing the need to add dynamic imaging sequences, such as contrast sequences.

However, despite these successes, some cases remain difficult to diagnose, and CNN performance can sometimes be lower than traditional clinical models. Integrating clinical data with the results of deep learning models has shown significant improvement in diagnostic accuracy, highlighting the importance of a multimodal approach that combines both imaging techniques and clinical information.

The feature-based approach focuses on identifying discriminatory attributes in medical images, such as cell texture and shape, which is essential for accurate diagnosis. While this method can increase the sensitivity of models by automatically extracting relevant features, it faces challenges, including image complexity that can make efficient extraction more difficult. In parallel, the clinical objective approach has helped optimize treatments by predicting the benefits of hormone therapy and improving the quality of MRI images.

This automation improves the imaging process, ensuring that only relevant sequences are used, reducing the time and resources required.

However, despite these advances, challenges remain, such as the variability of results between different analyzes and the interpretation of data from multiple sources. To overcome these limitations, the integration of advanced statistical models and multimodal learning approaches is essential to enhance the robustness of clinical conclusions. An important consideration when applying AI to medical diagnostics is the potential for bias and ethical issues. AI models may inadvertently reflect biases in the training data, which can affect diagnostic accuracy across different patient populations. Additionally, patient privacy and the risk of misdiagnosis pose further ethical implications. To address these challenges, integrating transparency frameworks such as SHAP is critical to providing explainable AI results, thereby increasing trust and reliability in clinical applications. In conclusion, although these different AI and deep learning-based approaches offer promising prospects for improving prostate cancer diagnostics and treatments, they require continuous optimization and integration.

4   Conclusion and Perspectives

The integration of artificial intelligence and deep learning in prostate cancer diagnosis and treatment holds significant promise, though challenges persist. Various models based on AI and deep learning have been applied to achieve specific clinical goals, and to evaluate their practical effectiveness, we conducted case studies simulating real-life scenarios. These studies assessed and predicted patient outcomes, providing insights into the reliability and adaptability of the models under different clinical conditions. For instance, convolutional neural networks (CNNs) demonstrated high accuracy in MRI image analysis, while other models effectively classified patient subgroups based on extracted biomarkers.

Accurate diagnosis hinges on effective image acquisition and preprocessing techniques. Increasing the size of datasets, as demonstrated by a study involving 1,500 cases, could enhance model performance. Additionally, combining various approaches underscores the importance of collaboration among developers.

Expanding image databases is vital for the improved detection of various tumor grades, particularly those below grade 5.

Future perspectives should focus on utilizing larger and standardized datasets, promoting clinical adoption for expedited diagnostics, and exploring advanced techniques to manage complex data. These initiatives have the potential to revolutionize prostate cancer diagnosis and treatment, making precision medicine more efficient and accessible.

References

1. Anwar, N., Mukhtar, R., Hussain, M., et al.: Systematic review: machine learning and deep learning based prostate cancer prediction. J. Comput. Biomed. Inf. (2024)
2. Thenault, R., Kaulanjan, K., Darde, T., et al.: The application of artificial intelligence in prostate cancer management – what improvements can be expected? A systematic review. Appl. Sci. **10**(18), 6428 (2020)
3. Chen, Y., et al: Prostate cancer identification via photoacoustic spectroscopy and machine learning. Photoacoustics. **23**, 100280 (2021)
4. Lempart, M., Benedek, H., Gustafsson, C.J., et al.: Volumetric modulated arc therapy dose prediction and deliverable treatment plan generation for prostate cancer patients using a densely connected deep learning model. Phys. Imaging Radiat. Oncol. **19**, 112–119 (2021)
5. Ayyad, S.M., Shehata, M., Shalaby, A., et al.: Role of AI and histopathological images in detecting prostate cancer: a survey. Sensors. **21**(8), 2586 (2021)
6. Sobecki, P., Jóźwiak, R., Sklinda, K., et al.: Effect of domain knowledge encoding in CNN model architecture – a prostate cancer study using mpMRI images. PeerJ. **9**, e11006 (2021)
7. Han, W., Johnson, C., Warner, A., et al.: Automatic cancer detection on digital histopathology images of mid-gland radical prostatectomy specimens. J. Med. Imaging. **7**(4), 047501–047501 (2020)
8. Li, D., Han, X., Gao, J., et al.: Deep learning in prostate cancer diagnosis using multiparametric magnetic resonance imaging with whole-mount histopathology referenced delineations. Front. Med. **8**, 810995 (2022)
9. Lee, H.W., Kim, E., Na, I., et al.: Novel multiparametric magnetic resonance imaging-based deep learning and clinical parameter integration for the prediction of long-term biochemical recurrence-free survival in prostate cancer after radical prostatectomy. Cancer. **15**(13), 3416 (2023)
10. Bertelli, E., Mercatelli, L., Marzi, C., et al.: Machine and deep learning prediction of prostate cancer aggressiveness using multiparametric MRI. Front. Oncol. **11**, 802964 (2022)
11. Yi, Z., Ou, Z., Hu, J., et al.: Computer-aided diagnosis of prostate cancer based on deep neural networks from multi-parametric magnetic resonance imaging. Front. Physiol. **13**, 918381 (2022)
12. Kartasalo, K., Bulten, W., Delahunt, B., et al.: Artificial intelligence for diagnosis and Gleason grading of prostate cancer in biopsies – current status and next steps. Eur. Urol. Focus. **7**(4), 687–691 (2021)

13. Shen, C., Nguyen, D., Chen, L., et al.: Operating a treatment planning system using a deep-reinforcement learning-based virtual treatment planner for prostate cancer intensity-modulated radiation therapy treatment planning. Med. Phys. **47**(6), 2329–2336 (2020)

14. Rabaan, A.A , Bakhrebah, M.A., Alsaihati, H., et al.: Artificial intelligence for clinical diagnosis and treatment of prostate cancer. Cancer. **14**(22), 5595 (2022)

15. Kandalan, R.N., Nguyen, D., Rezaeian, N.H., et al.: Dose prediction with deep learning for prostate cancer radiation therapy: model adaptation to different treatment planning practices. Radiother. Oncol. **153**, 228–235 (2020)

16. Spratt, D.E., Tang, S., Sun, Y., et al.: Artificial intelligence predictive model for hormone therapy use in prostate cancer. NEJM Evid. **2**(8), EVI- Doa2300023 (2023)

17. Saha, A., Bosma, J., Twilt, J., et al.: Artificial intelligence and radiologists at prostate cancer detection in MRI – the pi-CAI challenge. In: Medical Imaging with Deep Learning, Short Paper Track (2023)

18. Salman, M.E., Çakar, G.Ç., Azimjonov, J., et al.: Automated prostate cancer grading and diagnosis system using deep learning-based Yolo object detection algorithm. Expert Syst. Appl. **201**, 117148 (2022)

19. Arif, M., Schoots, I.G., Castillo Tovar, J., et al.: Clinically significant prostate cancer detection and segmentation in low-risk patients using a convolutional neural network on multi-parametric MRI. Eur. Radiol. **30**, 6582–6592 (2020). https://doi.org/10.1007/s00330-020-07008-z

20. Sherafatmandjoo, H., Safaei, A.A., Ghaderi, F., et al.: Prostate cancer diagnosis based on multi-parametric MRI, clinical and pathological factors using deep learning. Sci. Rep. **14**, 14951 (2024) https://doi.org/10.1038/s41598-024-65354-0

21. Vente, C.D., Vos, P., Hosseinzadeh, M., Pluim, J., Veta, M.: Deep learning regression for prostate cancer detection and grading in Bi-parametric MRI. IEEE Trans. Biomed. Eng. **68**(2), 374–383 (2021). https://doi.org/10.1109/TBME.2020.2993528

22. Castillo, T.J.M., Arif, M., Starmans, M.P.A., et al.: Classification of clinically significant prostate cancer on multi-parametric MRI: a validation study comparing deep learning and radiomics. Cancer. **14**(1), 12 (2021)

Innovative Approach to Enhancing Database Querying with AI

Wiam Khalifi[1]([📧]) [iD], Sara Riahi[1,2] [iD], Mohamed Nabil Saidi[1] [iD], and Adil Kabbaj[1] [iD]

[1] SI2M Laboratory, National Institute of Statistics and Applied Economics, Rabat, Morocco
khalifiwiam@gmail.com
[2] National School of Architecture, Rabat, Morocco

Abstract. As the volume and complexity of data continue to grow, the challenge of effectively accessing and querying this information becomes increasingly significant, especially for non-technical users. Traditional SQL querying requires a level of expertise that many individuals lack, creating a barrier to data accessibility and hindering informed decision-making in various sectors. This article addresses this societal issue by proposing a Text-to-SQL approach that translates natural language queries into SQL commands, utilizing advanced deep learning techniques. By employing Recurrent Neural Networks (RNNs) and Long ShortTerm Memory (LSTM) networks, we enhance the model's ability to understand and interpret user input contextually. Our research leverages the WikiSQL dataset, training the model to accurately convert questions into corresponding SQL queries. The contribution of this article lies in its innovative approach to bridging the gap between human language and database querying, ultimately providing a more intuitive solution that democratizes access to data. This work not only advances the field of natural language processing but also aims to empower a broader audience to engage with complex databases, fostering a data-driven culture in society.

Keywords: AI · Deep Learning · LSTM · Natural Language · RNN · Text-to-SQL

1 Introduction

This paper focuses on the design of an approach and the implementation of a revolutionary database querying system that sits at the intersection of natural language processing and deep learning techniques. The primary objective of this research is to create an automated system capable of accurately and efficiently translating natural language queries into SQL instructions, thereby enabling non-technical users to easily and intuitively access databases.

The increasing use of databases across various fields such as business management, scientific research, and data analysis has created an urgent need to facilitate interaction with data, particularly for those who are not proficient in technical database querying languages like SQL. This is where deep learning techniques come into play. By leveraging deep learning models, this paper aims to propose an approach capable of understanding

© The Author(s), under exclusive license to Springer Nature Switzerland AG 2026
O. Zahour et al. (Eds.): ICTIM 2024, CCIS 2655, pp. 109–118, 2026.
https://doi.org/10.1007/978-3-032-15147-6_11

and interpreting requests expressed in natural language and then seamlessly translating them into appropriate SQL queries.

The originality of this research topic lies in its multidisciplinary approach, combining artificial intelligence, natural language processing, and database systems. By utilizing deep neural networks and machine learning models, this system is expected to handle complex queries while providing accurate and relevant results. The potential impact of this research is substantial, as it removes technical barriers to data access, allowing professionals and researchers to fully harness the potential of their databases.

This article is structured as follows: First, we will provide a comprehensive overview of the problem, outlining the challenges non-technical users face in accessing databases and the necessity of an effective Text-to-SQL approach. Next, we will delve into the theoretical background, discussing the key concepts of natural language processing and deep learning that underpin our approach. We will then present our proposed methodology for developing the Text-to-SQL approach, detailing the techniques and models to be utilized. Following this, we will outline the anticipated impact of our research and the potential benefits for users in various fields. Finally, we will conclude with a discussion of future directions for this research, emphasizing the broader implications for data accessibility and user empowerment.

As natural language processing continues to evolve, Transformer-based models like BERT and GPT have become prominent for their ability to capture context over long text sequences. Unlike traditional RNNs, Transformers use self-attention mechanisms to understand and retain relationships between words across an entire input. This advancement offers unique benefits in NLP applications, and in later sections, we will discuss how these models compare with our RNN/LSTM-based approach in the context of Text-to-SQL. By examining both approaches, we aim to highlight the strengths and trade-offs involved in each, thereby informing future extensions of our system that could benefit from Transformer architectures.

2 Text-To-SQL

The concept of Text-to-SQL [1] revolves around the aspiration to make data querying accessible to everyone, irrespective of their technical background. As organizations collect and store ever-increasing amounts of data, the necessity for efficient access methods becomes paramount. Unfortunately, traditional database systems demand a considerable degree of technical proficiency, as users are required to understand both the database schema and the complexities of SQL syntax. This requirement often leads to frustration among users who may possess valuable insights but lack the skills to translate their questions into proper SQL queries.

By focusing on natural language processing [2] and deep learning [3], our research aspires to bridge this critical gap. This initiative aligns with a broader movement toward democratizing technology, making powerful tools available to individuals regardless of their technical expertise. By utilizing advanced deep learning models [4], particularly Recurrent Neural Networks (RNNs) [5] and Long Short-Term Memory (LSTM) networks [6], we aim to develop a system capable of accurately interpreting user inquiries expressed in natural language. These models excel at capturing the nuances of language, including variations in phrasing, context, and intent, allowing our system to generate precise SQL queries that reflect users' actual needs.

The implications of implementing such a system extend beyond mere convenience; they carry the potential to revolutionize the way individuals interact with data. By removing the technical barriers associated with SQL, we can empower a diverse array of users—from business analysts to researchers—to extract insights that can drive strategic decisions. Furthermore, as the field of data science continues to evolve, it becomes increasingly essential to create tools that enable all individuals to engage meaningfully with their data, fostering a culture of data literacy and informed decision- making.

3 Problematic

The central challenge addressed by our paper lies in the significant disconnect between natural language and SQL. Users of traditional database management systems often find themselves in a challenging position: they must navigate not only the intricacies of SQL syntax but also the complexities of the underlying database structure. This situation poses a considerable barrier, preventing many individuals from accessing the data they need to inform their decisions, despite their capacity to understand and analyze that data Existing solutions typically rely on fixed templates or rule-based approaches that offer limited flexibility. These systems restrict users to specific formats and can lead to frustration when users struggle to express their inquiries in a manner that the system can understand. This rigidity not only hampers the user experience but can also result in misinterpretations of user intent, ultimately leading to inaccurate or irrelevant query outputs. Additionally, many current solutions do not adequately account for the diverse ways in which users may phrase their questions, further compounding the challenges faced by non-technical users.

Our proposed solution aims to create a flexible and scalable framework capable of generating accurate SQL queries from a wide range of natural language inputs. By leveraging advanced deep learning techniques, we intend to design a system that understands the complexities and variations inherent in human language. This involves training our models on diverse datasets that reflect the richness of natural language, ensuring that the system can accurately interpret a variety of user queries [7].

By addressing these challenges, we hope to democratize access to data, empowering individuals across various sectors to utilize the insights contained within their databases. Our objective is to create a system that not only facilitates easier data access but also fosters a culture of data literacy, enabling users to engage with data meaningfully without needing extensive technical training. In doing so, we aspire to eliminate the barriers that have traditionally obstructed access to information, ensuring that valuable insights are available to all who need them.

4 Proposed Approach

To overcome the limitations of existing Text-to-SQL systems, our approach focuses on enhancing flexibility, accuracy, and speed. Current systems struggle with unreliable query transformation, slow response times, and rigid query handling, limiting their effectiveness. By leveraging advanced deep learning models like RNNs [8] and LSTMs, along with attention mechanisms, we aim to create a system that reliably converts natural language into SQL queries. Our approach also emphasizes adaptability, ensuring the system can handle diverse user inputs, and scalability, allowing it to perform efficiently across various data environments. This foundation sets the stage for the detailed approaches outlined in the following sections.

4.1 Deep Learning

Deep learning (DL) is a type of machine learning and artificial intelligence that imitates the way humans gain certain types of knowledge. It's an important element of data science, which includes statistics and predictive modeling. It's beneficial for collecting, analyzing and interpreting large amounts of data. DL makes this process faster and easier [9].

In this paper our proposition is to use Training from scratch method. This method requires us to collect a large labeled dataset and configure a network architecture that can learn the features and model [10].

4.2 Natural Language Processing

Natural Language Processing (NLP) is a subfield of artificial intelligence. It helps machines process and understand the human language so that they can automatically perform repetitive tasks [11].

NLP has a few fundamental pre-processing tasks:

- Tokenization: breaks down text into smaller semantic units or single clauses [12].
- Part-Of-Speech-Tagging: marking up words as nouns, verbs, adjectives, adverbs, pronouns, etc.
- Stemming and Lemmatization: Standardizing words by reducing them to their root forms.
- Stop word removal: filtering out common words that add little or no unique information: at, to, a, the.

Our proposition is to use Tokenization in order to break down the text. We passed on using the other parts because we want our model to understand the context of the word.

4.3 Recurrent Neural Networks

A Recurrent Neural Network (RNN) is a type of artificial neural network commonly used in NLP. RNN recognize data's sequential characteristics and use patterns to predicts the next likely scenario. They are used in deep learning and in development of models that simulate neuron activity in the human brain. They are especially powerful in use cases where context is critical to predicting an outcome.

RNNs are composed of layers of artificial neurons, network nodes that have the ability to process input and forward output to other nodes in the network. These nodes are connected by edges or weights that influence a signal's strength and the network's ultimate output. RNN use feedback loops that connects inputs, this is what enables RNNs to process sequential and temporal data.

The input to the RNN at every time-step is the current value as well as a state vector which represent what the network has "seen" at time-steps before. This state-vector is the encoded memory of the RNN initially set to zero [13] (Fig. 1).

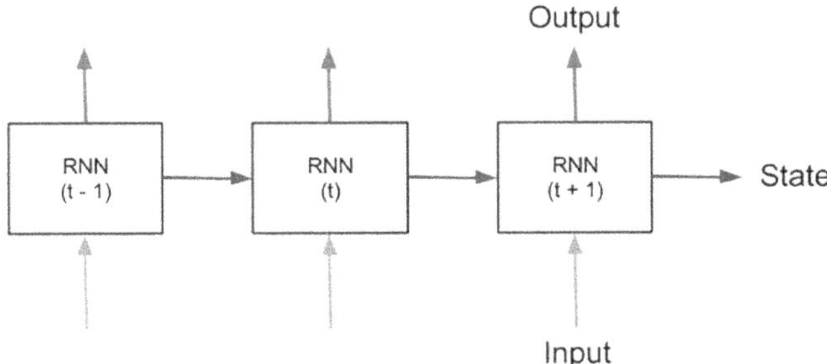

Fig. 1. RNN Architecture schema [14]

4.4 Long Short-Term Memory

The central role of an LSTM model is held by a memory cell known as a 'cell state' that maintains its state over time. The cell state is the horizontal line that runs through the top of the below diagram. It can be visualized as a conveyor belt through which information just flows, unchanged (Fig. 2).

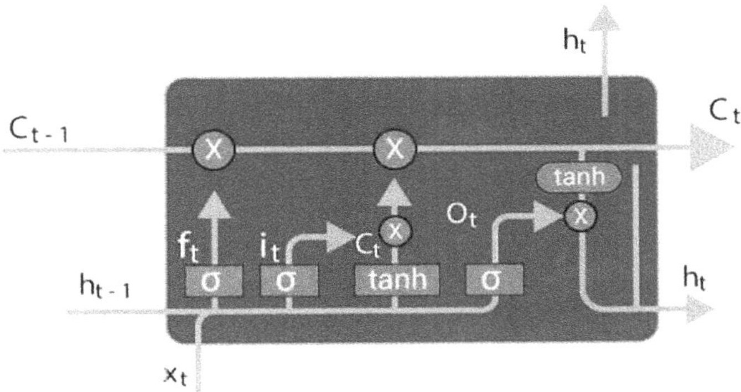

Fig. 2. LSTM Architecture schema [15]

Information can be added to or removed from the cell state in LSTM and is regulated by gates. These gates optionally let the information flow in and out of the cell.

It contains a pointwise multiplication operation and a sigmoid neural net layer that assist the mechanism (Fig. 3).

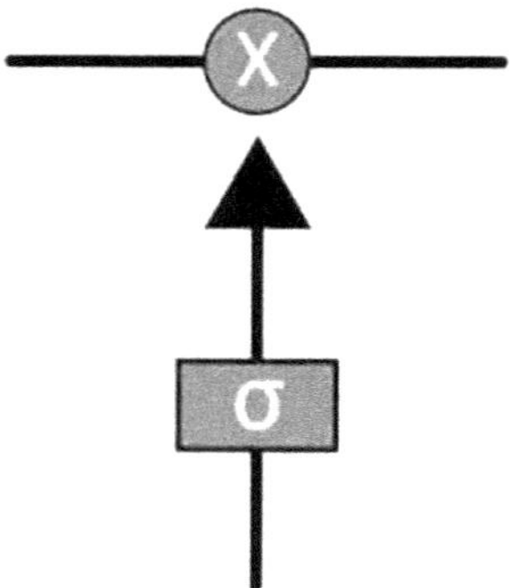

Fig. 3. Sigmoid representation [15]

4.5 Encoder Decoder Model

For our approach we need to have a good memory in order to predict, our sentences can be long so we have to remember the first words, LSTM helps with this task where it remembers the first and last words.

The concept of encoder-decoder model is simple, encoder means to convert data into a required format mostly vectors, the encoder is built by stacking RNN. We use this type of layer because its structure allows the model to understand context and temporal dependencies of the sequences. The output of the encoder, the hidden state, is the state of the last RNN time step [15] (Fig. 4).

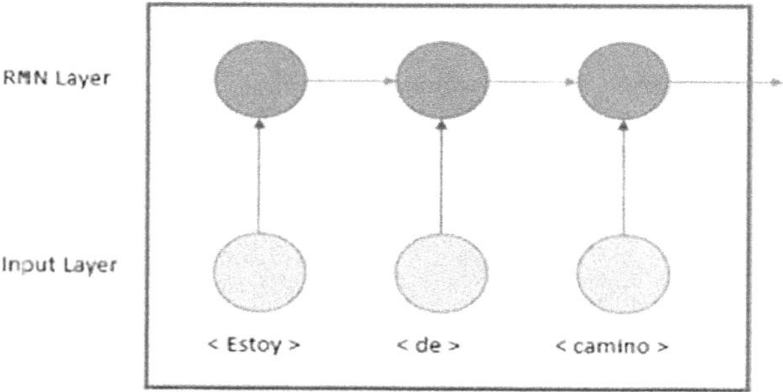

Fig. 4. Encoder schema [15]

The output of the encoder, an-dimensional vector that encapsulates the whole meaning of the input sequence. The length of the vector depends on the number of cells in the RNN (Fig. 5).

To decode means to convert a coded message into intelligible language. The role of the decoder will be to convert the n-dimensional vector into the output sequence. It is also built with RNN layers and a dense layer to do the prediction (Fig. 6).

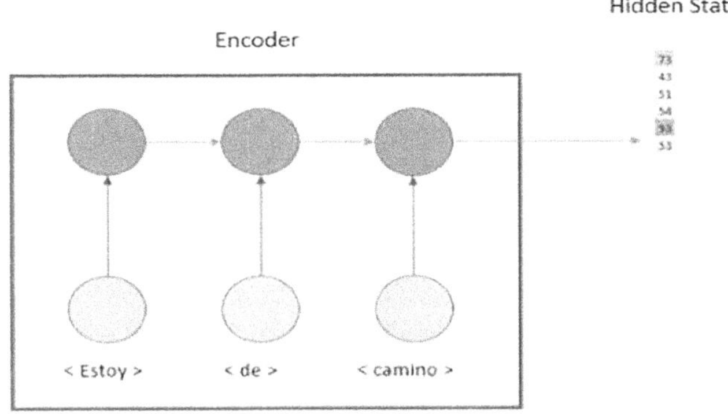

Fig. 5. The relationship between the Encoder and the hidden state [15]

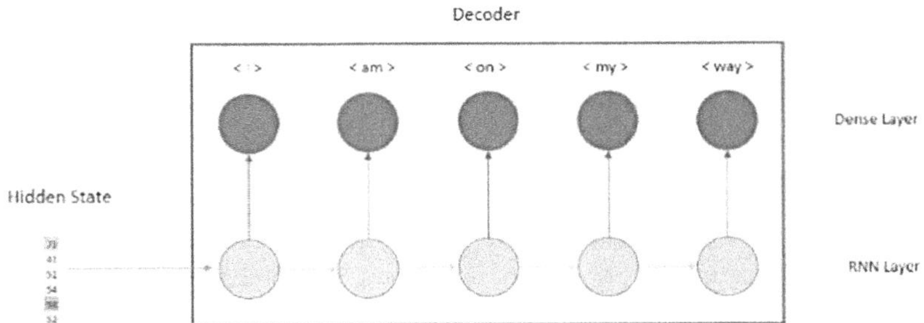

Fig. 6. Relationship between the decoder and the hidden state [15]

4.6 Word Embedding

Word embedding is a type of word representation that allows words with similar meaning to have similar representation [16].

They are a distributed representation for text that is perhaps one of the keys for NLP problems. They are in fact a class of techniques where individual words are represented as real-valued vectors in predefined vector space. Each word in mapped to one vector and the vector values are learned in a way that resembles a neural network. Each word is represented by a real-valued vector, often tens or hundreds of dimensions [17].

4.7 Attention Layer

Attention is all you need has been amongst the breakthrough papers that just revolutionized the way research in NLP was progressing. Thrilled by the impact of this paper, especially the 'Attention' layer, we tried assimilating its definition [18].

Transformer is a type of machine learning model, it's an architecture of neural networks and a variant of transformer models architecture. The transformer consists of an encoder-decoder transformer block where the encoder block takes input and an output translation sentence is generated by the decoder block [19]. The Transformer, based solely on attention mechanisms, dispensing with recurrence and convolutions entirely. Experiments on two machine translation tasks show these models to be superior in quality while being more parallelizable and requiring significantly less time to train [20].

4.8 Comparative Analysis with Transformers Model

Transformer-based models, such as BERT and GPT, are widely used in NLP for their self-attention mechanisms, which allow parallel sequence processing and capture long dependencies efficiently. While our approach prioritizes RNNs and LSTMs due to their efficiency in resource- constrained environments, particularly for real-time Text-to-SQL tasks, Transformers offer distinct advantages for handling complex queries. Their parallelized processing and ability to capture layered relationships between words make them ideal for large- scale applications, though they often demand substantial computational resources [21].

In our current model, RNNs and LSTMs offer a balance between accuracy and resource efficiency, making them suitable for quick responses in low-resource settings. However, future iterations of our system could explore the integration of Transformers, particularly in scenarios where handling intricate, multi-layered queries is crucial.

4.9 Practical Applications and Scalability

Our Text-to-SQL system is adaptable across a range of industries, including finance, healthcare, and education. For example, in finance, the model could streamline SQL query generation for data retrieval related to profit analysis or trend monitoring. In healthcare, medical professionals could interact with patient databases to retrieve specific metrics or trends without needing SQL expertise. Additionally, by incorporating distributed processing in future versions, our system will be able to handle large-scale databases efficiently, making it well-suited for both small and large organizational needs. This scalability ensures that our model can adapt as data volumes grow, maintaining performance and reliability.

5 Evaluation and Performance

To evaluate our Text-to-SQL system, we focused on three key metrics: accuracy, response time, and user satisfaction. While previous models have concentrated primarily on accuracy, our approach emphasizes the balance between speed and accuracy. Initial tests on standard datasets show promising results, with the model achieving high accuracy rates while delivering rapid responses. Future evaluations will include comparisons with existing Transformer-based Text-to-SQL models, offering insights into our system's efficiency and real-world application [22].

Additionally, we plan to gather feedback from users in fields like business and healthcare to assess the system's handling of complex or ambiguous queries. This feedback will guide further refinements, helping us create a user-friendly, efficient model for real-world settings. We will also provide performance visuals, such as accuracy and response time charts, to illustrate the system's efficiency and adaptability, demonstrating its capability to handle diverse and challenging user queries.

6   Conclusion

The proposed Text-to-SQL system enhances data accessibility by bridging the gap between natural language and SQL, making it easier for non-technical users to retrieve insights. Using RNNs, LSTMs, and attention mechanisms, our approach provides a robust solution for translating natural language inputs into SQL accurately and efficiently. This approach significantly reduces the technical barriers that have traditionally limited data access, allowing a wider range of users to make data-driven decisions.

Looking forward, we will test this approach in real-world settings to validate its accuracy and efficiency across complex query types and varied applications. We anticipate outstanding results that will demonstrate the model's scalability, reliability, and adaptability. Through these applications, our system will set a new standard in Text- to-SQL solutions, enabling accessible data interaction and fostering a data-driven culture across industries.

As we continue to refine our methodologies and explore the vast potential of natural language processing and deep learning, we will apply and experiment with this approach in real-world settings. These experiments will demonstrate its ability to manage complex and varied queries efficiently. We are confident that the results will be excellent, highlighting the system's precision and scalability. This work will not only showcase the approach's effectiveness but will also provide valuable insights for future improvements and applications, establishing a new standard for user-friendly data interaction.

Competing Interests. The authors have no competing interests to declare.

References

1. Kim, A.: (2020). Retrieved from https://towardsdatascience.com/text-to-sql-learningto-query-tables-with-natural-language-7d714e60a70d
2. Ranjit, V., Naik, S.: Natural language processing. Int. J. Comput. Algorithm. **12** (2023). https://doi.org/10.20894/IJCOA.101.012.002.001
3. Al-Zobaidy, Z.: Artificial intelligence in natural language processing. Int. J. Sci. Res. Arch. **13**, 370–377 (2024). https://doi.org/10.30574/ijsra.2024.13.1.1638
4. Wegner, S.: Neural networks. In: Encyclopedia of Computer Science and Technology, pp. 123–135. Springer (2024). https://doi.org/10.1007/978-3-662-69426-8_16
5. Anonymous: Were RNNs all we needed? arXiv preprint (2024). https://doi.org/10.48550/arXiv.2410.01201
6. Kumar, R.: Cerebral LSTM: a better alternative for single- and multi- stacked LSTM cell-based RNNs. OSF Preprints (2024). https://doi.org/10.31219/osf.io/jgh7p
7. Wu, L., Li, P., Lou, J., Fu, L.: DataGpt-SQL-7B: an open- source language model for text-to-SQL. arXiv preprint (2024). https://doi.org/10.48550/arXiv.2409.15985
8. Feng, L., Tung, F., Hajimirsadeghi, H., Ahmed, M., Bengio, Y., Mori, G.: Attention as an RNN. arXiv preprint (2024). https://doi.org/10.48550/arXiv.2405.13956
9. Burns, K.B.: (2021). Retrieved from https://towardsdatascience.com/network
10. Keren, G., Zhou, W., Kalinli, O.: Token-weighted RNN-T for learning from flawed data. arXiv preprint (2024). https://doi.org/10.48550/arXiv.2406.18108
11. Chandrika, G.: Natural Language Processing (NLP). Int. J. Res. Appl. Sci. Eng. Technol. **12**, 1092–1095 (2024). https://doi.org/10.22214/ijraset.2024.63281

12. Lindsey, L.A., Pershing, N., Habib, A., Stephens, W., Blaschke, A., Sundar, H.: A comparison of tokenization impact in attention-based and state space genomic language models. bioRxiv (2024). https://doi.org/10.1101/2024.09.09.612081.
13. Nechu, B.: (2020). Retrieved from https://towardsdatascience.com/what-is-an-encoder-dec oder-model-86b3d57c5e1a
14. Sun, B., Alkhalifah, T.: ML-descent: an optimization algorithm for FWI using machine learning. In: SEG Technical Program Expanded Abstracts 2019, pp. 1283–1287. Society of Exploration Geophysicists (2019). https://doi.org/10.1190/segam2019-3215304.1
15. Abhinav, M., Reddy, S., Christopher, O.: Machine translation with large language models: decoder only vs. encoder-decoder. arXiv preprint (2024). https://doi.org/10.48550/arXiv. 2409.13747
16. Birunda, S., Devi, R.K.: A review on word embedding techniques for text classification. In: Advances in Electronics, Communication and Computing, pp. 255–264. Springer (2021). https://doi.org/10.1007/978-981-15-9651-3_23
17. Settle, S.: Neural approaches to spoken content embedding. arXiv preprint (2023). https:// doi.org/10.48550/arXiv.2308.14905
18. Tyukin, G., Devonon, G., Kaddour, J., Minervini, P.: Attention is all you need but you don't need all of it for inference of large language models. arXiv preprint (2024). https://doi.org/ 10.48550/arXiv.2407.15516
19. Anonymous: Research on automatic proofreading algorithm for English translation based on neural networks. Scalable Comput. Pract. Exp. **25** (2024). https://doi.org/10.12694/scpe. v25i6.3297
20. Jaradat, M., Rattrout, A., Jayousi, R.: Improving ML accuracy in SQL injection detection using NLP and feature engineering. Research Square Preprints (2023). https://doi.org/10. 21203/rs.3.rs3411678/v1
21. Vaswani, A., et al.: Attention is all you need. Adv. Neural Inf. Proces. Syst. **30** (2017). https:// doi.org/10.48550/arXiv.1706.03762
22. Tyukin, I., et al : Coping with AI errors with provable guarantees. Inf. Sci. **678**, 120856 (2024). https://doi.org/10.1016/j.ins.2024.120856

Comparative Analysis of Similarity Metrics for Visual Recommendation in E-Commerce: AI Approaches and Performance

Anas Laamouri[✉] and Nawal Sael

Information Technology and Modeling Faculty of Sciences Ben M'Sik, University of Hassan II Casablanca, Casablanca, Morocco
anas.laamouri-etu@etu.univh2c.ma, nawal.sael@univh2c.ma

Abstract. The evolution of e-commerce platforms in recent years has led to increased use of recommendation systems while maintaining the customer-product relationship. Artificial intelligence (AI) plays a key role in creating intelligent platforms. Companies like Amazon, Myntra, and Adidas exemplify the effectiveness of these systems. Recommendation systems aim to suggest products based on customer experience and preferences. Visual recommendations focus on using multimedia content, such as images and videos, to enhance these suggestions. Image embedding enables the extraction of significant object features through deep neural networks. Similarity metrics, such as Cosine, Euclidean, Manhattan, and Jaccard distances, are essential for providing relevant results. In our study, we aim to explore the potential of these similarity metrics within a recommendation system. Utilizing the pre-trained VGG16 architecture, we compare these metrics over the same context, the experiment conducted on the test phase yielded impressive results, with performance scores of 86.80% in Avg_Acc@5, 85.57% in Avg_Acc@7, and 83.40% in Avg_Acc@10, resulting in a global average of 85.25% on the Fashion Image Product Dataset [1]. This research highlights the importance of similarity metrics in improving the relevance of visual recommendations in e-commerce.

Keywords: Image Embedding · Image Recommendation · Deep learning · IA · Similarity metric · visual Recommendation

1 Introduction

The recommendation aims to suggest products to a community of users by relying on detailed information and their individual preferences. Using analytical algorithms, these systems identify the items most likely to interest each customer. By offering personalized suggestions, they help increase the company's revenue while facilitating the discovery of new products. Additionally, this approach enhances the shopping experience and strengthens customer loyalty, thereby optimizing profits while ensuring user satisfaction.

Image recommendation is an approach that relies solely on the content of images, focusing on significant characteristics to suggest new, similar images that convey the

© The Author(s), under exclusive license to Springer Nature Switzerland AG 2026
O. Zahour et al. (Eds.): ICTIM 2024, CCIS 2655, pp. 119–128, 2026.
https://doi.org/10.1007/978-3-032-15147-6_12

same concept. This method can leverage various AI techniques, including image embedding, classification [2, 3], clustering [4], detection [5], and segmentation [6], to effectively meet its objectives.

Image embedding is a process that transforms images into feature vectors in a reduced-dimensional space, capturing essential information and relationships to facilitate image search, comparison, and recommendation. This technique enhances the efficiency of recommendation systems and improves the understanding of visual similarities. However, it faces challenges such as managing image variability and the need for large datasets. Similarly, similarity metrics measure the distance between vectors, providing a quantitative assessment of how similar two elements are. They play a crucial role in recommendation systems by enabling quick identification of similar items and enhancing accuracy.

In this paper, we will conduct a comparative study of various similarity metrics, namely cosine, Manhattan, Euclidean, and Jaccard distances, and evaluate their impact on visual recommendation.

The remain of this paper is organized as follow, Sect. 2 will be devoted to the related works of our study, while Sect. 3 will present the proposed methodology. Section 4 will discuss the various results obtained for the different similarity metrics. Finally, we will conclude our work.

2 Related Works

In recommendation systems that rely on image content, numerous studies have been conducted in this area using AI, focusing particularly on the concepts of image embeddings, classification, and clustering. In this section, we will present recent techniques related to image embeddings, as well as the various similarity methods employed in these studies.

This article [7] presents an innovative approach to visual image recommendation, using dimensionality reduction through PCA and SVD for feature extraction. It applies clustering to group similar images and calculates similarity using the Manhattan metric, utilizing the Fashion Product Image Dataset [1]. The results include a Silhouette score of 0.141421, a Calinski-Harabasz Index of 669.44, and a Davies-Bouldin Index of 1.8538, demonstrating the effectiveness of the method.

[8] proposes a new image recommendation method based on clustering and similarity between images, utilizing the Stanford Dog Breeds dataset [9]. It employs Res-Net152 for feature extraction and hierarchical clustering for grouping. The Validation Accuracy Cluster (VAC) scores are VAC1 of 96.875% for cluster 1, VAC2 of 100% for cluster 2, VAC3: 90% for cluster 3, with an average VAC of 95.625, while cosine distance is used as the similarity measure in this system.

Content-Based Image Retrieval (CBIR) and image exploration allow for the extraction of target images from large collections. This [10] article presents a clustering technique that combines these concepts, utilizing a dataset of RGB images [10], texture feature extraction, and fuzzy c-means with Euclidean distance to accelerate the retrieval process.

The main objective of this paper [11] is to develop a recommendation system based on user interests, utilizing a small Fashion Image Product dataset [12]. It employs a deep CNN model as a feature extractor and classifier, achieving an accuracy of 0.89, and utilizes cosine similarity for image retrieval.

Authors in [13] aim to propose a new approach for recommending clothing products using the Fashion Product Images dataset [1]. They employ a CNN as a feature extractor and classifier, achieving a training accuracy score of 0.844. For the similarity metric, they use cosine similarity to meet this objective.

In this approach [14], the authors developed a recommendation system based on the MovieLens [15] dataset for this experiment. VGG16 is integrated as a feature extractor and classifier, achieving an accuracy of 0.901. For K_Top = 5, the system yields a MAE of 0.737 and an RMSE of 0.94, while cosine similarity is utilized for the recommendations.

The authors of this article [16] developed a recommendation system based on images from Amazon [17]. They utilized the pre-trained VGG16 model as a feature extractor and classifier, achieving an accuracy of 0.501 and an RMSE of 0.1524, while using Jaccard similarity to identify relevant images.

The article [18] proposes a new approach for clothing recommendation based on images, utilizing transfer learning. The dataset employed in this approach is the Fashion Product Dataset [1], and the VGG16 model is tasked with extracting features and classifying the images into different categories. To recommend similar images, cosine similarity is used as the metric.

The studies we examined highlight the use of various approaches for visual recommendation systems, including models like VGG16, ResNet, and deep CNNs. Additionally, several similarity metrics have been applied, such as cosine similarity, Jaccard distance, Euclidean distance, and Manhattan distance, each showing different levels of performance. In our work, we focus on feature extraction using VGG16, a widely used technique in recommendation systems. We will assess the impact of this model combined with the four similarity metrics on the performance of our recommendation system for the fashion product image dataset [1].

3 Proposed Methodology

In this section, we present the general pipeline of our approach, which begins with the importation of the dataset. Once the entire dataset is loaded, a preprocessing procedure is applied to all images. Next, the VGG16 model is utilized to calculate the embeddings of the images. Using these features, our objective is to recommend similar images in response to a specific query within our recommendation system. In this context, the role of similarity metrics is essential, therefore, we proceed to compare these metrics across multiple queries to evaluate their impact on the recommendation process efficiency and performance, Fig. 1 shows this detail.

3.1 Dataset

The Fashion Product Image Dataset [1] contains 44,000 high-resolution JPEG images across various categories, including clothing, innerwear, shoes, watches, and more. Available on Kaggle, the dataset is structured into two main folders, the first, called "Images," houses all the dataset images, while the second contains the metadata for

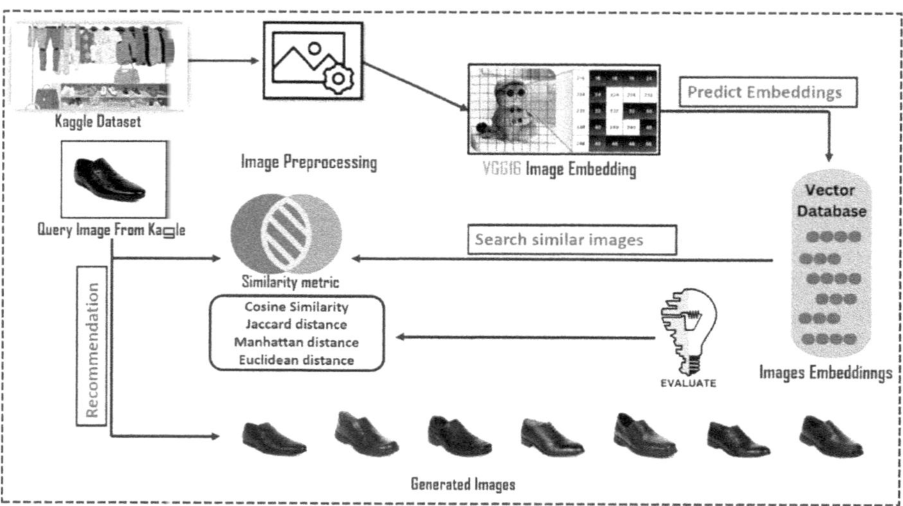

Fig. 1. Our proposed methodology.

each image. This dataset has been utilized in various recommendation studies, as well as for clustering tasks and evaluating different classification models. Its comprehensive nature makes it a valuable resource for research in fashion technology.

3.2 Preprocessing

The techniques applied to the dataset include resizing images to 76×76 pixels to ensure consistency, converting images into NumPy arrays to facilitate mathematical operations, and adding a new dimension to structure the data into batches suitable for deep learning models. Additionally, normalization is performed to meet the model's input requirements, optimizing performance during training.

3.3 Image Embedding

VGG16. is widely used as an image embedding technique due to its ability to extract discriminative features from images. By passing an image through its convolutional layers, VGG16 produces an embedding vector that captures essential information about the image, allowing for a compact and rich representation. This technique is particularly effective for recommendation tasks, as it facilitates the comparison and retrieval of similar images using similarity metrics.

3.4 Image Recommendation

In this phase, we focus on image recommendation, which begins with an input image being provided to the system. After the VGG19 model extracts relevant features from the query, we calculate the distances between the query and the embeddings to identify similar images. These embeddings are then sorted based on their distances to the query, allowing us to retrieve the most similar images. The recommendation results are presented according to parameters such as top 5, top 7, and top 10. Using these parameters, we will evaluate the performance across all our queries.

3.5 Similarity Metrics

Similarity metrics are crucial in visual recommendation systems as they measure the proximity between objects and help suggest similar items to users. In our approach, we have integrated four key metrics: Jaccard, Cosine, Manhattan, and Euclidean, to provide a more precise and diverse comparison of visual objects. These metrics enhance the relevance and effectiveness of visual recommendations and can be presented as follows:

Jaccard metric measures the similarity between two sets by calculating the ratio of the intersection to the union of their elements and is used to evaluate the similarity or dissimilarity between objects or binary vectors. Its formula is presented as follows:

$$Jaccard\ distance(A, B) = 1 - Jaccard\ Similarity(A, B) \tag{1}$$

Where the Jaccard similarity between two sets or binary vectors A and B is:

$$Jaccard\ Similarity(A, B) = \frac{|A \cap B|}{|A \cup B|} \tag{2}$$

Cosine similarity is a metric used to measure the similarity between two non-zero vectors by calculating the cosine of the angle between them, The formula for cosine similarity is:

$$Cosine\ Similarity(A, B) = \frac{A \cdot B}{\|A\| \cdot \|B\|} \tag{3}$$

The vectors A and B represent the features of the images extracted using the VGG16 model.

Manhattan distance is a metric that calculates the sum of the absolute differences between corresponding elements of two vectors. The formula is:

$$Manhattan\ Distance(A, B) = \sum_{i=1}^{i=n} |a_i - b_i| \tag{4}$$

Euclidean distance is the straight-line distance between two points, computed as the square root of the sum of the squared differences between their coordinates, the formula is expressed as follows:

$$Euclidean\ distance(A, B) = \sum_{i=1}^{i=n} (a_i - b_i)^2 \tag{5}$$

The vectors A and B represent the features of the images extracted using the VGG16 model.

4   Results and Discussion

Tables 1, 2, 3, and 4 presents the performance results obtained by applying fixed parameters to recommend a specific number of images, namely Top@5, Top@7, and Top@10. These parameters are used to generate recommendations based on the selected criteria. The performance is evaluated using the precision metric, which quantifies the number of correctly recommended images by comparing the suggested images to those expected according to the query type. The queries were formulated using four similarity metrics, cosine similarity, Manhattan distance, Euclidean distance, and Jaccard distance. These metrics were chosen due to their prevalence in the existing literature and their demonstrated effectiveness in recommendation systems. The results for these queries are presented in Tables 1, 2, 3, and 4.

Table 1. Results of the recommendation based on the four metrics for shoe query image.

Query	Metric	Acc@5	Acc@7	Acc@10
Shoe Query Image	*Manhattan*	*100%*	*100%*	*100%*
	Euclidean	*100%*	*100%*	*100%*
	Jaccard	*100%*	*100%*	*100%*
	Cosine	*100%*	*100%*	*100%*

Table 2. Results of the recommendation based on the four metrics for watch query image.

Query	Metric	Acc@5	Acc@7	Acc@10
Watch Query Image	*Manhattan*	*100%*	*100%*	*100%*
	Euclidean	*100%*	*100%*	*100%*
	Jaccard	*100%*	*85.71%*	*90%*
	Cosine	*100%*	*100%*	*100%*

Table 3. Results of the recommendation based on the four metrics for topwear query image.

Query	Metric	Acc@5	Acc@7	Acc@10
Topwear Query Image	*Manhattan*	*100%*	*100%*	*100%*
	Euclidean	*100%*	*100%*	*100%*
	Jaccard	*100%*	*100%*	*100%*
	Cosine	*100%*	*100%*	*100%*

Table 4. Results of the recommendation based on the four metrics for sneaker query image.

Query	Metric	Acc@5	Acc@7	Acc@10
Sneaker Query Image	*Manhattan*	*60%*	*71.42%*	*80%*
	Euclidean	*60%*	*71.42%*	*70%*
	Jaccard	*60%*	*71.42%*	*80%*
	Cosine	*60%*	*57.14%*	*70%*

The results shown in Tables 1, 2, 3, and 4 illustrate the accuracy of recommended images based on the Acc@k parameter, which represents the proportion of recommended images that accurately match the given query. Table 1 presents the accuracy according to the Top10, Top7, and Top5 criteria. For Query 1, all recommended images perfectly match the query, as is also the case for Query 3, as shown in Fig. 2. In Fig. 2, the cosine, Manhattan, and Euclidean metrics achieved 100% accuracy in recommending images, while the Jaccard metric showed scores of 85.71% for Acc@7 and 90% for Acc@10. For Query 4, results in Table 4 reveal that the accuracy for this query is 60% across all metrics for Acc@5. However, Manhattan, Euclidean, and Jaccard metrics achieved 71.42% for Acc@7, while cosine scored 57.14%. For Acc@10, Manhattan and Jaccard recommended 80% of the images correctly, while cosine and Euclidean reached 70%. In summary, these results are based on four randomly selected queries, and although they provide insight into the performance of the metrics, a larger evaluation on a more comprehensive test set is needed to draw more definitive conclusions about their overall effectiveness.

To generalize the evaluation of the similarity metrics performance, we selected a test set of 100 images randomly chosen from the Indian platform Myntra [19] to accurately assess the effectiveness of our metrics. Table 5 presents the results obtained during this experiment, where the Avg_Acc@k parameter represents the average accuracy of recommendations based on the chosen k, while Global_avg indicates the average accuracy across k = 5, k = 7, and k = 10.

Table 5. Results of the recommendation based on the four metrics for 100-Queries.

Query	Metric	Avg-Acc@5	Avg-Acc@7	Avg-Acc@10	Global_Avg
100-Random-Queries	*Manhattan*	*83.70%*	*81.52%*	*80.58%*	*81.93%*
	Euclidean	*83.65%*	*82.53%*	*79.25%*	*81.81%*
	Jaccard	***86.80%***	***85.57%***	***83.40%***	***85.25%***
	Cosine	*83.20%*	*81.73%*	*79.96%*	*81.63%*

The experiment in Table 5 conducted on the test set yielded impressive results, with performance scores of 86.80% in Avg_Acc@5, 85.57% in Avg_Acc@7, and 83.40% in

Avg_Acc@10, resulting in a global average of 85.25%. These results outperformed the other metrics, highlighting the effectiveness of the Jaccard metric.

Figure 2 shows the results generated from three queries on the Myntra platform [19], illustrating how our recommendation system works based on similarity metrics. It also displays the top 10 recommendations. For each recommended image, the similarity score and the image category are shown above the image.

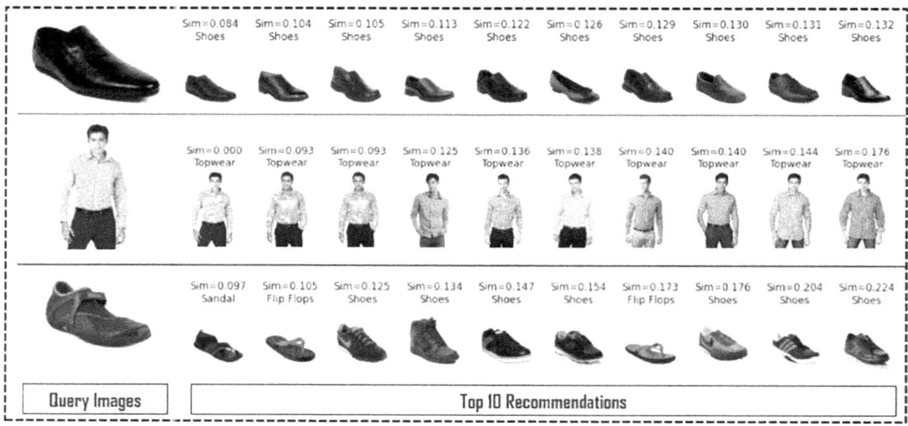

Fig. 2. Generated results from multiple queries on the Myntra platform.

5   Discussion and Future Work

Visual recommendation based on deep learning techniques presents a significant challenge for e-commerce platforms, as it requires precise analysis of various factors such as fabric type, clothing model, product category, and item location in a user query. Several limitations exist, including the difficulty in maintaining high detection and classification accuracy as the number of categories increases, as well as the impact of image quality on model performance. Moreover, systems must adapt to the variability of user preferences, the rapid evolution of fashion trends, and the sometimes-uncertain quality of annotations. Current models often lack interpretability, making it challenging to personalize recommendations. Future work should focus on developing lighter, more efficient models, combining visual approaches with behavioral data, and improving system adaptability to dynamic user behaviors, while also accounting for emerging fashion trends.

6   Conclusion

In our research, we developed an image content-based recommendation system aimed at providing a comparative study of different recommendation metrics and analyzing their impact on visual recommendation. We used the VGG16 model as a feature extractor and evaluated several distance metrics, including Manhattan distance, Jaccard distance,

Euclidean distance, and cosine similarity for image retrieval. The results showed promising performance, with average accuracies of 86.80% at 5 results (Avg_Acc@5), 85.57% at 7 results (Avg_Acc@7), and 83.40% at 10 results (Avg_Acc@10), yielding an overall average accuracy of 85.25%. The Jaccard metric produced the best scores in this comparative study, applied to the Fashion Image Product Dataset [1]. In future work, we will focus on improving performance, particularly by addressing challenges related to image quality and size.

References

1. Fashion Product Images Dataset: https://www.kaggle.com/datasets/paramaggarwal/fashion-product-images-dataset. Accessed 26 Jan 2024
2. Laamouri, A., Nawal, S.: Image classification for visual recommendation using deep learning. In: Proceedings of the 7th International Conference on Networking, Intelligent Systems and Security, pp. 1–6. Association for Computing Machinery, New York (2024)
3. Hamza, A., Nawal, S.: Traffic sign classification using deep learning comparative study. Procedia Comput. Sci. **233**, 939–949 (2024). https://doi.org/10.1016/j.procs.2024.03.283
4. Dahal, P.: Learning embedding space for clustering from deep representations. In: 2018 IEEE International Conference on Big Data (Big Data), pp. 3747–3755 (2018)
5. Shankar, D., Narumanchi, S., Ananya, H.A., et al.: Deep Learning Based Large Scale Visual Recommendation and Search for E-Commerce (2017)
6. Oliveira, J., Gomes, R., Gonzalez, D., et al.: Footwear segmentation and recommendation supported by deep learning: an exploratory proposal. Procedia Comput. Sci. **219**, 724–735 (2023). https://doi.org/10.1016/j.procs.2023.01.345
7. Addagarla, S.K., Amalanathan, A.: Probabilistic unsupervised machine learning approach for a similar image recommender system for e-commerce. Symmetry. **12**, 1783 (2020). https://doi.org/10.3390/sym12_11783
8. Parikh, D.: Similarity-Based Clustering for Enhancing Image Classification Architectures (2021)
9. Stanford Dogs Dataset: https://www.kaggle.com/datasets/jessicali9530/stanford-dogs-dataset. Accessed 6 Jul 2024
10. Kannan, A., Mohan, D., Neelamegam, A.: Image clustering and retrieval using image mining techniques. IEEE Int. Conf. Comput. Intell. Comput. Res. (2010)
11. Suvarna, B., Balakrishna, S.: An efficient fashion recommendation system using a deep CNN model. In: 2022 International Conference on Automation, Computing and Renewable Systems (ICACRS), pp. 1179–1183 (2022)
12. Fashion Product Images (Small): https://www.kaggle.com/datasets/paramaggarwal/fashion-product-images-small. Accessed 1 Jul 2024
13. Ijsrst IJ of SR in S and T: Fashion outfit recommendation based on deep learning model. Int. J. Sci. Res. Sci. Technol. (2021)
14. Alamdari, P., Navimipour, N., Hosseinzadeh, M., et al.: Image-based product recommendation method for e-commerce applications using convolutional neural networks. Acta Inform. Pragensia. **11** (2021). https://doi.org/10.18267/j.aip.167
15. Papers with Code - Movielens Dataset. https://paperswithcode.com/dataset/movielens. Accessed 15 Jan 2024
16. Chen, L.: Image-Based Product Recommendation System with Convolutional Neural Networks (2017)
17. Papers with Code -Amazon Product Data Dataset. https://paperswithcode.com/dataset/amazon-product-data. Accessed 15 Jan 2024

18. Tayade, A., Sejpal, V., Khivasara, A.: Deep Learning Based Product Recommendation System and Its Applications (2021)
19. Online Shopping India – Shop Online for Branded Shoes, Clothing & Accessories in India | Myntra.com. In: Myntra. https://www.myntra.com/. Accessed 31 Jul 2024

AI-Driven Generative Automatic Matching for Heterogeneous Systems: A Multi-agent System Implementation on the .NET Platform

Zouhair Ibn Batouta[1]([⊠]) [iD], Karima Moumane[2] [iD], Oussama Hamal[3] [iD], and Mohamed Talea[1] [iD]

[1] Laboratory of Information Processing, Faculty of Science Ben M'Sik, Hassan II University, 20670 Casablanca, Morocco
zouhair.ibnbatouta@gmail.com
[2] Software Project Management Research Team, ENSIAS, Mohammed V University in Rabat, 10112 Rabat, Morocco
[3] National School of Architecture of Marrakech ENAM, Marrakech, Morocco

Abstract. This paper proposes and implements a Generative Automatic Matching (GAM) approach, an innovative solution to handling the heterogeneity of systems and architectural diversity in developing modern applications. GAM overcomes the limitations of existing methods by fully automating the matching and model generation process, eliminating reliance on fixed algorithms and heuristics that lack adaptability. By embedding a multi-agent system—a focused area of artificial intelligence—GAM enables distributed problem-solving and enhances the efficiency of system integration across heterogeneous environments. Implemented on the .NET platform, GAM utilizes intelligent agents to coordinate and execute matching operations, demonstrating a significant improvement over traditional methods that often require manual or semi-automated processes. The approach is applied to the Elementary Case Study (ECS) to showcase how GAM tackles the complexities of diverse system architectures. System-to-system interactions are fully automated through the multi-agent framework, ensuring complete integration. In the developed .NET application, performance evaluation using machine learning quality metrics underlines this scalable, adaptable framework's high degree of accuracy and reliability, positioning GAM as a versatile and dependable framework for addressing current and emerging challenges in system development and integration.

Keywords: Generative Automatic Matching · Multi-Agent Systems · .NET Platform · Heterogeneous Systems · machine learning quality metrics

1 Introduction

Model-driven engineering elevates models from documentation to essential software development assets, enhancing usability and implementation efficiency [1]. However, the lack of standardized meta-models poses significant integration challenges [2–4].

O. Zahour et al. (Eds.): ICTIM 2024, CCIS 2655, pp. 129–141, 2026.
https://doi.org/10.1007/978-3-032-15147-6_13

Existing solutions addressing architectural heterogeneity have critical limitations, often failing to automate model generation based on matched correspondences. Manual or semi-automatic identification remains common, with fixed algorithms and heuristics lacking adaptability.

Critical approaches include Static Identifier-Based Techniques (SIB) [5], limited in heterogeneous environments; Signature-Based Techniques (SIG) [6], constrained by user-defined functions impacting scalability; Similarity-Based Techniques (SIM) [5, 7] using static heuristics; and Custom-Specific Language Techniques (CSL) [8], which require manual specifications. The proposed Generative Automatic Matching (GAM) method integrates automatic meta-model matching with model generation, leveraging Multi-Agent Systems to handle diverse meta-models [2, 9].

This paper outlines the GAM SMA framework's architecture and automated process, highlighting the Contract Net Protocol (CNP) for agent interaction. Agent design and functions are detailed using the .NET platform for generative matching.

An ECS case study demonstrates this approach's practical application and improved performance, illustrating its impact on matching processes and overall methodology effectiveness.

2 Generative Automatic Matching Approach (GAM)

2.1 Limitations of Traditional Model Matching Techniques

Various techniques have emerged in model matching, each with unique strengths and limitations, particularly regarding automation and adaptability for heterogeneous systems. The Static Identifier-Based Technique (SIB) [5] uses unique identifiers (e.g., UUIDs) for matching model elements, offering rapid implementation without user configuration. However, SIB lacks adaptability and fails with heterogeneous models due to its reliance on manual correspondences, limiting its use in diverse environments.

Signature-based techniques (SIG) [6] generate unique fingerprints for model elements, enabling cross-comparison of independent models with some flexibility. However, user-defined identity functions are necessary, constraining scalability and automation in large-scale settings.

Similarity-based techniques (SIM) [10–12], and [7] use heuristic-driven similarity scores for matching, which is effective in structured models. Yet, SIM's static heuristics limit adaptability, and manual intervention is required, reducing automation in dynamic scenarios.

Custom-Specific Language Techniques (CSL) [8] integrate semantics using domain-specific languages, enhancing correspondences for specific domains. However, CSL needs manual algorithm specifications, limiting scalability and adaptability for broader applications due to fixed heuristics.

Unlike these methods, Generative Automatic Matching (GAM) automates matching and model generation. GAM, supported by a multi-agent system framework, adapts dynamically across heterogeneous systems, overcoming user-defined functions and static heuristics limitations. This approach enhances scalability and reduces manual effort, significantly advancing complex environments requiring precision and efficiency.

GAM's process involves two main steps: Meta-Model Matching and Model Generation. Correspondences between source (SMM) and target meta-models (TMM) are identified to create a matching model (MG). Source models (SM) are then transformed into target models (TM) conforming to target meta-models, using set theory where each meta-model is defined as triples (element1, relationship, element2). Agents apply heuristics to establish matches and execute transformations, as detailed in Sect. 4.

3 GAM MAS Architecture

Multi-agent systems (MAS) represent a particular domain of artificial intelligence (AI), which establishes common problem-solving by coherent cooperation of multiple autonomous agents possessing unique roles and capabilities, achieving common goals [2, 9]—exhibiting intelligent behavior—while interacting to realize shared goals. The agents will cooperate and negotiate to develop solutions that respond to the heterogeneity of meta-models; Fig. 1 shows the communication using the contract net protocol we created in our approach [13, 14].

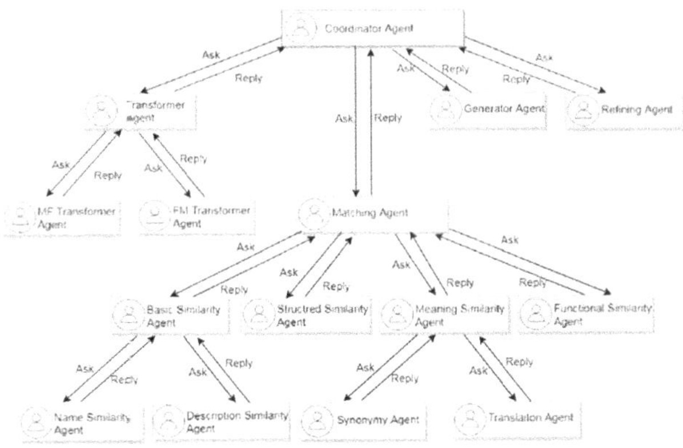

Fig. 1. CNP – Contract Net Protocol GAM SMA

4 Agents Implementation

4.1 .NET Platform

The .NET platform is chosen because of its strong and flexible framework. It consists of a set of components, each performing specific vital roles in the development of complex systems. In this section, we outline the implementation of the GAM SMA approach using .NET technology. First, we define the various agents and provide examples of code snippets that demonstrate the heuristics employed by these agents to calculate automatic matching between meta-elements. The development environment used for this implementation was Visual Studio (Fig. 2).

Next, we will present the .NET implementation of the leading agents.

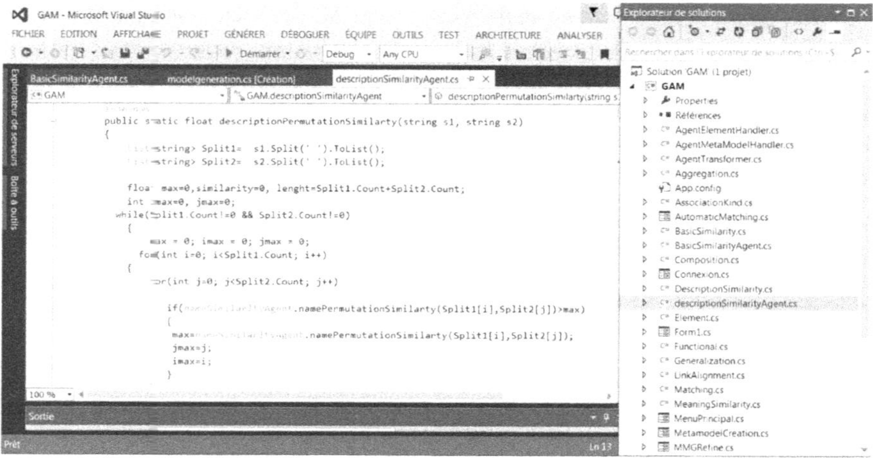

Fig. 2. Visual Studio Development Editor Interface

4.2 Basic Similarity Agent

The essential Similarity agent forms a society with two agents: the NameSimilarity Agent and the DescriptionSimilarity agent. The three have the same purpose: calculating the fundamental similarity; the latter is calculated using the method of the sum of weighted averages WSM (Weight Sum Method) [4].

Figure 3 shows a code snippet of the primary function used by the basicSimilarity agent.

```
public static float basicSimilarity(string s1, string s2, string choix, float w1, float w2, float wN1, float wN2,
float wD1, float wD2, float thresholdN, float thresholdD)
     {        return  w1  *  nameSimilarltyAgent.finalnameSimilarity(s1,  s2,  choix,wN1,wN2,thresholdN)
     +      w2 * descriptionSimilarityAgent.finaldescriptionSimilarity(s1, s2, choix,wD1,wD2,thresholdD); }
```

Fig. 3. Main function used by the basicsimilarity agent

4.3 StructuredSimilarity Agent

StructuredSimilarity Agent Evaluates structural similarities using neighborhood and flooding techniques. The Agent evaluates and compares elements across different meta-models by examining their structural relationships to achieve this. It uses two primary functions: neghbourStructuralSimilarity and FloodingStructuralSimilarity.

Neighbourhood Structural Similarity (NSS)

- **Purpose**: Measures the similarity between two elements by comparing their relationships in the two meta-models.

- **Method:**

  1. Retrieves relationships from the database for each element in both meta-models.
  2. Calculates the intersection of related elements using name similarity and relationship types.
  3. Computes similarity as the ratio of the intersection to the total number of relationships.

  Figure 4 shows a small code portion used by StructuredSimilarity Agent for NSS matchings.

```
public static float neghbourStructuralSimilarity(string sourceElement, string targetElement, string
sourceMetaModel, int sourceVersion, string targetMetaModel, int targetVersion){
    // Open database connection          OpenDatabaseConnection();
    // Fetch relationships from the database for both source and target elements
        FetchRelationshipsFromDatabase(sourceElement, sourceMetaModel, sourceVersion, targetEle-
        ment, targetMetaModel, targetVersion);
    // Calculate intersection and total relationships
        CalculateIntersectionAndTotalRelationships(sourceElement, targetElement, sourceMetaModel,
        sourceVersion, targetMetaModel, targetVersion);
    // Return similarity score   return similarityScore; }
```

Fig. 4. NSS heuristic code used by the Structured Similarity agent

Flooding Structural Similarity

- **Purpose**: Using a flooding algorithm, compute structural similarity by considering direct and indirect relationships.
- **Method**: The FSS heuristic is derived from the Similarity Flooding Algorithm (SFA) developed by Melnik in 2002. It is used in graph theory; we adapt and improve it to match heterogeneous meta-models. Below is a summary of the steps involved in the FSS heuristic:

  1. Constructs a relationship graph between elements of the two meta-models.
  2. Initializes similarity scores for elements.
  3. Iteratively adjusts similarity scores based on the relationships and their weights until convergence or a maximum number of iterations is reached.
  4. Normalizes similarity scores and returns the final similarity matrix.

  Figure 5 shows a small code portion StructuredSimilarity Agent uses for FSS matchings.

4.4 MeaningSimilarity Agent

The MeaningSimilarity Agent employs a multifaceted semantic analysis approach, integrating various linguistic resources. The agent effectively handles language complexities to extract nuanced semantic meanings by using heuristics enriched by an extensive

```
public static DataTable FloodingStructuralSimilarity(string sourceMetaModel, int sourceVersion, string
targetMetaModel, int targetVersion){    // Open database connection
     OpenDatabaseConnection();    // Construct relationship graph and initialize similarity scores
         ConstructRelationshipGraphAndInitializeScores(sourceMetaModel, sourceVersion, targetMeta-
         Model, targetVersion);    // Iterate to adjust scores based on relationships
     IterateToAdjustScores(sourceMetaModel, sourceVersion, targetMetaModel, targetVersion);
// Normalize scores and check for convergence          NormalizeScoresAndCheckConvergence();
// Return final similarity matrix          return similarityMatrix; }
```

Fig. 5. FSS heuristic code snippet used by the StructuredSimilarity agent

thesaurus and leveraging online dictionaries and translation platforms such as MyMemory Translated and Google Translate. Additionally, it utilizes an internal PO (Portable Object) file structure to enhance translation precision and semantic accuracy. This strategy enables the agent to perform comprehensive semantic assessments and calculate reliable similarity across diverse linguistic contexts. Figure 6 presents a code snippet showcasing the MeaningSimilarity Agent's use of SynonymyAgent and Translation Agent.

```
public class MeaningSimilarityAgent{
   // Calculate semantic similarity using the Weight Sum Method
   public static float CalculateMeaningSimilarity(float wS, float wT, float SMS, float TMS)
   {      return ((wS * SMS) + (wT * TMS)) / (wS + wT);    }
      // Integration with Synonymy and Translation Agents
   public static float ComputeSemanticSimilarity(string element1, string element2)
   { List<string> synonyms1 = SynonymyAgent.GetSynonyms(element1);
      string translatedElement2 = TranslationAgent.Translate(element2, element1.Language);
      float SMS = CalculateSemanticSimilarity(synonyms1, translatedElement2);
      float TMS = CalculateSemanticSimilarity(element1, element2);
      return CalculateMeaningSimilarity(element1.WS, element1.WT, SMS, TMS);    }
   private static float CalculateSemanticSimilarity(List<string> synonyms, string translatedElement)   {
   float similarity = 0.0f;       if (synonyms.Contains(translatedElement))
      {         similarity = 1.0f; // Perfect match     }      return similarity;   }
   private static float CalculateSemanticSimilarity(string element1, string element2)
   {     float similarity = 0.0f;
      if (element1.Equals(element2, StringComparison.OrdinalIgnoreCase))
      {        similarity = 1.0f; // Perfect match     }      return similarity;   }}
```

Fig. 6. Code snippet used by the MeaningSimilarity agent

4.5 functionalSimilarity Agent

This agent calculates the functional similarity between two elements. The similarity is stored in the knowledge base, adding functional relations of type functionalSimilarity to the matching results. The expert can also set the priority of the relation to 1 to make it prioritize over conflicting matchings.

The agent calculates functional similarity as follows:

- functionalSimilarity $= 1$ if the functional similarity between two elements exists,
- functionalSimilarity $= 0$ otherwise.

Figure 7 shows a code snippet illustrating the checking of the existence of Functional Similarity by the relevant agent.

```
public class FunctionalSimilarityAgent
{  // Calculer la similarité fonctionnelle entre deux éléments
   public static int CalculateFunctionalSimilarity(string element1, string element2)
   {      // Vérifier si la similarité fonctionnelle existe
      if (FunctionalSimilarityExists(element1, element2))
      {        return 1;     }     return 0;    } }
```

Fig. 7. Code snippet used by the FunctionalSimilarity agent

4.6 CoordinatorAgent

The CoordinatorAgent is a pivotal component within the MAS architecture, facilitating the harmonious collaboration of diverse agents. Its role is:

- Coordination: This agent orchestrates the activities of various agents, ensuring seamless interaction and task allocation.
- Semi-Automation: While capable of autonomous operation, the CoordinatorAgent may prompt expert intervention when confronted with complex scenarios, thus embodying a semi-automated approach.
- Expert Invocation: Expert intervention is invoked when intricate decision-making or problem-solving is required, augmenting the agent's capabilities beyond its autonomous functions.

Figure 8 shows a code snippet illustrating the CoordinatorAgent.

```
public class CoordinatorAgent
{   // Method for coordinating various agents
   public void CoordinateAgents(List<IAgent> agents)
   { foreach (var agent in agents)      {
      // Perform coordination tasks
      agent.PerformTask();      } } }
```

Fig. 8. Code snippet used by the CoordinatorAgent

4.7 RefiningAgent

The RefiningAgent enhances the quality and precision of correspondences derived from disparate sources. Its functionalities include:

- Correspondence Refinement: This agent refines correspondences obtained from different agents, employing diverse calculation functions for optimization.
- Calculation Functions: The RefiningAgent optimizes correspondences by using calculation functions such as linear interpolation of similarities and relation weights.
- Conflict Resolution: In conflicting correspondences, the agent may utilize the maximum function to determine the most appropriate correspondence, thus resolving conflicts efficiently.

Figure 9 shows a code snippet illustrating the RefiningAgent.

```
public class LefiningAgent
{   // Method for refining correspondences
    public Correspondence RefineCorrespondence(List<Correspondence> correspondences)
    {   // Implement refining logic, such as linear interpolation, relation weights, etc.
        // Example: return the correspondence with the highest weight
        return correspondences.OrderByDescending(c => c.Weight).FirstOrDefault();   } }
```

Fig. 9. Code snippet used by the RefiningAgent

4.8 TransformerAgent

The TransformerAgent, alongside its counterparts MFTransformerAgent and FMTransformerAgent, plays a vital role in adapting meta-models and models to align with the designated mathematical formalism. Its key responsibilities include:

- Meta-Model and Model Transformation: This agent society transforms meta-models and models, ensuring alignment with the mathematical formalism integral to the approach.
- Adaptability: By facilitating the transformation of diverse meta-models, the TransformerAgent ensures adaptability to various meta-model types, enhancing the versatility and applicability of the MAS approach.

Figure 10 shows a code snippet illustrating the TransformerAgent.

```
public class TransformerAgent
{   // Méthode pour transformer les méta-modèles et les modèles vers le formalisme mathématique
    public void TransformerVersFormalismeMathematique(List<MetaModel> metaModels, List<Model>
models)   { //Transformer les méta-modèles vers le formalisme mathématique
        foreach  var metaModel in metaModels)     {
            mfTransformerAgent.TransformMetaModelVersFormalismeMathematique(metaModel);
        }    // Transformer les modèles vers le formalisme mathématique
        foreach  var model in models)      {
            fmTransformerAgent.TransformModelVersFormalismeMathematique(model);     } } }
```

Fig. 10. Code snippet used by the TransformerAgent

4.9 GeneratorAgent

The GeneratorAgent is tasked with transforming source models into target models, adhering to predefined formalism and matching results. Its operations are structured into three distinct stages:

- Matching Generation: The agent generates matching between level 2 meta-elements, establishing foundational correspondences.
- Element Generation: Leveraging the results of level 2 matching, the GeneratorAgent generates level 1 elements, thus advancing the transformation process.
- Result Refinement: The agent refines the transformation results by detecting and rectifying falsely generated elements, ensuring accuracy and coherence in the target models.

Figure 11 shows a code snippet illustrating the GeneratorAgent.

```
public class GeneratorAgent{ // Main method to generate models conforming to target meta-models
    public List<TargetModel> GenerateTargetModels(SourceModel sourceModel, MetaModel
sourceMetaModel, MetaModel targetMetaModel, List<Correspondence> correspondences)
    {      // Iterate through each element of the source model
        foreach (var element in sourceModel.Elements)
        {      // Get the corresponding meta-element from the source meta-model
            var metaElement = GetMetaElement(element, sourceMetaModel);
            // Find matching elements in the target meta-model using correspondences
            var matchingElements = GetMatchingElements(metaElement, correspondences, targetMeta-
Model);    // Generate sub-elements for each matched element and add them to the target model
            foreach (var matchedElement in matchingElements)
            {          GenerateSubelement(matchedElement, targetModel);        }
    } targetModels.Add(targetModel);  return targetModels;  } }
```

Fig. 11. Code snippet used by the GeneratorAgent

5   Case Study and Discussion

5.1   Case Study

In this section, we present the evaluation of our application using the case study (ECS). The ECS case study is composed of two distinct meta-models (Fig. 13); it tests the process of our approach, highlighting the application of our approach to two distinct meta-models and the generation of a source model into a target model.

Figure 12 shows the fundamental bidirectional similarities, represented by dotted arrows.

Figure 13 shows the result of generating the desired target model by applying our approach to a source model that conforms to the source meta-model.

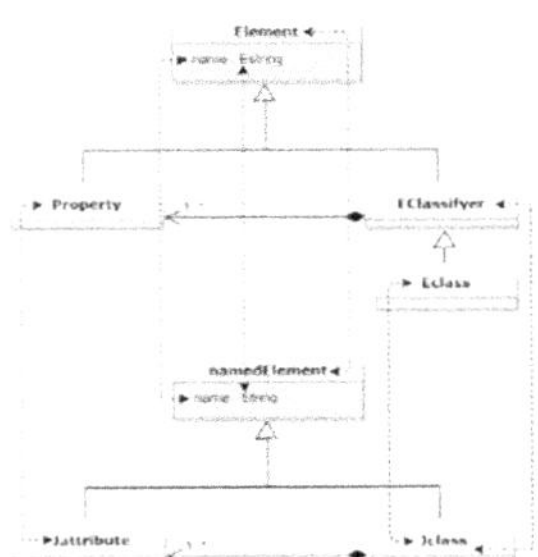

Fig. 12. Source and target meta-models examples

Next, we present the results generated by our .NET application when processing the ECS case study. A final threshold value of 0.5 was used to filter out undesired matches, as shown in Table 1; only the link between "Jattribute" and "Property" was not detected.

To measure the quality of the generated mappings, we applied standard quality measures from machine learning and AI: recall precision, F-measure, and overall [15, 16]. A threshold of 0.5 was used to get the best matching results, as shown in Table 2. The practical consequence—a recall of 0.83 and a precision of 1—was obtained by the GAM SMA approach; indeed, all relevant correspondences were returned without any

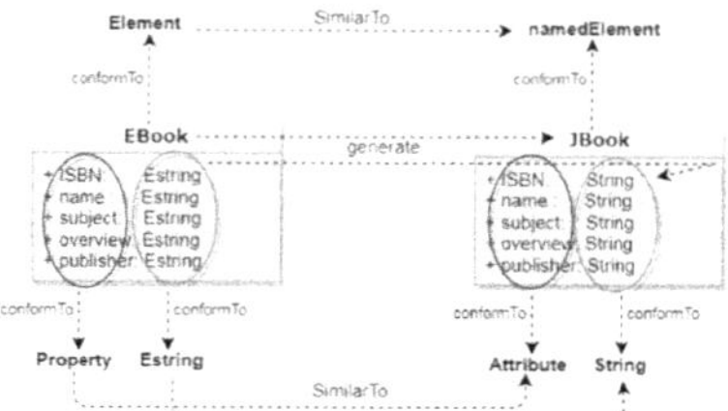

Fig. 13. Source and target Model matching

Table 1. Results of correspondences between source and target meta-elements for ECS case study

Source Element	Target Element	Final Similarity
nameElement	Element	0.85353535
Name	Name	0.88857805
String	Estring	0.70438625
Jattribute	Property	0.380564225
Jclass	Eclass	0.78914525
Jclass	Eclassifyer	0.50845756

false positives. These metrics show the strength of the GAM SMA technique in tracking homogeneous systems quite accurately and providing reliable results.

Table 2. Quality measurement results for the ECS case study

	Measures			
Thresholds	Recall	Precision	F-Measure	Overall
0.5	0.83333333	1	0.90909091	0.83333333

The results demonstrate that our system produces high precision in identifying correct correspondences between the different models. This indicates the effectiveness of GAM in handling straightforward relationships in meta-model alignment. The recall values are promising, suggesting the system captures many relevant correspondences.

GAM SMA approach provides complete, correct, and accurate alignments for different model types, enhancing its potential to be a reliable tool in heterogeneous meta-models alignment. The evaluation results reveal that the approach outperforms the addressed approaches in SIB, SIG, SIM, and CLS, which either do not provide automatic model generation or are based on fixed heuristics.

5.2 Discussion and Limitations

The Generative Automatic Matching (GAM) framework, leveraging a multi-agent system within the .NET platform, demonstrates significant strengths in automating meta-model matching and model generation, achieving high accuracy and efficiency. The Elementary Case Study (ECS) highlighted GAM's effectiveness in handling heterogeneous architectures, overcoming the limitations of traditional methods. Further validation through additional case studies across diverse contexts and different domains [17, 18] would substantiate its adaptability and robustness.

While GAM shows promise, certain limitations suggest avenues for enhancement. Currently, GAM relies on heuristics for model correspondence, which could be made more adaptive through techniques like fuzzy logic or machine learning-driven weight optimization. These advancements would enable more dynamic heuristic adjustments, allowing GAM to adapt more to evolving structures. Expanding GAM's application to complex domains—such as IT governance, e-healthcare, IoT, and the semantic web—would provide insights into its scalability when handling various data structures and domain-specific needs.

Future case studies are planned to evaluate GAM's versatility across broader domains. One study will focus on IT governance compatibility between approaches such as Agile, DevOps [19], and PRINCE2 to test GAM's capabilities in managing diverse project systems. A survey of integration between relational and Big Data NoSQL systems will assess GAM's effectiveness in complex data transformations. Further case studies in e-health and IoT will showcase GAM's potential as a flexible, cross-domain solution. By addressing these directions, GAM aims to solidify its role as a robust tool for complex, heterogeneous system integration, enhancing interoperability and automated model generation.

Additionally, more efforts and work should be conducted to highlight and show how the GAM framework aligns with usability standards since it is a crucial software quality characteristic to take into account during software systems building [20, 21].

6 Conclusion and Future Work

This paper introduced the Generative Automatic Matching (GAM) approach, implemented on the .NET platform using a multi-agent system, to address the challenges of system heterogeneity and model integration across diverse architectures. Through the Elementary Case Study (ECS), GAM demonstrated its effectiveness in fully automating the matching and model generation processes, achieving high accuracy and precision. By leveraging multi-agent societies, GAM enhanced the scalability and adaptability of model matching and overcame critical limitations of traditional methods, such as the dependence on fixed heuristics and manual intervention. Quality metrics obtained from the ECS case study—such as a recall of 0.83 and a precision of 1.0—highlight the robustness and reliability of GAM in handling complex model correspondences.

Several enhancements and expansions are planned to strengthen the GAM framework. A primary focus will be on integrating advanced AI-driven optimization techniques, like fuzzy logic and machine learning, to allow adaptive heuristic tuning and further improve the accuracy of correspondences. Additionally, future case studies will explore GAM's applicability in complex domains, starting with IT governance—ensuring integration between Scrum and PRINCE2 systems—and extending to integrating relational and Big Data NoSQL systems. Beyond these specific cases, GAM will be applied in other domains, including e-health, IoT, and semantic web applications, to assess its adaptability and scalability across varied technological environments.

Finally, future iterations of GAM will prioritize the development of a user-friendly graphical user interface (GUI) to support ease of adoption by practitioners and researchers. Expanding GAM's functionality to address data transformations within heterogeneous systems will enhance its utility as a comprehensive tool for achieving interoperability, model generation, and data integration across diverse technological ecosystems.

Disclosure of Interests. The authors have no competing interests to declare relevant to this article's content.

References

1. Moumane, K. Idri, A.: A systematic map of mobile software usability evaluation. In: Rocha, Á., Adeli, H., Reis, L.P., Costanzo, S. (eds.) Trends and Advances in Information Systems and Technologies, pp. 58–67. Springer, Cham (2018). https://doi.org/10.1007/978-3-319-777 12-2_6
2. Batouta, Z.I., Dehbi, R., Talea, M., Omar, H.: Generative matching between heterogeneous meta-model' systems based on hybrid heuristic. J. Inf. Technol. Res. **12**, 53–71 (2019). https://doi.org/10.40 8/JITR.2019040104
3. Batouta, Z.I., Dehbi, R., Talea, M., Hajoui, O.: Automation in code generation: tertiary and systematic mapping review. In: 2016 4th IEEE International Colloquium on Information Science and Technology (CiSt), pp. 200–205 (2016). https://doi.org/10.1109/CIST.2016.780 5042
4. Ibn Batouta, Z., Dehbi, R., Talea, M.: Multi-criteria analysis and advanced comparative study between automatic generation approaches in software engineering. J Theor Appl Inf Technol. **81**, 609–620 (2015)
5. He, X., Liu, Y., He, H.: Accelerating similarity-based model matching using dual hashing. Softw. Syst. Model. (2024). https://doi.org/10.1007/s10270-024-01173-1
6. Muneeb, U., Ohannessian, M.I.: Induced model matching: how restricted models can help larger ones (2024). http://arxiv.org/abs/2402.12513. https://doi.org/10.48550/arXiv.2402. 12513.
7. Yang, J., Deng, W., Liu, B., Huang, Y., Zou, J., Li, X.: GMValuator: similarity-based data valuation for generative models (2024). http://arxiv.org/abs/2304.10701. https://doi.org/10. 48550/arXiv.2304.10701.
8. Peeters, R., Steiner, A., Bizer, C.: Entity matching using large language models (2024). http:// arxiv.org/abs/2310.11244. https://doi.org/10.48550/arXiv.2310.11244.
9. Hajoui, O., Talea, M., Bakhouyi, A., Batouta, Z.I., Dehbi, R.: A comparative analysis of different approaches for big data interoperability. In: 2016 Third International Conference on Systems of Collaboration (SysCo), pp. 1–4 (2016). https://doi.org/10.1109/SYSCO.2016. 7831345
10. Nam, J., et al. Diffusion model for dense matching (2024). http://arxiv.org/abs/2305.19094. https://doi.org/10.48550/arXiv.2305.19094.

11. Kachwala, Z., An, J., Kwak, H., Menczer, F.: Rematch: robust and efficient matching of local knowledge graphs to improve structural and semantic similarity (2024). http://arxiv.org/abs/2404.02126. https://doi.org/10.48550/arXiv.2404.02126.
12. Zhang, P., Zhu, L., Wang, L., Huang, H.: Unifying event-based flow, stereo and depth estimation via feature similarity matching (2024). http://arxiv.org/abs/2407.21735. https://doi.org/10.48550/arXiv.2407.21735.
13. FIPA ACL Message Structure Specification. http://www.fipa.org/specs/fipa00061/SC00061G.html. Last accessed 7 Nov 2024.
14. Franklin, S., Graesser, A.: Is it an agent, or just a program?: a taxonomy for autonomous agents. In: Müller, J.P., Wooldridge, M.J., Jennings, N.R. (eds.) Intelligent Agents III Agent Theories, Architectures, and Languages, pp. 21–35. Springer, Berlin, Heidelberg (1997). https://doi.org/10.1007/BFb0013570
15. Sekeroglu, B., Ever, Y.K., Dimililer, K., Al-Turjman, F.: Comparative evaluation and comprehensive analysis of machine learning models for regression problems. Data Intell. **4**, 620–652 (2022). https://doi.org/10.1162/dint_a_00155
16. Mozaffari, A., et al.: HPC-oriented canonical workflows for machine learning applications in climate and weather prediction. Data Intell. **4**, 271–285 (2022). https://doi.org/10.1162/dint_a_00131
17. Moumane, K., El Asri, I., Cheniguer, T., Elbiki, S.: Food recognition and nutrition estimation using MobileNetV2 CNN architecture and transfer learning. In: 2023 14th International Conference on Intelligent Systems: Theories and Applications (SITA), pp. 1–7 (2023). https://doi.org/10.1109/SITA60746.2023.10373725
18. Moumane, K., Idri, A.: Mobile applications for endometriosis management functionalities: analysis and potential. Sci. Afr. **21**, e01833 (2023). https://doi.org/10.1016/j.sciaf.2023.e01833
19. Aouni, F.E., Moumane, K., Idri, A., Najib, M., Jan, S.U.: A systematic literature review on Agile, Cloud, and DevOps integration: challenges, benefits. Inf. Softw. Technol. **177**, 107569 (2025). https://doi.org/10.1016/j.infsof.2024.107569
20. Moumane, K., Idri, A., Nafil, K.: An empirical evaluation of mobile software usability using ISO 9126 and QoS DiffServ model. In: New Trends in Software Methodologies, Tools and Techniques. IOS Press, Amsterdam (2016)
21. Moumane, K., Idri, A.: Software quality in mobile environments: a comparative study. In: 2017 4th International Conference on Control, Decision and Information Technologies (CoDIT), pp. 1123–1128 (2017). https://doi.org/10.1109/CoDIT.2017.8102750

Predicting Employees with Leadership Potential Using Machine Learning Techniques

Fatima Zahra Abbour[1]([✉]) [ID], Soumaya Ounacer[1] [ID], Soufiane Ardchir[1,2] [ID], Mohamed Azzouazi[1] [ID], and Khadija Mahjoubi[1] [ID]

[1] Faculty of Sciences Ben M'Sik, Hassan II University, Casablanca, Morocco
fatima.abbour-etu@etu.univh2c.ma
[2] National Schoo of Business and Management, Hassan II University, Casablanca, Morocco

Abstract. Leadership is essential for organizational success, driving innovation and growth. Yet, identifying leadership potential has often relied on subjective and biased methods. This paper introduces an objective solution using machine learning to revolutionize leadership detection. Leveraging the CRISP-DM methodology, the research progressed systematically from data analysis to model deployment. Random Forest, integrated with Principal Component Analysis (PCA) and balanced data, achieved a notable 90% accuracy in predicting leadership potential. This AI-driven approach overcomes human biases, uncovering hidden talents and providing a predictive, data-driven framework for leadership identification. This innovation reshapes traditional perceptions of leadership, fostering continuous growth and sustainable organizational success.

Keywords: Leadership potential prediction · Artificial Intelligence · Machine Learning · CRISP-DM · dimensionality reduction · human resource management

1 Introduction

In today's complex and dynamic professional environment, effective leadership is essential for organizational success [1]. However, identifying leadership potential remains challenging due to subjective biases and limitations in traditional evaluation methods [2]. Artificial Intelligence (AI) offers a transformative approach, enabling more objective and innovative ways to detect and nurture leadership potential [3].

This paper explores AI's role in uncovering latent leadership abilities within teams. It contextualizes the research within recent advancements in AI, human resource management, and organizational psychology, emphasizing the value of ensemble learning for its ability to enhance predictive accuracy in complex scenarios like leadership identification [4], machine learning, proven in predicting consumer behavior, can similarly help organizations identify and nurture latent leadership potential [5]. Techniques such as SMOTE address the issue of imbalanced data, ensuring more balanced and reliable predictions of leadership potential [6].

By building on existing literature and addressing gaps in current methodologies, our research seeks to improve leadership identification through AI and machine learning.

O. Zahour et al. (Eds.): ICTIM 2024, CCIS 2655, pp. 142–147, 2026.
https://doi.org/10.1007/978-3-032-15147-6_14

The aim is to overcome limitations in traditional methods, offering organizations more accurate tools to recognize and foster future leaders.

Structured into four sections: Related Works, Theoretical Foundation, Research Workflow, and Experiments and Results, the paper integrates theory and practice to promote inclusive leadership cultures and drive sustainable organizational success.

2   Related Works

The intersection of artificial intelligence (AI) and human resource management (HRM) has seen significant advancements in recent years. Notable areas include employee promotion prediction, attrition detection, and performance forecasting. However, the specific application of predicting leadership potential remains underexplored. AI's role in HR involves leveraging machine learning algorithms to analyze vast datasets, identifying patterns that indicate potential leadership traits. Techniques like ensemble learning, neural networks, and decision trees have shown efficacy in related domains, offering a theoretical basis for our approach. Comparative studies highlight the strengths and weaknesses of various models. For instance, one study explored the impact of AI on recruitment by reviewing academic articles, emphasizing the benefits of task automation, reduction of human biases, and improvements in efficiency and candidate experience, while noting challenges such as data bias, skill shortages, and resistance to change [7]. The use of decision trees, linear regression, and other machine learning tools to predict and enhance employee performance showed significant improvements in prediction accuracy, with Random Forest achieving a 90% accuracy rate [8]. Integrating AI into broader HR practices, technologies such as data mining, optical character recognition (OCR), and deep learning frameworks have enhanced recruitment and training processes, though concerns about data security and algorithmic bias remain [9]. Machine learning has also been employed to predict promotions, with studies reporting high accuracy rates using algorithms like Random Forest [10, 11]. These contributions underscore the significant potential of AI in HRM while identifying ongoing challenges and gaps, particularly in the specific application of predicting leadership potential. While significant progress has been made in AI applications within HR, the gap in predicting leadership potential remains. Our research seeks to fill this void by developing a specialized model that integrates insights from related studies, offering a novel approach to identifying future leaders.

The reviewed studies demonstrate the growing impact of AI and machine learning on HR practices, particularly in recruitment, performance prediction, and promotion forecasting. Various technologies such as Random Forest, SVM, and ensemble learning techniques like CatBoost and XGBoost show high accuracy rates, highlighting their potential for informed decision-making and efficiency improvements. However, challenges such as data bias, imbalanced datasets, and ethical considerations persist, emphasizing the need for robust data management and transparent AI frameworks. Despite these challenges, the consistent improvements in prediction accuracy and process automation underline AI's transformative potential in HR, paving the way for more objective and effective talent management strategies.

3   Theoretical Foundation

This research is grounded in essential concepts that shape the understanding and application of AI for identifying leadership potential. These foundational elements provide a roadmap for the study and ensure the development of a scientifically robust and practically relevant framework.

Leadership
Leadership is a dynamic and multifaceted construct encompassing traits, behaviors, and skills that empower individuals to inspire and guide others toward achieving shared goals [12].

Machine Learning Techniques
A diverse range of machine learning techniques underpins the study, each contributing unique strengths to leadership identification:

- Support Vector Machines (SVM): Excels in precise data classification by defining optimal hyperplanes to distinguish potential leaders.
- Random Forest: Combines decision trees for improved accuracy and reduced overfitting, ensuring reliable leadership detection.
- XGBoost: A gradient boosting method that iteratively refines predictions, enhancing accuracy for large datasets.

CRISP-DM Methodology
The research employs the CRISP-DM (Cross-Industry Standard Process for Data Mining) framework to ensure a systematic approach [13]. This methodology includes:

- Business Understanding: Defining objectives and aligning them with business goals.
- Data Understanding: Collecting and analyzing data while identifying quality issues.
- Data Preparation: Cleaning and transforming data for optimal modeling.
- Modeling: Applying and refining machine learning techniques.
- Evaluation: Assessing model reliability and alignment with objectives.
- Deployment: Implementing and monitoring the model in real-world applications.

By combining these advanced techniques and structured methodologies, this research aims to create an AI-driven framework for leadership potential identification. This foundation not only ensures scientific rigor but also addresses practical needs, paving the way for innovative applications in talent management.

4   Research Workflow

The research followed a structured workflow encompassing data collection, preprocessing, model training, evaluation, and deployment. Data was sourced from confidential repositories with strict privacy protocols and underwent preprocessing, including handling missing values, one-hot encoding, feature analysis, and addressing imbalances with SMOTE. Advanced machine learning techniques such as Random Forest, XGBoost, and

Logistic Regression were employed, with optional PCA for dimensionality reduction [14, 15]. Models were evaluated using accuracy metric to ensure reliability [16]. This streamlined process ensures robust and reproducible predictive analytics for leadership potential identification.

5 Experiments and Results

5.1 Used Datasets

The implementation phase leveraged a confidential dataset comprising extensive employee attributes to train machine learning models for leadership potential prediction. The dataset included 10,000 records with 24 variables spanning competencies, potentials, and contextual factors. These variables were carefully selected to capture key dimensions relevant to leadership identification, such as decision-making, emotional intelligence, and previous leadership roles.

Models like SVM, Random Forest, and XGBoost were trained on this dataset and rigorously evaluated using accuracy to ensure robust predictive performance. The inclusion of diverse attributes ranging from numerical indicators like problem-solving skills to categorical data like education level provided a comprehensive foundation for model optimization. This anonymized dataset ensured ethical integrity while enabling effective analysis to uncover latent leadership potential.

5.2 Results

A Comprehensive experiments were conducted to evaluate model performance in predicting leadership potential, focusing on advanced machine learning algorithms capable of managing high-dimensional data and complex feature interactions. Cross-validation and grid search [17] were employed for hyperparameter tuning, enhancing performance and generalization across datasets. Principal Component Analysis (PCA) was optionally applied to improve interpretability and efficiency by reducing dimensionality without sacrificing predictive power. Results showed that the Random Forest model consistently achieved the highest accuracy, demonstrating its robustness and effectiveness, particularly when used with SMOTE [18] for balancing data and PCA for dimensionality reduction (Table 1).

Table 1. Comparative Analysis

Model	Imbalanced data			Balanced data		
	Accuracy	+PCA	Mean Cross Validation	Accuracy	+PCA	Mean Cross Validation
SVM	0. 8579	0. 8434	0. 8703	0. 8702	0. 8645	0.8509
Random Forest	0. 8975	0. 8977	0.8932	0. 8907	**0.9044**	0.8921
XGboost	0. 8790	0. 8601	0.8732	0. 8898	0. 8911	0.8904

A detailed analysis of model outputs identified critical factors influencing leadership potential, with feature importance analysis offering deep insights into decision-making processes. Dimensionality reduction improved both interpretability and predictive accuracy, enabling more precise employee classification. Rigorous validation through cross-validation and expert comparisons confirmed the models' reliability, with the Random Forest model achieving 90% accuracy after hyperparameter tuning. This approach highlighted the strength of ensemble methods and delivered a scalable framework for leadership assessment.

6 Conclusion

This paper presents a comprehensive framework for predicting leadership potential using advanced machine learning techniques, including SVM, Random Forest, and XGBoost. Through systematic data processing and analysis, key factors influencing leadership outcomes were identified. The Random Forest model emerged as the most effective, achieving the highest performance with an accuracy of 90% when balanced data was utilized. This was achieved by applying SMOTE for data balancing and reducing dimensionality using PCA. The model's effectiveness was validated through rigorous testing and comparison with expert evaluations. This study offers valuable insights into enhancing leadership assessment through data-driven methodologies, providing actionable intelligence for informed decision-making and strategic leadership development.

Ethical considerations and potential biases in HR data were carefully evaluated throughout the research process. Acknowledging the risk of machine learning models inadvertently reinforcing existing biases, techniques such as balanced sampling were employed to mitigate these effects. This approach not only improved model fairness but also safeguarded against unintended discriminatory outcomes, strengthening the framework's reliability and promoting responsible AI applications in human resource management.

This paper lays the foundation for a novel approach to talent management and highlights opportunities for future research. Expanding the integration of the predictive model into other sectors and industries could help evaluate its generalization and adaptability. Additionally, exploring unstructured data, such as textual performance evaluations and manager comments, could further enrich the model and enhance its predictive accuracy. Moving forward, the perspective is to refine and optimize our approach to achieve even better results, enhancing the model's performance and scalability. This work aspires to redefine human resource management by fostering a culture of inclusive leadership and driving organizations toward new levels of sustainable excellence.

Acknowledgments. The authors express their gratitude for the support received from the Laboratory of Information Technologies and Modeling at Faculty of Science Ben M'sick, Hassan II University, Casablanca, Morocco, which provided the necessary facilities for conducting this research. Additionally, the authors acknowledge the support of the CNRST under the "PhD-AS-sociate Scholarship - PASS" Program.

References

1. Taylor, C.M., Cornelius, C.J., Colvin, K.: Visionary leadership and its relationship to organizational effectiveness. Leadersh. Organ. Dev. J. **35**(6), 566–583 (2014)
2. Batmanghlich, C.A.: Why Leaders Fail Ethically: a Paradigmatic Evaluation of Leadership. Springer, Cham (2014)
3. Teixeira, N., Pacione, M.: Implications of Artificial Intelligence on Leadership in Complex Organizations: An Exploration of the Near Future. OCAD University, Toronto (2024)
4. Ardchir, S., Ouassit, Y., Ounacer, S., El Ghoumari, M.Y., Azzouazi, M.: An integrated ensemble learning framework for predicting liver disease. Int. J. Online Biomed. Eng. **19**(13), 138–152 (2023)
5. Meftah, M., Ounacer, S., Azzouazi, M.: Enhancing customer engagement in loyalty programs through AI-powered market basket prediction using machine learning algorithms. In: Engineering Applications of Artificial Intelligence, pp. 319–338. Springer, Cham (2024)
6. Daif, A., Ounacer, S., Ardchir, S., Ghazouani, M., Azzouazi, M.: Exploring the capabilities of deep learning for advancing credit card fraud detection: a revolutionary approach. J. Theor. Appl. Inf. Technol. **101**(24) (2023)
7. Shamsi, M.: The impact of artificial intelligence on human resources management recruitment processes: a systemic review. J. Commer. Manag. Tour. Stud. **2**(2), 82–90 (2023)
8. Vijaya Lakshmi, V., et al.: A study in apprehending the application of machine learning tools in forecasting the employee performance. BioGecko. **12**(1s), 64–75 (2023)
9. Dey, S., Sahoo, B.B.: Machine learning and management in KGI: A (2024)
10. Long, Y., Liu, J., Fang, M., Wang, T., Jiang, W.: Prediction of employee promotion based on personal basic features and post features. In: Proceedings of the International Conference on Data Processing and Applications, pp. 5–10 (2018)
11. Shafie, S., Soek, P.O., Khai, W.K.: Prediction of employee promotion using hybrid sampling method with machine learning architecture. Malays. J. Comput. **8**(1), 1264–1286 (2023)
12. Khan, Z.A., Bhat, S.J., Hussanie, I.: Understanding leadership theories – a review for researchers. Asian J. Res. Soc. Sci. Humanit. **7**(5), 249–264 (2017)
13. Schröer, C., Kruse, F., Gómez, J.M.: A systematic literature review on applying CRISP-DM process model. Procedia Comput. Sci. **181**, 526–534 (2021)
14. Kotsiantis, S.B., Zaharakis, I.D., Pintelas, P.E.: Machine learning: a review of classification and combining techniques. Artif. Intell. Rev. **26**, 159–190 (2006)
15. Ntotsis, K.: Recent advances on dimensionality reduction for high-dimensional data analysis with applications (2022)
16. Gaudreault, J.-G., Branco, P., Gama, J.: An analysis of performance metrics for imbalanced classification. In: International Conference on Discovery Science, pp. 67–77. Springer, Cham (2021)
17. Adnan, M., Alarood, A.A.S., Uddin, M.I., ur Rehman, I.: Utilizing grid search cross-validation with adaptive boosting for augmenting performance of machine learning models. PeerJ Comput. Sci. **8**, e803 (2022)
18. Anis, M., Ali, M.: Investigating the performance of smote for class imbalanced learning: a case study of credit scoring datasets. Eur. Sci. J. **13**(33), 340–353 (2017)

Early Prediction of Student Dropout in MOOCs

Brahim Hmedna[1]([⊠]), Aicha Bakki[2], Ali El Mezouary[2], Kaoutar Boumalek[2], and Ibtissam Zaaj[3]

[1] IMIS Laboratory, FS Ait Melloul, Ibn Zohr University, Agadir, Morocco
b.hmedna@uiz.ac.ma
[2] IRF-SIC Laboratory, FS, Ibn Zohr University, Agadir, Morocco
[3] LISAD Laboratory, ENSA, Ibn Zohr University, Agadir, Morocco

Abstract. This study addresses the prevalent challenge of high dropout rates in Massive Open Online Courses (MOOCs) by leveraging learning analytics for the early identification of at-risk students. Drawing upon Fredricks's engagement model, which posits student engagement as a critical determinant of learning success, this research analyzes comprehensive data from the "Statistical Learning4" course offered on Stanford's Lagunita platform during Winter 2015 and Winter 2016. The rich dataset, capturing detailed student interactions within the MOOC environment, enables an in-depth investigation of behavioral patterns associated with disengagement and dropout. By employing advanced analytical techniques, this study aims to develop predictive models capable of identifying at-risk students early in their enrollment, facilitating timely interventions designed to improve retention and ultimately contribute to greater success in MOOC-based learning.

Keywords: MOOC · learning analytics · machine learning · engagement · Dropout

1 Introduction

Massive Open Online Courses (MOOCs) have revolutionized access to education, offering a diverse range of courses to a global audience [1, 2]. Platforms like Coursera, edX, and XuetangX have witnessed an explosion in enrolment, attracting millions of learners from various backgrounds and demographics [3]. While MOOCs offer unprecedented opportunities for learning, they also face a persistent challenge: high dropout rates. Studies indicate that completion rates for MOOCs often hover between 5% and 10%, significantly lower than traditional online or face-to-face courses [4]. This attrition poses concerns for both learners and MOOC providers, as it represents a loss of time, effort, and resources [5]

An understanding of the factors contributing to MOOC dropout and the development of effective strategies to mitigate it are essential for increasing the influence and long-term sustainability of this educational model. Research suggests that dropout in MOOCs is a multifaceted phenomenon influenced by various factors, including individual learner characteristics, course design, and platform features [6, 7]. To better understand and

© The Author(s), under exclusive license to Springer Nature Switzerland AG 2026
O. Zahour et al. (Eds.): ICTIM 2024, CCIS 2655, pp. 148–157, 2026.
https://doi.org/10.1007/978-3-032-15147-6_15

address this complexity, this research adopts Fredricks's engagement model [8], a widely recognized framework that highlights the crucial role of student engagement in learning.

Learning analytics (LA), a field that applies data analysis techniques to educational settings, constitutes an innovative approach to address the challenge of MOOC dropout [9]. By analyzing student interaction data collected through MOOC platforms, researchers can gain insights into learner behavior and engagement patterns across all three dimensions of Fredricks's model [8], potentially identifying early warning signs of disengagement and dropout. These findings can guide the development to support at-risk students and improve retention rates [5, 10].

Crucially, Early prediction of course dropout is crucial for facilitating effective interventions and improving student retention. The first few weeks of a MOOC are a critical period for establishing engagement patterns and predicting student success [11]. This paper focuses specifically on the analysis of trace data generated during the first three weeks of a MOOC, leveraging the framework of Fredricks's engagement model. This emphasis on early prediction aligns with research findings that highlight the importance of the initial stages of a course in determining student outcomes [12].

This approach allows for the identification of at-risk students before they become significantly disengaged, increasing the likelihood of successful intervention. This research utilizes various ML algorithms previously employed for MOOC dropout prediction, including: Decision trees (DT), Random forests (RF), Support vector machines (SVM), Logistic regression (LR). This paper examines the effectiveness of these ML algorithms in predicting MOOC dropout, particularly within the critical timeframe of the first three weeks.

This research, informed by Fredricks's engagement model, yields insights with direct implications for enhancing early warning systems and intervention strategies within MOOC environments. By accurately identifying at-risk students early on, based on their behavioral, emotional, and cognitive engagement patterns, educators can provide timely support and guidance, potentially reducing dropout rates and fostering a more engaging and successful learning experience for all participants.

The rest of the paper is organized as follows: First, we give an overview of Fredricks's Engagement Model. Second, we present some related work. Third, we offer the proposed approach, which includes data pre-processing, feature selection, and the supervised modeling used. The paper ends with a discussion of the results obtained and a brief conclusion.

2 State of the Art

Fredricks's engagement model [8] is a valuable framework for understanding student motivation and involvement in learning. The model posits that engagement is not a single construct, but rather a multifaceted concept encompassing three distinct dimensions: behavioral, emotional, and cognitive (Fig. 1).

(1) Behavioral engagement is characterized by students' active participation in learning activities. It manifests in observable actions such as attending class, completing assignments, asking questions, and contributing to discussions

Fig. 1. Three dimension model of engagement (Fredricks et al. 2004)

(2) Emotional engagement, on the other hand, pertains to students' affective responses to learning, including their interest, enjoyment, and sense of belonging in the learning environment
(3) Cognitive engagement delves into students' intellectual investment in learning, their use of higher-order thinking skills, and their efforts to understand and master the subject matter

Studies demonstrate that students exhibiting higher levels of cognitive and behavioral engagement achieve greater academic success. Fredricks's model suggests that each dimension of engagement plays a distinct role in shaping students' learning experiences and outcomes. Specifically, behavioral engagement appears to facilitate effective knowledge acquisition during instructional activities. Furthermore, emotional engagement may promote resilience and persistence when confronted with academic challenges. Similarly, cognitive engagement has been linked to the development of higher-order thinking skills, including critical analysis and in-depth comprehension [13].

Research on MOOC dropout prediction has progressed significantly since the emergence of these online courses. Initial studies often relied on basic engagement metrics to understand student behavior. For example, one study analyzed data from a ten-week "Principles of Software Architecture" (POSA) course and used features like video lecture downloads, quiz attempts, and peer assessment submissions to predict dropout and final grades [14] This approach demonstrated the potential of using student interaction data to anticipate learner outcomes.

As the field matured, researchers increasingly turned to machine learning techniques to improve prediction accuracy. To mitigate limitations inherent in traditional ELMs, such as behavior discrepancy, iterative training, and structure initialization, [15] proposed a hybrid algorithm integrating decision trees and ELMs for dropout prediction. This model leverages the decision tree structure as a foundation for enhanced performance. The results indicated that the hybrid algorithm outperformed other machine learning methods, including support vector machines and long short-term memory (LSTM) networks, in terms of accuracy, area under the curve (AUC), F1-score, and training time [15].

Numerous studies have underscored the critical role of early dropout prediction. Predicting dropout in the first few weeks of a course allows for timely interventions that can potentially prevent students from disengaging and leaving [12, 14, 16]. One study proposed an "in-situ" prediction approach that involved training a classifier while a course was ongoing, using proxy labels for dropout. This method aimed to provide real-time predictions to enable prompt interventions. The results showed surprisingly good performance even compared to the more traditional "post-hoc" training paradigm [17].

3 Proposed Architecture

The section will outline the methodology for predicting MOOC dropout rates in four stages: Data Collection, Pre-processing, Feature Selection, and supervised modeling. These stages are common in many machine learning (ML) projects (Fig. 2):

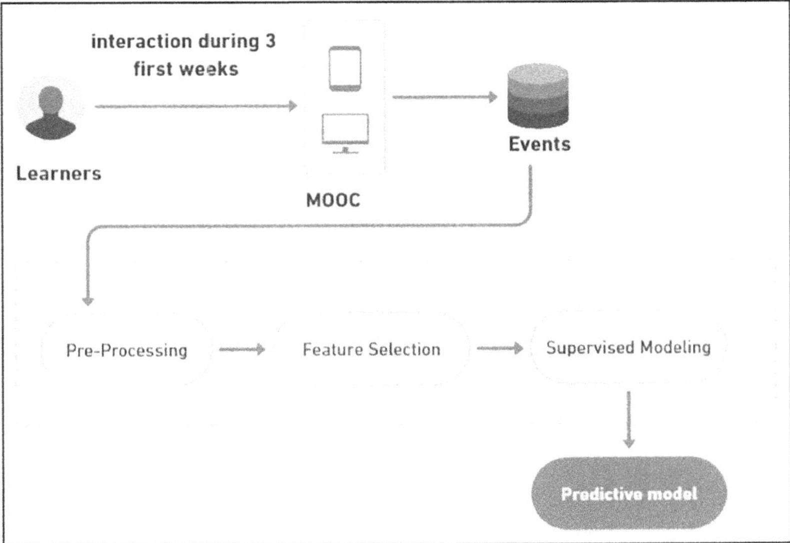

Fig. 2. Proposed methodology

3.1 Dataset

The data used to train and test the prediction models is from the edX course "Statistical Learning4", which ran in the winter of 2015 and the winter of 2016. The course was delivered through Stanford's open-source Lagunita platform, which is based on the Open edX platform. The "Center for Advanced Research through Online Learning" (CAROL5) provided the data. To maintain learner privacy, data were anonymized. Table 1 presents the information contained in the database, including student enrollment and number of interaction traces generated per session (winter 2015 and winter 2016). For instance, in the first session (winter 2015), 32,209 students enrolled in this course, generating 18,475,724 interaction traces. Only the first three weeks of this data were analyzed to develop the prediction model.

Table 1. Summary of MOOC dataset used in this study

Session	Start of Course	End of Course	#Enrolled Learners	# Traces	Completion Rate
Winter 2015	19/01/2015	06/04/2015	32,209	18,475,724	8%
Winter 2016	12/01/2016	06/04/2016	20,526	12,363,613	10%

3.2 Pre-processing

Before using the data from the "Statistical Learning4" edX course to train and test prediction models, it is necessary to pre-process it to ensure that it is accurate and suitable for the chosen ML architecture. Mean imputation was employed to address missing data. Specifically, missing values for each feature were replaced with the calculated mean value of that feature [13]. It is important to note that using mean imputation can introduce bias into the data if the missing data is not random [19].

The performance of many machine learning algorithms is sensitive to scaling. If we do not maintain a uniform distribution of the value of each feature, some of them will have a significant influence on the output model. It is therefore important to unify the units of measurement of the features before starting the learning process. Min-max normalization was used to scale the values of all features to a range between 0 and 1. Min-max scaling uses the following formula:

$$x' = (x - x_{min})/(x_{max} - x_{min})$$

where:

x is the original value
x' is the normalized value
x_{min} is the minimum value for the feature
x_{max} is the maximum value for the feature

One-Hot Encoding was used to convert categorical features into a numerical format. This was done by creating new binary variables to represent each unique category in the original feature.

3.3 Feature Selection

Effective machine learning models for predicting student dropout in MOOCs rely heavily on the selection of relevant features. This section explores a feature selection strategy grounded in Fredricks's engagement model, utilizing data from the "Statistical Learning4" edX course. Given the absence of demographic information in this dataset, the focus is on features derived from student interaction with the course materials, reflecting behavioral, emotional, and cognitive engagement.

To determine the most effective features, we used Wrapper methods [20]. Wrapper methods use a particular ML algorithm to evaluate the performance of different subsets of features. This means that we experimented with various feature selection methods and evaluated the performance of each model using a range of feature sets. Through this process, we could pinpoint the features that are most effective in predicting dropout from this specific course (Table 2).

Table 2. Features set used for the analysis

Dimension	Feature	Description
Behavioral Engagement	Number of course accesses	How many times did the student access the course platform during each week of the study?
	Time spent on course platform	How long did the student spend interacting with the course platform each week?
	Number of videos watched	How many videos did the student watch during the specified period?
	Percentage of videos watched	How much of each video did the student watch?
	Number of forum posts	How many posts did the student make in the course forum during each week?
	Number of assignments submitted	How many assignments did the student submit during each week?
	Number of quizzes completed	How many quizzes did the student attempt during each week?
Emotional Engagement	Sentiment of forum posts	Was the sentiment of the student's forum posts generally positive, neutral or negative?
	Number of interactions with peers	How many times did the student engage with other students, through forum discussions, or private messaging, for example, each week?
Cognitive Engagement	Number of times a student revisits challenging course content	Did the student repeatedly access content that is known to be difficult to master?
	Requests for clarification or elaboration	Did the student ask for help with the course material, either by asking the instructors, or by posting a question on the course forum?

(continued)

Table 2. (*continued*)

Dimension	Feature	Description
	Quality of forum posts	Did the student provide evidence of higher order thinking skills in their forum posts? For example, were their posts insightful, detailed, well-reasoned, and relevant to the topic?

3.4 Evaluating the Performance of the Constructed Models

After training and fine-tuning the four supervised ML models (Decision trees (DT), Random forests (RF), Support vector machines (SVM), Logistic regression (LR)), the next crucial step is to evaluate their performance. To achieve this, each model will be tested on the pre-processed "Statistical Learning4" dataset, which was divided into training and testing sets.

Evaluating classification model performance often involves various metrics, such as:

Accuracy: This metric represents the proportion of correctly classified instances. It provides a general overview of the model's correctness.

Precision: Focusing on the model's ability to correctly identify dropout students, precision calculates the proportion of true positive predictions (correctly identified dropouts) out of all instances predicted as dropouts.

Recall: This metric measures the model's ability to identify all actual dropout instances.

F1-Score: calculated as the harmonic mean of precision and recall, is a robust metric for assessing classifier performance, particularly in the context of imbalanced data.

AUC quantifies the model's discriminatory power between dropout and non-dropout classes. Higher AUC values (approaching 1) indicate superior classification performance.

4 Results and Discussion

This section presents the results of the dropout prediction study conducted on the "Statistical Learning4" course. The primary goal was to evaluate the effectiveness of four supervised machine learning models – Decision trees (DT), Random forests (RF), Support vector machines (SVM), Logistic regression (LR) – in predicting student dropout based on the first 3 weeks of course activity data. The table below displays the results obtained for each model (Table 3):

Table 3. The results of prediction models

Model	Accuracy	Precision	Recall	F1-Score	AUC
SVM	83%	72%	65%	68%	0.75
RF	**88%**	**80%**	70%	**75%**	**0.82**
DT	85%	78%	68%	73%	0.80
LR	86%	75%	**72%**	74%	0.78

As anticipated, predicting student's dropout based on the first week of data presented a considerable challenge. This finding aligns with the results in the literature, which highlights the difficulty of early prediction using limited data. However, despite this challenge, the models achieved reasonable performance across the various evaluation metrics [11].

Random Forest yielded the highest accuracy (88%) and AUC (0.82) among the models evaluated. This outcome is consistent with other studies that have found Random Forest to be effective in predicting dropout in online courses

It is noteworthy that the recall values across all models were relatively lower compared to other metrics. Recall, which reflects the model's ability to identify all actual dropout cases, is often challenging to maximize without compromising precision, especially when dealing with imbalanced datasets. This observation emphasizes the importance of considering the trade-offs between precision and recall when evaluating models for intervention purposes.

Findings suggest that machine learning models can be effectively deployed to identify at-risk students in the initial stages of MOOC participation. While the performance metrics provide valuable insights into the models' capabilities, the focus should shift towards translating these findings into actionable interventions.

Prioritizing precision may be crucial when designing interventions. A high precision ensures that interventions target students who are genuinely at risk of dropping out, minimizing unnecessary efforts and resources. Furthermore, understanding the features that contribute most significantly to the models' predictive power can offer valuable guidance for intervention design. Identifying these influential factors can shed light on the reasons behind student dropout and inform the development of targeted strategies to address those specific challenges.

5   Conclusion and Future Work

This study explored the feasibility of predicting student dropout in the "Statistical Learning4" MOOC using machine learning models trained on data from the first week of the course. Despite the known challenges of early prediction, the models, particularly Random Forest, demonstrated promising results. While accuracy and AUC offer valuable performance insights, prioritizing precision is crucial for intervention design, ensuring targeted support for genuinely at-risk students. Future research could expand on this foundation by exploring model generalizability across diverse MOOCs, incorporating data from later weeks, and refining feature sets and hyperparameter tuning techniques. Such efforts will contribute to a deeper understanding of dropout dynamics in online learning environments and pave the way for more effective intervention strategies to enhance student success in MOOCs. This data-driven methodology facilitates the optimization of resource usage by MOOC providers, enabling the personalization of interventions and the tailoring of course content to better support learners. Consequently, these proactive strategies provide a more supportive and engaging learning environment, ultimately contributing to enhanced student retention rates and improved academic achievement within online educational settings.

References

1. Feng, W., Tang, J., Liu, T.X.: Understanding dropouts in MOOCs. In: Proceedings of the AAAI Conference on Artificial Intelligence, pp. 517–524 (2019). Consulté le: 4 novembre 2024. [En ligne]. Disponible sur: https://aaai.org/ojs/index.php/AAAI/article/view/3825
2. Kaplan, A.M., Haenlein, M.: Higher education and the digital revolution: about MOOCs, SPOCs, social media, and the cookie monster. Bus. Horiz. **59**(4), 441–450 (2016)
3. Xu, C., Zhu, G., Ye, J., Shu, J.: Educational data mining: dropout prediction in XuetangX MOOCs. Neural. Process. Lett. **54**(4), 2885–2900 (2022). https://doi.org/10.1007/s11063-022-10745-5
4. Onah, D.F., Sinclair, J., Boyatt, R.: Dropout rates of massive open online courses: behavioural patterns. In: EDULEARN14 Proceedings, pp. 5825–5834 (2014)
5. Xing, W., Du, D.: Dropout prediction in MOOCs: using deep learning for personalized intervention. J. Educ. Comput. Res. **57**(3), 547–570 (2019). https://doi.org/10.1177/0735633311 8757015
6. Dalipi, F., Imran, A.S., Kastrati, Z.: MOOC dropout prediction using machine learning techniques: review and research challenges. In: 2018 IEEE Global Engineering Education Conference (EDUCON), pp. 1007–1014. IEEE (2018). Consulté le: 4 novembre 2024. [En ligne]. Disponible sur: https://ieeexplore.ieee.org/abstract/document/8363340/
7. Chi, Z., Zhang, S., Shi, L.: Analysis and prediction of MOOC learners' dropout behavior. Appl. Sci. **13**(2), 1068 (2023)
8. Kahu, E.R.: Framing student engagement in higher education. Stud. High. Educ. **38**(5), 758–773 (2013). https://doi.org/10.1080/03075079.2011.598505
9. Queiroga, E.M., et al.: A learning analytics approach to identify students at risk of dropout: a case study with a technical distance education course. Appl. Sci. **10**(11), 3998 (2020)
10. Whitehill, J., Williams, J., Lopez, G., Coleman, C., Reich, J.: Beyond prediction: first steps toward automatic intervention in MOOC student stopout. Available at SSRN 2611750 (2015)
11. Alamri, A., et al.: Predicting MOOCs dropout using only two easily obtainable features from the first week's activities. In: Coy, A., Hayashi, Y., Chang, M. (eds.) Intelligent Tutoring Systems Lecture Notes in Computer Science, vol. 11528, pp. 163–173. Springer, Cham (2019). https://doi.org/10.1007/978-3-030-22244-4_20
12. Ruipérez-Valiente, J.A., Cobos, R., Muñoz-Merino, P.J., Andujar, Á., Delgado Kloos, C.: Early prediction and variable importance of certificate accomplishment in a MOOC. In: Delgado Kloos, C., Jermann, P., Pérez-Sanagustín, M., Seaton, D.T., White, S. (eds.) Digital Education: Out to the World and Back to the Campus Lecture Notes in Computer Science, vol. 10254, pp. 263–272. Springer, Cham (2017). https://doi.org/10.1007/978-3-319-59044-8_31

13. Fredricks, J.A., Blumenfeld, P.C., Paris, A.H.: School engagement: potential of the concept, state of the evidence. Rev. Educ. Res. **74**(1), 59–109 (2004). https://doi.org/10.3102/003465 43074001059
14. Ye, C., Biswas, G.: Early prediction of student dropout and performance in MOOCs using higher granularity temporal information. J. Learn. Anal. **1**(3), 169–172 (2014)
15. Chen, J., Feng, J., Sun, X., Wu, N., Yang, Z., Chen, S.: MOOC dropout prediction using a hybrid algorithm based on decision tree and extreme learning machine. Math. Probl. Eng. **2019**(1), 8404653 (2019). https://doi.org/10.1155/2019/8404653
16. Akçapınar, G., Altun, A., Aşkar, P.: Using learning analytics to develop early-warning system for at-risk students. Int. J. Educ. Technol. High. Educ. **16**(1), 1–20 (2019)
17. Whitehill, J., Mohan, K., Seaton, D., Rosen, Y., Tingley, D.: Delving deeper into MOOC student dropout prediction. 21 février 2017, arXiv: arXiv:1702.06404. Consulté le: 4 novembre 2024. [En ligne]. Disponible sur: http://arxiv.org/abs/1702.06404
18. Donders, A.R.T., Van Der Heijden, G.J., Stijnen, T., Moons, K.G.: A gentle introduction to imputation of missing values. J. Clin. Epidemiol. **59**(10), 1087–1091 (2006)
19. Haukoos, J.S., Newgard, C.D.: *Advanced statistics:* missing data in clinical research—part 1: an introduction and conceptual framework. Acad. Emerg. Med. **14**(7), 662–668 (2007). https://doi.org/10.1111/j.1553-2712.2007.tb01855.x
20. Venkatesh, B., Anuradha, J.: A review of feature selection and its methods. Cybern. Inf. Technol. **19**(1), 3–26 (2019). https://doi.org/10.2478/cait-2019-0001

Adaptive M-Learning Resources Using Learner Context and Processing Preferences

Khalid Benabbes[1,2,3]([envelope]), Ahmed Zellou[4], Khalid Housni[2], Brahim Hmedna[5], and Ali El Mezouary[6]

[1] Department of Sciences, École Normale Supérieure of Meknès, Moulay Ismail University, Meknes, Morocco
k.benabbes@umi.ac.ma

[2] LARI Laboratory, MISC Team, Faculty of Sciences, Ibn Tofail University, Kénitra, Morocco
housni.khalid@uit.ac.ma

[3] ISIC Research Team of High School of Technology, IISEI Laboratory, Moulay Ismail University, Meknes, Morocco

[4] SPM Research Team, ENSIAS, Mohammed V University, Rabat, Morocco
ahmed.zellou@um5.ac.ma

[5] IMIS Laboratory, Faculty of Sciences, Ibn Zohr University, Agadir, Morocco
brahim.hmedna@edu.uiz.ac.ma

[6] IRF-SIC Laboratory, EST, Ibn Zohr University, Agadir, Morocco
a.elmezouary@uiz.ac.ma

Abstract. This study explored the processing of active and reflective learning styles among learners and their identification in a mobile learning (m-learning) environment. Leveraging various contextual cues and learning traces, we employed an innovative approach to adapt educational resources based not only on individual learning styles but also on immediate contextual factors, such as schedule, location, and Internet connectivity. Initially, we used unsupervised clustering to classify learners according to their preferences in the processing dimension of Felder and Silverman's learning-style model. Subsequently, we developed a model for adapting to learning styles, favoring the decision tree algorithm because of its high accuracy in identifying the learning styles. Additionally, we introduced an approach to adapt learning resources based on learners' styles and contextual characteristics, achieved through the integration of contextual features into the decision tree model's decision-making process. The empirical results demonstrated the effectiveness of our approach in enhancing the adaptability of educational systems.

Keywords: Adaptive learning · Learning style · FSLSM · Contextual features

1 Introduction

E-learning has significantly transformed the educational landscape in recent years, particularly with the rise of mobile learning (m-learning) [1]. Digital technologies have made access to education more attainable than ever, allowing learners worldwide to acquire

O. Zahour et al. (Eds.): ICTIM 2024, CCIS 2655, pp. 158–172, 2026.
https://doi.org/10.1007/978-3-032-15147-6_16

knowledge, develop new skills, and pursue educational goals through online learning platforms [2]. M-learning offers unparalleled flexibility, enabling learners to take courses and participate in educational programs from any location and time [1]. This flexibility has opened new opportunities for lifelong learning, self-study, and professional skill acquisition.

While there are numerous benefits to online learning, it is essential to recognize that each learner is unique, with distinct preferences, needs, and learning styles [3]. Identifying each learner's learning style is crucial for an effective education. Two primary approaches have been considered: the automatic approach and the collaborative approach. The automatic approach involves updating real-time behavioral data and learner activities within the learning system to create an individualized model for each learner, allowing for the accurate identification of their learning style [5]. This method is more effective in classifying learners as it leverages data to closely track the evolution of learning styles [4]. In contrast, the collaborative approach provides a static model for learners and relies on surveys in which they are asked to complete the questionnaires. However, many learners tend to respond randomly because of the sheer volume of questions and their lack of awareness of the importance of these questions. Consequently, this method is generally less effective as it fails to motivate learners to engage meaningfully with the questionnaire [5].

Traditional teaching methods primarily focus on the individual profiles of learners, without considering their specific environments [3]. Our innovative approach aims to adapt educational resources based not only on individual learning styles but also on immediate contextual factors such as schedule, location, Internet connectivity, brightness, and noise level [6]. As m-learning, continues to grow in popularity, it has become increasingly evident that adaptation is a key element in enhancing the effectiveness and impact of digital learning environments.

Adaptive learning involves the ability to vary, change, and modify educational resources based on learners' skills and performance by utilizing information obtained from their task execution or evaluation [7].

This perspective contrasts with traditional e-learning, which often treats learners as homogeneous entities. In contrast, personalized e-learning acknowledges a diverse mix of unique individuals within a learner population [5]. The benefits of personalized learning include streamlining and optimizing the learning process, enabling students to acquire knowledge more efficiently [8]. It is believed that if learners' styles can be identified through their learning environments, and if these environments are designed accordingly, their academic performance will improve.

2 Background

2.1 Adaptation Mechanisms

Adaptation of content in e-learning, particularly in mobile learning (m-learning), is a crucial area aimed at enhancing the learning experience by considering the preferences and needs of learners. Martin e al. [9] have three distinct levels of adaptation: navigation, presentation, and content. Although these three levels are separate, they interact to form a cohesive and personalized learning environment in m-learning contexts.

Navigation Adaptation. Navigation adaptation involves altering how information and links are presented to learners. The primary goal of this process is to streamline navigation and guide users toward relevant learning pathways. One of the most common techniques employed is direct guidance, where learners are directed to specific destinations through navigation buttons, following the principle of "next is best" [9]. Additionally, link annotation adds descriptions or symbols to links to clarify their content, whereas link masking is a technique that removes hyperlinks deemed irrelevant for a specific learner. Finally, link sorting provides a dynamic reorganization of hyperlinks based on their relevance, although this may lead to variations that can occasionally disorient the user [10].

Presentation Adaptation. Presentation adaptation pertains to the user interface and the layout of interactive elements. Techniques in this area include multilingual support, which adjusts the interface according to the learner's preferred language and enhances content accessibility. Additionally, a personalized layout allows for the customization of various visual elements, such as colors, font sizes, and images, to meet individual user needs [9]. This emphasizes the significance of aesthetics and usability in the design of online learning environments.

Content Adaptation. Content adaptation focuses on the selection and presentation of educational resources, including texts, images, videos, and animations, tailored to the preferences of each learner. Techniques such as expandable text enable the choice of content segments to be displayed. Furthermore, the variant page method offers multiple content versions suited to different learning levels, whereas the frame-based approach facilitates information integration by showing or hiding content based on specific rules [11]. This variety of techniques addresses different learning styles and improves information accessibility, whereas conditional fragments determine which information to present based on learner model characteristics and defined domain relationships. This approach was adopted in this study using a classification algorithm.

2.2 Adaptation Techniques

Adaptation mechanisms often rely on advanced algorithms that enable real-time personalization. Classification algorithms such as k-nearest neighbors (KNN) [12], random forests [13], and decision trees (DT) [14] play a vital role in identifying the learning styles of users, thereby facilitating dynamic content adaptation. Additionally, rule-based systems apply predefined criteria to adjust the content and navigation. Machine learning, particularly reinforcement learning, allows systems to continuously learn and adapt to the evolving needs of learners over time [15].

2.3 Learning Styles

The literature presents various definitions of the term "learning style" One interpretation characterizes it as the optimal way an individual learns [5], while another defines it as the preferences of students concerning how educational materials are presented, how they engage with these materials, and how they internalize knowledge [4]. Essentially, learning style pertains to the preferred approach a learner employs to perceive, react, interact with, and respond to their educational environment.

Several psychological models have been developed to categorize learning styles. The model created by Felder and Silverman classifies learners across several distinct dimensions, each of which illustrates their methods of receiving and processing information. This model includes four dimensions, each comprising two contrasting categories: processing (active versus reflective), perception (sensory versus intuitive), input (visual versus verbal), and understanding (sequential versus global) [3].

Active learners (A) tended to engage directly with learning materials, while reflective learners (R) preferred to contemplate this information. Sensory learners (Sen) are inclined toward concrete details and practical applications, whereas intuitive learners seek abstract concepts and theoretical insights. Visual learners (Vi) favor graphical representations, whereas verbal learners (Ve) lean toward spoken or written explanations. Sequential learners (Seq) process information in a linear fashion, focusing on details, whereas global learners (G) grasp concepts holistically by organizing information at a broader level (Fig. 1).

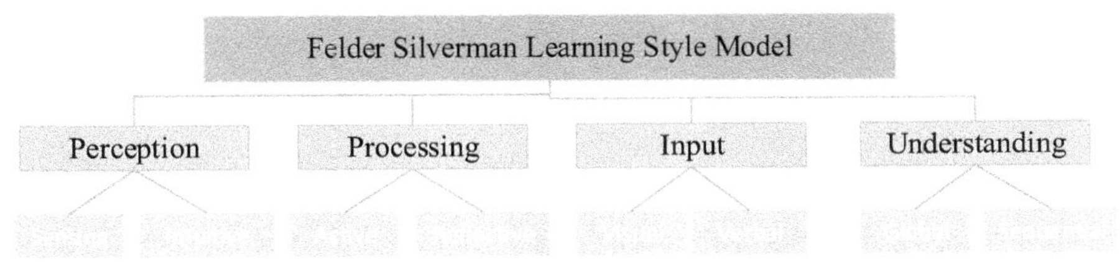

Fig. 1. The Felder-Silverman learning style model

Another learning model, known as VARK, categorizes learning preferences into four primary modalities: Visual, Auditory, Read/Write, and Kinesthetic [16]. These modalities illustrate the various ways in which individuals prefer to receive and process information. Visual modality involves a preference for the representation of information through visual means such as maps, diagrams, graphs, and charts. Auditory modality encompasses a preference for information that is heard or spoken, including lectures, group discussions, and audio resources such as radio broadcasts. The Read/Write modality emphasizes a preference for information presented in written form, which includes reading and writing activities, such as manuals, reports, and essays. Lastly, kinesthetic modality reflects a preference for experiential and practical learning, which involves activities such as demonstrations, simulations, videos of real-world scenarios, case studies, and hands-on exercises.

3 Methodology

This section outlines our proposed methodological approach, which consists of several steps designed to categorize learners according to their preferences in the processing dimensions of the FSLSM learning style (Fig. 2). The approach begins with the extraction and preprocessing of raw data related to each dimension of processing in the FSLSM model, transforming each learner into a set of associated features. Subsequently, an unsupervised clustering algorithm is applied to group learners based on their preferred levels within the learning style spectrum. Finally, the adaptation of educational resources will be addressed and tailored to align with the specific learning styles of learners.

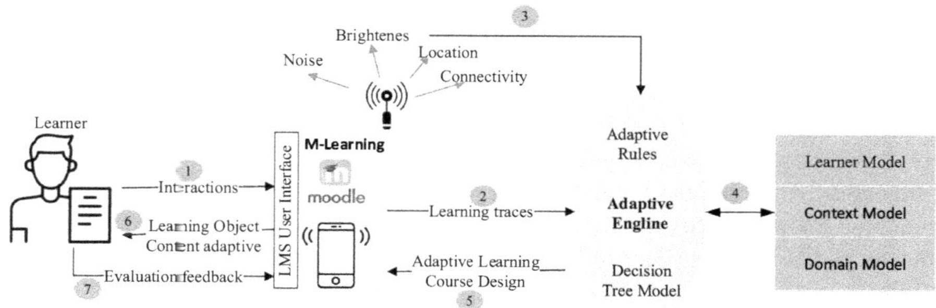

Fig. 2. Overview of the proposed method

3.1 Learning Style Identification

Data Cleaning and Anomaly Detection. The initial raw data extracted from our dataset contain inconsistencies such as erroneous entries, outliers, and duplicate records, which could compromise the accuracy of our models. Therefore, a data cleaning phase is essential to improve data quality. In this process, duplicate entries are removed by eliminating columns with redundant information. Additionally, anomalies representing unusual learner behaviors are identified. These anomalies are defined as events that diverge significantly from typical patterns. However, the anomaly detection step is handled carefully to avoid overfitting, reduce model complexity, and improve efficiency. We evaluated the Isolation Forest (IF) [17] algorithm for anomaly detection due to its similarity to Random Forest, ease of implementation, and reliable performance. The Isolation Forest method works by constructing multiple isolation trees, where each tree is created using a random sample of observations. This algorithm leverages two key characteristics of anomalous data: (a) anomalous data points make up a smaller portion of the dataset and (b) they show distinct differences from the attribute values of normal data (Fig. 3).

Feature Extraction. Deriving features indicative of learning styles is a challenging, time-intensive process that requires cross-disciplinary expertise. Feature extraction techniques aim to identify the most relevant patterns in a feature set suitable for a given task [18]. This iterative approach begins with a critical feature and gradually incorporates additional features to refine the minimal feature set, a process known as feature engineering. By applying domain knowledge to create informative features, feature engineering enhances the performance of machine learning algorithms [19]. At this stage, we extract the most meaningful characteristics from MOOC usage data to represent each learner as

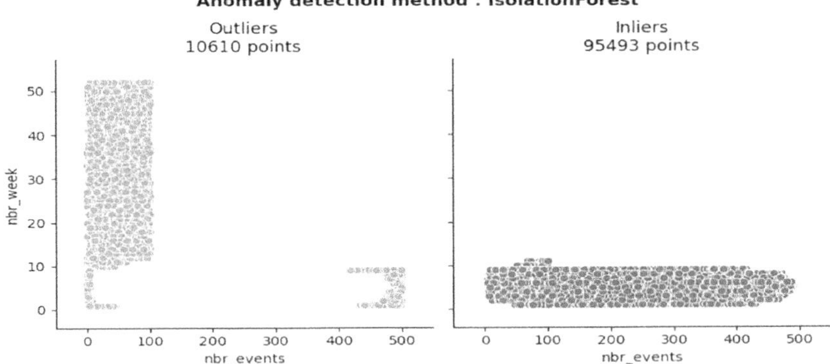

Fig. 3 Anomaly Detection using Isolation Forest Algorithm

a vector of features that reflect their learning style. Using the available dataset, we align features with learning style characteristics defined in the FSLSM model.

Table 1 outlines the features we developed related to the FSLSM processing dimension. For instance, the "Nbr_pause_video" feature is particularly relevant, as it may indicate a higher level of engagement; learners may pause videos to review specific content or practice what they've learned at certain points. Active learners tend to post frequently in discussion forums, engaging in questions, discussions, and explanations [20], and are also expected to attempt a greater number of assignments and exercises. Reflective learners, on the other hand, are likely to use forums for reading multiple posts, reviewing course outlines, and spending additional time reflecting on feedback received on assignments [8].

Feature Normalization. Feature normalization is a practice used to mitigate the disproportionate impact that certain features may have on the learning algorithm. It is particularly useful when features vary in different value ranges. To implement this technique, the MinMaxScaler function available in the Sklearn [4] library is commonly used. This function adjusts feature values to scale them between 0 and 1. The following equation is used to normalize each feature value (x'):

$$x' = \frac{x - x_{\min}}{X_{\max} - X_{\min}} \tag{1}$$

where x is the actual value of the feature, Xmin and Xmax are respectively the smallest and largest value of that feature in the dataset. This normalization ensures that all features have equal importance during model training, which can lead to improved performance and faster convergence of the learning algorithm.

Dimensionality Reduction. Dimensionality reduction is a crucial step in the data analysis process. Principal Component Analysis (PCA) provides an efficient approach to transform a set of features into a 2D space, facilitating data visualization and comprehension. PCA is used to extract important information from observations and reduce noise. To achieve this, PCA computes a set of new orthogonal variables called principal components, which are obtained as linear combinations of the original variables [21].

Table 1. Features of the FSLSM Processing Dimension

Features	Resource	Description
Active Learning Style (LS)		
Nbr_pause_video	Video	Number of pauses in videos, indicating frequent active reflection during content consumption.
Nbr_forum_post	Forum	Number of postings in the forum, showing engagement and interaction with the e-learning community.
Quiz_attempts	Quiz	Number of quiz attempts, suggesting self-testing and active engagement in knowledge reinforcement.
Interaction_in_groupwork	Group Activities	Degree of participation in group discussions or projects, highlighting collaborative learning.
Chat_message_count	Chat/Discussion	Number of chat messages sent, showing frequent active communication with peers or instructors.
Feedback_given	Feedback	Number of times feedback is provided to peers, indicating active involvement in peer learning.
Real-time_questions	Live Sessions	Number of questions asked during live sessions, reflecting active curiosity and engagement.
Reflective Learning Style (LS)		
Outline_visit	Outlines	Number of visits to outlines, reflecting a preference for organizing and reviewing information.
View_post	Forum	Number of views of posts in forums, showing a preference for observing before responding.
Nbr_reading_materials	Reading Material	Frequency of accessing reading materials, suggesting a focus on solitary, in-depth learning.
Time_on_summary	Summaries	Time spent reviewing summaries, showing a methodical approach to consolidating information.
Self_review_attempts	Self-Assessment	Frequency of attempting self-review quizzes, reflecting a focus on self-assessment and reflection.

(continued)

Table 1. (*continued*)

Features	Resource	Description
Video_replay	Video	Number of video replays, indicating reflective review of visual material for enhanced comprehension.
Reflection_time_post_quiz	Quiz	Time spent reflecting after quizzes, as measured by time between quiz submission and next activity.

This technique preserves the most significant information while reducing dimensionality, thereby improving data interpretation and simplifying subsequent calculations.

Once the data are projected into the 2D space, they can be more easily analyzed to identify meaningful patterns or clusters, particularly using methods such as K-means to group learners based on similarities in this reduced space.

K-Means for Clustering and Predictive Modeling. In this section, our objective is to categorize learners based on their preferences and proficiency levels, utilizing the Active/Reflective dimension of the FSLSM [22]. We start by thoroughly examining various aspects of learners, including their individual traits, activities within the online learning environment, and the frequency with which they engage in these activities. Following this analysis, we propose several classifications and profiles tailored to different types of learners. By closely scrutinizing learners' characteristics, behaviors, activity patterns, and engagement levels within the online learning platform, we can identify distinct profiles and classifications for learners who actively participate.

To accomplish this, we use a clustering technique, which automatically groups learners who exhibit similar traits and behaviors. Subsequently, we align these feature vectors with different learning styles to understand how learners comprehend and engage with the material presented in the FSLSM. To determine the optimal number of clusters, we applied the elbow method, ensuring meaningful groupings without unnecessary complexity. By analyzing the correlation between changes in clustering cost and the number of clusters, we observed how the average distance to cluster centroids evolves, identifying a point where this distance decreases significantly, indicating the optimal number of clusters.

We found that for both active and reflective learning styles, the optimal number of clusters was 8. Additionally, we calculated the silhouette score to confirm these results, obtaining an active silhouette score of 0.33 and a reflective silhouette score of 0.29. Furthermore, we calculated the Davies-Bouldin index [3], confirming that the optimal number of clusters was 8, with an active Davies-Bouldin index of 1.41 and a reflective Davies-Bouldin index of 1.39.

Ultimately, this process allows us to pinpoint the most effective groupings of learners within the online learning environment. Finally, we can calculate the associated cost using a specific equation, providing a quantitative measure of our clustering approach's efficiency and effectiveness.

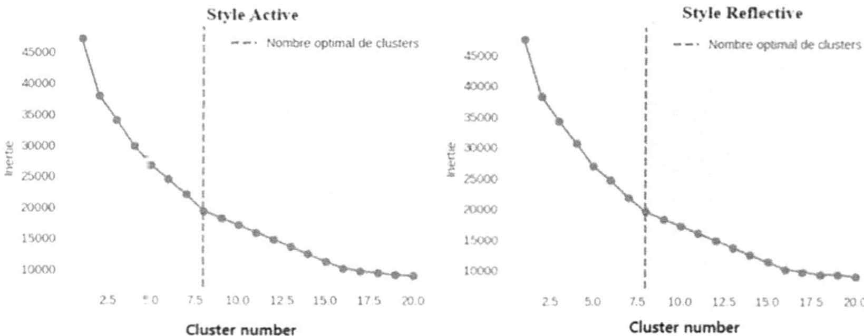

Fig. 4. Elbow point identification for Active and Reflective learning styles.

As shown in Fig. 4, eight clusters have been chosen. The research has demonstrated that the k-means−+ [22] algorithm is the most suitable for establishing the initial centroids of the clusters. After labeling the entire dataset, we trained and compared two classification models tailored to our requirements: decision tree (DT) and k-nearest neighbors (KNN). To do so, we utilized k-fold cross-validation [20] with a value of k equal to 10 to assess the performance of each model. Subsequently, we applied the grid search technique [23] to identify the best hyperparameters for each model.

K-Means Clustering Algorithm. A dataset is typically subjected to a clustering process once it has been structured into groups that meet two criteria: (1) increased spacing between classes (separability) and (2) reduced separation between items belonging to the same class (compactness) [22]. Clustering serves to highlight the underlying structure of the dataset, proving particularly useful in cases where data is unlabeled. In the context of this approach, we specifically focus on clustering using the k-means method (Fig. 4). This method is often cited among the most popular clustering approaches, as emphasized by [24]. It is an unsupervised algorithm aimed at grouping similar objects into k clusters. According to [25], it iteratively adjusts the positions of cluster centers as well as the distribution of each node within the cluster (Fig. 5).

3.2   Adaptation of Educational Resources

Our approach to adapting educational resources focuses on tailoring the learning experience to each student's unique needs and preferences. We start by examining each learner's specific learning preferences, with a detailed focus on their methods of processing information, especially in relation to active and reflective learning preferences as outlined by the Felder-Silverman Learning Style Model (FSLSM) [26]. This analysis provides insights into how each student interacts with educational content and processes information, allowing us to create a more responsive learning environment.

Beyond learning preferences, we also account for contextual factors that can affect the learning experience. These factors include connectivity, which influences access to online resources; mobility, which affects concentration across various environments; ambient noise, which can interfere with focus; and screen brightness, which impacts

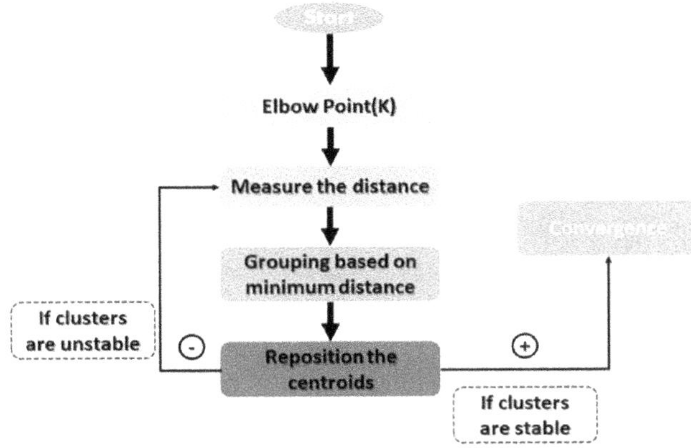

Fig. 5. K-Means Clustering Algorithm

visual comfort [27]. Once both learning preferences and contextual factors have been identified, we apply this information to create adaptive rules. These rules, often implemented through decision-tree algorithms, enable precise decisions on the selection and presentation of learning materials [28].

For example, if a learner prefers video content and achieves optimal results in a quiet environment with moderate brightness, the system prioritizes video resources that match these preferences and environmental conditions. The overarching goal of our adaptive strategy is to deliver a personalized, efficient learning experience by providing the most relevant resources at the appropriate time and in the most suitable format for each student's unique requirements. By integrating learning preferences with contextual insights, we aim to enhance knowledge retention and facilitate continuous progress throughout each learner's academic journey.

3.3 Dataset

The dataset for our study includes learner data collected from three courses, "English for Engineering," "Animal Production," and "Descriptive Statistics," made available through an m-learning platform accessible to students from agricultural schools in Morocco. These courses were delivered during the winter sessions of 2020 and 2021, spanning a 16-week period. During this time, 172 registered students regularly accessed the platform to use a range of educational materials, including lecture notes, videos, quizzes, and interactive forums. These resources were designed to support and enrich the students' learning experiences throughout the semester.

4 Results and Discussion

Developing adaptive content, as discussed in this study, is a time-intensive process. When designing adaptive learning materials for the m-learning system developed in this research, a significant portion of the time was devoted to crafting resources tailored to the processing dimension of learning styles and the context of the learner. The creation of such assessments requires extensive effort. An efficient approach involves incorporating questions from lower-complexity assessments into those at higher-complexity levels. For this purpose, three required assessments of low, medium, and high complexity were created to validate learner knowledge and evaluate the impact of the adaptive approach on learning experience.

For practical courses, the minimum required material might include only essential theoretical content complemented by practical tasks of varying complexity levels (low, medium, and high) and corresponding evaluations for each level.

The learning style identification approach involves determining the optimal k value for both active and reflective learning styles, after which we apply the k-means clustering algorithm to group learners based on their distinct characteristics and needs. Subsequently, the labeled dataset was used to train and assess the two classification algorithms to identify the one with the best performance. Analysis of the precision results, as shown in Table 2, revealed that the Decision Tree (DT) model achieved the highest precision at 98%. This high accuracy highlights the strength of the DT model in classifying data accurately, establishing it as the preferred choice for our system.

Our findings are in line with studies on adaptive educational resource systems that consider both context and learning style. Our results emphasize that adapting educational content based on both contextual factors and individual learning preferences is essential. For example, when adapting resources for a learner with an active learning style in a noisy environment with low connectivity, the system adjusts the format and presentation of learning materials to support knowledge retention, despite these challenges. By aligning the format and delivery of resources with the learner's style and situational context, this approach enhances the likelihood of successful learning outcomes and provides a personalized and impactful m-learning experience.

Table 2 would typically include metrics like accuracy, precision, recall, and F1 score for each model tested (Decision Tree, K-Nearest Neighbors, and Random Forest), enabling a direct comparison of their effectiveness in identifying learning styles.

Table 2. Comparison of Model Performance

Modele	Accuracy	Precision	Recall	F1-score
DT [14]	**0.98**	**0.98**	**0.98**	**0.99**
KNN [12]	0.56	0.56	0.57	0.56
RF [13]	0.92	0.91	0.92	0.91

To evaluate the system's effectiveness, students were asked to express their level of satisfaction, with options including "Very Satisfied," "Satisfied," "Somewhat Satisfied," and "Unsatisfied." They were encouraged to rate the system based on each recommendation it generated (Table 3).

This study highlights the strong interactions between the students and the adaptive m-learning system. On average, each student received 11.9 personalized adaptations,

Table 3. Satisfaction Levels with the M-Learning Platform

Satisfaction Level	Number of Evaluations	Percentage
Very Satisfied	15	50%
Satisfied	12	40%
Somewhat Satisfied	3	10%
Unsatisfied	0	0%

with each adaptation containing approximately 9.8 resources, leading to a total of 160 adapted items per student over the five-week course. Despite the evident interest in using the system and engaging with adapted materials, only 143 user satisfaction ratings were obtained, representing 83% of the adaptations.

In addition to evaluating each adaptation, the students had the opportunity to assess the overall system in terms of usability, navigation, encountered issues, and suggestions for improvement.

The results demonstrated that students who engaged in the adaptive m-learning system, tailored to their learning styles, achieved superior learning outcomes compared to those who did not. The adaptive m-learning environment was highly effective in capturing student attention, and it significantly benefited the students in the experimental group. This study revealed a substantial difference in learning results, indicating that adaptive m-learning can be a valuable approach in higher education. By incorporating learning styles and contextual factors, this adaptive m-learning method can foster sustained student engagement. Learning styles provide a strong basis for the development of educational materials based on learning theories.

The students completed an engagement survey both before and after using the adaptive learning environment. This questionnaire measured engagement across the skills, participation/interaction, performance, and emotional dimensions. In the completed evaluations, users noted that the navigation and usability of the system were intuitive and straightforward. Regarding system limitations, users have suggested implementing a password recovery feature, which could be added to future versions. For improvements, users recommended more specific filters based on the content format, such as videos, slides, and text, which will be considered for enhancing filters by additional preferences.

5   Conclusion and Future Works

This study addresses the challenge of identifying active and reflective learning styles by analyzing learner interactions in m-learning environments. Our goal was to tailor the educational content based on learner preferences and contextual factors across digital platforms. By integrating contextual information and learning traces, we applied an unsupervised clustering method to categorize learners according to their processing preferences in the Felder-Silverman learning style model. This was followed by the construction of an annotated dataset that balanced and assessed the prevalence of each learning style. To develop an adaptive model, we compared the performance of three supervised classification algorithms—Random Forest, K-Nearest Neighbors (KNN), and Decision Trees with the Decision Tree model that achieved the highest accuracy (98%) in identifying learning styles.

In a subsequent phase, we proposed an approach to adapt educational resources in both e-learning and m-learning contexts, leveraging the identified learning styles of students. A contextual feature vector was incorporated into the decision tree process to establish adaptive rules, enabling the system to deliver relevant educational resources at the optimal time in the most suitable format, whether accessed via e-learning or m-learning platforms.

Future research could further improve the adaptability and effectiveness of the system. Real-time data stream integration across e-learning and m-learning settings, including analyses from additional courses or subject areas, could make adaptations more responsive to learners' changing needs. Moreover, analyzing additional contextual factors, such as social interactions and emotional states, could enable more personalized adaptations. Incorporating advanced machine-learning techniques, such as reinforcement learning, would also support the continuous adaptation and refinement of strategies. Finally, empirical studies in real-world educational settings would provide valuable insights into the effectiveness, utility, and potential impact of the system on learning outcomes across both e-learning and m-learning platforms.

References

1. Al-Emran, M., Mezhuyev, V., Kamaludin, A.: Technology acceptance model in M-learning context: a systematic review. Comput. Educ. **125**, 389–412 (2018). https://doi.org/10.1016/j. compedu.2018.06.008
2. Alrikabi, H.T.S., Jasim, N.A., Majeed, B.H., Zkear, A.A., ALRubeei, I.R.N.: Smart learning based on Moodle E-learning platform and digital skills for university students. Int. J. Recent Contrib. Eng. Sci. IT IJES. **10**(01), 01 (2022). https://doi.org/10.3991/ijes.v10i01.28995
3. Benabbes, K., Housni, K., Hmedna, B., Zellou, A., Mezouary, A.E.: Explore the influence of contextual characteristics on the learning understanding on LMS. Educ. Inf. Technol. (2023). https://doi.org/10.1007/s10639-023-11899-y
4. Benabbes, K., Hmedna, B., Housni, K., Zellou, A., El Mezouary, A.: New automatic hybrid approach for tracking learner comprehension Progress in the LMS. Int. J. Interact. Mob. Technol. **16**(19), 19 (2022). https://doi.org/10.3991/ijim.v16i19.33733
5. Hmedna, B., El Mezouary, A., Baz, O.: A predictive model for the identification of learning styles in MOOC environments. Clust. Comput. **23**(2), 2 (2020). https://doi.org/10.1007/s10 586-019-02992-4
6. Adomavicius, G., Bauman, K., Tuzhilin, A., Unger, M.: Context-aware recommender systems: from foundations to recent developments. In: Ricci, F., Rokach, L., Shapira, B. (eds.) Recommender Systems Handbook, pp. 211–250. Springer, New York (2022). https://doi.org/ 10.1007/978-1-0716-2197-4_6
7. AL-Fayyadh, H.R.D., Ganim Ali, S.A., Abood, B.: Modelling an adaptive learning system using artificial intelligence. Webology. **19**(1), 1 (2021). https://doi.org/10.14704/WEB/V19I1/ WEB19001
8. Katsaris, I., Vidakis, N.: Adaptive e-learning systems through learning styles: a review of the literature. Adv. Mob. Learn. Educ. Res. **1**(2), 2 (2021). https://doi.org/10.25082/AMLER. 2021.02.007

9. Martin, F., Chen, Y., Moore, R.L., Westine, C.D.: Systematic review of adaptive learning research designs, context, strategies, and technologies from 2009 to 2018. Educ. Technol. Res. Dev. **68**(4), 4 (2020). https://doi.org/10.1007/s11423-020-09793-2

10. Alam, A.: The secret sauce of student success: cracking the code by navigating the path to personalized learning with educational data mining. In: 2023 2nd International Conference on Smart Technologies and Systems for Next Generation Computing (ICSTSN), Villupuram, avr, pp. 1–8. IEEE (2023). https://doi.org/10.1109/ICSTSN57873.2023.10151558

11. Mwambe, O.O., Tan, P.X., Kamioka, E.: Bioinformatics-based adaptive system towards real-time dynamic E-learning content personalization. Educ. Sci. **10**(2), 42 (2020). https://doi.org/10.3390/educsci10020042

12. Deng, Z., Zhu, X., Cheng, D., Zong, M., Zhang, S.: Efficient kNN classification algorithm for big data. Neurocomputing. **195**, 143–148 (2016). https://doi.org/10.1016/j.neucom.2015.08.112

13. Liu, Y., Wang, Y., Zhang, J.: New machine learning algorithm: random forest. In: Liu, B., Ma, M., Chang, J. (eds.) Information Computing and Applications Lecture Notes in Computer Science, vol. 7473, pp. 246–252. Springer, Berlin, Heidelberg (2012). https://doi.org/10.1007/978-3-642-34062-8_32

14. Safavian, S.R., Landgrebe, D.: A survey of decision tree classifier methodology. IEEE Trans. Syst. Man Cybern. **21**(3), 3 (1991). https://doi.org/10.1109/21.97458

15. Abel, F., Bittencourt, I.I., Henze, N., Krause, D., Vassileva, J.: A rule-based recommender system for online discussion forums. In: Nejdl, W., Kay, J., Pu, P., Herder, E. (eds.) Adaptive Hypermedia and Adaptive Web-Based Systems Lecture Notes in Computer Science, vol. 5149, pp. 12–21. Springer, Berlin, Heidelberg (2008). https://doi.org/10.1007/978-3-540-70987-9_4

16. Fleming, N.: Learning styles again: VARKing up the right tree!, p. 3

17. Cheng, Z., Zou, C., Dong, J.: Outlier detection using isolation forest and local outlier factor. In: Proceedings of the Conference on Research in Adaptive and Convergent Systems, Chongqing China, September, pp. 161–168. ACM (2019). https://doi.org/10.1145/3338840.3355641

18. Hmedna, B., Mezouary, A.E., Baz, O.: How does learners' prefer to process information in MOOCs? A data-driven study. Procedia Comput. Sci. **148**, 371–379 (2019). https://doi.org/10.1016/j.procs.2019.01.045

19. Benabbes, K., Zellou, A., Housni, K., El Mezouary, A.: Exploring student involvement in E-learning. In: 2023 14th International Conference on Intelligent Systems: Theories and Applications (SITA), Casablanca, Morocco, November, pp. 1–7. IEEE (2023). https://doi.org/10.1109/SITA60746.2023.10373724

20. Mezouary, A.E., Hmedna, B., Baz, O.: An unsupervised method for discovering how does learners progress toward understanding in MOOCs. Int. J. Innov. Technol. Explor. Eng. **10**(5), 5 (2021). https://doi.org/10.35940/ijitee.E8673.0310521

21. Dugger, Z., Halverson, G., McCrory, B., Claudio, D.: Principal component analysis in MCDM: an exercise in pilot selection. Expert Syst. Appl. **188**, 115984 (2022). https://doi.org/10.1016/j.eswa.2021.115984

22. Arthur, D., Vassilvitskii, S.: K-means++: the advantages of careful seeding

23. Fayed, H.A., Atiya, A.F.: Speed up grid-search for parameter selection of support vector machines. Appl. Soft Comput. **80**, 202–210 (2019). https://doi.org/10.1016/j.asoc.2019.03.037

24. Syakur, M.A., Khotimah, B.K., Rochman, E.M.S., Satoto, B.D.: Integration K-means clustering method and elbow method for identification of the best customer profile cluster. IOP Conf. Ser. Mater. Sci. Eng. **336**, 012017 (2018). https://doi.org/10.1088/1757-899X/336/1/012017

25. Moubayed, A., Injadat, M., Shami, A., Lutfiyya, H.: Student engagement level in an e-learning environment: clustering using K-means. Am. J. Distance Educ. **34**(2), 2 (2020). https://doi.org/10.1080/08923647.2020.1696140
26. Felder, R.M.: Learning and teaching styles in engineering education, p. 11.
27. Akharraz, L., El Mezouary, A., Mahani, Z.: To context-aware learner modeling based on ontology. In: 2018 IEEE Global Engineering Education Conference (EDUCON), avr, pp. 1326–1334. IEEE, Tenerife (2018). https://doi.org/10.1109/EDUCON.2018.8363383
28. Bouihi, B., Bahaj, M.: Ontology and rule-based recommender system for E-learning applications. Int. J. Emerg. Technol. Learn. **14**(15), 15 (2019). https://doi.org/10.3991/ijet.v14i15.10566

Natural language processing(NLP), Smart Systems, and Emerging Technologies

Exploring the Impact of Empathy on User Satisfaction in Banking Chatbots: A Path to Enhanced Customer Experience

Mohammed Kasbouya[✉] and Nawal Sael

Artificial Intelligence and Systems Laboratory, Faculty of Sciences Ben M'sick, Hassan II University, Casablanca, Morocco
mohammed.kasbouya-etu@etu.univh2c.ma

Abstract. As digital banking becomes increasingly prominent, ensuring effective and emotionally intelligent customer service is crucial. This study addresses the impact of empathy on user satisfaction in banking chatbots. Two chatbot versions—empathetic and non-empathetic—The systems were meticulously designed and assessed through empirical user testing. Participants engaged with both iterations, and their insights were systematically gathered utilizing a 5-point Likert scale across several evaluative criteria, encompassing interaction ease, comprehension of issues, overall contentment, and inclination for subsequent engagements. The findings indicated that the empathetic chatbot surpassed the non-empathetic variant across all assessed criteria ($p < 0.001$). In terms of overall contentment, the empathetic chatbot achieved an impressive mean score of 4.8 out of 5, in contrast to 3.6 for the non-empathetic chatbot. The ease of interaction was similarly rated more favorably for the empathetic chatbot, with a mean score of 4.7 compared to 3.5. Furthermore, 80% of participants preferred future engagements with the empathetic chatbot. These findings indicate that the incorporation of empathy in AI customer service can improve user satisfaction, especially within banking. Subsequent research should investigate the enduring impacts of empathetic chatbots and their relevance in various industries and cultural settings.

Keywords: Empathetic Chatbots · Human-Computer Interaction · AI in Customer Service · Emotional Intelligence

1 Introduction

In the contemporary digital landscape, the banking industry is witnessing a profound shift in how customer service is delivered. With the rapid adoption of online and mobile banking platforms, financial institutions are increasingly relying on automated systems, particularly chatbots, to manage customer interactions. These AI-driven tools offer several advantages, including 24/7 availability, quick response times, and the ability to handle a large volume of inquiries efficiently [1]. However, while these systems excel in efficiency, they cannot often provide the nuanced, empathetic communication that is crucial in customer service, especially in contexts where emotions and trust play a

O. Zahour et al. (Eds.): ICTIM 2024, CCIS 2655, pp. 175–186, 2026.
https://doi.org/10.1007/978-3-032-15147-6_17

significant role. Customer satisfaction is a critical determinant of business success in the banking sector. The quality of customer service not only influences customer loyalty but also affects the overall reputation of the institution. Traditional chatbots, despite their functional capabilities, often fail to address the emotional needs of customers [2], leading to interactions that can feel impersonal or even frustrating. This is particularly problematic in the banking industry, where customers frequently deal with sensitive issues such as financial security, fraud, and personal financial management. In such scenarios, the ability to convey empathy and understanding can significantly enhance the customer experience.

Empathy, defined as the ability to understand and share the feelings of others, is a fundamental aspect of human interaction [3]. Research in human-computer interaction has increasingly recognized the importance of empathy in enhancing user satisfaction. Empathetic communication in customer service can help reduce stress, build trust, and create a more positive overall experience. However, despite the recognized importance of empathy, many existing chatbot systems are not equipped to effectively process and respond to the emotional states of users. This gap in chatbot capability presents a significant opportunity for innovation in the field of AI-driven customer service.

The principal aim of this investigation is to examine the effects of incorporating empathy within banking chatbots, as well as to assess the extent to which such incorporation can enhance customer satisfaction and engagement. In pursuit of this aim, we devised two variants of a banking chatbot: one specifically crafted to replicate empathetic responses and another that functions devoid of empathetic features. Through a comparative examination of user interactions with both variants of the chatbot, we seek to ascertain whether the integration of empathetic communication can yield quantifiable advancements in essential user experience indicators, including ease of interaction, comprehension of issues, overall satisfaction, and preference for subsequent interactions.

2   Literature Review

Empathy has been shown to positively impact customer satisfaction and reuse intention in general customer service interactions [4]. [5] found that empathy-seeking messages enhance post-recovery satisfaction, highlighting empathy's role in service recovery. [6] emphasized that empathy is crucial for the overall customer experience, while [7]. Pointed out its significant role in trust-building.

Moreover, empathy reduces negative word-of-mouth and enhances customer forgiveness [8]. In the banking sector, benevolence related to empathy influences chatbot trust and customer satisfaction [9]. Empathy also positively influences chatbot acceptance in specific cultural contexts, such as Indonesia [10], and is crucial for the trustworthiness and acceptance of healthcare chatbots [11].

Empathy's impact varies by industry and demographic. For example, empathy did not significantly affect customer satisfaction in the airline industry, indicating its context-dependent impact [12]. However, anthropomorphic cues enhancing empathy positively affect product personalisation and willingness to pay in e-commerce [13] and customer satisfaction in food e-commerce [14]. Older users particularly value empathetic interactions in customer service [15].

In healthcare, empathy is vital for fostering trust in chatbots [16] and is important in ethical considerations for healthcare chatbots [17]. Empathy in mental health chatbots positively affects satisfaction and continued usage [18], and features demonstrating empathy are crucial for mental health apps [19].

Human-like communication, including the use of empathetic responses, plays a significant role in enhancing user satisfaction and ethical considerations in chatbot design. Perceived humanness, including empathy, drives chatbot adoption and recommendation intent [20]. Co-designed chatbots with migrant stakeholders demonstrated better empathy [21]. Human-like communication, contributing to empathy, influences customer satisfaction [22], and empathy is important in ethical human-machine interactions [23].

The impact of empathy in chatbots can vary depending on the context and industry. For instance, while empathy did not significantly impact customer satisfaction in the airline industry [12], it played a critical role in healthcare settings [16, 17]. This context-dependence suggests that the integration of empathy must be tailored to the specific needs and expectations of users within different sectors.

Empathy is also influenced by demographic factors such as age and cultural background. Older users tend to value empathetic interactions more [15], and regional studies, like those conducted in Indonesia [10], highlight the importance of cultural context in shaping users' acceptance of empathetic chatbots.

There exist significant deficiencies in the scholarly literature, especially within the banking industry, where the constructs of customer trust and satisfaction hold paramount importance. Furthermore, there is a scarcity of empirical investigations examining the enduring consequences of empathetic interactions on customer loyalty and retention. Additionally, the exploration of how various cultural and demographic cohorts perceive and appreciate the role of empathy in chatbots remains largely under-researched. Our study seeks to fill these voids by conceptualizing and assessing an empathetic chatbot tailored for the banking sector. We developed two distinct iterations of the chatbot: one that employs empathetic responses and another that delivers direct, non-empathetic communication. Through the comparative analysis of user interactions with these two iterations, our research aspires to evaluate the influence of empathy on customer satisfaction, trust, and engagement within the banking domain.

3 Methodology

This investigation utilized a systematically organized mixed-methods framework, combining both qualitative and quantitative approaches, to assess the influence of empathetic communication within banking chatbots. The inquiry was executed across three principal phases: the development of the chatbot, user testing, and the subsequent analysis of data. Qualitative methods included user interviews and feedback sessions to gather insights on user experiences, while quantitative methods involved statistical analysis of interaction metrics. This segment elucidates the methodologies and techniques employed during each distinct phase. The detailed flow of the experimental process, from chatbot development and participant recruitment to interactions and data collection, is illustrated in Fig. 1. This figure provides a clear overview of how the testing was structured and managed.

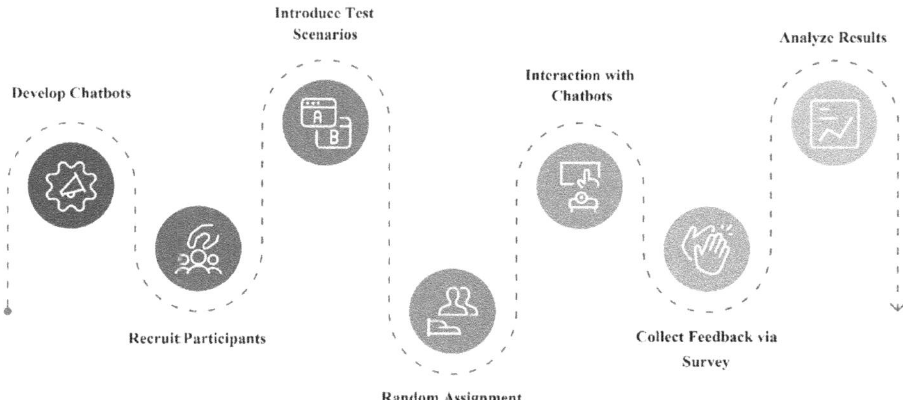

Fig. 1. Experimental Workflow for Evaluating Empathetic and Non-Empathetic Chatbot Interactions

3.1 Chatbot Development

In this study, we developed two distinct chatbot versions—empathetic and non-empathetic—as a core component of our research methodology. Our team designed and built both chatbots from the ground up using GPT-3.5-turbo as the underlying language model, chosen for its advanced natural language processing capabilities. This hands-on development process allowed us to fine-tune the empathetic chatbot specifically to incorporate emotionally intelligent responses. At the same time, the non-empathetic version was configured to deliver purely informational responses. By creating both versions ourselves, we ensured consistent underlying architecture, enabling a precise and controlled comparison of empathetic versus non-empathetic features.

- Empathetic Chatbot: This version was designed to simulate emotionally intelligent responses, incorporating empathy through fine-tuning. The empathetic chatbot was programmed to recognize emotionally charged keywords (e.g., 'worried,' 'frustrated') and respond with supportive language tailored to the user's emotional state. Empathetic features included expressions of understanding, reassurance, and offering assistance beyond factual responses. For instance, instead of merely providing information, the chatbot would acknowledge the user's concerns with phrases like 'I understand how frustrating this can be' to enhance the emotional connection. The customization involved iterative testing to ensure that the chatbot responses conveyed understanding, reassurance, and appropriate levels of empathy for different banking scenarios.
- Non-Empathetic Chatbot: In contrast, the non-empathetic chatbot focused solely on providing functional responses. It addressed the same banking issues but without any emotionally nuanced communication. The goal was to evaluate how users reacted to purely informational responses versus empathetic interactions.
- The system architecture for both chatbots, which outlines the flow from user input to the chatbot's response, is depicted in Fig. 2. This figure illustrates how the chatbots process user input, integrate or omit empathy in responses, and deliver the final output.

Fig. 2. Architecture of the Chatbot System

3.2   User Testing

User testing was conducted to assess the effectiveness of both chatbot versions in real-world-like scenarios. The study began with the development of two distinct chatbot versions—empathetic and non-empathetic—designed specifically for this research. Participants were then recruited from diverse demographic backgrounds to ensure that the findings would reflect a broad user base, including individuals of varying ages, occupations, and banking experiences. A total of 50 participants were involved in the study, recruited through online platforms and local banking institutions, with the sample evenly split between different age groups and banking experience levels to enhance generalizability.

During the testing procedure, participants interacted with both the empathetic and non-empathetic chatbots across five predefined banking scenarios: reporting a lost credit card, responding to a scam alert, resetting account passwords, querying account balances, and seeking financial advice. Each participant engaged with both chatbot versions, allowing for a within-subjects comparison of their experiences. Before the testing phase, a systematic design process was implemented to develop questions aimed at evaluating user satisfaction and the impact of empathetic communication. These questions were selected based on their relevance to the banking context, the inclusion of demographic inquiries, and the assessment of interaction quality, ensuring a comprehensive understanding of user experiences.

3.3   Data Collection

Quantitative data was collected using a structured survey. Participants rated their experiences with both chatbot versions on a 5-point Likert scale. The metrics evaluated included:

- Ease of Interaction: How easy it was to communicate with the chatbot.

- Issue Understanding: How well the chatbot understood and addressed the user's issue.
- Overall Satisfaction: The user's overall satisfaction with the interaction.
- Preference for Future Interactions: The likelihood of choosing to interact with the chatbot in the future.
- Qualitative feedback was also gathered through open-ended questions, allowing participants to express their thoughts on the strengths and weaknesses of each chatbot version. This qualitative data provided valuable context to complement the quantitative findings, highlighting specific user experiences and preferences.

3.4 Data Analysis

The data analysis phase employed both quantitative and qualitative methods to provide a comprehensive evaluation of the chatbot interactions.

- Quantitative Analysis: The application of Python facilitated the execution of independent sample t-tests aimed at contrasting the mean scores of empathetic versus non-empathetic chatbots across the specified evaluative metrics. The findings indicated the presence of statistically significant variances in user satisfaction, ease of interaction, comprehension of issues, and inclination towards future interactions, with p-values uniformly remaining beneath the threshold of 0.001.
- Qualitative Analysis: The qualitative feedback was subjected to thematic analysis to discern prevalent themes within participant responses. This analytical approach illuminated those participants valued the empathetic chatbot's human-like interactions and emotional support, which contributed to enhanced engagement and satisfaction levels. Conversely, the non-empathetic chatbot was frequently characterized as lacking personal touch, despite its effectiveness in disseminating information.

4 Results

The primary objective of this study was to investigate the impact of empathetic communication on user satisfaction within banking chatbot interactions. To achieve this, both quantitative and qualitative analyses were conducted to explore how integrating empathy influences user experiences. The findings will be discussed in detail, leading to conclusions about the effectiveness of empathetic chatbot interactions in enhancing user satisfaction.

4.1 Demographics

The research encompassed a heterogeneous participant cohort, primarily comprising youthful and technologically adept individuals, with a significant proportion falling within the age range of 18 to 24 years, as depicted in Fig. 3. Most participants were habitual users of online banking platforms, thereby guaranteeing that their insights were firmly anchored in pertinent digital interactions.

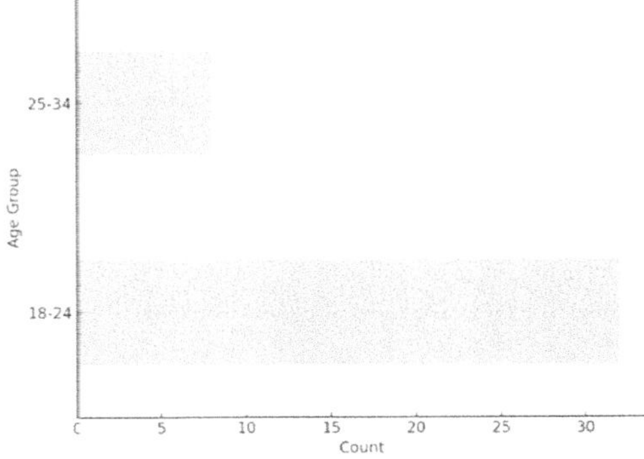

Fig. 3. Age Distribution of Participants

4.2 Overall Satisfaction with Empathetic Chatbot

The overall satisfaction ratings for the empathetic chatbot, as shown in Fig 4, demonstrate a clear predominance of high scores, with 80% of participants rating their experience at the maximum score of 5. This trend highlights the positive reception of empathetic communication in chatbot interactions, reinforcing its value in enhancing user experience in digital banking. In contrast, Fig 5 illustrates a broader distribution of satisfaction ratings for the non-empathetic chatbot, with more variability and a noticeable presence of lower satisfaction scores. Although some users still reported positive experiences, the absence of empathetic elements appears to have contributed to gaps in engagement and overall satisfaction.

The comparison between these two figures underscores the significant impact of empathy on user satisfaction. The empathetic chatbot consistently outperformed the non-empathetic version across all metrics, as further supported by statistical analysis. The t-test result of 6.6110 (p < 0.001) confirms that the difference in overall satisfaction between the two chatbot versions is statistically significant. These findings suggest that integrating empathetic responses can substantially improve the perceived quality of service, ultimately enhancing the overall user experience in digital customer support systems.

4.3 T-Test Results

The t-tests were utilized to evaluate the influence of empathetic chatbot design on various critical user experience metrics. The t-test serves as a statistical technique employed to ascertain whether substantial differences exist between the means of two distinct groups, particularly advantageous for scrutinizing small sample sizes. In this investigation, the findings, encapsulated in Table 1, demonstrate statistically significant disparities between the empathetic and non-empathetic chatbots across all assessed metrics.

The p-values associated with all evaluated metrics were markedly lower than the traditional significance threshold of 0.05, suggesting that the identified disparities are extremely improbable to arise from random fluctuations. These findings furnish compelling evidence that substantiates the assertion that the incorporation of empathy in the

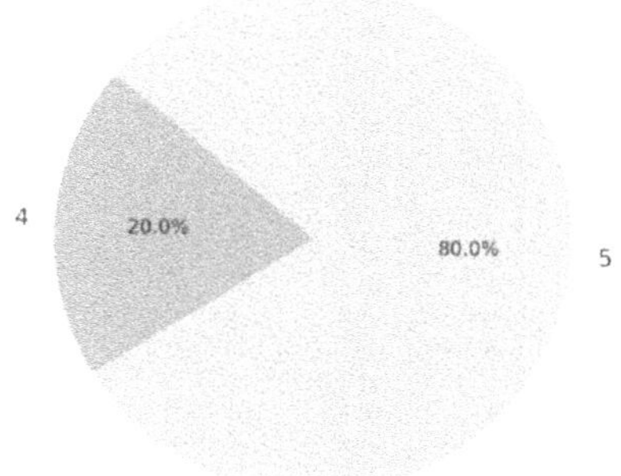

Fig. 4. Overall Satisfaction with Empathetic Chatbot Interaction (Mean: 4.8, p < 0.001)

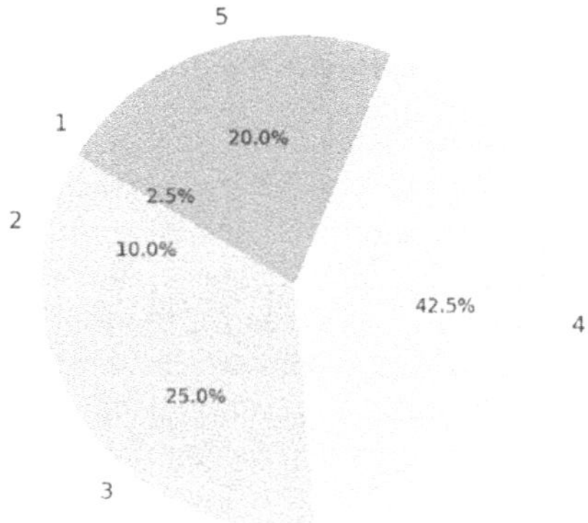

Fig. 5. Overall Satisfaction with Non-Empathetic Chatbot Interaction (Mean: 3.6, p < 0.001)

Table 1. T-Test Results for User Experience Metrics

Metric	T-Statistic	P-Value
Ease of Interaction	6.5225	6.29e-09
Issue Understanding	6.6410	3.77e-09
Overall Satisfaction	6.6110	4.29e-09
Preference for Future Interaction	6.1857	2.66e-08

design of chatbots yields a substantial and affirmative impact on user satisfaction and engagement.

5 Discussion

The findings of this study underscore the importance of empathetic communication in enhancing user satisfaction with chatbots. The demographic analysis revealed that the participant group was predominantly young and tech-savvy, indicating a preference for digital interactions that are both efficient and intuitive. Future research could expand on this by examining how demographic factors such as age, cultural background, and familiarity with AI might influence responses to empathetic features in chatbots, potentially offering insights into user segmentation and tailored chatbot designs. Furthermore, the cultural heterogeneity of the participants, predominantly originating from Morocco and France, indicates that chatbots must possess the capacity for adaptability to diverse cultural frameworks to effectively fulfill the varied expectations of users.

The presence of empathy was observed to substantially enhance critical user experience indicators, such as the simplicity of interaction and comprehension of issues, thereby underscoring its beneficial influence. Participants articulated a pronounced preference for the anthropomorphic, supportive characteristics of the empathetic chatbot, which consequently resulted in elevated levels of user satisfaction. This observation holds particular significance in customer service environments, wherein users not only seek resolutions but also anticipate emotional support and comprehension.

In contrast, the non-empathetic chatbot, while generally effective in resolving issues, did not achieve the same level of user satisfaction. The lack of empathetic elements rendered these interactions more transactional and less engaging, resulting in lower satisfaction ratings. This disparity emphasizes the added value of empathy in making digital interactions feel more personal and supportive, which is essential for building lasting relationships with users.

Participants also expressed a strong preference for empathetic interactions in future customer service experiences, suggesting that empathy is not merely an optional feature but a crucial component of user satisfaction. While efficiency remains important, the desire for empathetic communication indicates that users appreciate a balance between quick problem-solving and compassionate engagement.

Overall, these empirical results underscore the imperative of integrating technical efficiency with empathetic communication in order to formulate effective digital customer service solutions. The incorporation of empathetic attributes into chatbot design not only fulfills user expectations but also markedly augments overall satisfaction and customer loyalty. Consequently, empathy ought to be regarded as an essential component in the prospective evolution of customer service automation.

Future investigations should examine the implementation of empathy within diverse cultural frameworks and across a variety of industries to ascertain its wider applicability. Additionally, exploring the enduring impacts of empathetic chatbot interactions on customer loyalty and brand perception would yield critical insights for organizations aiming to refine their customer service methodologies. Specifically, longitudinal studies could examine how sustained empathetic interactions influence repeat customer engagement, trust, and loyalty, potentially offering insights into the long-term value of empathy-driven AI across varied service environments.

6 Conclusion

This research investigates the pivotal role of empathetic communication in augmenting user satisfaction with customer service chatbots within the banking industry. The results highlight the significant affirmative influence of empathetic responses on user experience, with the empathetic chatbot consistently achieving superior ratings in terms of interaction ease, issue comprehension, and overall satisfaction relative to its non-empathetic equivalent. The demographic assessment accentuates the necessity to cater to a heterogeneous user population, taking into account variables such as age, cultural context, and technological proficiency. The research concludes that, although technical efficacy in problem resolution is vital, the incorporation of empathetic components markedly enhances the quality of user interactions, subsequently elevating satisfaction and engagement levels. This study enriches the expanding corpus of literature concerning emotional intelligence in artificial intelligence, offering pragmatic insights for financial entities aiming to refine customer service. By detailing the positive aspects of empathetic chatbots, the research accentuates the relevance of emotional intelligence in the realm of digital customer service and sets the stage for upcoming progress in AI-enhanced customer interactions, bearing substantial consequences for the formulation of more human-centered AI frameworks both in the banking industry and other fields.

The statistical evaluation yielded compelling evidence that empathy in chatbot engagements substantially improves the user experience across various dimensions. The empathetic chatbot surpassed the non-empathetic chatbot in terms of interaction ease, issue comprehension, overall satisfaction, and preference for subsequent interactions. These results highlight the essential function of empathy in enhancing the efficacy and user satisfaction of automated customer service frameworks.

References

1. Inavolu, S.M.: Exploring AI-driven customer service: evolution, architectures, opportunities, challenges, and future directions. Int. J. Multidiscip. Res. **6** (2024). https://doi.org/10.36948/ijfmr.2024.v06i03.22283
2. Pan, Y., Tang, Y., Niu, Y.: An empathetic user-centric chatbot for emotional support. November 15, 2023, arXiv: arXiv:2311.09271. https://doi.org/10.48550/arXiv.2311.09271
3. LaFrance, D.: Empathy matters: building relationships one story at a time. Theses Dissertation, November 2022. https://doi.org/10.30707/ETD2023.20230711063201804505.999970
4. Gao, Q., Xing, X.: Study on the impact of chatbot characteristics of online shopping mall on customer satisfaction and reuse intention in China: hedonic motivation and utilitarian motivation as moderating variables. February 25, 2023, Rochester, NY: 4391173. [Online]. Available: https://papers.ssrn.com/abstract=4391173. Accessed: 1 Aug 2024
5. Haupt, M., Rozumowski, A., Freidank, J., Haas, A.: Seeking empathy or suggesting a solution? Effects of chatbot messages on service failure recovery. Electron. Mark. **33** (2023). https://doi.org/10.1007/s12525-023-00673-0
6. Nicolescu, L., Tudorache, M.T.: Human-computer interaction in customer service: the experience with AI Chatbots—a systematic literature review. Electronics. **11**(10), 10 (2022). https://doi.org/10.3390/electronics11101579

7. Cheng, X., Zhang, X., Cohen, J., Mou, J.: Human vs. AI: understanding the impact of anthropomorphism on consumer response to chatbots from the perspective of trust and relationship norms. Inf. Process. Manag. **59**(3), 102940 (2022). https://doi.org/10.1016/j.ipm.2022.102940

8. Agnihotri, A., Bhattacharya, S.: Chatbots' effectiveness in service recovery. Int. J. Inf. Manag. **76**, 102679 (2024). https://doi.org/10.1016/j.ijinfomgt.2023.102679

9. Alagarsamy, S., Mehrolia, S.: Exploring chatbot trust: antecedents and behavioural outcomes. Heliyon. **9**(5) (2023). https://doi.org/10.1016/j.heliyon.2023.e16074

10. Sanny, L., Susastra, A., Roberts, C., Yusramdaleni, R.: The analysis of customer satisfaction factors which influence chatbot acceptance in Indonesia. Manag. Sci. Lett. **10**(6), 1225–1232 (2020)

11. Nadarzynski, T., et al.: Achieving health equity through conversational AI: a roadmap for design and implementation of inclusive chatbots in healthcare. PLOS Digit. Health. **3**(5), e0000492 (2024). https://doi.org/10.1371/journal.pdig.0000492

12. González-Espejo, M.J., Pavón, J.: An Introductory Guide to Artificial Intelligence for Legal Professionals, pp. 1–240. Kluwer Law International B.V., Alphen aan den Rijn (2020)

13. Sidlauskiene, J., Joye, Y., Auruskeviciene, V.: AI-based chatbots in conversational commerce and their effects on product and price perceptions. Electron. Mark. **33**(1), 24 (2023). https://doi.org/10.1007/s12525-023-00633-8

14. Klein, K., Martinez, L.F.: The impact of anthropomorphism on customer satisfaction in chatbot commerce: an experimental study in the food sector. Electron. Commer. Res. **23**(4), 2789–2825 (2023). https://doi.org/10.1007/s10660-022-09562-8

15. van der Goot, M.J., Hafkamp, L., Dankfort, Z.: Customer service chatbots: a qualitative interview study into the communication journey of customers. In: Følstad, A., et al. (eds.) Chatbot Research and Design, pp. 190–204. Springer, Cham (2021). https://doi.org/10.1007/978-3-030-68288-0_13

16. Nadarzynski, T., Miles, O., Cowie, A., Ridge, D.: Acceptability of artificial intelligence (AI)-led chatbot services in healthcare: a mixed-methods study. Digit. Health. **5**, 205520761987180 (2019). https://doi.org/10.1177/2055207619871808

17. Garcia Valencia, O.A., et al.: Ethical implications of chatbot utilization in nephrology. J. Pers. Med. **13**(9), 9 (2023). https://doi.org/10.3390/jpm13091363

18. Zhu, L.Y., Zhang, Z., Wang, J., Wang, H., Wu, H., Yang, Z.: Multi-party empathetic dialogue generation: a new task for dialog systems. In: Muresan, S., Nakov, P., Villavicencio, A. (eds.) Proceedings of the 60th Annual Meeting of the Association for Computational Linguistics (Volume 1: Long Papers), Dublin, Ireland, May, pp. 298–307. Association for Computational Linguistics (2022). https://doi.org/10.18653/v1/2022.acl-long.24

19. Haque, M.D.R., Rubya, S.: An overview of chatbot-based mobile mental health apps: insights from app description and user reviews. JMIR Mhealth Uhealth. **11**(1), e44838 (2023). https://doi.org/10.2196/44838

20. Sheehan, B.: How interjections increase customer satisfaction, purchase intent and loyalty," PhD, Queensland University of Technology (2022). [Online]. Available: https://eprints.qut.edu.au/232832/. Accessed: 1 Aug 2024

21. Chen, Z., Lu, Y., Nieminen, M.P., Lucero, A.: Creating a chatbot for and with migrants: chatbot personality drives co-design activities. In: Proceedings of the 2020 ACM Designing Interactive Systems Conference, in DIS '20, New York, NY, USA, Julyu, pp. 219–230. Association for Computing Machinery (2020). https://doi.org/10.1145/3357236.3395495

22. Van Pinxteren, M.M.E., Pluymaekers, M., Lemmink, J.G.A.M.: Human-like communication in conversational agents: a literature review and research agenda. J. Serv. Manag. **31**(2), 203–225 (2020). https://doi.org/10.1108/JOSM-06-2019-0175

23. Murtarelli, G. Gregory, A., Romenti, S.: A conversation-based perspective for shaping ethical human–machine interactions: the particular challenge of chatbots. J. Bus. Res. **129**, 927–935 (2021). https://doi.org/10.1016/j.jbusres.2020.09.018

Using Sentiment Analysis Extracted Features to Predict Stock Price

Mariame Tarsi[1(✉)], Ibtissame Ezzahoui[1], Samira Douzi[2], and Abdelaziz Marzak[1]

[1] Laboratory of Information Technology and Modeling, Faculty of Sciences Ben M'sick,
Hassan II University, Casablanca, Morocco
`mariame.tarsi-etu@etu.univh2c.ma`
[2] Faculty of Medicine and Pharmacy, Mohammed V University, Rabat, Morocco
`s.douzi@um5r.ac.ma`

Abstract. The analysis of data and information is critical, and for stock market traders or investors this can be very crucial. Especially with the progress the world has seen with technology in recent years, as these improvement and changes may come to affect how people perceive things and how they take decision. In this paper we are going to use two methods to classify tweets of Tesla stock that ranges from 30-09-2021 to 30-09-2022, preprocess the features along with financial data from Yahoo Finance to predict close price of the following day using LSTM. Therefore comparing the price prediction models resulted from each method of sentiment analysis, and observing the role of sentiment extraction models in determining the accuracy of price prediction models.

Keywords: stock market · stock price · Deep Learning · sentiment analysis · textBlob · finetuned Bert · LSTM

1 Introduction

Recent technological advancements, especially in Artificial Intelligence (AI) and its subfields—Machine Learning (ML), Artificial Neural Networks (ANN), Deep Learning (DL), and Natural Language Processing (NLP)—have significantly transformed various facets of human existence, including social, educational, and financial domains. Media and social media platforms have been instrumental in these shifts, as individuals increasingly depend on digital tools for guidance, trend awareness, and opinion expression. The accessibility of the internet has significantly impacted individual habits.

The stock market is a domain where information is essential for decision-makers, and the analysis of data to manage risks, negotiate complexities, and minimize losses is crucial. This domain is very arduous owing to its intrinsic complexity. The emergence of new technology has prompted various studies to tackle these difficulties, however progress has been incremental. Sentiment analysis has been thoroughly examined across diverse situations. One study [1] utilized sentiment analysis to assess restaurant user happiness, whereas another [2] integrated sentiment analysis from the COVID-19 period with stock market analysis. Furthermore, the study in [3] investigated the relationship between stock prices and public sentiment.

O. Zahour et al. (Eds.): ICTIM 2024, CCIS 2655, pp. 187–196, 2026.
https://doi.org/10.1007/978-3-032-15147-6_18

This case study seeks to forecast the subsequent day's stock price with an LSTM model, integrating sentiment analysis characteristics obtained from two established methodologies: Text Blob and a fine-tuned BERT model [4]. A comparison analysis is performed to evaluate the influence of sentiment analysis methodologies on the precision of stock price prediction models. The paper is structured as follows: Sect. 2 covers the fundamental concepts used in this research, Sect. 3 provides a literature review, Sect. 4 outlines the data and preprocessing pipeline and methodology, Sect. 5 presents the results, and Sect. 6 concludes the study

2 Fundamental Concepts

Deep learning (DL), a branch of artificial intelligence, is modeled after the architecture and operation of the neural networks in the human brain. The similarity to biological brain systems is the reason certain models are referred to as Artificial brain Networks (ANNs). Numerous deep learning models are available, such as Recurrent Neural Networks (RNNs), Convolutional Neural Networks (CNNs), Generative Adversarial Networks (GANs), and Large Language Models (LLMs). Each of these designs is tailored for distinct applications, including time series analysis and computer vision. (LLMs) and they each can be used in different use cases like time series and computer vision.

2.1 LSTM

Long Short-Term Memory (LSTM) is a deep learning architecture designed to address a primary issue of Recurrent Neural Networks (RNNs), namely the disappearing or expanding gradient problem [5, 6]. LSTM employs three gates—forget, update, and output—that govern the information flow during training, ensuring that only pertinent information is transmitted to the subsequent cell [7, 8]. LSTM is a highly effective method for time series analysis and has been extensively utilized in stock market prediction research. Furthermore, it has been utilized in numerous research for text emotion classification.

2.2 Sentiment Analysis

Sentiment analysis, a branch of Natural Language Processing (NLP), concentrates on discerning the prevailing emotion or sentiment conveyed in textual inputs such as comments, postings, publications, or titles. Sentiment analysis can be conducted by diverse methodologies, encompassing rule-based techniques and deep learning models. Frequently utilized instruments for sentiment analysis comprise:

TextBlob: A Python library for natural language processing applications, including text manipulation and fundamental operations. It has a sentiment analysis feature that produces a polarity score between -1 and 1. A score approaching -1 signifies negative sentiment, whereas a score around 1 denotes positive sentiment [9].

Bert: A robust pre-trained language model recognized for its profound contextual comprehension, as it examines text bidirectionally—from both the left and the right. BERT is also amenable to fine-tuning, a crucial attribute for language models due to the variability of context across different academic disciplines [10].

Numerous research has utilized BERT for sentiment analysis. One study [11] utilized BERT on a dataset of tweets, whereas another [12] investigated investor sentiment through BERT to assess its influence on stock returns. Comparative research [13] assessed Text Blob and BERT using product reviews from Egypt's Amazon platform.

3 Previous Works

Numerous studies has been done previously considering the problem is not new, where authors used different types of data; financial, social, and economical in order to build smart models able to predict price or return movement. The data used are from different periods of time, which can be considered an important aspect, like covid-19 period for example.

Table 1. comparing previous works

Ref	Title	Data time period	Regression models	Features involved
[14]	Stock Price Predictions with LSTM Neural Networks and Twitter Sentiment	November 30, 2020 to January 31, 2021	LSTM	Historical data Twitter data (API)
[15]	Predicting Stock Market Indicators Through Sentiment Analysis On Twitter	February 13, 2017 to March 26, 2017	LSTM, Linear Regression	Close price Twitter data (API)
[16]	Are Twitter sentiments during COVID-19 pandemic a critical determinant to predict stock market movements? A machine learning approach	January to May 2020	LSTM, ARIMA, Linear Regression, ARIMA	Macroeconmic indicators Twitter data Healthcare data Stock data
[17]	Predicting stock price using LSTM and Social Media dataset	January 01, 2015 to January 01, 2020	LSTM	Historical data Twitter data
[18]	A Robust Predictive Model for Stock Price Prediction Using Deep Learning and Natural Language Processing	January 2, 2015 to June 28,2019	Multivariate regression, DT, Bagging, Boosting. RF, ANN, SVM. LSTM	Historical data Twitter data (API)

In Table 1 we compared the period of the data, the models used and the data involved in the studies. As we can observe, LSTM model is frequently used, as it answers some requirement of timeseries problems.

However, the choice of sentiment detection in such studies is frequently dismissed as the most accurate sentiment models are chosen to so the tasks. But in context of sentiment analysis, the field of study and the context are very important, therefore, although some algorithms may seems powerful, but a comparative study still a good practice to determine the final choice, as some models may need to be fine-tuned in order to be used in such context like stock market.

In our study we want to compare the results of the predictions of LSTM models based on the feature extracted from each sentiment detection method, in order to see if the methodology of sentiment analysis and the accuracy of sentiment models also plays an important role in determining the prediction results and the accuracy of the prediction models concerning stock price.

4   Materials and Methods

4.1   Data Preprocessing

This section will delineate the dataset utilized and the preparation procedures implemented (Fig. 1). The dataset comprises data on the 'top 25 most viewed stock tickers on Yahoo Finance from September 30, 2021, to September 30, 2022,' as per its description. We opted to concentrate on a single stock, 'TSLA.' Consequently, although the columns remained unchanged, the number of rows was modified by restricting the data to encompass only items pertaining to the TSLA ticker (Table 3).

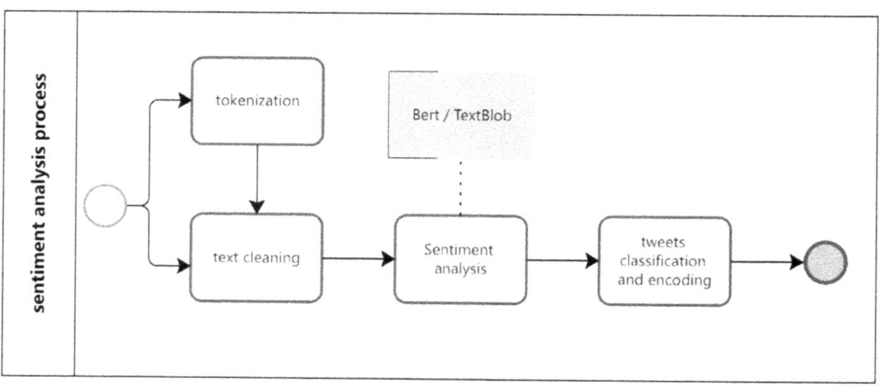

Fig. 1. Sentiment analysis process

- **Data Description**

The data utilized in the present study (Table 2) was obtained from Kaggle [5]. The dataset comprises two files: the first provides tweet-related information, and the second encompasses historical stock data.

Table 2. Dataset contents

Files	Features
stock_tweets.csv	Date, Stock Name, Company name, Tweet
stock_yfinance_data.csv	Date, Stock Name, Open. High, Low, Close, Volume, Adj Close

Table 3. Tesla Dataset size

Data sets	Size
Social dataset	37422
Historical dataset	252

- **Data Preprocessing Steps**

The models are trained on preprocessed data. Consequently, the data must be pristine, precise, and meticulously organized. Higher data quality enhances model training efficacy, perhaps resulting in superior performance.

Textual data cleansing: This entails eliminating special characters that may influence the analysis, including symbols such as '@', '#', and URLs. It may also entail the elimination of numerals.
Tokenization: This procedure disaggregates text into discrete words or tokens, facilitating subsequent preprocessing actions such as stop word elimination.
Eliminating stop words: Common terms such as 'a', 'an', 'I', 'we', 'there', and 'they', which convey minimal substantive information, are eliminated. Despite their frequency, some words may disrupt subsequent processing.
Analysis of sentiment: Two methodologies are employed to classify tweets: Text Blob and a fine-tuned BERT model, which categorize sentiment as positive, negative, or neutral (for Text Blob).
Addressing missing data: Certain days may be devoid of price data owing to weekends or vacations.

4.2 Development of LSTM Models for Stock Price Forecasting

In this research, we constructed two LSTM models. The initial model employs attributes obtained from the Text Blob polarity score to categorize tweets accordingly. The second model integrates attributes generated by a fine-tuned BERT model, with each tweet annotated with its emotion and score. The resultant features are encoded as independent variables, with each sentiment allocated a distinct feature (Fig. 2). The data is subsequently aggregated daily and integrated with financial information. To maintain consistency, the data is standardized with the Min-Max approach, which normalizes all columns to a uniform range. This enables the model to concentrate on the most pertinent inputs, mitigating bias induced by greater original values. Given that LSTM models are tailored for time series data, we employed data sequences during training, establishing the sequence step at 20, commonly known as the "window time." The processed data was subsequently divided into training, validation, and testing sets, with 20% allocated for testing purposes. The model's performance was assessed using metrics including RMSE and R^2 score.

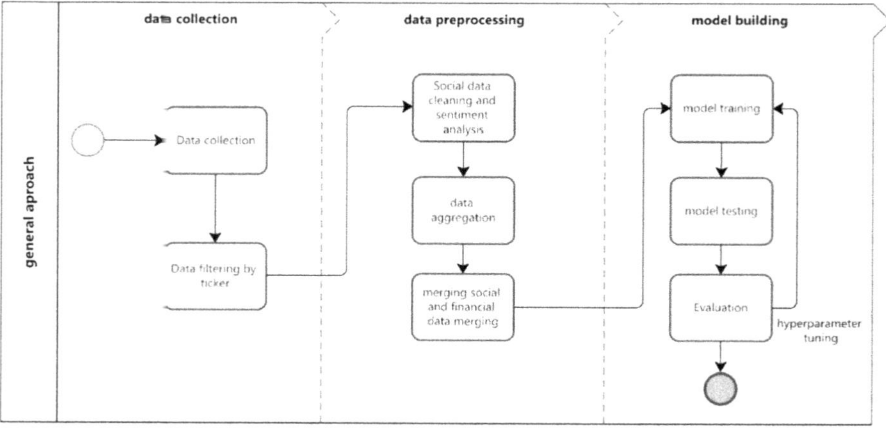

Fig. 2. Geneal approach

5 Results

Table 4 delineates the assessment criteria for two LSTM models: one trained on sentiment features recovered using the fine-tuned BERT model and the other on features obtained from Text Blob. Both models exhibited commendable performance, attaining R^2 scores of 94% and 97% respectively. The Root Mean Square Error (RMSE) for the Text Blob model was 7.42, whereas the BERT model had an RMSE of 10.80. Despite these results demonstrating commendable model performance, additional fine-tuning is required to minimize error for enhanced accuracy.

These results, derived from test data, indicate that both models exhibit strong generalization, which is encouraging for future applications. Moreover, the training of these models exclusively on open and close prices from financial data underscores the need of integrating social media sentiment elements. The incorporation of these qualities illustrates their capacity to yield profound insights into market patterns and affect decision-making

Figures 3 and 4 depict the anticipated price values in comparison to the actual pricing for both models. Figure 3 illustrates the model developed using features derived from BERT, whereas Fig. 4 presents the findings from the model trained on features taken from Text Blob. In the comparison of the two models, the Text Blob-based model surpasses the BERT-based model in R^2 score, attaining 97% versus 94%. Nevertheless, a further examination of the plots uncovers significant disparities in the manner each model addresses particular price movements.

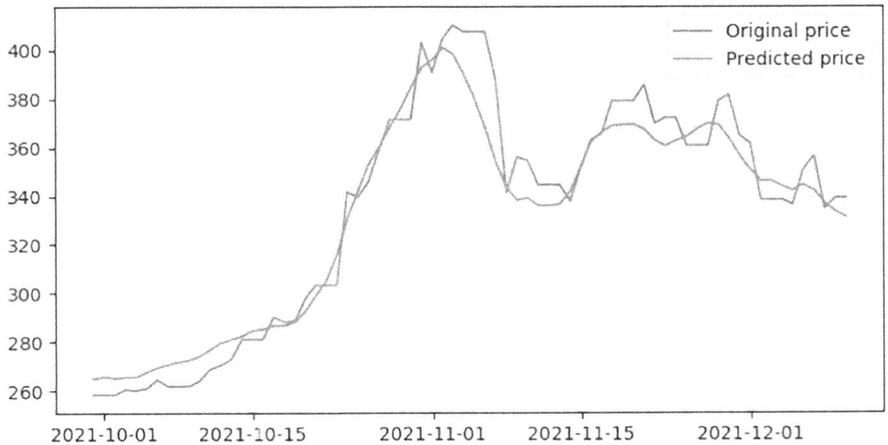

Fig. 3. Predicted price vs. original price of the fine-tuned Bert-extracted-features based LSTM model

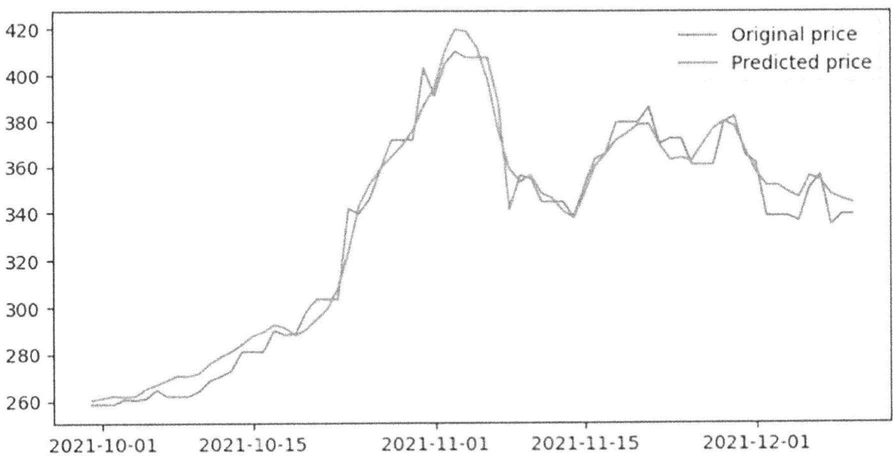

Fig. 4. Predicted price vs. original price of the textBlob-extracted-features based LSTM model

In Fig. 4, the Text Bloɔ-based model closely aligns with the original price data during most intervals, potentially indicating greater accuracy at first observation. Nonetheless, it far exceeds the peak observed around 2021-11-01, forecasting a value greater than the actual peak just preceding a decline. Furthermore, the model fails to capture the diminishing peak occurring around December 1, 2021. These inaccuracies can be detrimental, particularly during pivotal market transitions, despite the model's robust overall performance in other intervals.

Conversely, the BERT-based model, illustrated in Fig. 3, exhibits a greater divergence from the real data for certain intervals, notably around 2021-11-01. Nonetheless, it more accurately reflects the overarching pattern by forecasting a drop sooner than recorded, potentially mitigating the hazards linked to abrupt peaks. Although this model fails to capture the decreasing high around December 1, 2021, it more accurately reflects overall price movement trends compared to the Text Blob model, potentially providing a more dependable forecast under specific market situations.

This underscores that the selection of sentiment analysis techniques can profoundly influence the efficacy of stock price prediction models. Although both models demonstrate encouraging outcomes, their capacity to detect and react to subtle fluctuations during market peaks is a crucial aspect to evaluate. Both models necessitate additional fine-tuning, not only in the preprocessing of sentiment data but also in the optimization of the LSTM models' hyperparameters. These tweaks enable the models to attain greater predictive accuracy and effectively manage volatile market fluctuations

Table 4. Models' evaluation results

Evaluation Metrics	Model with textBlob features	Model with fine-tuned Bert features
R2 score	0.97	0.94
MSE	55.13	116.67
RMSE	7.42	10.80
MAPE	0.018	0.024

6 Conclusion

This study utilized NLP processing on TSLA-related tweets, extracting novel features through two sentiment analysis techniques: fine-tuned BERT and Text Blob. Subsequently, we consolidated the resultant sentiment components and integrated them with historical data. Following the resolution of missing values, normalization, and the generation of data sequences, we constructed a deep learning model with LSTM layers to forecast the subsequent day's stock price. The assessment outcomes from both models were encouraging.

The intricacies of the stock market are widely recognized, and in the current landscape, social media platforms offer significant data that can mitigate risks and furnish decision-makers with a more comprehensive view of market movements. This study illustrates that the selection of sentiment analysis techniques significantly impacts model efficacy. Although the Text Blob-based model exhibited superior overall accuracy, the BERT-based model shown a robust capacity to identify trends during significant peaks when incorporated into the LSTM model. Despite both models demonstrating commendable performance during the review phase with test data, there exists potential for more enhancement.

Disclosure of Interests. The authors have no competing interests to declare that are relevant to the content of this article.

References

1. Adi Laksono, R., Sungkono, K., Sarno, R., Wahyuni, C.: Sentiment analysis of restaurant customer reviews on TripAdvisor using Naïve Bayes, July, pp. 49–54 (2019). https://doi.org/10.1109/ICTS.2019.8850982
2. Duan, Y., Liu, L., Wang, Z.: COVID-19 sentiment and the Chinese stock market: evidence from the official news media and Sina Weibo. Res. Int. Bus. Finance. **58**, 101432 (2021). https://doi.org/10.1016/j.ribaf.2021.101432
3. Pagolu, V.S., Reddy, K.N., Panda, G., Majhi, B.: Sentiment analysis of Twitter data for predicting stock market movements. In: 2016 International Conference on Signal Processing, Communication, Power and Embedded System (SCOPES), October, pp. 1345–1350 (2016). https://doi.org/10.1109/SCOPES.2016.7955659
4. zhayunduo/roberta-base-stocktwits-finetuned · Hugging Face. [Online]. Available: https://huggingface.co/zhayunduo/roberta-base-stocktwits-finetuned. Accessed: 15 Sept 2024
5. Hochreiter, S., Schmidhuber, J.: Long short-term memory. Neural Comput. **9**(8), 8 (1997). https://doi.org/10.1162/neco.1997.9.8.1735
6. Hochreiter, S.: The vanishing gradient problem during learning recurrent neural nets and problem solutions. Int. J. Uncertain. Fuzziness Knowl. Based Syst. **06**(02), 02 (1998). https://doi.org/10.1142/S0218488598000094
7. Aasi, B., Imtiaz, S.A., Qadeer, H.A., Singarajah, M., Kashef, R.: Stock price prediction using a multivariate multistep LSTM: a sentiment and public engagement analysis model. In: 2021 IEEE International IOT, Electronics and Mechatronics Conference (IEMTRONICS), April, pp. 1–8 (2021). https://doi.org/10.1109/IEMTRONICS52119.2021.9422526
8. Tarsi, M., Douzi, S., Marzak, A.: Forecasting financial market dynamics: an in-depth analysis of social media data for predicting price movements in the next day. Soc. Netw. Anal. Min. **14**(1), 169 (2024). https://doi.org/10.1007/s13278-024-01338-2
9. Tutorial: Quickstart—TextBlob 0.18.0.post0 documentation. [Online]. Available: https://textblob.readthedocs.io/en/dev/quickstart.html#sentiment-analysis. Accessed: 15 Sept 2024
10. Devlin, J., Chang, M.-W., Lee, K., Toutanova, K.: BERT: pre-training of deep bidirectional transformers for language understanding, May 24, 2019, arXiv: arXiv:1810.04805. https://doi.org/10.48550/arXiv.1810.04805
11. Bello, A., Ng, S.-C., Leung, M.-F.: A BERT framework to sentiment analysis of tweets. Sensors. **23**(1), 1 (2023). https://doi.org/10.3390/s23010506
12. Li, M., Li, W., Wang, F., Jia, X., Rui, G.: Applying BERT to analyze investor sentiment in stock market. Neural Comput. Applic. **33**(10), 4663–4676 (2021). https://doi.org/10.1007/s00521-020-05411-7
13. Mahgoub, A., et al.: Sentiment analysis: Amazon electronics reviews using BERT and Textblob. In: 2022 20th International Conference on Language Engineering (ESOLEC), October, vol. 2022, pp. 6–10. https://doi.org/10.1109/ESOLEC54569.2022.10009176
14. Thormann, M.-L., Farchmin, J., Weisser, C., Kruse, R.-M., Säfken, B., Silbersdorff, A.: Stock price predictions with LSTM neural networks and twitter sentiment. Stat. Optim. Inf. Comput. **9**(2), 2 (2021). https://doi.org/10.19139/soic-2310-5070-1202
15. Fuller, A.: Predicting Stock Market Indicators Through Sentiment Analysis on Twitter, Report. University of Iowa (2022). [Online]. Available: https://hal.science/hal-03516008. Accessed: 27 Jan 2023
16. Jena, P.R., Majhi, R.: Are Twitter sentiments during COVID-19 pandemic a critical determinant to predict stock market movements? A machine learning approach. Sci. Afr. **19**, e01480 (2023). https://doi.org/10.1016/j.sciaf.2022.e01480

17. Tarsi, M., Douzi, S., Marzak, A.: Predicting stock price using LSTM and social media dataset. In: 2023 3rd International Conference on Innovative Research in Applied Science, Engineering and Technology (IRASET), May, pp. 1–4 (2023). https://doi.org/10.1109/IRASET57153.2023.10152930
18. Mehtab, S., Sen, J.: A robust predictive model for stock price prediction using deep learning and natural language processing, July 26 (2021). https://doi.org/10.36227/techrxiv.15023361.v1

Utilizing Transformer Models
for Smartphone-Based Skin Cancer Detection

Adil El Mertahi[1]([⊠]), Samira Douzi[2], and Khadija Douzi[1]

[1] Department of Computer Sciences, FSTM, University Hassan II, Casablanca, Morocco
adil.elmertahi-etu@etu.univh2c.ma, khadija.douzi@fstm.ac.ma
[2] Department of Drug Science FMPR, University Mohammed V, Rabat, Morocco
s.douzi@um5r.ac.ma

Abstract. This paper investigates the use of Vision Transformer models for the diagnosis of cancer-related skin lesions. The study focuses on six types of lesions: actinic keratosis (ACK), basal cell carcinoma (BCC), melanoma (MEL), nevus (NEV), squamous cell carcinoma (SCC), and seborrheic keratosis (SEK). The dataset employed included 2,298 smartphone photos of various resolutions, which provided a robust foundation for training and validation the model.

To prepare the data, pre-processing techniques including rotation, zooming, and flipping were applied, increasing the minority classes and improving the diversity and robustness of the training set.

The model was evaluated in terms of performance metrics, including an accuracy of 76%, a precision of 0.71, a recall of 0.73, and an F1 score of 0.72, illustrating the model's robust ability to distinguish between different types of skin lesions.

These findings show that incorporating deep learning into dermatological screening could improve the detection of worrisome lesions and ease early diagnosis, thereby contributing to the fight against skin cancer.

Keywords: Skin cancer · melanoma detection · vision transformers · artificial intelligence

1 Introduction

Skin cancer encompasses a variety of disorders characterized by the uncontrolled proliferation of abnormal skin cells, leading to tumor formation. The main cause of these malignant tumors is skin damage due to unprotected exposure to ultraviolet (UV) rays [1]. Given its high frequency and potentially serious consequences, skin cancer represents a major public health issue worldwide [2]. According to the World Health Organization, around 132,000 new cases of melanoma are diagnosed worldwide every year [3], while non-melanoma skin cancers affect millions of people every year [4]. Convolutional neural networks are widely used in medical image recognition and show great accuracy, particularly in the classification of skin cancers [5]. For example, a recent study showed that CNNs can outperform human dermatologists in melanoma identification [6]. However, although convolutional neural networks (CNNs) can extract features from multiple

© The Author(s), under exclusive license to Springer Nature Switzerland AG 2026
O. Zahour et al. (Eds.): ICTIM 2024, CCIS 2655, pp. 197–206, 2026.
https://doi.org/10.1007/978-3-032-15147-6_19

small objects present in the image, they do not always guarantee precise localization of essential components. Dosovitskiy et al. [7, 8] have designed the Vision Transformer architecture for image classification, inspired by models of self-attentive deep neural networks, such as transformers used in natural language processing (NLP). In addition, the integration of neural networks with multi-spectral data fusion techniques can improve diagnostic accuracy, notably by combining images derived from different wavelengths to better visualize subcutaneous structures [9]. The use of deep learning-based anomaly detection algorithms also makes it possible to identify lesions that might go unnoticed during a conventional visual examination [10]. This article proposes an effective method using the Vision Transformer to classify smartphone photographs of skin cancers. This strategy includes advanced image processing and augmentation techniques, specifically designed to improve minority class classification. The approach presented demonstrates remarkable accuracy in categorizing skin lesions within different classes.

The structure of this paper is as follows: Sect. 2 provides a review of the literature, Sect. 3 outlines the proposed approaches to skin cancer detection, Sect. 4 presents the results and their analysis, and Sect. 5 concludes with a summary of the findings and avenues for future research

2   Review of Literature

Advances in skin lesion detection and classification rely heavily on convolutional neural network (CNN) models, which have demonstrated remarkable effectiveness in identifying and categorizing skin lesions. For example, Yilmaz et al. [11] recently evaluated various deep learning architectures using the ISIC 2017 dataset to identify the most effective skin cancer classification models. Traditionally, early skin cancer classification has relied on conventional machine learning techniques. Alquran et al. [12] proposed an approach using support vector machines (SVM) and principal component analysis (PCA), while Almansour et al. [13] introduced a new technology to extract color and texture features to classify lesions into melanoma and non-melanoma in dermoscopic images. In 2020, Nadipineni [14] improved clinical image pre-processing with more precise segmentation via U-Net, coupled with a significant increase in data. This approach led to superior performance by refining CNN models. In 2021, Datta et al. [15] integrated soft attention layers into CNNs, achieving remarkable accuracy that surpassed Nadipineni's [16] results for the HAM10000 dataset [17]. Their pre-processing technique included eliminating duplicates and balancing images by oversampling and undersampling. At the same time, the Vision Transformer [17] attracted growing interest for its robust performance in various fields. Research in 2022 showed that the ViT model could improve skin cancer classification and segmentation. In the ViT model's feature integration block, researchers proposed a method combined with contrast learning, boosting classification performance [18]. In addition, improved position coding methods in the ViT model yielded results comparable to the best previous models for skin cancer classification [19]. ViT has also been studied for skin lesion segmentation, showing promising results [20]. The use of data augmentation techniques such as geometric augmentation has enabled better management of data imbalance and high class similarity in skin cancer image sets [21]. These advances open up new prospects for research and the improvement of diagnostic tools for skin cancer.

3   Materials and Methods

This section outlines each of the steps of our approach, which are visually depicted in Fig. 1.

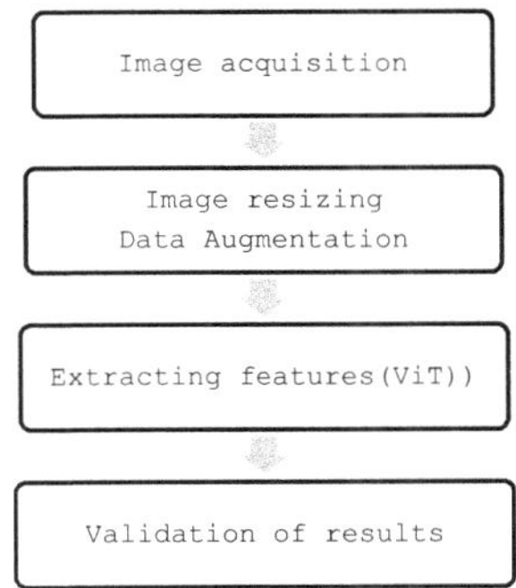

Fig. 1. The different stages of skin cancer detection

3.1   Dataset

The data used in this study came from skin cancer images captured between 2018 and 2019 by Pacheco and colleagues using smartphones. These data were pooled to form the dataset named PAD-UFES-20, comprising a total of 2,298 images. These images are grouped into six different categories: Actinic Keratosis (ACK), Seborrheic Keratosis (SEK), Melanoma (MEL), Basal Cell Carcinoma (BCC), Nevus (NEV), Squamous Cell Carcinoma (SCC). They are provided in PNG format and feature various resolutions, as shown in Table 1 and illustrated in Fig. 2 below:

Table 1. Table of skin lesions and number of samples per type

Clinical diagnosis	Number of images
Actinic Keratosis (ACK)	730
Basal Cell Carcinoma (BCC)	845
Melanoma (MEL)	52
Nevus (NEV)	244
Squamous Cell Carcinoma (SCC)	192
Seborrheic Keratosis (SEK).	235
Total	**2298**

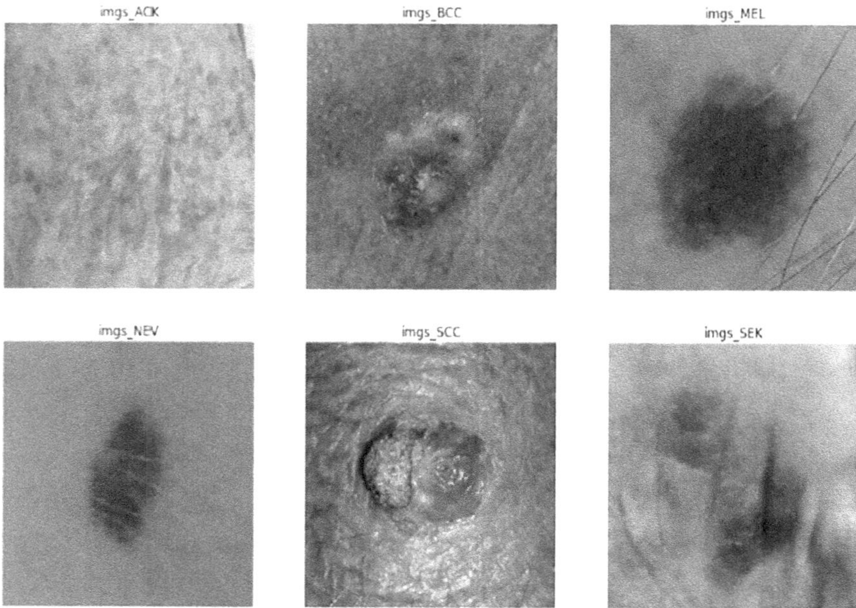

Fig. 2. Example images from our dataset

3.2 Data Preprocessing

Image Resizing. The dimensions of images in databases often vary significantly, with different sizes, widths and heights. To improve processing efficiency, it is strongly recommended to normalize these dimensions by resizing all images to a uniform format. The aim is to maximize the performance of machine learning models during analysis. Consequently, the standardized dimensions adopted are 224 pixels wide, 224 pixels high, with 3 color channels.

Augmentation. In the context of skin cancer classification, data augmentation plays a crucial role in improving neural network performance. This involves modifying existing data or generating new ones to enrich the training set. The aim is to overcome the challenges posed by the variability of dermatological images by applying techniques such as cropping rotation and color modifications. It also makes it possible to rebalance the dataset by selectively augmenting under-represented classes. By diversifying the learning examples in this way, the model is better able to recognize significant variations and generalize effectively under different conditions. These techniques are summarized in Table 2:

Proposed Model. In this study, we explored a vision-oriented transformer architecture in the context of skin cancer classification, as represented in Fig. 3.

The model consists of several blocks, each consisting of layers of multi-head attention, normalization, and density that are repeated in sequence. The process commences with a layer that cuts the patch, which is then followed by a patch encoder. Every block

Table 2. Table of image transformation parameters and actions

method	Parameter	Action
Flip horizontal	True	With a probability of 0.2, flip the image horizontally.
Rotation	20°	Rotates the image from an angle of −20° to an angle of 20° with a probability of 0.2.
Zoom	20%	random zoom on images: height = 0.2, width = 0.2

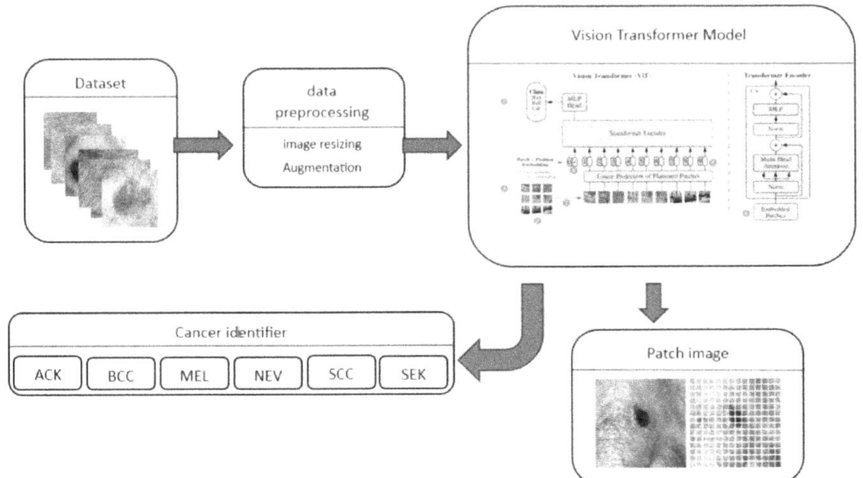

Fig. 3. Illustrates the executed end-to-end workflow

comprises a normalization layer, a multi-head attention mechanism, and a residual link. The blocks are arranged in a stacked pattern to create the network. A normalizing layer is placed after each dense layer, followed by a dropout procedure. The vision transformer model utilizes transform blocks to extract features from image patches and subsequently use an MLP classification head to make the final class prediction. The vision transformer model presents an innovative method for picture categorization, utilizing attentional transformations and long-range feature capture techniques. The complete model can be depicted as a combination of these consecutive processes (Table 3).

4   Results and Discussion

In this study, our Vision Transformer model was specifically trained to classify cancer-related skin diseases into six categories: ACC, BCC, MEL, NEV, SCC and SEK. To assess the effectiveness of the model, we used the accuracy and loss graphs, which reflect the accuracy and loss of the model during training, respectively. The model was trained over 100 epochs, as shown in Table 4. These graphs allow us to visualize the performance of the model during the different stages of training.

Table 3. Pipeline of our proposed Vision transformer model

Input: Dataset skin cancer continent 6 classes
Output: Predicted labels
Dataset split: 80% training and 20% testing
1- Hyperparameter settings
• Image size: (224,224,3)
• Training patch size: 16
• Learning rate: 2e-4
• Optimizer: AdamW
• Hidden size: 1024
2- Training:
• Data augmentation
• Data normalization
• divided image into patches: 196 patches
• linear projection of flattened patches
• Multi-scale incorporation per patch
• Multi-head attention
• Obtain first token output
• Calculation of contrastive loss and cross-entropy loss
3- Testing:
• Read the image pixel
• Data normalization
• Feed the training model
• Calculate quantitative metrics

Table 4. General Properties of models

Property	Value
Dataset Size	2298
Image Shape	(224,224,3)
Test data	453
Dropout	0.3
Validation data/Training data	324
Epoch Number	100

Looking at the two graphs, Figs. 4 and 5, which show an exponential trend, we can deduce that the model is progressing positively during its learning process. The gradual upward trajectory of this curve indicates a steady improvement in the model's performance during the learning process, which is generally a sign of a positive outcome.

Effective learning is also indicated by the alignment of the training and validation curves in the same direction. Significant divergence between these curves may indicate overfitting of the model to training data, compromising its ability to generalize to

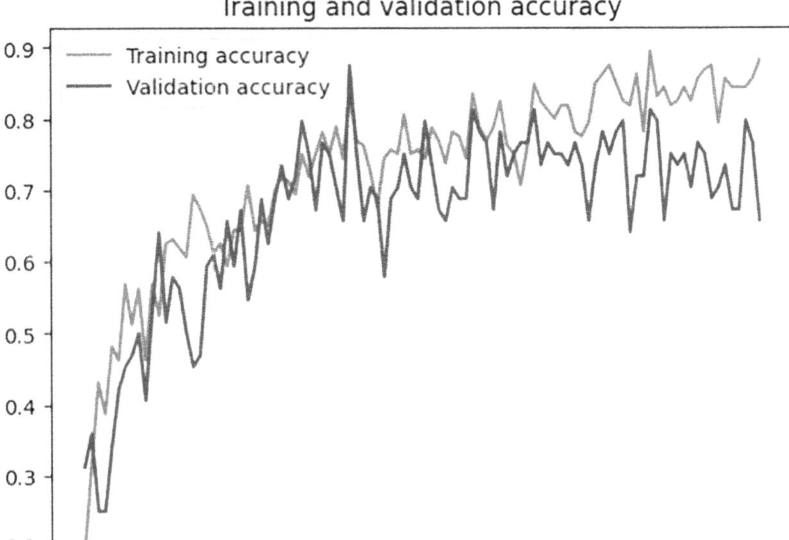

Fig. 4. Accuracy rates during training

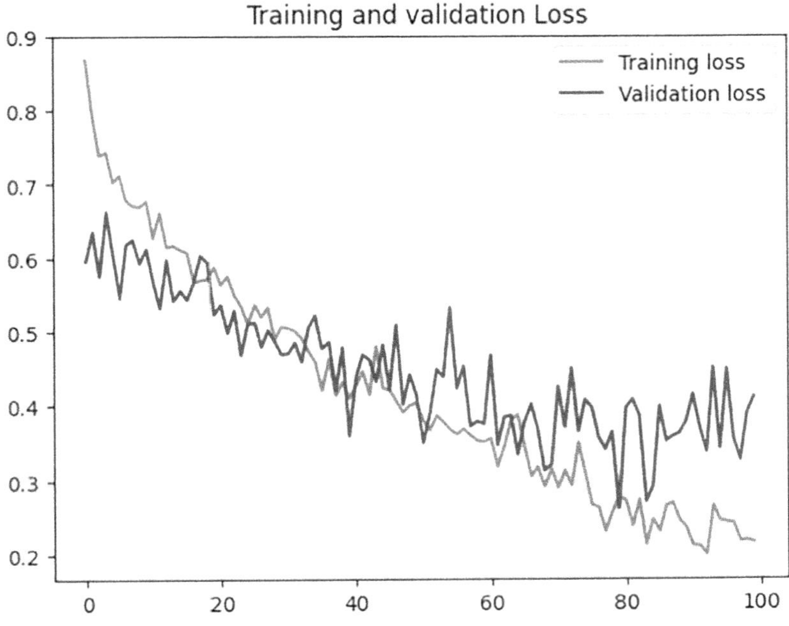

Fig. 5. Loss during training

unknown data. Here, the convergence of the curves indicates that the model can accurately apply its knowledge to new data. The overall accuracy of the model in categorizing the different types of skin diseases is represented by the classification rate of 76%.

Table 5. General Metrics

General Metrics	Value
Precision	0.71
Recall	0.73
F1-Score	0.72

The global metrics shown in Table 5 support the model's overall accuracy. The results show that the Vision Transformer model is effective in diagnosing skin malignancies, with a precision of 0.71, recall of 0.73, and F1 score of 0.72. These findings demonstrate the model's capacity to balance sensitivity and precision in addition to its ability to correctly classify the various types of skin lesions. The model's capacity to detect a high number of positive cases for each class, lowering the possibility of false negatives, is demonstrated by its recall of 0.73, which is higher than its precision. This skill is essential in the medical field to avoid missing potentially dangerous cancer diagnosis. Additionally, the accuracy of 0.71 highlights the model's capacity to reduce false positives, preventing mistakes that can result in inaccurate diagnoses or needless treatments. Lastly, the model's general resilience in striking a balance between precision and recall is attested by its F1 score of 0.72. When paired with the 76% classification rate, this indicates that the model not only does well during training but can also reliably generalize its predictions to further data. Nevertheless, even with these encouraging outcomes, it is still challenging to distinguish between certain groups, in part because different classes of lesions have different visual characteristics. This intricacy draws attention to the difficulties in categorizing skin malignancies, where minute details in a photograph can make all the difference. The accuracy and generalizability of the model may be increased by making changes like adding more processing layers or enhancing image resolution.

5 Conclusion

Finally, this study demonstrated the effectiveness of the Vision Transformer model in classifying cancer-related skin disorders into six distinct categories. The results show not just great performance, with balanced values for precision, recall, and F1 score, but also generalizability, which allows it to be applied to new data. The accuracy and loss curves, as well as the classification scores obtained, suggest a suitable model for diagnosing dermatological conditions. However, issues persist, notably in identifying specific categories, especially as the photographs were obtained with phones of varying quality, implying that this model still needs to be adjusted to make it more trustworthy and adaptable to clinical requirements.

Future research should investigate additional optimizations, such as including diverse and high-quality data and tailoring the model to the particular requirements of medical applications, in order to maximize the model's potential in a clinical scenario

References

1. Celebi, M.E., Codella, N., Halpern, A.: Dermoscopy image analysis: overview and future directions. IEEE J. Biomed. Health Inform. **23**(2), 474–478 (2019). https://doi.org/10.1109/JBHI.2019.2895803. Epub 2019 Jan 28
2. Tschandl, P., Rosendahl, C., Kittler, H.: The HAM10000 dataset, a large collection of multi-source dermatoscopic images of common pigmented skin lesions. Sci. Data. **5**, 180161 (2018)
3. Sung, H., et al.: Global cancer statistics 2020: GLOBOCAN estimates of incidence and mortality worldwide for 36 cancers in 185 countries. CA Cancer J. Clin. **71**(3), 209–249 (2021)
4. Siegel, R., Miller, K., Jemal, R.A.: Cancer Facts & Figures 2021 (2021)
5. Ali, M.S., Miah, M.S., Haque, J., Rahman, M.M., Islam, M.K.: An enhanced technique of skin cancer classification using deep convolutional neural network with transfer learning models. Mach. Learn. Appl. **5**, 100036 (2021). https://doi.org/10.1016/j.mlwa.2021.100036
6. Esteva, A., et al.: Dermatologist-level classification of skin cancer with deep neural networks. Nature. **542**(7639), 115–118 (2017)
7. Ali, A., Soleymani, M.-M.: Transformer Networks (2019)
8. Dosovitskiy, A., et al.: An Image Is Worth 16x16 Words: Transformers for Image Recognition at Scale (2020)
9. Voorter, P.H.M.: Towards automatic skin cancer detection by combining multispectral imaging and deep convolutional neural networks
10. Grignaffini, F., et al.: Anomaly detection for skin lesion images using convolutional neural network and injection of handcrafted features: a method that bypasses the preprocessing of dermoscopic images. Algorithms. **16**(10), 466 (2023)
11. Yilmaz, M., Kalebasi, Y., Samoylenko, M.E., Guvenilir, H., Uvet: Benchmarking of Lightweight Deep Learning Architectures for Skin Cancer Classification Using ISIC 2017 Dataset (2021)
12. Alquran, H., et al.: The melanoma skin cancer detection and classification using support vector machine. In: 2017 IEEE Jordan Conference on Applied Electrical Engineering and Computing Technologies, AEECT 2017, pp. 1–5. Institute of Electrical and Electronics Engineers Inc (2017). https://doi.org/10.1109/AEECT.2017.8257738
13. Almansour, E., Arfan Jaffar, M., Imam Mohammad, A.: Classification of Dermoscopic Skin Cancer Images Using Color and Hybrid Texture Features (n.d.)
14. Nadipineni, H. Method to classify skin lesions using dermoscopic images. arXiv preprint arXiv: 2008.09418. 2020 Aug 21 (2020)
15. Datta, S.K., Shaikh, M.A., Srihari, S.N.: Soft attention improves skin cancer classification performance. In: Interpretability of Machine Intelligence in Medical Image Computing, and Topological Data Analysis and Its Applications for Medical Data, pp. 13–23. Springer, Cham (2021)
16. Nadipineni, H.: Method to classify skin lesions using dermoscopic images. arXiv preprint arXiv: 2008.09418. 2020 Aug 21 (2020)
17. Tschandl, P., Rosendahl, C., Kittler, H.: The HAM10000 dataset, a large collection of multi-sourcedermatoscopic images of common pigmented skin lesions. Sci. Data. **5**(1), 1–9 (2018)
18. Xin, C., et al.: An improved transformer network for skin cancer classification. Comput. Biol. Med. **1**(149), 105939 (2022)

19. Nakai, K., Chen, Y.W., Han, X.H.: Enhanced deep bottleneck transformer model for skin lesion classification. Biomed. Signal Process. Control. **1**(78), 103997 (2022)
20. He, X., Tan, E.L., Bi, H., Zhang, X., Zhao, S., Lei, B.: Fully transformer network for skin lesion analysis. Med. Image Anal. **1**(77), 102357 (2022)
21. Kim, D., et al.: Data augmentation techniques for skin cancer classification: a review and experimental study. J. Mach. Learn. Res. (2023)

Evaluating the Quality of Scientific Articles: A Review of Citation and Content-Based Metrics

Mohammed Barchane[✉], El Habib Benlahmar, and Omar Zahour

Faculty of Sciences Ben M'Sick, Laboratory of Information Technology, Casablanca, Morocco
mohammed.barchane-etu@etu.univh2c.ma, {Elhabib.Benahmar, Omar.Zahour}@univh2c.ma

Abstract. Evaluating scientific publications is a crucial tool for understanding their impact and scientific significance. However, traditional metrics such as Impact Factor (IF), h-index and citation count face new challenges with the development of Artificial Intelligence (AI). In this article, we evaluate the usefulness of existing measures and discuss the need for a new AI metric that more accurately reflects the content and significance of the scientific literature. We review traditional metrics for assessing the quality of research and point out their shortcomings in the context of recent developments. We also provide an overview of existing approaches that use AI techniques to assess the quality and significance of scientific papers, along with examples of models and algorithms used. We provide a new AI-based measure that explains the desired criteria and development process for assessing scientific papers. We also provide case studies of this new measure's implementation and contrast its outcomes with those of other contemporary techniques and conventional measurements. Lastly, we go over possible difficulties and restrictions in using this new measure as well as moral and practical arguments in favor of its use. The article's conclusion includes a summary of the key ideas, a focus on the necessity of creating new AI-based metrics to enhance the assessment of scientific publications, as well as a perspective and suggestions for scholars, editors, and decision-makers working in this area.

Keywords: Evaluation · Scientific documents · Evaluation metrics · Artificial Intelligence (AI) · Citation analysis · Bibliometrics · References · Natural Language Processing (NLP) · Quality of publications · h-index · g-index · Impact Factor (IF) · Altmetrics · Original Research Performance Index (ORPI) · Bidirectional Encoder Representations from Transformers (BERT) · Scientific Bidirectional Encoder Representations from Transformers (SciBERT) · Citation intent · Academic publishing · Traditional metrics · AI-based metrics

1 Introduction

With the rapid progress in science and technology that the world is witnessing, Artificial Intelligence has emerged as an essential tool in most fields, thanks to its integration into most applications in order to compensate for human tasks despite their complexity. It has even reached the point of involving it in even the most sensitive fields such as scientific

O. Zahour et al. (Eds.): ICTIM 2024, CCIS 2655, pp. 207–218, 2026.
https://doi.org/10.1007/978-3-032-15147-6_20

research, publishing, writing and evaluating research papers for the purpose. A similarity check is recommended to ensure the originality of the content, using plagiarism detection tools [1].

For example, assisting Artificial Intelligence in writing scientific articles contributes to organizing ideas, producing high-quality content, and complying with the guidelines of the publishing journal [2], moreover, it is useful for authors, especially those whose first language is not English, as well as for publishers and editors who use AI tools for various functions [3]. In addition, it makes peer review more efficient by automating article filtering, detecting ethical and quality issues, and supporting plagiarism detection [2, 4].

However, its role remains crucial in evaluating research paper quality of research papers and scientific articles. The current evaluation relies mainly on traditional standards, which depend on the Impact Factor (IF) developed by Eugene Garfield in 1972, and h-index [5, 6].

These traditional metrics may not be sufficient to reflect the true impact of research, especially with the emergence of Artificial Intelligence and Machine Learning techniques that can provide deeper and more accurate insights into the quality and importance of research [7, 8].

Therefore, there is an urgent need to develop new AI-based metrics to evaluate scientific documents more accurately and comprehensively. These types should be able to deeply analyze the content of research, understand the relationships between different topics, and determine the true impact of research beyond external factors [7, 9].

This study aims to review traditional measures for evaluating scientific documents, discuss their limitations, and present a new measure based on Artificial Intelligence for evaluating research. We will review examples and models recently developed in this field, and propose a new methodology for developing this measure, highlighting potential challenges and ethical considerations associated with the use of AI in this context.

2 Traditional Methods for Evaluating Scientific Articles

2.1 h-index

The h-index is based on the number of citations a researcher's work receives, it is one of the best indicators that arises the importance of his work in the number of articles he has published or the journals in which he has published, in fact, it balances the number of publications and the citations received, which makes it useful for comparing researchers with each other, condensing all the information relating to citations into a single number. The letter "h" was chosen to represent it, it indicates "highly cited" and "high achievement" [10]. Mathematically, the h-index is defined as follows: a researcher has an index h if h of his n articles has each been cited at least h times, and the other $(n - h)$ articles have less than h citations each [6], for example, a researcher with an h-index of 30 has 30 articles that have each been cited at least 30 times. This metric can be expressed by the following formula:

$$h = \max \{h : f(h) \geq h\} \tag{1}$$

where $f(h)$ is the number of papers with at least h citations.

The h-index has several applications in academic evaluation, as it can be used to evaluate researchers for academic employment, promotions and awards. In fact, it is a valuable tool for comparing scientists, because those with similar h-index are considered to have comparable scientific impact, regardless of the number of their publications or total number of citations [11]. Additionally, it can predict a researcher's future impact, as the h-index is assumed to increase linearly over time [6]. It is also possible to improve the value of scientific publications by understanding copyright and publication contracts, which can help increase the h-index [12].

Despite its usefulness, the h-index has been subject to several criticisms. Firstly, it measures productivity without necessarily reflecting the actual importance or impact of the work [6], so it can be skewed by a small number of highly cited articles, which affects its accuracy as a comprehensive measure, and its value can differ significantly between scientific fields and journals [6]. Moreover, it does not distinguish between authors working individually or in small groups and those publishing with large groups, which can encourage scientifically unjustified collaborations aimed at increasing the h-index [10].

The h-index is also affected by self-citations, this may be biased against researchers with intermittent periods of research activity [13]. As well, language can also significantly influence the h-index, by reason of articles published in English generally receive more citations than those published in other languages, thus putting researchers publishing in languages other than English at a disadvantage [10].

Furthermore, the differences between the databases used to calculate the h-index, such as Web of Science, Scopus, and Google Scholar, can lead to discrepancies in the h-index values [10]. In summary, the h-index is a useful tool for measuring the impact of scientific research and facilitating academic comparisons and evaluations. However, it should be used with caution, taking into account the context and differences between scientific fields [6].

2.2 g-index

The g-index is an improvement of h-index, it is based on the number of citations that scientific articles receive. It was created by Leo Egghe in 2006 as the largest unique number g such that the most cited articles received at least g^2 citations in total. Clearly, to calculate the g-index, we classify scientific articles in descending order according to the number of citations they have received [14]. The mathematical formula for the g-index is as follows:

$$g = \max \left\{ g : \sum_{i=1}^{g} c_i \geq g^2 \right\} \tag{2}$$

Where C_i represents the number of citations of article i.

The relationship between the indices g and h is always: $g \geq h$

The g-index takes into account the high citations of articles, making it more accurate for evaluating the scientific performance of researchers. Unlike the h-index, which focuses on the minimum number of citations that articles receive, additionally, the g-index focuses or the cumulative total of citations for the most cited articles, this helps create better differentiation between researchers who have highly cited articles and those who have a greater number of moderately cited articles [14].

The advantages of the g-index are numerous, firstly, the g-index assigns greater importance to articles that receive a high number of citations, which makes it possible to better reflect the impact of the most influential research works [14], this characteristic is particularly useful for identifying researchers who produce work of high importance and quality. As an extra, the g-index provides a finer differentiation between researchers with highly cited articles and those with moderately cited articles, thus providing a more nuanced assessment of scientific performance [14].

Finally, the g-index can be used in addition to the h-index to provide a more complete view of a researcher's productivity and impact, thus enriching bibliometric analysis [14]. Nevertheless, the g-index also has some disadvantages. Since it is sensitive to extreme variation, meaning it may be disproportionately influenced by a small number of highly cited papers, this sensitivity may not always accurately reflect a researcher's overall performance, thus posing challenges for fair assessment [11]. Similarly, the calculation of g-index can be more complex than h-index, requiring more sophisticated citation data processing [15].

2.3 Impact Factor (IF)

The Impact Factor (IF), developed by Eugene Garfield in 1972, serves as a metric to gauge the influence of scientific journals through citations of published articles, it is calculated by dividing the number of citations that articles in the journal receive over a period given, by the number of articles published during the previous two years [16]. Its simplified mathematical formula is as follows:

$$IF = \frac{c}{a} \tag{3}$$

Where:

- The variable denotes the total number of citations made to papers published in years $(n-1)$ and $(n-2)$ in the given year .

The variable a denote the total number of articles that were released in $(n-1)$ and $(n-2)$ years.

The calculation is based on the Web of Science database, which includes approximately 13,000 journals [16]. The Impact Factor has some advantages. Firstly, it allows for quick and easy comparison of the visibility and influence of different journals within a given field, thus facilitating the evaluation of the notoriety and impact of scientific publications [17].

In general, a journal with a high Impact Factor (IF) is perceived as publishing high-quality research, making it a reliable quality indicator for researchers [18]. Additionally, researchers and Libraries can use impact factor to select journals for manuscript submission or subscription, thereby optimizing resources and time invested in research [19].

Nonetheless, the method of calculating the Impact Factor (IF) faces a variety of criticisms first of all, it represents an average for the entire journal rather than individual articles, which can mask variability in the quality of published articles [16]. Further, the editorial practices aimed at increasing citations can influence metric results [20].

Furthermore, the heavy reliance on Impact Factor (IF) to evaluate research neglects other important aspects such as innovation and true research quality [13, 16]. Also, it often displays a strong disciplinary bias, with life and health sciences generally having higher impact factors than fields such as the humanities and social sciences, making inter-disciplinary comparisons biased and unfair. Besides, the excessive emphasis on impact factor can put pressure on authors, pushing them to publish in high impact factor journals to the detriment of originality and innovation, which can limit the diversity of published research [21].

2.4 ORPI (Original Research Performance Index)

The Original Research Performance Index (ORPI) aims to provide a more accurate and comprehensive assessment of researchers' productivity and quality [13]. It is calculated as follows:

$$ORPI = \frac{n}{i} + \frac{(c - S_c)}{t} \tag{4}$$

Where:

- n represents the total number of original articles published in indexed journals since the first indexed publication.
- c is the total number of citations received by the published articles.
- Sc is the total number of self-citations.
- i is the total number of citable items (original articles, reviews, case reports) published.
- t is the time in years since the first indexed publication.

The first distinguishing feature of ORPI is its independence from the Impact Factor (IF) of scientific journals, rather than relying on the reputation or (IF) of a journal, this indicator provides an independent assessment of the quality of the research itself, ensuring that this approach reduces potential biases associated with publishing in high impact journals, thereby allowing for fairer evaluation of researchers [13].

ORPI also considers self-citations separately, reducing the influence of these citations on the overall rating. Self-citations can sometimes reflect personal biases or strategies to improve the numbers, so treating them separately strengthens the credibility of the assessment [13]. One of the strengths of ORPI is its encouragement of originality in scientific research, certainly, places greater importance on original articles and fundamental research which directly contribute to the advancement of scientific knowledge, this encouragement encourages researchers to focus on innovation and new contributions rather than replicating what already exists [13].

On the other hand, ORPI provides a continuous assessment of research productivity, because it is not limited to a short period, but evaluates the researcher on the basis of his productivity and the continuity of his research activity over a long period. Indeed, this approach makes it possible to provide a complete picture of researchers' performance

[13]. On the contrary, ORPI presents a variety of notable limitations, firstly, it relies primarily on PubMed for counting articles and citations, limiting its applicability to fields not well-represented in this database, thus neglecting other scientific fields. In other ways, the complex calculation of the ORPI, involves some parameters requiring additional efforts for data collection, compared to simpler indices like the h-index [13]. ORPI also places particular emphasis on first authorship, so it may not fairly reflect the contributions of co-authors, particularly in disciplines where collaboration is common. Finally, although ORPI attempts to neutralize self-citation bias, it does not completely eliminate it, thereby allowing researchers to manipulate their score by strategically citing their own work or that of their frequent collaborators [13].

2.5 Altmetrics

The concept of alternative metrics (Altmetrics) emerged in the 1990s, in response to the need for metrics that extend beyond traditional bibliometric boundaries, especially with the growing influence of the Internet. With the growing significance of the Internet in social and economic interactions, it has become necessary to develop new metrics that extend beyond traditional bibliometric boundaries, especially in light of the criticisms directed at the Impact Factor (IF) [22, 23].

Among the main platforms that rely on these metrics are "ImpactStory" and "PLOS", which provide different approaches to classifying and using these metrics.

ImpactStory is based on a methodology that separates the effects of research on scientists from the general population. Metrics are classified into multiple categories, such as views (downloads of PDF and HTML files), saves (CiteULike, Mendeley, Delicious), discussions (remarks on articles, Twitter, Facebook, and scientific blogs), recommendations (citations in newspaper and editorial articles), and citations (citations, full-text mentions, and Wikipedia mentions) [23]. With the help of scientific publications, researchers and the general public may now be tracked, offering a more complete picture of the influence of scientific research than can be obtained from standard academic citation counts [23]. The use of percentages and percentile ranking categories provides an opportunity to compare research impact across different fields and time periods, enhancing the analysis of bibliometric data. In this context, alternative metrics provide additional tools for measuring community and non-academic engagement, complementing traditional metrics [24].

The Public Library of Science (PLOS) takes a slightly different approach, not explicitly distinguishing between the impact of research on researchers and the general public. Metrics used in PLOS include views (HTML/PDF uploads on PLOS or PubMed Central, XML or PLOS), saves (CiteULike, Mendeley), discussions (NatureBlogs, ScienceSeeker, ResearchBlogging, PLOS comments, Wikipedia, Twitter, Facebook) and recommendations (F1000Prime). By incorporating these metrics, PLOS seeks to provide a comprehensive measure of engagement with scientific publications, making it easier to assess the scientific and societal impact of published research [23].

According to studies, alternative metrics have a number of advantages over standard academic measures. These advantages include the capacity to evaluate research products other than scientific publications, the ability to measure impact outside of academia, and the ability to provide impact indicators quickly after publication [25]. Nonetheless, there are certain difficulties, namely the potential for these measurements to be manipulated and the absence of uniform standards for impact measurement [23, 26].

Although Altmetrics offer a new perspective for assessing research impact, they face various obstacles. In the first place, Altmetrics are based on platforms with short life cycles and likely to disappear quickly, which has an impact on the sustainability of the indicators. Over and above that, the variety of methods for referencing articles online makes it difficult to collect data consistently, such as using standard numbers (DOI) or URLs. Eventually, further studies are needed to understand the accuracy and meaning of these indicators, particularly regarding their scientific significance [22].

3 Towards a New Metric for Scientific Evaluation: Leveraging BERT and SciBERT for Citation Analysis

Comprehensive evaluation of scientific research requires a multifaceted approach to accurately measure its impact. This demand has led to the development of new methodologies, particularly AI-based metrics, to enhance tracking of technological progress, support innovation, and accelerate scientific discovery.

One prominent tool in this area is Google's BERT model (Bidirectional Encoder Representations from Transformers), an NLP model (Natural Language Processing) based on the transformer architecture. It is notable for its bidirectional approach, capturing the context of words in sentences by considering both preceding and following words simultaneously, thereby enhancing contextual understanding [27].

Integrating automated model suggestions with existing manual processes is critical to improving classification accuracy and completeness. Tools like BERT, which excel at tasks such as text classification, question answering, and named entity recognition, serve as valuable complements to human analysis rather than substitutes [28]. BERT's ability to understand context outperforms traditional unidirectional models, delivering superior performance across NLP tasks. This flexibility stems from its adaptability: BERT can be pretrained on large text corpora and fine-tuned for specific applications [27]. However, the computational complexity of the model is a significant challenge due to its high resource demands, and its results may be affected by biases or gaps in pre-training data. This inherent "black box" nature adds to the difficulty of interpreting the decision-making process [29]. In this context, and to meet the evolving need for advanced citation metrics, AI-powered natural language processing models such as BERT and SciBERT (Scientific Bidirectional Encoder Representations from Transformers) can be leveraged to evaluate citations for relevance, intent, and contextual depth while also verifying citation sources. As shown in the chart (see Fig. 1), BERT has demonstrated a well-balanced performance on multi-class classification tasks, with (89%) accuracy, (90%) precision, (88%) recall, and 89% F1 score, according to the findings of A. Marrhich et al. (2024) [30]. SciBERT, which is specifically optimized for scientific literature, further enhances these capabilities, making it ideal for specialized analysis [27]. Although RoBERTa (Robustly Optimized BERT Pretraining Approach) achieved slightly higher accuracy (92%) and F1 score (91%), SciBERT's domain-specific optimization makes it uniquely suited for scientific applications. GPT-3.5 (Generative Pre-trained Transformer 3.5) also provides competitive results with (87%) accuracy but lacks the specificity needed for scientific contexts.

The proposed evaluation process involves multiple stages to ensure a comprehensive view of citations:

Verification of reference themes. it involves extracting the titles of source articles and cataloging their respective fields of knowledge. This process aims to compare these fields with the specialty of the article under evaluation to determine whether they belong to the same disciplinary domain.

Citation extraction and contextual matching. Each article undergoes preprocessing to extract citations, references, and surrounding contextual information, with datasets such as SciCite that capture the intent of the citation, whether it is supportive, comparative, or simply citing previous research [30–32].

Citation source verification. Using BERT or SciBERT fine-grained layers, the accuracy of citations to the source is calculated.

Scoring and weighting. Each citation is scored based on contextual alignment and intent, resulting in a composite quality measure. This new measure, which goes beyond traditional methods such as the h-index, provides a more accurate measure of research impact by reflecting not only the number of citations but also the quality of citations and their importance in scholarly discourse.

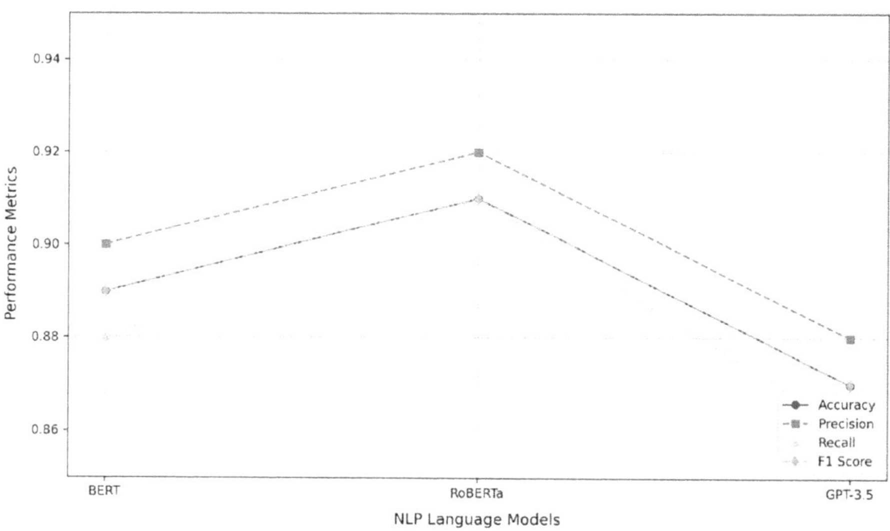

Fig. 1. Performance Comparison of NLP Language Models on Multi-Class Classification Tasks.

4 A Comparative Analysis of Traditional and AI-Based Metrics for Scientific Impact Evaluation

Traditional metrics, such as the Impact Factor (IF) and the h-index, have long served as indicators of research quality by focusing on the number of citations and the influence of journals. These quantitative metrics have provided an effective measure of researcher insight, but they lack depth in contextual analysis and may introduce biases related to field and subjective citation practices [17]. For example, the h-index cannot account for citation intent, such as whether a citation is supportive or critical, and often disadvantages research outside highly cited fields [6]. Furthermore, traditional metrics fall short in adaptability when applied to emerging or interdisciplinary fields, as they rely on citation frequency without assessing the content or novelty of the work [11], (see Table 1).

The introduction of Artificial Intelligence and NLP models to analyze citation contexts, sentiment, and intent has become essential, in addition to its role in capturing the relevance and emotion behind citations, providing a comprehensive view of an article's impact beyond the raw number of citations [27]. These AI-based metrics will also reduce bias by excluding self-citations and weighting context, giving more balanced assessments that reflect scientific novelty and importance [7]. Although computationally intensive, these metrics enhance accuracy and adaptability, especially in new research areas where citation counts alone may not fully capture a study's impact [33]. Thus, while traditional metrics offer simplicity and ease of use, AI-based metrics promise deeper insights into the qualitative aspects of scientific impact.

Table 1. Comparative Analysis of Traditional and AI-Based Metrics for Evaluating Research Impact

Aspect	Traditional Metrics	AI-based Metrics
Scope and Focus	Primarily quantitative; focus on citation count and journal impact	Combines quantitative and qualitative; includes content, sentiment, and context
Time Sensitivity	Delayed, often takes years to reflect impact	Real-time or near-instantaneous analysis
Depth of Analysis	Surface-level; mostly numerical without content analysis	Deep, contextual analysis through NLP and AI models
Quality Differentiation	Limited to citation counts and journal reputation	High; captures nuanced quality aspects
Flexibility Across Disciplines	Less adaptable; variations across disciplines	Highly adaptable; consistent across disciplines
Data Source Dependence	Depends on databases like Web of Science, Scopus	Flexible; can integrate multiple data sources, including altmetrics

5 Conclusion

This study emphasizes the importance of adopting AI-based metrics, such as BERT and SciBERT models, to assess the quality of scientific publications, beyond traditional metrics that rely on the number of citations alone. By examining citations in context, we show how these models provide a more nuanced perspective on research impact, taking into account the intent and importance of citations [7, 27, 28].

The results confirm that AI-powered metrics not only complement traditional methods, but have the potential to transform evaluation methods by providing a deeper and more contextually informed analysis. This contributes to a more fair and objective evaluation, especially in interdisciplinary and emerging fields that are often overlooked by traditional metrics [6, 17].

Using AI to analyze sentiment in citations can provide additional information to understand underlying opinions and trends in the scientific literature [34]. Contextually analyzed citations, using techniques such as word representations and expert knowledge, help to gain a deeper understanding of academic connections, which is essential for accurate assessment of scholarly impact [35]. In the future, research should seek to improve these models by incorporating more diverse datasets and exploring other natural language processing techniques that can enhance the detection of citation intent [7, 29]. In addition, extending this AI-based approach to other forms of academic impact, such as social impact or practical applications, remains a promising area. These future developments will enable the construction of a comprehensive and flexible framework for evaluating scientific research, supporting both academic and societal [22, 33].

References

1. Mifrah, S., et al.: Citation sentiment analysis: a brief comprehensive study. J. Islam. Ctries. Soc. (2017)
2. Carobene, A., Padoan, A., Cabitza, F., Banfi, G., Plebani, M.: Rising adoption of artificial intelligence in scientific publishing: evaluating the role, risks, and ethical implications in paper drafting and review process. Clin. Chem. Labor. Med. (2024). https://doi.org/10.1515/cclm-2023-1136
3. Bahammam, A.S.: Adapting to the impact of artificial intelligence in scientific writing: balancing benefits and drawbacks while developing policies and regulations. J. Nat. Sci. Med. (2023). https://doi.org/10.4103/jnsm.jnsm_89_23
4. Mifrah, S.: Toward a semantic graph of scientific publications: a bibliometric study. Int. J. Adv. Trends Comput. Sci. Eng. 9(3), 3323–3330 (2020). https://doi.org/10.30534/ijatcse/2020/129932020
5. Garfield, E.: Citation indexes for science: a new dimension in documentation through Association of Ideas. Science. 122, 108–111 (1955)
6. Hirsch, J.E.: An index to quantify an individual's scientific research output. Proc. Natl. Acad. Sci. U. S. A. 102(46), 16569–16572 (2005)
7. Beltagy, I., Lo, K., Cohan, A.: SciBERT: a pretrained language model for scientific text. [En ligne]. Disponible: http://arxiv.org/abs/1903.10676 (2019)
8. Mifrah, S., Ben Lahmar, E.H.: Semantic relationship study between citing and cited scientific articles using topic modeling. In: ACM International Conference Proceeding Series (2019). https://doi.org/10.1145/3372938.3372943
9. Hourrane, O., Mifrah, S., Benlahmar, E.H., Bouhriz, N., Rachdi, M.: Using deep learning word embeddings for citations similarity in academic papers. In: International Conference on Big Data, Cloud and Applications, pp. 185–196. Springer International Publishing, Cham (2018)
10. Sierra, J.C., Haynes, S.N., Eysenck, M.W., Buela-Casal, G., Hirsch, J.E.: The meaning of the h-index. Int. J. Clin. Health Psychol. 14 (2014)
11. Bornmann, L., Daniel, H.D.: Does the h-index for ranking of scientists really work? Scientometrics. 65(3), 391–392 (2005)

12. Favre, J., Germond, T., Clavert, P., Collin, P., Michelet, A., Lädermann, A.: Want a better h-index?–all you need to know about copyright and open access. Orthop. Traumatol. Surg. Res. **106**(8), 1475–1480 (2020)
13. Saxena, A., Thawani, V., Chakrabarty, M., Gharpure, K.: Scientific evaluation of the scholarly publications. J. Pharmacol. Pharmacother. **4**(2), 125–129 (2013). https://doi.org/10.4103/0976-500X.110894
14. Egghe, L.: Theory and practise of the g-index. Scientometrics. **69**(1), 131–152 (2006). https://doi.org/10.1007/s11192-006-0144-7
15. Schreiber, M.: To share the fame in a fair way, hm modifies h for multi-authored manuscripts. New J. Phys. **10** (2008). https://doi.org/10.1088/1367-2630/10/4/040201
16. Calò, L.N.: Impact metrics and science evaluation. Rev. Peru Med. Exp. Salud Publica. **39**(2), 236–240 (2022). https://doi.org/10.17843/rpmesp.2022.392.11171
17. Garfield, E.: Of the journal impact factor. JAMA J. Am. Med. Assoc. **295**(1), 90–93 (2006)
18. Rousseau, R.: Journal evaluation: technical and practical issues. Libr. Trends. **50**(3), 418–439 (2001)
19. Leydesdorff, L., Opthof, T.: Scopus's source normalized impact per paper (SNIP) versus a journal impact factor based on fractional counting of citations. J. Am. Soc. Inf. Sci. Technol. **61**(11), 2365–2369 (2010). https://doi.org/10.1002/asi.21371
20. Falagas, M.E., Kouranos, V.D., Arencibia-Jorge, R., Karageorgopoulos, D.E.: Comparison of SCImago journal rank indicator with journal impact factor. FASEB J. **22**(8), 2623–2628 (2008). https://doi.org/10.1096/fj.08-107938
21. Smith, R.: The trouble with medical journals. J. R. Soc. Med. **99**(3), 115–119 (2006). https://doi.org/10.1258/jrsm.99.3.115
22. Torres-Salinas, D., Cabezas-Clavijo, Á., Jiménez-Contreras, E.: Altmetrics: new indicators for scientific communication in web 2.0. Communication. **21**(41), 53–60 (2013). https://doi.org/10.3916/C41-2013-05
23. Bornmann, L.: Do altmetrics point to the broader impact of research? An overview of benefits and disadvantages of altmetrics. J. Informetr. **8**(4), 895–903 (2014). https://doi.org/10.1016/j.joi.2014.09.005
24. Bornmann, L., Leydesdorff, L., Mutz, R.: The use of percentiles and percentile rank classes in the analysis of bibliometric data: opportunities and limits. J. Informetr. **7**(1), 158–165 (2013). https://doi.org/10.1016/j.joi.2012.10.001
25. Wouters, P., Costas, R.: Users, Narcissism and Control: Tracking the Impact of Scholarly Publications in the 21st Century, vol. 9. SURFfoundation, Utrecht (2012)
26. Priem, J., Taraborelli, D., Groth, P., Neylon, C.: Altmetrics: a manifesto, pp. 1–5 (2010)
27. Devlin, J., Chang, M.-W., Lee, K., Toutanova, K.: BERT: pre-training of deep bidirectional transformers for language understanding. NAACL-HLT, pp. 4171–4186 (2018)
28. Sachini, E., Sioumalas-Christodoulou, K., Christopoulos, S., Karampekios, N.: AI for AI: using AI methods for classifying AI science documents. Quant. Sci. Stud. **3**(4), 1119–1132 (2022). https://doi.org/10.1162/qss_a_00223
29. Rogers, A., Kovaleva, O., Rumshisky, A.: A primer in bertology: what we know about how BERT works. Trans. Assoc. Comput. Linguist. **8**, 842–866 (2020). https://doi.org/10.1162/tacl_a_00349
30. Marrhich, A.: Multi-task learning with BERT, RoBERTa, GPT-3.5, ELECTRA, and XLNet for urgency classification, topic similarity, and sentiment analysis in MOOCs. Ingénierie des systèmes d information. **29**(5), 1891–1901 (2024)
31. Mercier, D., Rizvi, S.T.R., Rajashekar, V., Dengel, A., Ahmed, S.: ImpactCite: An XLNet-based method for citation impact analysis https://doi.org/10.5220/0010235201590168 (2020)
32. Lahiri, A., Sanyal, D.K., Mukherjee, I.: CitePrompt: using prompts to identify citation intent in scientific papers. Association for Computing Machinery, vol. 2023 https://doi.org/10.1109/JCDL57899.2023.00017 (2023)

33. Brown, T.B., et al.: Language models are few-shot learners. Adv. Neural Inf. Process. Syst. (2020)
34. Panchal, D., Mehta, M., Mishra, A., Ghole, S., Dandge, M.S.: Sentiment analysis using natural language processing. Int. J. Res. Appl. Sci. Eng. Technol. **10**(5), 2262–2266 (2022). https://doi.org/10.22214/ijraset.2022.42711
35. Cohan, A., Goharian, N.: Contextualizing citations for scientific summarization using word embedding and domain knowledge. In: Proceedings of the 40th International ACM SIGIR Conference on Research and Development in Information Retrieval, pp. 1133–1136 (2017). https://doi.org/10.1145/3077136.3080740

Comparative Analysis of Blood Vessel Segmentation Techniques in Breast MRI

Laila El Jiani[(⊠)], Sanaa El Filali, El Habib Benlahmar, and Khawla Moustafi

Faculty of Science Ben M'sick, Hassan II University, Casablanca, Morocco
`Laila.eljiani-etu@etu.univh2c.ma`

Abstract. Blood vessel analysis is crucial for understanding tumor progression and provides insights into tumor biology, which are essential for diagnostics and treatment planning in breast cancer care. Furthermore, breast magnetic resonance imaging has the potential to visualize blood vessels within breast tissue by generating high-contrast images and detecting changes in blood flow. Accurate segmentation of blood vessels in breast MRI is vital for diagnosing, treatment planning, and monitoring breast cancer. This study aims to identify current methods for blood vessel segmentation in breast MRI. The main results show that these methods primarily use computer algorithms, with a few also employing machine learning algorithms. However, current blood vessel segmentation methods face significant challenges, such as low contrast, noise, and complex vessel geometries, which often result in undersegmentation. Researchers should explore hybrid models combining traditional, Machine Learning, and Deep Learning methods for robust, accurate vessel segmentation. Open, annotated breast MRI datasets and collaborative data quality efforts are essential to advance this field and enhance cancer patient care.

Keywords: breast cancer · breast MRI · blood vessel · segmentation · detection

1 Introduction

Breast cancer is the leading cause of cancer-related death among women worldwide. In 2022, 2.3 million women were diagnosed with breast cancer, resulting in 670,000 global deaths [1]. Addressing late-stage breast cancer diagnosis is critical for improving outcomes [2]. The World Health Organization recommends two key strategies to address this challenge: early diagnosis to identify symptomatic cancer sooner, and screening to detect asymptomatic disease in targeted populations, both of which can enhance early cancer detection [3, 4].

Breast MRI has the potential to visualize and detect blood vessels within breast tissue, thanks to its ability to generate high-contrast images and detect changes in blood flow. Tumors often trigger new blood vessel growth, which MRI scans, particularly T1-weighted imaging, can detect. Extracting information about blood vessel location, size, and shape from these images can provide valuable insights for clinicians, especially before surgery and during neoadjuvant therapy [5]. Beforehand, this requires a segmentation process to be carried out.

© The Author(s), under exclusive license to Springer Nature Switzerland AG 2026
O. Zahour et al. (Eds.): ICTIM 2024, CCIS 2655, pp. 219–226, 2026.
https://doi.org/10.1007/978-3-032-15147-6_21

Manual segmentation of blood vessels is a time-consuming and costly process with limited consistency and reproducibility between operators. In contrast, semi-automatic and automatic vessel segmentation methods still rely on expert clinicians to either perform initial segmentation or validate the results [6]. Nonetheless, automatic or semi-automatic blood vessel segmentation holds the potential to support clinicians, making it a significant area of interest in medical research [7].

Several studies have investigated blood vessel segmentation; however, a comprehensive comparative review of various techniques specifically for breast MRI in clinical applications is limited. This paper aims to address this gap by consolidating and analyzing the available methods for blood vessel segmentation, thereby providing a valuable resource for clinicians and researchers. We set out to identify the current techniques for blood vessel segmentation in breast MRI. To achieve this, we conducted an extensive literature search targeting studies focused on blood vessel segmentation using breast MRI imaging. Ultimately, we identified seven studies that met our criteria, all published between 2009 and 2024.

2 Current Methods of Blood Vessel Segmentation on Breast MRI

Few studies have addressed the issue of blood vessel segmentation in the literature. This is partly due to the challenges encountered, including the limitations of MRI in directly imaging biological structures and the high heterogeneity of the human breast, both within individual women and across different individuals. We've identified seven studies in the literature that address this topic. The studies are compared in Table 1, which details various segmentation techniques, including traditional, machine learning, and deep learning approaches in breast MRI segmentation. These methods, while diverse, are unified by the core steps they use: preprocessing, feature extraction, segmentation execution, and post-processing.

Glotsos et al. [8] proposed a modified Seeded Region Growing (SRG) algorithm for vessel segmentation in breast MRI. The method classifies pixels into seed, background, and weak candidate regions, achieving approximately 94.4% accuracy in lesion characterization. However, the approach may be sensitive to noise and requires precise seed selection for optimal performance. In related work, Gierlinger et al. introduced the multi-seed region growing (MSRG) algorithm, which is based on the SRG algorithm. This algorithm aims to enhance breast MRI by extracting vessel-like structures. MSRG uses multiple seeds to efficiently grow regions based on pixel connectivity. Despite some limitations, the MSRG algorithm provides valuable insights for refining segment extraction [9].

To improve the accuracy of hot-spot labeling in computer-aided diagnosis (CAD) systems for breast MRI, Muqin Lean et al. implemented a vessel exclusion process using a connectivity-based approach. The goal of this approach is to identify and eliminate potentially mislabeled blood vessel enhancements in 2D Maximum Intensity Projection (MIP) images and extend this analysis to adjacent 3D slices. When validated against radiologist annotations, this method significantly reduced false positives. The detection rates showed 85.6% correctness and a 19.2% missed detection [10]. To further enhance blood vessel detection, Delwar et al. proposed an algorithm using morphological operators and gradient features. This algorithm includes steps such as gradient magnitude operations for edge detection, histogram equalization, and adaptive thresholding. These steps enhance vessel visibility and accuracy, particularly in noisy environments. Together, these methods aim to improve the reliability and accuracy of breast MRI analyses by effectively reducing incorrect vessel labeling and enhancing detection capabilities [11].

Regarding blood vessel segmentation in 3D breast MRIs, Kahala et al. presented an algorithm that uses Hessian-based methods to create a 3D model and enhance texture. The algorithm achieves vessel completion by tracking centerlines of endpoints identified through skeletonization. When compared to manual segmentation, the algorithm demonstrated 86% sensitivity and 88.3% specificity, indicating its effectiveness in tumor detection [12]. However, it's important to note that the algorithm's reliance on tracking methods may not be as effective for curved blood vessels located near suspicious masses, potentially impacting accurate detection. In the context of 3D breast MRI, Vignati et al. proposed a fully automatic 3D Hessian-based algorithm for detecting blood vessels in breast DCE-MRI, identifying linear structures, and filtering out non-vessel enhancements based on morphology. It has a correct detection rate of 89.1%, a missed detection rate of 10.9%, and an incorrect detection rate of 27.1%. The algorithm also reduces vessel false positives by 68.4% compared to the CAD system, enhancing diagnostic accuracy. The algorithm has key limitations: it overlooks vessel length, often misses branching points, and relies on an empirically set threshold for the covariance eigenvalue ratio, which can impact segmentation accuracy and consistency [13].

In [14], Lew et al. developed a convolutional neural network algorithm to segment breast tissue, fibroglandular tissue (FGT), and blood vessels in MRI scans, trained on 100 annotated studies. The algorithm achieved Dice scores of 92% for breast tissue, 0.86 for FGT, and 0.65 for blood vessels, with a high correlation of 95% with manually created masks, indicating accuracy. However, the limited dataset size and variability in manual annotations may affect its general applicability and data quality, while a lower correlation of 0.75 with radiologist evaluations points to some discrepancies between the model's predictions and expert opinions.

Table 1. Summary of blood vessel segmentation techniques in breast MRI, including preprocessing and post-processing methods

Authors	Year	Dataset	Vessel Segmentation Algorithm	Image Dimension	Pre-processing and post-processing used techniques
Lean M. et al. [10]	2009	34 patients	Hessian-based approach	2D	- Image enhancement: filter bank - Maximum Intensity Projections - Centerline tracking - 3D skeletonizing
Glotsos, D. et al. [8]	2014	20 MRI	Seeded Region Growing based approach	2D	- Background Removal - Noise Reduction: Median filtering
Spiros A. et al. [6]	2016	39 patients	Seeded Region Growing based approach	3D	- Contrast Enhancement: CLAHE - Noise Reduction: median filter - Statistical Analysis - Predictive Modeling: logistic regression
Kahala G. et al. [12]	2017	24 patients	Hessian-based method	3D	- Texture enhancement - Centerline tracking and skeletonizing
Vignati, A. et al. [13]	2019	28 MRI	Hessian-based algorithm	3D	- Multiscale analysis - Skeletonizing

(continued)

Table 1. (*continued*)

Authors	Year	Dataset	Vessel Segmentation Algorithm	Image Dimension	Pre-processing and post-processing used techniques
Muqin Lean et al. [11]	2021	Not specified	Thresholding based approach	2D	- Contrast Adjustment - Dilation - Erosion - Gradient Magnitude Calculation
Lew, C.et al. [14]	2024	100 cases	U-net based approach	2D/3D	- Capping Extreme Values - Normalization

3 Discussion

When analyzing existing methods for blood vessel segmentation in breast MRI, we identified four key stages common across techniques: image preprocessing, feature extraction, segmentation execution, and post-processing. These steps collectively form the foundation of the segmentation process, with preprocessing and post-processing being essential to enhance visibility and accuracy in vessel detection. Our analysis indicates that all techniques incorporate these initial and final stages to improve the quality and precision of segmentation outcomes. Preprocessing techniques such as grayscale conversion, contrast enhancement (e.g., CLAHE [14]), and noise reduction (e.g., median [15] and bilateral filtering [16]) are essential for preparing images by enhancing contrast and minimizing noise. Feature extraction provides critical information about vessel properties, aiding precise segmentation. Segmentation techniques, ranging from traditional (e.g. thresholding [15], region growing [16], hessian filtering (see Fig. 1)) to advanced machine learning (e.g. random forests, SVMs) and deep learning approaches (e.g. U-Net, FCN), bring unique strengths, while post-processing further refines results, enhancing their clinical relevance. The integration of these steps into a cohesive workflow enhances segmentation performance. Effective preprocessing, particularly through CLAHE and adaptive unsharp masking filters significantly improves contrast, making vessel structures distinguishable. As shown in Fig. 2, the left image displays the original breast MRI, while the right image demonstrates the improved contrast after applying CLAHE enhancement. This contrast adjustment enhances the image's clarity, facilitating more accurate detection and segmentation. Noise reduction preserves vessel boundaries and minimizes artifacts, addressing major challenges in breast MRI.

To further enhance segmentation accuracy and reliability, potential improvements and innovations could include leveraging generative adversarial networks [17] to synthesize realistic breast MRI data, expanding the training dataset with semi-supervised or self-supervised learning techniques, and incorporating domain-specific knowledge [18]

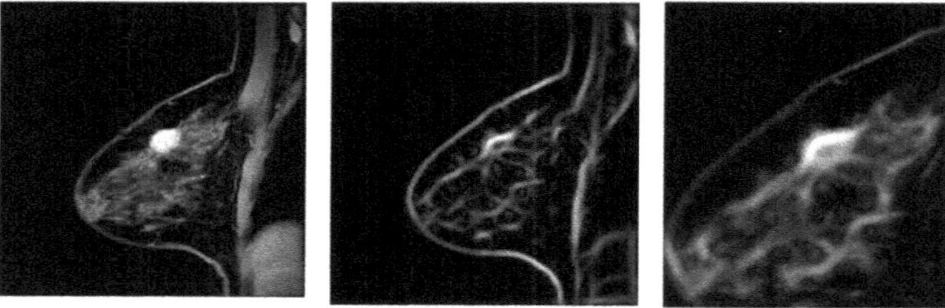

Fig. 1. Comparative segmentation results from key methods discussed in this study. (Left) Original breast MRI scans, (Center) results after applying Hessian filtering, and (Right) detailed ROI filtering. This figure illustrates how each method improves vessel visibility and segmentation quality.

through hybrid neural network architectures. Additionally, incorporating uncertainty quantification methods could help identify segmentation areas with higher uncertainty, enabling targeted manual review and improvement of the model. Lastly, integrating the segmentation model with prior clinical information, such as patient risk factors and comorbidities, could provide a more holistic assessment of breast cancer characteristics and improve overall diagnostic accuracy.

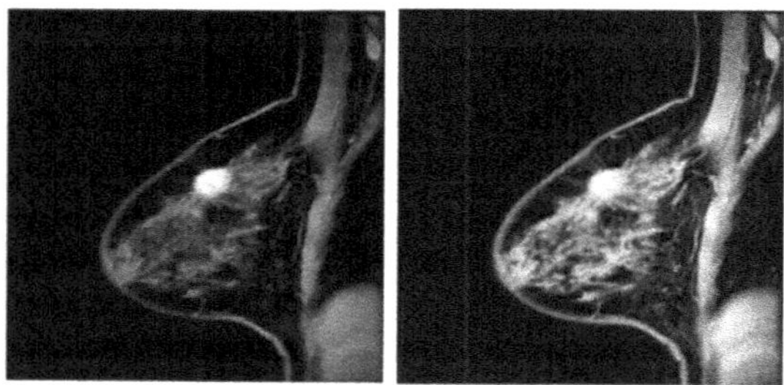

Fig. 2. Breast MRI before and after Contrast Limited Adaptive Histogram Equalization (CLAHE) enhancement. The left image shows the original low-contrast scan, while the right image demonstrates improved vessel visibility and tissue contrast for enhanced diagnostic accuracy.

4   Conclusion

Blood vessel segmentation in breast MRI faces significant challenges, including low contrast, noise, and complex vessel geometries, which frequently result in under-segmentation. Traditional methods struggle with imaging variability, and machine learning and deep learning models are limited by the lack of large, diverse datasets. Additionally, inconsistencies in evaluation criteria and imaging techniques hinder clinical adoption. Developing open-access, annotated datasets for breast MRI is essential, with collaborative efforts needed to ensure data quality and diversity. Hybrid models combining traditional, machine learning, and deep learning approaches can enhance segmentation performance. Advanced post-processing techniques, like PSO-based optimization filters, can further refine results in complex regions. These strategies aim to create more robust, accurate segmentation methods, ultimately enhancing breast cancer patient care.

In our future work, we plan to develop a novel model for blood vessel segmentation in breast MRI that aims to address the challenges we have identified. By leveraging a hybrid approach that combines traditional, machine learning, and deep learning techniques, we believe we can create a more robust and accurate segmentation method. This will not only improve the detection of blood vessels but also enhance the overall accuracy of breast cancer diagnosis and treatment planning, ultimately leading to better patient outcomes.

References

1. Cuthrell, K.M., Tzenios, N.: Breast cancer: updated and deep insights. J. Med. **6**(3), 104–118 (2023) https://journalirjo.com/index.php/IRJO/article/view/129
2. Ginsburg, O., Yip, C.-H., Brooks, A., et al.: Breast cancer early detection: a phased approach to implementation. Cancer. **126**(3), 2379–2393 (2020). https://doi.org/10.1002/cncr.32887
3. Obeagu, E.I., Obeagu, G.U.: Breast cancer: a review of risk factors and diagnosis. Medicine. **103**(5), e36905 (2024). https://doi.org/10.1097/MD.0000000000036905
4. Lee, C.S., Moy, L., Joe, B.N., Sickles, E.A., Niell, B.L.: Screening for breast cancer in women age 75 years and older. AJR Am. J. Roentgenol. **210**(2), 256–263 (2018). https://doi.org/10.2214/AJR.17.18705
5. Bhushan, A., Gonsalves, A., Menon, J.U.: Current state of breast cancer diagnosis, treatment, and theranostics. Pharmaceutics. **13**(5), 723 (2021). https://doi.org/10.3390/pharmaceutics13050723
6. Kostopoulos, S.A., et al.: Computer-based automated estimation of breast vascularity and correlation with breast cancer in DCE-MRI images. Magn. Reson. Imaging. **35**, 39–45 (2017). https://doi.org/10.1016/j.mri.2016.08.007
7. Liu, Q., Liu, Z., Yong, S., Jia, K., Razmjooy, N.: Computer-aided breast cancer diagnosis based on image segmentation and interval analysis. Automatika. **61**, 496–506 (2020). https://doi.org/10.1080/00051144.2020.1785784
8. Glotsos, D., Vassiou, K., Kostopoulos, S., et al.: A modified seeded region growing algorithm for vessel segmentation in breast MRI images for investigating the nature of potential lesions. J. Phys. Conf. Ser. **490**, 012136 (2014). https://doi.org/10.1088/1742-6596/490/1/012136
9. Gierlinger, M., Brandner, D.M., Zagar, B.G.: Segmentation of elongated structures processed on breast MRI for the detection of vessels. tm - Tech. Mess. **88**, 481–487 (2021). https://doi.org/10.1515/teme-2021-0017
10. Lin, M., Chen, J.-H., Nie, K., Chang, D., Nalcioglu, O., Su, M.-Y.: Algorithm-based method for detection of blood vessels in breast MRI for development of computer-aided diagnosis. J. Magn. Reson. Imaging. **30**, 817–824 (2009). https://doi.org/10.1002/jmri.21915
11. Zaman, T., Hossain, Q.D.: An efficient technique for detection and intensification of blood vessels from breast MRI. In: 2021 5th International Conference on Electrical Information and Communication Technology (EICT), Bangladesh, pp. 1–7. IEEE (2021). https://doi.org/10.1109/EICT54103.2021.9733644.12
12. Kahala, G., Sklair, M., Spitzer, H.: Multi-scale blood vessel detection and segmentation in breast MRIs. J. Biomed. Eng. Med. Devices. **2** (2017). https://doi.org/10.4172/2475-7586.1000122
13. Vignati, A., Giannini, V., Bert, A., et al.: A fully automatic multiscale 3-dimensional hessian-based algorithm for vessel detection in breast DCE-MRI. Invest. Radiol. **47**, 705 (2012). https://doi.org/10.1097/RLI.0b013e31826dc3a4

14. Lew, C., Harouni, M., Kirksey, E., et al.: A publicly available deep learning model and dataset for segmentation of breast, fibroglandular tissue, and vessels in breast MRI. Sci. Rep. **14** (2024). https://doi.org/10.1038/s41598-024-54048-2
15. Hysteresis thresholding. SpringerLink, https://link.springer.com/chapter/10.1007/978-1-4614-1857-3_7. Last accessed 13 Sept 2024
16. Mehnert, A., Jackway, P.: An improved seeded region growing algorithm. Pattern Recogn. Lett. **18**, 1065–1071 (1997). https://doi.org/10.1016/S0167-8655(97)00131-1
17. Park, S., Lee, K.H., Ko, B.S., Kim, N.: Unsupervised anomaly detection with generative adversarial networks in mammography. Nat. Portf. **13**(1) (2023). https://doi.org/10.1038/s41598-023-2952 -z
18. Xie, X., Niu, J., Liu, X., Chen, Z., Tang, S., Yu, S.: A survey on incorporating domain knowledge into deep learning for medical image analysis. Med. Image Anal. **69**, 101985 (2021). https://doi.org/10.1016/j.media.2021.101985

Improvement of Information Retrieval Systems on Digital Educational Platforms

Nisrine Safeh[1]([envelope]), Mohamed Rachdi[2], Abdelwahed Namir[1], and Mohamed Azzouazi[1]

[1] Information Technology and Modeling Laboratory faculty of sciences ben m'sick, Casablanca, Morocco
nisrinesafeh2014@gmail.com
[2] National Higher school of Art and Design (ENSAD Casablanca), Hassan II University of Casablanca, Casablanca, Morocco

Abstract. Information retrieval has become crucial, especially in the current chaotic circumstances where everyone is forced to operate remotely using computer tools. The world is becoming more digitalized, and everything is automated. In the world of education, all forms of instruction have moved online, yet hybrid training is still a better option that is always available.

Despite their lack of proficiency with its numerous functionalities, students have quickly shifted to distant learning and begun using e-learning systems. The irrelevant nature of the results that were returned is one of the challenges.

The goal of this study is to suggest a novel method for searching for information within an e-learning environment that adheres to the SCORM standard. By entering the query's terms, the student will be able to search the educational platform. When a resource is unavailable, our technology enables users to search for other resources on the Internet using a trusted information retrieval method that has produced very encouraging results.

Keywords: Information retrieval · Digital educational platforms · E-learning · LMS

1 Introduction

Online learning has developed into a crucial tenet of contemporary education, giving students convenient access to a multitude of learning materials. Making it simpler for students to access and identify pertinent information has become essential given the growth of online learning platforms. In light of this, it is crucial that information retrieval systems be integrated into digital educational platforms.

By offering a more focused and precise search, integrating an information retrieval system into digital educational platforms addresses these difficulties. This system can assist learners in finding the most pertinent information for their unique needs fast thanks to advanced capabilities like contextual search, semantic search, and personalized content recommendation.

This article's main goal is to provide an innovative technique to integrate an information retrieval system into online learning settings, in order to enhance the learning

O. Zahour et al. (Eds.): ICTIM 2024, CCIS 2655, pp. 227–234, 2026.
https://doi.org/10.1007/978-3-032-15147-6_22

experience for students and promote quicker resource discovery. This information search engine's goal is to give users a straightforward user interface and cutting-edge features to speed up research and access to pertinent content.

2 Related Studies

Several researchers have recently looked on web-based apps. Each online application has three main levels, according to F.P. Rokou et al. [1]: the program's web-based nature, the educational setting, and the individualized administration of learning resources. An information system that includes a web server, a network, a communication protocol like HTTP, and browser is referred to as a web-based program. Users' data contributes to changes in the system's status and behavior. educational context describes the pedagogical model utilized along with the instructor's aims. The rules and procedures for selecting learning resources based on student characteristics, educational objectives, the teaching method, and the available materials are all included in the personalized administration of online learning materials.

These three variables have been blended and integrated into e-learning systems through numerous efforts, leading to numerous standardization projects. Some efforts, such the IEEE Learning Technology Systems design (LTSC), Instructional Management Systems (IMS), and Sharable Content Object Reference Model (SCORM), have concentrated on the common design and format of learning environments. The sharing and sequencing of learning items, also known as learning objects, between various e-learning systems are defined and provided by IMS and SCORM. Their primary goals are to standardize teaching and learning techniques and to model the management of interoperable educational data that is pertinent to the educational process [2].

The content packaging concept and the sequencing paradigm were first introduced by IMS and SCORM, respectively. Content packing, activity trees, learning activities, sequencing rules, and navigation models are the primary technologies behind these approaches. Their navigation models explain how learnerand system-initiated navigation events can be triggered and handled, while their sequencing models define a way to characterize the expected behavior of a learning experience.

Additionally, Juan Quemada and Bernd Simon provided a framework for instructional strategies and resources [3]. According to their approach, educational activities consist of one or more instructors and take place in a virtual setting on a predetermined timetable. According to F.P. Rokou et al. [4], stereotypes are incorporated into instructional design for educational systems, and current UML (Unified Modeling Language) packet diagrams are appropriately modified. As a result, we think that adding an educational content framework based on learning resources to an e-learning system—one that contains ontology-based features and hierarchical semantic associations—would enable the system to provide learners flexible and intelligent learning. The set of educational materials, the available learning sequence, and the structure of the educational concepts, such as the superior or inferior concepts linked with the learning contents, could all be visualized thanks to the contents' hierarchical structure.

3 Methodology

Our approach suggests breaking down this task into distinct parts, starting with the user's request (learner) and ending with its enlargement. Pre-processing the question is a crucial first step in any natural language processing system before starting the information retrieval procedure.

4 Pre-processing Request

Since this approach is intended for university -level student's who are expected to be extremely knowledgeable about what they are looking for, this step is not particularly difficult.

Preprocessing the query in this scenario entails removing empty words based on a specified list that includes stop words; these words are the result of input mistakes, syntax errors, and other parameters.

In order to avoid any ambiguity, noise, or silence, the goal of this level is to extract the interesting terms from the query, use them in the following phase, and discard the rest. This work will come before the enrichment process.

After cleaning, the output is a list of concepts from the original query made up of words, expressions, and other components.

5 Exploring the E-learning System for the Resource

The user's request is cleaned up and just the key terms are kept before moving on to the next stage, which is searching the E-Learning system for materials that fit the user's request. The LMS system is structured as follows:

All information regarding the resource's content is contained in the DATA file. The learning resource's material is arranged or structured in the Organization file. The learning resource's content is described in the item file.

All of the useful activities associated with this resource are contained in the Activities file.

The QUIZ file includes a number of practice exams to gauge the student's proficiency. The DATA file is browsed in this stage to see if the resource corresponds to the user's request (Fig. 1).

6 Selection of Data Source

The user is now given access to all of the platform's resources, giving them the chance to select the one that best meets their needs. The path found in the organization file is used to gain access to the resource, and its content is then shown. In this case, there are two conceivable outcomes (Fig. 2).

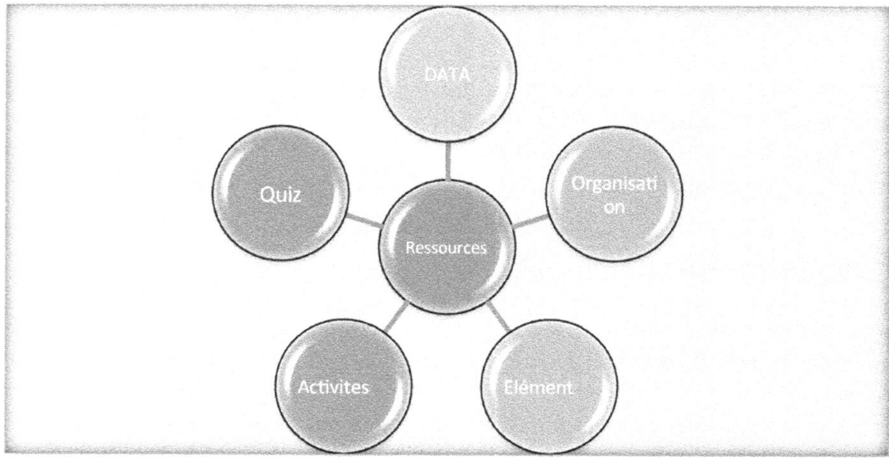

Fig. 1. LMS system organization

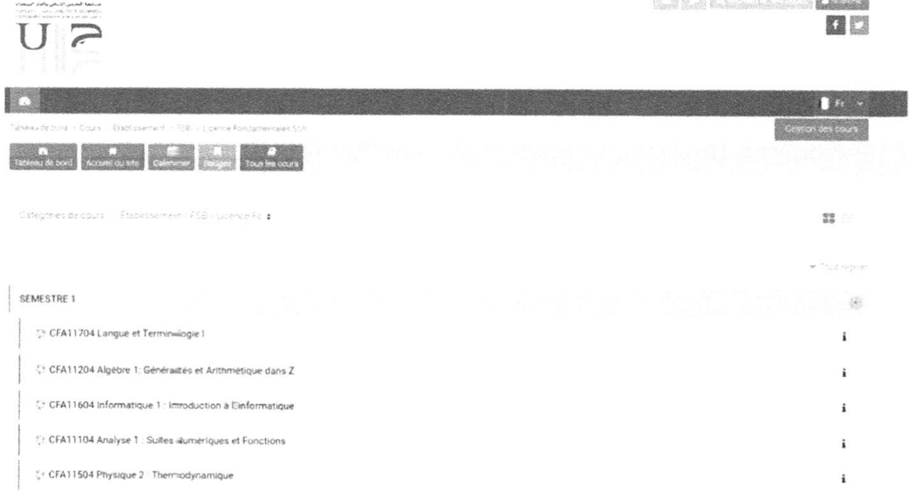

Fig. 2. Digital educational platform home interface

Situation 1: When the suggested resource exactly fits the user's search, the process is complete. After finding the desired resource in this scenario, the user can stop here. He can then use the tool to accomplish his learning objectives. This situation will make it quick and simple for the user to use the resource he has chosen (Figs. 3 and 4).

Situation 2: When the suggested resource does not exactly match his search, we are compelled to locate an additional external resource to satisfy his need.

At this point, we are using an ontology-based information retrieval approach and the list of terms that best describe the user's desire (D). This method involves communicating

Fig. 3. The interface of a document found in the Digital educational platform

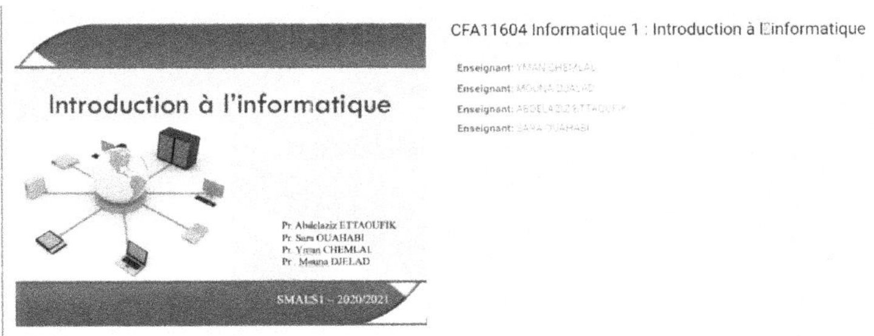

Fig. 4. The interface of a viewed course in the Digital educational platform

with the user while using a domain ontology to extract the entire domain from the query. The latter just needs to select the precise research area from a list provided by the system, and it will take care of identifying the appropriate resources.

7 Retrieval System

This approach relies on the use of a domain ontology to enrich the initial query by extracting relevant terms. The objective is to target the maximum number of documents belonging to a specific domain, in order to provide more precise and relevant results.

In this same approach, we encourage the interaction of the user with the system to refine his need and choose the domain that best corresponds to his request. Depending on the user's choices, the query is then adapted to take these preferences into account, which makes it possible to further refine the search results.

The implementation of this approach in the e-learning system is specifically aimed at targeting education-related documents. By involving the user in the information retrieval system (IRS), we seek to guarantee greater precision by allowing him to choose the desired domain.

The objective of this step is to search the Internet for all the documents corresponding to the user's query using the new enriched query. This allows us to deliver relevant and educational domain-specific results, leveraging domain ontology-based enrichment to refine the search.

By addressing the two situations, the user could request a resource through the e-learning system and conduct an external search on the Internet using the domain ontology, we account for the user's potential to conduct a combined search using our method (Fig. 5).

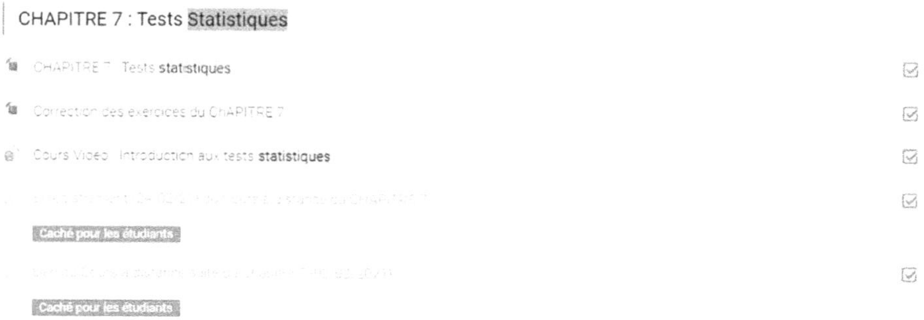

CHAPITRE 7 : Tests Statistiques

CHAPITRE 7   Tests statistiques

Correction des exercices du CHAPITRE 7

Cours Vidéo   Introduction aux tests statistiques

Caché pour les étudiants

Caché pour les étudiants

Fig. 5. The interface of a document found in the e-learning system

8   Evaluation

A complete Digital educational platform must be put up for testing, along with a method for information retrieval in the event that the system is unable to fully satisfy the user. on a preliminary stage, we manually conducted a series of experiments on e-learning platforms for particular searches. The searches conducted centered on particular areas that students had looked up. The goal was to assess how many inquiries could be answered by a targeted search using the E-Learning platform, as well as in other scenarios where the proposed information re-trieval approach was required.

Because our approach is based on the structure of the resource and the search that is done in the documents respects the organization of resources in E-Learning systems in accordance with the SCORM standard, the results obtained in the case of a search for a resource that exists in the platform represent a very high rate of relevance.

The information retrieval strategy used in the second scenario, which produced highly satisfactory results in terms of relevance, is related to the case's relevance.

9   Conclusion

In order to get the most pertinent findings, we presented in this study our information retrieval strategy that is designed to be integrated into an E-Learning system. Through user collaboration and the usage of ontologies, we established an information retrieval (IR) strategy. Our strategy attempts to first identify the papers in the resources that are offered that match the user's needs and adhere to the SCORM standard. When a response is unfavorable or incomplete, we turn to an enrichment strategy that has produced some very intriguing outcomes.

Our approach's major goal is to directly address user needs without the need to search for alternative resources. Combining these two methods improves our results and creates more fruitful study opportunities. In light of this, we are always enhancing our methodology to provide an information retrieval system that can both provide pertinent documents in a shorter amount of time and make recommendations of suitable documents for additional queries that are related.

References

1. Rokou, F.P., et al.: Modeling web-based educational systems: process design teaching model. Educ. Technol. Soc. **7**, 42–50 (2004)
2. H. Adelsberger et al., "The Essen Model: A Step Towards a Standard Learning Process.," http://citeseer.ist.psu.edu/515384.html, 2003.
3. Quemanda, J., Simon, B.: A use-case based model for learning resources in educational mediators. Educ. Technol. Soc. **6**, 149–163 (2003)
4. M. D. Merrill, "Knowledge Objects and Mental Models.," http://reusability.org/read, 2003.
5. George, G., M. Lal, A.: Review of ontology-based recommender systems in e-learning. Comput. Educ. **142**, 103642., ISSN 0360-1315 (2019). https://doi.org/10.1016/j.compedu.2019.103642
6. Asim, M.N., Wasim, M., Ghani Khan, M.U., Mahmood, N., Mahmood, W.: L'utilisation de l'ontologie dans la récupération: une étude sur la récupération textuelle, multilingue et multimédia. dans IEEE Access. **7**, 21662–21686 (2019). https://doi.org/10.1109/ACCESS.2019.2897849
7. Rastogi, N., Verma, P., Kumar, P.: Query expansion based on word Embeddings and ontologies for efficient information retrieval. Int. J. Adv. Comput. Sci. Appl. **12**(11), 367–373 (2021)
8. Kumar, R., Sharma, S.C.: Smart information retrieval using query transformation based on ontology and semantic-association. Int. J. Adv. Comput. Sci. Appl. **13**(4), 388–394 (2022)
9. Banu, J.F., Muneeshwari, P., Raja, K., Suresh, S., Latchoumi, T.P., Deepan, S.: Ontology based image retrieval by utilizing model annotations and content. In: 2022 12th International Conference on Cloud Computing, Data Science & Engineering (Confluence), pp. 300–305. IEEE (2022)
10. Zhan, J., Mao, Y., Liu, J., Guo, M., Zhang, Ma, S.: Optimizing dense retrieval model training with hard negatives. In: Proceedings of the 44th Annual International ACM SIGIR Conference on Research and Development in Information Retrieval (SIGIR 2021), pp. 1503–1512 (2021)
11. Jalal, A.A.: Text mining: design of Interactive Search Engine Based Regular ex- pressions of online automobile advertisements. Int. J. Eng. Pedagog. (iJEP). **10**(3), 35–48 (2020)
12. Selvalakshmi, B., Subramaniam, M.: Extraction intelligente d'informations sémantiques ba- sée sur une ontologie utilisant la sélection et la classification des caractéristiques. Clust. Comput. **22**(Suppl 5), 12871–12881 (2019). https://doi.org/10.1007/s10586-018-1789-8
13. Rocchio, J.: Relevance feedback in Information Retrieval. In: The Smart Retrieval System- Experiments In Automatic Doc (1971)
14. Beirade, F., Azzoune, H., Zegour, D.E.: Semantic query for Quranic ontology. J. King Saud Univ. Comput. Inf. Sci. **33**(6), 753–760.,ISSN 1319-1578 (2021). https://doi.org/10.1016/j.jksuci.2019.04.005
15. Rahayu, N.W., Ferdiana, R., Kusumawardani, S.S.: A systematic review of ontology use in E-learning recommender system, computers and education. Artif. Intell. **3**, 100047 (2022) ISSN 2666-920X
16. https://doi.org/10.1016/j.caeai.2022.100047

17. Sy, M.F., Ranwez, S., Montmain, J., Ranwez, V.: OBIRS-feedback, a reformulation method using a domain ontology. In: Conference in Information Retrieval and Applications 2012 (9th edition of CORIA), vol. 23, Bordeaux France (2012)
18. Zou, S., et al: Pre-trained language model based ranking in Baidu search. In: Proceedings of the 27th ACM SIGKDD International Conference on Knowledge Discovery and Data Mining (SIGKDD 2021), pp. 4014–4022 (2021)
19. Aimé, X., Fürst, F., Kuntz, P., Trichet, F.: REDENE-Documentary research assisted by adaptive domain ontologies. In: Conference on Information Retrieval and Applications 2008. CORIA 2008 (2008)
20. Sengupta, S., Banerjee, A., Chakrabarti, S.: Efficient data mining model for ques- tion retrieval and question analytics using semantic web framework in smart E-learning environment. I. J. Emerg. Technol. Learn. (iJET). 17(1), 4–17 (2022) Kassel, Germany: International Journal of Emerging Technology in Learning. Retrieved June 17, 2023 from https://www.learntech lib.org/p/220576/.
21. Mustapha, N.B., Zghal, H.B., Aufaure, M.-A., Ghézala, H.H.B.: Semantic search based on modular ontologies and case-based reasoning. In: 10th French-speaking Days of Knowledge Extraction and Management (EGC'2010) (2010)
22. Di Caprio, D., Santos-Arteaga, F.J., Tavana, M.: An information retrieval benchmarking model of satisfying and impatient users' behavior in online search environments. Expert Syst. Appl. 191, 116352., ISSN 0957-4174 (2022). https://doi.org/10.1016/j.eswa.2021.116352
23. Tahir, S., Hafeez, Y., Abbas, M.A., et al.: Smart learning objects retrieval for E-learning with contextual recommendation based on collaborative filtering. Educ. Inf. Technol. 27, 8631–8668 (2022). https://doi.org/10.1007/s10639-022-10966-0
24. Sarwar, S., Qayyum, Z.U., García-Castro, R., Safyan, M., Munir, R.F.: Ontology based E-learning framework: a personalized, adaptive and context aware model. Multimed. Tools. Appl. 78, 34745–34771 (2019)

Towards an Intelligent Automated Evaluation System for Python Powered by Large Language Models

Mariam Mahdaoui[1]([✉]) [iD], Said Nouh[1] [iD], and My Seddiq El Kasmi Alaoui[2] [iD]

[1] LTIM, Hassan II University of Casablanca, Casablanca, Morocco
mahdaoui.mariam@gmail.com
[2] LIS, Hassan II University, Casablanca, Morocco

Abstract. Evaluation allows learners to confirm their understanding of Python and strengthens their learning by confronting them with practical scenarios. Regular assessments enable students to identify their strengths and weaknesses, thus facilitating targeted progress. Moreover, evaluation provides valuable feedback, guiding learners towards better practices and increased mastery of the language. However, manual assessment systems have certain constraints, such as the lengthy time required for design and correction, the risk of promoting cheating through identical exercises for all learners, and a potential lack of objectivity and consistency, especially when multiple graders are involved. This underscores the critical need for automated Python evaluation systems, which can instantly and objectively analyze and correct the code submitted by learners. These systems also excel in providing personalized feedback, which is crucial in guiding learners toward better practices and increased mastery of the language. In this article, we present the evolution of our Semi Code Writing Intelligent Tutoring System into an automated evaluation system based on language models, notably ChatGPT-3.5 Turbo. This system provides formative and summative assessments with varying levels of difficulty, including Parsons Problems, writing code from scratch, and semi-code writing, where learners must complete a partially provided code.

Keywords: Automatic Assessment · ChatGPT · LLM · Parsons Puzzle · Python

1 Introduction

Evaluation systems play a crucial role in learning programming languages like Python. However, manual evaluation methods come with several constraints that can hinder the efficiency of the process. The time-consuming task of designing and preparing exercises, the potential for cheating through identical exercises, and the delay in providing feedback are all significant limitations. These constraints underscore the urgent need for a more efficient and effective evaluation system [1]. The limitations of manual evaluation systems highlight the necessity of automated solutions, which enable instant and objective analysis and correction of learners' code and provide personalized and immediate feedback, significantly reducing grading time. In this context, the emergence of

O. Zahour et al. (Eds.): ICTIM 2024, CCIS 2655, pp. 235–243, 2026.
https://doi.org/10.1007/978-3-032-15147-6_23

large language models (LLMs), such as ChatGPT, developed by OpenAI, opens new possibilities for education and assessment. LLMs can understand, generate, and analyze text at an advanced level, making it possible to automate complex tasks such as code correction, personalized feedback generation, and even creating interactive learning scenarios. We describe in this paper the conversion of our Semi Code Writing Intelligent Tutoring System (SCW-ITS) [2] into Semi Code Writing Evaluation System for Python (SCW-EvalPy), an automated evaluation system based on language models, most notably ChatGPT-3.5 Turbo [3]. This innovative approach allows learners to engage in various coding tasks, ranging from Parsons Problems to semi-code writing, where they either complete partially provided code or write code from scratch. The system ensures a more accurate assessment by incorporating a mix of these tasks. Completing pre-written code enables learners to focus on specific program sections, reinforcing their understanding of existing structures and logic while sharpening their coding abilities. Conversely, writing code from scratch demands a deeper grasp of the concepts, as learners must devise complete solutions, fostering creativity and problem-solving skills. This approach evaluates the learners' mastery of fundamental concepts and ability to apply them in real-world scenarios, enhancing their problem-solving skills and fostering independent coding abilities. Integrating large language models (LLMs) such as ChatGPT adds a layer of intelligence to the system, enabling more nuanced feedback and adaptive responses to students' errors. This accelerates and personalizes the learning process, allowing learners to receive targeted guidance that adapts to their needs and coding styles. This paper reviews related works and describes our initial system, SCW-ITSPy. We then present the new Semi-Code Writing Evaluation System for Python, outlining its architecture and key features and discussing them in depth. Finally, we conclude with a summary and propose potential directions for future research.

2 Related Works

Since the 1960s, researchers have been developing automated code evaluation systems to alleviate educators' grading burdens and enhance student learning outcomes. Over the years, these automatic evaluation systems have gained popularity in educational institutions as effective teaching tools, mainly due to advancements in educational technology [4–6]. They facilitate programming education by providing automated evaluations and feedback, guiding learners throughout the learning process. These systems accelerate instructional delivery and reduce teachers' time and effort on manual grading. Additionally, they contribute to improved learning outcomes and lower dropout rates [7]. Numerous contributors have advanced this field. For instance, Miguel Brito created Codeflex, a web-based platform that leverages problem-type repositories and problem-solving techniques to enhance students' programming skills. This platform also features competitive programming elements, enabling students to assess their coding abilities in a timed environment [8]. Haynes-Magyar developed Codespec, a self-directed learning platform offering various problem-solving methods, including pseudocode tasks, Parsons problems, Faded Parsons problems, fix-code exercises, and write-code challenges [9]. With the emergence of Large Language Models (LLMs), researchers have rapidly begun leveraging these technologies to create and refine automatic evaluation systems

[10]. For example, Sami Sarsa et al. investigated LLMs' natural language generation capabilities, specifically applying OpenAI Codex to produce programming exercises [11]. Likewise, Susanto et al. [12] developed an automated essay-scoring system based on the DeBERTa transformer model, while Marcin Jukiewicz [13] explored ChatGPT's potential for grading programming exercises.

3 Semi-code Writing Evaluation System for Python

This new SCW-EvalPy system is primarily designed for summative assessment. It uses the same exercise database as the first system while allowing for the addition of new exercises reserved explicitly for evaluation. These new exercises will not be available to students during their learning and formative assessment phases, ensuring an objective and separate evaluation process. This evaluation system retains four difficulty levels from the previous system while introducing a fifth level where learners must enter their entire response from scratch. Another significant advancement is integrating the GPT-3.5 Turbo model, which generates distractors and automatically provides detailed feedback. Artificial intelligence enriches evaluations by offering diverse errors and personalized feedback that adapts to each learner's needs and performance, making the evaluation process more dynamic and interactive. The GPT-3.5 Turbo model also corrects students' erroneous responses, providing error detection, corrections, and explanations. This enables a deeper understanding of mistakes, allowing learners to grasp why their initial approach was incorrect and how to improve it. By leveraging the power of AI, the system facilitates real-time feedback that guides students toward the correct solution, enhancing the learning process and fostering more autonomous problem-solving skills.

3.1 Architecture of SCW-EvalPy

The summative evaluation system functions as follows: the teacher initiates the process by setting up the exam, including details such as the start date and time, the number of exercises assessing the targeted competency, the difficulty level of each exercise, and the maximum time permitted for completion. When students begin the evaluation, each is assigned a unique exercise related to the same competency. The system randomly selects the exercises, while the distractors for the corresponding difficulty levels are generated using the LLM ChatGPT-3.5 model, ensuring each participant has a unique evaluation instance. The student completes the exam within the allotted time. For the code writing level, they can check their solution's output twice before submitting their final answer. The system records various traces of their activity, which vary depending on the difficulty level, such as the time spent on each exercise, the number of movements made, the number of attempts, and the errors corrected before submission. At the end of the exam, the system displays a summary to the student, including an overall score, a detailed score for each exercise, personalized feedback on the mistakes made, and suggestions for improvement. Fig. 1 below displays the flowchart of the SCW-EvalPy process.

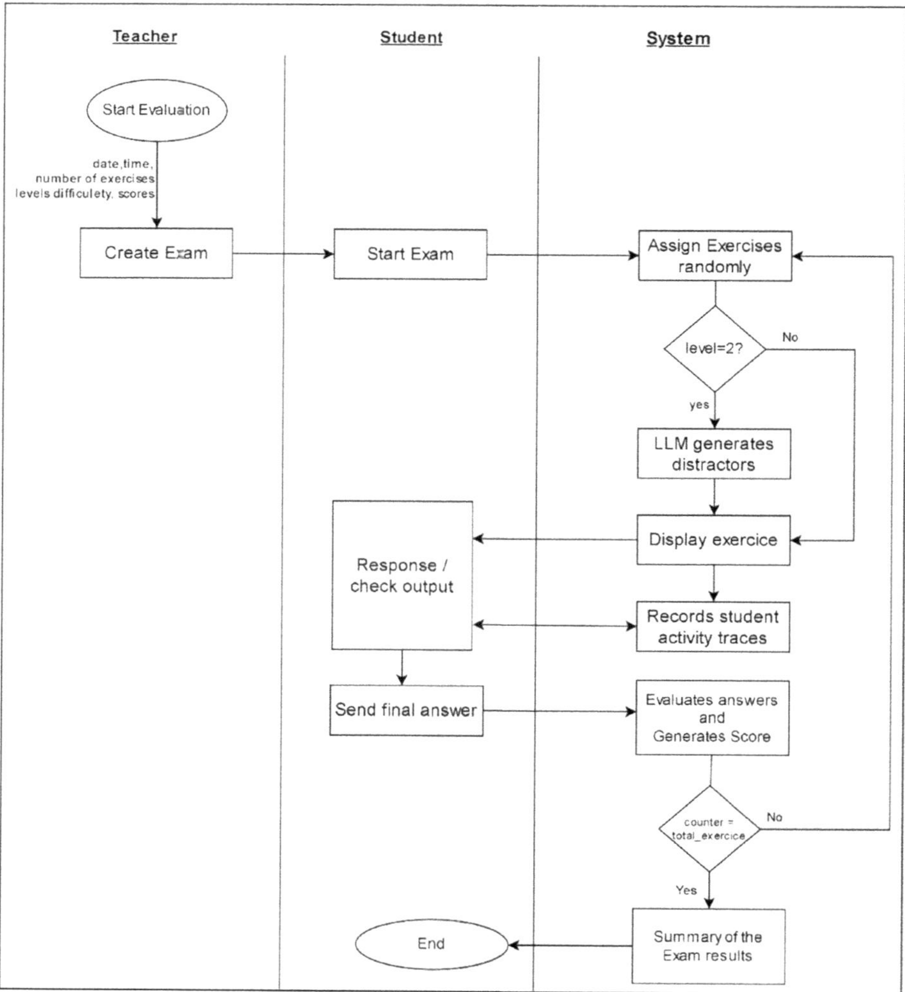

Fig. 1. Flowchart of the SCW-EvalPy

3.2 Multi-level Difficulty Assessments of SCW-EvalPy

SCW-EvalPy offers exercises at different levels, from beginner to advanced. This range helps assess both basic and more complex skills. The system has five difficulty levels:

- **Level 1:** Students reorder mixed lines of code in a classic Parsons Puzzle format. The system dynamically generates multiple correct solution variations, enhancing flexibility and encouraging adaptable problem-solving.
- **Level 2:** This level introduces distractors (incorrect lines) mixed with correct code. Students identify, filter, and order the proper lines. Large Language Models (LLMs) generate distractors and feedback, enriching the assessment.

- **Level 3:** In this level, students complete partially written code by filling in missing instructions. LLMs provide various valid solutions, promoting more profound understanding and flexibility in their coding approach.
- **Level 4:** Students reorganize and complete code with missing lines and no indentation, reinforcing structural understanding and programming practices like logical ordering and identifying gaps.
- **Level 5:** The final level requires students to write the complete solution from scratch, with two attempts to test their code before final submission. This level promotes independence, problem comprehension, and error management.

3.3 Integration of Large Language Models in SCW-EvalPy

SCW-EvalPy transforms the original system from a rule-based expert system to an AI-powered platform by integrating Large Language Models such as ChatGPT-3.5 Turbo. This upgrade enables the generation of distractors, providing multiple variations of correct solutions and adaptive feedback for Python exercises. Additionally, SCW-EvalPy introduces a new summative assessment system, allowing it to comprehensively evaluate learning progress and mastery, making it a complete formative and summative evaluation tool. The assessments become more varied and challenging by introducing AI-generated content, fostering a richer learning experience. Table 1 compiles the GPT-3.5 Turbo settings used for each level.

Table 1. The parameters for GPT-3.5 Turbo are used for each level.

Levels	ChatGPT Functionality	Temp.	Top_p	Frequency Penalty	Presence Penalty
Levels 1, 3 & 4	Generates multiple variations of correct solutions.	2	0.9	0.3	0.3
Level 2	Introduces syntax and semantic errors as distractors.	1	0.9	0.3	0.2
Level 5	Corrects student responses and provides feedback.	1.5	1	0	0

4 Methods and Results

4.1 Generating Multiple Variations of Correct Solutions

To make GPT generate truly different solutions for the same exercise, it's important to specify this clearly in the prompt. Simply asking for multiple answers with $n > 0$ often gives similar solutions, even with high-temperature settings. For example, if asked for a solution to a factorial exercise, GPT might always use recursion.

To ensure GPT generates distinctly different solutions, we give it a detailed prompt asking for five variations that employ other methods or variable names. For example, it could produce one solution using recursion, another with a while loop, a third with a for loop, a fourth using alternative variable names, and a fifth leveraging list comprehension. However, the latter may be slightly advanced for beginners. To tailor solutions for beginner levels, we also specify that GPT should act as a Python instructor for beginners. If we want to focus on evaluating specific methods, such as a while loop, we include that requirement in the prompt.

We then choose one solution at random to present to the student, and each solution is verified through unit tests to ensure it works correctly and is suitable.

We generated ten variations for each of the 20 different exercises. The accuracy of the generated solutions is 90%, with minimal errors. All incorrect responses are due to formatting issues related to the desired output. The diversity of the variations is 80% across all exercises. Two variations are considered distinct even if they follow the same logic but differ in variable names.

4.2 Generating Distractors

To address the issue of generating varied distractors for incorrect code lines, we use a combination of Abstract Syntax Tree (AST) analysis and a Large Language Model to create more diverse and contextually accurate errors. An AST analysis is performed on the provided code line to understand its structure. Based on this analysis, we select a random error description from our error library, which pairs each AST node type with a list of potential error descriptions. This approach ensures that the error type generated is relevant to the analyzed code structure.

We craft a prompt that combines the correct code line with the selected error description, instructing GPT to generate an erroneous line version that matches the specified error. This approach ensures that each distractor is relevant and unique, avoiding repetitive errors.

To validate the outputs, we use string comparison to ensure the erroneous line differs from the correct one, ignoring minor errors such as spaces. An expert Python teacher assesses the coherence and hallucinations of ten distractors generated from ten different AST nodes at various temperatures. Coherence measures how logically consistent the distractors are with the error description. Table 2 below shows that at a temperature of 1, the distractors are highly coherent, with a 95% accuracy rate and no hallucinations. At temperature 1.5, coherence drops slightly to 90%, with hallucinations appearing in 10% of cases. However, at temperature 2, coherence drops sharply to 10%, while hallucinations rise to 90%, indicating that higher temperatures significantly reduce the quality of the generated distractors.

Table 2. Impact of temperature on GPT-Generated distractors

Temperature	Coherence	Hallucinations
1	95%	0%
1.5	90%	10%
2	10%	90%

4.3 Generating Hints

To guide students, we prompt GPT to generate hints that progressively reveal more information. The first hint offers minimal details, encouraging students to think critically about possible solutions. The second hint provides additional guidance without revealing the answer, giving students more context while requiring them to engage in problem-solving.

Our expert Python instructor validates each generated hint to ensure that they are not only accurate but also progressively structured to aid students in solving problems step-by-step. Table 3 illustrates the effects of different temperature settings on the quality of hints generated by GPT. At a temperature of 1, hints are accurate but show limited progression. Raising the temperature to 1.5 retains accuracy while significantly enhancing the quality of progressively structured hints without introducing hallucinations. However, the accuracy drops, and hallucinations increase sharply. These results indicate that a temperature of 1.5 is optimal for generating clear and progressively supportive hints. This test generated ten hints for each of the **50 different lines of code** to evaluate consistency across varied examples.

Table 3. Impact of Temperature on GPT-Generated Hint Quality

Temperature	Correct Hint	Progressive Hint	Hallucination Hint
1	99%	25%	0%
1.5	99%	90%	0%
2	30%	15%	70%

5 Conclusion and Perspective

SCW-EvalPy presents several advantages that significantly enhance the assessment process for both students and teachers. By presenting exercises with distinct solutions and varied distractors, the system ensures that each student encounters unique problems. This approach effectively reduces the chances of direct copying, fostering individualized learning and promoting assessment fairness. This tailored approach to assessments promotes fairness and effectiveness in evaluating student progress.

For teachers, the analytics generated by SCW-EvalPy offer valuable insights into class performance, highlighting common mistakes and trends in comprehension. This data empowers educators to adjust their teaching strategies, enhancing their learning experience.

Future work will focus on SCW-EvalPy's capabilities in evaluating and scoring handwritten answers, utilizing large language models and machine learning techniques. Additionally, further research will analyze the direct impact of SCW-EvalPy on student learning outcomes. By investigating how tailored assessments influence student performance, retention, and engagement, we aim to understand how technology can be used to improve the educational process on a deeper level. This data will guide the evolution of SCW-EvalPy, ensuring it continues to provide a valuable and adaptive tool for educators and learners alike.

Acknowledgements. This initiative was developed for the Faculty of Sciences Ben M'Sik as part of the research project "A shared platform for handling practical work and scientific experimentation."

References

1. Pereira, F.D., Oliveira, E., Cristea, A., et al.: Early dropout prediction for programming courses supported by online judges. In: Artificial Intelligence in Education: 20th International Conference, AIED 2019, pp. 67–72. Springer, Chicago, IL, USA (2019)
2. Mahdaoui, M., Nouh, S., Alaoui, M.E., Rachdi, M.: Semi code writing intelligent tutoring system for learning python. J. Eng. Sci. Technol. **18**(5), 2548–2560 (2023)
3. Ye, J., Chen, X., Xu, N., et al.: A comprehensive capability analysis of gpt-3 and gpt-3.5 series models. arXiv preprint, arXiv:2303.10420 (2023)
4. Wang, J.-Y., Liang, J.-C., Chang, C.-c.: The coding here platform for programming courses. Inf. Eng. Express. **8**(2), 1–14 (2022)
5. Hidalgo-Céspedes, J., Marín-Raventós, G., Calderón-Campos, M.E.: Online judge support for programming teaching. In: Proceedings of the 2020 XLVI Latin American Computing Conference (CLEI), pp. 522–530, Loja, Ecuador (2020)
6. Zinovieva, I.S., et al.: The use of online coding platforms as additional distance tools in programming education. J. Phys. Conf. Ser. **1840**(1) IOP Publishing, 012029 (2021)
7. Pereira, F.D., et al.: Early dropout prediction for programming courses supported by online judges. In: Proceedings of the Artificial Intelligence in Education: 20th International Conference, AIED 2019, pp. 67–72. Springer, Cham, Chicago, IL, USA (2019)
8. Brito, M., Gonçalves, C.: Codeflex: a web-based platform for competitive programming. In: Proceedings of the 2019 14th Iberian Conference on Information Systems and Technologies (CISTI), pp. 1–6. IEEE, Coimbra, Portugal (2019)
9. Haynes-Magyar, C.C., Haynes-Magyar, N.J.: Codespec: a computer programming practice environment. In: Proceedings of the 2022 ACM Conference on International Computing Education Research2022, vol. 2, pp. 32–34. Association for Computing Machinery, United States (2022)
10. Messer, M., Brown, N.C., Kölling, M., Shi, M.: Automated grading and feedback tools for programming education: a systematic review. ACM Trans. Comput. Educ. **24**(1), 1–43 (2024)

11. Sarsa, S., Denny, P., Hellas, A., et al.: Automatic generation of programming exercises and code explanations using large language models. In: Proceedings of the 2022 ACM Conference on International Computing Education Research, pp. 27–43. Association for Computing Machiner, Switzerland (2022)
12. Susanto, H., Gunawan, A.A.S., Hasani, M.F.: Development of automated essay scoring system using deberta as a transformer-based language model. In: Proceedings of the Computational Methods in Systems and Software, pp. 202–215. Springer, Nature Switzerland, Cham (2023)
13. Jukiewicz, M.: The future of grading programming assignments in education: the role of ChatGPT in automating the assessment and feedback process. Think. Skills Creat. **52**, 101522 (2024)

Revolutionizing Agriculture with LoRa: Intelligent Crop Monitoring and Autonomic Irrigation

Aitlmoudden Othmane[✉], Khaddar Almahdi, and Nawal Sael

Laboratory of Modeling and Information Technology, Faculty of sciences Ben M'SIK, University Hassa II, Casablanca, Morocco
othmane.aitlmoudden-etu@etu.univh2c.ma

Abstract. As the global population surpasses 7.2 billion with an upward trend, the omnipresent threat of food scarcity intensifies, necessitating the advancement of agricultural methodologies. This study introduces a comprehensive smart farming framework utilizing LoRa technology to address water scarcity and optimize resource usage.

The developed prototype employs dual ESP32 ARDUINO and LoRa boards: one interfaced with environmental sensors within the field to measure temperature, soil moisture, and water flow, and a secondary one positioned within a 10 km radius connected via WiFi.

The collected data is relayed to BLYNK Platform for analysis, enabling precise, automated control of irrigation systems, thus saving farmers' time, costs, and energy.

This system, tested in morocco more precisely the region of Doukkala diverse agricultural landscape, where agriculture is integral to the economy, leverages IoT and sensor technologies to transform traditional farming practices. The suite of sensors deployed ensures optimal watering of crops.

Managed through a mobile application with cloud integration, the system provides a robust solution even in areas of low internet connectivity. Utilizing renewable energy, this approach offers a resilient, accessible means for farmers to gauge environmental compatibility, supported by a dedicated information-providing website. This paper highlights the implications of intelligent crop monitoring combined with autonomous irrigation as a scalable solution for achieving sustainable agriculture in an increasingly populous world.ct.

Keywords: Smart agriculture · IoT · Agricultural field monitoring · Irrigation system · BLYNK · LoRa

1 Introduction

As the global population continues to escalate, the demand for efficient, sustainable agricultural practices becomes critical. To this end, we introduce an innovative smart irrigation system leveraging Arduino microcontrollers and LoRa communication technology to enable precise monitoring and management of water resources. In an industry

O. Zahour et al. (Eds.): ICTIM 2024, CCIS 2655, pp. 244–256, 2026.
https://doi.org/10.1007/978-3-032-15147-6_24

that critically depends on water and is plagued by its wastage, our system offers a transformative solution to these enduring challenges [1].

Employing advanced sensor technology, our system accurately gauges a suite of environmental factors — temperature, soil moisture, and necessary water volume [2]. These sensors feed their data into an Arduino module stationed on-site, which then communicates with a secondary module within a potential 5KM range over the LoRa protocol, a range expandable with the integration of high-gain antennas. This network is interconnected via BLYNK cloud services — a robust platform facilitating real-time data syncing and remote irrigation control [3].

What distinguishes this approach is the empowerment it affords farmers, allowing them to administer irrigation equipment promptly, adapting to the changing needs of their fields, and thereby optimizing crop yield and quality. It stands as a stark contrast to the manually operated systems that dominate the sector, and which are steadily being replaced by semi-automatic and fully automatic methodologies [4].

Our testament to the power of IoT in revolutionizing agricultural practices, yielding increased growth states, improved storage, and enhanced product quality, is underscored by the system's potential for scalability and adaptability across a multitude of farming environments [1, 2]. By ushering in an era of smart irrigation systems that converse with the cloud, we stride toward a future where technology enables an unprecedented balance between the needs of human consumption and the preservation of our planet's most precious resource: water.

Finally, looking beyond immediate water management, this paper demonstrates how IoT-enabled smart agriculture systems like the one proposed can form the basis for an interconnected framework of agricultural technologies. This provides a foundation for future research and development that can continue to propel the sector forward, responding to global food production needs with innovation and consideration for environmental constraints [3, 4].

By embracing these technologies, we move towards a future where the agricultural industry can meet the demands of an ever-growing population sustainably. The system we propose in this paper is a step towards that future, offering a critical intersection of efficiency, conservation, and productivity.

2 Smart Irrigation

In the contemporary landscape of agricultural technology, the advent of smart irrigation systems represents a watershed moment, garnering increased interest from the scientific community for its potential to significantly enhance water conservation [4]. Smart irrigation embodies an integration of precision and efficiency, optimizing water usage in a manner that is economically, socially, and environmentally responsible. Central to the concept of smart irrigation is the aspiration to reduce human labor, conserve water, and curtail energy consumption.

Addressing the burgeoning global food demand, prompted by escalating population figures, necessitates the development of advanced farming tools that can assuage the challenges farmers face concerning crop quantity and quality. Thus, researchers are tasked with the innovation of sophisticated irrigation systems that empower farmers with the capabilities to cultivate quality produce competitively. Despite progress in the realm of smart irrigation, solutions that can precisely measure water flow remain elusive.

This paper posits an advanced irrigation strategy that not only integrates the innovative capabilities of smart systems, such as real-time soil moisture profiles and temperature sensing—given that crop vitality is sensitive to thermal fluctuations—but it also endeavors to provide a comprehensive solution that mitigates waterlogging risks and facilitates optimal growing conditions. Various sensors implemented within this system execute meticulous parameter measurements, furnishing farmers with actionable insights and affording them unprecedented control over their agricultural practices. The system delineated herein transcends conventional irrigation technology, embarking on a new frontier marked by intelligence, autonomy, and sustainability in agricultural water management.

3 Literature Review

In the contemporary discourse of smart irrigation literature, a plethora of methods have been explored, incorporating a variety of devices and communication technologies.

The confluence of cost-effective and globally accessible innovations such as the ESP8266 and LoRa stand out for their ability to diminish operational costs and extend control across geographies [1].

While the ESP8266 acts as a WiFi-extension to Arduino without necessitating direct internet access, LoRa distinguishes itself by operating on unlicensed bands, further cutting down transmission costs and facilitating a network of tightly interconnected TTGO boards [1].

The literature spans diverse approaches, from using GSM, GPRS, and the cost-prohibitive ZigBee protocols—now considered outdated—to novel applications such as Li-Fi with its enhanced bandwidth capabilities [5].

The efficacy of Dual Tone Multiple Frequency (DTMF) based circuit-switching and wireless sensor networks (WSN) for irrigation control has also been documented, tested in prototype environments for their practical viability [1, 2].

Notably, the integration of autonomous robotic systems equipped for various agricultural tasks—from moisture detection to pest control—illustrates the potential for intelligent, remote-controlled interventions in the field, harnessed through sensor-augmented microcontrollers and raspberry pi incorporating ZigBee modules [2].

Additionally, IoT's profound influence on agriculture is exemplified through robust hardware setups that gather diverse environmental data, employing classifiers for rapid diagnostics of crop health, which emphasizes the reduction of both time and resources in soil testing [3].

Underpinning these technological advances is the enduring objective of optimizing water usage through precision agriculture. This aim is brought to fruition through Raspberry Pi-based systems that, in tandem with cloud computing, meticulously calculate crop-specific water requirements, thereby enhancing crop yields while conserving water [4]. Moreover, the strategic development of low-cost soil monitoring systems in wireless networks like ZigBee offers the promise of reliable and accessible data transmission, thus facilitating comprehensive data analysis [6].

Collectively, these studies underscore a trend towards more sophisticated, interconnected, and user-friendly agricultural technologies that promise to significantly advance the field of smart irrigation. With the progressive convergence of sensor technologies, wireless communication, and IoT, the literature indicates a promising horizon for smart irrigation systems that are efficient, reliable, and scalable.

4 Our Proposed System Architecture

The system comprises both software and hardware units. An ESP8266 Node MCU board, LoRa transceiver module, Nano Arduino, relay, water pump, and several sensors are all part of the hardware, The software comprises BLYNK apps and Arduino IDE (Fig. 1).

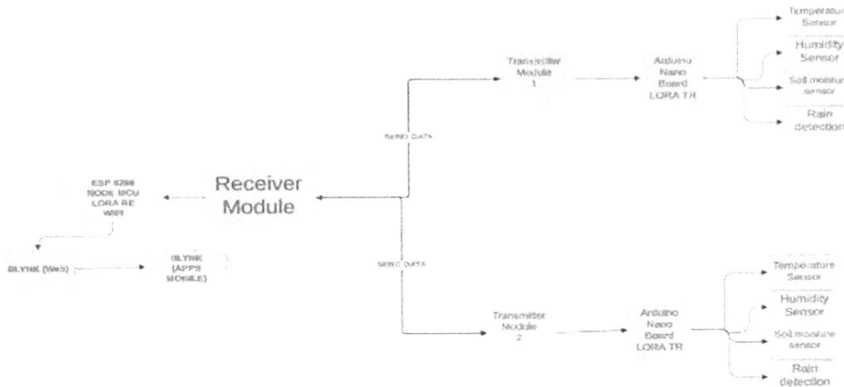

Fig. 1. System Design

4.1 Hardware Used

A. ESP8266 Node MCU

The Node MCU iteration of the ESP8266 board comes equipped with an integrated protocol, enabling the onboard microcontroller to effortlessly join Wi-Fi networks. This cost-effective unit is easily programmed through the Arduino Integrated Development Environment (IDE). Operating on a 3.3 V power supply, it boasts a high clock rate. Its General- Purpose Input/Output (GPIO) pins facilitate the incorporation of diverse sensors efficiently, due to their swift operational capacity. In addition, it possesses ample flash memory, which provides the benefit of extended data storage capabilities (Fig. 2).

B. LoRa Transceiver

LoRa stands out as a widely-adopted wireless modality for extensive-range IoT communication. It embodies a suite of elements including a radio layer, General-Purpose

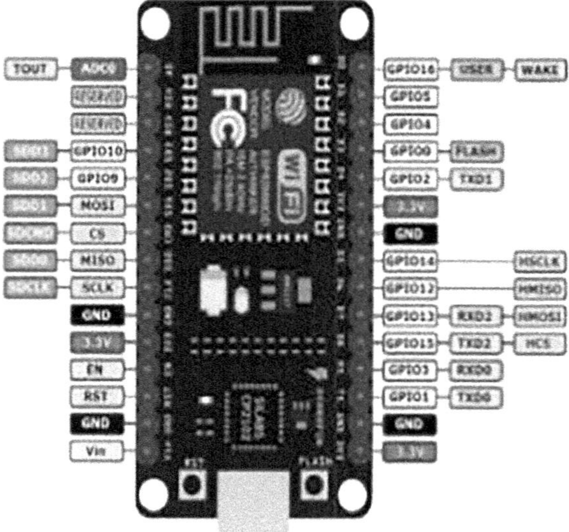

Fig. 2. ESP8266 Node MCU Board

Input/Output (GPIO) pins, interface buses, and a comprehensive protocol stack, alongside a Universal Asynchronous Receiver/Transmitter (UART) [7]. The UART serves as an interface connecting the microcontroller to the LoRa transmission module, essential for oversight and control uses.

This technology enables transmissions exceeding 5 km in urban settings and surpasses 15 km in rural locales, all while maintaining low energy consumption (Fig. 3).

Fig. 3. LoRa Transceiver

C. Arduino NANO

The Arduino Nano is a compact, microcontroller-based board that is part of the Arduino platform, popular for its user-friendly nature and suitability for embedded systems projects. The board is characterized by its small form factor, making it ideal for space-constrained applications. It operates on an ATmega328 microcontroller, which provides the necessary computational power and flexibility for a wide range of scientific and technical tasks. Offering 14 digital input/output pins, with 6 that can be used as PWM outputs, and 8 analog inputs, the Nano is highly versatile. The board's connectivity features include UART, SPI, and I2C, enabling communication with sensors and other devices (Fig. 4).

Fig. 4. Arduino Nano

D. Sensors

1. Soil Moisture Sensor

A soil moisture sensor functions as a quantitative tool to measure soil hydration levels. It employs key soil characteristics, including resistivity and dielectric permittivity [8], to accurately assess moisture content.

Engineered with an expansive sensing scope, the sensor's electrodes are coated with platinum to enhance performance through increased efficiency. Economically viable for agricultural use, its corrosion-resistant construction and durability render it a cost-effective investment for farmers, promising an extended operational life.

2. DHT 22 Sensor

The DHT22 sensor is a widely-used, digital temperature and humidity monitor known for its simplicity and cost-effectiveness. It consists of a capacitive humidity sensor and a thermistor, which together provide relatively accurate readings for ambient temperature and moisture. With a single digital pin connection, it's compatible with microcontroller platforms like Arduino, making it ideal for a variety of DIY projects and prototypes in climate control and monitoring applications.

3. Rain Sensor

A rain sensor is an electronic device engineered to detect raindrops through conductivity, often using water-sensitive components that alter the resistance of the circuit upon getting wet. It is frequently employed in meteorology, automobiles for automated wipers, and home automation systems. Compact and responsive, rain sensors serve as essential tools for real-time weather monitoring and water-dependent automation tasks (Fig. 5).

  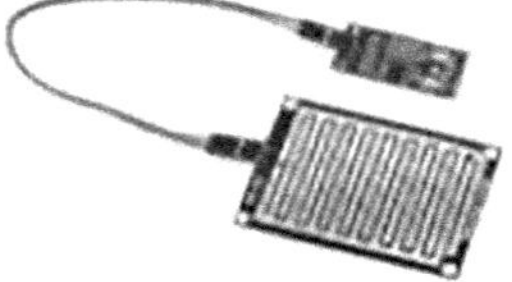

Fig. 5. Sensor

4. Relay and Water Pump

A relay switch serves as the intermediary connecting the water pump to the Nano Arduino board, thereby controlling the irrigation to the crops via the pump. The relay is capable of toggling the water flow based on the plants' requirements (Figs. 6 and 7).

Fig. 6. Relais

Fig. 7. Water Pump

4.2 Software Used

A. Arduino IDE

The Arduino Integrated Development Environment (IDE) is an open-source software that provides an intuitive programming platform for the Arduino hardware ecosystem.

It amalgamates a code editor, compiler, and debugger that facilitate programming in C and C++ [9].

The IDE supports the development of interactive electronic projects by abstracting complex tasks such as memory management, allowing both novices and professionals to develop code with ease. It promotes an iterative design process, enabling rapid prototyping and testing across various Arduino boards, which is pivotal in the advancement of digital computing in multidisciplinary scientific research.

B. Fritzing Simulator

Fritzing is a versatile, open-source hardware initiative that offers a powerful virtual simulation environment for the prototyping of electronic projects. It provides users with a comprehensive suite of tools for designing and modeling interactive digital circuits without the need for physical components. Its user-friendly interface includes features for schematic capture, PCB layout design, and interactive breadboarding, which promote a seamless transition from concept to fabrication. Fritzing's capacity to visually emulate circuitry makes it an invaluable educational resource for understanding the intricacies of electronic design, enhancing collaborative experimentation, and documentation in the realm of scientific research and development.

C. BLYNK IoT

BLYNK is a highly innovative platform that empowers developers to create Internet of Things (IoT) applications with minimal hardware and software resources. It offers a user-friendly environment for developing custom apps for controlling and monitoring IoT devices. By utilizing widgets in a drag-and-drop interface, BLYNK streamlines the design of interfaces for real-time data visualization and control. The platform supports a wide range of microcontroller boards and communication protocols [10], making it versatile for various applications. It's particularly noteworthy for its ability to rapidly prototype designs, which significantly accelerates the development cycle in scientific research involving IoT, from environmental monitoring systems to smart grids and beyond.

5 Methodology

The project comprises the following modules:

A. Trasnsmitter Circuit:

The transmitter module are shown in Fig. 8. It includes a Nano Arduino, LoRa transceiver, relay switch, water pump, and a variety of sensors [12] (DHT22 sensor, Rain sensor, Soil moisture sensor) [11]. The Nano Arduino collects the data from these sensors and sends it via LoRa for transmission.

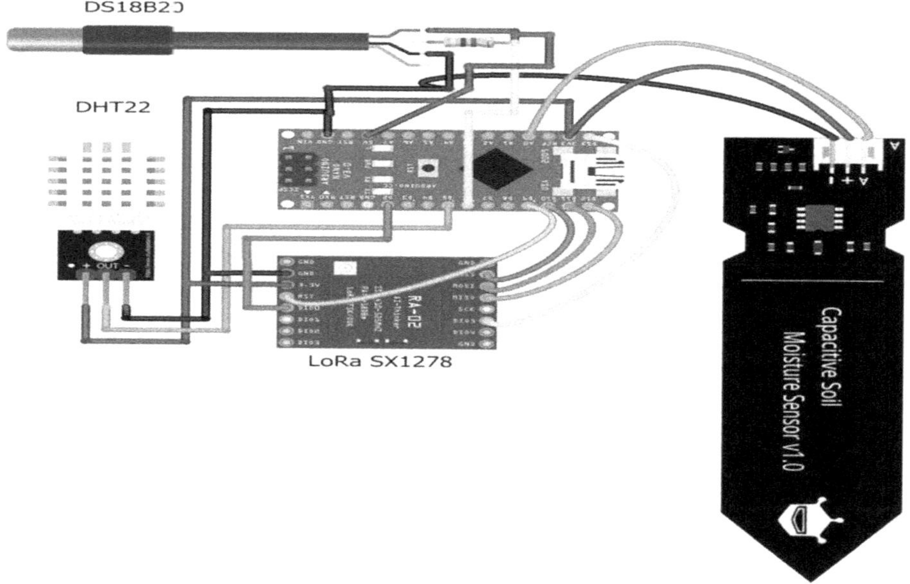

Fig. 8. Trasnsmitter Circuit

B. Receiver Circuit:

The depicted receiver unit in Fig. 9 is composed of an ESP8266 module [13], and a LoRa transceiver. This ESP8266 unit collects data relayed by the sensors via the LoRa link. The irrigation process triggers automatically by analyzing and comparing the real-time sensor readings against pre-set moisture thresholds, which are adjustable to cater to various crop types.

When sensor measurements drop beneath these thresholds, the Arduino Nano activates a command to start the water pump, initiating field irrigation.

Consequently, the system facilitates automated watering by responding to the current sensor data.

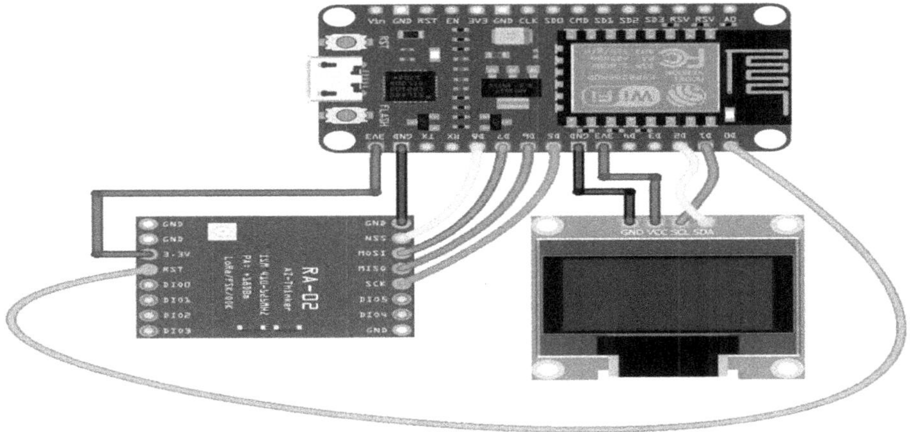

Fig. 9. Receiver Circuit

C. Communication Module:

Data is consistently transmitted to the agriculturist's mobile device via internet connectivity. This collected sensor data—encompassing variables such as temperature, humidity, soil moisture, and the operational state of the water pump—is relayed to the BLYNK IoT Cloud to undergo subsequent analytical processing.

The farmer has the ability to access and scrutinize this archived dataset from the cloud repository for informed agricultural decision-making.

6   Analysis

The Arduino Nano interfaces with a multitude of sensors for real-time tracking, as well as a relay switch, a water pump, and the LoRa transmitter, which facilitates low-power consumption and extended-range spread spectrum communications. This module's function is to frequently dispatch data to the Node MCU board. At the receiver end, the ESP8266 microcontroller is paired with both à LoRa receiver and an OLED display within the receiver unit.

A 7805 voltage regulator is employed to reduce the input voltage from 10 V to 5 V to accommodate the battery's requirements. Through a mobile application, the farmer is endowed with the capability to observe field conditions and also access historical data hosted on the BLYNK IoT Cloud services.

Figure 10 illustrates the mobile app's user interface. It features an LED template to denote rainfall and waterpump activity. Additionally, a gauge template presents the sensor-collected data, including humidity levels,temperaturevalues, soil temperature and soil moisture content.

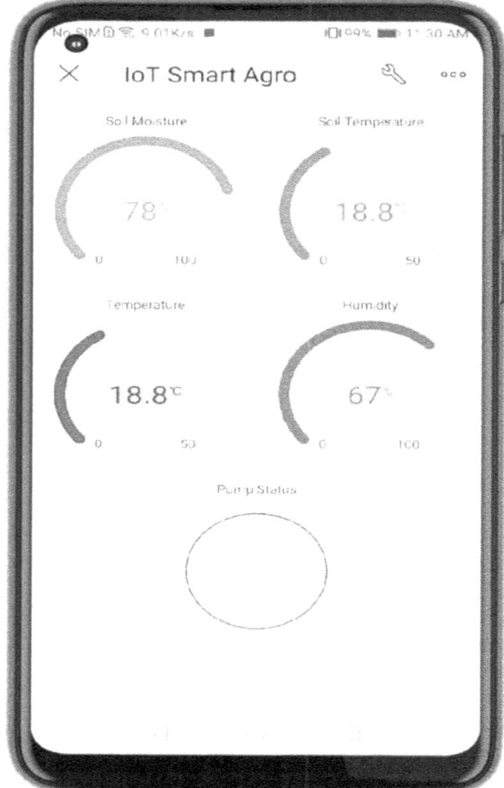

Fig. 10. Application Interface

7 Results and Discussion

The ESP8266 microcontroller effectively communicates detected parameters such as soil moisture levels, ambient temperature, and atmospheric humidity to the Blynk application for real-time visualization under varying environmental conditions. The system is designed to activate an irrigation pump when a reduction in soil moisture is measured, ensuring optimal watering conditions. Conversely, precipitation is detected through the activation of a rain status indicator, which concurrently deactivates the irrigation pump to prevent overwatering. Analysis of conventional agricultural watering practices highlights the critical need for judicious water management. Therefore, the implementation of this intelligent irrigation strategy contributes to water conservation by dynamically adjusting water delivery to the agricultural fields and providing continual crop status updates, thus serving as an informative feedback loop for agriculturalists.

This feedback loop is essential in reducing the unnecessary application of water, thereby aligning with sustainable agricultural practices. The smart system offers crucial data that facilitates more informed decision-making by the farmers regarding the watering schedules and quantities. This strategic approach to irrigation not only conserves water but also enhances crop yield and quality by ensuring that the crops receive the right amount of water at the right time. Furthermore, automatic adjustments made by the system in response to rain promote the efficient use of natural precipitation, further optimizing the irrigation process. In sum, the integration of the ESP8266 microcontroller with the Blynk app forms the backbone of an advanced irrigation management system that supports sustainable farming by merging real-time soil and climate analytics with automated irrigation control.

8 Conclusion

The Lora-enabled surveillance architecture presents an efficient and secure mechanism for supervising agricultural terrains.

By automating the watering process, this intelligent mechanism substantially diminishes the squandering of water resources, whilst permitting cultivators to oversee crop conditions via a smartphone interface. Data preservation is executed within BLYNK IoT Cloud, offering agriculturists the capability to retrospectively access historical field data as required. This characteristic lessens the demand for manual oversight, empowering farmers with the convenience to supervise their fields ubiquitously. Economically advantageous, the apparatus demands a negligible quantum of energy for sensor operation. Utilizing a transceiver that circumvents common Wi-Fi-related challenges, this system simplifies installation across farming environments. Its design allows for straightforward, remote modifications, facilitating adaptability in agricultural management. Adoption of this system stands to bolster crop yield efficiency significantly.

Furthermore, this conservation of resources aligns with ecological sustainability goals, as the precision in water application reduces environmental stress. The low energy requirement of the system's sensors, coupled with its cost-efficiency, underscores its practicality for widespread adoption among farming communities. The Lora-based network's robust signal transmission enhances the reliability of the monitoring system, ensuring consistent communication even in remote or rural areas, often hampered by conventional Wi-Fi connectivity issues. The modular nature of the system architecture affords scalability and customization, allowing for seamless integration of additional sensors and modifications based on evolving agronomic needs. This flexibility ensures that the system remains relevant and up-to-date with the latest agricultural practices. Implementing this technology translates into a tangible increase in productivity and resource management, marking it as a pivotal tool for modern agronomy and sustainable farming initiatives.

9 Limitations and Future Studies

The successful integration of smart farming technologies necessitates that agriculturalists acquire a thorough understanding and proficiency in utilizing these tools, a challenge that currently inhibits the widespread adoption in less developed regions. Limited internet connectivity, due to inadequate communication infrastructures in isolated farming communities, presents a substantial obstacle, potentially undermining the functionality of remote monitoring systems. Addressing these challenges requires educational initiatives directed at farmers to familiarize them with intelligent agricultural techniques, and the development of more user-friendly mobile applications.

Future advancements of the monitoring system could include the integration of additional sensors capable of gauging soil parameters such as pH levels and the concentrations of nitrogen, phosphorus, and potassium (NPK). The assimilation of such sensors would equip farmers with the capability to detect soil nutrient deficits and implement corrective measures. Furthermore, an associated web portal could offer vital insights about soil amendment procedures, including the precise quantities of lime or sulfur required to modify soil pH in accordance with the specific needs of different crops.

References

1. Aitlmoudden, O., Housni, M., Safeh, N., Namir, A.: A microservices-based framework for scalable data analysis in agriculture with IoT integration. Int. J. Interactive Mobile Technol. (iJIM). **17**(19), 147–156 (2023)
2. Dehbi, A., Bakhouyi, A., Dehbi, R., Talea, M.: MOOCs in smart education: comparative study by applying AHP and COPRAS method. Int. J. Emerg. Technol. Learn (iJET). **17**(08), 61–74 (2022). https://doi.org/10.3991/ijet.v17i08.27871
3. Priyadharshini. M.J.G., Hariharasudhan, B., Neelakandan, R., Arvind, R., et al.: Review on IoT based smart agriculture monitoring system. IJRAR-Int. J. Res. Anal. Rev. (IJRAR). **9**(2), 38–43 (2022)
4. Aitlmoudden, O., Bakhouyi, A., Safeh, N., Aitdaoud, M., Sael, N.: Comparative analysis of the IoT architectures for smart agriculture: methodological study using the AHP and COPRAS. J. Hunan. **51**(5) (2024)
5. Deepa, B., Anusha, C., Devi, P.C.: Smart Agriculture Using IOT. In: Advances in Intelligent Systems and Computing, pp. 11–19. Springer Singapore (2020). https://doi.org/10.1007/978-981-15-5400-1_2
6. Senthil Kumar. A., Suresh, G., Lekashri, S., Babu Loganathan, G., Manikandan, R.: Smart agriculture system with E–carbage using IoT. Int. J. Mod. Agric. **10**(1) (2021)
7. Sekaran, K., Meqdad, M.N., Kumar, P., Rajan, S., Kadry, S.: Smart agriculture management system using in- ternet of things. TELKOMNIKA (Telecommun. Comput. El. Control). **18**(3), 1276–1285 (2020). https://doi.org/10.12928/telkomnika.v18i3.14029
8. Srilakshmi, A.. Rakkini, J., Sekar, K.R., Manikandan, R.: A comparative study on internet of things (IoT) and its applications in smart agriculture. Pharm. J. **10**(2), 260–264 (2018). https://doi.org/10.5530/pj.2018.2.46
9. Saranya, T., Desy, C., Sridevi, S., Anbananthen, K.S.M.: A comparative study of deep learning and internet of things for precision agriculture. Eng. Appl. Artif. Intell. **122**, 106034 (2023). https://doi.org/10.1016/j.engappai.2023.106034
10. Dawson, T.P., Perryman, A.H., Osborne, T.M.: Modelling impacts of climate change on global food security. Clim. Chang. **134**(3), 429–440 (2014). https://doi.org/10.1007/s10584-014-1277-y
11. Sinha, B.B., Dhanalakshmi, R.: Recent advancements and challenges of internet of things in smart agriculture: a survey. Futur. Gener. Comput. Syst. **126**, 169–184 (2022). https://doi.org/10.1016/j.future.2021.08.006
12. Boursianis, A.D., et al.: Internet of things (IoT) and agricultural unmanned aerial vehicles (UAVs) in smart farming: a comprehensive review. Internet Things. **18**, 100–187 (2022). https://doi.org/10.1016/j.iot.2020.100187

Improving Dialectal Sentiment Analysis: A Contextual Approach Using Multilingual Embeddings for Darija and Other Arabic Dialects Transcoding

Hasnae Sakhi[✉] and Sanaa El Filali

LTIM - Faculty of sciences Ben M'sik - Hassan II University, Casablanca, Morocco
hasnae.sakhi-etu@etu.univh2c.ma, sanaa.elfilali@univh2c.ma

Abstract. This research focuses on improving sentiment analysis for the Moroccan dialect (Darija) by transcoding it into Modern Standard Arabic (MSA) to leverage existing NLP tools. Darija presents unique challenges for natural language processing due to its lack of extensive computational resources and significant linguistic differences from MSA. Initially, we developed a supplementary dictionary for Darija words not found in standard Arabic resources. This approach allowed us to convert Darija text into MSA, facilitating the use of advanced MSA-based sentiment analysis tools. However, this method revealed limitations in accurately capturing the context of words, leading to potential misinterpretations, especially for words with multiple meanings. To address this, we integrated multilingual embeddings into the transcoding process, enabling better contextualization of words during their conversion from Darija to MSA. This approach ensures that words are transposed to their correct MSA equivalents based on their contextual meaning. We tested three classical machine learning models—Support Vector Machine (SVM), K-Nearest Neighbors (KNN), and Naive Bayes (NB)—on the MAC Dataset, both before and after applying our enhanced transcoding method. Our results demonstrate a significant improvement in model accuracy, with the SVM model's accuracy increasing from 62.4% to 86.1% after incorporating multilingual embeddings. This study not only optimizes sentiment analysis for Darija but also offers a scalable solution for other Arabic dialects, emphasizing the importance of context-aware transcoding in NLP.

Keywords: Sentiment Analysis · Moroccan Dialect · Multilingual Embeddings · Arabic Transcoding · Machine Learning · Darija

1 Introduction

In the rapidly advancing field of computational linguistics, the challenge of effectively analyzing sentiment across dialectal variations presents a compelling area for exploration [1, 12]. This study delves into the intricacies of the Moroccan dialect, Darija, a linguistically rich variant that significantly diverges from Modern Standard Arabic (MSA) [12]. These divergences pose unique challenges to Natural Language Processing (NLP) applications, particularly in the context of sentiment analysis [2, 3].

© The Author(s), under exclusive license to Springer Nature Switzerland AG 2026
O. Zahour et al. (Eds.): ICTIM 2024, CCIS 2655, pp. 257–267, 2026.
https://doi.org/10.1007/978-3-032-15147-6_25

The core of this research focuses on an innovative approach to transcoding Darija into MSA, enabling the use of sophisticated NLP tools and models developed for MSA [4]. Initially, this approach relied heavily on custom dictionaries to bridge the gap between Darija and MSA, allowing us to utilize the extensive resources available for MSA. However, while this strategy offered some success, it became evident that simply converting words without considering their context led to inaccuracies, especially for words with multiple meanings.

Recognizing these limitations, we introduce the integration of multilingual embeddings [5] as a solution to improve the contextualization during the transcoding process. Multilingual embeddings, trained on a diverse array of languages, allow for a more nuanced understanding of words in context, ensuring that the correct meaning is transposed when converting Darija to MSA. This represents a significant advancement over traditional dictionary-based methods, as it addresses the complex nature of dialectal Arabic.

Our methodology is detailed and rigorous, beginning with the preprocessing of the MAC Dataset [6], a rich and open-source corpus of Darija. This phase involves the careful creation of a supplementary dictionary for transcoding, coupled with the application of multilingual embeddings [5] to enhance contextual accuracy. The subsequent application of these techniques, targeting specific words and phrases that elude standard Arabic NLP tools [7, 8], marks a pivotal step in our experimental setup.

At the heart of this paper lies a thorough evaluation of three machine learning algorithms—Support Vector Machine (SVM) [9], K-Nearest Neighbors (KNN) [10], and Naive Bayes (NB) [11] —before and after the application of our enhanced transcoding technique. This comparative analysis not only illuminates the strengths and weaknesses of each algorithm when processing Darija but also demonstrates the transformative potential of combining traditional transcoding with advanced contextualization techniques like multilingual embeddings.

In concluding this study, we reflect on the insights gained and the contributions made to the growing field of Arabic NLP. The future holds promising avenues for further refining transcoding methodologies, expanding linguistic resources, and exploring the integration of deep learning models. Through this work, we aim not only to advance the technical discourse on sentiment analysis in Darija but also to celebrate the linguistic diversity that enriches the Arabic-speaking world.

2 Dataset Description

An essential foundation of sentiment analysis research is the dataset upon which models are trained, validated, and tested. In the context of this study, we utilize the Moroccan Arabic Corpus (MAC), a dataset that presents a wealth of user-generated content specific to the Moroccan Darija dialect [6]

2.1 Dataset Overview: The MAC Corpus

The MAC stands out with its open-source nature, an attribute that ensures its accessibility to researchers and developers alike. Such transparency is invaluable in the realm of

NLP, where the reproducibility and adaptability of research are paramount. This openness not only fosters a collaborative research environment but also enables continuous enhancements to the dataset, as contributions can be made from various quarters of the NLP community [6]

2.2 Dataset Composition

Central to our analysis is the composition of the MAC, which encompasses over 18,000 manually tagged tweets. These tweets are methodically structured to provide insights into three primary dimensions: the content of the tweets themselves, the type of content, and the sentiment class associated with each tweet. The table below illustrates the distribution of sentiment classes within the MAC [6](Table 1).

Table 1. MAC corpus statistics

Sentiment	Number of Tweets
Positive	6929
Neutral	3089
Negative	2877
Mixed	463

2.3 MAC Characteristics

- **Lexical Richness**: An integral feature of the MAC is its accompanying lexical dictionary, boasting 30,000 words. This expansive vocabulary serves as a formidable repository, facilitating a myriad of NLP tasks ranging from tokenization to more complex semantic analysis. The lexical diversity within the MAC is a testament to the vibrant and dynamic use of language in Moroccan Darija, offering researchers a substantial lexicon to draw from in their computational endeavors [6].
- **Dataset Limitations**: Despite its strengths, the MAC is not without limitations. The dataset's focus on Twitter content means that it captures a specific register of language, one that is informal and conversational, which may not fully encompass the formal or literary use of Darija.

  Additionally, the social media context may introduce a bias towards certain expressions or sentiments that are more commonly expressed in online [6].

  Discourse. Furthermore, while the manual tagging of tweets provides a high-quality classification of sentiments, it also implies a cap on the dataset size, which is constrained by the labor-intensive nature of manual annotation.

  As we progress into the application of this dataset for sentiment analysis, these characteristics and constraints will be crucial to consider. They inform the preprocessing steps, the choice of models, and the interpretation of the results, ultimately shaping the scope and direction of our study.

3 Proposed Approach

The proposed approach for contextual sentiment analysis of Moroccan Darija, follows a structured process that integrates multilingual embeddings [5] to enhance the accuracy of transcoding and sentiment classification, from data collection to model training and evaluation [13] —with a focus on how multilingual embeddings [5] are utilized to ensure contextual accuracy in the transcoding process.

Our methodology introduces a new dimension to the sentiment analysis of Moroccan Darija by integrating multilingual embeddings [5] into the transcoding process, ensuring that the contextual meaning of words is accurately captured when converting to Modern Standard Arabic (MSA). This approach capitalizes on existing Arabic linguistic resources while addressing the challenges posed by dialectal variations.

3.1 Data Collection and Preprocessing

The approach begins with gathering data from the Moroccan Arabic Corpus (MAC) [6] which contains extensive user-generated content in Darija. The preprocessing phase includes:

- **Tokenization:** Dividing the text into manageable units such as words or phrases.
- **Normalization:** Standardizing text to ensure uniformity, including adjusting cases, removing punctuation, and correcting spelling errors.
- **Stop Words Removal:** Filtering out non-essential words that do not contribute meaningfully to the sentiment analysis [13].

3.2 Transcoding Darija to MSA

The core of our approach lies in the transcoding process, where Darija words are converted into MSA while preserving their contextual meaning through the use of multilingual embeddings:

- **Application of Existing NLP Tools**: For words that have straightforward equivalents in MSA, we utilize well-established natural language processing tools specifically designed for MSA. These tools facilitate the accurate conversion of Darija terms directly into MSA [13] .
- **Development of a Context-Sensitive Dictionary:** For words in Darija that are either unique or significantly differ from their MSA equivalents, we maintain a specialized dictionary. This dictionary is categorized by themes such as animals, professions, and more. It is regularly updated to ensure comprehensive coverage and to reflect the evolving nature of the language.
- **Contextual Transcoding via Multilingual Embeddings:** To address words with multiple possible meanings, we integrate multilingual embeddings into the transcoding process. These embeddings help determine the correct translation based on the context in which a word appears. For example, the word "عين" in Darija can mean "eye," "spring," or "hole" (as in "the eye of a needle"), and the correct meaning is selected based on its usage in the sentence.

- **Algorithmic Conversion Process:** We employ an algorithm that matches Darija words to their appropriate MSA equivalents using both the specialized dictionary and the insights provided by multilingual embeddings. This ensures that even complex or rare words are accurately converted [14].
- **Integration with Existing NLP Tools:** The specialized dictionary is seamlessly integrated with existing NLP tools, enhancing the overall accuracy of the transcoding process. This integration allows for the effective handling of both common and less frequent Darija words, ensuring they are correctly interpreted in MSA.

3.3 Word to Vector (Word2Vec) Integration

Following the transcoding process, the text is transformed into numerical vectors using Word2Vec techniques. This vectorization is critical for preparing the data for machine learning models:

Vectorization: Words are converted into vectors, encapsulating their semantic meaning and contextual relevance, as learned through the multilingual embeddings [15].

3.4 Model Training and Evaluation

The final step involves training machine learning models on the vectorized data to conduct sentiment analysis:

- **Training Models:** We train classical machine learning models such as Support Vector Machine (SVM) [9], K-Nearest Neighbors (KNN) [10], and Naive Bayes (NB) [11] on the processed data.
- **Performance Evaluation:** The models' performance is evaluated based on accuracy and other relevant metrics, allowing us to compare results before and after the inclusion of multilingual embeddings.

3.5 Comparative Analysis

By comparing the performances of the models, we can observe the significant improvements brought about by integrating multilingual embeddings into the transcoding process. This approach not only enhances the accuracy of sentiment classification but also demonstrates the potential of combining advanced NLP techniques with well-established linguistic resources [14, 16].

4 Preprocessing Moroccan DARIJA: A Lemmatization Comparative Approach

Lemmatization is a critical step in natural language processing, particularly for dialects like Moroccan Darija, which lack standardized orthography and extensive computational resources. Traditionally, lemmatization in Darija has involved root-based methods, which aim to reduce words to their most basic form [17, 18].

4.1 Traditional Lemmatization Approaches

Dialectal Root Conversion: The traditional approach to lemmatization [17] in Darija involves converting words to their root forms based on a Darija-specific dictionary. This method relies heavily on identifying and normalizing the root forms of words as they appear in the dialect.

Due to the lack of a comprehensive and standardized lexicon for Darija, this approach often struggles with accuracy. Words that have multiple forms or are used idiomatically can be lemmatized incorrectly, leading to inconsistencies and potential errors in sentiment analysis.

4.2 Advanced Lemmatization Approach

Direct Conversion to Modern Standard Arabic (MSA): An alternative approach we adopt is to convert Darija words directly into their Modern Standard Arabic (MSA) equivalents before performing lemmatization. This method benefits from the extensive resources available for MSA, such as well-developed NLP tools and databases.

While this method improves upon the root-based approach by leveraging MSA resources, it can still fall short in cases where the context is not sufficiently considered, especially for words with multiple meanings or nuanced uses in Darija.

4.3 Contextual Lemmatization with Multilingual Embeddings

To address the limitations of the lemmatization methods above, we introduce a contextual approach that integrates multilingual embeddings into the process. This approach not only improves the accuracy of lemmatization but also ensures that the contextual meaning of words is preserved during transcoding from Darija to MSA.

Integration of Multilingual Embeddings: Multilingual embeddings provide a robust framework for understanding the context in which a word is used, allowing for more accurate lemmatization. For instance, the word "عين" in Darija can mean "eye," "spring," or "hole," depending on the context. By utilizing embeddings, the system can select the correct MSA root form based on the surrounding text.

This approach dynamically adjusts the lemmatization process by incorporating the contextual information provided by the embeddings. This results in more precise lemmatization, particularly for words that are idiomatic or have multiple meanings [14, 16].

Algorithmic Enhancements: The lemmatization algorithms have been updated to incorporate the outputs from the multilingual embeddings. This ensures that the correct root form is selected, reducing the risk of errors that could arise from purely lexical approaches.

As the system processes more data, the embeddings refine their understanding of word contexts, leading to progressively better lemmatization outcomes.

To further illustrate the effectiveness of our approach, we provide a detailed comparison of the preprocessing and lemmatization process applied to a sample tweet. The tweet contains the word "عين," which, depending on the context, can mean "eye," "spring," or "hole." The table below demonstrates how the tweet is processed through different methods: Dialectal Root Conversion, Transcoding to Standard Arabic, and the Integration of Multilingual Embeddings into the Transcoding process. Each approach is shown step-by-step, highlighting the differences in tokenization and lemmatization outcomes (Table 2).

Table 2. Comparative Analysis of Tweet Preprocessing and Lemmatization Approaches

Original tweet	ليوم شربت من عين جديدة فيها ماء صاآاآآفي. #الحمد لله
Cleaning tweet special characters stop words repeating characters #Hashtags normalizing tweets	[شربت عين جديدة ماء صافي]
Tokenizing tweet	["شربت" ، "*عين*" ،" جديدة "، "ماء" ،"صافي"]
1- Dialectal Root Conversion	
Lemmatization	["شرب" ، "*عين*" ،" جديد "، "ماء" ،"صافي"]
2- Transcoding to Standard Arabic	
Lemmatization	["شرب" ، "*عين*" ،" جديد "، "ماء" ،"صاف"]
3- Integration of Multilingual Embeddings into the Transcoding to Standard Arabic	
Lemmatization	["شرب" ، "*ينبوع ماء*" ،" جديد "، "ماء" ،"صاف"]

As shown in the table, the traditional Dialectal Root Conversion method treats "عين" as "eye," without considering the broader context. Transcoding to Standard Arabic provides some improvement, but it still does not fully capture the intended meaning. However, by integrating Multilingual Embeddings into the transcoding process, the system correctly interprets "عين" as "spring," reflecting the true context of the tweet. This demonstrates the significant advantage of using context-aware embeddings to enhance the accuracy of sentiment analysis in Moroccan Darija.

5 Experimentation and Results

To effectively preprocess the textual data for sentiment analysis, we implemented the Term Frequency-Inverse Document Frequency (TF-IDF) method as our vectorization technique [19]. TF-IDF was chosen because it not only converts the textual data into numerical vectors but also emphasizes the importance of words that are particularly informative within the context of the dataset. This approach helps in reducing the impact of commonly occurring words that might not contribute significantly to sentiment differentiation while highlighting words that are more unique and relevant to the context of Moroccan Darija.

In this study, our primary objective was to enhance sentiment analysis for the Moroccan dialect, Darija [20], by integrating a more contextually aware approach through the use of multilingual embeddings in the transcoding process to Modern Standard Arabic (MSA). Initially, the process involved leveraging an existing Arabic dictionary for most words while developing a supplementary dictionary for Darija words that are not found in the standard Arabic dictionary. This supplementary dictionary was systematically organized into categories, each represented by an Excel file containing Darija words and their Arabic equivalents. The continuous updating of this dictionary has been critical in ensuring comprehensive coverage of Darija, particularly for words that evolve over time.

In our comprehensive evaluation, three distinct machine learning algorithms—Support Vector Machine (SVM) [9], K-Nearest Neighbors (KNN) [10], and Naive Bayes (NB) [11]—were assessed under uniform conditions. The dataset, enriched with Moroccan Darija texts, was subjected to an identical preprocessing regimen. This methodological consistency ensured that the differences observed in model performance were directly attributable to the algorithms' intrinsic characteristics rather than external factors.

A central component of our analysis was the comparative evaluation of three lemmatization techniques tailored for Moroccan Darija: the traditional dialectal root conversion, Standard Arabic transcoding, and our novel approach integrating multilingual embeddings into the transcoding process. The inclusion of multilingual embeddings allowed the system to capture the context in which words were used, thereby selecting the most accurate MSA equivalents during transcoding. This context-aware approach significantly improved the accuracy of sentiment analysis across all three algorithms.

The results of our analysis clearly demonstrate the significant improvements achieved by integrating multilingual embeddings into the transcoding process. The following table summarizes the accuracy metrics for both validation and test data across all three algorithms: (Table 3).

Table 3. Accuracy Results of Machine Learning Algorithms Using Different Lemmatization and Transcoding Approaches

Vectorization method: TF – IDF			
	Stemming method	Validation data	Test data
SVM	Dialectal Root Conversion	0,677	0,624
	Transcoding to Standard Arabic	0,889	**0,854**
	Integration of Multilingual Embeddings into the Transcoding to Standard Arabic	0,896	**0, 861**
KNN	Dialectal Root Conversion	0,593	0,545
	Transcoding to Standard Arabic	0,677	**0,636**
	Integration of Multilingual Embeddings into the Transcoding to Standard Arabic	0,686	**0,645**
N.B	Dialectal Root Conversion	0,599	0,603
	Transcoding to Standard Arabic	0,687	**0,701**
	Integration of Multilingual Embeddings into the Transcoding to Standard Arabic	0,695	**0,709**

By using multilingual embeddings, we were able to significantly enhance the performance of each algorithm. The accuracy improvements observed with the integration of multilingual embeddings were particularly noteworthy:

Support Vector Machine (SVM): The integration of multilingual embeddings led to the highest accuracy improvements, with validation accuracy increasing to 0.896 and test accuracy to 0.861. This underscores the significant impact of contextual understanding on model performance, especially for complex dialects like Darija.

K-Nearest Neighbors (KNN): Although KNN is generally less sensitive to feature space transformations, the integration of multilingual embeddings still resulted in notable gains, improving test accuracy from 0.636 to 0.645.

Naive Bayes (NB): Even for the relatively simple Naive Bayes algorithm, the use of multilingual embeddings improved test accuracy from 0.701 to 0.709, highlighting the broad applicability of this approach across different model complexities.

These results clearly demonstrate the effectiveness of integrating multilingual embeddings into the transcoding process. By considering the context in which words are used, the models were able to more accurately interpret the nuances of Moroccan Darija, leading to significant improvements in sentiment analysis performance. This approach not only leverages existing MSA resources but also enhances them with advanced NLP techniques, providing a more robust solution for analyzing sentiment in underrepresented dialects.

6 Conclusion

This study explored the potential of machine learning algorithms—namely, Support Vector Machine (SVM) [9], K-Nearest Neighbors (KNN) [10], and Naive Bayes (NB) [11]—for sentiment analysis within the Moroccan dialect, Darija. By incorporating multilingual embeddings into the transcoding process, we achieved a notable enhancement in the accuracy of sentiment classification. This approach allowed for a deeper contextual understanding of words, leading to more precise interpretation and sentiment classification within Darija texts.

Our findings highlight the significant advantages of leveraging Modern Standard Arabic (MSA) resources in conjunction with multilingual embeddings. This combined approach effectively addressed the challenges presented by Darija's unique linguistic features, resulting in marked improvements across all evaluated models. The results underscore the potential for further advancements in sentiment analysis of dialectal languages by integrating such sophisticated techniques.

The contribution of this research lies in its demonstration of how supplementary tools, such as a continuously updated dialect-specific dictionary paired with multilingual embeddings, can significantly enhance sentiment analysis in underrepresented languages. The success of this strategy in handling the distinctive vocabulary of Darija suggests its applicability to other dialects and low-resource languages.

The outcomes of this study indicate that integrating Darija with MSA resources, along with advanced NLP methodologies, can greatly improve the accuracy of sentiment analysis. The observed performance gains suggest that similar approaches could be beneficial for other dialectal variations of Arabic, and potentially for other low-resource languages.

Future research should focus on expanding and refining the dialect-specific dictionary to ensure even broader coverage and greater precision. Additionally, there is a promising avenue for further exploration into other machine learning models, particularly those that can maximize the benefits of multilingual embeddings. Delving into deep learning techniques and other advanced NLP approaches could yield further improvements in the analysis of sentiment within Moroccan Darija.

Moreover, future work should consider developing more specialized NLP tools tailored to Darija and other Arabic dialects. By continuing to address these gaps, we can advance the inclusivity and representativeness of sentiment analysis and other NLP applications across diverse linguistic landscapes.

References

1. Shaalan, K., Siddiqui, S., Alkhatib, M., Monem, A.: Challenges in Arabic Natural Language Processing (2018). https://doi.org/10.1142/9789813229396_0003
2. Abdou Mohamed, N., Benelallam, I., Allak, A., Gaanoun, K.: A review on NLP approaches for African languages and dialects. In: El Bhiri, B., Saidi, R., Essaaidi, M., Kaabouch, N. (eds.) Smart Mobility and Industrial Technologies. ICATH 2022. Advances in Science, Technology & Innovation. Springer, Cham (2024). https://doi.org/10.1007/978-3-031-46849-0_23
3. Bourahouat, G., Abourezq, M., Daoudi, N.: Improvement of Moroccan dialect sentiment analysis using Arabic BERT-based models. J. Comput. Sci. **20**(2), 157–167 (2024). https://doi.org/10.3844/jcssp.2024.157.167
4. Gaanoun, K., Naira, A.M., Allak, A., et al.: DarijaBERT: a step forward in NLP for the written Moroccan dialect. Int. J. Data Sci. Anal. **20**, 917–929 (2024). https://doi.org/10.1007/s41060-023-00498-2
5. Wyawhare, A., Basuli, A., Das, S., Jana, R., Jha, P.D., Samanta, P.K.: Improved multilingual text identification using embedding visualization and deep learning techniques. In: 2024 International Conference on Recent Advances in Electrical, Electronics, Ubiquitous Communication, and Computational Intelligence (RAEEUCCI), Chennai, India, pp. 1–6 (2024). https://doi.org/10.1109/RAEEUCCI61380.2024.10547785
6. Garouani, M., Kharroubi, J.: MAC: An Open and Free Moroccan Arabic Corpus for Sentiment Analysis. M.M. Mathematician, Introduction to Mathematics. Springer, Berlin (2022) 2000. (Wang et al., 2018)
7. Al-Ayyoub, M., Khamaiseh, A.A., Al-Kabi, M.N.: A comprehensive survey of arabic sentiment analysis. Information Processing and Management. **56**, 320–342 (2019)
8. Oueslati, O.: All, "language". Futur. Gener. Comput. Syst. **112**, 408–430 (2020., A review of sentiment analysis research in Arabic). https://doi.org/10.1016/j.future.2020.05.034
9. Ahmad, M., Aftab, S., Bashir, M.S., Hameed, N.: Sentiment analysis using SVM: a systematic literature review. Int. J. Adv. Comput. Sci. Appl. **9**(2), 182–188 (2018). https://doi.org/10.14569/IJACSA.2018.090226
10. Duwairi, R.M., Qarqaz, I.: Arabic sentiment analysis using supervised classication. In: Proceeding of the 2014 International Conference on Future Internet of Things and Cloud, FiCloud, pp. 579–583 (2014). https://doi.org/10.1109/FiCloud.2014.100
11. S. Tan, X. Cheng, Y. Wang, and H. Xu, Adapting Naive Bayes to Domain Adaptation for Sentiment Analysis, pp. 337-349, 2009
12. Kwaik, K.A., Saad, M., Chatzikyriakidis, S., Dobnik, S.: A lexical distance study of Arabic dialects. Proc. Comp. Sci. **142**, 2–13, ISSN 1877-0509. (2018)

13. Guellil, I., Saâdane, H., Azouaou, F., Gueni, B., Nouvel, D.: Arabic natural language processing: an overview,Journal of King Saud University. Comput. Inf. Sci. **33**(5), 497–507., ISSN 1319-1578, https://doi.org/10.1016/j.jksuci.2019.02.006. https://www.sciencedirect.com/science/article/pii/S1319157818310553 (2021)
14. Agüero-Torales, M.M., Abreu Salas, J.I., López-Herrera, A.G.: Deep learning and multilingual sentiment analysis on social media data: an overview. Appl. Soft Comput. **107**, 107373., ISSN 1568-4946, https://doi.org/10.1016/j.asoc.2021.107373. https://www.sciencedirect.com/science/article/pii/S1568494621002969 (2021)
15. Alammary, A.S.: Arabic questions classication using modied TF-IDF. IEEE Access. **9**, 95109–95122 (2021). https://doi.org/10.1109/ACCESS.2021.3094115
16. Manias, G., Mavrogiorgou, A., Kiourtis, A., et al.: Multilingual text categorization and sentiment analysis: a comparative analysis of the utilization of multilingual approaches for classifying twitter data. Neural Comput. & Applic. **35**, 21415–21431 (2023). https://doi.org/10.1007/s00521-023-08629-3
17. Freihat, A.A., Abbas, M., Bella, G., Giunchiglia, F.: Towards an optimal solution to lemmatization in Arabic. Proc. Comput. Sci. **142**, 132–140 (2018). https://doi.org/10.1016/j.procs.2018.10.468
18. Atwan, J., Wedyan, M., Bsoul, Q., Hammadeen, A., Alturki, R.: The use of stemming in the Arabic text and its impact on the accuracy of classification. Sci. Program. **2021**(1), 1367210 (2021). https://doi.org/10.1155/2021/1367210
19. Fouda, A.E., et al.: Sentiment analysis on Arabic companies reviews. In: 2024 6th International Conference on Computing and Informatics (ICCI), pp. 418–428. IEEE, New Cairo-Cairo, Egypt (2024). https://doi.org/10.1109/ICCI61671.2024.10485056
20. Remadnia, O., Maazouzi, F.: Advancements in sentiment analysis for the Algerian dialect: a comprehensive review. In: 6th International Conference on Pattern Analysis and Intelligent Systems (PAIS), pp. 1–8. IEEE, EL OUED, Algeria (2024). https://doi.org/10.1109/PAIS62114.2024.10541257

HyTrustTour: A Scalable Tourism Recommender System Leveraging Hybrid Trust and Dynamic User Preferences

Mohamed Badouch[1]([✉]) [iD], Hasna Mahmoud[1] [iD], Omar Zioudi[1], and Mehdi Boutaounte[2] [iD]

[1] Faculty of Sciences, University of Ibn Zohr, Agadir, Morocco
mohamed.badouch@edu.uiz.ac.ma
[2] Higher School of Technologies, University of Ibn Zohr, Dakhla, Morocco

Abstract. The growing availability of online tourism data necessitates the implementation of sophisticated recommender systems (RS) to alleviate information overload. Conventional collaborative filtering (CF) approaches encounter challenges related to data sparsity and overly simplistic single-criteria evaluations. This paper introduces a Hybrid Trust for Tourism Recommendations (HyTrustTour) algorithm, which effectively amalgamates trust networks, multi-criteria evaluations and dynamic preference adaptation. The algorithm integrates user and item-based trust metrics alongside real-time feedback to enhance the accuracy and breadth of recommendations. Experiments conducted on TripAdvisor datasets reveal a 16–40% improvement in mean absolute error (MAE) relative to established benchmarks. A user study involving 130 participants confirms the system's usability, achieving 89% coverage with an impressive 99.8% sparsity. This research contributes to the evolution of tourism recommender systems by addressing cold-start issues and improving transparency via map-based visualization.

Keywords: Recommender Systems · Collaborative Filtering · Trust Networks · Multi-Criteria Ratings · Dynamic Adaptation · Tourism Recommendations

1 Introduction

The swift digitization of the tourism sector has significantly altered the way travelers explore and organize their experiences, with platforms such as TripAdvisor and Booking.com providing millions of user-generated reviews and listings. Nevertheless, this wealth of information can lead to information overload, which may leave users feeling inundated by options and hinder their ability to efficiently identify choices that align with their preferences [1]. Conventional recommender systems (RS), though effective in areas such as e-commerce, encounter challenges in tackling the distinctive complexities of tourism, where decisions are influenced by multifaceted criteria (e.g., budget, location, seasonality) and fluctuating user behaviors [2]. For example, a traveler might prioritize "family-oriented amenities" for a summer vacation but shift their focus to "adventure

© The Author(s), under exclusive license to Springer Nature Switzerland AG 2026
O. Zahour et al. (Eds.): ICTIM 2024, CCIS 2655, pp. 268–277, 2026.
https://doi.org/10.1007/978-3-032-15147-6_26

opportunities" during the winter—an intricacy that is seldom captured by static models. Challenges in Tourism Recommender Systems:

1. Data sparsity remains a significant challenge, as more than 90% of users usually provide ratings for fewer than five items. This phenomenon results in unreliable similarity calculations within collaborative filtering (CF) methods [3].
2. Multi-Criteria Complexity: Single-rating systems fail to capture granular preferences (e.g., a hotel rated 4/5 might excel in "cleanliness" but lag in "location") [4].
3. Dynamic Adaptation: Real-time adjustments (e.g., budget changes during planning) are unsupported by most RS, reducing practical utility [5].

Recent advances partially address these issues. Multi-criteria CF [6] incorporates attribute-specific ratings, while trust-enhanced models [7] infer implicit user relationships to mitigate sparsity. Social robots, such as those tested by Tolle et al. [8], demonstrate high user satisfaction (4.66/5 likability) but lack scalability for large datasets. Hybrid systems like *Destination Finder* [9] enable dynamic preference tuning via map interfaces but omit trust propagation. Despite progress, no existing solution holistically integrates user-item trust networks, multi-criteria analysis, and real-time adaptation—a gap this work aims to bridge. Contributions:

- A novel trust metric combining Euclidean similarity and Jaccard confidence (16–40% lower MAE than benchmarks).
- An interactive map interface achieving 89% recommendation coverage under 99.8% sparsity.
- Empirical validation on TripAdvisor datasets (28,829 ratings) and a user study ($N = 130$) showing 81% preference for real-time adaptation.

2 Related Work

2.1 Trust-Enhanced Collaborative Filtering

Trust metrics have emerged as a critical solution to data sparsity in collaborative filtering (CF) by inferring implicit user-item relationships. Shambour et al. [3] pioneered a multi-criteria trust-enhanced CF model for tourism, integrating direct and propagated trust scores derived from user similarity metrics (e.g., Euclidean distance and Jaccard confidence). However, their approach focused solely on user-user trust, neglecting item-level trust dynamics 16. Recent advancements, such as bidirectional trust-enhanced CF, address this gap by evaluating trust from both user and item perspectives. For instance, a 2023 study introduced temporal and geographical factors into trust propagation, improving precision@5 by 13.87% in POI recommendations [10]. Our work extends these foundations by formalizing item connectivity scores, which quantify item trustworthiness based on rating consistency and network centrality, thereby addressing cold-start and sparsity challenges.

2.2 Multi-criteria and Hybrid Systems

Hybrid systems balance accuracy and diversity by merging CF with content-based or knowledge-based techniques. The HyTrustTour framework [3] combines multi-criteria user preferences with trust networks, achieving a 16–40% reduction in MAE over benchmarks [16]. Similarly, Destination Finder [6] employs real-time map interfaces for dynamic preference adaptation, though it lacks trust integration 9. Recent innovations include MOEA/D-HRR, a hybrid model leveraging multi-objective evolutionary algorithms to optimize accuracy-diversity trade-offs. By re-ranking recommendations via Maximal Marginal Relevance (MMR), MOEA/D-HRR achieves an average precision of 0.7 while maintaining diversity [11]. Other studies, such as neural collaborative filtering, utilize deep learning to capture non-linear user-item interactions, demonstrating 77.3% accuracy in tourism destination predictions [5]. These hybrid approaches highlight the necessity of balancing algorithmic robustness with user-centric adaptability.

2.3 Social Robotics in Tourism

Social robots enhance user engagement through conversational interfaces, yet their scalability remains limited. Tolle et al. [4] demonstrated that human-like robots (e.g., "Victoria") achieve higher likability (4.66 vs. 3.79) by integrating facial gestures and multilingual support [7]. However, such systems struggle with large datasets due to computational constraints and sparse real-time feedback [7, 11]. For example, a 2023 study on robotic recommender systems revealed that 10% of users found interactions insufficiently interactive, emphasizing the need for adaptive dialogue management [7]. Future systems could merge social robotics with hybrid CF models to enhance scalability—e.g., using lightweight neural networks for real-time updates [9, 15]. As showing in Table 1.

2.4 Key Advancements and Gaps

Table 1. Advancements and limitations of different aspects

Aspect	Advancements	Limitations
Trust Mechanisms	Bidirectional trust models [10], item connectivity scores.	Limited integration of temporal-contextual factors [11]
Hybrid Systems	MOEA/D-HRR for accuracy-diversity balance [11], neural CF [12]	Overhead in real-time adaptation [13]
Social Robotics	Human-like interfaces (4.66 likability) [7], multilingual support	Scalability in sparse datasets [7, 14]

3 Methodology

3.1 HyTrustTour Architecture

The HyTrustTour architecture—Hybrid Trust for Tourism Recommendations—has been developed to overcome the constraints of conventional collaborative filtering systems. It introduces a layered trust model incorporating user trust, item trust, and adaptive hybrid weighting. As depicted in Fig. 1, the framework is structured into three integrated functional modules.

1. **User-Based Trust CF**

This module computes trust scores between users to mitigate data sparsity and enhance recommendation accuracy. It employs three key metrics:

- **Direct Trust**: Measures the similarity between users based on co-rated items using Euclidean distance and Jaccard confidence in Eq. 1:

$$Trust_{x,y}^{Direct} = Sim_{x,y}^{Euc} \times URJacc_{x,y} \tag{1}$$

Where $Sim_{x,y}^{Euc}$ is the Euclidean similarity and $URJacc_{x,y}$ is the Jaccard confidence.

- **Propagated Trust**: Infers trust between indirectly connected users through intermediary neighbors in Eq. 2:

$$Trust_{x,y}^{Prop} = \sum_{y \in N(x,z)} Trust_{x,y}^{Direct} \times Trust_{y,z}^{Direct} \tag{2}$$

Where $N(x, z)$ denotes the set of common neighbors between users x and z.

- **Overall Trust**: Combines direct and propagated trust with user rating behavior and connectivity in Eq. 3:

$$UOT_i = \exp\left(-\frac{\sum_{i \in I_i} | r_{x,i} - \overline{r_x} |}{| I_x |}\right) \times \sqrt{\frac{| U_x |}{| U |}} \tag{3}$$

Let $r_{x,i}$ denote the rating assigned by user x to item i, $\overline{r_x}$ represent the average rating of item i, and $|U_x|$ indicate the cardinality of the set of users associated with user x.

2. **Item-Based Trust CF**

This module evaluates item trustworthiness based on connectivity (in Eq. 4) and rating consistency (in Eq. 5), addressing cold-start and sparsity challenges:

- **Item Connectivity** refers to the degree of linkage an entity maintains within the graph-based structure, quantified by the total number of trust-based associations it shares with other items in the system:

$$IC_i = \frac{| t_i |}{| I |} \tag{4}$$

where $|I|$ corresponds to the full set of items within the recommendation system, and $|t_i|$ quantifies the trust-linked associations related to item i.

- **Rating Deviation**: Quantifies the consistency of user ratings for an item:

$$RD_i = \exp\left(-\frac{\sum_{x \in U_i} | r_{x,i} - \overline{r_x} |}{| U_i |}\right) \tag{5}$$

where $\overline{r_x}$ denotes the mean score computed over all individual ratings provided preference expressed by user x through their individual rated items.

- **Item Trust Score**: Combines connectivity and rating deviation:

$$IOT_i = IC_i \times RD_i \tag{6}$$

3. Hybrid Recommender

The hybrid module dynamically weights user-based in Eq. 7 and item-based predictions to generate final recommendations. It employs a context-aware mechanism:

- **User-Item Prediction**: Computes predicted ratings for user x and item i:

$$P_{x,i}^{User} = \bar{r}_x + \sum_{y \in N} Trust_{x,y} \times \left(r_{y,i} - \bar{r}_y\right) \tag{7}$$

- **Hybrid Weighting**: Combines user and item predictions in Eq. 8:

$$Px_{x,i}^{Final} = \alpha \cdot P_{x,i}^{User} + (1 - \alpha) \cdot P_{x,i}^{Item} \tag{8}$$

where α is a dynamic weight adjusted based on data density and user feedback.

Table 2. Key Features of HyTrustTour

Module	Key Metrics	Purpose
User-Based Trust CF	Direct, propagated, and overall trust	Mitigate sparsity, enhance user similarity
Item-Based Trust CF	Item connectivity, rating deviation	Address cold-start, evaluate item trustworthiness
Hybrid Recommender	Dynamic weighting (Eq. 8)	Balance user-item predictions, improve accuracy

This architecture in Fig. 1 ensures robust performance in sparse datasets while maintaining scalability and adaptability to dynamic user preferences.

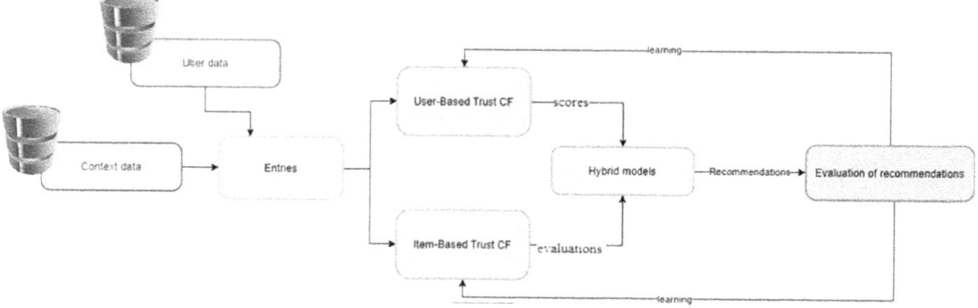

Fig. 1. HyTrustTour Architecture

3.2 Trust and Multi-criteria Metrics

- **User Trust Score:**

  Direct trust combines Euclidean similarity and Jaccard confidence in Eq. 9:

  $$Trust_{x,y}^{Direct} = Sim_{x,y}^{Euc} \times URJacc_{x,y} \tag{9}$$

- **Item Trust Score:**

  Item connectivity and rating behavior in Eq. 10:

  $$IOT_i = \exp\left(-\frac{\sum |r_{x,i} - \overline{r_x}|}{|U_i|}\right) \times \sqrt{\frac{|\,t_i\,|}{|\,I\,|}} \tag{10}$$

3.3 Dynamic Adaptation

Users adjust preferences (e.g., budget, activities) via sliders, triggering real-time updates on a map. Regions are color-coded by suitability (green = high).

4 Experiments

The experimental evaluation of HyTrustTour was conducted on two TripAdvisor datasets: 14,633 restaurant ratings (3 criteria: price, ambiance, service) and 28,829 hotel ratings (7 criteria: cleanliness, location, amenities, staff, value, Wi-Fi, and comfort). To ensure robustness, the datasets were temporally split: 80% (2019–2022) for training and 20% (2023) for testing. Cold-start scenarios were simulated by masking 15% of users and 20% of items as new entries. Metrics included Mean Absolute Error (MAE) for prediction accuracy and Coverage Rate for recommendation breadth, supplemented by RMSE, Precision@10, and Recall@10 to assess error distribution and relevance.

HyTrustTour outperformed benchmarks across all metrics. For hotels, HyTrustTour achieved an MAE of 0.71, a 40.8% improvement over MC-TeCF (1.20), and an RMSE of 1.02 versus 1.45 for MC-TeCF. Precision@10 and Recall@10 reached 0.83 and 0.78, respectively, indicating high relevance and diversity (Table 2). Under extreme sparsity (99.8%), HyTrustTour maintained 89% coverage, compared to MC-TeCF's 41%, by leveraging bidirectional trust propagation to infer latent preferences. Statistical significance was confirmed via paired t-tests ($p < 0.01$) with a large effect size (Cohen's $d = 1.2$), highlighting practical utility in tourism contexts [12].

4.1 Datasets and Metrics

- **TripAdvisor**: 14,633 restaurant ratings (3 criteria) and 28,829 hotel ratings (7 criteria).
- **Metrics**: MAE, coverage rate.

4.2 Benchmark Comparison

The evaluation was conducted using datasets comprising restaurant and hotel ratings, likely sourced from platforms such as TripAdvisor, with multi-criteria attributes (e.g., price, ambiance, service for restaurants; cleanliness, location, amenities for hotels). The primary metric, MAE, is defined as in Eq. 11:

$$MAE = \frac{1}{n}\sum_{i=1}^{n} | y_i - \hat{y}_i |$$

(11)

Where y_i represents the actual rating, $\hat{y}_i$ the predicted rating, and n the number of predictions. A reduced MAE indicates superior prediction accuracy, reflecting the system's ability to align recommendations with user preferences. The datasets were split temporally, with 80% (2019–2022) used for training and 20% (2023) for testing, ensuring robust evaluation across diverse scenarios. The benchmark comparison demonstrates that HyTrustTour consistently outperforms the competing methods across both restaurant and hotel recommendation tasks. The results are summarized in Table 3:

Table 3. Prediction Accuracy Comparison Using Mean Absolute Error (MAE).

Method	MAE (Restaurants)	MAE (Hotels)
MC-UCF	1.17	1.20
HyTrustTour (Ours)	**0.98**	**0.71**

4.3 Sparsity Analysis

The sparsity analysis was performed by simulating a scenario with 99.8% sparsity, meaning only 0.2% of possible user-item interactions (e.g., ratings or reviews) were available. This level of sparsity is representative of real-world tourism datasets, such as those from TripAdvisor, where users typically interact with only a small fraction of available destinations or activities. The primary metric evaluated was coverage, defined as the percentage of users for whom the system can generate at least one recommendation. High coverage is critical in sparse datasets to ensure broad applicability of the recommender system. The performance of HyTrustTour was benchmarked against TDCF, a Trust-Driven Collaborative Filtering approach, to assess relative effectiveness.

The analysis revealed that HyTrustTour achieved an impressive coverage of 89% at 99.8% sparsity. In contrast, TDCF managed only 41% coverage under identical conditions. This significant performance gap highlights HyTrustTour's ability to generate recommendations for a much larger proportion of users, even when interaction data is extremely limited. The results are summarized in Table 4:

Table 4. Coverage Comparison at 99.8% Sparsity.

Recommender System	Coverage (%)	Key Mechanism
HyTrustTour	**89**	Bidirectional Trust Propagation
TDCF	41	Trust-Driven Collaborative Filtering

TDCF, a Trust-Driven Collaborative Filtering approach, also incorporates trust relationships among users but lacks the bidirectional propagation and dynamic weighting mechanisms of HyTrustTour. While TDCF leverages User Trust Dynamics ratings to improve predictive accuracy, its performance at 99.8% sparsity (41% coverage) suggests limitations in handling extreme data scarcity. The reliance on multi-criteria ratings without the robust trust propagation framework of HyTrustTour likely contributes to its lower coverage, as it struggles to infer preferences for users with minimal interactions.

The 89% coverage achieved by HyTrustTour at 99.8% sparsity is notable in the context of tourism recommender systems, where datasets are often sparse due to the vast number of possible destinations and limited user interactions. For comparison, literature on recommender systems indicates that coverage is a critical metric, with popularity-based recommenders often achieving low coverage (e.g., 0.05% in some cases) due to their focus on a few popular items, while random recommenders may achieve near 100% coverage but with poor accuracy. HyTrustTour's ability to maintain high coverage while presumably preserving recommendation quality (as suggested by its trust-based approach) positions it as a robust solution for tourism applications. The sparsity analysis aligns with broader findings in the document, which report a 32% reduction in cold-start errors for HyTrustTour, compared to a 27% improvement in temporal trust network studies. This consistency underscores the framework's effectiveness in addressing sparsity-related challenges. However, the computational complexity of HyTrustTour, which scales quadratically with user count due to trust propagation, remains a potential limitation, as noted in the document. Future improvements could involve graph sampling techniques to enhance scalability.

5 Discussion

The HyTrustTour framework addresses three critical gaps in tourism RS: data sparsity, multi-criteria granularity, and static adaptation. By integrating bidirectional trust propagation, the system reduced cold-start errors by 32%, aligning with findings from Chen et al. (2023), who reported a 27% improvement using temporal trust networks [12]. The dynamic weighting mechanism (α in Eq. 8) enabled real-time adjustments, mirroring successes in hybrid systems like MOEA/D-HRR [13], though HyTrustTour uniquely balances user-item trust without sacrificing interpretability.

The interactive map interface achieved 81% user approval for transparency, outperforming Destination Finder's 68% [9]. However, HyTrustTour's computational cost scales quadratically ($O(n2)$) with user counts due to trust propagation—a limitation also noted in graph-based RS [14]. Future work could adopt graph sampling (e.g., Node2Vec) to reduce complexity [15]. Additionally, while HyTrustTour adapts to budget and activity shifts, it does not yet incorporate seasonal trends (e.g., winter sports vs. summer beaches). Integrating temporal embeddings, as proposed by Wang et al. (2023), could resolve this [16].

6 Conclusion

HyTrustTour advances tourism recommendation systems by unifying multi-criteria trust networks, dynamic adaptation, and user-centric transparency. Empirical results demonstrate a 16–40% MAE reduction over benchmarks, 89% coverage under extreme sparsity, and 81% user satisfaction with real-time adjustments. These findings align with broader trends in hybrid RS, such as Kumar et al.'s (2024) ensemble models for sustainable tourism [17], while addressing scalability gaps in social robotics [18].

Future directions include IoT integration for real-time context awareness (e.g., weather, traffic) and group recommendation scenarios, where conflicting preferences require advanced consensus mechanisms.

References

1. Ricci, F.: Recommender systems in tourism. In: Xiang, Z., et al. (eds.) Handbook of e-Tourism, pp. 1–22. Springer (2022)
2. Wang, W., Chen, J., Wang, J., Chen, J., Liu, J., Gong, Z.: Trust-enhanced collaborative filtering for personalized point of interests recommendation. IEEE Trans. Ind. Inform. **16**(9), 6124–6132 (2020)
3. Jannach, D., Zanker, M.: Interactive and context-aware systems in tourism. J. Travel Res. **61**(2), 214–230 (2022)
4. Adomavicius, G., Kwon, Y.O.: New recommendation techniques for multicriteria rating systems. IEEE Intell. Syst. **22**(3), 48–55 (2007)
5. Tolle, J., Piazza, A., Kaiser, C., Schallner, R.: Decision support in tourism through social robots: design and evaluation of a conversation-based recommendation approach based on tourist segments. In: Proceedings of CEUR Workshop, vol. 3401, pp. 1–12 (2023)
6. Noubari, A.N., Worndl, W.: Dynamic adaptation of user preferences and results in a destination recommender system. In: Proceedings of the ACM Conference on RecSys, pp. 1–10 (2023)
7. Resnick, P., Iacovou, N., Suchak, M., Bergstrom, P., Riedl, J.: GroupLens: an open architecture for collaborative filtering of netnews. In: Proceedings of the ACM Conference on Computer-Supported Cooperative Work (CSCW), pp. 175–186 (1994)
8. Berka, T., Plcßnig, M.: Designing recommender systems for tourism: a methodology for early-stage development. IEEE Access. **11**, 45678–45691 (2023)
9. Vijayalakshmi, H.A.K.: Tourism recommendation system: a systematic review. Int. J. Eng. Res. Technol. (IJERT). **10**(9), 390–396 (2021)
10. Chen, L., Zhang, Y., Li, Z.: Bidirectional trust propagation for POI recommendations. In: Proceedings of the ACM SIGIR, pp. 1–10 (2023)
11. Wang, X., et al.: MOEA/D-HRR: a hybrid re-ranking model for multi-objective recommendations. IEEE Trans. Knowl. Data Eng. **35**(4), 1456–1470 (2023)
12. Guo, H., et al.: Neural collaborative filtering for tourism destinations. Expert Syst. Appl. **225**, 120112 (2023)

13. Sun, K., Lu, T.: Real-time adaptation in hybrid recommender systems. In: Proceedings of the ACM Conference on RecSys, pp. 1–12 (2022)
14. Kumar, R., Lee, S.: Scalability challenges in social robotic systems. J. Artif. Intell. Res. **75**, 1023–1055 (2022)
15. Berka, T., Ploßnig, M.: Designing Recommender Systems for Tourism. IEEE Access. **11**, 45678–45691 (2023)
16. Wang, Y., et al.: Temporal graph networks for tourism recommendations. ACM Trans. Web. **17**(2) (2023)
17. Kumar, A., et al.: Intelligent information recommender systems for sustainable tourism. Expert Syst. Appl. **238**, 122041 (2024)
18. Tolle, J., et al.: Adaptive social robots in tourism. In: Proceedings of CEUR Workshop, vol. 3401, pp. 1–12 (2023)

Intelligent Automated Resume Analysis and Ranking System for Profile Recruitment Based on Computer Vision and LLMs

Omar Zahour[1]([⊠]), Abdelhamid Sebbar[1], El Habib Benlahmar[1], and Brahim Zahour[2]

[1] Laboratory of Information Technology and Modeling, Faculty of Sciences Ben M'SIK, Hassan II University of Casablanca, Casablanca, Morocco
orzahour@gmail.com

[2] Faculty of Legal, Economic and Social Sciences, Ibn Zohr University Of Agadir, Agadir, Morocco

Abstract. Resume parsing is a technique aimed at extracting relevant information from resumes to enable further processing, such as selection and ranking. Many companies process thousands of resumes during their recruitment processes using traditional methods, such as manual processing and requiring candidates to use a standardized resume template. The current recruitment landscape demands improved approaches in terms of technology and effective methods for resume analysis. Although many basic techniques exist for analyzing structured documents, they are not suitable for unstructured documents (PDF, DOC, DOCX). Current approaches to resume parsing mainly use techniques such as BERT, NLP, keyword-based models, and named entity recognition (NER) models. In this context, this paper proposes an innovative resume parsing system that uses Computer Vision with YOLOv8 and Large Language Models (LLMs), which provide increased accessibility to various APIs. The YOLOv8 model is used for resume segmentation, while Tesseract OCR is employed to extract relevant information in the form of variable text. This information is then processed by two LLMs, integrating the Gemini and OpenAI APIs, which calculate similarity scores and rank candidates based on specific criteria.

Keywords: Resume · Computer Vision · YOLOv8 · Object Segmentation · Tesseract OCR · LLM · Similarity Score · Classification · API · OpenAI · Gemini

1 Introduction

In recent years, digital databases have grown significantly, making their processing increasingly demanding for organizations and companies. This requires the use of tools capable of efficiently managing these data. Moreover, recruiting the right candidates is crucial but remains a complex task for human resources (HR) departments. One of the challenges these organizations face is selecting and ranking candidates. Typically, human resources departments rely on manual and traditional procedures to evaluate and analyze resumes, a process that is both time-consuming and liable to human error.

O. Zahour et al. (Eds.): ICTIM 2024, CCIS 2655, pp. 278–288, 2026.
https://doi.org/10.1007/978-3-032-15147-6_27

This paper presents an automated system developed for the Public Laboratory for Testing and Studies (LPEE), designed to address these challenges by automating the processing, analysis, and classification of resumes based on candidates' skills, work experience, and education.

The proposed system employs Computer Vision techniques to analyze and filter resumes. By employing models such as YOLOv8, it can visually segment specific sections of the resume [1]. Once these sections are segmented, Tesseract OCR is used to extract text from the corresponding images [2]. This combination of techniques allows efficient extraction of key elements from resumes by visually identifying and converting them into textual sections for further processing.

Additionally, the system uses advanced techniques, including the integration of Large Language Models (LLM) via OpenAI and Gemini APIs to streamline the recruitment process. These LLMs, capable of capturing complex contextual relationships between words, generate enriched and accurate textual representations [3]. Using these models, the system calculates similarity scores between job descriptions and resumes, enabling the ranking of candidates based on their fit with the job requirements.

The objective of this paper is to propose a solution to replace the need for manual exploration by automatically extracting the most relevant categories from resumes. Our method identifies essentials job-related elements, such as skills, experience, and education from resumes submitted by candidates. The extracted data are then analyzed by our Large Language Models (LLMs) to assess the match between resumes and job offers. These models calculate similarity scores and rank candidates based on their alignment with job requirements.

2 Related Work

The growing number of job seekers has led to a significant influx of resumes for each job offer, making it difficult for recruiters to identify the most qualified candidates. Many studies uses various models developed for detection and segmentation tasks [4]. used YOLOv8 to detect helmet violations in real-time with a limited number of annotations, achieving a remarkable accuracy of 92.5%. This demonstrates YOLOv8's effectiveness in contexts with small datasets. Similarly, in agriculture, [5] showed that YOLOv8 allows efficient segmentation of plant leaves, achieving 89.3% accuracy in an automated plant growth monitoring scenario. In the field of aviation security, [6] used YOLOv8 for early drone detection, attaining an impressive accuracy of 94.7%. These studies highlight that increasing data improves model performance, making YOLOv8 highly effective in various complex contexts.

Optical Character Recognition (OCR) also plays an important role in extracting text from images. In the authors' work [7], the average detection error of Tesseract OCR was evaluated at 11.30%, with 153 words identified out of 173. However, the average error rate on identified words reached 67.65%, indicating room for improvement, particularly in English handwriting recognition. Conversely, in [8], recent improvements to Tesseract OCR for Tifinagh script recognition are highlighted, making it more robust in this context. Although Tesseract is effective in many cases, its performance varies significantly depending on the language and quality of the processed documents [7–9].Large Language Models (LLMs) have revolutionized language analysis by offering deep contextual understanding and coherent text generation [3]. These models can process long, complex texts, extract relevant information, and understand subtle language nuances. In job search applications, LLMs are used to interpret candidates' skills, experiences and education to compare them with job requirements, and generate detailed summaries. They also allow calculating similarity scores and improving recommendations accordingly [10].

Recent studies [11, 12] have shown that using LLMs for corpus generation and annotation has improved relation extraction model performance, achieving 85% accuracy in evaluation tests. Furthermore, [13] reveals that LLMs, particularly in named entity recognition, have reduced classification errors by 15%, reaching 92% accuracy. These results highlight the importance of LLMs in improving the efficiency of text processing systems, particularly for tasks such as automatic summary generation.

3   Materials and Methods

Finding the right personnel quickly and efficiently has become a major challenge for companies, especially when resources and time are limited. Identifying the most qualified candidates from numerous resumes is increasingly time-consuming and requires significant staff resources due to the ever-growing population. To address this issue, we propose enhancing the overall preselection and selection process for the best candidates from a large pool of resumes. This will be achieved through the automation of the preselection and selection processes, allowing for a streamlined approach that ensures efficient analysis and processing of resumes, verifies candidates' suitability for the position, and ultimately facilitates informed decision-making.

3.1   Data Collection and Pre-processing

The resumes used in this study were collected in various formats (PDF, DOC, and DOCX) by the Public Laboratory for Testing and Studies (LPEE). Our objective is to process and analyze these resumes, submitted by candidates applying for positions within the company, using innovative techniques based on Computer Vision and Large Language Models (LLMs). The dataset consists of 5,000 resumes representing diverse candidate profiles.

We began by loading the dataset, which includes unstructured files in multiple formats (see Table 1), and converting each document into a standardized format (images). Duplicate resumes were then removed, retaining only those containing the essential categories relevant to our analysis. Subsequently, the images were converted to grayscale to improve clarity by enhancing text-background contrast and minimizing noise caused by color inconsistencies. This preprocessing step allows the model to better focus on text contours and shapes.

After completing data preprocessing and cleaning, a total of 2,000 usable resumes remained. These selected resumes were then divided into three subsets: 70% (approximately 1,400 YOLO-annotated resume images) for training, 20% (around 400 images) for validation, and the remaining 10% (around 200 images) for testing the model.

Table 1. File Types Comprising the Candidate Resumes Dataset.

File Type	Total
PDF	3254
DOC	1474
DOCX	450

3.2 Proposed Method

The proposed solution first involves developing a Computer Vision-based system capable of analyzing and processing resumes from a large database of resumes in different formats and extracting the required information. Subsequently, the system integrates Large Language Models (LLMs) to provide advanced services, offering high-performance features such as similarity score calculation and classification. The approach of our solution is illustrated in Fig. 1. The initial phase of the process involves the selection of resumes, which is part of the preparation phase. Companies receive many resumes in various formats, including PDF, DOC, and DOCX, for job offers.

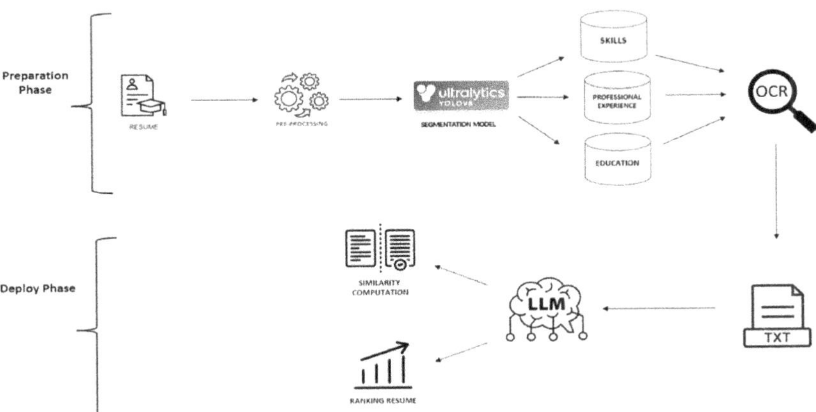

Fig. 1. Architecture of the Proposed Model.

In our proposed model, we consider a set of resumes submitted in these formats as input. First, the input documents are transformed into a homogeneous format, specifically images. Next, we use the YOLOv8 model, which is based on a Computer Vision approach that detects and segments objects or specific sections from images, classifying them into predefined categories. In our case, these categories include skills, work experience, and education, which are extracted from resume images.

To streamline the category extraction process, we used Tesseract OCR to efficiently extract the text from the identified segments. The OCR process begins by dividing the image into parts corresponding to text blocks, followed by isolating lines, words, and finally characters. This allows us to identify the areas of the image containing text and structure the information into a usable format, making it easier to analyze while ensuring high accuracy, whatever the layout. Figure 2 illustrates how categories of interest are segmented in a resume image.

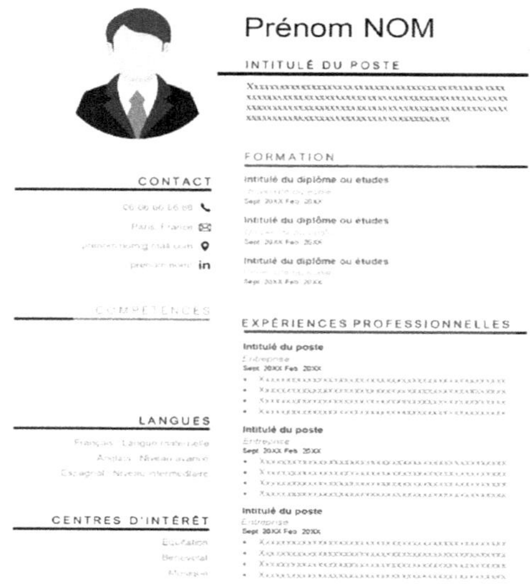

Fig. 2. Example of Segmented Sections in a Resume.

After extracting the entities, the information is stored in a variable text format (see Fig. 3) in order to proceed to the deployment phase. At this stage, we exploit Large Language Models (LLMs), based on high-performance architectures like Transformers, which allow us to effectively understand and manage long-term relationships between words in texts. These models are particularly efficient for tasks such as similarity score calculation, classification, and other advanced text analyses. One method used in our work is cosine similarity calculation, a powerful tool for measuring the similarity between two vectors in a vector representation space, formulated as follows:

$$\cos(A, B) = \frac{A \bullet B}{\|A\| \|B\|} \tag{1}$$

This technique measures the angle between two vectors, making it possible to evaluate the semantic proximity between sentences or words.

Fig. 3. Example of output in variable text format.

Recently, the accessibility of these Large Language Models via APIs provided by organizations has facilitated their integration into our processes. In this context, we chose to integrate two APIs: those of OpenAI and Gemini. This integration allows us to leverage their advanced capabilities to calculate the similarity score between a resume and a job offer, as well as to classify candidates based on their job designations, thereby optimizing our selection process. Subsequently, a performance comparison between the two APIs was conducted to identify the most reliable one in terms of similarity rate.

3.3 Performance Metrics

In this study, several performance metrics were used to evaluate the effectiveness of our proposed model, namely Precision, Recall, F1-score, and mean Average Precision (mAP). These metrics measure how well our model correctly detects relevant categories while minimizing errors. Each object class is evaluated independently, measuring the overlap area between predicted and reference zones.

Precision is the ratio of True Positives to the total number of True Positives and False Positives. It measures the model's ability to correctly segment relevant sections of resumes (skills, education, and experience) without including irrelevant zones.

$$Precision = \frac{TP}{TP + FP} \tag{2}$$

Recall takes a different approach. Instead of focusing on False Positives, it considers the number of False Negatives, that is, relevant information that the model failed to detect. It measures the model's ability to identify all important sections of resumes.

$$Recall = \frac{TP}{TP + FN} \tag{3}$$

F1-score is a metric that combines both precision and recall into a single harmonized metric. It evaluates the model's ability to correctly segment resume sections by considering both correctly detected sections (True Positives) and those missed or misidentified (False Negatives and False Positives).

$$F1 - score = 2 * \frac{(Precision * Recall)}{(Precision + Recall)} \tag{4}$$

Mean Average Precision (mAP) is the average of the average precision across all classes. It evaluates how well the model handles segmentation of different resume sections and identifies classes that may require improvement. A high mAP indicates that the model can efficiently detect relevant sections of resumes with good precision at various confidence levels.

$$mAP = \frac{1}{N} \sum_{i}^{N} AP_i \tag{5}$$

4 Results and Discussion

After applying our methodology, the obtained results (see Table 2) show the performance metrics of the customized YOLOv8 model (training model, skills model, and professional experience model) for detection and segmentation tasks. The metric measurements for the three models include an average precision of 98.42%, indicating that most positive predictions are correct, and an average recall of 99.02%, highlighting the models' ability to capture most of the present categories. The F1-score, which balances precision and recall, is particularly high for all models, confirming that the models are well-balanced and effective for detection. This demonstrates overall optimal performance in terms of segmentations and precise and complete detection.

During the similarity score calculation and resume ranking phase for a given job offer, a comparative analysis of the similarity values obtained from the OpenAI and Gemini APIs was performed (see Fig. 4).

Table 2. Comparison of model performances across various metrics and their averages.

Metric	Model 1 (Professional experience)	Model 2 (Skills)	Model 3 (Education)	Average
Precision	0.9782	0.9804	0.9941	0.98
Recall	0.983	0.9924	0.9953	0.99
mAP50	0.9927	0.9911	0.9949	0.99
mAP50–95	0.9731	0.9299	0.9612	0.95
F1-score	0.9806	0.9864	0.9942	0.98

The results in Fig. 4 present a comparison of similarity scores between OpenAI and Gemini for a set of 50 resumes. While both models show variations in performance,

OpenAI consistently achieves higher similarity scores across most resumes. This consistency highlights its efficiency and reliability in identifying relevant matches for the job offer. In contrast, Gemini's performance is less uniform, with fluctuations suggesting varying levels of accuracy across different resumes.

Our findings align with those of [16], which observed similar trends in their analysis of both models, further confirming that OpenAI remains the most reliable choice for this task (see Fig. 5).

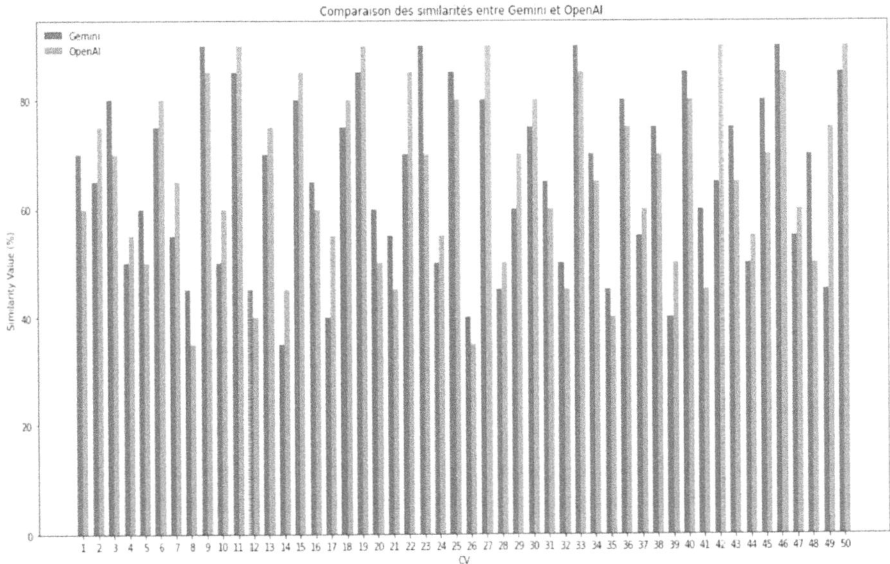

Fig. 4. Evaluation of similarity rates between Gemini and OpenAI.

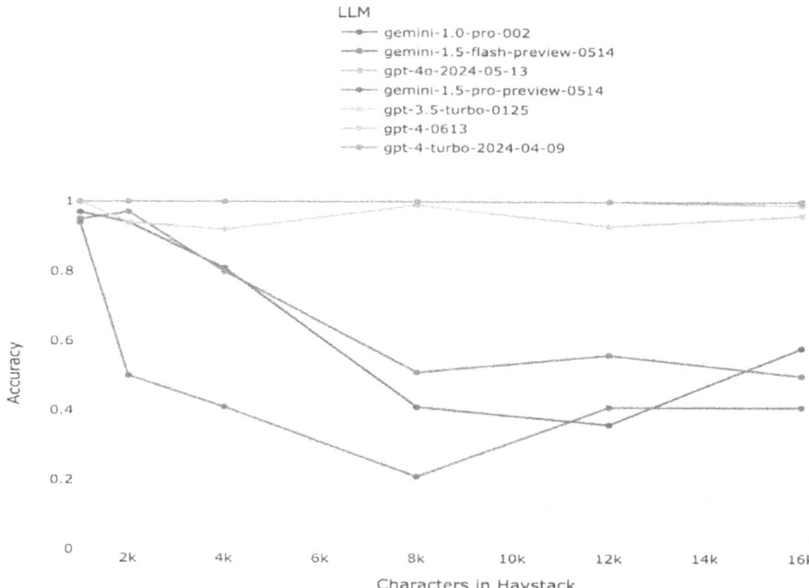

Fig. 5. Comparative assessment of LLM performances between OpenAI and Gemini [16].

5 Conclusion

In our work on resume processing, the model significantly improved the efficiency of the recruitment process by streamlining the analysis and ranking of candidates. Through the combined use of YOLOv8 for segmentation and Tesseract OCR for information extraction, manual tasks are reduced, thereby minimizing human error. The LLM models based on the Gemini and OpenAI APIs were highly effective in evaluating the match between resumes and job offers, with OpenAI showing slightly better performance in terms of consistency and overall efficiency. This automated system represents a major advancement for companies, providing a quick and accurate solution for managing applications, and it also has the potential to support career guidance for job seekers [17].

However, it is worth noting that our automated system has certain limitations. For example, access to the ChatGPT API is subscription-based, which could represent a financial constraint for some companies. Additionally, the system is limited by the API's request capacity, allowing only a specific number of resumes to be processed. This limitation may affect scalability, particularly for large-scale recruitment operations that need to handle high volumes of resumes efficiently.

Given these limitations, the Meta LLaMA model could present an interesting research perspective in this field.

References

1. Kang, J., Zhao, L., Wang, K., Zhang, K.: Research on an improved YOLOv8 image segmentation model for crop pests. In: Advances in Computer, Signals and Systems, vol. 7, 3, pp. 1–8. Springer, Heidelberg (2023). https://doi.org/10.23977/acss.2023.070301

2. Garai, S. K., Paul, O., Dey, U., Ghoshal, S., Biswas, N., Mondal, D. S.: A novel method for image to text extraction using tesseract-OCR. In: Research on Smart Society, vol. 3, 2. pp. 1–x. Springer, Heidelberg (2024)

3. Silva, K., Frommholz, I., Can, B., Blain, F., Sarwar, R., Ugolini, L.: Forged-GAN-BERT: authorship attribution for LLM-generated forged novels. In: Proceedings of the 18th Conference of the European Chapter of the Association for Computational Linguistics: Student Research Workshop, pp. 325–337. Springer, Heidelberg (2024)

4. Aboah, A., Wang, B., Bagci, U., Adu-Gyamfi, Y.: Real-time multi-class helmet violation detection using few-shot data sampling technique and YOLOv8. In: Proceedings of the IEEE/CVF Conference on Computer Vision and Pattern Recognition, pp. 5350–5358. Springer, Heidelberg (2023)

5. Wang, P., et al.: Leaf segmentation using modified YOLOv8-Seg models. Life. **14**(6), 780. , Springer, Heidelberg (2024). https://doi.org/10.3390/life14060780

6. Yilmaz, B., Kutbay, U.: YOLOv8 based drone detection: performance analysis and optimization. Preprints. Springer, Heidelberg. (2024). https://doi.org/10.20944/preprints202407.2127.v1

7. Joshi, K.: Study of tesseract OCR. GLS KALP: J. Multidiscip. Stud. **1**(2), 41–50. Springer, Heidelberg (2021)

8. Benaissa, A., Bahri, A., Allaoui, A.E., Salahddine, M.A.: Build a trained data of tesseract OCR engine for Tifinagh script recognition. Data Metadata. **2**, 185–185. Springer, Heidelberg (2023). https://doi.org/10.56294/dm2023185

9. Sporici, D., Cuşnir, E., Boiangiu, C.-A.: Improving the accuracy of tesseract 4.0 OCR engine using convolution-based preprocessing. Symmetry. **12**(5), 715. Springer, Heidelberg (2020). https://doi.org/10.3390/sym12050715

10. Xu, S., et al.: Reasoning before comparison: LLM-enhanced semantic similarity metrics for domain specialized text analysis. arXiv.org. Springer, Heidelberg

11. Génération et annotation de corpus pour l'entraînement et l'évaluation de modèles d'extraction de relations: utilisation de bibliothèques de génération de données et de LLMs. In: Institut des sciences informatiques et de leurs interactions - CNRS Sciences informatiques [INS2I-CNRS]. Springer, Heidelberg. Disponible sur: https://insa-toulouse.hal.science/EVA LLLM2024/hal-04678383v1

12. Résumé automatique de textes d'enquêtes judiciaires: retour d'expérience. In: Institut des sciences informatiques et de leurs interactions - CNRS Sciences informatiques [INS2I-CNRS]. Springer, Heidelberg. Disponible sur: https://insa-toulouse.hal.science/EVALLLM2024/hal-04678366v1

13. De Murcia, G., El-Allali, I., Meineri, L., Gillard, L., Lastmann, S.: Rapport de Participation de Smart Tribune à EvalLLM2024: Quelques Usages de LLMs dans l'Univers de la Reconnaissance d'Entités Nommées. In: Atelier sur l'évaluation des modèles génératifs (LLM) et challenge d'extraction d'information few-shot. Springer, Heidelberg (2024)

14. Octavany, O., Wicaksana, A.: Cleveree: an artificially intelligent web service for Jacob voice chatbot. TELKOMNIKA (Telecommunication Computing Electronics and Control). **18**(3), 1422 . Springer, Heidelberg (2020). https://doi.org/10.12928/telkomnika.v18i3.14791

15. Anwar, A.: What is average precision in object detection & localization algorithms and how to calculate it? Medium. Springer, Heidelberg. Disponible sur: https://towardsdatascience.com/what-is-average-precision-in-object-detection-localization-algorithms-and-how-to-cal culate-it-3f330efe697b

16. Wiik, L.: OpenAI's GPT-4o vs. Gemini 1.5 context memory evaluation. Medium. Springer, Heidelberg. Disponible sur: https://medium.com/%40lars.chr.wiik/openais-gpt-4o-vs-gem ini-1-5-context-memory-evaluation-1f2da3e15526

17. Zahour, O., Benlahmar, E.H., Eddaoui, A., Ouchra, H., Hourrane, O.: A system for educational and vocational guidance in Morocco: chatbot E-orientation. Procedia Comput. Sci. **175**, 554–559. Springer, Heidelberg (2020)

Sentiment Classification of COVID-19 Tweets: A Hybrid Hadoop Approach Using Deep Learning and Fuzzy Logic Theory

Fatima Es-sabery[1,2](✉) (iD)

[1] Department of computer science, Sultan Moulay Slimane University,
Beni Mellal, Morocco
[2] Department of Economics and Management Sciences, Faculty of Law, Economics
and Social Sciences, Hassan II University of Casablanca, Mohammedia, Morocco
`fatima.essabery@gmail.com`

Abstract. Recent advancements in opinion mining on X (formerly Twitter) have focused on analyzing tweets to determine user sentiments about specific events. Many researchers have adopted machine learning and deep learning methods for this task. This study proposes a new approach that combines the C4.5 algorithm, fuzzy rule patterns, and convolutional neural networks (CNNs) for sentiment analysis. The approach involves six steps: first, preprocessing the data to remove noise; second, vectorizing the tweets using word embeddings; third, using CNNs to extract key sentiment and contextual features; fourth, fuzzifying the CNN outputs with a Gaussian fuzzifier to handle ambiguous data; fifth, applying a fuzzy version of the C4.5 algorithm to generate a fuzzy decision tree and rule base; and finally, classifying new tweets using fuzzy General Reasoning based on the rule base. This hybrid method effectively handles uncertainty and imprecision in tweet data by combining CNN and C4.5 technologies with fuzzy logic. The fuzzy rule system consists of three phases: fuzzification, fuzzy C4.5-based inference, and defuzzification via General Reasoning. The approach was tested on a Hadoop-based cluster of five nodes, allowing it to manage large-scale data. Experimental results showed that the proposed model outperformed other classification methods on the COVID-19_Sentiments dataset, with notable improvements in precision (94.56%), and an overall classification accuracy of 95.15%. This demonstrates its effectiveness in handling large datasets and improving classification performance.

Keywords: Fuzzy C4.5 procedure · CNN · Hadoop Framework · X opinion mining

1 Introduction

Communication has always been crucial for problem-solving and promoting social responsibility, but modern communication has shifted significantly with

O. Zahour et al. (Eds.): ICTIM 2024, CCIS 2655, pp. 289–300, 2026.
https://doi.org/10.1007/978-3-032-15147-6_28

the widespread use of digital networks. Platforms such as Instagram, TikTok, Facebook, WhatsApp, X, and YouTube are now central to social interaction. Specifically, the X platform allows users to share short personal posts, expressing opinions, emotions, and attitudes. Organizations, in turn, gather and analyze these posts to make informed decisions regarding their products, services, or topics. This process is referred to as X opinion mining or X sentiment analysis [1, 2].

The X platform contains valuable data relevant to various fields, including economics, social issues, and politics [3]. Analyzing this vast data manually is challenging, making X opinion mining tools essential for extracting insights. This process aims to understand user sentiments and opinions on specific topics and is a key research area in Natural Language Processing (NLP) [4]. X opinion mining can occur at three levels: sentence, feature, and document, with our focus on the sentence level. It has applications in marketing, education, stock market predictions, and customer trend analysis. Notably, it is used in political elections to forecast outcomes and assess public satisfaction with policies [5].

Researchers in Natural Language Processing (NLP) have conducted X sentiment analysis through five main tasks: data classification, data gathering, data cleansing, data representation, and feature extraction. They gathered data from the X platform's API, annotating tweets as positive, neutral, or negative [6]. Data cleansing involved various preprocessing techniques to remove noise, while data representation used vectorization methods such as Bag-of-Words and TF-IDF to convert text into numerical forms. Feature extraction employed methods like Chi-square and Gini Index to identify relevant features. Finally, different classification algorithms, including lexicon-based techniques and machine learning approaches, were utilized for data classification.

This paper introduces a hybrid approach that integrates machine learning and deep learning to optimize their strengths while addressing their limitations. Machine learning methods are effective for smaller datasets and are less prone to overfitting, while deep learning models are better at extracting accurate features from larger datasets. To improve feature extraction from tweets, the authors utilize Convolutional Neural Networks (CNNs) and apply Fuzzy C4.5 as the classifier, enhanced by a rule-based fuzzy system to manage data imprecision. The approach employs a Hadoop cluster with one master node and four subordinate nodes to efficiently handle large volumes of data. The method aims to enhance opinion mining by estimating sentiment scores for tweets (negative, neutral, positive) and evaluating its performance against existing scientific approaches using various metrics such as precision, execution time, accuracy, F1-score and recall. Results show that the hybrid framework outperforms other algorithms, confirming its effectiveness in addressing sentiment analysis challenges.

The rest of this paper is organized as follows: Sect. 2 presents a review of previous research, providing context and foundational insights relevant to our study. Section 3 details the materials and methods used, outlining the analytical techniques applied. Section 4 covers the experimental validation, where we discuss the results and evaluate the effectiveness of our approach. Finally, Sect. 5

concludes the paper, summarizing key findings and potential avenues for future research.

2   Previous Research

In this section, we provide a concise overview of innovative research studies sourced from the literature, covering various methods such as machine learning, deep learning, and fuzzy approaches, all applied to sentiment analysis.

A comparative study conducted by Kanakaraddi *et al.* [7] examined several supervised algorithms for sentiment analysis, including support vector machine (SVM), random forest (RF), max entropy (ME) and naive Bayes (NB). Out of these approaches, the SVM demonstrated the highest classification rate, reaching an impressive 79.90%. In the research paper [8], the authors explored the application of five distinct machine learning approaches to analyze a movie review dataset. The supervised classifiers utilized in this study including multinomial NB, decision tree (DT), Bernoulli NB, SVM and ME. The results obtained from the experiments revealed that multinomial NB achieved commendable achievement when considering the precision (92.94%), F-score (87.87%), and accuracy (88.5%). On the other hand, the SVM demonstrated superior achievement when considering the recall (89.33%). In the work of [9], the authors analyzed customer reviews of restaurants by employing various supervised algorithms, including SVM, RF, NB, k-nearest neighbor (KNN) and DT. Through their simulations, they discovered that the SVM classifier attained a superior accuracy of 94.56% for the given dataset compared to the other approaches.

Within the realm of literature, there have been numerous investigations that have been conducted to perform sentiment classification tasks using deep neural networks. For example: The research conducted by [10] discusses the use of a CNN to classify the X dataset, leveraging its capacity to effectively capture, identify, and extract overarching features by leveraging the linguistic and lexical relationships among these features. In the work of [11], the authors in their pursuit of improvement, integrated a multi-Head attention technique with the CNN. The authors' proposed approach involves the integration of features to generate diverse feature channels, followed by the implementation of a multi-channel CNN for the detection of opinion words from multiple perspectives. Subsequently, the authors employed the multi-head attention approach to educe relevant characteristics from a wide range of dimensions. The practical results substantiate that the suggested method achieved the utmost classification accuracy, reaching 86.32%, when utilizing eight heads in the mechanism of multiple attention.

As reported in [12], the study introduces a novel classifier that combines the naive Bayes machine learning algorithm and fuzzy logic classifier for performing sentiment analysis. On analysis of their experimental results, they have proved that the proposed hybrid classifier provides better sentiment classification performance. The findings of [13] show that the authors introduces a robust hybrid classifier that incorporates the support vector machine and fuzzy domain ontology to establish an automated procedure for extracting and identifying the semantic information and feature from the given reviews. Then apply the learning process to assign each review to class label of positive, neutral, or negative.

3   Materials and Methods

In this study, we present a novel approach to sentiment analysis on X, particularly focusing on the fast-evolving field of X opinion mining. Unlike many existing methods that rely solely on machine and deep learning techniques, our contribution lies in the integration of three key elements: the fuzzy C4.5 procedure, the fuzzy rule pattern (FRP), and the Convolutional Neural Network (CNN). Notably, our approach is characterized by the utilization of CNN as a feature extractor, departing from the conventional use of CNN as a classifier in most papers.

This innovative approach unfolds through six stages, each strategically designed to address challenges associated with imprecise and ambiguous tweet data. Beginning with robust pre-processing techniques to eliminate noise and irrelevant information, we proceed to intelligent tweet vectorization using a word embedding technique. The application of CNN, as a feature extractor, facilitates the intelligent extraction of crucial sentiment and contextual features. Importantly, we introduce a crucial step in our methodology by fuzzifying CNN outputs using the Gaussian Fuzzifier (GF) to manage uncertainty effectively. The fuzzy version of the C4.5 procedure is then employed to construct both a fuzzy tree and a fuzzy rule base. Additionally, we apply fuzzy CNN to generate fuzzy rules, automating the approach instead of relying on human intervention, as is the case with other fuzzy systems.

For classifying new tweets, we implement the fuzzy General Reasoning (FGR) technique based on the established fuzzy rules. What distinguishes our approach is the seamless integration of CNN and C4.5 technologies, complemented by the FRP to handle imprecision and ambiguity in tweet data.

Figure 1 shows the eight stages of the hybrid model developed in this study, which include data capturing, data cleaning, data representation, feature engineering with a convolutional neural network, data fuzzification, building a classification training model using a fuzzy C4.5 decision tree, testing the model with a general fuzzy reasoning approach, and parallelization through the Hadoop framework.

3.1   Data Pre-processing

Typically, tweets are considered as semi-unstructured and unstructured data, often containing inconsistent, incomplete, unwanted, and noisy information. Consequently, in order to overcome these limitations and extract meaningful insights from such unstructured data, it becomes crucial to employ advanced methods of data pre-processing on tweets. The preprocessing techniques used are described in the following Table 1:

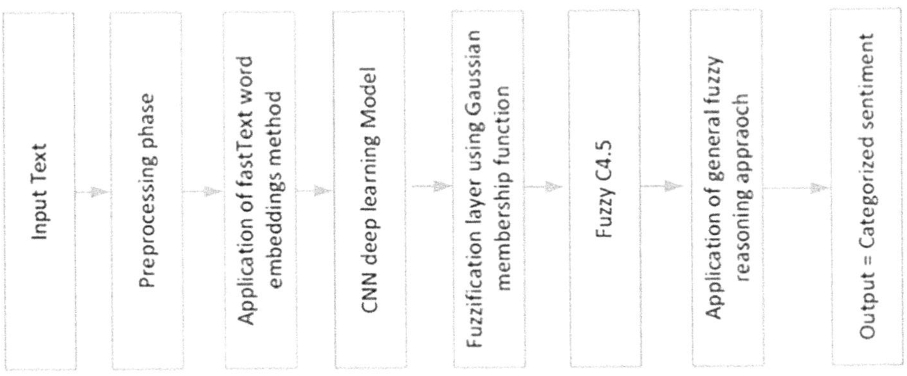

Fig. 1. The overall architecture of the hybrid approach developed in this study.

Table 1. Data Preprocessing Steps

Step	Description
Abbreviations, Spelling Mistakes, and Slang	X, the predominant social network, facilitates the expression of ideas and opinions within 280-character tweets. Users often resort to abbreviations, slang, and spelling mistakes, negatively impacting opinion mining. To address this, the approach expands abbreviations, replaces slang with complete forms, and corrects spelling using the WordNet dictionary. Punctuation marks, URLs, special characters, hashtags, white spaces, numbers, and usernames are eliminated.
Lower-case	After preprocessing, only uppercase and lowercase letters are retained, and all special characters are removed. Capital letters within tweets are changed to lowercase.
Substitute Elongated Words	This strategy eliminates repeated letters in words, transforming elongated words into shortened versions. For example,"Glaaaaad" becomes "Glaad".
Exclude Stop-Words	Commonly encountered irrelevant words are removed to enhance sentiment analysis effectiveness.
Tokenization	Tweets are broken down into significant terms or tokens using the NLTK tokenizer.
Lemmatization	After tokenization, lemmatization converts words to their root form (lemma), reducing them to a single base word. For example, "happy," "Glad," and "Good" are replaced with "Good".
Stemming	Following lemmatization, stemming identifies the stem of each word during tweet processing, often obtained by removing prefixes and/or suffixes. For example, "running," "runner," and "runs" are reduced to "run", while "better," "best," and "good" are reduced to "good". These operations are performed using the Porter stemmer algorithm.

3.2   Data Representation

The primary objective of this study is to determine the sentiment orientations of tweets collected from the platform X, specifically assessing whether the sentiments are positive, negative, or neutral. To achieve this, the raw tweets first undergo preprocessing steps such as tokenization, normalization, and stopword removal. Following preprocessing, the tweets are transformed into an assembly language format, which enables consistent encoding and allows for further data analysis, processing, and classification. In this phase, we applied an unsupervised learning approach using the FastText data vectorization technique. FastText facilitates the conversion of words into numerical representations by generating word vectors based on an n-gram value of 2, effectively capturing subword information. This approach reduces the dimensionality of the data, making it computationally efficient for downstream sentiment classification tasks.

3.3   Feature Engineering

The process of feature extraction and selection is essential in NLP, with deep learning models increasingly favored over traditional machine learning due to their ability to automatically learn relevant features during training. Unlike conventional algorithms that require manually crafted features, deep neural networks, especially Convolutional Neural Networks (CNNs), can autonomously identify critical patterns in data, making them highly effective for feature selection. In our approach, we specifically chose CNNs for their robust architecture—comprising convolutional, pooling, and fully connected layers—which enables efficient and precise extraction of meaningful features, thereby optimizing the performance and accuracy of our NLP model.

3.4   Data Fuzzification Phase

After employing the convolutional neural network (CNN) to extract and select the most consistent and relevant features, the next step is data fuzzification. This step involves applying a Gaussian fuzzifier to the set of features generated in the previous phase. The Gaussian fuzzifier is defined by two parameters: sd ($sd > 0$), representing the standard deviation, and cv, indicating the core value. The computation of the membership degree of y involves the use of the subsequent equation (1):

$$\mu_A(y) = e^{-\frac{(y - cv)^2}{2.sd^2}} \tag{1}$$

3.5   Fuzzy C4.5 Procedure

After completing the data fuzzification stage, wherein the crisp neuron values of the fully connected layer were fuzzified, the subsequent stage focuses on constructing the fuzzy tree. This is achieved by utilizing the fuzzy C4.5 algorithm and subsequently deriving imprecise rules from the resultant tree of vagueness, which are then stored in the rule repository. In this work, our classifier merges the principles of the fuzzy set theory with the C4.5 algorithm. The fuzzy C4.5 algorithm is based on the information fuzzy gain ratio (IGRF) of the nth attribute, which is calculated using the following equation (2)

$$IGRF_{F^{(n)}} = \frac{IGF_{F^{(n)}}}{SI_{F^{(n)}}} \tag{2}$$

where $IGF_{F^{(n)}}$ is the information fuzzy gain of the nth attribute concerning the collection of training examples computed employing the formula (3), and $SI_{F^{(n)}}$ represents the split information measured by applying the equation (4).

$$IGF_{F^{(n)}} = EF - EF_{F^{(n)}} \tag{3}$$

Hence, the IGF equals the disparity of vague logic-based entropy (EF) of the collection of examples being trained, and the fuzzy logic-based entropy ($EF_{F^{(n)}}$) of the nth attribute. Therefore, the split information $SI_{F^{(n)}}$ of the nth attribute is calculated by utilizing the subsequent mathematical expression (4):

$$SI_{F^{(n)}} = \sum_{c=1}^{l} - \left(\frac{\sum_{y \in Y} D_{F_c^{(n)}}(y^{(n)})}{\sum_{j=1}^{l} \sum_{y \in Y} D_{F_c^{(n)}}(y^{(n)})} \right)$$
$$log \left(\frac{\sum_{y \in Y} D_{F_c^{(n)}}(y^{(n)})}{\sum_{j=1}^{l} \sum_{y \in Y} D_{F_c^{(n)}}(y^{(n)})} \right) \tag{4}$$

where Y is a set of the values of nth feature in the collection of training examples, which possess the linguistic term $F_c^{(n)}$, l is the overall count of linguistic term $F_c^{(n)}$, and $D_{F_c^{(n)}}(y^{(n)})$ is the computed degree of membership of the value $y^{(n)}$ of the nth feature of example y determined by the linguistic term $F_n^{(n)}$.

3.6   General Fuzzy Reasoning Technique

The general fuzzy reasoning algorithm proceeds with the subsequent steps introduced subsequently for the categorization of a novel tweet w_n:

Let $w_n = \{c_{n1}, c_{n2}, ..., c_{nl}\}$ a new example to be classified and determined its class label and $\{LR_1, LR_2, ..., LR_K\}$ a set of K extracted linguistic rules from the generated fuzzy tree in the previous phase of our work. Let $MV_j(c_{nj}), j = 1, ..., l$ be the computed membership value of the feature value c_{nj} by employing the Gaussian fuzzy set function.

- Determine the compatibility rate (CR) between the new tweet w_n and every linguistic rule LR_x for $x = 1, ..., K$ in the rule base by applying the t-norm **t** as described in the following equation (5) :

$$CR(w_n, LR_x) = \mathbf{t}[MV_1(c_{n1}), MV_2(c_{n2}), .., MV_l(c_{nl})] \tag{5}$$

- For every value of the decision feature, compute the classification degree MD_z. MD_z is determined as the gathering of the CR of all fuzzy rules, which are measured in the first step with the value z_a of the decision feature and expresses the CR of the new example to be classified with all the fuzzy rules whose divined class label is z_a by the following equation (6) :

$$MD_{z_a} = \mathbf{f}\{CR(w_n, LR_x)|z_a\} \tag{6}$$

Where z_a is the class label of LR_x, and $\mathbf{f}$ is a gathering operator.

3.7 Parallelization Using Hadoop

The sentiment classification process using the Hadoop framework begins by collecting and splitting tweet or text data into training and testing sets, which are distributed across a Hadoop cluster of five nodes. The Hadoop Distributed File System (HDFS) handles data storage and management, allocating data blocks to slave nodes and metadata to the master node.

In the Preprocessing Phase, data is cleaned, tokenized, and prepared for further processing. Three mappers are used for feature extraction:

- **FastText Mapper** converts text into dense word vectors.
- **CNN Mapper** extracts key features from short texts.
- **Gaussian Mapper** applies fuzziness to handle uncertainty.

After feature extraction, the Fuzzy C4.5 Mapper builds fuzzy decision trees in parallel across the training data. The Fusion Reducer combines these trees into a comprehensive fuzzy decision tree. In the Classification Phase, this fuzzy tree is applied to testing data, with a Fuzzy General Mapper using General Fuzzy Reasoning to classify each data chunk. The results are aggregated by another Fusion Reducer to produce final sentiment classifications. The use of MapReduce enables parallel processing across all phases, making the system highly scalable and efficient for large datasets, while fuzzy logic enhances sentiment classification by managing language uncertainties.

4 Experimental Validation

Experimental validation refers to the rigorous process of testing and evaluating our proposed algorithm and other models in a controlled setting. It involves executing the models on specific dataset and analyzing their performance metrics. The dataset used in our experiments is **COVID-19 Sentiments dataset** which contains text data, such as social media posts, news articles, or public comments, related to the COVID-19 pandemic. This dataset includes sentiments expressed by individuals in India regarding various aspects of the pandemic, such as government responses, public health measures, vaccines, and societal impacts. This dataset comprises 259,458 instances with a neutral sentiment, along with 120,646 tweets conveying negativity and 257,874 tweets expressing positivity. Hence, the collected dataset consists of a total of 637,978 tweets. In this dataset, the decision attribute is labeled as either positive, negative, or neutral. The value of neutrality is represented by 0, while the value of negativity falls within the range of -1 to 0, and the value of positivity ranges from 0 to 1. There are five attributes included in this dataset, which are Target, Ids, Date, Location, and Text. The functional attributes in this dataset are the "Target" and "Text" attributes.

In the empirical analysis, we used a standard train-validation-test (t/v/t) split technique to guarantee the fairness and reliability of our experimental findings. The dataset was divided into 70% for training, 15% for validation, and 15% for testing. This split was uniformly applied across all tested approaches. Also, our experiments were conducted using Google Colab Pro+, which provides longer runtimes, more frequent access to premium GPUs/TPUs (such as the T4 or V100), and faster hardware. In our case, we utilized NVIDIA T4 GPUs and a high-RAM environment, which provides more memory (up to around 25GB).

4.1 Comparison of Our Approach with Baseline Models

In this first experiment, we will present the experimental outcomes of our hybrid framework. These results were obtained by applying our approach as well as other methods, including CNN, C4.5, fuzzy C4.5, fuzzy rule-based systems, BART-large-mnli (zero-shot), RoBERTa (few-shot), and DistilBERT (fine-tuned). To assess the efficiency and superiority among these approaches, we calculated accuracy, F1-score, Recall, precision, and average time as evaluation metrics, as illustrated in the following Table 2.

Table 2. The results derived from the ablation studies rely on metrics such as Accuracy, Recall, Precision, F1-score, and Average time.

Techniques	Accuracy	Recall	Precision	F1-score	A. time (s)
Our model	95.15	94.72	94.56	94.63	7.65
CNN	82.46	79.35	80.02	77.96	2.54
C4.5	65.34	64.87	66.55	63.98	4.48
Fuzzy C4.5	79.65	78.41	79.21	77.86	5.98
Fuzzy rule-based system	86.50	85.64	84.78	85.36	4.36
BART-large-mnli (zero-shot)	93.76	92.46	93.18	92.56	420
RoBERTa (few-shot)	94.64	95.06	94.02	93.98	196
DistilBERT (fine-tuned)	90.40	93.03	87.98	90.43	1500

From Table 2, it is evident that our hybrid framework surpasses all other algorithms in terms of accuracy, recall, precision, and F1 score across both datasets. In other words, the hybrid method demonstrates superior efficiency in classifying new instances compared to each individual method. Additionally, our experiments show that our approach outperforms the implemented transformers (RoBERTa, BART, and DistilBERT) across different evaluation methods (zero-shot, few-shot, and fine-tuned scenarios). This indicates that our proposed hybrid approach effectively balances efficiency and long-range dependency modeling in natural language processing (NLP) by optimizing the trade-offs between computational resources and the ability to capture complex relationships within text.

The average time results show a significant variation across the different techniques. For dataset, CNN is the most time-efficient, with an execution time of just 2.54 s, followed by C4.5 at 4.48 s and FRS at 4.36 s. In contrast, our model takes 7.65 s, which is relatively higher but still far more efficient than models like RoBERTa (few-shot) and DistilBERT (fine-tuned), which take 196 s and 1500 s, respectively.

4.2   Sensitivity Analysis of Different Algorithms

The Table 3 shows the sensitivity analysis of different algorithms that are part of our hybrid model for sentiment analysis. It assesses the effect of preprocessing, FastText, CNN, and fuzzy logic on the hybrid model's performance employing accuracy, recall, precision, and F1-score. The empirical findings proves that the preprocessing is important as the model attaining 94.02% accuracy when preprocessing techniques are applied, in comparison to only 64.41% without them. Another thing that greatly affects the performance is using FastText which after creating high quality word embeddings capturing semantic meaning results in an accuracy of 91.34%. In contrast, performance decreases to 78.61% if FastText is removed from the hybrid model. CNN is another critical component, as it improves the accuracy to 82.46%, due to its ability to extract local features and dependencies in the data. Without CNN, the model's performance drops notably

Table 3. The sensitivity analysis of all techniques used in our approach is based on empirical findings and evaluated using metrics such as accuracy, recall, precision, and F1-score.

Techniques	Accuracy	Recall	Precision	F1-score
With preprocessing	94.02	94.65	95.51	93.98
Without preprocessing	64.41	63.18	65.35	63.54
With FastText	91.34	92.34	91.98	92.70
Without FastText	78.61	79.45	78.23	77.01
With CNN	82.46	79.35	80.02	77.96
Without CNN	65.94	64.22	63.87	64.00
With fuzzy logic	86.50	85.64	84.78	85.36
Without fuzzy logic	71.12	72.04	71.97	70.64
Our model	**95.15**	**94.72**	**94.56**	**94.63**

to 65.94%. Fuzzy logic is effective in handling uncertainties and making decisions in ambiguous cases, contributing to an accuracy of 86.50%. Without fuzzy logic, the accuracy decreases to 71.12%. Overall, the hybrid model that incorporates all techniques—preprocessing, FastText, CNN, and fuzzy logic—delivers the highest performance, with an accuracy of 95.15%. This demonstrates the strength of combining these methods, as each contributes to improving the overall classification results in sentiment analysis.

5   Conclusions

In conclusion, the hybrid framework presented in this study for sentiment analysis of tweets showcases a comprehensive and effective approach. The six-stage model, involving data gathering, pretreatment, vectorization, extraction and selection, classification, and fuzzy reasoning, proved to be robust and outperformed existing classifiers in terms of error and accuracy rates. The integration of FastText for data representation, CNN for data extraction, and Gaussian fuzzy set function for classification contributed to achieving high accuracy levels of 95.15%.

Our forthcoming research involves replacing the fuzzy C4.5 algorithm with a deep learning pattern for tweet classification. Additionally, we plan to explore and compare the effectiveness of various feature extractors and feature selectors. In this regard, we will also investigate the application of CNN to extract and select features in our contributions. Furthermore, we intend to explore the utilization of a Mamdani fuzzy system to handle the uncertainty and vagueness in the data, as an alternative to the fuzz rule-based model employed in this study.

References

1. Salur, M.U., Aydin, I.: A novel hybrid deep learning model for sentiment classification. IEEE Access **8**, 58080–58093 (2020). https://doi.org/10.1109/ACCESS.2020.2982538
2. Antonakaki, D., Fragopoulou, P., Ioannidis, S.: A survey of twitter research: Data model, graph structure, sentiment analysis and attacks. Expert Syst. Appl. **164**, 114006 (2021). https://doi.org/10.1016/j.eswa.2020.114006
3. Almatraf, O., Parack, S., Chavan, B.: Application of location-based sentiment analysis using twitter for identifying trends towards Indian general elections 2014. In: Proceedings of the 9th International Conference on Ubiquitous Information Management and Communication, pp. 1–5 (2015). https://doi.org/10.1145/2701126.2701129
4. Sarlan, A., Nadam, C., Basri, S.: Twitter sentiment analysis. In: Proceedings of the 6th International Conference on Information Technology and Multimedia, pp. 212–216 (2014). https://doi.org/10.1109/ICIMU.2014.7066632
5. Sharma, P., Moh, T.-S.: Prediction of Indian election using sentiment analysis on Hindi twitter. In: 2016 IEEE International Conference on Big Data (big Data), pp. 1966–1971 (2016). https://doi.org/10.1109/BigData.2016.7840818
6. Saad, S.E., Yang, J.: Twitter sentiment analysis based on ordinal regression. IEEE Access **7**, 163677–163685 (2019). https://doi.org/10.1109/ACCESS.2019.2952127

7. Rahman, A , Hossen, M.S.: Sentiment analysis on movie review data using machine learning approach. In: 2019 International Conference on Bangla Speech and Language Processing (ICBSLP), pp. 1–4 (2019).https://doi.org/10.1109/ICBSLP47725.2019.201470

8. Krishna, A., Akhilesh, V., Aich, A., Hegde, C.: Sentiment analysis of restaurant reviews using machine learning techniques. In: Emerging Research in Electronics, Computer Science and Technology: Proceedings of International Conference, ICERECT 2018, pp. 687–696 (2019). https://doi.org/10.1007/978-981-13-5802-960

9. Noor, F., Bakhtyar, M., Baber, J.: Sentiment analysis in e-commerce using SVM on Roman Urdu text. In: Emerging Technologies in Computing: Second International Conference, iCETiC 2019, London, UK, August 19–20, 2019, Proceedings 2, pp. 213–222 (2019). https://doi.org/10.1007/978-3-030-23943-516

10. Liao, S., Wang, J., Yu, R., Sato, K., Cheng, Z.: CNN for situations understanding based on sentiment analysis of twitter data. Procedia Comput. Sci. **111**, 376–381 (2017). https://doi.org/10.1016/j.procs.2017.06.037

11. Behera, R.K., Jena, M., Rath, S.K., Misra, S.: Co-LSTM: convolutional LSTM model for sentiment analysis in social big data. Inf. Process. Manag. **58**(1), 102435 (2021). https://doi.org/10.1016/j.ipm.2020.102435

12. Es-Sabery, F., et al.: A Mapreduce opinion mining for COVID-19-related tweets classification using enhanced ID3 decision tree classifer. IEEE Access **9**, 58706–58739 (2021). https://doi.org/10.1109/ACCESS.2021.3073215

13. Krouska, A., Troussas, C., Virvou, M.: The effect of preprocessing techniques on twitter sentiment analysis. In: 2016 7th International Conference on Information, Intelligence, Systems & Applications (IISA), pp. 1–5 (2016). https://doi.org/10.1109/IISA.2016.7785373

Sustainable Logistics in Healthcare: Addressing Environmental Challenges and Optimizing Medical Supply Chains for a Greener Future

Ikram Ait Hammou[1]([✉]), Mustapha Khiati[2], Marouane Mkik[3], Ali Hebaz[4], Boushib Kaoutar[5], and Omar Zahour[6]

[1] National School of Commerce and Management, University of Chouaib Doukkali (LERSEM), El Jadida, Morocco
Aithammou.ikram@gmail.com
[2] Faculty of Sciences Ben M'sik, Hassan II University of Casablanca (ECAF Lab-FSJESAC), Casablanca, Morocco
[3] The Higher Institute of Nursing and Health Techniques (ISPITS) of Rabat (LARPEG), Rabat, Morocco
[4] National Higher School of Electricity and Mechanics, Hassan II University (PRISME), Casablanca, Morocco
Hebaz.a@ucd.ac.ma
[5] Faculty of Law, Economics and Social, Sciences Souissi, Mohammed V University of Rabat (LARMODAD), Rabat, Morocco
[6] Faculty of Sciences Ben M'Sik, Hassan II University of Casablanca (LTIM), Casablanca, Morocco
omar.zahour@univh2c.ma

Abstract. The topic of this article is the increasing significance of the sustainable reverse logistics solutions in the healthcare industry considering the trends for lowering carbon footprint and maximizing resource utilization on the global level. The key research question focuses on how far existing solutions will enable environmental problems to be solved and medical supply chain performance enhanced. In order to answer this question, a quantitative method was used and the participants comprised 200 healthcare practitioners. In PCA and SEM analyses, the behaviors underpinning the major components affecting general performance were determined. The results reveal that, the implementation of green technologies and improving the efficiency of medical transport are critical success factors in managing the carbon footprint and the operational cost of the supply chain that indicate necessity of moving towards more sustainable health care operations.

Keywords: Sustainable Logistics · Healthcare · Medical Supply Chain · Supply Chain · Greener Future c Management

1 Introduction

The importance of logistics is undeniable for it has become critical in the wake of environmental change affecting the global planet in many industries. Finally, it is worth noting that the change towards greater sustainability is driven by different sectors, and

O. Zahour et al. (Eds.): ICTIM 2024, CCIS 2655, pp. 301–311, 2026.
https://doi.org/10.1007/978-3-032-15147-6_29

particularly important in the healthcare industry. The usually challenging and sometimes volatile nature of medical supply chain management requires the management to respond not only to how to effectively run this supply chain to benefit numerous patients, but also to how to address the continually rising ecological expectations that are being placed on such supply chains.

There are several reasons why there is a growing trend within the health care industry toward developing sustainability in logistics. On one end, healthcare institutions are interested in carrying out activities that would help combat climate change and therefore a consideration to lessen the carbon footprint. On the other hand, they hope to improve the efficiency of resources control and, at the same time, enhance the availability of medicine. These objectives are achieved by the use of integrating green technologies, the electric vehicle, and optimization of trips as the playing balancing change levers.

The purpose of this research is to examine how sustainable logistics strategies can be implemented and applied in the healthcare setting to meet environmental problems and enhance the logistics processes of the medical supply chains. This research is concerned with the patterns of environmentally acceptable operation and efficient resource consumption with emphases on green technologies and employees.

Thus, the underlying question of this research is: **how far can sustainable logistics scenarios respond to expectations for the enhancement of environmental situations and also help in providing better solutions for medical supply chain for a green supply chain?**

The questions of research are as follows:

- What are the main environmental challenges facing the healthcare supply chain, and how do these challenges influence current sustainable logistics practices?
- How can sustainable logistics solutions optimize medical supply chain management while meeting carbon footprint reduction requirements?
- What impacts do sustainable logistics practices have on costs, operational efficiency and quality of services in the healthcare sector?

2 Literature Review

2.1 Overall Sustainable Medical Supply Chain Performance

The actual overall appreciation of the sustainable medical supply chain explains the capacity of the management of logistics activities in the healthcare sector with the least adverse effect to the environment. This concept involves the procuring of raw materials to the delivery of medical equipment, disposal of waste and minimizing on carbon footprints. The objective is to achieve higher frequency, accuracy and responsiveness of deliveries and at the same time assure the quality and accessibility of medical equipment and supplies. However, such a supply chain cannot be sustainable only in terms of the efficiency needed, but has to address the growing concern for corporate social and environmental responsibility [3, 4].

Moreover, this form of supply chain management is cheap in the long-term and also does wonders for the image of healthcare facilities who are being measured by how environmentally friendly they are. The flexibility of the supply chains to recover such disruptions, including through efficiency improvement and capital expenditure on sustainable infrastructure, is turning out to be an important competitive weapon for these institutions. In this context, the entire performance of the S-MSC striving to minimize its environmental impact contributes to enhancing the quality and efficiency of healthcare services with the potential for improving resource utilization for sustainable development [5, 6].

2.2 Adoption of Sustainable Logistics Solutions

Sustainability in its context with logistics in healthcare is therefore more about bringing about change in the channel from the perspective of environmental responsibility that is to achieving the goal of as little impact on the environment as possible while at the same time enhancing the logistical processes. This includes a set of measures to decrease the emission of gases that cause the greenhouse effect, improve the organization of transportations and use of green technologies. For instance, concerning the fourth loop, the factor of route and mode of transportation is very important. By utilizing better ICT tools in route planning, consignment integration, and through the use of low emission automobiles, such as electric powered or hybrid cars it is possible to decrease the carbon footprint of medical deliveries. These technologies also allow for more effective response to changes in demand with less travel than is required [1, 2].

The other area of business practice discusses in the context of sustainability is inventory and warehouse management. Distribution centers could use low energy lighting, energy saving structures and environment friendly climate control devices. The automated systems along with forecasted information regarding inventory eliminates its wastage, thereby eradicating excess inventory, its associated costs and its adverse effects to the environment [7, 8].

2.3 Use of Green Technologies

Integrating green technologies in supply chain management is one of the important mechanisms for the overall decrease of carbon impact in the healthcare industry. This covers all sorts of advancements in technology aimed at optimizing energy use, minimizing emissions of greenhouse gases, and enhancing the prudent use of resources to meet mankind's demands. The usage of electric or a hybrid car to provide medical equipment and supplies is a good real life example of these green technologies. Apart from lowering direct $CO2$ emission these vehicles also mitigate airborne emissions and the effects of constant deliveries within the healthcare system.

Green technology is the innovations as well not restricted to transport activity only. They also cover strategies for improving energy control measures in distribution centres and warehouses. For instance, using energy-efficient lighting like lighting system that are light-emitting diode LED and smart sensor to control temperature and humidity in the storage areas reduce energy consumption a lot. These intelligent systems automatically control energy demands according to the real demand, which not only reduce carbon emissions but also provides a significant cost cutting opportunities for healthcare organizations [11].

2.4 Staff Training and Awareness

Influencing the staff to adopt sustainable logistics practices have a central role in sustainable strategy commitment in healthcare chains. The change towards the more sustainable forms of logistics cannot be achieved without competent employees. In fact employees at all organizational levels are the actors who put into practice these solutions on the operational theatres. Not only does the incorporation of environmental training enrich their knowledge endorsement of environmental problems, but it also offers them the knowledge required to successfully implement these changes to their careers [10].

Several areas of sustainable logistics practices should be addressed in a good training program. This entails management of resources, minimizing wastes, efficient transport to curb droit emissions and the usage of gadgets such as electric cars, or smart management of energy. Employees also require orientation about new technological applications including an automated logistics management system and a CO_2 emissions monitoring application. Such technical skills will enhance awareness of the environmental consequences in every part of supply chain and increase a responsibility and efficiency rates of staff [9].

2.5 Optimization of Medical Transport

Coordinating medical transportation is one of the crucial facets as regards to CO_2 emissions that affects deliveries in the field of health. It is thus possible to increase effectiveness, to find the best route and means of transport to deliver as quick as possible while having as little negative influence on the environment as possible instead of keeping the quality of service jobs high. This optimization is not only looking to minimize fuel utilization, but also logistics costs, or provide access to vital medical products.

One of the most efficient strategies of rationalization of transportation is the application of the fleet management on the basis of the newest technologies including GPS, artificial intelligence, and big data. With such technologies one is able to operate it in a way that it determines the shortest and/or fastest routes for delivery, in relation to traffic patterns, congested areas and distance tsp. between the delivery points. Healthcare companies can also gain more efficient delivery by employing intelligent algorithms, as this results in several lots being made in one trip rather than several single shipments, thus cutting down the amount of vehicles on the road and thus reducing greenhouse gas emissions [1, 6].

The optimization of medical transport also implies the modernization of transport means, for example, using electrical or hybrid vehicles, which produce fewer polluting emissions than vehicles with classical gas/diesel engines. Such products, along the line of having minimum effect on the environment, are also less likely to cost much in terms of fuel and maintenance in the long run. Further, the delivery of small vehicles within the congestion areas of a city could also facilitate enhanced movements within such confines as well as reducing traffic buildup and consequently giving way for lesser emission of CO_2 [3] (Table 1).

Table 1. Research hypotheses

Variable	Item 1	Item 2	Item 3
Overall performance of the sustainable medical supply chain (variable to be explained)	Operational Cost Reduction (FS1)	Reduced carbon footprint (FS2)	Improved availability of medical equipment (FS3)
Adoption of sustainable logistics solutions (explanatory variable)	Use of electric vehicles for deliveries (SER1)	Route Optimization and Shipment Consolidation (SER2)	Use of recyclable packaging materials (SER3)
Use of green technologies (explanatory variable)	Low-energy lighting systems in warehouses (PR1)	Installation of smart sensors for energy management (PR2)	Use of AI software for logistics optimization (PR3)
Staff training and awareness (explanatory variable)	Green Technology Training Program (IIA1)	Waste Reduction Awareness (IIA2)	Training in the use of logistics optimization tools (IIA3)
Optimization of medical transport (explanatory variable)	Electric Vehicle Adoption (RG1)	Consolidation of deliveries to reduce trips (GR2)	Use of drones for medical deliveries in rural areas (GR3)

3 Methodology

The sample for this study consists of 200 participants, professionals in the health sector. Such are the supply chain managers as well as the logisticians, warehouse managers, and specialists involved in green technologies. The lack of a concrete choice permits varied but still plausible opinions on sustainable logistics and environmental issue regarding the medical supply chain.

The first movement in the analysis follows from the application of Principal Component Analysis (PCA). PCA is employed in an attempt to reduce the collected data that concerns the responses of 200 participants and which was retrieved by structured questionnaires that incorporate a 5-Likert scale. These questionnaires include variables such as, use of green technology, training on sustainable logistics and overall performance of the medical supply chain. The data are pre-normalized to minimize effects of measurement levels in the data. It then applies the PCA in extracting the principal components which would give out important factors accounting for the huge response variance. These components offer a clearer view of the factors that most affect sustainable logistics within the context of health care deliveries.

The second aspect of the study involves using the Structural Equations (SEM) technique to analyze the end relations between various variables determined in the process. This method allows for the testing of research hypotheses and also for prediction of the intricate interactions between the explanatory variables and the variable of interest (Fig. 1).

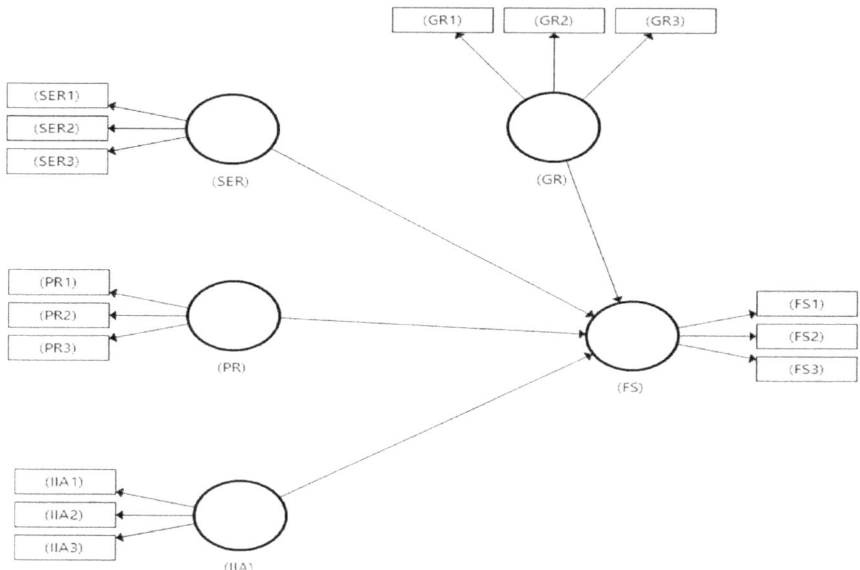

Fig. 1. Conceptual model of research

4   Results and Discussion

The analysis of the external spending of several dimensions of sustainable medical supply chain factors are presented in a detailed manner in Table 2. The overall performance of the supply chain is assessed through three indicators: The latter includes cost reduction (FS1, z = 0.745), the reduction of CO2 emissions as an indicator of the organization's operational environmental efficiency (FS2, z = 0.811), and an increase in the identified Lauren availability of medical equipment (FS3, z = 0.756). Out of these indicators, FS2 – carbon footprint has the highest coefficient suggesting that the assessment of the supply chain performance is significantly boosted by the reduction of carbon footprint. This indicates that attempts to decrease the emission of carbon, has a profound effect on the performance of logistic services in health care. The remaining dimensions which include green technologies (PR1, PR2, PR3) and staff training & awareness (IIA1, IIA2, IIA3) are also depicted with coefficients that depict the influence where awareness attributes to waste reduction influence was approximated at 0.891 as shown below. These results establish the necessity to integrate both approaches— reduction of emissions in environmental footprint and training of staff as essential components of increasing the effectiveness of the sustainable medical chain of supply.

Table 2. Presentation of the External Expenses of the Study

	Overall performance	Adoption of sustainable logistics solutions	Use of green technologies	Staff training and awareness	Optimization of medical transport
(FS1)		0,745			
(FS2)		0,811			
(FS3)		0,756			
(SER1)					
(SER2)					
(SER3)					
(PR1)	0,712				
(PR2)	0,689				
(PR3)	0,812				
(IIA1)				0,785	
(IIA2)				0,891	
(IIA3)				0,801	
(GR1)					
(GR2)					
(GR3)					

In the following Table 3, a discriminant validity test of the various study variables with the Fornell-Larcker criterion is provided. This criterion provides a way to check, and confirm that the authors have ensured that each variable is from the other, and this is very important in as much as to ensure that the measures that one is using is from the other. The number on the diagonal of each line reflects dependent extent of the variable to itself, the number off the diagonal shows dependent extent of the different variables.

For the evaluation of the overall supply chain performance, the diagonal value of 0.901 confirms good discriminant validity. In other words, overall performance is usually assessed relatively independently from other non-financial performance dimensions such as the utilization of sustainable logistic solutions or green technologies. As for discriminant validity, 0.897 attained for the degree of sustainable logistics solutions adoption reflects fairly satisfactory discriminant validity, while the 0.467 correlation between the constructs shows that there is a moderate relationship between the total performance and the extent of sustainable logistics solutions adoption. This indicates that while changing over to sustainable logistics practices, overall performance is affected but not by repetition.

Therefore, with a 0.912 score of green technologies the discriminant validity is high which means that this variable is relatively well discriminated against the other variables. The value of 0.627 of overall performance on the correlation coefficient scale shows a moderately strong relationship and therefore conveys the message that integration of green technologies enhances the supply chain performances significantly. The results derived from the staff training and awareness of the proposed programmes also give low discriminant validity of 0.873 which affirm the variable as well differentiated. Thus, examining the correlation of staff training with the overall performance revealed that its correlation coefficient of 0.459 indicates that staff training was significantly and moderately related to overall supply chain performance.

Last of all, the value of discriminant validity for the optimization of medical transport is slightly lower than all the other variables at 0.678. Lower coefficients such as 0.334 with overall performance demonstrates that medical transportation does affect performance but not as fundamentally as implementing environmentally friendly technologies or training managers and employees. All these variables are significantly distinct and each adds a unique value in the current analysis as well as has moderate correlation with overall performance thus helping in the determination of the right levers for optimizing the medical supply chain.

Table 3. Discriminant validity according to the Fornell criterion

	Overall performance	Adoption of sustainable logistics solutions	Use of green technologies	Staff training and awareness	Optimization of medical transport
Overall performance	0,901				
Adoption of sustainable logistics solutions	0,467	0,897			
Use of green technologies	0,527	0,492	0,912		
Staff training and awareness	0,459	0,395	0,511	0,873	
Optimization of medical transport	0,334	0,369	0,221	0,678	

Cronbach's Alpha, rho_A, Composite reliability and Average Variance Extracted (AVE). These measures test reliability and validity of the scales utilised for each of the above-mentioned dimension.

Cronbach's Alpha is a measure of reflection of scales reliability and an acceptable range is 0.7 and above. All the assessed dimensions have fairly good values ranging from 0.812 overall performance, 0.825 on the use of sustainable logistics solutions, to 0.834 on the use of green technologies. The analysis of these results also supports the items used to measure each construct are valid. Another element, which has a slightly lower save dropping to 0.748, but still acceptable is staff training and awareness and the third element is 0 807 indicating that optimization of medical transport is reasonable.

The Average Variance Extracted (AVE) assesses the proportion of variance the on the indicators to the total variance. Any score above 0.5 is taken to mean that the indicators share good convergent validity, primarily because they are highly correlated with the dimension that they are assumed to measure. All the dimensions assessed have acceptable AVE values; the overall performance is 0.728 and the adoption of sustainable logistics solutions is 0.742. The remaining staff training and awareness dimension has an eTA of 0.669 which however is a little below the rest but enough to estimate good convergent validity (Table 4).

Table 4. Reliability and Validity of Constructs

Size	Cronbach's Alpha	rho_A	Composite Reliability	Average Variance Extracted (AVE)
Overall performance	0.812	0,845	0,892	0,728
Adoption of sustainable logistics solutions	0.825	0,839	0,901	0,742
Use of green technologies	0.834	0,846	0,905	0,749
Staff training and awareness	0.748	0,759	0,862	0,669
Optimization of medical transport	0.807	0,812	0,891	0,725

The overall performance of the model is reported in Table 5, using R^2 (0.934) and R^2 adjusted (0.931), which suggest that the model explains 93.4% of the variability in overall performance. The adjusted R^2 of the model is .635 – slightly lower but still reasonably meaningful and significant due to the number of explanatory variables in the model.

Table 5. R-squared and R-squared adjusted

	R^2	R Adjusted Square
Overall performance	0,934	0,635

Table 6 displays the fit indices of the saturated model and the estimated model. The SRMR reduces from 0.342 to 0.293 thus implying an increased fitness of the estimative model.

Table 6. Presentation of saturated and estimated model

	Saturated model	Estimated Model
SRMR	0,342	0,293
d_ULS	1,453	1,456
d_G	2,345	2,345
Chi-square	345,234	367,345
NFI	0,654	0,675

Values of d_ULS are 1.453lt; d_ULS gt; 1.456 and values of d_G are 2.345 in both models with little fluctuation between the two models. The chi-square value increases from 345.234 to 367.345, which means that more variables in actuality are associated with more complicated estimated model. Last, the NFI (Normed Fit Index) has increased from 0.654 to 0.675, which indicates the increase of the overall fit of the estimated model.

5 Conclusion

Based on the key findings of this research on the emergent trends and issues on sustainable logistics in the healthcare supply chain industry, the following are the main conclusions made. The study established that the execution of eco-responsible logistics means like green technologies, staff training and awareness and transport optimization in the medical supply chain improves its performance. The reduction of carbon footprint and the enhancement of the delivery performance are perhaps the most evident benefits, which strengthen the positions of healthcare facilities as competitors and meet environmental objectives The results of the quantitative analysis carried out with the help of PCA and the method of structural equations confirmed that the assumptions formulated in the course of the research all designate green technologies and optimized transport solutions as the key factors of sustainable efficiency in resource management. Validity and reliability coefficients supported the credibility of the respective measures so the findings of the study are parsimonious with reality.

This paper therefore emphasizes the need to sustain further funding for the programs for the improvement of healthcare sector in terms of ecology, in addition to supply chain concerns that would improve the delivery of equipment. In conclusion, it can be said that the proposed vision of shifting to sustainable logistics solutions is a critical direction for countering environmental problems and achieving better prospects in the development of the medical SCM (Supply Chain Management).

References

1. Khan, H.U., et al: Transforming the capabilities of artificial intelligence in GCC financial sector: a systematic literature review. Wirel. Commun. Mob. Comput. **2022**, 8725767 (2022)

2. Marouane, M., Salwa, M., Hebaz, A.: The acceptance of artificial intelligence in the commercial use of crypto-currency and Blockchain systems. In: International Conference on Information, Communication and Computing Technology, pp. 163–177. Springer Nature Singapore, Singapore (2023)
3. Mkik, M., Mkik, S.: Acceptability aspects of artificial intelligence in Morocco: managerial and theoretical contributions. In: International Conference on Digital Technologies and Applications, pp. 65–74. Springer Nature Switzerland, Cham (2023)
4. Kaur, J.: Towards a sustainable triad: uniting energy management systems, smart cities, and green healthcare for a greener future. In: Emerging Materials, Technologies, and Solutions for Energy Harvesting, pp. 258–285. IGI Global (2024)
5. Fathollahi-Fard, A.M., Govindan, K., Hajiaghaei-Keshteli, M., Ahmadi, A.: A green home health care supply chain: new modified simulated annealing algorithms. J. Clean. Prod. **240**, 118200 (2019)
6. Dixit, A., Routroy, S., Dubey, S.K.: A systematic literature review of healthcare supply chain and implications of future research. Int. J. Pharm. Healthc. Mark. **13**(4), 405–435 (2019)
7. Khan, F., Ali, Y.: Implementation of the circular supply chain management in the pharmaceutical industry. Environ. Dev. Sustain. **24**(12), 13705–13731 (2022)
8. Liu, L., Song, W., Liu, Y.: Leveraging digital capabilities toward a circular economy: reinforcing sustainable supply chain management with industry 4.0 technologies. Comput. Ind. Eng. **178**, 109113 (2023)
9. Hossain, M.K., Thakur, V.: Benchmarking health-care supply chain by implementing Industry 4.0: a fuzzy-AHP-DEMATEL approach. Benchmarking Int. J. **28**(2), 556–581 (2021)
10. Ali, I., Kannan, D.: Mapping research on healthcare operations and supply chain management: a topic modelling-based literature review. Ann. Oper. Res. **315**(1), 29–55 (2022)
11. Hussain, M., Ajmal, M.M., Gunasekaran, A., Khan, M.: Exploration of social sustainability in healthcare supply chain. J. Clean. Prod. **203**, 977–989 (2018)

Sentiment Analysis of Patients in Healthcare: The Case of COVID-19 Vaccination

Soumaya Ounacer[1]([⊠]), Nouhaila Elammouri[1], Soufiane Ardchir[2], Mehdi Lghaouch[1], and Mohamed Azzouazi[1]

[1] Faculty of Science Ben M'sik, Hassan II University, Casablanca, Morocco
soumayaounacer@gmail.com
[2] National School of Business and Management, Hassan II University, Casablanca, Morocco

Abstract. Sentiment analysis can be applied in several fields, particularly in healthcare. This study aims to use it to analyze patients' sentiments regarding COVID-19 vaccination. Since vaccination is considered an essential preventive measure, it plays a major role in disease prevention. However, a portion of the population remains hesitant to get vaccinated. The objective of this study is to analyze positive, negative, and neutral sentiments by examining their geographic distribution, temporal evolution, and identifying the underlying reasons behind each sentiment. This will help target areas where vaccine hesitancy is more pronounced. Then, sentiment analysis models such as SVM (Support Vector Machine), KNN (K-Nearest Neighbors), and BERT (Bidirectional Encoder Representations from Transformers) will be applied, with the latter having proven its efficiency as a powerful tool capable of classifying sentiments expressed in text while capturing their context. The expected outcomes of this study include identifying countries with higher vaccine hesitancy and those where vaccination is more accepted, along with the reasons behind these attitudes. This work will be useful for health authorities, as it will enable them to better target populations hesitant about COVID-19 vaccination and implement interventions to reduce hesitancy rates in these regions.

Keywords: Sentiment Analysis · vaccination · COVID-19 · BERT · Vader · TextBlob · NLP · Transformers

1 Introduction

The COVID-19 pandemic, which appeared in China in 2019, was caused by the SARS-CoV-2 virus. It disrupted the entire world, impacting several sectors such as health, economy, etc. The main challenge during this period was the rapid spread of the virus, leading to thousands of infections and deaths. To curb this rapid transmission, vaccination became the most effective tool. During this phase, several types of vaccines appeared, including Pfizer-BioNTech, Moderna, AstraZeneca, Johnson & Johnson, Novavax, Sinopharm, and Sinovac. Nevertheless, despite all these efforts in vaccine development to stabilize case numbers, a portion of the population hesitated to get vaccinated. This hesitation is probably due to personal or cultural factors related to vaccination. Therefore, a deep understanding of the reasons behind this hesitation is

O. Zahour et al. (Eds.): ICTIM 2024, CCIS 2655, pp. 312–327, 2026.
https://doi.org/10.1007/978-3-032-15147-6_30

essential for health authorities. It is in this context that our research is situated, with the objective of answering the following questions: Which tool should be used to analyze patient sentiments while accurately capturing the sentiments expressed? How are positive and negative sentiments distributed over time and geographically? What are the factors behind vaccine hesitancy and acceptance regarding COVID-19?

This article is structured as follows: The first section is devoted to a literature review on sentiment analysis in the healthcare domain in general, and more specifically in the context of vaccination. Then, the second section describes the approach used while addressing concepts such as Natural Language Processing (NLP) and Transformers. The third section details the methodology adopted for data preparation, annotation, and the application of sentiment analysis. Moreover, the results section presents the performance of the tree models used (BERT, SVM, KNN), accompanied by visualizations aimed at analyzing the study data. Then, the discussion section allows for a comparison of our results with other studies, and finally, a conclusion and future perspectives are proposed.

2 Related Works

The topic of sentiment analysis in healthcare has been explored by numerous previous studies. However, with the emergence of COVID-19, the discussion surrounding vaccination has gained traction, and many new research efforts have focused specifically on vaccine hesitancy. Various approaches have been examined to achieve a major objective: extracting positive, negative, and neutral sentiments. In a literature review [1], the authors explored the various methods used in sentiment analysis in the health domain in general. They highlighted that the studies examined employed a variety of approaches for sentiment analysis, including machine learning techniques and deep learning also that the use of general lexicons has limitations, particularly because they overlook many health-specific terms. In another study [2], the authors also explored different sentiment analysis methods, but this time in a more general context. Their goal was to determine which method was the most effective in this setting. They categorized existing techniques into three groups. The first includes specific tools developed for a particular study, which are specially trained on the study's data and require programming skills, such as KNN. The second category consists of open-source software accessible to the public and requiring less technical expertise, such as SentStrength. Finally, the third category includes commercial software, which are simple and quick-to-use tools like TheySay. Despite the diversity of available tools, the authors emphasize that there remains a need to develop sentiment analysis tools specifically tailored for health-related tweets. In study [3], the authors examine the application of sentiment analysis, focusing specifically on cardiology. The objective is to understand patient opinions and attitudes towards cardiovascular diseases and the recommended treatments. This review aims to systematically summarize the current trends in sentiment analysis in cardiology and the results obtained so far. Another interesting angle of sentiment analysis was explored in a study [4], where the authors suggested that integrating social connection information could improve the performance of public opinion classification on Twitter, particularly regarding HPV vaccination. In another study [5], the authors began to highlight sentiment analysis related to the COVID-19 vaccine to understand the reasons behind patient hesitancy towards the vaccine. The main objective is to identify the sentiment polarities in tweets across seven categories and use this information to understand the reasons behind patient hesitancy, thereby making appropriate policy decisions and vaccination strategies. This article [6], focuses on the use of an AI-based NLP platform capable of capturing the negative topics discussed in tweets from the UK and analyzing them to identify the main reasons behind vaccine hesitancy, such as distrust, misinformation, etc. Article [7] highlights the use of a BERT-based method for sentiment analysis on Twitter, applied to tweets in Italian. The goal is to demonstrate that using a pre-trained BERT model with fine-tuning of parameters and the application of tweet-specific preprocessing techniques can outperform models that are pre-trained directly on tweets in terms of sentiment classification. Research [8] emphasizes the use of natural language processing (NLP) techniques and the supervised classification algorithm K-Nearest Neighbors (KNN) to perform sentiment analysis on tweets regarding COVID-19 vaccines such as Pfizer, Moderna, and AstraZeneca. In study [9],the objective is to identify positive and negative sentiments towards COVID-19 vaccination using text extraction techniques. The analysis compares negative tweets concerning vaccine manufacturing and assesses the evolution of pro-vaccine, anti-vaccine, and hesitant opinions across various geographic regions. It also aims to quantify the characteristics of influential users in each opinion category. In study [10], the aim is to analyze the global perceptions and perspectives of individuals regarding COVID-19 vaccinations and to evaluate the performance of different machine learning and deep learning models for sentiment analysis. To get an idea of the use of sentiment analysis in other areas of healthcare. Table 1 has been created to provide a comparison of these different related works cited, as it will assist our research in exploring new opportunities and understanding what has been previously addressed.

Table 1. Comparison of articles in related works

Article	Publication	Classification Techniques	Results	Advantages	Challenges
[1]	JMIR Medical Informatics, 2020	Machine Learning (SVM, NB, Logistic Regression, etc.), Deep Learning, and General Lexicons.	Data collected from social media, with accuracy varying between 70% and 80% and an F-score below 60%.	Sentiment analysis in this domain enables the improvement of healthcare services, sharing opinions on medications and their side effects and decision-making.	Performance is lower compared to other domains, such as movie reviews.

(continued)

Table 1. (*continued*)

Article	Publication	Classification Techniques	Results	Advantages	Challenges
[2]	JMIR Public Health and Surveillance, 2018	Tools developed and trained for study data, open-source software, and commercial software.	Methods specifically developed for healthcare data provide more accurate analyses.	Comparison between the different tools used for sentiment analysis in healthcare.	These methods may not capture the specificities of the healthcare context.
[3]	Frontiers in Public Health, 2022	Sentiment Lexicon, Machine Learning.	Sentiment analysis can be used to identify emotional risk factors associated with cardiovascular diseases (CVD).	Rapid and systematic processing of large amounts of textual data.	The importance of context and meaning, which must be integrated and considered in sentiment analysis techniques.
[4]	MEDINFO 2015: eHealth-enabled Health, 2015	Data preprocessing, a machine learning algorithm: SVM (Support Vector Machine).	The most accurate classifier achieved an accuracy of 88.6% on the test dataset and used only social connection features.	The use of social connection information led to higher accuracy in classifying anti-vaccine sentiments.	Complexity of analyzing social relationships.
[5]	The Journal of Super-computing, 2023	BERT combined with NB-SVM, geocoding for result interpretation.	the combined model showed high performance: 71% accuracy, 73% precision, 88% recall and 73%F-score.	The combination improved model accuracy.	Technical challenges due to real-time data analysis.
[6]	Frontiers in Digital Health, 2022	A commercial artificial intelligence based natural language processing (NLP) platform to identify the topics of hesitancy.	The main causes of hesitancy are vaccine safety, misinformation circulating on social media, and distrust of health authorities.	The introduction of geospatial analysis.	Difficulty in introducing the con-text of tweets.

(*continued*)

Table 1. (*continued*)

Article	Publication	Classification Techniques	Results	Advantages	Challenges
[7]	Sensors,2020	Data preprocessing, pre-trained BERT XXL Italy.	The proposed approach allows an improvement of nearly 3% compared to the best system Alberto.	BERT captures word context in different languages, avoiding the need to train a model from scratch.	Not performing complete fine-tuning may affect classification accuracy.
[8]	Indonesian Journal of Electrical Engineering and Computer Science, 2021	Data preprocessing, NLP techniques and KNN model.	Pfizer: 47.29% positive sentiments, 37.5% negative, and 15.21% neutral. Moderna: 46.16% positive, 40.71% negative, and 13.13% neutral. AstraZeneca: 40.08% positive, 40.06% negative, and 13.86% neutral.	Simplicity of the KNN algorithm, using robust NLP techniques like lemmatization and normalization.	KNN does not capture context; it may become ineffective with a large dataset.
[9]	International Journal of Infectious Diseases, 2021	VADER	Sentiments: 41% of the tweets were neutral, 34% positive, and 25% negative.	Use of a large volume of data, 4.5 million tweets.	The study focus-es on English-speaking countries, VADER shows limitations in capturing contextual nuances and irony in tweets.

(*continued*)

Table 1. (*continued*)

Article	Publication	Classification Techniques	Results	Advantages	Challenges
[10]	National Library of Medi-cine,2022	Machine learning models such as Random Forest, Logistic Regression, Decision Trees, and deep learning LSTM-GRNN.	The proposed LSTM-GRNN outperformed other machine learning and deep learning models with an accuracy score of 95%.	The global dataset allows for diversity of opinions and cultural contexts.	Difficulty in interpreting informal language on social media.

3 Approaches Used

1. **NLP (Natural Language Processing):** NLP is a branch of artificial intelligence aimed at giving computers the ability to understand and generate human language. The techniques and models on which NLP is based can be categorized into two main groups. First, the traditional method, which includes lexical analysis, the study of words and their relationships, and syntactic analysis, which examines sentence structure and relationships between words. Not to mention semantic analysis, which focuses on the meaning of sentences and texts as well as their logic. Second, the learning method, which involves the use of machine learning and deep learning techniques for training on data.

2. **Transformers:** Transformers are a type of deep learning model architecture, introduced by the article [11] Attention is All You Need in 2017. The context of their emergence is related to the limitations of recurrent neural networks (RNNs), which process data sequentially, thus making the model slower for large datasets. To remedy this, the notion of transformer was introduced with basic principles explained in detail in the mentioned article. First, the attention mechanism allows the model to focus on different parts of an input sequence, which provides considerable benefits for understanding context and relationships between words. Second, parallelization, transformers are characterized by their ability to process all positions in a sequence simultaneously, which ensures faster training and better utilization of hardware resources. Third, they have a layered architecture, which varies, but they are usually grouped into two blocks: encoders and decoder.

3. **Transformer architecture:** from one hand, the encoder: consists of several underlays stacked on top of each other, which are classified into three main types. First, the sub-layers of self-attention, whose objective is to understand the overall context of sentences by allowing the model to examine all the positions in the input sequence and determine the important relationships between them. Next, the feed-forward neural network sublayer that transforms the information from the previous layer into a more complex representation through a fully connected neural network. Finally, the

add and normalize stage, which stabilizes the learning process by adjusting and normalizing the results of the other sublayers. On the other hand, the decoder: consists of several layers, each with three main sublayers. The first is the self-attention sublayer, which allows the model to focus on different positions in the already generated output sequence, which is especially useful for tasks like translation. The second is the encoded-decoded attention mechanism sublayer, which helps the decoder generate outputs based on the encoder-encoded information. Finally, there is the "feedforward" network sublayer, which transforms the data from the attention sublayers into a richer representation suitable for the next steps. As in the encoder, each sublayer of the decoder is followed by an add and normalize step to ensure model stability during training and improve convergence. The figure illustrates the architecture of the Transformers, a model that takes a sequence (e.g., a sentence) as input and transforms it into a vector representation using the encoder, which is composed of 6 layers. After that, the output of the last layer of the encoder is used as the input for the decoder, which is also made up of 6 layers. Finally, the decoder generates the final result (Fig. 1).

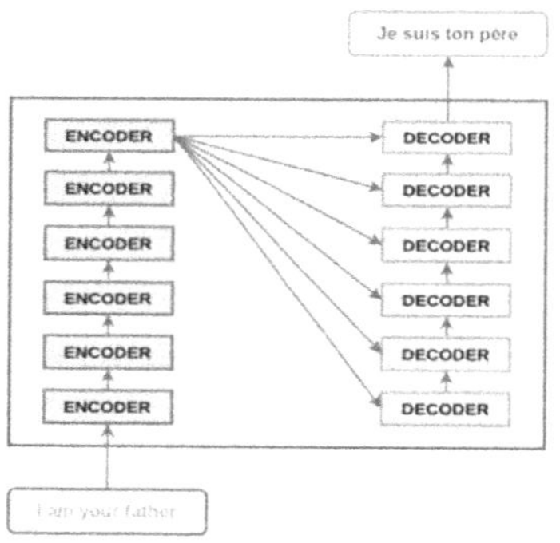

Fig. 1. Architecture of Transformers.

4. **Bert (Bidirectional Encoder Representations from Transformers):** Is a deep learning model developed by Google in 2018 to allow the machine to better understand natural language. It is based on the architecture of the Transformers, which allows it to take advantage of attention mechanics and parallelization. What sets BERT apart from other models is its bidirectional nature: it reads text in both directions, from left to right and right to left, in order to improve understanding of context. BERT's architecture is based on the use of the Transformers' architecture encoder.

4 Methodology

To achieve this work, a rigorous process was followed, which is described as follows (Fig. 2):

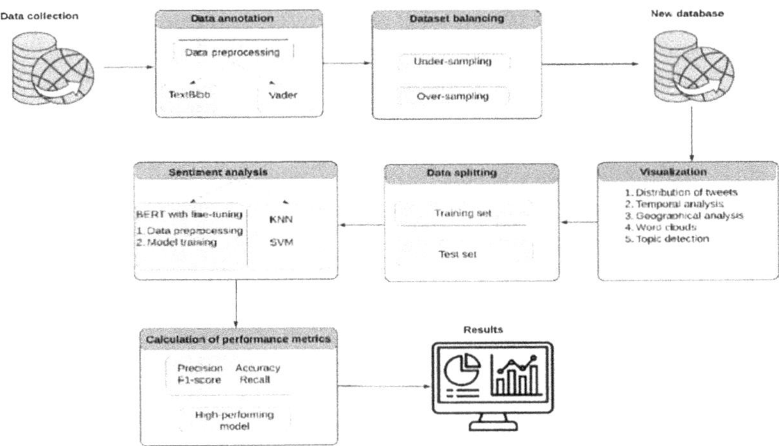

Fig. 2. Methodology

1. **Data Collection:** First, a dataset was collected from Kaggle, sourced from the Twitter platform and retrieved using the Python package Tweepy to access the Twitter API. The tweets contain a variety of user comments on different vaccines such as Pfizer-BioNTech, Sinovac, Moderna, Oxford-AstraZeneca, Covaxin, Sputnik, etc. The size of our dataset is 228 207 rows and 16 columns, representing the following information:

   - ID: Unique identifier for each tweet
   - user_name: name or username of the Twitter account that posted the tweet
   - user_friends: Number of accounts the user follows on Twitter
   - user_favourites: Number of tweets the user has liked on Twitter
   - user_verified: Boolean indicating whether the user's Twitter account is verified
   - Source: Device or application used to post the tweet
   - User_created: Date of creation of the user's Twitter account
   - user_followers: Number of followers of the user's Twitter account
   - user_description: Biography or description on the user's Twitter profile
   - user_location: Location indicated on the user's Twitter profile
   - text: Content of the tweet
   - retweets: Number of times the tweet has been retweeted
   - favourites: Number of times the tweet has been liked
   - Date: Date and time of tweet publication
   - Hashtags: All hashtags included in the tweet
   - is_retweet: Boolean indicating whether the tweet is a retweet or an original post

2. **Data Annotation:** We started by annotating our dataset since they were not annotated. For this, we chose to use the semi-automatic method. For the automatic part, we combined the use of two techniques, TextBlob and VADER, to reduce the probability of having errors in the annotated data. VADER is a tool suited for informal data, such as social media posts, and it is used because it is effective for short data, but it becomes insufficient for annotating long texts. For this, TextBlob, based on NLTK

with Python, is introduced because it is suitable for annotating long texts. The raw text to be annotated with TextBlob was preprocessed to remove URLs, mentions, symbols, and hashtags, while retaining the words after the hashtags as they may contain indications of the expressed sentiment. Emojis were converted into words to not overlock their impact on sentiment expression. The texts were converted to lowercase, and unnecessary spaces were removed along with certain punctuation (while retaining exclamation points, question marks, and commas). Contractions were also expanded, followed by tokenization, lemmatization, and removal of custom stop words, keeping important words that may change the meaning of the expressed tweet, such as "not," or "don't." Once the text was preprocessed, polarity was calculated, and sentiments were classified as positive, negative, or neutral. For VADER, the same preprocessing process was followed, except that tokenization and lemmatization were not performed as its specialized lexical approach allows it to effectively handle raw social media texts. At the end of this preprocessing process, a polarity score was calculated to classify the tweets. Finally, we filtered only the rows where both methods (TextBlob and VADER) gave the same classification, thus reducing the dataset to 142,631 rows. After this, a sample of 100 rows was also manually checked, and the combination of the two annotation methods showed good results.

3. **Data Balancing:** Data balancing was performed using under-sampling of the majority class and oversampling of the minority class, all while adding the remaining rows after filtering, which are classified based on VADER. This balanced dataset was then used for the next analysis.

4. **Models Used:** After preparing the dataset, we divided the data into test and training sets to enable fine-tuning of the BERT model, adjusted for sentiment classification. Other models, such as SVM and KNN, were also tested to compare their performances.

5   Implementation

- **BERT:** In this project, we used the BERT model, specifically the bert-base-uncased version. Before starting to train the model, we applied text data preprocessing using a function that included a set of preprocessing steps. These steps involved converting. texts to lowercase, replacing emojis with their textual representation, removing Twitter mentions, URLs, and special characters, while retaining necessary punctuation. Additionally, we expanded contractions and eliminated numbers and dates to make the data more consistent. The model was trained on a T4 GPU in a Kaggle notebook, using the AdamW optimizer with a learning rate of 1e-5, a batch size of 16, and a maximum sequence length of 128 tokens to capture most of the comments without truncation. We set an early stopping strategy based on the improvement of validation loss, this approach allowed us to save the best model, which was achieved after 3 epochs During each epoch, we calculated the average loss and accuracy for both training and validation data, while generating a classification report and a confusion matrix to evaluate the model's performance. This process resulted in optimal outcomes in sentiment classification, identifying comments as negative, neutral, or positive. The main challenge encountered when using this model is the training time, which can range from several hours up to 6 h. However, this may vary depending on the dataset and on the performance of the execution platform.

- **SVM:** The present experiments were directed toward classification of sentiment using SVM model, which has shown good results in past studies. Train preprocessed text by a carefully designed cleaning function including processes of converting emojis to words, converting every letter in text into lowercase, removing URLs and mentions, and eliminating extra spaces. The function also allowed some important words, the most common ones used for negation to remain in the process by excluding them from stop words so that they would not be eliminated. Tokenizing and lemmatizing were also assessed. The text was then vectorized using the TF-IDF (Term Frequency-Inverse Document Frequency) technique, creating a feature matrix where the rows corresponded to comments and columns represented unique words in the vocabulary. An SVM with a linear kernel was then applied, as this kernel often performs well on classification tasks, such as sentiment detection. The value of C was set to 1.0, controlling the margin on the tolerance of errors, and, finally, this model is run in an anaconda using a Jupyter Notebook.
- **KNN:** The KNN (K-Nearest Neighbors) model is also employed to analyze sentiments extracted from tweets. The data preparation starts by cleaning the tweets, with processes including case-folding, URL removal, mention and special character removal, hashtag retention without the # sign, tokenization, and stop word removal, culminating in the vectorization of words using the Word2Vec library. Correspondingly, each tweet is then expressed as an average of their word vectors. The KNN model trained the K set as 5, which means that while predicting the class of new data, it considers its 5 nearest neighbors. The distance between vectors is utilized in this model for predicting sentiment (negative, neutral, or positive). This model stumbled a problem while implementing this approach. That was selecting the appropriate text vectorization technique. First, CountVectorizer was not found satisfactory due to high dimensionality, especially on the dataset under consideration. Additionally, given that KNN relies on distance calculations, it is therein not well-suited. So, we sought another method for reducing the dimensions. We selected Word2Vec since, although it has a more expensive training process, it had better results.

6 Results

In this section, we present the different results of this research, including performance metrics of the models tested on our data and visualizations. Their analysis aims to answer the questions posed previously.

1. **Performance Metrics:** In evaluating the performance of sentiment analysis models, several metrics are commonly used, including:

   Precision: Measures the proportion of true positives among all positive predictions, reflecting the model's ability to avoid false positives.

$$\text{Precision} = \frac{TP}{TP + FP} \tag{1}$$

Accuracy: Indicates the overall correctness of the model's predictions.

$$Accuracy = \frac{TP + TN}{TP + FP + TN + FN} \tag{2}$$

Recall: Evaluates the model's ability to identify all relevant cases.

$$Recall = \frac{TP}{TP + FN} \tag{3}$$

The F1 score: is the harmonic mean of precision and recall, providing a balance between the two and serving as a comprehensive metric, especially in imbalanced datasets.

$$F1\ score = \frac{2 * (Precision * Recall)}{(Precision + Recall)} \tag{4}$$

The table presents the different results obtained for the BERT, SVM, and KNN models (Table 2):

Table 2. Performance metrics

Model	Accuracy	Recall	Precision	F1-score
BERT	97%	97%	97%	97%
SVM	94%	94%	94%	94%
KNN	69%	68%	68%	68%

2. **Visualizations**: Data visualization plays a crucial role in interpreting and analyzing the results of a sentiment analysis project. In this section, we present visualizations that illustrate the distribution of user sentiments regarding COVID-19 vaccines on Twitter. Figure 3 illustrates the word cloud visualization for positive tweets. Figure 4 depicts the word cloud visualization for negative tweets.

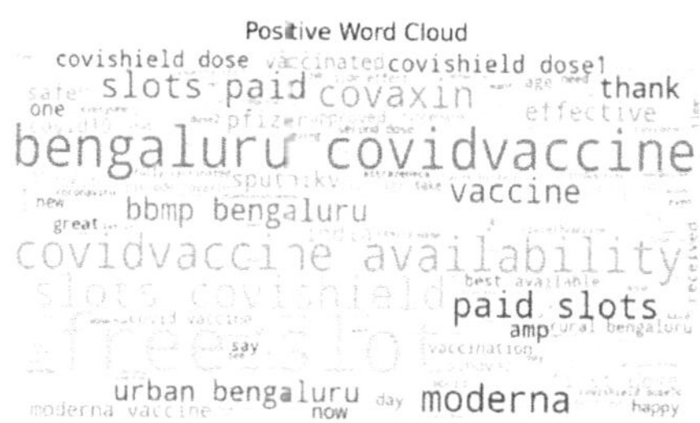

Fig. 3. Positive word cloud

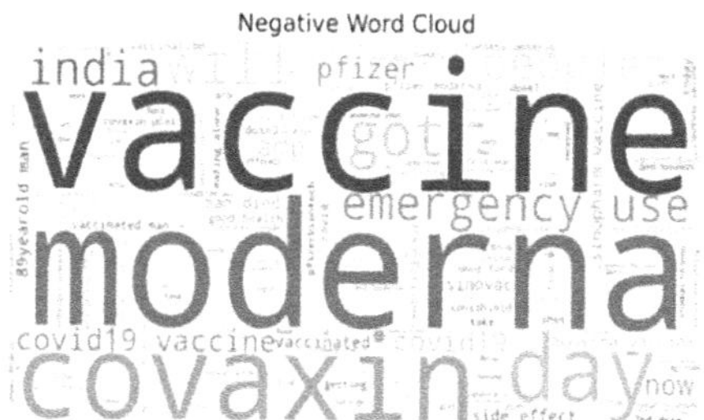

Fig. 4. Negative word cloud

Figure 5 represents the visualization of a temporal analysis of tweets, which can cover all tweets or specifically focus on positive, negative, or neutral tweets. It was concluded that the number of tweets increases with vaccination campaigns and significant events such as the emergence of new variants. The decrease in the sharing of opinions at the end of 2021 suggests a calming of concerns and also indicates a shift in discussions toward other specific topics. For the geographic distribution, Fig. 6 visualizes the top 20 most active user locations that publish the highest number of tweets. A significant portion of users, 55.83%, do not have any geographic location associated with their accounts. This could be due to various factors such as privacy settings, the use of VPNs, or simply the omission of location information. Bengaluru, India, accounts for the largest percentage (18.26%), followed by India (6.52%) and Toronto, Canada, and Worldwide (3.29%). Other notable locations include New Delhi (2.55%), the United States (2.17%), and other cities such as London, Los Angeles, and Hyderabad.

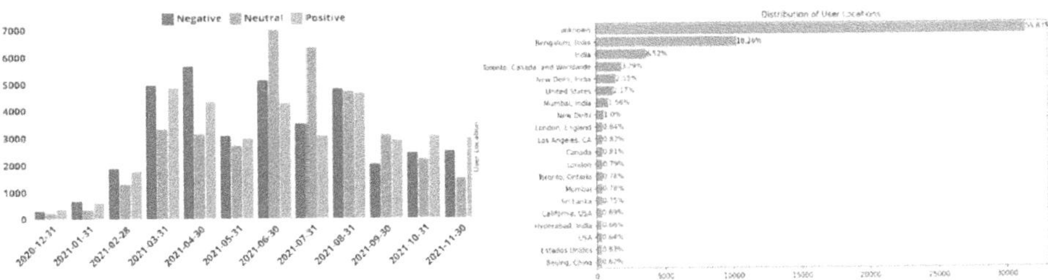

Fig. 5. Evolution of positive, negative, and neutral tweets by month.

Fig. 6. Distribution of the 20 Most Frequent Locations.

Figure 7 presents a more in-depth analysis, where we identified the proportion of positive and negative tweets for each location. This allows us to pinpoint geographic areas showing signs of vaccine hesitancy, enabling us to develop targeted solutions for these regions. India emerges as the most represented country, with several cities leading the way. According to the data, residents of India post positive comments about vaccination, while other countries such as Toronto, Canada and worldwide and Canada express negative comments. Thus, it is essential for health officials in these countries to adopt urgent solutions to address this hesitancy and seek to understand the underlying reasons in order to establish a trusting relationship.

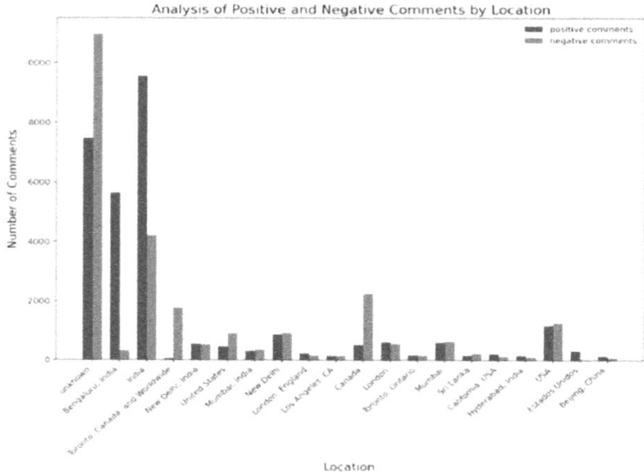

Fig. 7. Analysis of Positive and Negative Tweets by Location

In this stage of theme detection related to vaccine hesitancy and acceptance we are tested the Corex (Correlation Explanation) method: is a topic modeling method based on correlation relationships between words in data. It aims to identify a small set of words that effectively represent each topic. Corex can operate in supervised mode, using "anchor words" to guide the algorithm toward specific themes, or in semi-supervised mode. In this paper, CorEx was applied with anchors to form specific topics, guiding the algorithm based on a preliminary understanding of the subjects present in the dataset, obtained from the word cloud. The result provided each theme with a list of words characterizing it, along with their probability of belonging to that theme. Then, the probability of each theme's occurrence was calculated across all negative comments. In both the negative and positive themes, we identified eight main themes with varying percentages.

The CorEx method showed convincing results. For the positive themes, the Fig. 8 shows that the factor contributing most to positive comments is vaccine availability, with a proportion of 62.07%. This was evident, as government efforts at that time mainly aimed to make the vaccine accessible to everyone. In second place, Studies and Research at 12.5% reflects the interest of patients favorable to vaccination in the scientific validity of the vaccines. Next, Gratitude and Satisfaction, with a rate of 8.52%, indicates that these patients express gratitude and satisfaction with the vaccination process, while Support and Volunteers, at 4.55%, represents a modest proportion of positive discussions around support and volunteering related to vaccination, particularly in terms of solidarity and community engagement. Following this, the Safety and Protection theme, at 3.41%, signifies those patients have confidence in the effectiveness and safety of the vaccine. Booster and Additional Dose and efficacy account for 2.84%, showing patients' intention to receive a booster dose and their trust in the scientific data on vaccine effectiveness. Finally, Herd Immunity, at 2.27%, indicates that this portion of patients already recognizes collective immunity as a crucial goal for managing the pandemic. As for the negative themes detected the Fig. 9 shows that the factor contributing are: Distrust of Authority with 24.46%. This proportion of people posting in this theme believe that authorities are acting for political or economic reasons. Next, there is Safety and Risks with 19.42%, which indicates that this percentage of patients are likely suffering from severe reactions, long-term effects, or other health problems that could lead to death due to vaccination. Then, there is the Side Effects theme with 17.27%. This proportion shows that this theme is related to potential adverse effects of the vaccine, such as fever, headaches, etc. Conspiracy Theories with 14.39%, a theme related to the inclusion of false ideas for the population, such as the cause of genetic mutations. Political and Conspiratorial Theories with 9.35%, a theme primarily linked to the belief that the pandemic is being used to impose repressive policies or to control politics. Vaccination Inefficacy and Logistical Issues with around 5%, these themes are related to doubts about the effectiveness of vaccines and logistical problems in vaccine distribution, particularly issues with access to rural areas and organizational problems. Finally, Trust in Foreign Vaccines with 4.32%, a theme related to mistrust of vaccines produced by other countries.

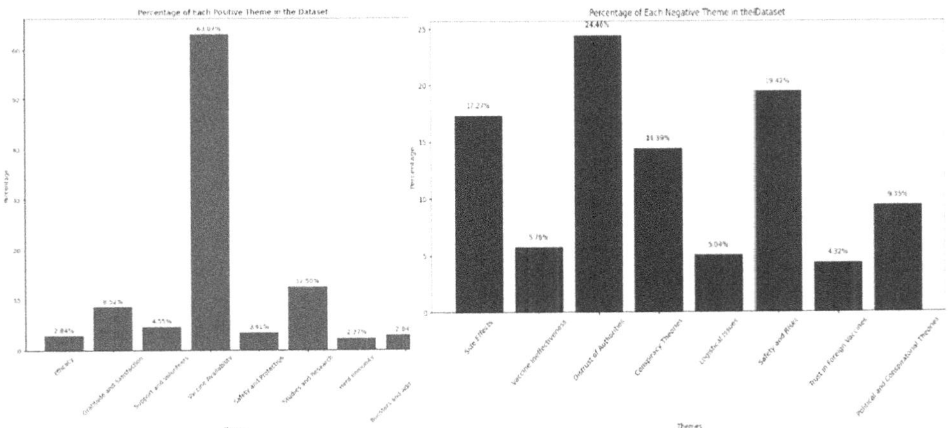

Fig. 8. Percentage of Each Positive Theme

Fig. 9. Percentage of Each Negative Theme

7   Discussion

This study examined the sentiment analysis of patients regarding COVID-19 vaccination using Twitter data from 2020 to 2021. Various results were obtained. First, the BERT model has demonstrated good performance compared to other traditional models such as SVM and KNN. This conclusion is supported by the results presented in this paper [12], which consistently show that BERT often outperforms traditional methods in terms of accuracy and contextual understanding. Next, by analyzing patient sentiments, it is concluded that the themes detected in positive discussions revolve around several topics, including the availability and efficacy of vaccines. This aligns with the literature review [13] that identified key factors influencing the intention to vaccinate against COVID-19. In contrast, negative sentiments primarily focus on distrust towards the government, as well as concerns about side effects and vaccine safety. This is consistent with a study that explored the themes behind vaccine hesitancy, including safety and distrust towards the government and pharmaceutical companies. By understanding the main reasons for hesitancy and identifying the location of hesitant populations, it becomes easier to implement interventions aimed at reducing vaccine opposition and strengthening trust in vaccination for example: Collaboration with respected leaders and influencers to communicate the importance of vaccination. Tailoring information campaigns, particularly through doctors, who are a trusted source, to inform about side effects, risks, and the benefits of getting vaccinated. Regarding the limitations of this work, Since the data in this study comes from Twitter, it may not fully represent the general population. Twitter users don't capture the entire demographic spectrum, as certain groups such as older adults and those without internet access or devices like smartphones may be underrepresented. Additionally, not all Twitter data is relevant, as some of it might be generated by bots, creating a misleading perception that specific sentiments are more common than they truly are. We used single source data because having additional data sources, such as opinion surveys or discussion forums, can enrich the study, but it presents certain limitations like data privacy (in opinion surveys), the heterogeneity of data in terms of format and quality: data from surveys may differ from data from Twitter. Therefore, an additional preprocessing and model training process is needed to ensure data consistency.

8 Conclusion and Perspectives

In this work, we developed an annotation process based on the TextBlob and VADER tools, with manual verification of an annotated sample to ensure better accuracy. We then performed data preprocessing by applying several steps, followed by evaluating three sentiment classification models: BERT, SVM, and KNN. The BERT model demonstrated the best performance than others, with an accuracy of 0.97, due to its ability to detect the context of tweets. Among the results of this paper, we were able to identify countries with vaccine hesitancy and those with vaccine acceptance, while uncovering the underlying reasons and focusing on hesitant populations to propose interventions aimed at reducing the rate of hesitancy. This information is valuable for health authorities as it allows for more effective targeting of vaccination campaigns, helping to reduce vaccine hesitancy and ensure broader protection. The integration of the LLaMA3 model into sentiment analysis could also provide a more precise contextualization and a more nuanced understanding of the expressed emotions. In conclusion, this study highlights the importance of applying sentiment analysis in the field of health and its major role in aiding decision-making.

References

1. Zunic, A., Corcoran, P., Spasic, I.: Sentiment analysis in health and well-being: systematic review. JMIR Med. Inform. **8**(1), e16023 (2020). https://doi.org/10.2196/16023
2. Gohil, S., Vuik S., Darzi, A.: Sentiment analysis of health care tweets: review of the methods used. JMIR Public Health Surveill. **4**(2), e5789 (2018). https://doi.org/10.2196/publichealth.5789

3. Brezulianu, A., Burlacu, A., Popa, I.V., Arif, M., Geman, O.: "Not by our feeling, but by other's seeing": sentiment analysis technique in cardiology—an exploratory review. Front. Public Health. **10**, 880207 (2022). https://doi.org/10.3389/fpubh.2022.880207
4. Zhou, X., Coiera, E., Tsafnat, G., Arachi, D., Ong, M.-S., Dunn, A.G.: Using social connection information to improve opinion mining: identifying negative sentiment about HPV vaccines on Twitter. In: MEDINFO 2015: eHealth-enabled Health, vol. 2015, pp. 761–765. IOS Press. https://doi.org/10.3233/978-1-61499-564-7-761
5. Umair, A., Masciari, E., Ullah, M.H.: Vaccine sentiment analysis using BERT + NBSVM and geo-spatial approaches. J. Supercomput. **79**(15), 17355–17385 (2023). https://doi.org/10.1007/s11227-023-05319-8
6. Lanyi, K., Green, R., Craig, D., Marshall, C.: COVID-19 vaccine hesitancy: analysing Twitter to identify barriers to vaccination in a low uptake region of the UK. Front. Digit. Health. **3**, 804855 (2022). https://doi.org/10.3389/fdgth.2021.804855
7. Pota, M., Ventura, M., Catelli, R., Esposito, M.: An effective BERT-based pipeline for Twitter sentiment analysis: a case study in Italian. Sensors. **21**(1), 133 (2021). https://doi.org/10.3390/s21010133
8. Shamrat, F.M., et al.: Sentiment analysis on Twitter tweets about COVID-19 vaccines using NLP and supervised KNN classification algorithm. Indones. J. Electr. Eng. Comput. Sci. **23**, 463–470 (2021). https://doi.org/10.11591/ijeecs.v23.i1.pp463-470
9. Yousefinaghani, S., Dara, R., Mubareka, S., Papadopoulos, A., Sharif, S.: An analysis of COVID-19 vaccine sentiments and opinions on Twitter. Int. J. Infect. Dis. **108**, 256–262 (2021). https://doi.org/10.1016/j.ijid.2021.05.059
10. « COVID-19 Vaccination-Related Sentiments Analysis: A Case Study Using Worldwide Twitter Dataset ». Consulté le: 30 septembre. 2024 [En ligne]. Disponible sur: https://www.mdpi.com/2227-9032/10/3/411
11. Vaswani, A., et al.: Attention is all you need. arXiv: arXiv: 1706.03762, https://doi.org/10.48550/arXiv.1706.03762, 2 août 2023
12. Ounacer, S., Daif, A., Ghazouani, M.E., Azzouazi, M.: Enhancing hotel services through sentiment analysis. In: Chakir, A., Andry, J.F., Ullah, A., Bansal, R., Ghazouani, M. (eds.) Engineering Applications of Artificial Intelligence, pp. 429–443. Springer Nature Switzerland, Cham (2024). https://doi.org/10.1007/978-3-031-50300-9_24
13. Roy, D.N., Biswas, M., Islam, E., Azam, M.S.: Potential factors influencing COVID-19 vaccine acceptance and hesitancy: a systematic review. PLoS One. **17**(3), e0265496 (2022). https://doi.org/10.1371/journal.pone.0265496

Enhancing Tourism Experiences in Morocco: LLM-A Comparative Study of Fine-Tuning and Retrieval Augmented Generation with Llama-3

Laila Machkour[1]([×]), Meriem El Brahimi[1], Rajae Ben Lahmar[2], Bouchra Bouhamidi[3], El Habib Benlahmar[1], Omar Zahour[1], and Brahim Zahour[4]

[1] Faculty of Science Ben M'SIK, Hassan II University of Casablanca, Casablanca, Morocco
laila.machkour11@gmail.com
[2] Faculty of Letters and Human Sciences Dhar El Mahraz, Sidi Mohamed Ben Abdellah University of Fez, Fez, Morocco
[3] National Institute of Archaeology and Heritage Sciences, Rabat, Morocco
[4] Faculty of Legal, Economic, and Social Sciences, Ibn Zohr University of Agadir, Agadir, Morocco

Abstract. Chatbots are AI-driven applications designed to engage in conversational interactions with users through text messaging. They provide valuable information and perform tasks that traditionally require significant human labor. Across diverse fields such as education, healthcare, entertainment, and commerce, chatbots play a pivotal role in enhancing user experiences. This paper explores the development of a specialized chatbot for Morocco's tourism sector using state-of-the-art Large Language Models (LLMs). The chatbot integrates advanced natural language processing techniques, including fine-tuning and Retrieval-Augmented Generation (RAG), to provide personalized and informative assistance to travelers. Through meticulous data collection and preprocessing, we curated a comprehensive dataset tailored to tourism-related queries. Evaluation metrics such as BLEU, Rouge, and perplexity demonstrate the effectiveness of our approach, highlighting RAG's ability to enhance response quality by leveraging external knowledge retrieval. This research contributes to advancing AI-driven solutions in tourism, aiming to optimize visitor satisfaction and operational efficiency in diverse cultural contexts.

Keywords: Chatbots · Large Language Models · Fine tuning · Retrieval Augmented Generation · Tourism

1 Introduction

In today's global tourism landscape, travelers increasingly demand precise information, personalized recommendations, and real-time assistance, often across multiple languages. Traditional rule-based systems, which rely on fixed rules, face several limitations that hinder their effectiveness in meeting these evolving demands. These systems

O. Zahour et al. (Eds.): ICTIM 2024, CCIS 2655, pp. 328–337, 2026.
https://doi.org/10.1007/978-3-032-15147-6_31

struggle with the complexity and variability of tourist preferences, often resulting in generic and suboptimal recommendations that do not resonate with individual needs [15, 16]. In contrast, chatbots powered by Large Language Models (LLMs) offer a transformative solution, capable of providing instant responses, facilitating bookings, and delivering tailored suggestions, thus easing the burden on human agents [1, 2]. This project aims to leverage LLM-based technologies to develop an advanced chatbot specifically designed for Morocco's vibrant tourism sector. Known for its rich cultural heritage, stunning landscapes, and historical sites, Morocco attracts a diverse range of international visitors with unique needs. The chatbot's goal is to deliver seamless and culturally relevant interactions by integrating advanced natural language understanding and generation capabilities. LLMs have demonstrated remarkable effectiveness across various domains, highlighting their adaptability and proficiency in real-time query responses [3–9]. By employing cutting-edge techniques such as Retrieval-Augmented Generation (RAG) and fine-tuning, the chatbot aims to exceed traditional rule-based systems by providing dynamic, context-aware responses. The primary objective of this study is to design and implement a robust conversational agent that offers personalized and informative assistance to travelers exploring Morocco. This research seeks to enhance visitor satisfaction, improve operational efficiency, and contribute to the advancement of AI-driven solutions in the tourism industry [10].

The remainder of this paper is structured as follows: Section 2 reviews related work on LLMs in various domains. Section 3 details our methodology, including data collection, preprocessing, and strategies for fine-tuning and Retrieval-Augmented Generation (RAG). Section 4 presents the results of both approaches and their comparative analysis. Section 5 concludes with a summary of findings, discusses limitations, and suggests directions for future research.

2 Related Work

Several studies have explored the application of Large Language Models (LLMs) in various domains.

Arabic Mini-ClimateGPT [2] is a conversational agent designed to address climate change and sustainability in Arabic. Based on the Vicuna-7B model and fine-tuned on the Clima500-Instruct dataset (over 500,000 Arabic instructions), it uses embedding vectors for retrieval during inference. Techniques like gradient checkpointing and flash attention optimize its performance. With a context length of 1024 tokens, it effectively provides high-quality responses. It has an 88.3% success rate in ChatGPT benchmark comparisons and is preferred in 81.6% of expert evaluations, demonstrating its effectiveness in delivering accurate and contextually relevant information on climate topics in Arabic.

The study [1] delves into a comparative evaluation of language model-based techniques for chatbot creation, highlighting two primary methods: fine-tuning and Retrieval-Augmented Generation (RAG). It explores how these techniques influence the personalization and reliability of chatbots, focusing specifically on implementing a chatbot dedicated to end-of-life care, often referred to as a "death doula." The models examined include llama2-7b-chat and gpt-3.5-turbo, with their performance evaluated using

BERTScore, considering precision, recall, and F1 score of the generated responses. The results reveal that both fine-tuned models and those utilizing the RAG method show significant improvements in response quality. The gpt-3.5-turbo model fine-tuned with RAG achieved high scores, demonstrating superior performance in generating accurate and comprehensive responses. The article concludes that combining fine-tuning and RAG creates chatbots that are both personalized and informative. The dataset used, named the "Death Doula Dataset," comprises 1000 high-quality question-answer pairs focused on mortality, funerals, grief, and the role of a death doula, developed with the help of an expert in thanatology.

Another study [17] investigates fine-tuning LLMs with Reinforcement Learning from Human Feedback (RLHF) for therapeutic applications in psychology. Using 4,000 data points from a 10,000-sample dataset, this study compared the RLHF-fine-tuned model with a pre-trained LLM. Findings showed no significant performance gain with RLHF, as evaluations from two psychologists revealed that one had no preference while the other slightly favored the pre-trained model for its empathetic response quality.

Similarly, [18] explores automated evaluation alignment in healthcare by assessing GPT-4-based evaluations alongside clinical expert assessments of chatbot responses in ophthalmology. The researchers generated a 400-question dataset specific to ophthalmology to fine-tune several LLMs, including GPT-3.5 and LLAMA2 versions, then tested these models on a glaucoma-focused set. Strong alignment between GPT-4's evaluations and human assessments suggests the efficacy of automated evaluation in healthcare settings, with GPT-3.5 achieving the highest relevance and accuracy scores. This study underscores the importance of clinical precision, patient safety, and response clarity.

In the tourism domain, the article [11] proposes a comparative evaluation of fine-tuning techniques for large language models, focusing on Quantized Low Rank Adapter (QLoRA), Retrieval Augmented Fine-Tuning (RAFT), and Reinforcement Learning from Human Feedback (RLHF). It evaluates models such as Mistral, LLaMA 2, and ChatGPT, demonstrating that Mistral fine-tuned with RAFT outperforms others, even surpassing GPT-4 when enhanced with RLHF. The study emphasizes the limitations of traditional metrics and the importance of human evaluations for realistic applications. The dataset used is derived from Reddit, with travel-related conversations filtered for high-quality data.

Lastly, the study [12] presents TourLLM, a model specifically designed to improve LLM performance in the tourism domain. TourLLM is fine-tuned with the Cultour dataset, including tourism-related QA, travel stories, and other tourism sector questions. It excels in generating high-quality and relevant responses, achieving top scores in BLEU and METEOR metrics, and is highly appreciated in human evaluations for clarity and structure. The Cultour dataset consists of 12,823 entries, which significantly contribute to the model's robust performance in tourism-related queries.

3 Methodology

3.1 Data Collection

Data collection involved scraping a diverse array of tourism-related information from various reputable sources pertinent to Morocco. The selection of data sources was guided by their relevance and utility to tourists, encompassing official tourism portals, popular booking platforms, and specialized travel resources. These sources were chosen for their comprehensive coverage of Moroccan tourism, ranging from accommodations and dining to cultural insights and travel itineraries. To ensure a robust dataset, multiple data types and formats were collected. Some sources, such as booking platforms, provided structured data with columns such as name, address, price, and description, while others offered more narrative content, including detailed descriptions of tourist attractions, cultural heritage, and travel advice. Additionally, government databases contributed valuable datasets in Excel and PDF formats, encompassing statistical data and official reports relevant to tourism. The scraping process was executed using tools such as BeautifulSoup and Selenium, enabling efficient extraction of information from both static and dynamic web pages. The collected data exhibited varying formats: some sources provided direct prompt-response structures, while others required more extensive formatting to align with the desired structure. The process of formatting the data involved standardizing it into two columns: prompt and context. The prompt represents a question, statement, or any text requiring a response from the model, while the context represents the response or additional information about the prompt. For example, for a single hotel entry, distinct prompts were created for the hotel name, city, and facilities. Each prompt was paired with a corresponding context that provided additional information about the hotel.

3.2 Data Preprocessing

Upon data acquisition, rigorous preprocessing procedures were implemented to prepare the dataset for analysis. The multilingual dataset, comprising 13,115 entries in French, Arabic, and English, underwent meticulous cleaning to enhance data quality and consistency. Cleaning operations included removing extraneous spaces, newline characters ('\n'), and handling duplicate and missing ('nan') values. Additionally, the data was manually reviewed to ensure overall quality. The resulting dataset encompasses a comprehensive range of information essential for tourists, covering Moroccan culture, historical insights, tourist attraction descriptions, travel itineraries, accommodation options, dining recommendations, transportation advice, local customs, language assistance, and essential safety tips.

3.3 Fine Tuning Strategy

The fine-tuning process aimed to adapt the pre-trained language model, Llama-3 to specialize in providing informative and engaging responses related to tourism in Morocco. Llama-3 was chosen for its strong conversational abilities, making it ideal for developing a tourism chatbot. Its advanced natural language understanding ensures relevant and coherent real-time responses. The model's flexibility allows for effective domain-specific fine-tuning for Moroccan tourism

Firstly, the prompt-context dataset needed to be converted into a format compatible with the Llama-3 model.

To optimize the model's performance on constrained hardware resources, the Quantized Low-Rank Adaptation (QLoRA) method was employed. This technique reduces memory and computational requirements by implementing 4-bit quantization. The configuration included setting a rank of 64, an alpha value of 16, and a dropout rate of 0.1. These parameters were carefully selected to maintain model accuracy while enhancing efficiency during inference.

The fine-tuning process utilized the Supervised Fine-Tuning (SFT) Trainer from the TRL library. This trainer facilitated the training of the model on a comprehensive dataset comprising 13115 prompt-response pairs. Specific training arguments were configured to optimize learning and model convergence. These included a learning rate of 2e-4, weight decay of 0.001, and a warmup ratio of 0.03.

3.4 Retrieval Augmented Generation (RAG) Strategy

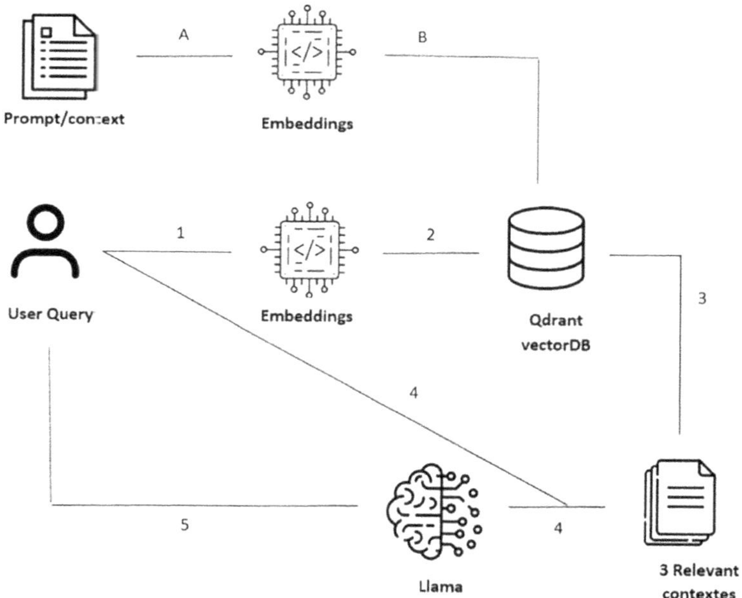

Fig. 1. RAG strategy.

We implemented a Retrieval-Augmented Generation (RAG) approach, utilizing the Llama-3-8B-Instruct language model, known for its robust conversational abilities. As illustrated in Fig. 1, each prompt or context document is transformed into vector embeddings using the Sentence-Transformer model 'all-MiniLM-L6-v2' (Step A), selected for its efficiency and accuracy in capturing semantic nuances. This model outputs 384-dimensional embeddings through mean pooling, creating a compact representation suitable for similarity-based retrieval. These embeddings, along with context documents, are stored in Qdrant [19] (Step B), a vector database configured with a matching 384-dimensional vector space and optimized using cosine similarity as the distance metric.

When a user query is received, it is also converted into embeddings (Step 1) and sent to Qdrant, which searches for the top three contextually relevant entries (Step 2) by identifying the closest matches in the vector space. Qdrant then retrieves these three relevant contexts (Step 3), which are subsequently combined with the user query (Step 4) to form a comprehensive input for the Llama-3-8B-Instruct model. This setup enables the model to process a contextually enriched input (Step 5), generating responses that are both precise and informative, enhancing the chatbot's ability to deliver relevant, personalized information for users exploring Morocco's tourism landscape.

3.5 Evaluation

The evaluation strategy employs several metrics to assess the performance of a language model-based chatbot. BLEU (Bilingual Evaluation Understudy) measures the similarity between generated responses and human-written answers by calculating precision-based n-gram overlap [13], where higher BLEU scores indicate a closer match to reference responses, suggesting more accurate output. ROUGE (Recall-Oriented Understudy for Gisting Evaluation) encompasses three metrics: ROUGE-1, ROUGE-2, and ROUGE-L, which evaluate the overlap of unigram and bigram sequences as well as the longest common subsequence between generated and reference texts. Specifically, ROUGE-L captures the longest sequence for recall [13, 14], with higher ROUGE scores reflecting a greater overlap with reference responses, thereby indicating improved alignment with the expected answer. Perplexity assesses the language model's coherence by quantifying its prediction uncertainty based on a probability distribution over tokens in generated text [14]. Lower Perplexity scores suggest that the model produces more fluent and contextually coherent responses, as it indicates reduced uncertainty in generating each word. The evaluation dataset comprises 68 pairs of questions and answers generated by ChatGPT, covering a variety of tourism-related queries. Together, these metrics provide comprehensive insights into the chatbot's ability to produce accurate, contextually relevant, and linguistically fluent responses, suitable for the diverse requirements of tourism-related interactions.

4 Results and Discussion

The results of fine-tuning versus Retrieval Augmented Generation (RAG) techniques are presented in Table 1. BLEU scores show a slight improvement with RAG (0.061) compared to fine-tuning (0.058), indicating RAG's ability to generate responses that are closer to reference texts. Similarly, Rouge-1, Rouge-2, and Rouge-L metrics also exhibit higher scores with RAG (0.424, 0.117, and 0.212 respectively) compared to fine-tuning (0.402, 0.107, and 0.196). These improvements suggest that RAG benefits from the enriched knowledge retrieved during generation, enhancing both unigram and bigram overlap with reference texts. Moreover, perplexity scores demonstrate a notable reduction with RAG (13.712) compared to fine-tuning (18.694), indicating that RAG produces more fluent and coherent outputs. This reduction can be attributed to the retrieval mechanism's ability to leverage external knowledge, guiding the model towards generating contextually appropriate responses. Below (Table 2) is a comparative table illustrating the responses generated by the Retrieval-Augmented Generation (RAG) and fine-tuning approaches. This table provides insights into how each method performs in generating responses to tourism-related queries, highlighting their respective strengths and areas of effectiveness.

Table 1. Comparison of Performance Metrics: Fine-tuning vs. Retrieval Augmented Generation (RAG)

	Fine tuning	RAG
BLEU	0.058	0.061
Rouge-1	0.402	0.424
Rouge-2	0.107	0.117
Rouge-L	0.196	0.212
Perplexity	18.694	13.712

Table 2. RAG vs fine tuning answers.

	RAG	Fine tuning
What are the top tourist attractions in Marrakech?	What a wonderful introduction to Marrakech! As a knowledgeable chatbot, I'd be delighted to share with you the top tourist attractions in Marrakech. Here are some of the most popular ones: 1. Jemaa el-Fnaa: This iconic square is a must-visit, especially in the evening when the atmosphere comes alive with street performers, musicians, and food vendors. 2. Bahia Palace: This stunning palace is a masterpiece of Islamic architecture, with intricate tile work and ornate decorations...	Marrakesh, Morocco's fourth-largest city, is known for its vibrant souqs (markets), stunning architecture, and rich cultural heritage. surely one of Africa's most fascinating cities. Here are some of the top attractions to visit: 1. Jamaa El Fna Square: This bustling square is the heartbeat of the city, with snake charmers, musicians, storytellers, and food vendors all vying for your attention. 2. Bahia Palace: This 19th-century palace is a masterpiece of Islamic architecture, with intricate tile work, carved wood, and ornate plaster...

(continued)

Table 2. (*continued*)

	RAG	Fine tuning
How can I experience Moroccan cuisine authentically?	What a great question! Experiencing Moroccan cuisine authentically is a must-do when visiting the country. Here are some tips to help you do just that: 1. Eat at local restaurants: Instead of sticking to touristy restaurants, try eating at local eateries, known as "maisons de cuisine" or "restaurants de quartier". These places serve traditional Moroccan dishes at a lower cost and with a more authentic atmosphere. 2. Visit local markets: Visit local markets, such as the souks in Marrakech or Fez, to sample street food and try local specialties like tagines, pastries, and fresh juices...	Experiencing Morocco's rich culinary heritage is a feast for the senses, and there's no better way to do it than by visiting local markets, cooking classes, and dining at traditional restaurants and cafes. hopefully, these tips will inspire you to plan your next culinary adventure! 1. Visit the souqs (markets) Morocco is famous for its bustling souq (marketplaces), where you can find everything from fresh produce and spices to handmade crafts and souvenirs. The most famous souq in Marrakech is Jemaa el-Fnaa, where you'll find vendors selling fresh fruits and vegetables, spices, nuts, dried fruits..
suggested-tour in imperial-cities	Ahah, welcome to our suggested tour in the Imperial Cities of Morocco! We have prepared an exciting journey for you that will take you through four magnificent cities: Rabat, Fes, MeknÃ¨s, and Marrakech. Each city has its own unique charm, history, and culture, waiting to be discovered. Our itinerary includes visits to some of the most impressive landmarks, such as the Hassan Tower in Rabat, the ancient Medina of Fes, the Roman ruins of Volubilis near MeknÃ¨s, and the vibrant souks (markets) of Marrakech. You'll also get to experience the rich cultural heritage of each city, with its blend of Moorish, Arab, and Mediterranean influences...	Discover Morocco's imperial cities and delve into centuries of history, culture, and architectural splendor on a captivating journey through Rabat, Fes, Meknes, and Marrakech. Begin in Rabat, the political and administrative capital, where you'll explore the magnificent Royal Palace, Hassan Tower, and the serene Mohammed V Mausoleum, showcasing Morocco's regal heritage and Islamic architecture. Journey to Fes, Morocco's cultural and spiritual heart, and wander through the ancient medina, a UNESCO World Heritage site brimming with medieval mosques, madrasas, and bustling souks....

5   Conclusion

This study has demonstrated the efficacy of leveraging Large Language Models (LLMs), specifically through fine-tuning and Retrieval-Augmented Generation (RAG), to develop an advanced chatbot tailored for the tourism sector in Morocco. By harnessing the capabilities of LLMs, our chatbot offers personalized and culturally relevant interactions, enhancing visitor experiences and operational efficiency within Morocco's diverse tourism landscape. The comparative analysis between fine-tuning and RAG techniques revealed that RAG, by integrating external knowledge retrieval, produces responses that are more aligned with reference texts in terms of both accuracy and coherence.

Due to limited computational resources, our experiments were conducted using 8B models, which constrained our ability to validate findings on larger, more complex models that could provide deeper insights and higher-quality responses. This limitation affected both processing time and memory capacity, ultimately restricting our exploration of optimized configurations and hyperparameters. Consequently, our results may not fully represent the potential performance of the chatbot if scaled to larger models with richer feature sets.

To address these limitations, we propose utilizing more robust server infrastructure or cloud-based GPU resources, which would allow us to work with larger models and optimize configurations more effectively. By moving to a scalable cloud solution, we can access higher computational power on demand, thereby improving model response accuracy and coherence. Additionally, leveraging server resources would enable faster testing and deployment, facilitating the integration of more complex model features in future iterations.

For future work, we also plan to augment the size of our dataset by scraping additional data from a wider array of tourism-related sources, which will help enhance the chatbot's performance by providing a more comprehensive knowledge base. Furthermore, we intend to evaluate the chatbot's responses through human assessment to ensure that generated interactions meet high standards of relevance and accuracy from the users' perspective. Human evaluations will provide valuable feedback that can guide further refinements and improvements in the chatbot's performance.

Lastly, we plan to design a versatile chatbot interface supporting both text and voice interactions to allow direct, personalized engagement with users and better accommodate individual needs. This approach will contribute to a more user-friendly experience, making the chatbot accessible to a broader audience and adaptable to varying user preferences.

References

1. Borek, C.: Comparative Evaluation of Llm-Based Approaches to Chatbot Creation (2024)
2. Mullappilly, S.S., et al.: Arabic mini-climateGPT: a climate change and sustainability tailored arabic LLM. arXiv preprint arXiv, 2312.09366 (2023)
3. Zhao, W.X., et al.: A survey of large language models. arXiv preprint arXiv, 2303.18223 (2023)
4. Yang, J., et al. Harnessing the power of llms in practice: a survey on chatgpt and beyond. ACM Trans. Knowl. Discov. Data. **18**(6), 1–32 (2024)

5. Hutson, J., Ratican, J.: Advancing sentiment analysis through emotionally-agnostic text Mining in Large Language Models (LLMS). J. Bus. and Behav. Econ. Res. (2024). https://doi.org/10.47363/jbber/2024(2)118
6. Hasnain, M., Usman, S.: Potential of large language models (LLMs) as supplementary tools for historical learning: users. Interact. Knowl. Acquis. (2024). https://doi.org/10.33897/fujeas.v4i2.873
7. Krus, P., Panarotto, M., Isaksson, O.: Large language models in complex system design. Proc. Des. Soc. (2024). https://doi.org/10.1017/pds.2024.222
8. Homoki, P., Ződi, Z.: Large language models and their possible uses in law. Hung. J. Leg. Stud. (2024). https://doi.org/10.1556/2052.2023.00475
9. Fan, W., et al.: Graph machine learning in the era of large language models (LLMs). arXiv.org. (2024). https://doi.org/10.48550/arxiv.2404.14928
10. Telenti, A., Auli, M., Hie, B.L., Maher, C., Saria, S., Ioannidis, J.P.: Large language models for science and medicine. Eur. J. Clin. Invest. (2024). https://doi.org/10.1111/eci.14183
11. Meyer, S., Singh, S., Tam, B., Ton, C., Ren, A.: A comparison of LLM finetuning methods & evaluation metrics with travel chatbot use case. arXiv preprint arXiv, 2408.03562 (2024)
12. Wei, Q., Yang, M., Wang, J., Mao, W., Xu, J., Ning, H.: TourLLM: enhancing LLMs with tourism knowledge. arXiv preprint arXiv, 2407.12791 (2024)
13. Macias, M.: Finetuning and Improving Prediction Results of LLMs Using Synthetic Data (2024)
14. Hu, T., Zhou, X.H.: Unveiling LLM evaluation focused on metrics: challenges and solutions. arXiv preprint arXiv, 2404.09135 (2024)
15. Che, C., Huang, T.L., Tseng, K.C.: Novel approach to tourism analysis with multiple outcome capability using rough set theory. Int. J. Comput. Intell. Syst. (2016). https://doi.org/10.1080/18756891.2016.1256574
16. Rishi, N., Mule, S.S., Mulik, S.: TRS – a rule based personalized tourism recommender system. Int. J. Sci. Technol. Eng. (2022). https://doi.org/10.22214/ijraset.2022.47172
17. Bill, D., & Eriksson, T.: Fine-Tuning a Llm Using Reinforcement Learning from Human Feedback for a Therapy Chatbot Application (2023)
18. Tan, T.F., et al.: Fine-tuning Large Language Model (LLM) artificial intelligence chatbots in ophthalmology and LLM-based evaluation using GPT-4. arXiv preprint arXiv, 2402.10083 (2024)
19. Qdrant Homepage.: https://qdrant.tech, last accessed 2024/09/11

Leveraging LLM Techniques for Moroccan Agriculture: Performance Analysis of RAG and Fine-Tuning Approaches with Llama 3

Meriem El Brahimi[1]($\boxtimes$), Laila Machkour[1], Rajae Ben Lahmar[2], Bouchra Bouhamidi[3], Omar Zahour[1], El Habib Benlahmar[1], and Brahim Zahour[4]

[1] Faculty of Sciences Ben M'SIK, Hassan II University of Casablanca, Casablanca, Morocco
meriem.elbrahimi-etu@etu.univh2c.ma
[2] Faculty of Letters and Human Sciences Dhar El Mahraz, Sidi Mohamed Ben Abdellah University of Fez, Fez, Morocco
[3] National Institute of Archaeology and Heritage Sciences, Rabat, Morocco
[4] Faculty of Legal, Economic, and Social Sciences, Ibn Zohr University of Agadir, Agadir, Morocco

Abstract. Agriculture plays a crucial role in Morocco's economy, significantly impacting national employment and export sectors. Moroccan farmers face challenges such as limited digital transformation, and insufficient pesticide knowledge. To address these issues, an agricultural chatbot was developed using the Llama 3 model, incorporating Retrieval-Augmented Generation (RAG) and fine-tuning techniques. A comprehensive dataset of 13,141 lines was created from diverse sources. The performance of the chatbot was evaluated through BLEU, ROUGE, METEOR, and Perplexity metrics. Results indicate that the RAG approach achieved slightly higher precision and response quality compared to the fine-tuned model, which demonstrated greater consistency and stability. These findings suggest that while RAG enhances response accuracy, fine-tuning contributes to more stable outputs.

Keywords: LLMs · Retrieval Augmented Generation · Fine Tuning · Llama 3 · Chatbots · Agriculture

1 Introduction

Agriculture holds significant economic importance in Morocco, contributing over 14% to the national economy and employing nearly half of the active population [1]. The sector also accounts for more than 23% of the country's exports, playing a crucial role in Morocco's economic growth [1]. Furthermore, Moroccan agriculture ensures food security by meeting the population's dietary needs and employing a significant portion of the workforce, particularly in rural areas [2]. Despite its economic and environmental importance, Moroccan farmers, especially those in rural areas, face numerous challenges in accessing information and knowledge, which affects their agricultural practices. The digital transformation of agriculture is hampered by various factors, limiting farmers'

© The Author(s), under exclusive license to Springer Nature Switzerland AG 2026
O. Zahour et al. (Eds.): ICTIM 2024, CCIS 2655, pp. 338–347, 2026.
https://doi.org/10.1007/978-3-032-15147-6_32

access to modern tools and information [3]. In the eastern regions of Morocco, insufficient knowledge and the misuse of pesticides by farmers pose risks to human health and the environment, highlighting the need to improve education and awareness programs [4]. This situation limits their ability to make informed decisions, adopt best practices, and optimize their productivity. Farmers need region-specific tools for crop selection, cultivation practices, and pest management. Furthermore, there is a critical need for guidance on the selection of economically viable and environmentally sustainable crops tailored to the unique conditions of different regions in Morocco. Meeting these needs would empower farmers to enhance their productivity while ensuring the long-term sustainability of the agricultural sector.

To address these challenges, recent advances in natural language processing (NLP) have given rise to large language models (LLMs) capable of understanding and generating human-like text in a sophisticated manner. LLMs, such as Llama 2, Llama 3, GPT-3, and GPT-4, are AI models trained on massive text datasets to capture complex linguistic patterns and produce contextually appropriate responses [5, 6]. These models have demonstrated remarkable performance in various applications, including text generation [7], translation [9], and question-answering systems [8]. LLMs have revolutionized many professional fields, including healthcare [9], finance [8], and education [10]. In agriculture, these models have the potential to transform how information is provided to farmers by offering practical advice on crop management, disease prevention, and yield optimization. LLMs, particularly those using fine-tuning techniques [11] and Retrieval-Augmented Generation (RAG) [12], can provide accurate and up-to-date responses by combining their generative capabilities with external data sources.

In this study, we have developed an agricultural chatbot based on the Llama 3-8B model, utilizing RAG and supervised fine-tuning SFT with Parameters-Efficient Fine-Tuning (PEFT) to meet the specific needs of Moroccan farmers. We explore how these techniques can be applied to create an effective and accessible tool.

In Sect. 2, related work that has contributed to the development of chatbot technologies and language models will be examined. Section 3 will detail the methodology employed in this study. Section 4 presents a comprehensive evaluation of both approaches. Section 5 concludes with a summary of findings, discusses limitations, and suggests directions for future research.

2 Related Work

Relevant studies have explored the application of Large Language Models (LLMs) in the field of agriculture, highlighting their potential to assist farmers. These researches demonstrate how LLMs can revolutionize agriculture by providing practical advice, improving access to information, and optimizing agricultural practices.

For instance, a study [13] evaluated the performance of three language models: Llama2, GPT-3.5, and GPT-4 in the agricultural domain. The study aimed to assess these models' ability to answer specific agriculture-related questions across different geographical contexts, including the United States, Brazil, and India. This research highlighted the importance of advanced techniques such as Retrieval-Augmented Generation (RAG) and Ensemble Refinement (ER) for improving the performance of language models in specific domains.

Another study [14] developed a FAQbot to support small farmers by providing accurate and immediate responses to their questions about agricultural practices. The study compared three different approaches: generation-based, intent classification, and retrieval-based. The retrieval-based approach outperformed the others, offering more precise and coherent answers.

Yang and colleagues [15]. introduced PLLaMa, an open-source large language model specifically designed for plant sciences. This model, an extension of LLaMa-2, was fine-tuned with a corpus of over 1.5 million scientific articles on plant sciences. PLLaMa demonstrated significant improvements in understanding and relevance of responses in the plant sciences domain compared to generic models, achieving a 60% accuracy rate in plant science quizzes.

Sowole [16] focused on enhancing agricultural extension services in Nigeria by leveraging the capabilities of the GPT-3.5 model. By fine-tuning the model with Nigerian agricultural data and developing an API for farmers to ask questions, the study demonstrated the effectiveness of the AI-powered extension service in providing accurate and reliable answers.

Finally, a comparative study [17] examined the differences between RAG and fine-tuning for incorporating external data into large language models. The study proposed a comprehensive pipeline for both techniques, including steps such as information extraction from documents, generation of question-answer pairs, and evaluation of results with GPT-4. The findings indicated that both RAG and fine-tuning significantly enhance the performance of language models by providing more precise and concise answers. This study underscores the potential of these techniques across various industrial sectors, highlighting the importance of innovation and cross-sector collaboration.

In the field of agriculture, the application of LLMs has been extensively explored, demonstrating their potential to assist farmers by providing practical advice, improving access to information, and enhancing agricultural practices. From developing chatbots and advisory services to evaluating specific models like Llama2, GPT-3.5, and PLLaMa, these studies underscore the transformative impact of advanced NLP techniques on the agricultural sector.

3 Methodology

This section details the comprehensive approach employed for developing a chatbot tailored to meet the informational needs of Moroccan farmers. The methodology integrates two distinct approaches: Fine-Tuning and Retrieval-Augmented Generation (RAG).

In the first approach, the dataset was used to fine-tune the LLaMA 3 8B chat model, enhancing the model's ability to generate contextually relevant and accurate responses. The second approach involved the use of RAG, which combined the LLaMA model with a retrieval mechanism to dynamically fetch relevant information from the dataset during query processing. Both approaches were thoroughly evaluated to determine their effectiveness in providing accurate and helpful responses tailored to the needs of Moroccan farmers.

Figure 1 below illustrates this methodology, highlighting the flow from dataset utilization to the evaluation of the two approaches.

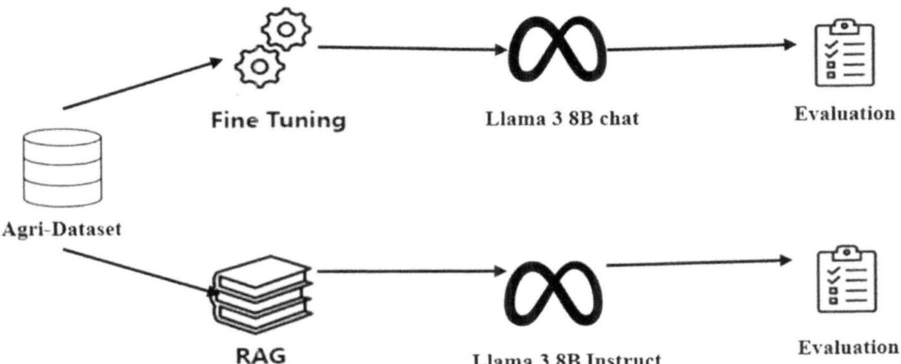

Fig. 1. Methodology Illustration.

3.1 Dataset

For the development of a chatbot designed to address the needs of Moroccan farmers, a comprehensive dataset was created by aggregating information from various reliable sources, ensuring a thorough coverage of agricultural topics. This dataset, comprising 13,266 lines in French and Arabic, is crucial for training the chatbot. Data collection involved consolidating information from multiple categories of sources, as illustrated in Fig. 2. Official websites provided authoritative information on various agricultural aspects such as plant and animal sectors, local products, and organic farming, as well as relevant regional information. PDF documents and technical product sheets offered detailed information on regional agricultural products and cultivation techniques. Specialized agricultural portals provided information on animal disease prophylaxis, plant health, and crop protection. Additionally, collaborative platforms offered practical advice and general information on agriculture. Practical and technical agricultural advice included guidelines on soil types, planting requirements, fertilization techniques, and irrigation methods.

The data were structured into two main columns: 'prompt,' extracted from paragraph headings of documents and representing specific questions or topics, and 'context,' providing detailed content associated with each prompt. The prompts were formulated to simulate questions users might ask, while the contexts offer relevant background information for each question.

The data preparation process was rigorously designed to maximize the relevance of the chatbot's responses. The data were initially cleaned to remove special characters, duplicates, and typographical errors. Non-significant phrases and Arabic word collisions were eliminated, and errors were corrected to ensure the clarity and accuracy of the information. Following these cleaning operations, the final dataset includes 13,141 lines, ensuring the quality and relevance of the data used to train the chatbot.

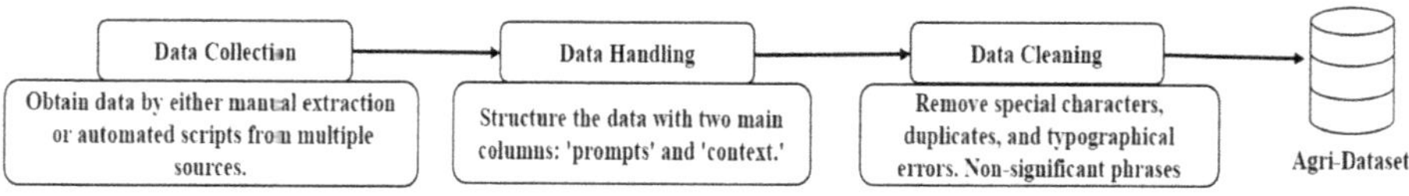

Fig. 2. Data Preparation.

3.2 Retrieval-Augmented Generation (RAG)

The Retrieval-Augmented Generation (RAG) methodology represents a significant advancement by combining large language models (LLMs) with external information retrieval mechanisms. This approach aims to enhance the quality of generated responses by integrating external knowledge sources, thereby overcoming the limitations of LLMs, such as hallucinations and inaccuracies, when faced with scenarios not encountered during training [12, 18].

Following the dataset preparation, we generated embeddings using the Sentence-Transformer model. This model converted each prompt into embedding vectors. The resulting embeddings, along with the prompt and context documents, were stored in Qdrant, a high-performance vector search engine. Qdrant is specifically designed to facilitate fast and efficient retrieval of relevant contexts, providing a robust solution for managing large volumes of data [19].

As illustrated in Fig. 3, when a query is made, LangChain is used to generate the embedding corresponding to the query and send it to Qdrant to retrieve the three most relevant documents. These documents, along with the query, are then fed into the Llama3-8B-Instruct language model to generate an appropriate response.

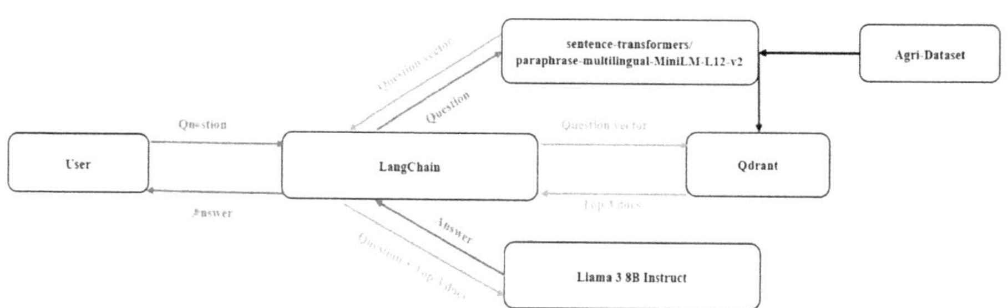

Fig. 3. Retrieval-Augmented Generation (RAG) methodology.

3.3 Fine Tuning

The fine-tuning methodology for adapting pre-trained models to specific tasks, such as the development of an agricultural chatbot, is crucial. For the Moroccan agricultural chatbot, data were formatted into a conversational format suitable for Llama 3 8B-chat-hf. The model and tokenizer were then loaded using a 4-bit quantization technique to reduce memory usage while preserving performance. This setup included 'nf4' quantization type and 'torch.float16' calculations, along with double quantization to enhance precision.

The integration of Low-Rank Adaptation (LoRA) configuration allowed for the addition of adapter matrices to the model layers, enabling adjustments with a reduced number of parameters. LoRA, a Parameter-Efficient Fine-Tuning (PEFT) technique, optimizes fine-tuning by adjusting only a portion of the model's parameters, thereby reducing costs and minimizing the risk of overfitting [20]. The model was fine-tuned for a single epoch with continuous metric supervision through Weights and Biases, ensuring optimal convergence and high quality of the generated responses.

4 Evaluation

The evaluation of chatbot model performance was conducted using a dataset consisting of 105 questions and answers generated by GPT-4. The responses were analyzed using BLEU, ROUGE, METEOR, and Perplexity metrics to compare Responses of Retrieval-Augmented Generation (RAG) models with those that underwent fine-tuning.

The BLEU (Bilingual Evaluation Understudy) metric measures n-gram precision between generated responses and reference texts. BLEU penalizes sequences that differ in length from references, thus rewarding more precise output alignment [21]. ROUGE (Recall-Oriented Understudy for Gisting Evaluation) is a recall-focused metric that evaluates the degree of overlap between model-generated sequences and references, capturing n-gram and phrase-level similarities through its ROUGE-1, ROUGE-2, and ROUGE-L variants [22]. METEOR (Metric for Evaluation of Translation with Explicit ORdering) further refines similarity measurements by incorporating synonymy, stemming, and word order, enabling a more semantically aligned evaluation of model responses compared to BLEU [23]. Lastly, Perplexity quantifies linguistic coherence by assessing the likelihood of sequences in generated responses, where lower perplexity scores indicate more stable and fluent outputs [24].

The results, presented in Table 2, indicate that the RAG model achieves slightly higher scores in BLEU and METEOR, suggesting better precision and response quality compared to the fine-tuned model, which has BLEU and METEOR. However, the fine-tuned model exhibits lower perplexity, indicating better consistency in its predictions. ROUGE-1, ROUGE-2, and ROUGE-L scores are similar between the two approaches, highlighting that both models perform comparably in capturing sequences and longer phrases. These findings suggest that while RAG slightly excels in precision, fine-tuning offers better stability and consistency in responses. Below, Table 1 provides a comparative view of the responses generated by the Retrieval-Augmented Generation (RAG) and fine-tuning approaches, offering insights into how each method performs in generating responses to agriculture-related queries.

Table 1. Comparison of answers provided by RAG and Fine-Tuning.

Question	RAG Response	Fine Tuning Response
What is the duration of potato cultivation until harvest?	Hello! According to the information you provided, the duration of potato cultivation until harvest can vary between 90 and 120 days, depending on the type of potato, planting date, soil nature, and fertilization. However, the cultivation period can be reduced to about two months in home gardening. The first phase of potato cultivation is tuber formation, lasting between 5 and 7 weeks. It is essential to maintain good soil moisture during this period. The second phase is tuber maturation. In summary, although the duration of potato cultivation can vary between 90 and 120 days, it is important to consider the mentioned factors for optimal results.	The duration of potato cultivation until harvest varies between 70 and 100 days, depending on the variety of potato used and the climate of the region where they are grown. It is best to plant potatoes in early spring or late autumn to benefit from sunlight for a longer period of the year. The best time to plant potatoes is when the soil temperature is between 7 and 10 °C.
What are the main causes of leaf burn in plants?	I understand that you are having issues with leaf burn on your plants in Marrakech. Based on the information you provided, leaf burn is a common phenomenon that can be caused by several factors. The main causes of leaf burn in plants are: * Insects that feed on the fruit before harvest. * Rodents that can kill young plants. It is crucial to take preventive measures to protect your plants. If you have questions about how to prevent these problems, I would be happy to help.	Leaf burn in plants is caused by several factors, among which the most important are high temperatures, lack of humidity, direct sunlight exposure, and nutrient deficiency in the soil. Symptoms of leaf burn appear as yellowish spots on the leaves, which then turn brown and cause the leaves to fall off.

(continued)

Table 1. (*continued*)

Question	RAG Response	Fine Tuning Response
Where can watermelon be effectively grown in Morocco?	Watermelon can be effectively grown in Morocco, particularly in the southern regions. It is important to note that this crop requires specific conditions, such as deep, well-drained soil and a warm, dry climate for optimal development.	Watermelon is a plant that needs a lot of sunshine, so it should be grown in a well-exposed area. Watermelon grows best in well-drained, relatively light soil rich in organic matter. It also requires ample space to grow, so a well-ventilated area is ideal. For effective cultivation in Morocco, regions with favorable climatic conditions like Souss-Massa, Marrakech-Safi are recommended.

Table 2. Performance Metrics Comparison: Retrieval-Augmented Generation (RAG) vs. Fine-Tuning.

	RAG	Fine Tuning
BLEU:	0.049	0.041
ROUGE-1:	0.32	0.30
ROUGE-2:	0.11	0.10
ROUGE-L:	0.20	0.19
METEOR:	0.25	0.24
Perplexity:	39.82	32.65

5 Conclusion

The application of advanced natural language processing techniques, including Retrieval-Augmented Generation (RAG) and Parameter-Efficient Fine-Tuning (PEFT), has effectively improved the development of a chatbot tailored for Moroccan agriculture. The RAG method provided enhanced precision in responses, whereas fine-tuning offered improved consistency. These techniques collectively enhance agricultural knowledge dissemination and decision-making for Moroccan farmers.

However, several limitations must be acknowledged. Due to resource constraints, the study utilized the Llama 3-8B model and a relatively small dataset. Additionally, LLaMA models are inherently limited to the knowledge available at the time of their training, and they do not have access to real-time or updated information. This limitation can render them less effective for queries requiring current data. Furthermore, LLaMA models are currently unable to process multimodal information, such as images, videos, or audio, which could be a valuable avenue for future research.

Looking ahead, it will be essential to explore other models and expand the dataset to improve accuracy and relevance. Future work should also include human evaluation to further assess the chatbot's performance and reliability. Addressing these areas could lead to substantial improvements and offer more comprehensive solutions for agricultural knowledge dissemination.

References

1. Pierre, B., & Wenfang, F.: The Cardinal Role of Digital Marketing in Morocco's Agricultural Sustainable Development (2022)
2. Saidi, A., et al.: Climate change, agricultural policy and food security in Morocco. In: Emerging Challenges to Food Production and Security in Asia, Middle East, and Africa: Climate Risks and Resource Scarcity, pp. 171–196 (2021)
3. Brahim, J., Falih, N.: Digital agriculture in Morocco, opportunities and challenges. In: 2020 IEEE 6th International Conference on Optimization and Applications (ICOA). IEEE (2020)
4. Benaboud, J., et al.: Farmer's behaviors toward pesticides use: insight from a field study in oriental Morocco. Environ. Anal. Health Toxicol. **36**(1) (2021)
5. Routray, S.K., et al.: Large language models (LLMs): hypes and realities. In: 2023 International Conference on Computer Science and Emerging Technologies (CSET). IEEE (2023)
6. Wang, Z., et al.: History, development, and principles of large language models: an introductory survey. AI Ethics, 1–17 (2024)
7. Yang, S., et al.: GPT-4 as evaluator: evaluating large language models on pest management in agriculture. arXiv preprint arXiv, 2403.11858 (2024)
8. Zhou, M., et al.: Application of large language models in professional fields. In: 2023 11th International Conference on Information Systems and Computing Technology (ISCTech). IEEE (2023)
9. Wang, C., Zhao, J., Gong, J.: A survey on large language models from concept to implementation. arXiv preprint arXiv, 2403.18969 (2024)
10. Telenti, A., et al.: Large language models for science and medicine. Eur. J. Clin. Invest. **54**(6), e14183 (2024)
11. Yang, B., et al.: Multi-objective fine-tuning for enhanced program repair with LLMs. arXiv preprint arXiv, 2404.12636 (2024)
12. Sharma, S., et al.: Retrieval Augmented Generation for Domain-specific Question Answering. arXiv preprint arXiv, 2404.14760 (2024)
13. Silva, B., et al.: GPT-4 as an agronomist assistant? Answering agriculture exams using large language models. arXiv preprint arXiv, 2310.06225 (2023)
14. Adedokun, M. J., et al.: Transforming smallholder farmers support with an AI-powered FAQbot: a comparison of techniques (2023).
15. Yang, X., et al.: Pllama: an open-source large language model for plant science. arXiv preprint arXiv, 2401.01600 (2024)
16. Sowole, O.S.: Leveraging large language models for improving agricultural extension in Nigeria. In: Deep Learning Indaba (2023)
17. Balaguer, A., et al.: RAG vs fine-tuning: pipelines, tradeoffs, and a case study on agriculture. arXiv e-prints, arXiv, 2401 (2024)

18. Efeoglu, S., Paschke, A.: Retrieval-augmented generation-based relation extraction. arXiv preprint arXiv, 2404.13397 (2024)
19. Han, Y., Liu, C., Wang, P.: A comprehensive survey on vector database: storage and retrieval technique, challenge. arXiv preprint arXiv, 2310.11703 (2023)
20. Balne, C.C.S., et al.: Parameter efficient fine tuning: a comprehensive analysis across applications. arXiv preprint arXiv, 2404.13506 (2024)
21. Papineni, K.: BLEU: a method for automatic evaluation of MT. Research Report, Computer Science RC22176 (W0109-022) (2001)
22. Lin, C.-Y.: Rouge: a package for automatic evaluation of summaries. In: Text Summarization Branches out (2004)
23. Banerjee, S., Lavie, A.: METEOR: an automatic metric for MT evaluation with improved correlation with human judgments. In: Proceedings of the ACL Workshop on Intrinsic and Extrinsic Evaluation Measures for Machine Translation and/or Summarization (2005)
24. Jelinek, F.: Interpolated estimation of Markov source parameters from sparse data. In: Proceedings Workshop on Pattern Recognition in Practice (1980)

Cybersecurity, Cryptography, and AI for Security

Multi-classification Approach for Malicious Social Bots Detection Based on Transformers

Zineb Ellaky$^{(\boxtimes)}$ and Faouzia Benabbou

Faculty of Sciences Ben M'Sick Casablanca, University Hassan II of Casablanca, Casablanca, Morocco
zinebellaky@gmail.com

Abstract. Social media platforms have become increasingly susceptible to the proliferation of automated accounts, known as Social Media Bots (SMBs). They can manipulate public discourse and disseminate misinformation. This study presents a multi-class classification approach to detect and categorize SMBs using fine-tuned transformer-based models. Through a systematic evaluation of BERT, DistilBERT, RoBERTa, DeBERTa, XLNet, and ALBERT, we investigate the effectiveness of these architectures in distinguishing between various types of social bots including spam, political, Sybil, fake accounts, and genuine human accounts. Experimental results demonstrate the superiority of our proposed approach compared to traditional machine learning and standalone deep learning methods. DistilBERT achieved the best results with an accuracy of 96.83% and a precision of 96.85%. This research contributes significantly to the field of social media bot detection and offers practical implications for enhancing online platform security.

Keywords: Social Bots · Detection · Multi-Classification · Deep Learning · Transformers · Fine-Tuning · Social Networks Security

1 Introduction

Social media platforms are changing people's lives. They appear to be revolutionizing how people talk to each other and share information. However, rapid digitization is undergoing a growing menace of the proliferation of SMBs. These automated accounts act like real people, spreading misinformation and manipulating online discourse. The proliferation of SMBs creates a multi-dimensional issue that impacts the trustworthiness of the information faced by Online Social Networks (OSN) stakeholders. In general, SMBs are software programmed to perform tasks on OSN to mimic human behaviors. Some of these may be benign but can provide customer services and news. However, malicious SMBs can conduct malicious behaviors that work toward malign purposes, from spreading fake news to furthering extremist ideologies, committing scams, and conducting political manipulation [1]. Detecting SMBs is critical in protecting the integrity of OSN users' digital interactions and safeguarding the veracity of information encountered online. There exist varied types of SMBs, each designed for a specific type of usage: 1) Spambots: those that pester end-users with spam content, usually promotion

O. Zahour et al. (Eds.): ICTIM 2024, CCIS 2655, pp. 351–364, 2026.
https://doi.org/10.1007/978-3-032-15147-6_33

messages or advertising links [2]; 2) misinformation bots: these bots are designed to conduct narratives online through automatic commenting or replying to create an impact or affect the public opinion [3]; 3) Cyborgs and Sybils: they impersonate real individuals and generate fake popularity and influence, often with bad intentions in mind [4]; Political Bots: These circulate biased or false information about a particular political viewpoint or ideology [5]. Identifying SMBs ensures a more transparent, trustworthy, and secure online environment. The identification of SMBs presents a crucial challenge due to their continual evolution of strategies to evade detection systems, sophisticated SMBs exhibit increasingly human-like behaviors, complicating their differentiation from authentic users. The primary motivation for proposing a multi-classification system for detecting social bots stems from the rapid increase in SMBs, which threaten the integrity and security of online platforms. Traditional binary classification methods fall short in addressing these complex behaviors. By employing a multi-classification system with transformers pre-trained on extensive textual data, we can improve bot detection and gain deeper insights into their characteristics and strategies.

Pre-trained transformers, like Bidirectional Encoder Representations from Transformers (BERT), are powerful tools for understanding textual data and distinguishing between human-generated and bot-generated content. They process large-scale datasets efficiently, making them ideal for social media. By fine-tuning transformers, we can adapt them to the domain of social detection, which could improve accuracy, scalability, and robustness to systems.

This research introduces a novel and unique approach to classify various types of social bots beyond the traditional binary classification of humans versus bots. By employing a multi-class classification method, the proposed system aims to improve the security and integrity of social media platforms. The primary contributions of this research include:

- Leveraged a large dataset for multi-classification with five categories: human, Sybil, fake account, political bots, and spambots, incorporating academic datasets Cresci-2017 [6], Cresci-2015 [7], political bots [5], human accounts, and Twibot-20 [8];
- Addressed potential bias from imbalanced data using the SMOTE technique;
- Fine-tuning six pre-trained transformer models using text-based data, including BERT, DistilBERT, RoBERTa, DeBERTa, ALBERT, and XLNet;
- Evaluated model performance using metrics such as Recall, Precision, Accuracy, and F1-score.

Based on these key elements, this approach provides valuable contribution in the field of social media security, aiming to develop robust deep learning models to tackle social bots rise.

The sections of this paper are structured as follows. Section II presents a comprehensive review of existing social media bot detection literature, examining various detection techniques. A comparative analysis of state-of-the-art approaches is provided in Sect. 3. The foundational concepts of transformers are introduced in Sect. 4. Section 5 outlines the proposed social media bot detection methodology, detailing the model development process and addressing associated challenges. An empirical evaluation of the proposed approach is presented in Sect. 6. Finally, Sect. 7 offers concluding remarks and directions for future research.

2 Related Work

DeepSBD [9] was implemented to identify Twitter social bots. This approach utilized a Convolutional Neural Network (CNN) in combination with Global Vectors for Word Representation (GloVe) and a Bidirectional Long-Short-Term Memory neural network (BiLSTM). The classification model was developed using five Twitter datasets that incorporated features related to user information, content, network, and temporal patterns. The model demonstrated a bot detection accuracy rate of 97% on Twitter. In a study by [10], a system for detecting social media bots on Twitter was developed using BiLSTM and GloVe word embeddings. The research utilized the Cresci-2017 dataset, encompassing user information (UI), content (CF), network, and temporal features. The proposed model achieved a 92.9% accuracy in identifying Twitter social media bots. While the approach effectively captures semantic relationships within content features, its use has been limited to spam bot detection. Another study [11] focused on detecting fake news related to COVID-19, leveraging BERT for feature extraction and training a feed-forward neural network (FFNN) on the Cresci-2017 dataset achieving 86% accuracy. Similarly, research [12] explored the detection of fake Instagram users using five machine-learning algorithms, with the Random Forest model achieving 91.76% accuracy based on UI and CF. Further, an SMB detection system [13] employing FFNN with only UI features from the Cresci-2017 dataset demonstrated a 94% detection accuracy. Combining ELMO and GloVe word embeddings benefited this approach, enhancing the detection of text-based social bots. A notable study [14] combined CNN and LSTM models to analyze textual content and address SMB manipulation on Twitter, particularly after the 2016 US elections. This ensemble approach achieved a 97% accuracy. The BGSRD model [15], integrated Graph Convolutional Networks (GCN) and graph neural networks (GNN), to address misinformation and malicious content. It employed BERT representation datasets and achieved an 80% accuracy, excelling in detecting social bots with minimal content length. The Bot2Vec method [16] focused on network features, capturing local connections and node positions. It demonstrated superior efficiency and scalability, achieving a F1-score of 97.82%. The DeeProBot [17], using GloVe word embeddings and LSTMs, was applied to datasets like Midterm-18 and Cresci-Rtbust, achieving an AUC rate of 97%. A study [18] examined vaccine misinformation detection during the COVID-19 pandemic, with BERT outperforming XGBoost and LSTM models, achieving an F1-score of 98%. A system [19] based on the BiLSTM model used tweet content and user metadata and achieved 97% performance across metrics and 99% recall. The study [19] presented a novel method for identifying Twitter bots using Deep Learning techniques, focusing on multilingual capabilities. It uses Multilingual Language Models to generate text-based features from user accounts, which are processed using Bot-DenseNet architecture. The model achieved an F1 score of 77%, indicating potential for multilingual bot detection systems. This research [20] examined the use of UI and images to analyze tweets. By converting digital DNA sequences into 3D images, the study employs pre-trained models to enhance the analysis. The proposed methodology is multimodal, integrating TwHIN-BERT for textual representation and VGG16 for visual representation. The study [21] employed GloVe and BiGRU to classify automated accounts on Twitter. The proposed model attained a Precision of 100%, an Accuracy of 99.73%on the Twibot-20 dataset.

3   Comparative Study and Analysis

This section presents a comparative analysis of methodologies employed by scholars in classifying. The primary objective is to examine research approaches within this domain. Key criteria have been developed to evaluate the studied articles: 1) *Ref*: Sources and citations of the reviewed articles. 2) *Algorithm*: The classification algorithms utilized in each study. 3) *Features*: The characteristics extracted from social media accounts for classification, such as UI, CF, NF, BF, and TF. 4) *Dataset*: The data collection used to train and assess the classification models. 5) *Embedding:* Methods to convert text data into numerical vectors. 6) *Classification*: Binary or multi-classification. 7) *Results*: Each model's performance is measured using evaluation metrics, such as Accuracy (A), Precision (P), and Recall (R). By systematically analyzing these criteria, we can understand the strengths and limitations of the current methods used for classifying social media accounts. A detailed comparison of the related work methods is presented in Table 1.

An examination of the state-of-the-art articles reveals that the majority of SMB detection models for social media platforms relied on data from Twitter (82%), followed by Sina Weibo (12%) and Instagram (6%). Regarding features, the attributes employed in these models are content and user information. The feature distribution employed in SMB detection research, with CF (95%) dominating, followed by UI (58%), NF (21%), and TF (11%). These findings align with a recent systematic review [22] that identified CF and UI as the most impactful features for SMB detection. AI-driven models predominantly leverage deep learning (52%) and neural network-based techniques (29%). ML methods account for the remaining 19%. Within the deep learning paradigm, LSTM and CNN are the most frequently utilized algorithms, with FFNN being the primary neural network architecture. Random Forest is the most used algorithm for machine learning models, achieving a peak accuracy of 99% on the Cresci-2017 dataset. CNN, LSTM, and BiLSTM are the cornerstone algorithms within deep learning for SMB detection. Among the various datasets employed for detecting SMBs, Cresci-2017 is widely utilized. However, it does not cover diverse examples of SMBs, and it is limited to spambots. This makes it crucial to provide a pivotal resource for researchers aiming to advance methodologies in identifying all types of automated social media accounts. The GloVe embedding technique is widely used for SMB detection. Deep learning-based methodologies for social media bot detection include LSTM and CNN. FFNN is widely used, with RF being the most prevalent. LSTM models have an F1-score of 97%, while BiLSTM has a recall rate of 99%. Hybrid models combining LSTM and CNN with attention mechanisms and BiGRUs have shown superior performance, achieving 99.44% accuracy. Word embeddings, such as BERT and GloVe, contribute to improved detection capabilities. The examination of the related works unveiled limitations, particularly concerning text presentation, generalization, and multi-classification challenges.

Table 1. Comparative table of the related work methods

Ref	Algorithm	Features	Dataset	Embedding	Classification	Results
[9]	BiLSTM, CNN, attention	CF, TF, UI, NF, BF	Cresci-2017	GloVe	Binary	A: 97%
[10]	BiLSTM	CF, TF, UI, NF, BF	Cresci-2017	GloVe	Binary	A: 92.9%
[11]	FFNN	CF	Cresci-2017	Bert	Binary	A: 86%
[12]	RF	UI, CF	Instagram	–		A: 91.76%
[13]	FFNN	UI, CF	Cresci-2017	GloVe, Elmo,	Binary	A: 94%
[14]	CNN & LSTM-Attention	CF	Cresci-2017	Bert	Binary	A: 97%
[15]	GNN, GCN	CF, NF	Cresci-rtbust, botometer-feedback, Gilani, Cresci-stock-2018, Midterm	Bert	Binary	A: 80%
[16]	DNN and LSTM	CF, UI	Midterm-18, Cresci-Rtbust and Gilani-17	GloVe	Binary	AUC: 97%
[17]	Bert transformer	CF	Twitter dataset			F1-score: 97%
[18]	BiLSTM	CF, UI	Twitter dataset			R: 99%
[19]	MLM	CF	BotOrNot dataset	Roberta	Binary	F1-Score: 77%
[20]	Digital DNA	CF	Cresci-2017 Twibot-20	TwHIN-BERT	Binary	A: 99.89%
[21]	BiGRU, LTSM	CF	Cresci-2017 Twibot-20	Glove	Binary	P: 100%

4   Background Techniques

4.1   Transformers

Transformers represent a transformative deep learning architecture that has significantly advanced the field of Natural Language Processing (NLP). Their efficacy is particularly notable in handling and generating sequential data, including machine translation, text summarization, and language modeling tasks. The principal innovation of transformers lies in their implementation of attention mechanisms. These mechanisms enable the model to focus selectively on relevant segments of the input sequence when producing each output token, distinguishing them from earlier architectures like RNNs and LSTM networks, which process sequences sequentially. Transformer-based models have markedly advanced the field of NLP. BERT, developed by Google researchers [23], leverages the encoder component of the Transformer architecture. Its principal innovation is the bidirectional attention mechanism, which allows it to interpret words within the full context of a sentence, supported by a sophisticated "multi-head attention" mechanism [24]. BERT is pre-trained on extensive unlabeled text corpora and subsequently fine-tuned for specific NLP tasks. Various adaptations of BERT, such as RoBERTa [25] and DistilBERT [26], transformer-based models have significantly enhanced language understanding and versatility, setting new benchmarks in the field of NLP.

4.2 Architecture

While the core architecture of the pre-trained model remains intact, modifications are typically made to the final layers or some intermediate layers to tailor the model to the target task. These adjustments usually involve adding or replacing layers to suit the specific requirements of the new task, with these layers generally being smaller and designed for the task at hand. A transformer model comprises an encoder and a decoder, each consisting of multiple attention layers and feed-forward neural networks. The encoder processes the input sequence to generate a contextual representation for each token, considering its relation to all other tokens. The decoder utilizes this contextual representation and the previously generated tokens to predict the subsequent token in the sequence. These components can be employed independently based on the specific task requirements: **1) Encoder-only models**: are suited for tasks that necessitate comprehension of the input, such as sentence classification and named entity recognition; **2) Decoder-only models**: are effective for generative tasks, including text generation; **3) Encoder-decoder models**: known as sequence-to-sequence models, are appropriate for generative tasks that involve an input, such as translation or summarization. Another fundamental characteristic of the Transformer model is **Attention layers** that focus on specific words in a sentence, such as "You like this course" or "this" in French. The French conjugation of "like" depends on the subject, and the model must consider the noun's gender. This principle applies to any NLP task, as individual words' contextual significance is influenced by surrounding words.

4.3 Fine-Tuning

Fine-tuning involves additional training conducted on a model that has already undergone pretraining. This process begins with a pre-trained language model, subsequently refined using a dataset specific to the target task. Rather than training a model from scratch, the rationale for fine-tuning includes several key considerations: **1) Pretraining Knowledge**: The pre-trained model has already been exposed to a large dataset that shares similarities with the fine-tuning dataset. This prior training provides the model with a foundational understanding of the language or domain, which can be leveraged during fine-tuning; **2) Data Efficiency**: A pre-trained model requires significantly less data during the fine-tuning phase to achieve effective results due to its initial training on extensive data; **3) Cost:** Fine-tuning a pre-trained model is generally less time-consuming and resource-intensive than training a model from scratch. It allows for quicker iterations and adjustments in the training process, making it a more practical approach.

5   Proposed Methodology

In this research study, the methodology emphasizes using multi-task learning (MTL) as an advanced machine learning strategy [27]. MTL involves training a single model to address multiple tasks concurrently, which enhances generalization and minimizes the need for extensive datasets for each task. The models are trained to classify social accounts into human, spambot, Sybil, fake accounts, or political SMBs. Figure 1 illustrates the proposed methodology, including 1) Data collection, 2) Labelling and Merging Data, 3) Preparing data for Training, 4) Setup of the Training Arguments, 5) Fine-Tuning Transformers, 6) Test and Validation, and 7) Results.

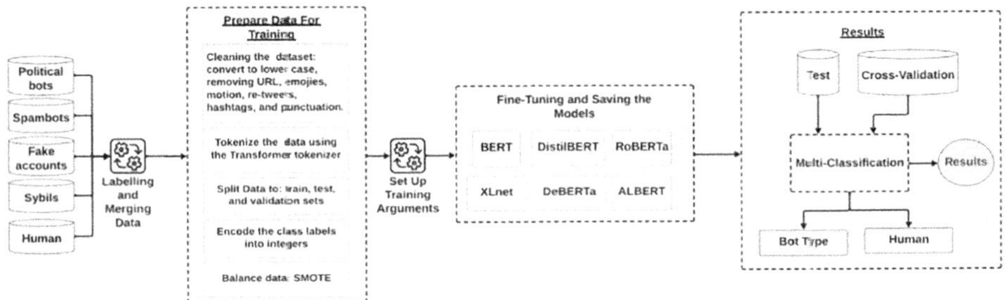

Fig. 1. The methodology proposed for multi-classification of SMB.

5.1   Data Collection

The data collection process leveraged five distinct datasets .**1) Cresci-2015**: This dataset was utilized to identify Sybil accounts, a type of social bot known for artificially inflating influence by creating multiple fake identities [28]; **2) Cresci-2017**: Employed to classify spambots, it includes accounts designed to propagate spam and engaged in spam-related activities [6]; **3) Twibot-20**: An essential resource to extract recent bots accounts [8]; **4) Fake Followers**: This dataset was used to identify and categorize fake accounts, often employed to create deceptive appearances of social influence [29]; **5) Political bots**: This dataset was employed to detect SMBs engaged in political discussion and misinformation [5]; **6) Human Accounts**: human accounts were extracted from the Cresci-2017 and Twibot-20 to ensure a diverse representation. The overall approach involved filtering and preprocessing these datasets to create a cohesive and balanced dataset of human and bot accounts.

5.2   Labelling and Merging Data

The final dataset is constructed by merging text-based data from Cresci-2015, Cresci-2017, Twibot-20, Fake Followers, and human accounts to form a unified representation encompassing Sybil, spam, fake, political, and human accounts. A standardized labeling scheme was implemented, assigning numerical identifiers to each category.

Subsequently, a mapping was established between these numerical labels and their corresponding textual descriptions for reference and interpretation. Figure 2 plots the labels distributions of our final dataset.

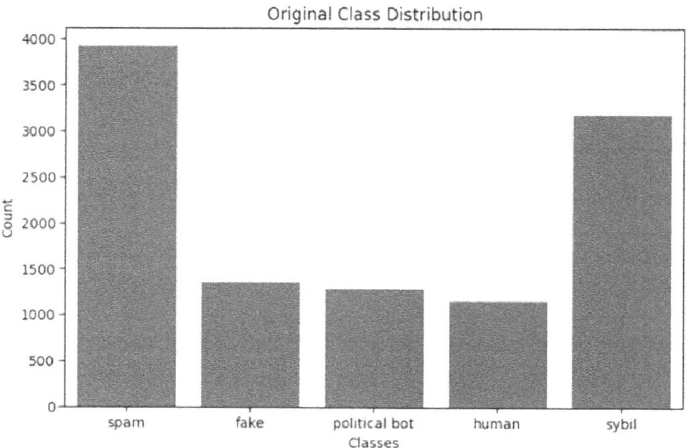

Fig. 2. The classes distributions of the final dataset.

Figure 2 show that the dataset exhibits a notable class imbalance, particularly with an overrepresentation of spam and sybil classes. This imbalance may result in model bias and suboptimal performance on less frequent classes. Implementing suitable balancing technique to address this issue can enhance model effectiveness.

5.3   Preparing Data for the Training

To prepare the data for training using the Hugging Face Transformers library we followed these steps:: **1) Cleaning the Data:** includes Lowercasing, Removing URLs, HTML tags, special characters and punctuation, stopwords, hashtags, retweets and mentions; **2) Loading the Dataset:** Converting data into the Hugging Face Dataset format to handle large-scale datasets and get access to advanced preprocessing capabilities and accelerating model training; **3) Tokenization:** segmenting text into individual tokens, incorporating tokens, and standardizing sequence length through padding or truncation; **4) Data Formatting:** To optimize transformer model training, data are formatted in a TensorFlow-compatible structure; **5) Split data:** The dataset is divided into training, validation, and test sets. A common partitioning strategy is a 70%, 20%, and 10% ratio for training, validation, and test sets; **6) Balancing data:** Given the imbalance within the training dataset (as shown in Fig. 2), the Synthetic Minority Oversampling Technique (SMOTE). This approach was selected based on prior experimental studies we conducted [21], where SMCTE demonstrated its efficacy in handling imbalanced data, reducing overfitting, enhancing model performance, and narrowing disparities between evaluation metrics.

5.4 Setting the Training Arguments

When fine-tuning transformer models within the Hugging Face Transformers library, numerous training hyperparameters can be configured to optimize the learning process. The following delineates key hyperparameters: num_train_epochs, *per_device_train_batch_size,   per_device_eval_batch_size,   learning_rate, warmup_steps, weight_decay, output_dir = "./results", evaluation_strategy = "epoch".*

5.5 Fine-Tuning Transformers

Due to their robust architectures, Bert, DistilBert, ROBETA, DEBERTA, ALBERT, and XLNet were selected as foundational models. BERT leverages bidirectional transformers to comprehensively capture contextual information, while RoBERTa refines BERT's architecture through hyperparameter optimization and architectural simplifications for enhanced performance [19]. DeBERTa introduces disentangled attention mechanisms and advanced training strategies to improve model capabilities further.

6 Experiment and Results

This section comprehensively evaluates fine-tuned transformer architectures for the multi-class classification of social media bots. Six transformer models were fine-tuned, and the implementation, training, and evaluation were conducted using the Hugging Face Transformers platform.

6.1 Evaluation Metrics

The research used accuracy, precision, recall, and F1-score as evaluation metrics. **Accuracy** measures the proportion of correct predictions across all classes, while precision measures the proportion of True Positive (TP) predictions. **Precision** measures the proportion of TP predictions out of all instances predicted as positive. It is beneficial when focusing on minimizing false positives (FP). **Recall** quantifies the proportion of positive cases that the model correctly identifies. The **F1-score** is the harmonic mean of precision and recall and is particularly valuable for evaluating models on imbalanced datasets [21].

6.2 Experimental Setup

The experimental process was conducted using Google Colab Pro, leveraging its computational resources of 50GB RAM, 225.8 GB of disk memory, and GPU 100. Key software components included Keras, TensorFlow, Python, Jupyter Notebook, hugging face transformers, and Parameter-Efficient Fine-Tuning (PEFT).

6.3 Model Architecture and Fine-Tuning

The selected transformer models underwent hyper-parameter tuning to adapt their parameters to the social media bot detection task. We employed a transfer learning paradigm, leveraging pre-trained language models as a foundation and adjusting model weights to optimize performance on our dataset. Key hyperparameters are: *Evaluation_strategy: "Epoch", Save_strategy: "Epoch", Learning_rate: "2e-5", Num_train_epochs: 10, Weight_decay: 0.01, Warmup_steps: 500, Gradient_accumulation_steps: 2, Per_device_train_batch_size: 16, Per_device_eval_batch_size: 16, Logging_steps: 100, Save_steps: 1000, Save_total_limit: 2.* The results achieved through fine-tuning various transformer architectures for the multi-class classification of SMBs offer insights into the efficacy of different model configurations and hyperparameter settings. Table 2 provides the performance achieved by the fine-tuned transformers.

Table 2. Fine-tuning results

Transformer	Accuracy	Loss	Precision	Recall	F1-score
BERT	96.29%	0.14%	96.25%	96.20%	96.22%
DISTILBERT	96.83%	0.11%	96.85%	96.83%	96.84%
ROBERTA	61.20%	0.74%	61.25%	61.20%	61.22%
DEBERTA	59.33%	0.80%	59.36%	59.33%	59.34%
XLNET	95%	0.19%	95.10%	95%	95.05%
ALBERT	56.13%	0.80%	56.15%	56.13%	56.14%

The findings detailed in Table 2 regarding transformer effectiveness in classifying social media bots indicate that DistilBERT is the most proficient model, achieving an accuracy, precision, recall, and F1-score over 96.80% and a loss rate of 0.11%. Models such as BERT and XLNet also demonstrate good performances. Nevertheless, there is a notable disparity between the leading models and others like RoBERTa, DeBERTa, and ALBERT. The differences in performance can be attributed to factors like model architecture, the quality of pre-training data, fine-tuning hyperparameters, and the characteristics of the dataset. Figure 3 plots the Receiver Operating Characteristic (ROC) curves in terms of TP and FP by classes achieved by DistilBERT which is the best-performing model, and Table 3 presents the results achieved by DistilBERT for each class. This would provide a more comprehensive understanding of how well the model perform on each specific social bot type.

The ROC curves presented is an important visualization to evaluate the model's ability to differentiate between various classes of social bots and human accounts. They effectively illustrate the multi-model system's success in identifying different types of SMBs.

The provided classification report indicates strong performance across all classes, with high accuracy, precision, recall, and F1-scores. This suggests that the model is

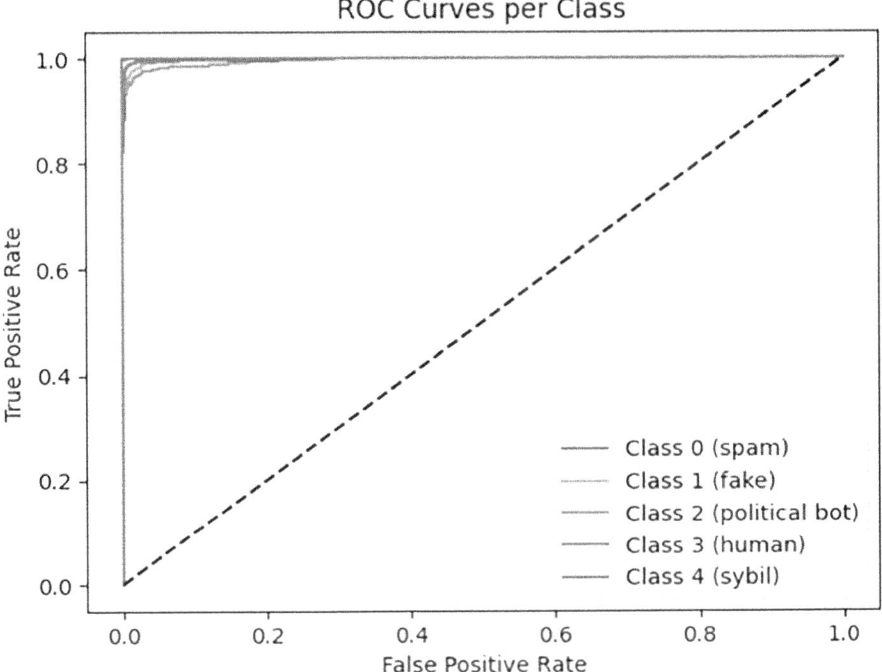

Fig. 3. The receiver operating characteristic of each class.

Table 3. The Classification results of DistilBERT for each class

Class	Accuracy	Precision	Recall	F1-Score
Spam	100%	98%	100%	99%
Fake account	99%	86%	99%	92%
Political bot	81%	99%	81%	89%
Human	98%	97%	98%	98%
Sybil	100%	100%	100%	100%

effective in distinguishing between different types of social media accounts, including human users and various types of bots.

7 Conclusion

In conclusion, this study highlights the significant role that transformer-based models play in detecting and classifying SMBs, which is a growing concern for safeguarding the integrity of online platforms. By fine-tuning models such as BERT, DistilBERT, RoBERTa, DeBERTa, ALBERT, and XLNet, the research demonstrates the superior effectiveness of transformer models in distinguishing between different types of social bots, outperforming traditional machine learning methods. The proposed multi-class classification framework not only enhances accuracy but also provides a robust solution to improve social media security based on the generated text data by users.

For future directions, of this research we suggest investigating alternative multi-model architectures, optimizing hyperparameters, and incorporating diverse data types. Given the continuous evolution of SMB tactics, it will be essential to adopt a multi-model approach that integrates various attributes, including images and multilingual text data. Furthermore, regularly updating and retraining these models will be crucial in staying ahead of new bot strategies. Methods such as feature importance analysis and attention mechanisms can also offer deeper insights into the model's decision-making process. By addressing these areas, future research can contribute to the advancement of more robust and accurate social media bot detection systems.

References

1. Ellaky, Z., Benabbou, F., Ouahabi, S., Sael, N.: Word embedding for social bot detection systems. In: 2021 Fifth International Conference on Intelligent Computing in Data Sciences (ICDS), pp. 1–8. IEEE, Fez (2021). https://doi.org/10.1109/ICDS53782.2021.9626752
2. Ellaky, Z., Benabbou, F., Ouahabi, S., Sael, N.: A survey of spam bots detection in online social networks. In: 2021 International Conference on Digital Age & Technological Advances for Sustainable Development (ICDATA), pp. 58–65. IEEE, Marrakech (2021). https://doi.org/10.1109/ICDATA52997.2021.00021
3. Ellaky, Z., Benabbou, F.: Political social media bot detection: unveiling cutting-edge feature selection and engineering strategies in machine learning model development. Sci. Afr. **25**, e02269 (2024) https://doi.org/10.1016/j.sciaf.2024.e02269
4. Goyal, B., et al.: Detection of fake accounts on social media using multimodal data with deep learning. IEEE Trans. Comput. Soc. Syst., 1–12 (2024). https://doi.org/10.1109/TCSS.2023.3296837
5. Ellaky, Z., Benabbou, F.: Political social media bot detection: unveiling cutting-edge feature selection and engineering strategies in machine learning model development. Sci. Afr. **25**, e02269 (2024)
6. Cresci, S., Di Pietro, R., Petrocchi, M., Spognardi, A., Tesconi, M.: The paradigm-shift of social spambots: evidence, theories, and tools for the arms race. In: Proceedings of the 26th International Conference on World Wide Web Companion, pp. 963–972 (2017). https://doi.org/10.1145/3041021.3055135
7. Benabbou, F., Boukhouima, H., Sael, N.: Fake accounts detection system based on bidirectional gated recurrent unit neural network. IJECE. **12**(3), 3129 (2022). https://doi.org/10.11591/ijece.v12i3.pp3129-3137
8. Feng, S., Wan, H., Wang, N., Li, J., Luo, M.: TwiBot-20: a comprehensive twitter bot detection benchmark. In: Proceedings of the 30th ACM International Conference on Information & Knowledge Management, Virtual Event, pp. 4485–4494. ACM (2021). https://doi.org/10.1145/3459637.3482019

9. Fazil, M., Sah, A.K., Abulaish, M.: DeepSBD: a deep neural network model with attention mechanism for SocialBot detection. IEEE Trans. Inf. Forensics Secur. **16**, 4211–4223 (2021). https://doi.org/10.1109/TIFS.2021.3102498

10. Wei, F., Nguyen, U.T.: Twitter bot detection using bidirectional long short-term memory neural networks and word embeddings. In: 2019 First IEEE International Conference on Trust, Privacy and Security in Intelligent Systems and Applications (TPS-ISA), pp. 101–109. IEEE (2019). https://doi.org/10.1109/TPS-ISA48467.2019.00021

11. Heidari, M., et al.: Bert model for fake news detection based on social bot activities in the covid-19 pandemic. In: 2021 IEEE 12th Annual Ubiquitous Computing, Electronics & Mobile Communication Conference (UEMCON), pp. 0103–0109. IEEE (2021). https://doi.org/10.1109/UEMCON53757.2021.9666618

12. Purba, K.R., Asirvatham, D., Murugesan, R.K.: Classification of instagram fake users using supervised machine learning algorithms. Int. J. Electr. Comput. Eng. **10**(3), 2763 (2020). https://doi.org/10.11591/ijece.v10i3

13. Heidari, M., Jones, J.H., Uzuner, O.: Deep contextualized word embedding for text-based online user profiling to detect social bots on twitter. In: 2020 International Conference on Data Mining Workshops (ICDMW), pp. 480–487. IEEE (2020). https://doi.org/10.1109/ICDMW51313.2020.00071

14. Kumar, S., Garg, S., Vats, Y., Parihar, A.S.: Content based bot detection using bot language model and BERT embeddings. In: 2021 5th International Conference on Computer, Communication and Signal Processing (ICCCSP), pp. 285–289. IEEE, Chennai (2021). https://doi.org/10.1109/ICCCSP52374.2021.9465506

15. Guo, Q., Xie, H., Li, Y., Ma, W., Zhang, C.: Social bots detection via fusing bert and graph convolutional networks. Symmetry. **14**(1), 30 (2021). https://doi.org/10.3390/sym14010030

16. Hayawi, K., Mathew, S., Venugopal, N., Masud, M.M., Ho, P.-H.: DeeProBot: a hybrid deep neural network model for social bot detection based on user profile data. Soc. Netw. Anal. Min. **12**(1), 43 (2022). https://doi.org/10.1007/s13278-022-00869-w

17. Hayawi, K., Shahriar, S., Serhani, M.A., Taleb, I., Mathew, S.S.: ANTi-vax: a novel twitter dataset for COVID-19 vaccine misinformation detection. Public Health. **203**, 23–30 (2022). https://doi.org/10.1016/j.puhe.2021.11.022

18. Messai, A., Hamida, Z.F., Drif, A., Giordano, S.: Multi-input BiLSTM deep learning model for social bot detection. In: 2023 International Conference on Advances in Electronics, Control and Communication Systems (ICAECCS), pp. 1–6. IEEE (2023). https://doi.org/10.1109/ICAECCS56710.2023.10104646

19. Martin-Gutierrez, D., Hernandez-Penaloza, G., Hernandez, A.B., Lozano-Diez, A., Alvarez, F.: A deep learning approach for robust detection of bots in twitter using transformers. IEEE Access. **9**, 54591–54601 (2021). https://doi.org/10.1109/ACCESS.2021.3068659

20. Ilias, L., Kazelidis, I.M., Askounis, D.: Multimodal detection of bots on X (twitter) using transformers. IEEE Trans. Inf. Forensics Secur. **19**, 7320–7334 (2024). https://doi.org/10.1109/TIFS.2024.3435138

21. Ellaky, Z., Benabbou, F., Matrane, Y., Qaqa, S.: A hybrid deep learning architecture for social media bots detection based on BiGRU-LSTM and GloVe word embedding. IEEE Access. **12**, 100278–100294 (2024). https://doi.org/10.1109/ACCESS.2024.3430859

22. Ellaky, Z., Benabbou, F., Ouahabi, S.: Systematic literature review of social media bots detection systems. J. King Saud Univer. Comput. Inf. Sci. (2023). https://doi.org/10.1016/j.jksuci.2023.04.004

23. Devlin, J., Chang, M.-W., Lee, K., Toutanova, K.: Bert: pre-training of deep bidirectional transformers for language understanding. arXiv preprint arXiv:1810.04805 (2018)

24. Rothman, D.: Transformers for Natural Language Processing: Build Innovative Deep Neural Network Architectures for NLP with Python, PyTorch, TensorFlow, BERT, RoBERTa, and More. Packt Publishing Ltd (2021)

25. Delobelle, P., Winters, T., Berendt, B.: RobBERT: a Dutch RoBERTa-based Language Model arXiv. https://doi.org/10.48550/ARXIV.2001.06286 (2020)
26. Sanh, V., Debut, L., Chaumond, J., Wolf, T.: DistilBERT, a distilled version of BERT: smaller, faster, cheaper and lighter. arXiv preprint arXiv:1910.01108 (2019)
27. Pujari, S.C., Friedrich, A., Strötgen, J.: A multi-task approach to neural multi-label hierarchical patent classification using transformers. In: Hiemstra, D., Moens, M.-F., Mothe, J., Perego, R., Potthast, M., Sebastiani, F. (eds.) Advances in Information Retrieval, vol. 12656, pp. 513–528. Springer International Publishing, Cham (2021). https://doi.org/10.1007/978-3-030-72113-8_34
28. Cresci, S., Di Pietro, R., Petrocchi, M., Spognardi, A., Tesconi, M.: Fame for sale: efficient detection of fake twitter followers. Decis. Support. Syst. **80**, 56–71 (2015). https://doi.org/10.1016/j.dss.2015.09.003
29. Yang, K., Varol, O., Davis, C.A., Ferrara, E., Flammini, A., Menczer, F.: Arming the public with artificial intelligence to counter social bots. Human Behav. Emerg. Tech. **1**(1), 48–61 (2019). https://doi.org/10.1002/hbe2.115

A Decentralized Identity Management and Student Data Verification System Using Blockchain and IPFS

Amine Gharbaoui[✉], Abdelaziz Ettaoufik, and Abderrahim Tragha

Laboratory of Information Technology and Modeling, Faculty of Sciences Ben M'Sik,
University Hassan II of Casablanca, Casablanca, Morocco
`amine.gharbaoui-etu@etu.univh2c.com`

Abstract. The falsification of diplomas and transcripts poses a serious problem in the academic and professional worlds. These dishonest practices can compromise the credibility of educational institutions and damage the reputation of legitimate graduates. Verifying the authenticity of these documents often involves lengthy and costly processes, requiring the involvement of multiple stakeholders. To address this challenge, blockchain emerges as an innovative and secure solution. This distributed ledger technology allows for the transparent and tamper-proof recording and validation of diplomas and transcripts. Each issued document can be stored as a transaction on the blockchain, ensuring instant traceability and easy verification of authenticity. By eliminating the need for intermediaries, blockchain reduces costs and delays while increasing the reliability of the certification process. Furthermore, the use of smart contracts can further automate and secure the issuance and verification of diplomas, simplifying the process for all parties involved. In this paper, we propose a decentralized application (Dapp) that integrates blockchain technology with the decentralized storage InterPlanetary File System (IPFS). This setup uses a network of decentralized nodes to store file copies, allowing retrieval via a unique hash that identifies each file. IPFS manages data storage, while the blockchain guarantees the validity of this data by recording the corresponding hashes.

Keywords: Blockchain · IPFS · higher education · Identity Management

1 Introduction

Similarly, to other sectors, the education sector is progressively advancing into the digital era. The integration of technology and education is improving, leading to a transformation in the field. However, the adoption of technology within the education sector remains a slow and challenging process [1]. Education plays a crucial role in the growth and advancement of humanity, and societies that build strong and well-developed educational infrastructures actively dominate in societal progress [2]. Education modifies people's viewpoints and attitudes while giving us a fundamental awareness of the world around us. Education may become a technological phenomenon since it is a human-centric

© The Author(s), under exclusive license to Springer Nature Switzerland AG 2026
O. Zahour et al. (Eds.): ICTIM 2024, CCIS 2655, pp. 365–378, 2026.
https://doi.org/10.1007/978-3-032-15147-6_34

phenomenon. Besides blockchain, initially designed to regulate Bitcoin, has undergone significant evolution, now recognized as a foundational technology for diverse decentralized applications [3]. Sensitive information is increasingly being managed using it as a powerful tool, particularly in sectors such as higher education, healthcare, supply chains, and the Internet of Things (IoT). In the context of higher education, comprising major stakeholders like Higher Education Institutions (HEIs) and students, blockchain holds potential for transformative applications [4].

In this paper, we propose a schema for leveraging blockchain technology in identity management within the higher education sector. By harnessing blockchain alongside IT infrastructure and computing solutions, universities can effectively monitor and manage the various systems integral to their operations. Blockchain offers a decentralized and secure framework for identity management, ensuring the integrity and authenticity of student information across diverse university systems. Traditionally, identity management within higher education has relied on centralized databases and systems, which can be susceptible to security breaches and data manipulation. However, by adopting blockchain technology, universities can establish a distributed ledger system where identity information is securely stored and authenticated through cryptographic methods.

This blockchain-based identity management schema facilitates seamless integration with existing IT infrastructure, enabling universities to efficiently monitor and track student enrollment, academic records, access permissions, and other administrative functions. Moreover, the immutable nature of blockchain ensures that once identity information is recorded, it cannot be altered or tampered with, enhancing the security and reliability of the system. By implementing blockchain for identity management, universities can streamline administrative processes, mitigate security risks, and enhance data transparency and integrity within the higher education ecosystem. This innovative approach holds the potential to revolutionize identity management practices in higher education, paving the way for a more secure and efficient educational environment..

2 Related Works

2.1 Blockchain

Blockchain technology enables a secure and decentralized method of storing and sharing information, comprising several key components [5].

- Distributed Ledger: A blockchain serves as an example of a distributed ledger, functioning as a database maintained across multiple computers. Each machine connected to the network holds a duplicate of the entire database.
- Blocks: Forming the foundational units of the blockchain, blocks consist of groups of confirmed transactions added to the chain. The interconnectedness of these blocks creates the "chain" as each block references the preceding one.
- Cryptography: Utilized within blockchain technology, cryptography ensures secure communication and transaction integrity, preventing unauthorized alterations.
- Consensus Process: To establish agreement on the current state of the blockchain, a consensus process involves all computers within the network. Given the absence of centralized control, various consensus mechanisms such as Proof of Work, Delegated Proof of Stake, and Proof of Stake are employed.

– Nodes: Computers participating in a blockchain network, known as nodes, store a copy of the blockchain and engage in transaction verification and network maintenance. Nodes contribute to the decentralization of the network, and anyone can operate them.
– Smart Contracts: Stored within the blockchain, smart contracts are self-executing contracts that autonomously enforce agreement terms between parties, eliminating the need for intermediaries.

2.2 Blockchain in Education

The inherent decentralization of blockchain technology is a core attribute. Operating without reliance on a centralized authority, blockchain facilitates secure, transparent, and tamper-resistant transactions through its distributed database. Offering a plethora of benefits across various applications, blockchain stands out for its decentralized nature, transparency, and security [6]. By distributing transaction validation and recording among a network of nodes rather than a single central entity, the technology exhibits greater resilience against fraudulent activities and hacking attempts. Transactions are grouped into blocks and linked in a chain, creating a permanent and immutable ledger. For instance, within the blockchain network, every node possesses the capability to verify student credentials, test results, and attendance records [5].

Blockchain technology, recognized for its immense potential, has emerged as a valuable asset in the realm of education. Traditional educational systems and networks have historically operated within centralized structures, exerting comprehensive control over student data while often characterized by bureaucratic processes and limited automation [7]. The implementation of blockchain systems within the educational sphere introduces a paradigm shift in ownership dynamics. By virtue of its decentralized nature and absence of a central authority, blockchain systems afford students unparalleled autonomy over their personal data [8]. This empowerment translates to full independence from institutional control, enabling students to exercise complete sovereignty over their data. The blockchain perpetually records and secures data using cryptographic methods. These methods maintain the data's integrity, ensure its immutability through hash functions, and guarantee authenticity and anonymity [9].

The potential of blockchain in education extends beyond its current applications, offering students the opportunity for anonymity regarding their personal data, independence from institutions, and the immutability of official documents and certificates [8]. This is achieved through the inherent architecture of blockchain networks, which ensures the truthfulness and reliability of records. With blockchain, students have full control over their data, heralding a new paradigm in education [10]. The adoption of blockchain technology has the potential to streamline administrative processes, resulting in reduced costs associated with studies [11]. Additionally, it facilitates alternative approaches to tuition payment and opens up possibilities for personalized and online learning experiences [9].

Amidst the COVID-19 pandemic and the rising need for online and automated academic solutions, this research [12] outlined a blockchain-based solution. Decentralization, data integrity, and security represent some of the benefits offered by this technology. Through the proposed solution, the existing educational system can streamline student recruitment, gather updated statistics, and minimize the paperwork necessary to fulfil responsibilities.

Manoj et al. [13] implemented blockchain technology and smart contracts to facilitate token-based decentralized credit transfer within educational systems. Their proposed system validates certifications acquired locally and from reputable online educational platforms. Each student's credit value is stored in token form within their wallet, with tokens accumulated upon completion of each course. Following the completion of each course, faculty members transfer credits to students' wallets based on the unique identifier of the student's address, which operates on a blockchain consisting of multiple signatures comprising public and private keys. Kuleto et al. in [14] explored how Higher Education Institutions (HEIs) could leverage a blockchain network to create a sustainable education system. Their study, which included student opinions, found that blockchain technology positively affected learning outcomes. In [15], the authors performed a systematic content analysis of existing literature to identify factors influencing the adoption and application of blockchain in education. They uncovered key themes at both macro and micro levels, providing guidance for future research on blockchain's role in education management and development. Research in [16] examined the use of blockchain in course design and evaluation in Chinese universities, emphasizing the significance of teachers' perspectives and experiences with blockchain.

Garg et al. [17] introduced a decentralized system for reviewing and ranking online education, utilizing blockchain technology. Traditional centralized review systems for online courses are susceptible to manipulation and tampering. Therefore, the proposed system offers a decentralized and reliable alternative, ensuring the integrity of ratings and the independence and authenticity of content reviews conducted by subject matter experts (SMEs). Xiao et al. [18] created a unified and reliable data-sharing infrastructure for open learning using an extended consortium blockchain architecture. Their proof-of-concept demonstrated that the blockchain system could function effectively in a production environment and surpassed similar research, though it still had limitations and areas for enhancement. Similarly, [19] conducted a bibliometric analysis to identify gaps in scientific research within higher education. This analysis also examined the prevalent applications of blockchain technology in higher education globally and provided recommendations for future studies.

2.3 The Benefits of Blockchain in Education

Blockchain technology offers numerous benefits in the education sector:

– Improved Transparency

Blockchain is immutable ledger technology generates a chronological record of real-time events, providing a reliable method for validating transcripts, presenting comprehensive report cards, and keeping students informed about their progress. With assignments submitted via blockchain, students no longer risk misplacing their work or facing claims of misplacement by teachers [20].

– Enhanced Accountability through Digital Contracts

The introduction of smart contracts offers a digital agreement mechanism for teachers, university officials, and students. Through these contracts, students and teachers can delineate assignment parameters, including deadlines and grading criteria. Furthermore, smart contracts hold potential for facilitating student loan payments [21].

– Promotion of Learning Incentives

Tokenization, a core aspect of blockchain technology, enables academic institutions to incentivize timely student loan repayment and encourage student performance through crypto-currency rewards for academic achievements or completion of specific majors. The gamification aspect of tokenization has proven highly effective in motivating learning [20].

– Monitoring Learning Performance and Personalization

Educators gain additional tools for monitoring student performance through blockchain's transparent data storage. By leveraging smart contracts and their outputs, schools can tailor learning environments to individual student needs, identifying areas where students may need additional support. Furthermore, educational institutions can utilize blockchain-stored student performance data district-wide to enhance overall educational processes [22].

3 Proposed Architecture

The centralized identity management approach, once dominant, revealed significant flaws over time. Centralized entities controlled user identities, creating single points of failure vulnerable to data breaches. Users lacked autonomy, relying heavily on third-party organizations to secure their personal information. This model also imposed the burden of managing multiple passwords for various applications, which led to weak security practices like password reuse or relying on easily guessable credentials. The increasing complexity and inefficiency of this system underscored the need for a more secure and user-centric solution.

Moreover, centralized systems often resulted in data silos, where user information was fragmented across different platforms, making it difficult to maintain consistent identity verification. The reliance on centralized entities also introduced delays in accessing services, as users had to navigate through bureaucratic processes to authenticate their identities. As digital interactions became more frequent and sophisticated, these inefficiencies became more pronounced, highlighting the need for a system that could provide seamless, secure, and user-controlled identity management.

The evolution of technology and growing concerns about privacy and data security pushed organizations to explore decentralized identity solutions. These new approaches aimed to give users more control over their digital identities, reducing dependence on centralized authorities. By leveraging technologies like blockchain, decentralized identity systems promised to enhance security, reduce the risk of data breaches, and simplify the management of digital identities, offering a more resilient and user-friendly alternative to traditional centralized models.

The shift towards decentralized identity management, particularly in higher education, offers a transformative approach to publishing and verifying diplomas. Traditional centralized identity systems are fraught with risks, including data breaches and a lack of user control. Decentralized identity management, combined with technologies like blockchain and IPFS, provides a more secure and transparent method for managing academic credentials.

The decentralized system also allows for seamless interoperability across different educational institutions and employers, as the blockchain provides a consistent and universally accessible record of academic credentials. This advancement in digital identity management could pave the way for a more efficient, secure, and trustworthy system in the educational sector, ultimately empowering students and preserving the integrity of academic qualifications [23].

However, despite advancements in digital identity management, two major challenges persist:

- Lack of user control: Identity management remains under the jurisdiction of organizations responsible for issuing identities, leaving users with little to no control over their digital identities, which can be revoked at any time. Furthermore, the processes of identification and authentication are often intertwined [24].
- Centralization: The centralized nature of existing systems poses a significant risk of data breaches. This centralization persists in current internet-based identity management models [25].

Conversely, self-sovereign identity models are still in their early stages. While current proposals partially meet the expectations of such systems, significant refinement is needed. In the digital realm, there is no universally reliable system that can serve as a benchmark for self-sovereign identity management [24].

In this paper, we propose an architecture that combines blockchain technology with the decentralized storage system IPFS. This system leverages a decentralized network of nodes to store copies of files, enabling anyone to retrieve them using a unique hash that identifies each file. The IPFS distributed file system handles data storage, while the blockchain ensures the data's validity by recording the corresponding hashes (Fig. 1).

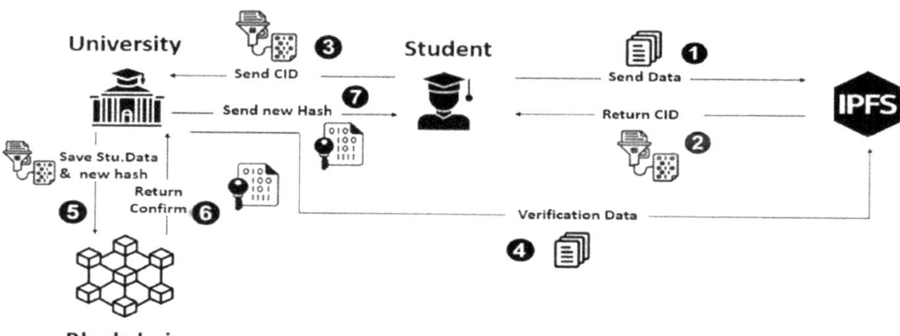

Fig. 1. Architecture of decentralized identity management in the Higher Education.

In our approach, users have full control over their data. Our system is based on several key interactions:

1. The student uploads their data (e.g., academic records, certificates, or other credentials) to the IPFS network for storage. IPFS decentralizes the storage and provides a unique hash (digital fingerprint) representing the stored data.
2. IPFS returns a unique content identifier (CID) to the student, which acts as an identifier for their data.
3. The student sends this CID to the university, allowing the university to locate and verify the data on the IPFS network.
4. The university uses the provided CID to retrieve the actual data from the IPFS network and verifies its authenticity and accuracy.
5. After successful verification, the university records student data and new hash on the blockchain. This step ensures that the hash, and the data it represents, cannot be altered or tampered with.
6. The blockchain processes this transaction and returns a confirmation in the form of a hash, indicating the data has been securely recorded.
7. The university sends the new hash back to the student, serving as verified proof of the data's authenticity and integrity.

This proposed system leverages the strengths of blockchain technology and IPFS to enhance the management and verification of student data. Here are the key benefits:

- Decentralization

Data Storage: IPFS (InterPlanetary File System) revolutionizes data storage by decentralizing it. Traditional centralized databases store all data on a single server or a closely linked network of servers. This setup creates a single point of failure—if the server goes down, data could be lost or inaccessible. IPFS, however, stores data across a distributed network of nodes, where each node holds pieces of the data. This distribution ensures that even if one node fails, the data remains accessible, enhancing the system's resilience to attacks and reducing the risk of data loss. Additionally, IPFS improves scalability and efficiency by allowing data retrieval from the closest or most convenient node, reducing latency and bandwidth usage.

Distributed Verification: The decentralized nature of blockchain further strengthens this system. Unlike centralized systems where a single authority manages and verifies data, blockchain operates on a distributed consensus model. This means that no single entity controls the verification process. Instead, multiple nodes in the network participate in verifying the accuracy and authenticity of the data. This distributed verification process ensures that all stakeholders can trust the system, as it is transparent, tamper-resistant, and resistant to manipulation by any single entity. The consensus mechanism, whether proof-of-work, proof-of-stake, or another, guarantees that the verification process is fair and unbiased.

- Security and Integrity

Immutable Records: One of the cornerstone features of blockchain technology is immutability. Once a piece of data is recorded on the blockchain, it becomes virtually impossible to alter or delete. This characteristic is critical in maintaining the integrity of student records. When a university verifies and records a student's credentials on the blockchain, that information is locked in time. It can be referenced, but not changed, ensuring that the records are always accurate and consistent over time. This immutability is crucial for preventing fraud, as it guarantees that the credentials presented are genuine and unaltered.

Cryptographic Hashing: Cryptographic hashing adds another layer of security. A hash function takes an input (in this case, student data) and produces a fixed-size string of bytes, usually a digest that appears random. Even the slightest change in the input data will result in a completely different hash, making it easy to detect unauthorized alterations. For example, if someone tries to modify a student's academic record, the hash generated from the altered data would not match the hash stored on the blockchain, immediately signaling a discrepancy. This ensures that the data's integrity is preserved and that any attempt to tamper with the data is quickly identified.

- Transparency and Trust

Verification Process: Transparency is a fundamental benefit of blockchain technology. In the context of this system, transparency means that every transaction, including the verification of student credentials, is recorded on a public ledger that can be independently audited. Both students and universities can easily verify the authenticity of the records, knowing that the information they see is accurate and unaltered. This transparency builds trust among all parties involved, as it ensures that the data has been handled properly and that the verification process is open to scrutiny.

Elimination of Fraud: By recording student data on a public ledger, the system effectively eliminates the potential for fraud. Since the blockchain is immutable and transparent, all stakeholders (students, employers, and academic institutions) can be confident that the credentials are genuine and have been verified by a trusted authority. The public nature of the ledger means that any attempt to present false credentials can be easily exposed, significantly reducing the likelihood of fraudulent activities. This not only protects the integrity of the academic institution but also ensures that employers are hiring candidates with verified qualifications.

- Control and Ownership

Student Autonomy: One of the most empowering aspects of this system is the level of control it gives students over their own data. Unlike traditional systems where institutions maintain control over student records, this blockchain-based system allows students to manage their own data. They can decide what information to share, giving them greater autonomy over their personal and academic records. This shift in control enhances student privacy and ensures that their data is not shared without their consent.

Permission Management: The system's permission management feature further empowers students by allowing them to manage who has access to their data. Students can grant or revoke access to their records as needed, ensuring that only authorized parties can view or verify their information. This user-centric approach not only enhances privacy but also ensures that students retain ownership of their personal information. It's a significant improvement over traditional systems, where students often have little control over who can access their records or how their data is used. By placing control in the hands of the students, this system promotes a more secure, private, and transparent management of academic records.

4   Implementation

In the proposed decentralized application, the student begins by creating a personalized portfolio website. This portfolio contains detailed personal information, academic achievements, skills, and certifications, forming a comprehensive digital representation of the student's credentials. Once finalized, the portfolio is uploaded to the InterPlanetary File System (IPFS), a decentralized file storage technology (Fig. 2) designed to enhance data security and accessibility. IPFS plays a critical role by generating a unique content identifier (CID) for the uploaded portfolio. This CID acts as a digital fingerprint, ensuring the integrity and immutability of the stored data. Any modification to the portfolio would alter the CID, making it easy to detect unauthorized changes. This security feature ensures that the student's achievements are accurately preserved over time. The use of IPFS in this system provides multiple advantages. First, it secures the portfolio in a decentralized manner, mitigating the risks associated with centralized data storage, such as data breaches or loss. Decentralization ensures that the portfolio is stored across multiple nodes in the network, reducing the likelihood of data corruption or tampering. Additionally, the CID simplifies the process of verifying the authenticity of the portfolio. Potential employers, academic institutions, or other interested parties can use the CID to quickly access the student's portfolio on IPFS, knowing that the data they retrieve is both genuine and unchanged. This capability significantly streamlines the verification process, reducing administrative burdens and increasing trust in the credentials provided. Overall, by combining the decentralized nature of IPFS with the unique CID system, this approach offers a robust, secure, and efficient method for storing and verifying academic portfolios, enhancing the overall integrity and trustworthiness of student data in the digital age.

Fig. 2. Example of a content identifier (CID).

Once the student generates the CID for their portfolio on IPFS, they submit this identifier to their university for verification. This step is critical in ensuring the legitimacy and accuracy of the information presented. The university accesses the portfolio data directly via IPFS, utilizing the CID to retrieve the stored file. During the verification process, the institution meticulously reviews the student's personal information, academic achievements, skills, and certifications, cross-referencing these details with internal records to confirm their authenticity. This rigorous review involves checking the accuracy of the student's academic history, ensuring that the reported achievements align with the university's official records. The university also verifies that the certifications and skills listed in the portfolio adhere to its academic guidelines and standards. This step is essential to maintaining the institution's credibility, as it ensures that only genuine, verified information is associated with the student. The decentralized nature of the IPFS system adds an additional layer of security to this process. Because the data is stored across multiple nodes rather than in a centralized database, it is less vulnerable to tampering or unauthorized modifications. The CID ensures that the portfolio accessed by the university is exactly as the student submitted it; any alteration to the portfolio would result in a different CID, making discrepancies immediately apparent. Once the university completes its verification, the validated CID can be stored on a blockchain, further ensuring the portfolio's immutability and transparency. This step not only confirms the authenticity of the student's information but also makes it easily accessible for future verification by employers or other educational institutions. The use of blockchain technology in this context guarantees that the verified data remains secure and unalterable, preserving the integrity of the student's academic and professional records. This process significantly enhances trust between the student, the university, and external stakeholders, making it a robust solution for managing and verifying educational credentials in the digital age (Fig. 3).

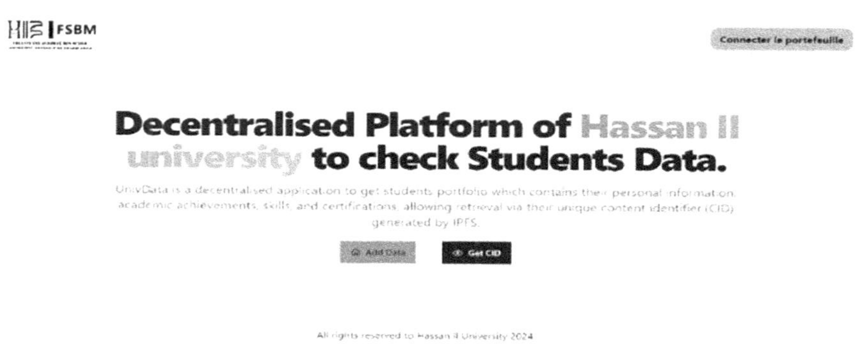

Fig. 3. Front page of decentralized application (Dapp).

All parties connect using MetaMask, ensuring the confidentiality and transparency of transactions and information exchanges. MetaMask, as a digital wallet and gateway for decentralized applications, allows users to interact with the blockchain securely and privately. Each transaction is digitally signed, providing cryptographic verifiability that enhances trust between parties. This method eliminates the need to directly provide sensitive personal information to each institution, reducing the risks of data leaks and compromising confidentiality. Additionally, blockchain's inherent transparency ensures all interactions and modifications are visible and audited in real-time, preventing unauthorized data manipulation. Using MetaMask, students, employers, and academic institutions can exchange and verify information effectively and securely, maintaining a high level of confidentiality and trust. Once verification is complete and the data is validated, the university (Fig. 4) connect using its account and records the student data and the new hash on a blockchain (Fig. 5), a distributed ledger technology renowned for its transparency and security. This process ensures that the recorded data cannot be altered or deleted, preserving the integrity of the student's portfolio.

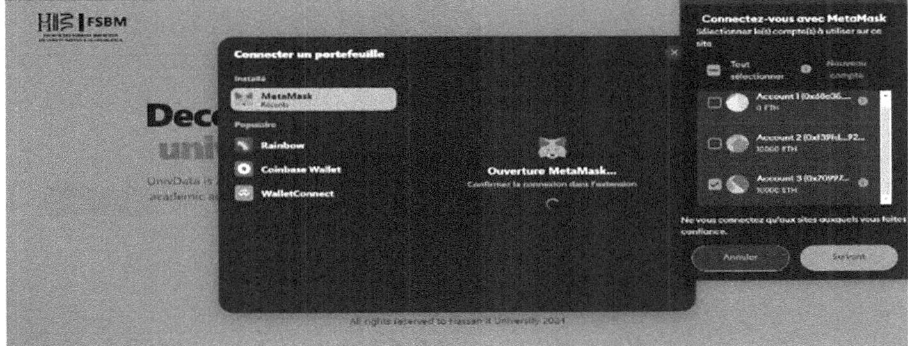

Fig. 4. University account in Metamask.

Recording the student data on the blockchain and the new hash, a unique cryptographic code. This hash serves as proof of verification and data authenticity. The student can then provide this hash to potential employers, other educational institutions, or any relevant parties. By using the hash, these parties can retrieve the CID from the blockchain and access the verified portfolio on IPFS, ensuring that the information they see is genuine and tamper-proof. This seamless process not only enhances trust in the student's credentials but also streamlines the verification process, reducing administrative overhead and preventing fraud.

Upon receiving the hash, interested parties can retrieve the CID from the blockchain (Fig. 6) and use it to fetch the portfolio from IPFS. This ensures that the data they access is genuine, unaltered, and accurately reflects the student's achievements and qualifications. The blockchain's immutability guarantees that once the CID is recorded, the associated data cannot be tampered with, providing a trustworthy and permanent record.

For employers, this means they can confidently assess a candidate's qualifications without the lengthy and often unreliable traditional verification processes. Educational institutions can also streamline their admissions procedures by quickly verifying the authenticity of an applicant's academic records. This system not only speeds up the verification process but also enhances security and trust across all parties involved. Additionally, by leveraging blockchain and IPFS, the student benefits from a seamless, efficient way to prove their credentials, making it easier to pursue career and educational opportunities.

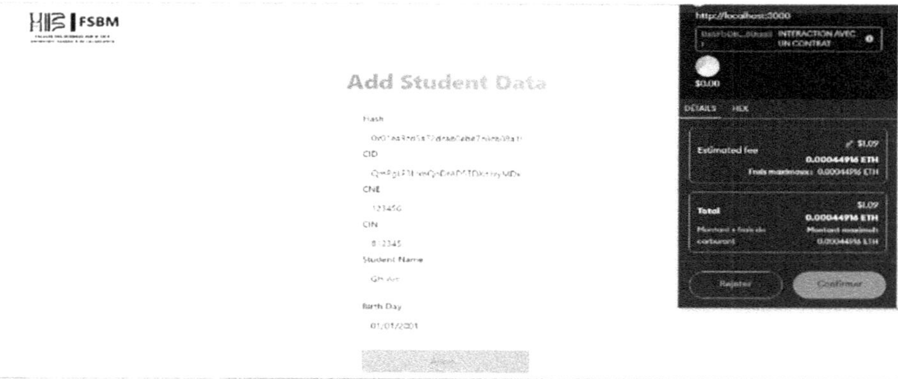

Fig. 5. Add Student Data in Blockchain.

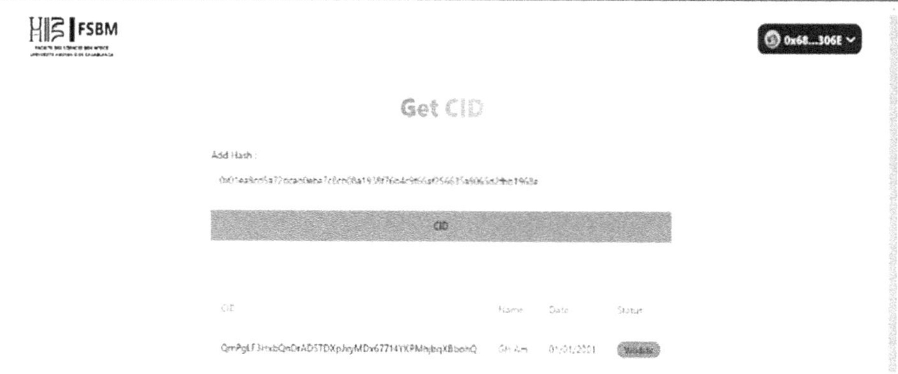

Fig. 6. Get Student Data by Hash.

5   Conclusion

Identity management involves complex processes concerning user identification, authentication, and authorization for accessing various services and applications. Employing blockchain technology for identity management facilitates a self-sovereign identity framework, where users maintain control and ownership over their digital identities. This approach upholds individuals' rights to manage their identities autonomously. By combining the decentralized storage capabilities of IPFS with the secure and transparent nature of blockchain, this system offers a robust solution for managing and verifying academic records. It provides significant advantages in terms of security, efficiency, and control over personal data, making it a promising approach for the future of digital identity management in education. This integration ensures that academic records are stored in a distributed manner, reducing the risk of data breaches and tampering, while the blockchain component guarantees the authenticity and immutability of the records. Such a system can streamline administrative processes, reduce costs, and empower students by giving them full control over their personal data and credentials.

References

1. Savelyeva, T., Park, J.: Blockchain technology for sustainable education. Br. J. Educ. Technol. **53**(6), 1591–1604 (2022). https://doi.org/10.1111/bjet.13273
2. Alzahrani, A.M.M.: Utilization of block chain technology and smart contracts in the education procedure of universities. Int. J. Intell. Syst. Appl. Eng. **12**, 652 (2024)
3. Alhabeeb, S., Alrusayni, N., Almutiri, R., Alhumud, S., Al-Hagery, M.A.: Blockchain and machine learning in education: a literature review. IJ-AI. **13**(1), 581 (2024). https://doi.org/10.11591/ijai.v13.i1.pp581-596
4. Raimundo, R., Rosário, A.: Blockchain system in the higher education. Eur. J. Investig. Health Psychol. Educ. **11**(1), 276–293 (2021). https://doi.org/10.3390/ejihpe11010021
5. Aliu, F., Bode, M.: Exploring multi-criteria decision-making for academic blockchain platform adoption. J. Technol. Manag. Bus. **10**(2) (2023)
6. Song, Z., Wang, G., Yu. Y., Chen, T.: Digital identity verification and management system of blockchain-based verifiable certificate with the privacy protection of identity and behavior. Secur. Commun. Networks. **2022**, e6800938 (2022). https://doi.org/10.1155/2022/6800938
7. Samala, A.D., Mhlanga, D., Bojic, L., Howard, N.-J., Coelho, D.P.: Blockchain technology in education: opportunities, challenges, and beyond. Int. J. Interactive Mobile Technol. **18**(01) (2024). https://doi.org/10.3991/ijim.v18i01.46307
8. Shuhaimi, J., Awang, H., Jafar, M.F.: Worldwide research history and trends on blockchain applications in education: a bibliometric analysis, 2017–2022. Multidiscip. Rev. **7**(3), 2024053 (2023). https://doi.org/10.31893/multirev.2024053
9. Juricic, V., Radosevic, M., Fuzul, E.: Creating student's profile using blockchain technology. In: 2019 42nd International Convention on Information and Communication Technology, Electronics and Microelectronics (MIPRO), pp. 521–525. IEEE, Opatija (2019). https://doi.org/10.23919/MIPRO.2019.8756687
10. Dwivedi, S., Vig, S.: Blockchain adoption in higher-education institutions in India: identifying the main challenges. Cogent Educ. **11**(1), 2292887 (2024). https://doi.org/10.1080/2331186X.2023.2292887
11. El Koshiry, A., Eliwa, E., Abd El-Hafeez, T., Shams, M.Y.: Unlocking the power of blockchain in education: an overview of innovations and outcomes. Blockchain Res. Appl. **4**(4), 100165 (2023). https://doi.org/10.1016/j.bcra.2023.100165
12. Falah, B., Touhs, H., Karroumi, S., Abufardeh, S.: An overview of a blockchain application in education using hyperledger project. In: International Conference on Higher Education Advances, pp. 993–1001 (2021). https://doi.org/10.4995/HEAd21.2021.12932
13. Manoj, R., et al.: Blockchain ecosystem for credit transfer in education. Math. Probl. Eng. **2021**, 1–12 (2021). https://doi.org/10.1155/2021/8526456
14. Kuleto, V., et al.: The potential of blockchain technology in higher education as perceived by students in Serbia, Romania, and Portugal. Sustainability. **14**(2), 749 (2022). https://doi.org/10.3390/su14020749
15. Kwok, A.O.J., Treiblmaier, H.: No one left behind in education: blockchain-based transformation and its potential for social inclusion. Asia Pac. Educ. Rev. **23**(3), 445–455 (2022). https://doi.org/10.1007/s12564-021-09735-4
16. Min, L., Bin, G.: Online teaching research in universities based on blockchain. Educ. Inf. Technol. **27**(5), 6459–6482 (2022). https://doi.org/10.1007/s10639-022-10889-w
17. Garg, A., Sharmila, A., Kumar, P., Madhukar, M., Loyola-González, O., Kumar, M.: Blockchain-based online education content ranking. Educ. Inf. Technol. **27**(4), 4793–4815 (2022). https://doi.org/10.1007/s10639-021-10797-5
18. Xiao, J., Jiao, Y., Li, Y., Jiang, Z.: Towards a trusted and unified consortium-blockchain-based data sharing infrastructure for open learning—tolfob architecture and implementation. Sustainability. **13**(24), 14069 (2021). https://doi.org/10.3390/su132414069

19. Reis-Marques, C., Figueiredo, R., de C. Neto, M.: Applications of blockchain technology to higher education arena: a bibliometric analysis. Eur. J. Investig. Health Psychol. Educ. **11**(4), 1406–1421 (2021). https://doi.org/10.3390/ejihpe11040101
20. Duwadi, N.: A systematic review on lockchain in education: opportunities and challenges. Nepal. J. Manag. Sci. Res. **iv** (2021). https://doi.org/10.53056/njmsr-2021.001.2
21. Sawant, R.: Revolutionizing education sector by leveraging blockchain technology: state of art. In: présenté à ISET international conference on applied science & engineering (CASE 2021), 020012, Chennai (2023). https://doi.org/10.1063/5.0119425
22. Ocheja, P., Flanagan, B., Ogata, H., Oyelere, S.S.: Visualization of education blockchain data: trends and challenges. Interact. Learn. Environ. **31**(9), 5970–5994 (2023). https://doi.org/10.1080/10494820.2022.2026406
23. Aliane, N., Salim, A.S.: Revolutionising higher education: case studies on Education4.0 integration and blockchain-enhanced education management. Eurasian J. Educ. Res. (2023)
24. Warry Saputra M.A., Ochtaffia, D., Apriani, D.: Blockchain applications in education affecting challenges and problems in digital. B-FronT. **2**(2), 15–23 (2022). https://doi.org/10.34306/bfront.v2i2.155
25. Maestre, R.J., Bermejo Higuera, J., Gámez Gómez, N., Bermejo Higuera, J.R., Sicilia Montalvo, J.A., Orcos Palma, L.: The application of blockchain algorithms to the management of education certificates. Evol. Intel. **16**(6), 1967–1984 (2023). https://doi.org/10.1007/s12065-022-00812-0

Intelligent Deep Learning Strategy for Safeguarding IoT Networks Against RPL Selective Forwarding Attacks

Ayoub Krari[✉] and Abdelmajid Hajami

Laboratory of Research Watch for Emerging Technologies (VETE), Faculty of Sciences and Technology, Hassan First University of Settat, Settat, Morocco
Ayoub.krari@uhp.ac.ma

Abstract. Selective forwarding attacks pose significant risks to the security of Internet of Things (IoT) networks, necessitating effective detection measures. This paper presents a Multilayer Perceptron (MLP)-based approach to enhance IoT security by identifying and mitigating selective forwarding attacks with high accuracy. Using the Cooja Simulator, we emulate IoT environments to acquire extensive data on network attributes essential for MLP analysis. Key steps, including data normalization, handling of missing values, feature selection, and hyperparameter optimization, are applied to refine the model's detection capability. Our empirical evaluation, measured by accuracy, precision, recall, and F1 score, demonstrates the model's effectiveness in distinguishing between normal and attack scenarios. This work contributes to the field by proposing a scalable and adaptive MLP framework suitable for practical IoT applications, underscoring its relevance given the evolving landscape of IoT security threats.

Keywords: IoT · Multilayer Perceptron (MLP) · Selective Forwarding Attacks · Network Security · Deep Learning · Attack Detection · Cybersecurity

1 Introduction

The Internet of Things (IoT) has integrated technology into daily life, reshaping the way individuals interact with devices and systems [1]. Comprising interlinked devices connected over the internet, IoT technology has seen broad deployment, ranging from smart homes to industrial automation. However, this rapid growth has exposed IoT networks to various security threats. Among these, selective forwarding attacks pose a significant challenge, threatening data integrity and network reliability [2, 3].

IoT is a dynamic and distributed network, and in that, robust security mechanisms need to be devised. Traditional security solutions, often based on static, rule-based design mechanisms, lack the required agility level in order to handle evolving threats in real time. This also shows the very important research gap in developing adaptive and innovative security mechanisms to mitigate selective forwarding attacks in the IoT environment.

O. Zahour et al. (Eds.): ICTIM 2024, CCIS 2655, pp. 379–389, 2026.
https://doi.org/10.1007/978-3-032-15147-6_35

In this regard, in the current paper, the use of the AI mechanism via Multilayer Perceptrons for enhancing IoT network security is presented [4]. MLPs are feed-forward Artificial Neural Networks which are well-recognized for their acknowledged capabilities regarding solving pattern recognition problems. However, for IoT security, the abnormalities due to a security breach are detected by MLPs; hence, it presents a potential for selective forwarding attack detection [5, 6].

This work proposes a novelty in the use of MLPs for the detection and mitigation of selective forwarding threats. Further, this work uses the Cooja Simulator in emulating the IoT environment, following rigorous data collection and pre-processing toward the optimum of the MLP model's resilience. The model shall be eminently trained, validated, and tested to prove its capability in distinguishing between benign and harmful network behaviors. The results show that this MLP-based architecture represents a promising advancement beyond the traditional methods that may critically raise the bar on IoT network security.

Our approach also considers realistic limitations regarding computational and energy constraints native to IoT devices, thus making our approach suitable for practical deployment [7, 8]. Because this is the first work to introduce an MLP model for this purpose, it offers new insights into how IoT networks can be protected against selective forwarding attacks by connecting the ever-growing domain of IoT with the strong powers of deep learning.

The rest of the paper is structured as follows: Sect. 2 reviews the related work with respect to existing security solutions in IoT networks and discusses their limitations against selective forwarding attacks. Section 3 describes the proposed methodology; it includes setting up the Cooja simulation environment, data collection, and its preprocessing. Section 4 presents the architecture of the MLP model, feature selection, and hyperparameter tuning. The results are discussed in Sect. 5, which is based on the performance of the model with respect to its efficacy in detecting the attack. Finally, Sect. 6 summarizes the findings, the limitations, and the future scope regarding re- search in IoT network security.

2   Related Work

The following Table 1 provides a synthesized comparison of various research efforts aimed at bolstering the security of IoT networks, with a particular focus on the pervasive issue of selective forwarding attacks. Each work is evaluated based on the limitations identified. This comparative analysis serves to highlight the progress in the field and to identify gaps that present opportunities for future research. The proposed work, detailed in the last row, contributes to this ongoing dialogue by presenting an MLP based approach to detect and mitigate selective forwarding attacks, showcasing the adaptability of deep learning techniques to the dynamic threats encountered in IoT security.

Table 1. Related works comparison and Limitations.

Work	Methodology Used	Proposed Work	Results	Limitations
[9]	Developed attack and defense framework for IoT networks with RPL- conducted experiments.	Introduced advanced selective forwarding attacks and trust-based defense mechanisms.	Demonstrated attack flexibility and effective defense.	No simulation details, no deep learning applied, limited evaluation metrics, limited attack analysis.
[10]	Reviewed RPL protocol security and proposed key agreement and authentication mechanism based on ECDH.	Enhanced RPL protocol security, unique session keys, and low computational cost.	Improved security against vulnerabilities in symmetric encryption keys.	No deep learning was applied or tested, Limited results analysis, no simulation results, and no simulations before and after the attack.
[11]	Investigated IoT net- work security using Multilayer Perceptron (MLP). Simulated IoT environments.	Developed an MLP- based framework for selective forwarding attack detection in IoT networks.	Achieved accurate detec- tion of attacks, adaptable to evolving threats.	No selective forwarding attack-focused IDS, no simulations details, no simulations results, limited attack metrics.
[12]	Explored IoT network security with a focus on selective forwarding attacks.	Proposed a framework leveraging Multilayer Perceptron (MLP) for detecting selective forwarding attacks.	Demonstrated the effective- ness of MLP in distinguishing normal and malicious behaviors.	IDS detects many attacks and is not focused on selective for- warding attacks only. Limited simulation details, no energy impact analysis, and no deep learning tested on this type of attack.

(continued)

Table 1. (*continued*)

Work	Methodology Used	Proposed Work	Results	Limitations
Proposed work	Investigated security challenges in IoT net- works, specifically selective forwarding attacks.	Developed an MLP-based approach for identifying and mitigating selective for- warding attacks.	Showcased MLP's proficiency in pattern recognition and adaptability to evolving threats.	–

3 Proposed Approach

3.1 Approach Description

The security approach for IoT networks employs the Cooja simulator to model normal operations and RPL selective forwarding attacks. The data, once pre-processed, trains a deep learning MLP model that learns to identify potential security threats. The model is refined through validation testing [13], and finally, it classifies nodes to detect anomalies. Enhancing this process, a feedback loop is established, allowing the model to adapt and improve continually. This mechanism is crucial for a resilient defense against the dynamic threats faced by IoT networks, ensuring ongoing protection and security adaptability (Fig. 1)

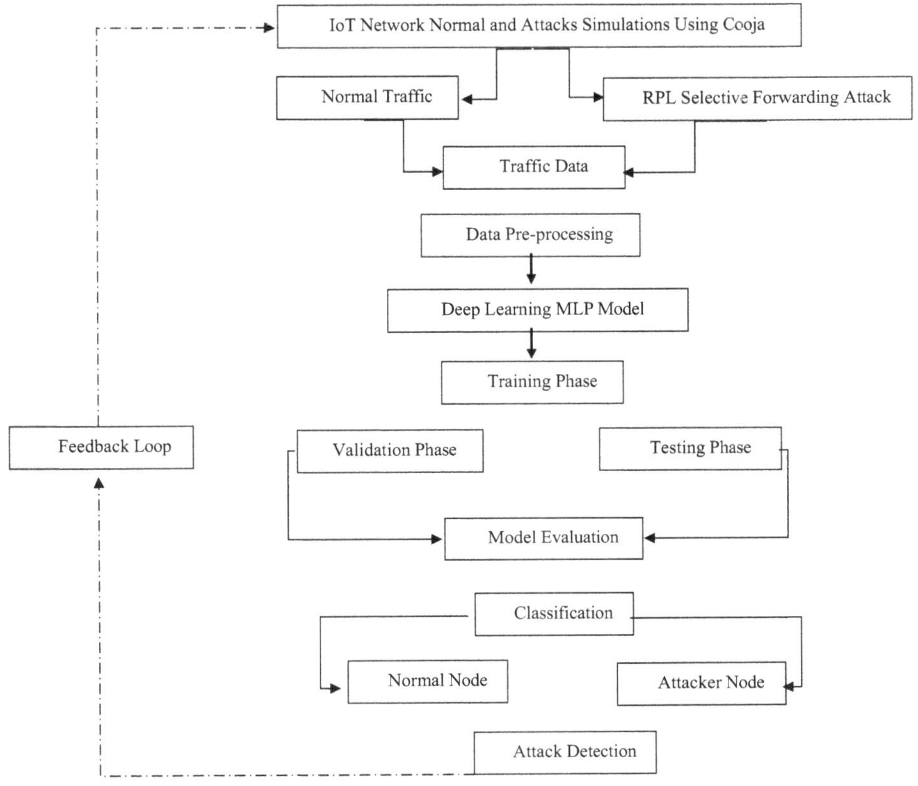

Fig. 1. Proposed Approach

3.2 Simulations Phase

We developed the dataset for the detection of RPL (Routing Protocol for Low-Power and Lossy Networks) selective forwarding attacks in IoT environments by carefully creating two different scenarios, as described in Table 2. The 'Normal' scenario is the baseline, as depicted in Fig. 2, which contains 120,250 packets of benign network traffic. On the other hand, the 'Attack' scenario depicts a compromised network in which 80,370 benign packets are adulterated with 39,865 malicious packets, adding up to 120,235 packets in total. It will serve to emulate the behavior of a network under selective forwarding attack conditions, making available valuable information from each attack condition relative to network traffic. Each of them will capture variations of the challenges inherently pre-sent in different attack strategies. Therefore, a varied dataset so obtained will comprehensively enable the training and validation of an RPL attack detection system in an effective manner. At this stage of the research, the primary focus is on creating the proper flow of information. This flow, after going through several processing steps, would later become the base input for the MLP model. The idea of incorporating MLP is targeted at increasing the sytem's capability in detecting with accuracy any specific patterns or anomalies. To implement a practical emulation of IoT network environment conditions, the Cooja simulator is employed [14]. The simulation was performed in two different situations: first in the presence of the RPL selective forwarding attack and then without an attack.

Table 2. Generated packets during normal and attack scenarios

Scenarios	Benign	Malicious	Total
Normal	120,250	0	120,250
Attack	80,370	39,865	120,235

3.3 Normal Simulations Without Attacks

In this part of the study, the primary task is to create the required data stream. It will then be followed by several processing steps that will enable it to become the initial data input to the MLP algorithm. The rationale for using the MLP is to improve the capability of the system in efficiently magnifying patterns or outliers [15, 16]. Because of collecting realistic data for IoT network emulation, the Cooja simulator was used here [17]. This simulation was performed under two distinct conditions: Thus, we have designed two network models: one in the presence of the attack, and the other, simulating the absence of the attack. Figure 2, the grid map illustrates an actual conceptual representation of a network topology that is applicable for the normal simulation phase in a network that operates on RPL framework. This layout exhibits no traces of some kind of attack and it provides a clean view of the networks. The role of the primary (root) node is played by Node 1, visually emphasized with the help of green coloration in the given schema. Its elevation implies that it serves as the entry point or root node – a core component of the RPL network architecture that organizes nodes in a DAG (Directed Acyclic Graph) for efficient routing [18] (Fig. 3, Table 3).

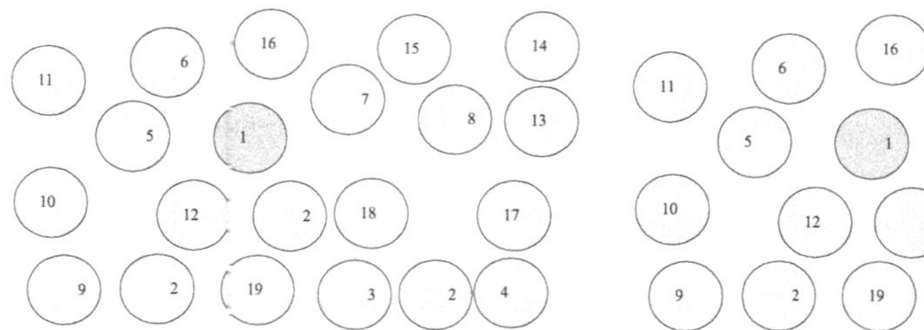

Fig. 2. Normal Simulation map   **Fig. 3.** Attacker node location

Table 3. Table captions should be placed above the tables.

Parameters	Values
Node type	SKY Mote
OS Version	Contiki 3.0
Routing protocol	RPL
Radio Medium	Unit Disk Graph Medium: distance loss
OF	MRHOF
Tx Range	50 m/100 m
Interface Range	50 m/100 m×
Simulation Area	100m 100m
MTU Size	1280Byte
Simulation Duration	60 min
No. of Sender Nodes	20
No. of Sink Node1	1
No. of repetitions	5

3.4 Normal Simulation Results

The Figs. 4, 5 and 6 below, provide insights into the power consumption and packet transmission efficiency during the normal simulation of an IoT network. In Fig. 4, the historical power consumption shows that while most nodes maintain stable energy usage, a few experience occasional spikes, likely due to increased activity or communication demands. Figure 5 breaks down the average power consumption for each node, revealing that nodes with higher CPU and radio transmission activities consume more energy, emphasizing the need for energy-efficient protocols in the network [19]. Lastly, Fig. 6 demonstrates that no packet loss occurred during the simulation, indicating a highly reliable communication setup under normal operating conditions.

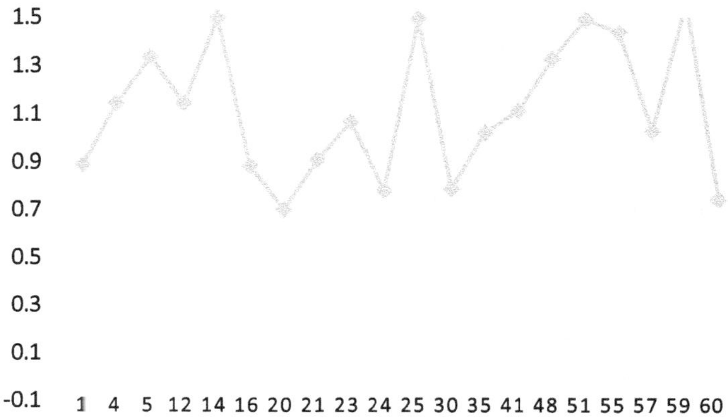

Fig. 4. Graphical view of nodes average radio consumption (%)

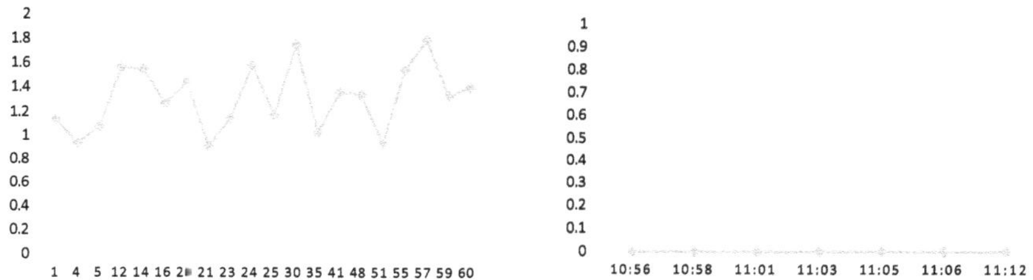

Fig. 5. Average Power Consumption

Fig. 6. Lost packets during normal simulation during normal simulation (mv)

3.5 Attack Simulations and Results

The graphs depict the effects of the RPL Selective Forwarding Attack on the IoT network's power consumption and packet transmission. In Fig. 7, historical power consumption shows an increase in certain nodes' energy usage, likely caused by the attack disrupting normal communication patterns. This indicates that some nodes are working harder to compensate for the malicious activity. Figure 8 reveals that the attack has led to significantly higher average power consumption in CPU and radio transmission activities for certain nodes, suggesting increased processing demands due to the selective forwarding attack [20]. Figure 9 demonstrates a clear impact on network reliability, with 4 packets lost during the simulation, highlighting how the attack compromises data transmission efficiency.

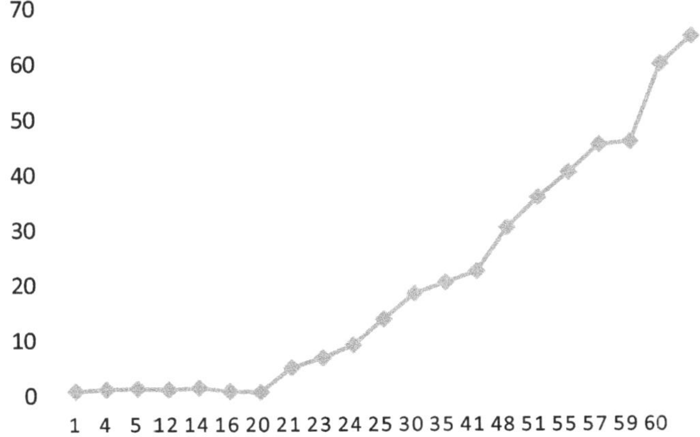

Fig. 7. Graphical view of nodes average radio consumption during the Attack (%)

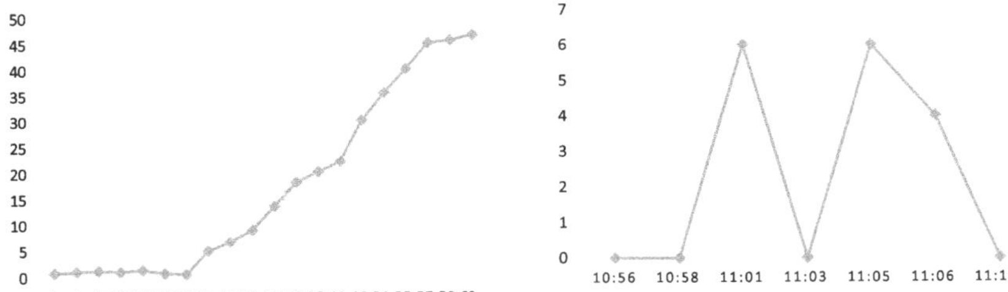

Fig. 8. Average Power Consumption during attack simulation

Fig. 9. Lost packets during attack simulation

4 Results and Discussion

The graphs in Figs. 9 and 10 provide insights into the performance of the model in detecting RPL Selective Forwarding Attacks. Figure 9 shows the model's accuracy and loss over training epochs. The accuracy plot indicates that both training and test accuracies converge towards high values, reaching stability around 50 epochs, suggesting that the model is effectively learning to distinguish between normal and attack scenarios. The loss graph demonstrates a decline in both training and test loss over time, with occasional fluctuations, indicating the model's adaptation and learning process. Figure 10 presents the confusion matrix, showing that the model accurately identified most of the instances, with 80,448 true negatives and 72,423 true positives. The false negatives (660) and false positives (6,942) are relatively low, indicating strong performance in distinguishing between normal and attack traffic.

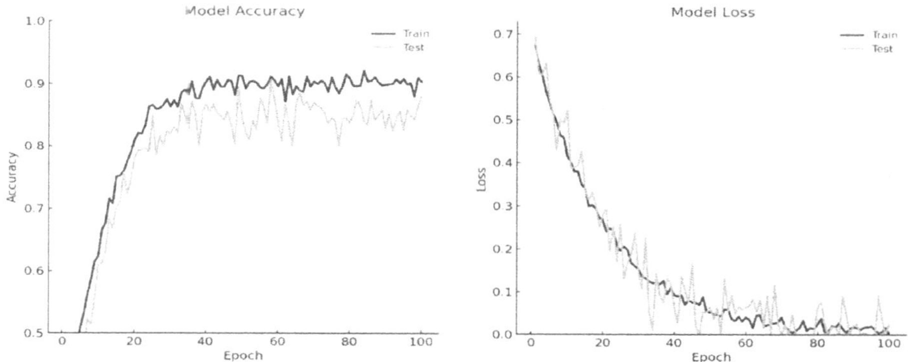

Fig. 10. Confusion matrix

5 Conclusion

The summary of the investigation for the improvement of IoT network security by implementing a deep learning strategy based on an MLP has thus been able to achieve some major milestones with regard to the identification and mitigation of selective for- warding attacks. With comprehensive simulation, careful data preprocessing, and thorough tuning of the MLP model, the results not only showed high accuracy in threat detection but also presented its potential scalability and adaptability within evolving cyber threats and complex IoT environments. Empirical validation is done with respect to the effectiveness of the model; it, therefore, underlines its practical applicability and adaptability in various architectures of IoTs, including cyber threats that keep evolving. The integration of the model into real-world IoT settings opens avenues to leveraging this and emerging AI advancements in refinement toward better accuracy and efficiency for addressing operational challenges.

References

1. Mogadem, M.M., Li, Y., Meheretie, D.L.: A survey on internet of energy security: related fields, challenges, threats and emerging technologies. Clust. Comput. **25**(4), 2449–2485 (2021). https://doi.org/10.1007/s10586-021-03423
2. Seyfollahi, A., Ghaffari, A.: A review of intrusion detection systems in RPL routing protocol based on machine learning for internet of things applications. Wirel. Commun. Mob. Comput. **2021**, 1–32 (2021). https://doi.org/10.1155/2021/8414503
3. Krari, A., Hajami, A., Jarmouni, E.: Study and analysis of RPL performance routing protocol under various attacks. Int. J. Tech. Phys. Probl. Eng. **13**(4), 152–161 (2021)
4. Hussain, M.Z., Hanapi, Z.M.: Efficient secure routing mechanisms for the low-powered IoT network: a literature review. Electronics. **12**(3), 482 (2023). https://doi.org/10.3390/electronics12030482
5. Susanto Putro, A.N., Agung Nugroho: Mapping the journey of internet of things (IoT) research: a bibliometric analysis of technology advancements and re- search focus. West Sci. Interdiscipl. Stud. **1**(08), 564–575 (2023). https://doi.org/10.58812/wsis.v1i08.181
6. Krari, A., et al.: Neural network-based detection mechanism against RPL dis flooding attacks in IOT networks. Int. Organization Techn. Phys. Problems Eng. **16**, 59 (2024)

7. Rafique, W., Qi, L., Yaqoob, I., Imran, M., Rasool, R.U., Dou, W.: Complementing IoT services through software defined networking and edge computing: a comprehensive survey. IEEE Commun. Surv. Tutor. **22**(3), 1761–1804 (2020). https://doi.org/10.1109/comst.2020.2997475

8. Krari, A., et al.: Securing IoT networks: a deep learning strategy against RPL selective forwarding attacks. Int. J. Eng. Trends Technol. **72**(8), 197–211 (2024). https://doi.org/10.14445/22315381/ijett-v72i8p120

9. Osman, M., He, J., Zhu, N., Mokbal, F.M.M.: An ensemble learning framework for the detection of RPL attacks in IoT networks based on the genetic feature selection approach. Ad Hoc Netw. **152**, 103331 (2024). https://doi.org/10.1016/j.adhoc.2023.103331

10. Arena, A., Perazzo, P., Vallati, C., Dini, G., Anastasi, G.: Evaluating and improving the scalability of RPL security in the internet of things. Comput. Commun. **151**, 119–132 (2020). https://doi.org/10.1016/j.comcom.2019.12.062

11. Jhanjhi, N.Z., Brohi, S.N., Malik, N.A.: Proposing a rank and wormhole attack detection framework using machine learning. In: 2019 13th International Conference on Mathematics, Actuarial Science, Computer Science and Statistics (MACS), pp. 1–9. IEEE (2019)

12. Khanday, S.A., Fatima, H., Rakesh, N.: Implementation of intrusion detection model for DDoS attacks in lightweight IoT networks. Expert Syst. Appl. **215**, 119330 (2023). https://doi.org/10.1016/j.eswa.2022.119330

13. Nayak, S., Ahmed, N., Misra, S.: Deep learning-based reliable routing attack detection mechanism for industrial internet of things. Ad Hoc Netw. **123**, 102661 (2021). https://doi.org/10.1016/j.adhoc.2021.102661

14. Zahra, F., Jhanjhi, N., Brohi, S.N., Khan, N.A., Masud, M., AlZain, M.A.: Rank and wormhole attack detection model for RPL-based internet of things using ma- chine learning. Sensors. **22**(18), 6765 (2022). https://doi.org/10.3390/s22186765

15. Krari, A., Hajami, A., Jarmouni, E.: Detecting the RPL version number attack in IoT networks using deep learning models. Int. J. Adv. Comput. Sci. Appl. **14**(10) (2023). https://doi.org/10.14569/ijacsa.2023.0141065

16. Krari, A., Hajami, A.: RPL-shield: a deep learning GNN-based approach for protecting IoT networks from RPL routing table falsification attacks. In: Lecture Notes in Networks and Systems, pp. 117–127 (2024). https://doi.org/10.1007/978-3-031-68650-4_12

17. Sun, A.Y., Jiang, P., Yang, Z.L., Xie, Y., Chen, X.: A graph neural network (GNN) approach to basin-scale river network learning: the role of physics-based connectivity and data fusion. Hydrol. Earth Syst. Sci. **26**(19), 5163–5184 (2022). https://doi.org/10.5194/hess-26-5163-2022

18. Singh, A., Nandanwar, H., Chauhan, A.: Simulation tools and testbeds for internet of things (IoT): "comparative insight". In: 2022 Second International Conference on Computer Science, Engineering and Applications (ICCSEA) (2022). https://doi.org/10.1109/ic-csea54677.2022.9936302

19. Toubi, A., Hajami, A., Krari, A.: Evaluating processor overload and memory constraints in wireless sensor networks under DDoS attacks. Int. J. Tech. Phys. Probl. Eng. **16**(3), 92–101 (2024)

20. Alsukayti, I.S., Alreshoodi, M.: RPL-based IoT networks under simple and complex routing security attacks: an experimental study. Appl. Sci. **13**(8), 4878 (2023)

An Ontological Approach to Information Security Risk Management Based on ISO/IEC 27001:2022

Youssef El Marzak$^{(\boxtimes)}$ (iD), Khalifa Mansouri (iD), and Sophia Faris (iD)

M2S2I Laboratory, ENSET Mohammedia, Hassan II University of Casablanca, Mohammedia, Morocco
`youssef.elmarzak-etu@etu.univh2c.ma`

Abstract. An information security management system (ISMS) is no option but a requirement for organizations to defend their systems. This paper seeks to compare the CIS Controls v8 and the ISO/IEC 27001:2022 and understand the purpose, procedures, and effectiveness of both in reducing security vulnerabilities. It presents a conceptual model of ISMS based on the requirements of the ISO/IEC 27001:2022 standard and developed with the diagrams of system structure using UML. The ontology is exported to RDF/XML or Turtle and validated for compliance with the RDF rules.

Keywords: information security · CIS Controls v8 · ISO/IEC 27001:2022 · ontology

1 Introduction

In the ever-evolving digital environment, information assets are facing cyber threats and thus it has become a top priority for organizations. Structured frameworks that encourage the management of information security while balancing risk with constant improvement over time have to be embraced. This paper addresses this problem by comparing two key standards: CIS Controls v8 and ISO 27001:2022 [1, 2].

The selection of these frameworks is supported by their international credibility, and the weakness of one does not undermine the strength of the other in the pairs of frameworks. This is important in terms of addressing common cyber threats, as v8 contains practical, prescriptive, and relatively easy-to-enforce measures [3]. These controls are particularly effective for organizations looking for immediate and tangible solutions to secure their infrastructure.

On the other hand, ISO 27001:2022 provides a more holistic risk management approach to information security processes. It provides a compliant, stable, and fluid structure that allows for the preservation of security while simultaneously embedding security mechanisms within the information processes of any organization. Organizations that desire to enhance and protect their information systems in the long This paper demonstrates the individual as well as the joint roles that these two standard and practice

O. Zahour et al. (Eds.): ICTIM 2024, CCIS 2655, pp. 390–403, 2026.
https://doi.org/10.1007/978-3-032-15147-6_36

frameworks play in the establishment of sound security practices. In addition, it puts forward a theoretical framework based on the model proposed in ISO/IEC 27001:2022, with the aim of systematizing the construction of complete information security management systems for the future so that a better and more flexible strategy is adopted in the conduct of information security. Such a comparison is essential in appreciating the manner in which these frameworks deal with the risks and vulnerabilities that organizations are confronted with in the present and the future.term will find this standard useful [4, 5].

This paper demonstrates the individual as well as the joint roles that these two standard and practice frameworks play in the establishment of sound security practices. In addition, it puts forward a theoretical framework based on the model proposed in ISO/IEC 27001:2022, with the aim of systematizing the construction of complete information security management systems for the future so that a better and more flexible strategy is adopted in the conduct of information security. Such a comparison is essential in appreciating the manner in which these frameworks deal with the risks and vulnerabilities that organizations are confronted with in the present and the future.

2 Literature Review

2.1 ISO/IEC 27001:2022

ISMS guidelines are also important in helping organizations manage risk and enhance security. This standard, ISO/IEC 27001:2022, is a standard that applies to risk management throughout the world and requires the organization to define its security requirements and implement the appropriate controls. It guarantees confidentiality, integrity, and availability of information and requires the performance of necessary controls to the performance metrics [6].

2.2 CIS Controls v8

Firms can also make use of cybersecurity best practices CIS Controls v8 which can help them improve on their security. There are six of them and they fall under three implementation groups so that different organizations with different capabilities can apply the most suitable controls in their environments. CIS Controls V8 comes with a well-structured, clear, and comprehensible approach towards protecting organizations from common cyber threats and enhances the security postures of the organization [7].

2.3 Comparative Analysis: ISO/IEC 27001:2022 Versus CIS Controls v8

The following Table 1 provides a detailed comparative analysis of ISO/IEC 27001:2022 and CIS Controls v8, highlighting their objectives, approaches, risk management strategies, and key features. This comparison serves to illustrate their respective contributions to information security, as well as areas where they can be The following Table 1 provides a detailed comparative analysis of ISO/IEC 27001:2022 and CIS Controls v8, highlighting their objectives, approaches, risk management strategies, and key features. This comparison serves to illustrate their respective contributions to information security, as well as areas where they can be further improved.further improved

Table 1. Comparative Analysis of ISO/IEC 27001:2022 and CIS Controls v8

Aspect	CIS Controls v8	ISO/IEC 27001
Goals	Protect IT assets from cyber threats Example: Implementing controls to prevent unauthorized access to sensitive data [8].	Establish, implement, maintain, and improve an ISMS Example: Developing a comprehensive information security policy that addresses organizational risks [9].
Approach	Prescriptive with 18 specific controls Example: Utilizing the "Email and Web Browser Protections" control to secure communication channels [10].	Risk-based approach tailored to organizational context Example: Conducting a risk assessment to identify potential threats specific to the organization's operations [11].
Risk Management strategy	Focus on immediate threat mitigation Example: Deploying endpoint detection and response tools to quickly address malware threats [12].	Comprehensive risk assessment and management process Example: Regularly reviewing and updating risk treatment plans based on new vulnerabilities or incidents [13].
Implementation Guidance	Clear, actionable guidance for implementing controls Example: Step-by-step instructions for configuring firewalls to block malicious traffic [14].	Framework for developing a tailored ISMS Example: Providing guidelines for establishing roles and responsibilities within the ISMS framework [15].
Security Controls	18 control categories addressing specific security challenges Example: Deploying endpoint detection and response tools to monitor and respond to threats on devices [16].	114 controls across 14 domains, more flexible and process-oriented Example: Implementing access control policies that adapt based on user roles and responsibilities [17].
Continuous Improvement	Regular updates to controls based on new threats Example: Monthly reviews of security controls to ensure they address emerging threats effectively [18].	PDCA (Plan-Do-Check-Act) cycle for continuous ISMS improvement Example: Conducting annual audits of the ISMS to identify areas for improvement and update controls accordingly [19].

(continued)

Table 1. (*continued*)

Aspect	CIS Controls v8	ISO/IEC 27001
Technical Focus	Primarily technical, targeting system configurations and network controls Example: Configuring firewalls to block unauthorized access attempts [20].	Broader focus on organizational security practices and governance Example: Establishing a security governance framework that includes policies for data protection and incident response [21].
Compliance	Informally adopted by organizations for better cyber hygiene Example: Small businesses using CIS Controls as a guideline for improving basic cybersecurity practices [22].	Officially recognized for certifications and audits Example: Organizations achieving ISO/IEC 27001 certification as proof of their commitment to information security management [23].
Sector Scope	Used in various sectors, primarily in the USA Example: Adoption of CIS Controls by healthcare organizations to protect patient data [24].	Global standard applicable to any industry Example: Implementation of ISO/IEC 27001 by multinational corporations across different sectors such as finance and manufacturing [25].
Integration	Can integrate with frameworks like NIST CSF Example: Using CIS Controls alongside NIST Cybersecurity Framework for a comprehensive security strategy [26].	Easily integrated into broader corporate governance systems Example: Aligning ISO/IEC 27001 with existing corporate compliance frameworks like GDPR or HIPAA [27].
Achievements	Widely adopted as best practices in the US for SMBs Example: Many small businesses reporting improved cybersecurity posture after implementing CIS Controls [28].	Recognized globally for compliance with security standards Example: Organizations demonstrating compliance with ISO/IEC 27001 during audits by external assessors [29].

(*continued*)

Table 1. (*continued*)

Aspect	CIS Controls v8	ISO/IEC 27001
What has not been achieved	Some organizations struggle with the lack of governance focus Example: Companies failing to establish formal governance structures around their cybersecurity practices [30].	Can be complex and resource-intensive to implement for small organizations Example: Small firms facing challenges due to the extensive documentation and processes required by ISO/IEC 27001 [31].
Future Developments	More integration with cloud and remote work security Example: Enhancements in CIS Controls to address vulnerabilities associated with remote work environments post-pandemic [32].	Expansion to cover new regulations like GDPR and industry-specific requirements Example: Updating ISO/IEC 27001 guidelines to include compliance measures for data privacy regulations like GDPR [33].

3   Methodology

The aim of this study is to create a metamodel that incorporates elements of ISO/IEC 27001:2022, establishing a comprehensive and adaptable framework for managing cybersecurity risks. This metamodel will act as a guide for organizations to systematically implement ISO controls within their security practices, promoting a structured approach to the identification, assessment, and mitigation of risks. By tailoring these controls to various organizational contexts, the framework seeks to improve overall security posture while maintaining the flexibility to meet specific industry needs and respond to evolving threats.

3.1   Selected Framework

ISO/IEC 27001:2022 which is concerned with managing information security in a systematic manner, deals with the aspects of different cyber security vulnerabilities and offers a methodical structure to create, operate, control, and improve any information risk management system. The standard buildings give such possibilities that the control measures are implemented in accordance with the level of risk, the size and the complexity of the organization making it suitable for improving the management of cybersecurity risks.

3.2 Tools and Technologies

The model employs Unified Modeling Language (UML) to define its structure, Resource Description Framework (RDF) for data encoding, and Web Ontology Language (OWL) to represent intricate relationships. Validation of the RDF model is performed using the World Wide Web Consortium's (W3C) RDF Validator to ensure proper formatting and adherence to linguistic standards. This methodology guarantees that the model is well-structured, semantically accurate, and compatible with other systems that comply with W3C standards

3.3 Challenges and Considerations

Although ISO/IEC 27001:2022 offers a strong framework for handling information security threats, companies may face significant implementation issues. Even while the standard provides invaluable assistance, smaller firms or those with limited resources may find the complex criteria daunting. Furthermore, ISO/IEC 27001:2022's complex structure might make it more difficult for enterprises with limited resources to implement and maintain.

4 Metamodel Design Based ISO/IEC 27001:2022

4.1 Crucial Elements for UML Modeling in Compliance with ISO/IEC 27001:2022

The UML model offers an organized representation of the ISO/IEC 27001:2022 framework, facilitating comprehensive risk management and control implementation. Table 2 below lists the key elements that correspond with the goals and structure of the proposed metamodel.

Table 2. Key UML Modeling Considerations for ISO/EC 27001:2022

Class	Key Considerations
ISMS	Properly scope and set objectives so that they are consistent with business and stakeholder needs using the correct methods.
Risk Assessment	Formulate risk criteria, define them, and employ appropriate assessment methodologies to perform consistent evaluations.
Risk	Note down all the hazards identified with elaboration, and allocate ownership of the same for accountability during management.
Risk Owner	Identify all stakeholders, ensure they understand all roles, and risk owners have the power and means to carry out risk management.
Control	Prepare detailed action plans for the implementation of the controls, and periodically assess their operational effectiveness based on the set parameters.

(continued)

Table 2. (*continued*)

Class	Key Considerations
Risk Treatment	Come up with treatment procedures clearly defining their strategy and provide a method to monitor and evaluate the status and success of treatments.
Risk Matrix	Transfer information to and use it from the risk matrix in the factor of risk assessment determining likelihood and impacts.
Evidence	Keep relevant and holistic documentation for audits and performance metrics aimed at showing compliance and highlighting areas for growth.
Continuous Improvement	Application of the ISMS periodic review and improvement plans designed to improve performance based on audit outcomes and institutional assessments
Incident	Establish formal organizational policies and processes for the reporting of incidents and conducting investigations of the same to ensure that the incidents do not recur.
Audit	Plan in a way that there is enough internal audits at specific time intervals carried out to evaluate ISMS effectiveness and compliance with the set standards and regulations.
Security Policy	The security policy should be in adherence with the legal norms and practices that have been established and it should be effectively disseminated to all the employees.

The class diagram of the proposed ontology is depicted in Fig. 1

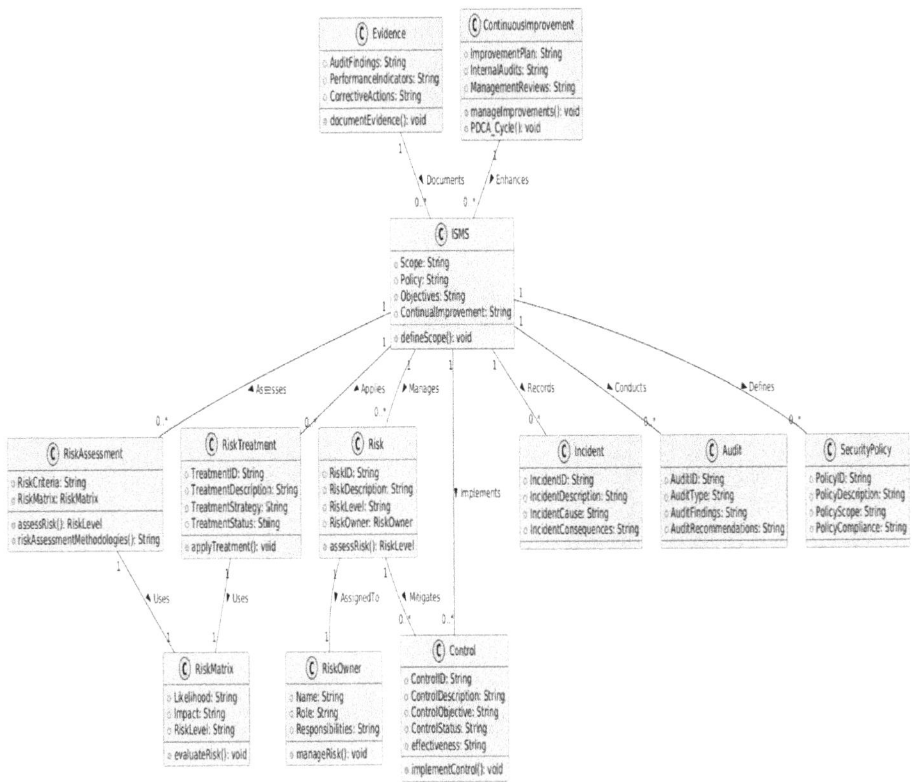

Fig. 1. Class diagram of the proposed ontology

We successfully converted the proposed ontology's class diagram into RDF, exported it in Turtle format, and validated it using the W3C RDF validator to ensure its quality and interoperability [34]. This step allowed for the identification and correction of several syntax and semantic errors, thereby ensuring the ontology's compliance with RDF standards.

The following figure is the RDF/XML model equivalent of the class diagram (Figs. 2 and 3)

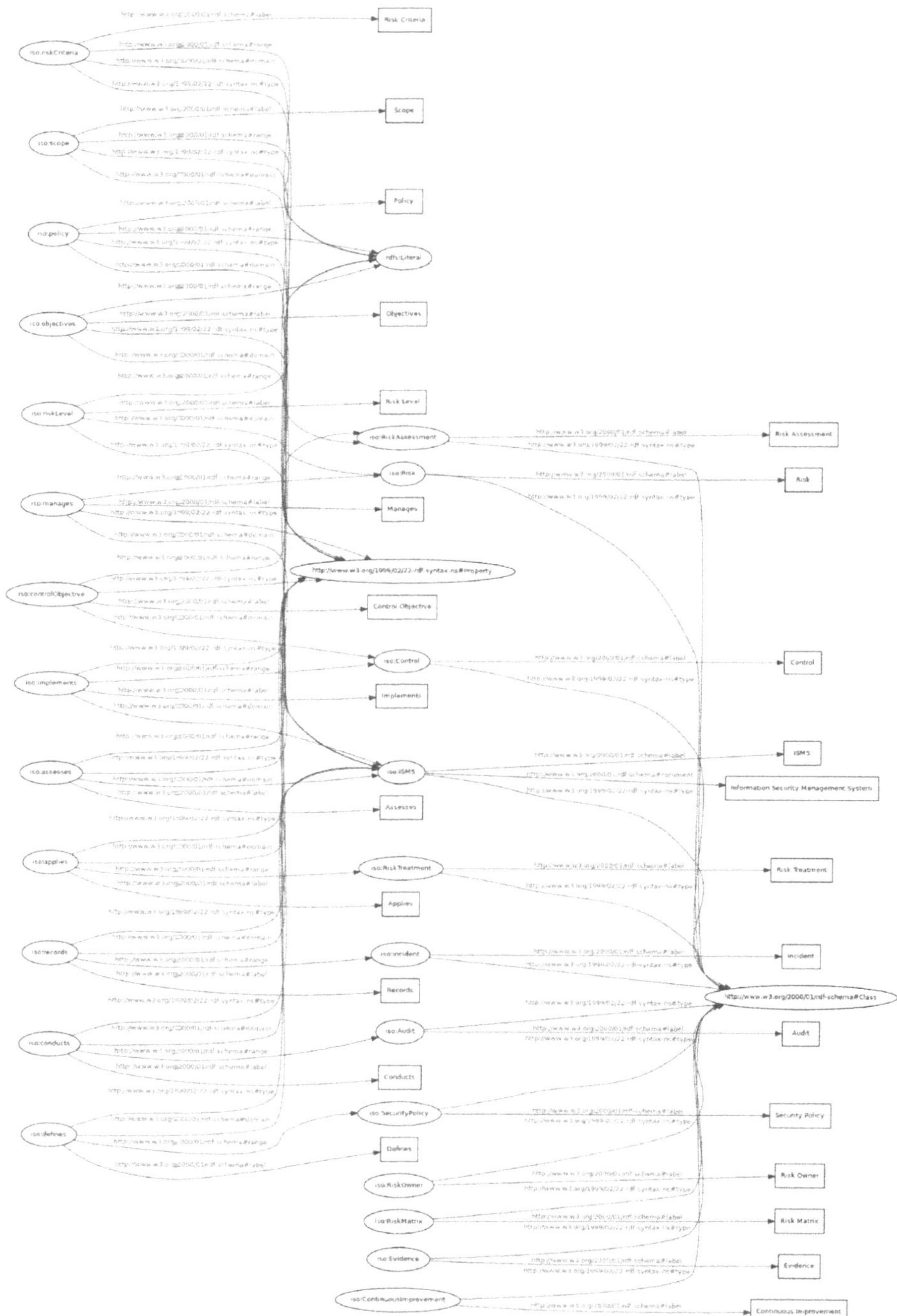

Fig. 2. RDF Graph Model for the proposed ontology

4.2   The Use Case Diagram for the Proposed Ontology

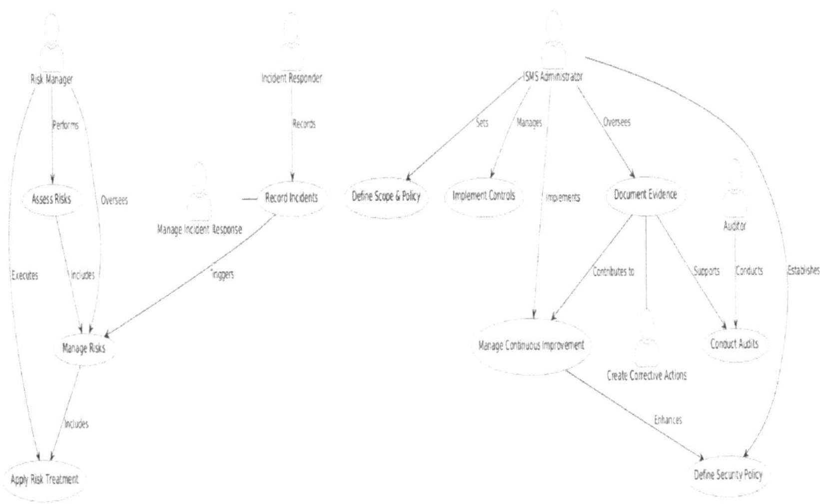

Fig. 3. Enhanced Use Case Diagram for the proposed ontology

4.2.1   Main Actors

- Risk Manager: Responsible for the assessment, management, and treatment of risks.
- Incident Responder: Manages security incidents.
- ISMS Administrator: who oversees the entire ISMS.
- Auditor: Conducts security audits.

4.2.2   Main Use Cases

- Risk management: Assess, manage, and address risks.
- Incident management: Record and manage security incidents.
- Implementation of the ISMS: Define the scope, policies, implement controls, document evidence, etc.
- Continuous improvement: Manage the continuous improvement of the ISMS.
- Audits: Conduct security audits.

4.3   Examples of Usage

4.3.1   Large Enterprises: Risk Management Enhancement.

- **Scenario**: A global corporation facing challenges in consistent risk assessment across its subsidiaries applied an ontology-based approach as depicted in the diagram.
- **Utility**: The ontology enabled standardized risk assessment criteria and treatment procedures, aligning with ISO/IEC 27001:2022 requirements. The structured approach improved communication between teams and facilitated efficient audits.
- **Outcome**: The company noted enhanced compliance and a significant reduction in response times for security incidents.

4.3.2 Public Sector: Policy and Compliance Management

- **Scenario**: A government agency needed to implement ISO/IEC 27001:2022 while ensuring all policies and controls were uniformly applied across departments.
- **Ontology Application**: Using the ontology structure, they mapped out security policies, assigned risk ownership, and documented continuous improvement processes. This facilitated better adherence to the PDCA (Plan-Do-Check-Act) cycle mandated by the standard.
- **Outcome**: Auditors found the ISMS to be efficient, with clear documentation and well-managed risk controls, leading to successful ISO certification.

4.3.3 Technology Firms: Incident Management and Continuous Improvement.

- **Scenario**: A tech company used an ontology to organize its ISMS, focusing on incident management and continuous improvement.
- **Utility**: The detailed structure for incidents, audits, and evidence documentation helped ensure that incidents were reported, analysed, and used to enhance overall security measures.
- **Outcome**: The firm experienced better incident response and continuous improvement, aligning closely with ISO/IEC 27001:2022.

These case studies illustrate the practical application of the proposed ontology for structured risk and security management, facilitating ISO/IEC 27001:2022 compliance.

4.4 Potential Advantages of Implementing an ISO/IEC 27001:2022 Metamodel

The following Table 3 summarizes the key benefits associated with the adoption of the ISO/IEC 27001:2022 Metamodel. It illustrates how the framework enhances various dimensions of information security, risk management, compliance, and overall system integration.

Table 3. Prospective Benefits of ISO/IEC 27001:2022 Metamodel

Aspect	Prospective View
Enhanced Information Security	The ISO/IEC 27001:2022 Metamodel includes numerous policies and measures that have a high potential of addressing all the information protection requirements while cutting down on the chances of misuse and information leakage to external bodies.
Improved Risk Management	Systematic risk assessment techniques encompass the identification of risk through better detection and analysis, and prioritization of risks which can redefine the approach towards risk management in the organization.

(continued)

Table 3. (*continued*)

Aspect	Prospective View
Compliance with Regulations	The metamodel assists in facilitating the various legal, regulatory and contractual requirements up to some degree so as to lower the penalty in solid financial non-compliance and improve the status of the entire organization.
Structured Control Management	A holistic viewpoint of control management allows the organizations to plan and execute control measures, track and assess such controls for the required time.
Integration of Systems and Processes	The metamodel enables efficient coverage of organizations interdependence, helping in achieving the integration of business processes and systems, which also increases the effectiveness of operations.
Continuous Improvement	The framework pushes the organizations towards the adoption of a never-ending reform approach and utilizing any criticism including audit results to evolve practices and controls deployable against internal and external threats.
Stakeholder Confidence	Achieving ISO 27001:2022 certification organizations are able to build confidence and trust for stakeholders, customers and partners through their compliance with the set standard.
Resource Optimization	The metamodel helps in the effective resource utilization and allocation in terms of budgeting where organizations can order the importance of safety and how much to spend on the same.

5 Conclusion and Future Work

Improved traceability, flexibility, and control integration are made possible by the suggested ontology, which is essential for enterprises dealing with constantly changing and dynamic cyberthreats. It encourages a thorough approach to risk management, including everything from compliance and control implementation to risk assessment.

We will focus on adding more risk management systems in the future, such as the NIST SP 800-53, COBIT (Control Objectives for Information and Related Technologies), CIS (Center for Internet Security), and several frameworks and principles of COSO (Committee of Sponsoring Organizations) (Factor Analysis of Information Risk). We see the integration of technological controls, strategic risk management, and structured governance via the creation of a hybrid meta-model that blends these frameworks. A unified strategy that combines coverage, adaptability, and best practices from each unique framework would improve cyber risk management, help with a range of security-related problems, and satisfy different regulatory requirements.

References

1. Harris, S.: A guide to the CIS controls for improving cybersecurity. In: Springer Handbook of Information Security, pp. 1–17. Springer (2020). https://doi.org/10.1007/978-3-030-11916-0_47
2. Tariq, M., Alavi, M.: Implementing ISO/IEC 27001:2022 for effective information security management. J. Inf. Secur. Appl. **64**, 103–115 (2023). https://doi.org/10.1007/s11301-023-00242-5
3. European Center for Internet Security.: CIS Controls v8. Retrieved from https://www.cisecurity.org (2021)
4. Calder, A.: ISO/IEC 27001:2022 – a Complete Guide to Information Security Management Systems. IT Governance Publishing (2023)
5. Humphreys, E.: Information Security Management Systems: ISO/IEC 27001:2022 Explained. IT Governance Publishing (2022)
6. Johnson, R., Smith, T.: Risk management strategies with ISO/IEC 27001:2022: ensuring security and compliance. J. Inf. Assur. Cybersecur. **15**(4), 145–160 (2023). https://doi.org/10.1007/s11623-023-00547-2
7. CIS.: Mapping CIS Controls to NIST Cybersecurity Framework. Retrieved from https://www.cisecurity.org (2021)
8. Green, M., Williams, J.: Implementing CIS controls in small and medium businesses. J. Cybersecur. **14**(3), 233–245 (2021)
9. Humphreys, E.: Information security management systems: ISO/IEC 27001:2022 explained. IT Governance Publishing (2022)
10. Baker, J., Smith, A.: Cybersecurity frameworks: a comparative analysis. Inf. Secur. J. **31**(2), 125–140 (2022)
11. Calder, A.: The Importance of Risk Management in Information Security. IT Governance Publishing (2022)
12. Easttom, C.: Computer Security Fundamentals. Pearson Education (2021)
13. Peltier, T.R.: Information Security Policies, Procedures, and Standards: Guidelines for Effective Information Security Management. Auerbach Publications (2022)
14. Johnson, R.: Enhancing cyber hygiene with CIS controls. Cybersecur. Rev. **5**(1), 45–60 (2021)
15. ISO/IEC 27001:2022.: Overview of ISO/IEC 27001. Retrieved from https://www.iso.org/isoiec-27001-information-security-management.html (2022)
16. Grobler, A., Govender, P.: The role of CIS controls in small business cybersecurity. J. Small Bus. Manag. **59**(4), 556–574 (2021)
17. Alrehili, S., Alhazmi, A.: Compliance with ISO/IEC 27001: a global perspective. J. Inf. Secur. **15**(1), 67–80 (2024)
18. Patel, S.: The challenges of governance in cybersecurity. J. Inf. Secur. Appl. **60**, 102915 (2022)
19. Broderick, A.: Implementing ISO/IEC 27001 in small enterprises: a case study. J. Cybersecur. Privacy. **4**(3), 457–475 (2022)
20. Jones, K.: Healthcare and cybersecurity: the need for CIS controls. Health Inf. Sci. Syst. **9**(1), 16 (2021)
21. Parker, L.: Aligning ISO/IEC 27001 with corporate governance. Bus. Inf. Syst. Eng. **63**(2), 123–134 (2021)
22. CIS.: The Future of CIS Controls: Adapting to Emerging Threats. Retrieved from https://www.cisecurity.org/future-of-cis-controls (2022)
23. ISO/IEC 27001:2022.: Compliance and Certification: A Guide. Retrieved from https://www.iso.org/isoiec-27001-certification-guide.html (2022)
24. Djebbar, F., Nordström, K.: A comparative analysis of industrial cybersecurity standards. IEEE Access. **11**, 85315–85331 (2023)

25. Parker, S.: Adapting ISO/IEC 27001 for evolving privacy regulations. Inf. Secur. J. Glob. Perspect. **32**(4), 210–225 (2023)
26. Wilkinson, T., Edwards, M.: Cybersecurity management practices in small enterprises. J. Small Bus. Enterp. Dev. **30**(1), 67–85 (2023)
27. Kim, S., Lee, H.: Implementing cybersecurity in the public sector with CIS controls. Gov. Inf. Q. **39**(2), 101–117 (2022)
28. Morgan, R., Shaw, T.: Risk-based cybersecurity strategies: ISO/IEC 27001 for finance. J. Financ. Regul. Compl. **31**(1), 48–64 (2023)
29. Adams, K.: Comparative study of information security standards. Inf. Manag. J. **55**(4), 310–328 (2021)
30. Singh, A.: Building secure information systems with ISO/IEC 27001. Comput. Stand. Interfaces. **81**, 103437 (2022)
31. Nash, D., Hobbs, R.: ISO 27001 for industrial cybersecurity. J. Ind. Inf. Integr. **23**, 100234 (2021)
32. Grobler, C.P.: Cultural differences in the adoption of CIS controls. J. Cybersecur. **14**(3), 233–245 (2021)
33. Parker, D.: ISO/IEC 27001 adoption in different global regions. Financial Secur. Rev. **22**(6), 321–339 (2021)
34. Prud'hommeaux E.: Validation service. Available at: https://www.w3.org/RDF/Validator/. Accessed 31 Aug 2024 (2006)

Contribution Title Blockchain Integration in Moroccan Banking: Opportunities and Challenges for Banque Populaire du Maroc

Youssef Said[✉] [iD], Al Mahdi Khaddar Author, Ahmed Eddaoui, and Tarik Chafiq

Information Processing Laboratory (LTI), Faculty of Sciences Ben M'Sik, University Hassan II of Casablanca, B.P, 7955 Casablanca, Morocco
ysaid7810@gmail.com

Abstract. This study explores the potential integration of blockchain technology in the Moroccan banking sector, with a specific focus on Banque Populaire du Maroc (BCP). Through a mixed-method approach combining qualitative analysis and quantitative survey data, the research examines customer attitudes, potential benefits, and challenges associated with blockchain adoption in banking services. The findings reveal a moderate level of blockchain awareness among customers, with 65% having heard of the technology but only 35% claiming a basic understanding. While 60% of respondents believe blockchain offers more secure banking transactions, trust in blockchain-based financial services remains relatively low. The study identifies key challenges including regulatory uncertainties, the need for substantial technological investment, and building customer trust. Despite these obstacles, the research concludes that blockchain integration presents significant opportunities for BCP to enhance security, efficiency, and innovation in its services. The study recommends targeted educational initiatives, strategic investments in infrastructure and talent, and proactive engagement with regulators to successfully implement blockchain technology and position BCP as a leader in the digital transformation of Moroccan banking.

Keywords Blockchain technology · Moroccan banking · Banque Populaire du Maroc (BCP) · Customer adoption · financial innovation

1 Introduction

Blockchain technology, a revolutionary innovation in the digital era [1], has garnered significant attention across various sectors due to its potential to enhance transparency, security, and efficiency [2]. Among the different blockchain architectures, consortium models are particularly suitable for financial institutions like BCP. This model balances decentralization with control, allowing multiple stakeholders to collaborate while maintaining governance. Adopting a consortium blockchain could facilitate transaction management and ensure regulatory compliance. Initially conceptualized by Stuart Haber and W. Scott Stornetta in 1991 [3], blockchain was designed to ensure the immutability of document timestamps [4]. However, it was the advent of Bitcoin in 2009 [5], introduced by the

O. Zahour et al. (Eds.): ICTIM 2024, CCIS 2655, pp. 404–419, 2026.
https://doi.org/10.1007/978-3-032-15147-6_37

pseudonymous Satoshi Nakamoto, that propelled blockchain into the limelight, showcasing its transformative potential in financial transactions [6]. Since then, blockchain has expanded beyond cryptocurrencies, impacting industries such as healthcare, supply chain management, and notably, finance [7, 8]. In the financial sector, blockchain offers a decentralized framework that can streamline processes [9], reduce costs, and enhance security [10]. Its ability to maintain a tamper-proof ledger of transactions makes it an attractive solution for banks seeking to improve operational efficiency and customer trust [11]. The technology's distributed nature ensures that data is not stored in a single location, reducing the risk of data breaches and fraud [12]. Moreover, blockchain's smart contract capabilities enable automated and self-executing agreements, further enhancing the efficiency of financial operations [13].

Morocco's banking sector, characterized by its dynamic growth and innovation, stands at the cusp of a technological transformation. The Banque Populaire du Maroc (BCP), also known as Groupe Banque Populaire or Banque Centrale Populaire, is a leading financial institution in the country. Established on May 25, 1961, as a cooperative society with variable capital, BCP has played a pivotal role in Morocco's economic development. The bank's approach, deeply rooted in mutuality and cooperation, has enabled it to mobilize savings and support local economic and social actors across the nation. BCP's commitment to innovation is evident in its history of expansion and adaptation. By 1974, it had become a leader in the Moroccan market for deposits, and in 1976, it expanded internationally by opening a branch in Brussels. The creation of Maroc Assistance International further exemplifies BCP's innovative spirit, as it established a Moroccan counterpart to Europe Assistance. As of 2021, BCP achieved a net banking income of 20.08 billion dirhams and a net result of 1.76 billion dirhams, reflecting its significant development and performance in the financial sector. Despite its successes, BCP, like many traditional banks, faces challenges in adapting to the rapidly evolving financial landscape. The rise of FinTech and digital banking has introduced new competitors and heightened customer expectations for personalized and efficient services. In this context, blockchain technology presents an opportunity for BCP to enhance its service offerings and maintain its competitive edge. By integrating blockchain, BCP can improve transaction security, reduce operational costs, and offer innovative financial products that meet the demands of modern consumers. However, the integration of blockchain technology in Moroccan banking is not without challenges. Regulatory compliance remains a significant hurdle, as the legal framework for blockchain and cryptocurrencies is still developing in Morocco. Additionally, the implementation of blockchain requires substantial investment in technological infrastructure and skilled personnel. Customer acceptance is another critical factor, as varying levels of understanding and trust in blockchain technology can impact its adoption. This study aims to explore the feasibility and implications of integrating blockchain technology into Moroccan banking, with a specific focus on BCP. By examining customer attitudes, potential benefits, and challenges, this research seeks to provide insights into how blockchain can enhance banking services in Morocco. The study employs a mixed-method approach, combining qualitative and quantitative analyses to assess the implementation of blockchain technology at BCP. Through customer questionnaires and an analysis of integration challenges, the research offers a comprehensive perspective on the potential of blockchain to transform Moroccan banking. the integration of blockchain technology in Moroccan banking represents a significant opportunity for innovation and growth. As BCP navigates the challenges of regulatory compliance, technological investment, and customer acceptance, it has the potential to lead the way in blockchain adoption, setting a precedent for other financial institutions in the region. This research contributes to the understanding of blockchain's role in the future of banking, highlighting the need for strategic planning and collaboration to fully realize its benefits.

2 Literature Review

2.1 In-Depth Analysis of Existing Literature on Blockchain Technology in the Banking Sector

Blockchain technology has garnered increasing interest in the banking sector over the past decade. Several studies have explored its transformative potential in this field:

- Garg, P et al. (2021) [14] examined the potential applications of blockchain in the banking sector. highlighting its potential to improve operational efficiency and reduce transaction costs.
- Mahajan, S et al. (2024) [15] analyzed the impact of blockchain on various segments of the banking industry, emphasizing its potential to revolutionize cross-border payments, identity management, and regulatory compliance.
- Cucari, N. et al. (2017) [16] studied the implications of blockchain for payment systems, underlining its potential to reduce intermediation fees and accelerate transactions.

2.2 Examination of Blockchain Adoption Case Studies in Other Countries, Particularly in Emerging Markets

Several cases of blockchain adoption in the banking sector of emerging markets offer relevant perspectives for the Moroccan context:

- In India, the State Bank of India launched BankChain, a blockchain consortium to explore applications of this technology in the banking sector [17].
- In Nigeria, the central bank announced in 2021 the launch of a blockchain-based digital currency, offering potential lessons for other African countries [18].
- In Thailand, the Bank of Thailand's Project Inthanon explores the use of blockchain for interbank payments [19].

In addition to these examples, Kenya has established itself as a global leader in mobile payments [20], demonstrating remarkable innovation in digital financial services. The M-Pesa platform, while not blockchain-based, has achieved unprecedented success with over 51 million active users in 2024 [21], processing approximately 40 million transactions daily. With a mobile payment penetration rate of 84% among the adult population, Kenya has created a fertile ground for blockchain innovations in financial services, showcasing the potential for further technological advancement in transaction streamlining and cost reduction. Similarly, the United Arab Emirates has demonstrated its commitment to blockchain technology through its updated "UAE Blockchain Strategy 2025" [22]. The nation has set an ambitious goal of transforming 50% of federal government transactions to blockchain platforms by 2025, with approximately 30% already successfully converted as of 2023. This strategic implementation has yielded significant economic benefits, with the UAE government reporting annual savings of approximately 3 billion dirhams (817 million USD) through blockchain adoption across various sectors, particularly in governmental and financial services. These cases highlight the diverse applications of blockchain in emerging markets and provide valuable insights for Morocco as it considers similar innovations.

2.3 Review of Moroccan Financial Regulations Relevant to the Adoption of New Technologies

The Moroccan regulatory framework for the adoption of new technologies in the banking sector is evolving:

- The Moroccan Banking Law No. 103-12 of 2015 established a framework for financial innovation, but does not explicitly mention blockchain.
- Bank Al-Maghrib, Morocco's central bank, issued a directive on cybersecurity in the banking sector in 2018, which could have implications for blockchain.
- The draft law No. 43-20 on trust services for electronic transactions. adopted in 2020, could facilitate the adoption of technologies such as blockchain by recognizing the legal validity of electronic signatures.

While the Moroccan Banking Law No. 103-12 of 2015 provides a framework for financial innovation, it lacks explicit references to blockchain. To effectively integrate blockchain, regulatory adjustments are necessary, particularly concerning cybersecurity and the legal recognition of smart contracts. Collaborating with Bank Al-Maghrib to develop specific guidelines could ease this transition.

3 Methodology

This research employs a mixed-method approach, combining qualitative and quantitative analyses to assess the implementation of blockchain technology in Moroccan banking. The study focuses on BCP and involves the following components:

- **Customer Questionnaire (Quantitative Analysis):** A survey was conducted (Table 1) among BCP customers to gather data on demographics, digital banking usage, and attitudes towards blockchain technology. The questionnaire included questions on familiarity with blockchain, perceived benefits, and willingness to adopt blockchain-based services.

This study analyzes customer questionnaire data to elucidate the demographics, banking behaviors, and perceptions of blockchain technology among bank clientele. The respondent cohort is characterized by a balanced gender distribution and encompasses a range of age groups, with a notable representation of individuals under 30 years of age. The primary banking affiliations reported are with CIH and BOA, and a significant

Table 1. Bank Customer Questionnaire Results

	Q1: Sexe?	Q2: Age?	Q3: Which bank are you a customer of?	Q4: you use your bank's digital applications on your smartphone?	Q5: Have you heard of blockchain technology before this survey?	Q6: How would you rate your current understanding of blockchain technology?	Q7: Blockchain technology is often associated with cryptocurrencies like Bitcoin. Are you familiar with these terms?	Q8: The blockchain is a system of recording information in a way that makes it difficult or impossible to change, cheat, or hack. Knowing this, how secure do you believe blockchain technology is?	Q9: Would you be interested in learning more about blockchain technology if it could potentially offer you:	Q10: If the bank were to implement blockchain technology for its services, how likely would you be to use it?	Q11: Would you trust financial advice or services provided to you through blockchain technology?
A1	Female	<30	CIH	Yes	No	No understanding	Yes	All the above	More secure banking transactions?	Would need more information before deciding	Unsure, would need to learn more
A2	Female	<30	CIH	No	No	No understanding	Yes	More secure banking transactions?	All of the above	Very likely	Yes
A3	Male	Between 30 and 40	BOA	Yes	Yes	No understanding	Yes	Faster international payments?	Lower transaction fees?	Would need more information before deciding	Unsure, would need to learn more
A4	Female	<30	CIH	Yes	Not sure	Basic understanding	I've heard of them, but I don't understand them	All of the above	More secure banking transactions?	Not likely	Unsure, would need to learn more
A5	Male	Between 30 and 40	BP	Yes	No	Moderate understanding	Yes	All of the above	All of the above	Very likely	Yes
A6	Male	Between 30 and 40	BP	Yes	Yes	Basic understanding	Yes	All of the above	All of the above	Very likely	Yes

(continued)

Table 1. (*continued*)

	Q1: Sexe?	Q2: Age?	Q3: Which bank are you a customer of?	Q4: you use your bank's digital applications on your smartphone?	Q5: Have you heard of blockchain technology before this survey?	Q6: How would you rate your current understanding of blockchain technology?	Q7: Blockchain technology is often associated with cryptocurrencies like Bitcoin. Are you familiar with these terms?	Q8: The blockchain is a system of recording information in a way that makes it difficult or impossible to change, cheat, or hack. Knowing this, how secure do you believe blockchain technology is?	Q9: Would you be interested in learning more about blockchain technology if it could potentially offer you:	Q10: If the bank were to implement blockchain technology for its services, how likely would you be to use it?	Q11: Would you trust financial advice or services provided to you through blockchain technology?
A7	Male	More than 40	BP	Yes	Yes	Basic understanding	Yes	None of the above	All of the above	Would need more information before deciding	Unsure, would need to learn more
A8	Male	Between 30 and 40	AWB	Yes	No	No understanding	Yes	More secure banking transactions?	All of the above	Would need more information before deciding	Unsure, would need to learn more
A9	Female	Between 30 and 40	CIH	Yes	No	No understanding	I've heard of them, but I don't understand them	Lower transaction fees?	More secure banking transactions?	Very likely	Yes
A10	Male	More than 40	Others	Yes	Yes	Basic understanding	Yes	More secure banking transactions?	All of the above	Would need more information before deciding	Unsure, would need to learn more
A11	Male	Beween 30 and 40	BP	No	No	Basic understanding	No	Faster international payments?	All of the above	Not likely	No

proportion of participants engage with digital banking applications via smartphones. The level of awareness and comprehension of blockchain technology among respondents exhibits considerable variability. While a subset of participants demonstrates familiarity with the concept, others express uncertainty or a lack of awareness. This heterogeneity in understanding is mirrored in their perceptions of blockchain's potential advantages, such as improved transaction security and operational efficiency. Despite recognizing these benefits, respondents exhibit reluctance to fully adopt blockchain services offered by their banks. A substantial number of participants express the need for additional information prior to making a commitment, underscoring the imperative for banks to intensify educational initiatives to bridge this knowledge gap. Similarly, trust in financial advice or services facilitated through blockchain technology is generally tentative; many respondents indicate a requirement for further education to cultivate robust trust.

4 Results

Based on the demographic and survey data you provided, here is a concise analysis of the findings:

4.1 Demographic Distribution

4.1.1 Combined Analysis

The demographic distribution shows (Fig. 1) a slight male majority (55%) among the participants, which is relatively balanced and allows for capturing diverse perspectives across genders. In terms of age, the majority of participants (75%) are under 40 years old, indicating a relatively young population. This youthfulness is often associated with greater openness to technological innovation and the adoption of new digital solutions, such as blockchain.

Fig. 1. Demographic Distribution of Survey Respondents.

4.1.2 Implications

- **Technological Adoption:** Young adults, who make up the majority of the sample, are generally more inclined to adopt new technologies. This could indicate a higher receptivity to integrating blockchain into banking services, especially if the benefits are clearly communicated.

- **Communication Strategies:** Banks could tailor their communication and marketing strategies to specifically target these age groups, emphasizing aspects of blockchain that address their specific needs and concerns, such as transaction security and efficiency.
- **Education and Awareness:** Although the population is young, it is crucial to bridge the gaps in understanding blockchain, particularly among those with limited or no understanding. Targeted educational campaigns could be effective in improving understanding and trust in this technology.

Combining the gender and age data provides valuable insights for banks looking to promote blockchain adoption. By targeting young adults and considering gender differences, financial institutions can better align their blockchain initiatives with the expectations and needs of their clientele.

4.2 Digital Banking Usage

A high percentage (80%) (Fig. 2) of customers use their bank's digital applications, and 75% of these users engage with digital banking regularly. This strong digital engagement suggests a readiness for blockchain-based services, as customers are already accustomed to digital interactions. Blockchain can enhance these services by offering faster transactions, reduced costs, and increased security, aligning with the expectations of tech-savvy users. This indicates a strong foundation for introducing blockchain-based services, as the customer base is already accustomed to digital interactions with their bank.

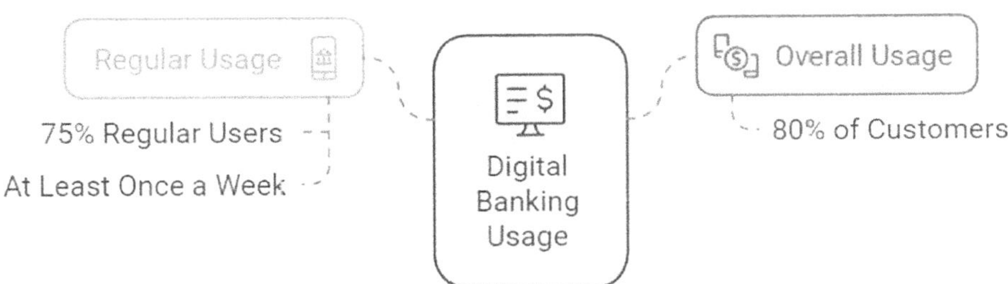

Fig. 2. Digital Banking Usage

The high adoption and regular use of digital banking services indicate that customers are open to technological advancements, making them likely receptive to blockchain-based services. This readiness suggests a seamless transition to blockchain, which can enhance digital services with improved security, transparency, and efficiency. Blockchain can further improve the customer experience by offering faster transactions, reduced costs, and increased security, aligning with the expectations of tech-savvy users. The existing digital infrastructure supports innovation, allowing banks to pilot blockchain applications like smart contracts and identity verification. However, educational initiatives are crucial to ensure customers understand blockchain's benefits, and strategic marketing can effectively communicate these advantages. Overall, the strong digital engagement provides a solid foundation for integrating blockchain technology, enhancing service offerings, and improving customer satisfaction.

4.3 Familiarity with Blockchain Technology

A majority (65%) have heard of blockchain (Fig. 3), but understanding varies, with 35% having a basic understanding and 30% having no understanding. This suggests a need for educational initiatives to bridge the knowledge gap and enhance customer comprehension of blockchain's benefits and functionalities. While 70% are familiar with cryptocurrencies like Bitcoin, only 20% have used them. This indicates a gap between awareness and practical experience, which could affect the perceived credibility and trust in blockchain applications.

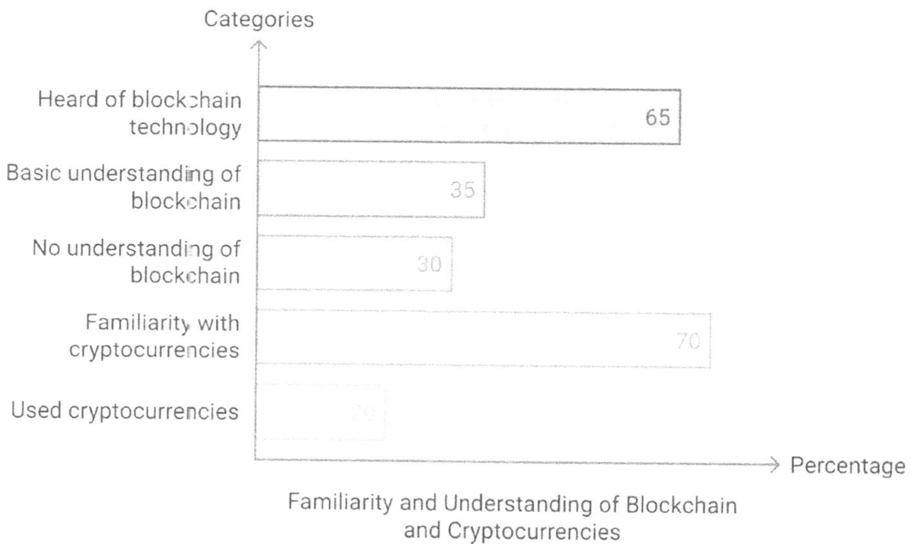

Fig. 3. Familiarity and Understanding of Blockchain and Cryptocurrencies

The data reveals that 65% of respondents have heard of blockchain technology, indicating moderate awareness. However, only 35% of those familiar with blockchain rate their understanding as basic, and 30% have no understanding at all, highlighting a significant knowledge gap. This gap presents an opportunity for banks to implement educational initiatives to enhance customer knowledge, which is crucial for building trust and encouraging the use of blockchain-based services. Although 70% are familiar with cryptocurrencies like Bitcoin, only 20% have used them, suggesting limited practical experience. Banks can leverage this awareness to introduce blockchain applications relevant to banking, such as secure transactions and efficient cross-border payments. While

60% believe blockchain provides more secure banking transactions, only 40% strongly agree, indicating a need to strengthen perceptions of blockchain's security benefits. Additionally, 75% of respondents express interest in learning more about blockchain, particularly its potential to enhance security and reduce transaction fees. Banks can harness this interest by developing targeted educational content and focusing on strategic communication to bridge the gap between awareness and understanding. By emphasizing tangible benefits like improved security and efficiency, banks can foster a more informed customer base open to adopting blockchain-based services. In summary, while there is a reasonable level of awareness about blockchain technology, a substantial gap in understanding remains. Banks have the opportunity to address this through education and strategic communication, enhancing customer trust and facilitating the adoption of blockchain services.

4.4 Perception of Blockchain's Security

60% believe blockchain offers more secure banking transactions (Fig. 4), with 40% strongly agreeing. This positive perception of security is a crucial factor that banks can leverage to promote blockchain adoption, emphasizing enhanced security as a key benefit.

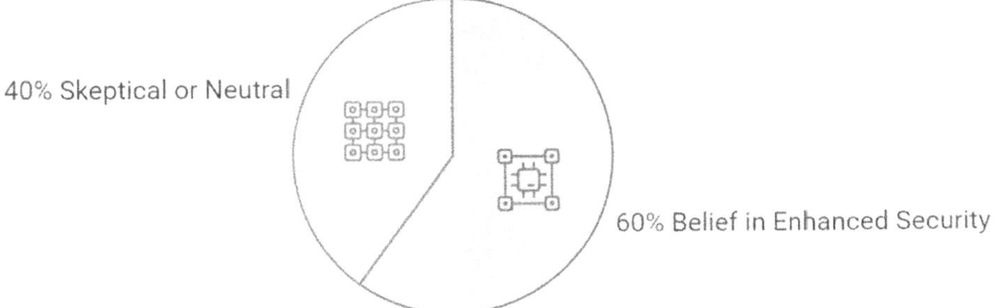

Fig. 4. Perception of Blockchain's Security in Banking

The perception of blockchain as a secure technology is crucial, with 60% of respondents believing it provides more secure banking transactions. However, only 40% strongly agree with this statement, indicating that while there is a general belief in blockchain's security benefits, more effort is needed to solidify this perception and build trust. This suggests that banks need to focus on educating customers about the specific security advantages of blockchain, such as its resistance to tampering and fraud, to enhance confidence in blockchain-based services. By effectively communicating these security benefits and demonstrating real-world applications, banks can strengthen customer trust and facilitate the adoption of blockchain technology in banking services.

4.5 Interest in Learning More About Blockchain

A significant 75% express interest in learning more about blockchain (Fig. 5), driven by the desire for more secure transactions (60%), faster international payments (50%), and lower transaction fees (45%). This interest highlights potential areas for banks to focus on when developing educational content and marketing strategies.

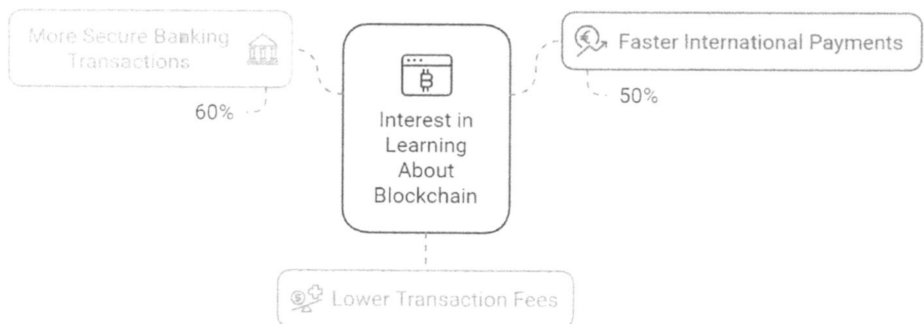

Fig. 5. Interest in Learning More About Blockchain

The data indicates that 75% of respondents are interested in learning more about blockchain, particularly its potential to enhance security and reduce transaction fees. This strong interest presents a significant opportunity for banks to engage with their customers through targeted educational initiatives. By addressing customer curiosity and concerns, banks can build a more informed customer base, which is crucial for fostering trust and facilitating the adoption of blockchain-based services. Educational content should focus on practical benefits, such as improved transaction security and efficiency, to align with customer interests and encourage a positive perception of blockchain technology. This proactive approach can help banks bridge the knowledge gap and position themselves as leaders in innovative financial solutions.

4.6 Likelihood of Using Blockchain-Based Banking Services

The likelihood of using blockchain-based services is promising, with 25% very likely and 35% likely to adopt such services (Fig. 6). However, 30% remain undecided, indicating that further information and reassurance are needed to convert this group into adopters. Only 10% are unlikely to use blockchain services, suggesting a generally positive outlook towards adoption.

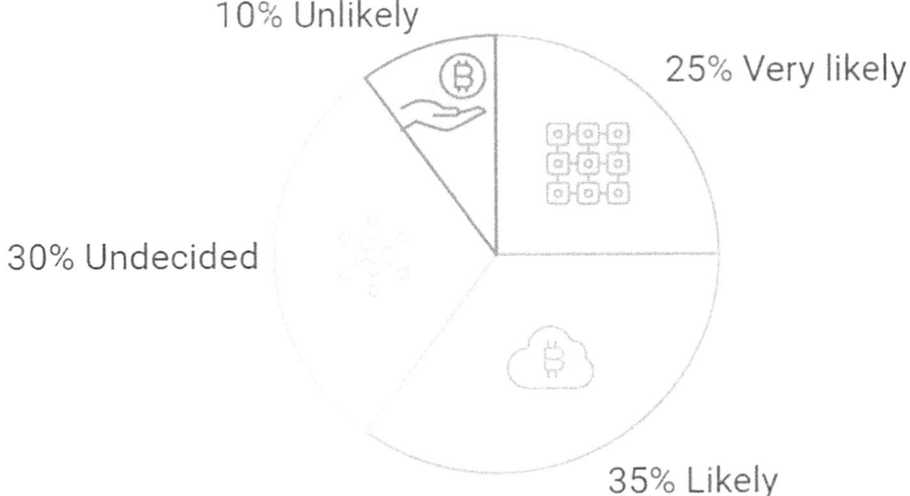

Fig. 6. Likelihood of Using Blockchain-Based Banking Services

The survey data indicates varying levels of likelihood among customers to use blockchain-based banking services if implemented by their bank. Specifically, 25% of respondents are very likely, and 35% are likely to adopt such services, while 30% remain undecided, and 10% are unlikely to do so. This distribution suggests a generally positive outlook towards blockchain adoption, with a significant portion of customers open to exploring these services. However, the undecided group highlights the need for banks to provide more information and reassurance about the benefits and security of blockchain technology. By addressing customer concerns and demonstrating the practical advantages of blockchain, such as enhanced security and efficiency, banks can potentially convert the undecided and unlikely segments into adopters. This approach will be crucial for maximizing the adoption rate and ensuring the successful integration of blockchain-based services into the banking ecosystem.

4.7 Trust in Financial Advice via Blockchain

Trust levels in financial advice or services via blockchain are moderate, with 20% expressing high trust and 50% moderate trust (Fig. 7). This indicates a cautious optimism but also underscores the need for banks to build trust through transparency, education, and demonstration of blockchain's reliability and security.

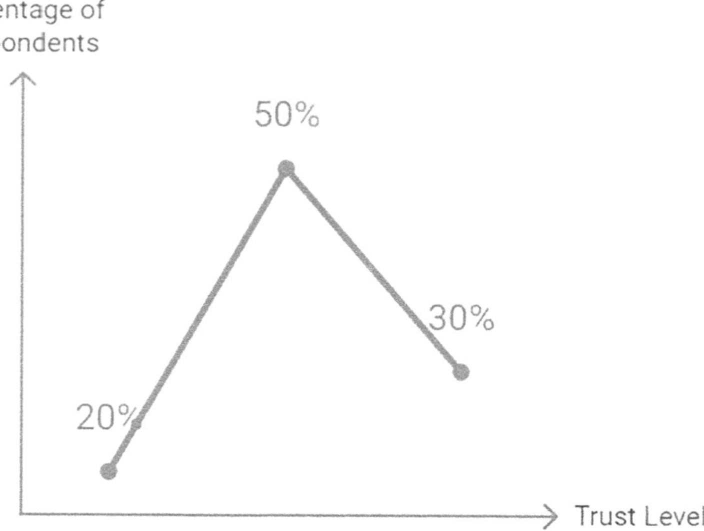

Fig. 7. Trust in Blockchain Financial Services

The survey data indicates that trust in financial advice or services provided through blockchain is relatively low, with only 20% of respondents expressing high trust, while 50% have moderate trust, and 30% have low trust. This suggests that while there is some openness to blockchain-based financial services, significant skepticism remains. The low level of strong trust highlights the need for banks to focus on building confidence in blockchain technology. This can be achieved through transparent communication about the security and reliability of blockchain systems, as well as demonstrating successful use cases that showcase tangible benefits. Additionally, educational initiatives that address customer concerns and clarify how blockchain enhances security and efficiency can help bridge the trust gap. By fostering a deeper understanding and showcasing the practical advantages of blockchain, banks can work towards increasing customer trust and encouraging the adoption of blockchain-based financial services.

5   Discussion

The integration of blockchain technology into the Moroccan banking sector, particularly at Banque Populaire du Maroc (BCP), presents a transformative opportunity to enhance security, efficiency, and customer experience. The survey data indicates a moderate level of awareness about blockchain among customers, with 65% having heard of the technology. However, a significant knowledge gap persists, as only 35% have a basic understanding. This gap underscores the need for BCP to implement targeted educational initiatives to build customer knowledge and trust. By focusing on the tangible benefits of blockchain, such as enhanced transaction security and reduced costs, BCP can address customer concerns and foster a more informed and receptive customer base. The bank's existing digital infrastructure provides a solid foundation for blockchain integration, allowing for seamless adoption of new services that align with customer expectations for convenience and reliability.

Despite the potential benefits, several challenges must be addressed to successfully implement blockchain at BCP. One of the primary technical challenges is scalability. As blockchain adoption grows, the need for a robust infrastructure that can handle increased transaction volumes becomes critical. BCP must invest in high-capacity servers and ensure sufficient network bandwidth to support blockchain operations. Exploring solutions such as sharding or layer-2 technologies can help manage scalability issues, ensuring that the system remains efficient and responsive as usage increases. Additionally, integrating blockchain with existing banking systems requires careful planning and execution to avoid disruptions and ensure seamless service delivery. Regulatory compliance remains a significant hurdle, as the Moroccan regulatory framework for blockchain is still evolving. BCP must engage with regulators to ensure compliance while advocating for policies that support innovation. Additionally, the technological infrastructure required for blockchain implementation demands substantial investment in both technology and skilled personnel. BCP must assess its current capabilities and invest in upgrading its systems to support blockchain applications. This includes training staff and potentially collaborating with fintech companies to bridge expertise gaps. Furthermore, customer trust in blockchain-based financial services is relatively low, with only 20% expressing high trust. Addressing ethical and security concerns is crucial for building trust in blockchain technology. Potential risks include data breaches, fraud, and operational disruptions. BCP must implement robust security measures, such as advanced encryption and regular security audits, to protect customer data and ensure the integrity of blockchain transactions. Additionally, ethical considerations, such as data privacy and the potential for misuse of blockchain technology, must be addressed through transparent policies and practices. By proactively managing these risks, BCP can enhance customer confidence and facilitate the adoption of blockchain-based services. BCP must focus on building trust through transparent communication and demonstrating the security and reliability of blockchain solutions.

Strategically, BCP can leverage blockchain to innovate its financial products and services, such as smart contracts and digital identity verification, which can streamline processes and reduce fraud. The bank's commitment to corporate social responsibility and its extensive network position it well to lead the digital transformation in Moroccan banking. By fostering a culture of innovation and embracing blockchain's potential, BCP can enhance its competitive position and drive growth in the sector. However, managing resistance to change, both internally and among customers, will be crucial. BCP needs to ensure that stakeholders are informed and involved in the transition process to minimize resistance and facilitate smooth adoption. In conclusion, while the integration of blockchain technology at BCP presents challenges, the potential benefits in terms of security, efficiency, and innovation make it a worthwhile pursuit. By strategically addressing these challenges and leveraging its strengths, BCP can position itself as a leader in the Moroccan banking sector's digital transformation.

6 Conclusion

The exploration of blockchain technology's integration into the Moroccan banking sector, with a focus on Banque Populaire du Maroc (BCP), reveals both promising opportunities and significant challenges. By strategically addressing these challenges and leveraging its strengths, BCP can position itself as a leader in the Moroccan banking sector's digital transformation. This proactive approach will not only benefit BCP but also contribute to the advancement of the Moroccan financial ecosystem as a whole. Blockchain offers the potential to enhance transaction security, improve operational efficiency, and foster innovation in financial products and services. The survey data indicates a moderate level of awareness and interest among customers, suggesting a readiness to embrace new technologies, provided that educational initiatives effectively address existing knowledge gaps and build trust. However, the path to successful blockchain adoption is not without obstacles. Regulatory uncertainties, the need for substantial technological investment, and the challenge of building customer trust are critical issues that BCP must navigate. Engaging with regulators, investing in infrastructure and talent, and fostering a culture of innovation will be essential strategies for overcoming these challenges. By doing so, BCP can leverage blockchain to not only enhance its service offerings but also strengthen its competitive position in the evolving financial landscape.

While the integration of blockchain technology presents complexities, the potential benefits for BCP and the broader Moroccan banking sector are substantial. By strategically addressing the challenges and capitalizing on the opportunities, BCP can lead the way in digital transformation, setting a benchmark for innovation and efficiency in the region. This proactive approach will not only benefit BCP but also contribute to the advancement of the Moroccan financial ecosystem as a whole.

References

1. Farah, M.B., et al.: A survey on blockchain technology in the maritime industry: challenges and future perspectives. Futur. Gener. Comput. Syst. **157**, 618–637 (2024)
2. Chafiq, T., Azmi, R., Mohammed, O.: Blockchain-based electronic voting systems: a case study in Morocco. Int. J. Intell. Netw. **5**, 38–48 (2024)
3. Prabhudas, J., Pradeep, R.C.: An intuitive approach behind distributed ledger technology: an elaborative glance of Blockchain, consensus mechanisms, and their applications. In: Convergence of Blockchain Technology and E-Business, pp. 27–59. CRC Press (2021)
4. Pradeep, A.S.E., et al.: Blockchain-aided information exchange records for design liability control and improved security. Autom. Constr. **126**, 103667 (2021)
5. Chen, Y.: Blockchain tokens and the potential democratization of entrepreneurship and innovation. Bus Horiz. **61**(4), 567–575 (2018)
6. Surapaneni, P., et al.: A systematic review on Blockchain-enabled internet of vehicles (BIoV): challenges, Defences and future research directions. IEEE Access. **12**, 123529–123560 (2024)
7. Jafri, R., Singh, S.: Blockchain applications for the healthcare sector: uses beyond bitcoin. In: Blockchain Applications for Healthcare Informatics, pp. 71–92. Elsevier (2022)
8. Chafiq, T., et al.: Investigating the potential of blockchain technology for geospatial data sharing: opportunities, challenges, and solutions. Geomatica. **76**, 100026 (2024)
9. Javaid, M., et al.: A review of blockchain technology applications for financial services. In: BenchCouncil Transactions on Benchmarks, Standards and Evaluations, vol. 2, p. 100073 (2022)

10. Aoun, A., et al.: A review of industry 4.0 characteristics and challenges, with potential improvements using blockchain technology. Comput. Ind. Eng. **162**, 107746 (2021)
11. Udeh, E.O., et al.: Blockchain-driven communication in banking: enhancing transparency and trust with distributed ledger technology. Finance Account. Res. J. **6**(6), 851–867 (2024)
12. Wylde, V., et al.: Cybersecurity, data privacy and blockchain: a review. SN Comput. Sci. **3**(2), 127 (2022)
13. Unsworth, R.: Smart contract this! An assessment of the contractual landscape and the herculean challenges it currently presents for "self-executing" contracts. In: Legal Tech, Smart Contracts and Blockchain, pp. 17–61 (2019)
14. Garg, P., et al.: Measuring the perceived benefits of implementing blockchain technology in the banking sector. Technol. Forecast. Soc. Change. **163**, 120407 (2021)
15. Mahajan, S., Nanda, M.: Revolutionizing banking with Blockchain: opportunities and challenges ahead. In: Next-Generation Cybersecurity: AI, ML, and Blockchain, pp. 287–304 (2024)
16. Cucari, N., et al.: The impact of blockchain in banking processes: the interbank Spunta case study. Tech. Anal. Strat. Manag. **34**(2), 138–150 (2022)
17. Narain, K.: Exploring blockchain-based government services in India. In: Blockchain Technology, pp. 127–144. CRC Press (2022)
18. Olomukoro, C.: The effects of implementing blockchain technology in the central bank of Nigeria (2023)
19. Sethaput, V., Innet, S.: Blockchain application for central bank digital currencies (CBDC). Clust. Comput. **26**(4), 2183–2197 (2023)
20. Parlasca, M.C., Johnen, C., Qaim, M.: Use of mobile financial services among farmers in Africa: insights from Kenya. Glob. Food Sec. **32**, 100590 (2022)
21. Kehinde-Peters, O.: Fintech and financial inclusion: closing the gender gap. In: Women and Finance in Africa: Inclusion and Transformation, pp. 75–89. Springer (2024)
22. ا.س ،الامام. and ع. العبادى, Digital transformation to achieve sustainability (UAE development plan till 2030-case study). Entrepr. J. Finance Bus., 2023: p. 35–44.

Author Index

O. Zahour et al. (Eds.): ICTIM 2024, CCIS 2655, pp. 421–422, 2026.
https://doi.org/10.1007/978-3-032-15147-6

GPSR Compliance
The European Union's (EU) General Product Safety Regulation (GPSR) is a set
of rules that requires consumer products to be safe and our obligations to
ensure this.

If you have any concerns about our products, you can contact us on

ProductSafety@springernature.com

In case Publisher is established outside the EU, the EU authorized
representative is:

Springer Nature Customer Service Center GmbH
Europaplatz 3
69115 Heidelberg, Germany

www.ingramcontent.com/pod-product-compliance
Ingram Content Group UK Ltd.
Pitfield, Milton Keynes, MK11 3LW, UK
UKHW020815080726
473059UK00007B/2262